WITHDRAWN

Handbook of
The Psychology of Aging

The Handbooks of Aging

Consisting of Three Volumes

Critical comprehensive reviews of
research knowledge, theories, concepts, and issues

Editor-in-Chief
James E. Birren

Handbook of the Biology of Aging
Edited by Edward L. Schneider and John W. Rowe

Handbook of the Psychology of Aging
Edited by James E. Birren and K. Warner Schaie

Handbook of Aging and the Social Sciences
Edited by Robert H. Binstock and Linda K. George

Handbook of
The Psychology of Aging

Third Edition

Editors
James E. Birren and K. Warner Schaie

Associate Editors
Margaret Gatz, Timothy A. Salthouse, and Carmi Schooler

Editorial Coordinator
Donna E. Deutchman

Academic Press, Inc.

Harcourt Brace Jovanovich, Publishers

San Diego   New York   Berkeley   Boston   London   Sydney   Tokyo   Toronto

Copyright © 1990 by Academic Press, Inc.
All Rights Reserved.
No part of this publication may be reproduced or transmitted in any form or by
any means, electronic or mechanical, including photocopy, recording, or any information storage and retrieval system, without permission in writing from the
publisher.

Academic Press, Inc.
San Diego, California 92101

United Kingdom Edition published by
Academic Press Limited
24–28 Oval Road, London NW1 7DX

Library of Congress Cataloging-in-Publication Data

Handbook of the psychology of aging / edited by James E. Birren,
K. Warner Schaie. -- 3rd ed.
    p. cm.
  Includes bibliographies and indexes.
  ISBN 0-12-101280-8 (alk. paper)
  1. Aging--Psychological aspects.
I. Birren, James E. II. Schaie, K. Warner (Klaus Warner), Date.
[DNLM: 1. Aged--psychology. 2. Aging. WT150 H236]
  BF724.55.A35H36 1990
  155.67--dc20
DNLM/DC
for Library of Congress   89-15061
                                                            CIP

Printed in the United States of America
90 91 92 93   9 8 7 6 5 4 3 2 1

Contents

Part Two
Influences of Behavior and Aging

Part Three
Behavioral Processes in Aging

Part Four
Applications to the Individual and Society

Contributors

Numbers in parentheses indicate the pages on which the authors' contributions begin.

Edward Anderson (21), Department of Human Development and Family Studies, Texas Tech University, Lubbock, Texas 79409

Toni C. Antonucci (103), Institute for Social Research, University of Michigan, Ann Arbor, Michigan 48106

Vern L. Bengtson (404), Andrus Gerontology Center, University of Southern California, University Park, Los Angeles, California 90089

Betty A. Birren (3), California Council on Gerontology and Geriatrics, Pacific Palisades, California 90272

James E. Birren (3, 45, 222), Borun Center for Gerontological Research, UCLA School of Medicine, Los Angeles, California 90024

Mindy J. Blum (404), Department of Psychology, University of Southern California, Los Angeles, California 90089

Elizabeth A. Bosman (446), Psychology Department, University of Waterloo, Waterloo, Ontario, Canada N2L 3G1

John Cerella (201), Veterans Administration Medical Center, Research Service, Bedford, Massachusetts 01730

Neil Charness (446), Psychology Department, University of Waterloo, Waterloo, Ontario, Canada N2L 3G1

Gene D. Cohen (359), National Institute on Aging, Bethesda, Maryland 20892

Roger A. Dixon (258), Department of Psychology, University of Victoria, Victoria, British Columbia, Canada V8W 2Y2

Robert E. Dustman (135), Veterans Administration Medical Center, Neuropsychology, Salt Lake City, Utah 84148

Jeffrey W. Elias (79), Department of Psychology, Texas Tech University, Lubbock, Texas 79409

Merrill F. Elias (79), Department of Psychology, University of Maine, Orono, Maine 04469

Penelope K. Elias (79), Beech Hill Enterprises, Inc., Mount Desert, Maine 04660

Rita Emmerson (135), Veterans Administration Medical Center, Neuropsychology, Salt Lake City, Utah 84148

James L. Fozard (150), National Institute on Aging, Gerontology Research Center, Longitudinal Studies Branch, Baltimore, Maryland 21224

Margaret Gatz (404), Department of Psychology, University of Southern California, Los Angeles, California 90089

Rose C. Gibson (103), Institute for Social Research, University of Michigan, Ann Arbor, Michigan 48106

Priscilla Gilliam MacRae (183), Department of Sports Medicine, Pepperdine University, Malibu, California 90265

David F. Hultsch (258), Department of Psychology, University of Victoria, Victoria, British Columbia, Canada V8W 2Y2

Margaret Hellie Huyck (124), Department of Psychology, Illinois Institute of Technology, Chicago, Illinois 60616

James S. Jackson (103), Institute for Social Research, University of Michigan, Ann Arbor, Michigan 48106

Alfred W. Kaszniak (427), Department of Psychology, University of Arizona, Tucson, Arizona 85721

Donald H. Kausler (171), Department of Psychology, University of Missouri-Columbia, Columbia, Missouri 65211

Douglas C. Kimmel (489), Department of Psychology, City College and the Graduate School, City University of New York, New York, New York 10031

Nathan Kogan (330), The New School for Social Research, New York, New York 10003

M. Powell Lawton (464), Philadelphia Geriatric Center, Philadelphia, Pennsylvania 19141

Leah L. Light (275), Department of Psychology, Pitzer College, Claremont, California 91711

J. J. McArdle (21), Department of Psychology, University of Virginia, Charlottesville, Virginia 22901

Gerald E. McClearn (67), Center for Developmental and Health Genetics, Pennsylvania State University, University Park, Pennsylvania 16802

Joan M. McDowd (222), Department of Psychology, University of Southern California, Los Angeles, California 90089

Harry R. Moody (489), Brookdale Center on Aging, Hunter College, City University of New York, New York, New York 10010

Patricia A. Parmelee (464), Clinical Research Center, Philadelphia Geriatric Center, Philadelphia, Pennsylvania 19141

Robert Plomin (67), College of Health and Human Development, Pennsylvania State University, University Park, Pennsylvania 16802

Patricia N. Prinz (135), Department of Psychiatry and Behavioral Sciences, University of Washington, Seattle, Washington 98195

Sara H. Qualls (375), Department of Psychology, University of Colorado at Colorado Springs, Colorado Springs, Colorado 80933

Timothy A. Salthouse (310), School of Psychology, Georgia Institute of Technology, Atlanta, Georgia 30332

K. Warner Schaie (291), Department of Human Development and Family Studies, The Pennsylvania State University, University Park, Pennsylvania 16802

Carmi Schooler (347), Laboratory of Socio-Environmental Studies, NIMH, Bethesda, Maryland 20892

Johannes J. F. Schroots (45), TNO Institute of Preventive Health Care, 2300 AC Leiden, The Netherlands

Dean Keith Simonton (320), Department of Psychology, University of California, Davis, California 95616

Michael A. Smyer (357), Department of Human Development and Family Studies, College of Health and Human Development, The Pennsylvania State University, University Park, Pennsylvania 16802

Waneen W. Spirduso (183), Physical and Health Education, University of Texas, Austin, Texas 78712

Diana S. Woodruff-Pak (234), Department of Psychology, Temple University, Philadelphia, Pennsylvania 19122

Steven H. Zarit (375), Department of Human Development and Family Studies, College of Health and Human Development, The Pennsylvania State University, University Park, Pennsylvania 16802

Foreword

The present volume is one of three Handbooks now in their third edition: *Handbook of the Biology of Aging; Handbook of the Psychology of Aging;* and *Handbook of Aging and the Social Sciences.* Because of the growth in research on aging, there has been an accelerated need to collate and interpret existing information. Thus, the decision was made to accelerate the publication of the third edition of these handbooks to reflect this expansion in research.

The growth of the National Institute on Aging and sponsorship of research by the National Institute of Mental Health and the Administration on Aging has stimulated needed research. Phenomena of aging cut across many scientific fields. It is impossible to represent all of the material that is relevant in one volume. We focus on three major sources of influence on aging: the biological, the psychological, and the social. Perhaps in a strict sense, one should view aging as an ecological phenomenon dependent upon the influences of genetics, physical and social environments, and individual behavior.

It is hoped that these volumes will be consulted across scientific areas to trace some of the pathways of aging through the matrix of scientific information and disciplinary orientation. It is expected that sci-

entific personnel, graduate students, and professionals will find the volumes useful. The availability of the information in the convenient form of the handbooks also may stimulate new courses of instruction and seminars on aging as well as provide easy access to the research literature.

The series editor wishes to thank the editors of the individual volumes, Robert H. Binstock, Linda K. George, John W. Rowe, K. Warner Schaie, Edward L. Schneider, and the associate editors, Caleb E. Finch, Margaret Gatz, Victor W. Marshall, George M. Martin, Edward J. Masoro, George C. Myers, Timothy A. Salthouse, Carmi Schooler, and James H. Schulz. The series editor is grateful to these editors for their cooperation in the successful completion of this publication adventure. Thanks are owed to Donna E. Deutchman for developing the plan for the third edition and coordinating the relationship with the publisher.

There is little doubt from the reading of these volumes that the subject matter of aging has become more sophisticated and also mainstream in many scientific disciplines. It is hoped that the handbooks' publication will motivate continued attention to research on aging and the well-being of the elderly in our society.

James E. Birren

Preface

The purpose of this handbook is to provide an authoritative review and reference source for the scientific and professional literature on the psychology of adult development and aging. It is designed to serve as a definitive reference source for graduate students, researchers, and professionals. The basic behavioral processes are covered in the volume to attempt to describe and explain changes in behavior and capacities that occur with advancing age as revealed in research. The explanations of the phenomena involve a wide range of factors, including biological influences, disease, and social influences such as generational differences and historical events. The chapters are intended to be comprehensive but do not necessarily review or refer to all publications on a specific point. In contrast to an annual review, the present chapters attempt to present a more systematic organization of information. Not only was the intention of this handbook to organize information in a convenient form, it is also designed to serve more systematic purposes and to focus on crucial theoretical or methodological problems.

The origin of the present third edition can be traced back to the *Handbook of Aging and the Individual*, published in 1959. Since then, the volume of published literature has dramatically expanded. The influence of the National Institute on Aging, the National Institute of Mental Health, the Administration on Aging, as well as many foundations has encouraged the growth of an area of knowledge that in 1959 was pioneering in character.

Research on the psychology of aging continues to be in an expanding phase. Also, there is a marked change in the academic setting. Whereas once the psychology of aging was a marginal topic not commonly found in the repertoire of teaching and research in departments of psychology, it is now increasingly becoming mainstream. Some departments have more than one faculty member with specialties in the subject matter. New positions are opening in both the academic arenas and the applied areas. This bodes well for the future intellectual prosperity of the field.

While it is devoted primarily to the understanding of phenomena of aging, it is hoped that this volume will lead to an improvement in the conditions and quality of human life. The editors note with pleasure the collegial cooperation that was elicited in preparing this handbook. The production of this volume was accompanied by prime motivation, high cooperation, and high academic standards.

Along with the fact that the psychology of aging has come to be a mainline concern in psychology departments, there has been a shift toward more theoretically oriented research. In the pioneering stage of the psychology of aging, there were many "look-and-see" investigations that helped to map out the territory. We now seem to be shifting into a phase when crucial experiments are wanted rather than descriptive ones. Thus, in the present chapters one finds more emphasis on systematic explanation.

Although the 1977 first edition of the present volume was comprehensive, the demand for space in the face of increasing publication costs now requires more selectivity. There are topics covered in the first and second editions but not represented in the present one because we felt that there had been insufficient progress since the previous handbook editions. For this reason, the reader is encouraged to consult the previous two editions for the treatments of particular topics.

Furthermore, there has been an editorial policy of enlisting new authors to prepare reviews on topics previously covered to get a turnover in perspective. Thus, the interested reader should consult previous editions to get alternative perspectives on material which is updated in the present volume. Not only does an improved perspective emerge, but an historical feeling will be experienced for shifting emphases in research.

In the second edition, two new parts were added to the handbook which dealt with "psychological applications to the individual" and "psychological applications to society." There were nine chapters written under this rubric which represented the outreach from the laboratory to society. This was done not only to point out the implications of research for application, but also to encourage the backflow of topics from "real life issues" to the laboratory. The editors believe that the intellectual prosperity of psychology depends upon the movement of information to and from basic research and application. In the current volume, there are fewer chapters in this area. But, one will note that there are fewer chapters in the book as a whole since there is continuing pressure to make the volume manageable in size. One adaptation to the pressures was to create chapters which are both full length and half length in character. This has no relationship to a presumed importance of a topic. It is intended to reflect the extent of recent research activity in the particular area.

The editors wish to thank the associate editors, Margaret Gatz, Timothy Salthouse, and Carmi Schooler, for their assistance in planning the book, selecting topics and authors, and spending hours in reviewing the chapters. Each chapter was read in its first and second draft by two persons. The editors also wish to thank the authors for their commitment to scholarship and producing the original drafts and final copies on schedule. We are pleased that this handbook was assembled and produced according to schedule.

The editors also wish to thank the editorial coordinator, Donna E. Deutchman, for her professional handling of the book and its obligations from its beginning. She coordinated the scheduling, nudged and urged the authors and editors to keep to the calendar, and she edited each chapter with care to reduce inadvertent errors and best express the authors' intentions. We also thank Alice Zeehandelaar for her patience and skill in ensuring that manuscripts, telephone messages, and correspondence did not go astray.

The psychology of aging is an area in which researchers and professionals have much to contribute to advances in knowledge gained through research, as well as to applications for enhancing the quality of life for millions of mature persons and for the well-being of our society. The contributors and editors trust that this edition as well as the previous ones will advance the organization of research, teaching of the subject matter of adult development and aging, and improvement of human services.

James E. Birren
K. Warner Schaie

Part One

Theory and Measurement in the Psychology of Aging

One

The Concepts, Models, and History of the Psychology of Aging

James E. Birren and Betty A. Birren

I. Introduction

The purpose of this chapter is to trace the origins of the study of the psychology of aging and its concepts, leading to a description of its present state. *Psychology* is described as the science of behavior. As this volume shows, this embraces a broad spectrum of subject matter such as sensation, perception, learning, memory, intellectual abilities, motivation, emotions, personality, attitudes, motor movements, and social relationships.

A simple definition of the psychology of aging is that it is the study of the changes in behavior that characteristically occur after young adulthood. A fuller definition of aging introduced the idea of typical changes with time: "Aging . . . refers to an orderly or regular transformation with time of representative organisms living under representative environments (Birren, 1988, p. 160). Excluded in this concept of aging are age-associated disease disorders such as Huntington's Chorea, and Alzheimer's and Parkinson's disease. Also excluded are such environmental effects

as starvation, exposure to a toxic environment, or war trauma. These produce atypical outcomes not experienced by most persons over the course of life. In an earlier handbook, Birren (1959b, p. 5) said, "In scientific discourse, the core meaning of aging implies a determinant chain of events occupying a significant part of the life span after maturity." Thus, a statement about the psychology of aging also involves a statement about time and directions usually shown in the organization of behavior. Imbedded in the concept of aging are the implications of such terms as *characteristic, typical patterns of change,* and *entrainment.* The latter refers to the coalescing of influences on behavior over time.

Aging implies something that is associated with chronological age but not identical with it. Aging is used both as a label for an independent variable to explain other phenomena and as a dependent variable that is explained by other processes. Because the term *aging* is often used in a global sense to refer to all interindividual age differences and intraindividual age

Handbook of the Psychology of Aging, Third Edition
Copyright © 1990 Academic Press, Inc. All rights of reproduction in any form reserved.

Obviously until recently, psychology did not embrace the implications of aging as part of the broader science. Although the American Psychological Association established a division on Maturity and Old Age in 1946, it did not establish a journal on aging until 1985, almost 40 years after the founding of the *Journal of Gerontology*.

Because it evolved outside the traditional core of psychology, the psychology of adult development and aging may have had the advantage of avoiding some of its intellectual biases. One of the biases that persists is the separation of social and biological psychologies. Although psychology is both a biological and a social science, that is, behavior is organized as a result of both influences, psychology for the most part has departmentalized or continued to separate the biological and the social components of behavior and has tended to neglect their interactions. Unfortunately, this separation does not encourage the study of adult development and of aging in which changes in behavior result from biological and social influences as well as from their interactions.

IV. The Emergence of Developmental Psychology

There was a small stream of research on aging during the latter part of the nineteenth century (see Birren, 1961). For example, in 1884 Galton gathered behavioral data on 9,337 males and females aged 5 to 80 years, at a health exposition in London. To measure the degree of association of variables with age, he devised what is most likely the first index of correlation. By 1931 Walter Miles was able to publish a review on the psychology of aging in the *Proceedings of the National Academy of Science,* "Measures of Certain Human Abilities Throughout the Life Span," and in 1933 he followed it with a longer paper on life span changes.

Between 1900 and 1940 only a small amount of research was done on the adult phase of life span, although research on child development expanded rapidly. It is to the emergence of child development that we turn to look for some of the roots of current thought in the psychology of aging.

G. S. Hall had written *Adolescence* in 1904, a book about the child's transition to adulthood. In 1910, G. M. Whipple published a manual of mental and physical tests. In 1914, it was expanded to two volumes. Whipple described it as "a book of directions, compiled with special reference to the experimental study of school children in the laboratory or classroom" (Whipple, Part II, 1915, p. 79). The first of the two 1915 volumes listed over 500 references, of which 37% were published before 1900. By 1931 the field of child psychology was sufficiently developed to warrant a *Handbook of Child Psychology.* In his introduction, Carl Murchison observed: "The field of child psychology is almost as old as is the field of experimental psychology" (Murchison, 1931, p. ix).

The psychology of aging trailed child psychology by almost 50 years, and very few researchers or scholars gave much attention to the psychological issues of later life until after World War II. By contrast, there was already a Bureau of Child Study in the Chicago school system before 1900 that was reporting systematic investigations of psychological measurements of children.

It is easy to form an impression that during the heyday of expansion of research on child development following World War I, most psychologists came to regard the child as an *end product* rather than as part of an ongoing course of the human life span. Implicit, perhaps, was the idea that the organism reaches its highest form of development by late adolescence, and there is little substance of scientific interest afterward. When the APA's Division on Maturity and Old Age (later renamed Division on Adult Development and Aging) was organized in 1946, many of its leaders believed that the Division of Developmental Psychology, which was concerned with children, would merge with it. This has not happened, and most investigators of the various phases of the life span appear to have at most only loose intellectual ties with each other.

For the most part, *developmental psychology*, scientifically and professionally has remained *child psychology*. However, a few early leaders in the study of child development did turn their attention to the psychology of aging later in their careers. Among these were G. S. Hall, Lewis Terman, Charlotte Bühler, Sidney Pressey, Irving Lorge, Harold E. Jones, and John E. Anderson. The latter two were early directors of institutes of child study founded in the 1920s. Sidney Pressey was the first psychologist to publish a book that dealt with developmental psychology covering the entire life span including "the adult and older years" (Pressey, 1939).

The assertive separation of psychology from philosophy in the early twentieth century was accompanied by an emphasis on experimental studies of learning. Contributing to this era were advances in classical conditioning, for example, Pavlov's studies, and later, the operant conditioning of behaviorists (B. F. Skinner). The "building block" of organized behavior was considered to be the conditioned response. It was as though many psychologists were convinced that by discovery of the principles of learning they would have a complete understanding of how behavior is organized. This influence was more dominant in child psychology than in the psychology of adults because the latter has matured more recently, in an intellectually more permissive atmosphere. Here the reminder is offered that learning by itself has never created a child nor an old person.

Behaviorism ruled out explanations in terms of both covert mental and physiological functions. In his book on animal awareness, Griffin (1970) listed a series of concepts that fell into the behaviorists' disfavor. Among these were *attention* and *intention*. Attention most assuredly is a precondition for learning and cognition. It is of interest to note that the 1987 *Handbook of Physiology* contains a chapter on attention (Heilman, Watson, Valenstein, & Goldberg, 1987) that depends upon the concept *intention*, a term excluded by behaviorism from the repertory of psychology.

In his *History of Psychology*, Peters (1962) made the point that "behaviorism is to be criticized not simply for its restrictive and outworn conception of scientific method; it is also to be criticized for having a very naive and inadequate view of what constitutes behavior" (p. 703). Riegel (1978), with reference to behaviorism, pointed out that in its purview "only the outer conditions and movement became the object of study" (1978, p. 27). He further maintained that the traditions of experimental and social psychology led to the study "of the individual and the group in a developmental vacuum" and that both "were founded in synchronic or 'timeless' thinking" (1978, p. 23). *Synchronic* refers to a state of the organism at only one point in time in contrast to comparing the state at two or more points in time—diachronic. Given this historical background, it is not surprising that experimental psychologists were vague and uninterested in the directions of behavior.

The growth of sophisticated experimental methods within psychology seems to have been accompanied by a tacit conviction that good research methods equal good theory. One of the few psychologists who incorporated the issues of developmental psychology into general psychology was J. R. Kantor (1959). He attempted to develop what he called an *interbehavioral psychology* that related behavior

both to its biological and social antecedents. For example, he commented about
early maturity and late life:

Developments during maturity consist primarily of augmentation of equipment through
individual contacts with novel and various
stimulus objects. The period of advancing age
marks a recurring susceptibility to biological
conditions, primarily of the devolutional sort.
At the same time, psychological equipments
are developed at the close influence of changes
in the social, occupational, and economic life
conditions. (Kantor, 1959, p. 167)

Kantor's view portrays a shifting nature
of influences on behavior and suggests
that he believed that biological influences
are dominant in early childhood, decline
in maturity, and then rise again in importance in later life.

V. Perspectives on Developmental Psychology

Although child psychology of the early
twentieth century was questing for broad
generalizations about development, psychology had another mission, to separate
itself and show itself to be different from
philosophy, its traditional university part-
ner. This separation was brought about at
the expense of emphasizing methods of
collecting data and of minimizing theory.
For example, Murchison's 1931 *Handbook of Child Psychology* has no section
devoted to theory, nor is the term *theory*
listed in the comprehensive subject index.
Child psychology, itself, was obviously influenced by the *zeitgeist* to be methodologically sophisticated but theoretically limited.

In the 1931 *Handbook of Child Psychology,* John E. Anderson stated the case for
rigor of method. "In the history of any science there can be discerned two trends,
one consisting of the main body of fact and
generalization, slowly but surely accumulated, which in the course of time becomes
welded into a substantial and integrated
field of knowledge, and the other consisting of the methods and techniques by
means of which problems are attacked."
Further, "problems, techniques, and results cannot be sharply differentiated. A
problem, however stated, does not become
a scientific problem until a method of at-
tack can be set up" (Anderson, 1931, p. 1).
These statements demonstrate the traditional emphasis on defining psychological
problems in terms of the methods of collecting data, *operationalism.* With such an
emphasis, however, it is possible to blur
the distinction between methods of collecting data, interpretations of the data,
and the underlying questions being asked.
A good theoretical question can encourage
methodological development. However,
as stated, the divorce of psychology from
philosophy had the effect of encouraging
operationalism.

A. The Concept of Development

The concept of development has received
scrutiny by several psychologists leading
to a listing several of its essential ideas: "1)
the organism conceived as a living system;
2) time; 3) movement over time toward
complexity of organization; 4) 'hier-
archization,' or the comprehension of
parts or part-systems into larger units or
'wholes'; and 5) an end state of organization which is maintained with some stability of self-regulation" (Harris, 1957, p.
3). Maier (1969) stated that development
was originally a biological term having to
do with physical growth and change in
structure over time. However, he also said
that in the psychological sense, "development relates to socio-psychological development. Development in this sense refers
to an integration of constitutional and
learned changes which make up an individual's ever-developing personality"
(Maier, 1969, p. 3).

Salkind (1985) said, "we can think of
development as a progressive series of
changes that occurs in a predictable pat-

tern as a result of an interaction between biological and environmental factors." This statement does not distinguish changes that occur in early life from those that occur in late life. Development might be regarded as progressing up to a phase of maximum differentiation after which dedifferentiation begins to occur (Schmidt & Botwinick, 1989).

Development, as scientists have defined it, implies changes in the organization of behavior from simple to complex forms, from small to large repertoires of behaviors, from fixed ways of responding to demands and needs to large repertoires of behaviors that can be strategically chosen. This suggests that development ends at no specific time and that the organism may continue to differentiate behaviors long after physical maturity, and move toward increasing complexity with concurrent differentiation and dedifferentiation (Schroots, 1988).

B. Theories of Development

In 1967, A. L. Baldwin published *Theories of Child Development*. Included in his review were the ideas of Heider, Lewin, Piaget, Freud, Werner, and Parsons. Baldwin stated that there were six scientific theories of child development significant enough to discuss. He also discussed behaviorist or conditioning (S-R) theories. His conclusion after reviewing these theories in some detail was that they were found to have a "patch work quality. The six becoming concerned with different aspects of child development more than they are focused on different explanations of the same behavior" (Baldwin, 1967). He added that the field of child development is in part a theory of behavior and action and in part a theory of change in behavior. This is relevant to the view in this chapter that the state of current theory in the psychology of aging, which borrows from existing islands of psychology, consists essentially of statements about how different aspects of behavior are organized, and

avoids theoretical statements about how behavior changes over time.

Development theories fall into several general types: (1) Maturational theories that emphasize biological unfolding of the organism with sequences of behavior explained in terms of the evolved genetic pattern of the species, the genome. (2) Social-personality theories that involve the development of the individual personality and its early formation in family relationships and later peer influences. (3) The development of behavioral controls over instincts that is the subject matter of psychoanalytic theory. (4) Behaviorism, which emphasizes learning and assumes that the nervous system begins as a *tabula rasa* for which learning determines the organization of behavior. And (5) the development of cognition that involves the emergence of a sequence of stages that provides a basis for differentiation and increasing complexity. In this latter theoretical explanation, the organism plays an active role in the outcomes of events, in contrast to a passive role in behaviorism.

To the preceding theoretical orientations another might be added, (6) the ecological orientation in which the behavioral tendencies of an organism result from the biological background of the organism and its interactions with a particular environment (Bronfenbrenner, 1977).

An organismic–ecological model appears to be a potentially useful perspective for understanding adult behavior. Baldwin said, "the Lewinian conceptualization of the differences between the children and adults is one of the few such descriptions that occur in the literature of child psychology" (Baldwin, 1967, p. 583).

In Baldwin's view, only Werner and Lewin were interested in the nature of development itself as opposed to the changes in specific aspects of behavior. With regard to Lewin, he said, "only Lewin gave even passing attention to the nature of the developmental process and he also adopted differentiation as a primary developmental concept" (Baldwin, 1967, p. 585). Baldwin noted that even the terms most commonly used in psychology, such as *stimulus* and *response*, avoid the implication that there is an organism that is active and mediating the environment and behavior.

Baldwin's summary of developmental theories was somewhat optimistic: "In retrospect, the theories do not turn out badly. In many ways they support each other, and in total, suggest a kind of proto-theory of child development which, although obviously incomplete, badly defined, and surely wrong in some respects is a feasible and workable basis for further research and for more refined theory building" (Baldwin, 1967, p. 599). However, this suggests that students of aging need to recognize that they cannot depend upon "hand-me-up" theories of child development to organize information about adult life.

An important contribution to concepts about development has come from dialectical psychology (Riegel, 1978). Salkind (1985) discussed the impact that dialectical thinking has had upon developmental psychology, in which the result of crises is viewed as releasing positive and negative forces leading to developmental progression. He noted that there are four categories of developmental progression: (1) inner-biological, (2) individual-psychological, (3) cultural-psychological, and (4) outer-physical (Salkind, 1985, p. 243). Generally, these are the same categories involved in adult transformations, although perhaps the relative contributions of these influences shift with age. For example, in later life, health and disease probably exercise a greater influence on behavior than they do in the developing child or young adult.

One difference in concepts of aging compared with concepts in child development is the impact of contemporary neuroscience. Early theories of child de-

velopment appeared before there was much known of the physiology and biochemistry of the human brain. We now suspect that there may be as many as 50 different neurotransmitters in the brain and that behavior is modulated by many of them. It seems unlikely that any future theory of aging can fail to take into account concepts derived from the growth of the neurosciences. This is not meant to imply an exclusive biological determination of aging but to say that the pattern of behavioral changes seen in adults is influenced by a wide range of factors, including the structure and function of the brain itself, which was little known in the early days of psychology.

VI. The Emergence of a Psychology of Aging

As previously noted, one of the earliest books on the psychology of aging was G. S. Hall's *Senescence: The Second Half of Life*, published in 1922. His book is a rather complete review of what was then known about aging, including writings from biological sciences, social sciences, and general literature. The 518 pages of his book are essentially a description of the empirical "forest" of aging, psychological, biological, physiological, medical, historical, literary, and behavioral. Hall clearly provided a developmental point of view in the foreword: "It is hoped that the data here garnered and the views propounded may help to a better and more correct understanding of the nature and functions of old age, and also be a psychologist's contribution to the long-desired, but long-delayed science of gerontology" (Hall, 1922, p. v.).

On a poetic note, Hall suggested that there is a clarity of the mind in late life, "an 'Indian Summer' that should be both expected and utilized to the utmost for this is a precious bud of vast potentialities. . . . It brings a new poise and a new perspective of values and hence a new orientation and newer and deeper insights into essentials" (Hall, 1922, p. 434). Hall distributed a questionnaire to an undetermined number of persons in New England, probably about 200. One of his questions was, "Did you experience an 'Indian Summer' of revived energy before the winter age began to set in?" (Hall, 1922, p. 347). He reported that only five subjects responded yes to this question and that most of the subjects felt themselves going on about as before with no change, save a gradual abatement of energy.

Although he attempted to give a comprehensive review of the literature on late life, it is clear that in 1922 this literature was much more sparse than was the literature on children. For Hall, the experience of aging was a matter of walking up the hill of life toward maturity and then walking carefully down the other side toward old age. His view is simply stated: "To learn that we are really old is a long, complex, and painful experience. Each decade the circle of Great Fatigue narrows around us, restricting the intensity and endurance of our activities" (Hall, 1922, p. 366).

Although Hall carried out one of the earliest empirical investigations of death, one of Western society's major taboos, research on death and dying did not really attract much interest for another 40 years. It is perhaps to the psychology of death that Hall gave his greatest attention, as demonstrated in the 79 pages of his 1922 book that he devoted to the subject. He contrasted curiosity about death and the death wish with the fear of death itself. However, he did not deal with death as an aspect of aging but as a developmental issue unto itself. "Thus the wish for and belief in immortality is at bottom the very best of all possible auguries and pledges that man as he exists today is only the beginning of what he is to be and do" (Hall, 1922, p. 515). In this passage, Hall shows his conviction that man is an evolving social creature as well as a self-concerned

organism. Probably Hall should be classed as an early cognitive developmentalist because he believed, as did Quetelet, that humans can aspire to further advances by thought and volitional effect. Although Hall did not present a theory of adult development and aging, he surveyed the territory in which such theories could develop.

The next major book in the field was Cowdry's 1939 *Problems of Ageing*. It includes chapters on many more aspects of aging than do contemporary books. It begins with chapters on plants, followed by chapters on protozoa and invertebrates, then insects and vertebrates. Then, after extensive treatment of the various organ systems, there are chapters on the psychological and clinical material and finally, one on the social urgency of research, all arranged in a simple to complex hierarchy. The mere fact that Cowdry's book was published in its comprehensive form represents a conviction held in the late 1930s that there were some holistic principles of aging to be derived by considering living systems in their entirety. Enthusiasm for holistic views of aging, however, has since declined markedly.

In the second edition of Cowdry's book, L. K. Frank wrote about the orderliness of changes with age: "Since almost all living organisms pass through a sequence of changes, characterized by growth, development, maturation, and finally senescence, ageing presents a broad biological problem" (Frank, 1942, p. XV). Frank later distinguished two views of aging; the first regards aging as an evolutionary process that operates cumulatively as an inevitable modification of the physiology of the organism; the other view regards aging as resulting from the accumulated effects of infections, traumas, nutritional inadequacies, and accidents. In the introduction to the first edition of *Problems of Ageing*, the philosopher John Dewey stated a paradox about development continuing in an aging individual:

The underlying problem, both scientifically and philosophically, it seems to me is that of the relationship of ageing and maturing. We are at present more or less in the unpleasant and illogical condition of extolling maturity and depreciating age. It seems obvious without argument there is some connection between the two; that we cannot separate the processes of maturing from those of aging even though the two processes are not identical. . . . That there should be a gradual wearing down of energies, physical and mental in the old age period, it seems reasonable to expect upon biological grounds, that maturing changes at some particular age into incapacity for continued growth in every direction is a very different proposition. (Dewey, 1939, p. XXXI)

Dewey's statement about the paradox of concurrent development and aging has usually been met by insulating conceptual issues and separately publishing material on the psychology, biology, and sociology of aging. The implication of Dewey's comment is that the individual can be increasingly wise and mature while at the same time increasingly biologically vulnerable and likely to die. Some psychologists prefer to do research on successful aging or the "up" side of life without questioning the nature of its entrainment with concurrent biological degradation. The puzzle of expressing this in a systematic or theoretical way remains as a fundamental issue for the psychology of aging.

It was not until almost 40 years after child study centers were started that research centers for the study of older adults were organized. The first of these was the Gerontology Research Center of the National Institutes of Health, which had its origins in discussions held in 1940, although it did not become active until 1946. About the same time, the Gerontological Society of America, the American Geriatrics Society, and the Division on Maturity and Old Age of the APA were established. After the end of World War II, an "adolescent" growth spurt occurred in the subject matter of the psychology of aging.

The first handbook on the psychological aspects of aging (Birren, 1959a) was published 28 years after the first handbook of child psychology. Its chapters show a persistent quality of psychology as being like islands of information organized according to their own assumptions and rules, for example, perception, learning, and personality with few bridging concepts between various aspects of behavior. At present, psychology has more information about the separate aspects of behavior than about how aspects of behavior are integrated or coordinated in regulating behavior. Even within the psychology of aging, few scholars seem to be interested in the organization of behavior in relation to aging, and therefore study changes in specific aspects of behavior. How behavior is organized over the life span is a more powerful question than simply how behavior becomes organized; the latter question seems static.

Perhaps few contemporary psychologists are as optimistic as was Quetelet in 1835 about the ease of discerning general laws governing the way humankind grows up and grows old. Indeed, most investigators of aging are avoiding the complexity of the phenomena and few attempt to deal with more than one microsystem of the organism.

VII. Complexity and Theories of Aging

One view of aging is that so much happens to organisms over the course of life that there is no determinant organization of aging; rather, it is essentially a consequence of chance events or noise. In this view, aging is a random process of change in an organism that develops in a deterministic way but thereafter becomes a victim of random degradations induced by the "slings and arrows of existence." This view of aging holds that the changes in the structures and functions of organisms are regulated by forces that arise outside of natural selection. It implies that an aging organism runs out of control of the developmental program of the genome. For example, "the organism ultimately dies of old age because it is now an unstable system which is provided with no further sequence of operational instructions and in which divergent processes are no longer coordinated to maintain function" (Comfort, 1956, p. 189). In this view, the organism progresses from an ordered state of programmed development to a disordered, chaotic state in old age, with decreased power of survival.

It seems more reasonable to expect that there are wide ranges of states that are not continually interacting (Birren, 1959b, p. 35). Anatomy of function and discontinuity in relationships (particularly quantity-bounded relationships) contribute to the complexity of aging of the human organism (Yates, 1982). Thus in terminal illness the incapacity associated with the period of terminal decline need not have been an influence over many previous years. Age changes, for example, in blood flow, blood pressure or body temperature, may not show a relationship to behavior until a critical value is reached. Presumably with advancing age, critical thresholds may become exceeded, and perhaps the boundary thresholds themselves change (Yates, 1988).

In accounting for complex human behavior, G.S. Hall's simple hill model of the course of human life, with development going uphill and aging going downhill, seems adequate to express what we now know. There are aspects of the adult organism that lose information and undergo increased entropy (disorder) at the same time that other systems gain information and demonstrate decreased entropy (increased organization). At present, there does not appear to be sufficient conceptual depth in the field to embrace this complexity (Schroots, 1988). There is growing recognition that theoretical advances are re-

quired (Birren & Bengtson, 1988; Schaie & Schooler, 1989), along with methodological sophistication (Schaie, Campbell, Meredith, & Rawlings, 1988).

VIII. The Status of Theory and Explanation of Aging

A. The Role of the Brain in Aging

The evolution of the primate brain has been marked by the attainment of a relatively large brain weight in relation to body size and total body weight. Sacher (1959) analyzed the relationship of the brain/body weight ratio to the longevity of organisms across species and found a remarkably high correlation. That is, brain size in relation to body size is a good predictor of the length of life of a species. This suggests that as complex nervous systems evolved, more efficient regulatory controls over bodily processes were provided for survival than were provided with small nervous systems, favoring survival of a species through high reproductivity but less through capacity for learning.

The brain is sometimes described as consisting of many organs, rather than as being a single organ. Thus the human brain is the primary physiological regulator of metabolic processes, endocrine activities, blood pressure, and temperature, as well as being responsible for the assembly and execution of complex behaviors. It is composed of support cells, glia, and neurons. The neurons are perhaps the most important cells of the body with regard to aging because after their reproduction by division in the fetal brain, the same neurons remain with us the rest of our lives. With their regulatory role, neurons are in a key position to disseminate information ranging from the accumulation of experience (memory) to endocrine interrelations, and to serve as a basic pacemaker of changes in aging.

Because of its dual role in regulating behavior and metabolic processes, the evolution of the complex nervous system is of great significance for the behavioral sciences. The brain influences the survival of vertebrates and also makes possible learning, storage of memories, and complex new behavior. Yet, in the context of its survival advantage, it may also be an evolutionary commitment to the pattern of aging. This raises the point that the long-living cells, the fixed postmitotic cells, particularly the brain neurons, although contributing to our remarkable longevity, also carry with them the germ of our demise by their loss of ability to replicate. Experiments currently conducted on transplanting cells into the brain from adrenal or other tissues for purposes of restoring function will undoubtedly point to the degree of reversibility of aging of vegetative and behavioral functions of the brain. Also, cell transplants have been used in hamsters to alter circadian rhythms, which points to the existence of a "master clock" in a particular nucleus, the suprachiasmic. Evidence from such research will increasingly define a richer biological background for studies of behavioral aging.

B. The Current Context

One of the strengths of the psychology of aging as a scientific endeavor is the diversity of its subject matter and methods. There appears to be an openness to accept contributions from a wide range of psychological investigations as well as from adjacent sciences. This bodes well for the future intellectual prosperity of the field. In 1977, Riegel believed that there was a convergence of science in gerontology and that gerontology had become the "intellectual vanguard for the behavioral and social sciences" (Riegel, 1977a, p. 88). He also believed that there was a convergence on a dialectical interpretation of life span development, that is, the outer determinants of behavior via social psychological and sociological influences and the interbiological foundations of behavior. He pointed out that an investigator who wants to integrate data on aging must analyze, and presumably explain, synchronization of sequences or their lack of synchronization over the adult years.

One of the pressures for theory is the current growth of the field, which is marked by an exponential growth in publications. About 500 items in psychological gerontology were published up to 1945. The literature doubled in each 10-year interval thereafter (Riegel, 1977a, p. 93). One consequence of this exponential growth of research and publications on the psychology of aging is that there has not been time to integrate concepts and findings. Also, the early psychologists entering the field had their previous experience in other areas of psychology. It is thus reasonable that they interpreted phenomena of aging in the light of theories of the subdisciplines of their backgrounds. As more investigators mature who have their primary research experience in the "phenomena of aging," it is to be expected that there will be more attempts at integration.

One of the influences on the expansion of research and the growth of publications has been the increased support of research on aging by federal agencies such as the National Institute on Aging, the National Institutes of Mental Health, the Administration on Aging, and others. Programmatic interests of the agencies as well as the rising economic implications of an aging population have not encouraged integrative theory.

Diffusion of interest in integrative theory of developmental processes results in part from the history of the National Institute of Child Health and Human Development (NICHD) in relation to the later established National Institute on Aging (NIA). When the NICHD was created in 1963, it reflected the life span point of view of its first director, Robert A. Aldrich, that it is necessary to look at processes throughout the life span and then apply what has been learned for the benefit of individuals of particular age levels. However, professional specialization and the preoccupations of investigators of specific age levels made it difficult to embrace the full life span in one institute. Social pressure led to the creation of the National Institute on Aging in 1975, only 12 years after the founding of the NICHD.

Professional services tend to be organized around the age of the population served, that is, fetus, newborn, preschool, school-aged children, adolescents, young adults, the middle aged, and old adults. This undoubtedly has had an influence on the research-knowledge generating system and on the relatively low interest in the development of theory and integration of knowledge across age levels.

C. Some Basic Questions

With the growth of interest in aging, there has been an increasing concern with the question, "How does behavior become organized over time?" In terms of the growth of psychology as a science, its early phase concentrated on establishing the building blocks of behavior. Perhaps psychology is now entering a later phase that will emphasize the interrelationship of these blocks over time. In this regard, one may regard the questions raised by the psychology of aging as a scientific advance in that they are broader and more dynamic than those of general psychology.

Another general question to be asked is, "What are the circumstances under which behavior becomes disorganized over time?" This question underlies research attempting to account for deficits in individuals. Given the increased frequency of deteriorative conditions in the elderly,

such as dementia, depression, cardiovascular and cerebrovascular disease, more professional emphasis is now placed on identifying the conditions of health and disease, in which behavior becomes disorganized.

IX. Integrative Theory

This *Handbook* reflects the current particulate or atomistic state of knowledge and the chapters present a great range of types of phenomena that may show changes of function with age that represent increases, declines, or stability. Furthermore, some of the phenomena may be reversible and others, irreversible. Given the early state of the science, it is not surprising that stereotypes and polar attitudes exist in society toward and by the aged. The aged can be regarded alternatively as kind or grouchy, wise or senile, active or inactive, or productive or a drain on the economy (see Crockett & Humbert, 1987). At the same time, the life satisfaction of older adults appears higher than that of young adults in many countries of the world (Butts & Beiser, 1987). Although we are learning more about age and abilities, the environments that favor or disadvantage older adults are not yet amenable to systematic explanation. Environments that require the use of experience and crystallized intelligence favor the performance of older adults. Salthouse (1987) pointed to the value of specific experience for the older person if it can translate into a current environmental task. Thus he noted "the molar equivalence or molecular decompensation of the performance of older adults." For example, older persons may show better memory for details after reading written texts; on the other hand, they may show less recall for main ideas (Meyer, 1987). Obviously, this differential pattern in performance must be placed in a broader context of the capacities of the organism and the requirements of its environment.

One term increasingly used in relation to aging is *compensation*. The older organism is presumed to maintain performance by compensating for deleterious changes in component processes. An older person may be expected to adapt to an environment if it requires previously learned skills and the opportunity of developing strategies for minimizing the consequences of deficits. However, a theory of compensation awaits future effort.

There seems to be little doubt that redundancy is the friend of the old. Specific experience and the opportunity for self-pacing of tasks favors the performance of older adults. On the other hand, external pacing embarrasses the older adult because of the tendency toward a molar slowing of behavior and diminished fluid intellectual abilities. The question of the ecological validity of psychological tests, the prediction of performance in real-life situations from laboratory or test assessments, is a current concern. Tests often do not measure lifelong adaptive styles and strategies or specific experience. Thus the assessment of an individual in an highly technical medical setting with a view to diagnosis will not be a very satisfactory predictor of the capacity of that individual for managing daily life in an independent residence. In addition to ecological validity of tests, there is an evolving ecological perspective in the psychology of aging that looks at the environmental context of the individual as well as at the individual's historical background and adaptive strategies.

Perlmutter, Adams, Berry, Kaplan, and Person (1987) have pointed out that older persons may react subjectively to memory performance that may further limit their ability. That is, memory failures may be a bigger threat to the self-esteem of an older person than to a younger adult. This leads to the proposition that there will be new views in the psychology of

aging of the dynamic organization of abilities and the antecedents of change as well as new views of the organization of acquired information.

Comprehensive research designs looking at the factor structure of both states and traits can include physiological, psychological, and social variables in the same matrix. An attempt to do this for age and attention was undertaken by Stankov (1988). His results indicated that in the later years, attentional processes, presumably related to physiological states, are highly related to fluid abilities but not significantly to crystallized abilities. Such designs not only continue in the style of experimental psychology by taking apart the organism to see the elements of behavior, but they also expand their objectives to examine how behavior becomes organized over long periods in the service of the living organism. In a similar way, the experiments on cognitive training by Willis and Schaie (1986) will lead to the delineation of what is modifiable and the extent to which it can be generalized to other areas of behavior.

Current methodological sophistication combined with an ecological approach to the life span seems to hold the potential for addressing some of these large questions of general interest, such as factors involved in individual longevity; predisposition to disease; the increasing longevity of women compared with men; social class; differences in habits of smoking, exercise, and diet; and patterns that lead to increasing or decreasing productivity with age and the demonstration of creativity and wisdom.

The emergence of integrative theory in the psychology of aging has been slow, perhaps because of the inherent complexity of the subject matter; underlying philosophical or ideological factors also may have been operating. An attempt to encourage theory development about change in the adult organism over the life span was undertaken through a year-long seminar at the Unversity of Southern California in 1986–1987 (Birren & Bengtson, 1988). Concepts from the humanities, the biological sciences, psychology, and the social sciences were juxtaposed.

Parallel to this effort on theory is an attempt to explore how advances in research impact on theory building. Schaie (1988) discussed research methodology and its influence on theory in three modes: (1) instrumentation, (2) research design, and (3) techniques of analysis. He examined two methodological developments that he believed have influenced theory, the age-cohort model in research design and confirmatory factor analysis in model testing. This suggests that theory building follows from sound methodological innovation in research (Salthouse, 1988). A complementary pathway also exists in which asking strong questions prompts methodological advances (Birren, 1988).

The present generation of psychologists has been trained either as social scientists or as biological scientists. This does not fit well the requirements of an ecological point of view and theory in which how we grow up and grow old is to be explained not only in terms of the human genome but in terms of the physical and social environments in which our heredity is expressed. Such a synthesis requires not only methodological sophistication and resources but investigators who are receptive to collaboration with other scientists.

One broad conception of the life span is in terms of the organism's capacity for self-regulation made possible by a highly developed nervous system (Birren, 1988, p. 161). In childhood, the individual moves in the direction of attaining increasing self-regulation in the biological, social, and psychological domains. As a result, the mature individual becomes more capable of regulating physiological processes and social interactions, as well

as internal behavioral processes such as thinking, emotions, and choices in the directions of behavior. Late in life, the capacity for self-regulation can be compromised but also compensated for. Perhaps with concepts such as these, we can explore aging with greater potential for robust generalizations about the genome's expression in particular physical and cultural environments.

Aging is a transformation of the structures and functions of the organism with a resulting decline in self-regulating biological, social, and behavioral capacities. It seems obvious that aging must proceed on the basis of the developmental processes that have evolved in the species and set limits for ontogeny in response to environmental characteristics. For these reasons Birren (1988) described his theoretical view of *aging as a counterpart of development;* closely related to development but not identical with it.

X. Conclusion

One cannot help but be impressed with the extensive recent growth of the research literature on the psychology of aging. It seems likely that merely out of the desperation of drowning in data, scholars and researchers will begin to develop theoretical and conceptual contributions that will provide an integrative matrix for our findings. This volume is itself a factor in reducing the patchwork quality of the subject.

Psychology itself is far from being an integrated science. To some extent this fragmentation was abetted by the past dominance by behaviorism that stressed *operationalism,* the definition of behavior in terms of the operations used in gathering the data. With the lessening of the influence of behaviorism and with encouragement of input from the adjacent disciplines of biology and sociology, it seems likely that the next decade will be an active one for theory. Contributions may also be expected from other sciences dealing with concepts of time and description of aging of complex systems.

In the previous edition of the *Handbook of the Psychology of Aging*, a metaphorical statement was used to express the significance of time in the organization of natural phenomena. "Time is the messenger of the gods, a messenger who passes through space, matter, and minds" (Birren & Cunningham, 1985, p. 3). This places time in a pervasive role in the organization and explanation of phenomena.

If an appropriate view of the human organism is that of a clock shop rather than of a single clock (see Schroots & Birren, this volume), future studies will be required to identify the conditions under which these clocks become autonomous or entrained. In terminal decline and in disease, there is entrainment in which previously autonomous processes become interlocked. When boundary conditions are exceeded, new relationships not continuous with the earlier states emerge. It is perhaps from such perspectives that the next phase of the psychology of aging may pursue its quest for broad causal relationships sought by Quetelet over a century and a half ago.

If the psychology of aging is as fertile a field of science as this volume suggests, general psychology will surely be heavily influenced by its dynamism. Furthermore, the principles of introductory psychology in the future will be taught in terms of development and aging rather than in terms of static elements of behavior.

References

Anderson, J. E. (1931). The methods of child psychology. In C. Murchison (Ed.), *A handbook of child psychology* (pp. 1–27). Worcester, MA: Clark University Press.

Baldwin, A. L. (1967). *Theories of child development.* New York: Wiley.

Bertalanffy, L. V. (1962). *Modern theories of development: In introduction to theoretical biology.* New York: Harper.

Birren, J. E. (Ed.). (1959a). *Handbook of aging and the individual.* Chicago: University of Chicago Press.

Birren, J. E. (1959b). Principles of research on aging. In J. E. Birren (Ed.), *Handbook of aging and the individual* (pp. 3–42). Chicago: University of Chicago Press.

Birren, J. E. (1961). A brief history of the psychology of aging. *The Gerontologist, 1,*69–77, 127–134.

Birren, J. E. (1988). A contribution to the theory of aging: As a counterpart of development. In J. E. Birren & V. L. Bengtson (Eds.), *Emergent theories of aging* (pp. 153–176). New York: Springer.

Birren, J. E., & Bengtson, V. L. (Eds.) (1988). *Emergent theories of aging.* New York: Springer.

Birren, J. E., & Cunningham, W. R. (1985). Research on the psychology of aging. In J. E. Birren & K. W. Schaie (Eds.), *Handbook of the psychology of aging,* 2nd Ed. (pp. 3–34). New York: Van Nostrand Reinhold.

Birren, J. E., & Renner, V. J. (1977). Research on the psychology of aging: Principles and experimentation. In J. E. Birren & K. W. Schaie (Eds.), *Handbook of the psychology of aging* 1st Ed. (pp. 3–38). New York: Van Nostrand Reinhold.

Birren, J. E., & Schroots, J. J. F. (1984). Steps to an ontogenetic psychology. *Academic Psychology Bulletin, 6,*177–190.

Bonner, J. T. (1958). *The evolution of development.* London & New York: Cambridge University Press.

Bronfenbrenner, U. (1977). Towards an experimental ecology of human development. *American Psychologist, 32,*513–531.

Buhler, C., Keith-Spiegel, P., & Thomas, K. (1973). Developmental psychology. In B. B. Wollman (Ed.), *Handbook of general psychology* (pp. 861–917). Englewood Cliffs, NJ: Prentice-Hall.

Butts, D. S., & Beiser, M. (1987). Successful aging: A theme for international psychology. *Psychology and Aging, 2,* 87–94.

Carmichael, L. (Ed.) (1946). *Manual of child psychology.* New York: Wiley.

Carmichael, L. (1951). Antogenetic development. In S. S. Stevens (Ed.), *Handbook of experimental psychology* (pp. 281–303). New York: Wiley.

Charness, N. (1988). The role of theories of cognitive aging: Comment on Salthouse. *Psychology and Aging, 3,* 17–21.

Comfort, A. (1956). *The biology of senescence.* London: Routledge & Kegan Paul.

Cowdry, E. V. (Ed.) (1939). *Problems of aging.* Baltimore: Williams & Wilkins.

Cowdry, E. V. (Ed.) (1942). *Problems of aging* (2nd ed.). Baltimore: Williams & Wilkins.

Crockett, W. H., & Humbert, M. L. (1987). Perceptions of aging and the elderly. *Annual Review of Gerontology and Geriatrics, 7,* 217–241.

Cunningham, W. R. (1987). Intellectual abilities and age. *Annual Review of Gerontology and Geriatrics, 7,* 117–134.

Dewey, J. (1939). Introduction. In E. V. Cowdry (Ed.), *Problems of ageing* (pp. XXVI–XXXIII). Baltimore: Williams & Wilkins.

Flugel, J. C., & West, D. J. (1964). *A hundred years of psychology.* London: Duckworth.

Frank, L. K. (1942). Foreword. In E. V. Cowdry (Ed.),*Problems of ageing* (pp XV–XXV). Baltimore: Williams & Wilkins.

Griffin, D. (1970). *Animal structure and function.* New York: H. R. & W.

Gruman, G. J. (1966). A history of ideas about the prolongation of life. *The American Philosophical Society Transactions, 56* (Part 9).

Hall, G. S. (1904). *Adolescence* (2 Vols.). New York: Appleton.

Hall, G. S. (1922). *Senescence: The second half of life.* New York: Appleton.

Harris, D. B. (Ed.) (1957). *The concept of development.* Minneapolis: University of Minnesota Press.

Hearnshaw, L. S. (1964). *A short history of British psychology.* London: Methuen.

Heilman, K. M., Watson, R. T., Valenstein, E., & Goldberg, M. E. (1987). Attention: Behavior and neural mechanisms. In V. B. Mountcastle, F. Plum, & S. R. Geiger (Eds.), *Handbook of physiology: Section 1: Neurophysiology* (pp. 461–481). Bethesda, MD: American Physiological Society.

James, W. (1900). *Psychology.* New York: Holt.

James W. (1902). *Talks to teachers on psychology.* New York: Holt.

Kantor, J. R. (1959). *Interbehavioral psychology.* Bloomington, IN: Principia Press.

Koch, S. (1959). *Psychology: A study of science.* New York: McGraw Hill.

Maier, H. W. (1969). *Three theories of child development.* New York: Harper.

Meyer, J. F. (1987). Reading comprehension and aging. In K. W. Schaie (Ed.), *Annual Review of Gerontology and Geriatrics, 7,* 93–115. New York: Springer Publishing Co.

Miles, W. R. (1931). Measures of certain abilities throughout the life span. *Proceedings of the National Academy of Sciences U.S.A. 17,* 627–633.

Miles, W. R. (1933). Age and human ability. *Psychological Review, 40,* 99–123.

Murchison, C. (Ed.) (1931). *A handbook of child psychology.* Worcester, MA: Clark University Press.

Perlmutter, M., Adams, C., Berry, S., Kaplan, M., & Person, D. (1987). Aging and memory. In K. W. Schaie (Ed.), *Annual Review of Gerontology and Geriatrics, 7,* 57–92. New York: Springer.

Peters, R. S. (1962). *Brett's history of psychology,* London: Allen & Unwin.

Pressey, S. L. (1939). *Life: A psychological survey.* New York: Harper.

Quetelet, M. A. (1835). Sur l'homme, et le développement de ses facultés. Paris: Bachelier (translated into English and published in Edinburgh in 1842; reprinted under the title, *A treatise on man,* in 1968 by Burt Franklin, New York).

Riegel, K. F. (1977a). History of psychological gerontology. In J. E. Birren & K. W. Schaie (Eds.), *Handbook of the psychology of aging* (pp. 70–102). New York: Van Nostrand Reinhold.

Riegel, K. F. (1977b). *The psychology of development and history.* New York: Plenum.

Riegel, K. F. (1978). *Psychology mon amour.* Boston: Houghton Mifflin.

Rowe, J. W., & Kahn, R. L. (1987). Human aging: Usual and successful. *Science, 237,* 143–149.

Royce, J. R. (1973). The present situation in theoretical psychology. In B. B. Wolman (Ed.), *Handbook of general psychology* (pp. 8–21). Englewood Cliffs, NJ: Prentice-Hall.

Sacher, G. A. (1959). Relation of lifespan to brain weight and body weight in mammals. *CIBA Foundation Colloquia on Ageing: The Lifespan of Animals*, pp. 115–133.

Salkind, N. J. (1985). *Theories of human development*. New York: Wiley.

Salthouse, T. A. (1987). The role of experience in cognitive aging. In K. W. Schaie (Ed.), *Annual Review of Gerontology and Geriatrics*, 7. New York: Springer Publishing Co.

Salthouse, T. A. (1988). Initiating the formalization of theories of cognitive aging. *Psychology of Aging*, 3, 3–16.

Schaie, K. W. (1988). The impact of research methodology on theory building in developmental sciences. In J. E. Birren & V. L. Bengtsen (Eds.), *Emergent theories of aging* (pp. 41–57). New York: Springer.

Schaie, K. W., Campbell, R. T., Meredith, W., & Rawlings, S. C. (Eds.) (1988). *Methodological issues in aging research*. New York: Springer.

Schaie, K. W., & Schooler, C. (Eds.) (1989). *Social structure and aging: Psychological processes*. Hillsdale, NJ: Erlbaum.

Schaie, K. W., Willis, S. L., Hertzog, C., & Schulenberg, J. E. (1987). Effects of cognitive training on primary mental ability structure. *Psychology and Aging*, 2, 233–242.

Schmidt, D. F., & Botwinick, J. (1989). A factorial analysis of the age de-differentiation hypothesis. In V. L. Bengtson & K. W. Schaie (Eds.), *The course of later life: Research and reflection* (pp. 87–92). New York: Springer.

Schroots, J. J. F. (1988). In growing, formative change and aging. In J. E. Birren & V. L. Bengtson (Eds.), *Emergent theories of aging* (pp. 299–329). New York: Springer.

Schroots, J. J. F., & Birren, J. E. (1988). The nature of time: Implications for research on aging. *Comprehensive Gerontology* (in press).

Stankov, L. (1988). Aging, attention and intelligence. *Psychology and Aging*, 3, 59–74.

Stevens, S. S. (Ed.) (1951). *Handbook of experimental psychology*. New York: Wiley.

Whipple, G. M. (1910). *Manual of mental and physical tests*. Baltimore: Warwick & York.

Whipple, G. M. (1914, 1915). *Manual of mental and physical tests. Part I: Simpler processes, Part II: Complex processes*. Baltimore: Warwick & York.

Willis, S. L., & Schaie, K. W. (1986). Training the elderly on the ability factors of spatial orientation and inductive reasoning. *Psychology and Aging*, 1, 187–194.

Wolman, B. B. (Ed.) (1973). *Handbook of general psychology*. Englewood Cliffs, NJ: Prentice-Hall.

Woodworth, R. S. (1938). *Experimental psychology*. New York: Holt.

Yates, F. E. (1982). Outline of a physical theory of physiological systems. *Canadian Journal of Physiology and Pharmacology*, 60, 217–248.

Yates, F. E. (1988). The dynamics of aging and time: How physical action implies social action. In J. E. Birren & V. L. Bengtson (Eds.), *Emergent theories of aging* (pp. 90–127). New York: Springer.

Two

Latent Variable Growth Models for Research on Aging

J. J. McArdle and Edward Anderson

I. Introduction

This chapter is a discussion about old research designs on aging and novel longitudinal data analyses. We present a small set of data on aging, including multiple age cohorts measured on multiple variables, and we analyze these data using some new mathematical and statistical modeling techniques. These analyses demonstrate how some new models might be used to provide answers for some old developmental questions. We discuss some limitations and extensions of these data designs and modeling analyses for our understanding of aging processes.

A. Previous Handbook Chapters

Previous volumes of the *Handbook of Aging* contained special chapters devoted to methodology. Schaie (1977) presented details on the complexities of introducing rigorous experimental design features into studies of aging. Of special relevance here is Schaie's call for "naturalistic controls for explanatory alternatives to the age dif-

ference hypothesis" (p. 42). Nesselroade (1977) pursued change concepts based on multivariate methods: "The appeal of the multivariate orientation . . . can be recognized at . . . the definition of pertinent concepts, especially change-related ones, as profiles or patterns of a set of measures, rather than in terms of single measures" (p. 59). Nesselroade also clarified the crucial distinctions between "invariance and stability of factors, and pattern versus level differences" (p. 65).

In the second *Handbook of Aging*, Nesselroade and Labouvie (1985) combined both quasi-experimentation and multivariate perspectives. They suggested "developmental/gerontological research and theory are defined as the study of behaviors B, that can be systematically linked to age, A, for some selected age interval . . . and some selected individuals, *i*. Descriptively, the functions *Bi(A)* expressing such relationships represent sets that are ordered along the age dimension" (p. 46). In the same volume, Schaie and Hertzog (1985) extended some of their earlier work to include linear structural equa-

Handbook of the Psychology of Aging, Third Edition
Copyright © 1990 Academic Press, Inc. All rights of reproduction in any form reserved.

tion models based on "maximum likelihood methods for testing structural hypotheses about the form of observed covariance matrices." At several points they also suggested that "it may well be timely to delve further into the complexities of what has become know as 'functional age'—that is, the substantiation of an age related but substantively grounded index" (p. 64).

The organization and form of this chapter follows the methodology chapters presented in the two prior *Handbook of Aging* volumes. Most of these prior ideas are restated and used here, especially the definition of aging as a functional relation between age and behavior. Except for a few classic sources, we only cite research published in the 1980s. Much of the work we use emphasizes the mixture of the recent advances in *structural equation modeling* (abbreviated as SEM) with *functional models of development*.

B. Linear Structural Equation Model Building·

The acronym LISREL has become a popular way to label all SEM-related research, but it actually refers to a popular computer program used for SEM analyses (in Joreskog & Sorbom, 1979, 1986; but see Fraser & McDonald, 1988). The mixture of classical SEM theory with the new LISREL program has spurred a lot of interest in longitudinal data analysis (e.g., Nesselroade & Baltes, 1979). The SEM approach allows the rigorous specification and estimation of developmental theory in terms of variables and their relations. Recent examples in aging are overviewed by Campbell and Mutran (1982), Hertzog (1987), and Alwin (1988). These presentations describe standard LISREL models, and these kinds of articles are useful as prerequisites for this discussion.

Most of the prior SEM presentations are based on the simultaneous analysis of factor analytic measurement models and

time-series structural models. Only a few recent models also include factor mean changes over time (e.g., Horn & McArdle, 1980; Joreskog, 1979). In broad terms, these SEM organizations allow tests of the patterns of changes in the coefficients over time, and SEM or LISREL is usually discussed as:

Causal modeling, or structural-equation analysis, is being developed rapidly by sociologists, economists, psychologists, and statisticians. . . . The main purpose of such techniques is to build and test causal representations of phenomena that are not experimentally tractable. (Baltes, Cornelius, & Nesselroade, 1979, p. 83)

C. The Developmental Function Approach

Figure 1A presents a plot of some research data to be analyzed here. These data plot a single measurement of intellectual ability measured on four age groups over a 12-year longitudinal study (from Botwinick & Siegler, 1980). It follows that the SEM we might choose to analyze these data would be based on some aspect of the longitudinal time flow, the ages at testing, and other variables. Latent variable cross-lagged SEMs for these kinds of cohort-sequential data have been presented by Horn and McArdle (1980). But when we have these kind of data we often ask, "What else can be done with longitudinal SEM?" As we will show here, there are many choices we can make about the longitudinal structural models of developmental change and growth.

One theme we can follow comes from the well-known research, "The Age Variable in Psychological Research" by Wohlwill (1970, 1973). In this work, Wohlwill weaves an interesting tale about developmental methods that has implications for most SEM research on aging:

The widespread tendency [is] to consider age as an independent variable, comparable to others employed in differential research, and to

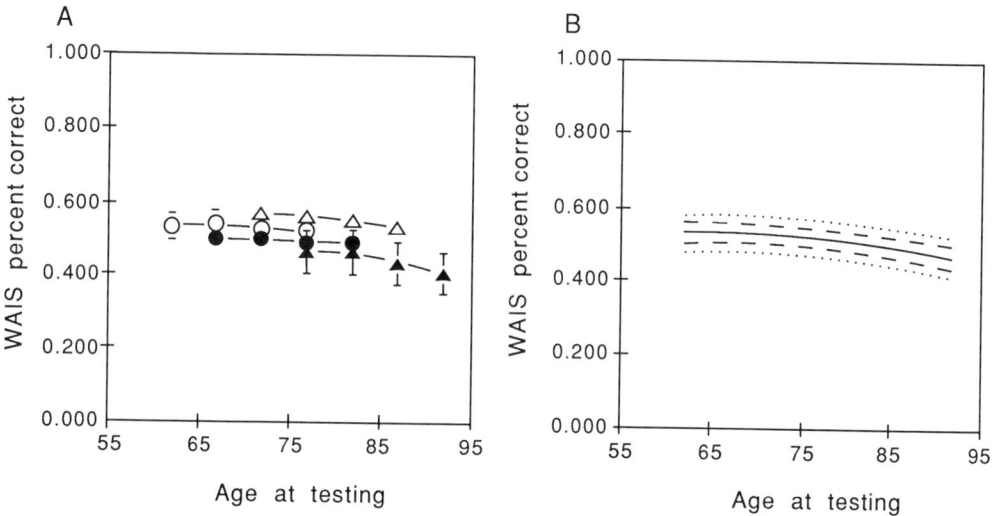

Figure 1 Selected longitudinal data and models. (A) TOTAL-WAIS scores for four groups (from Botwinick and Siegler, 1980; data in Table I). (B) A convergent latent growth curve (Model #Fa of Table II).

study age *differences* rather than age *changes*. An alternative view is presented, which treats developmental questions as analogous to other phenomena involving changes in behavior over time. Age is looked at as a dimension along which behavior changes are to be traced, forming part of the definition of the dependent variable in developmental studies. This dependent variable is to be defined in terms of specified aspects or parameters of the function describing the changes which occur with age for a given behavioral variable. (Wohlwill, 1970, p. 49)

Following this view we might be interested in plotting a functional relation between individual behavioral changes and age. Figure 1B is a plot of a theoretical model of this kind of developmental function. In this model the group average curve over age is indicated by the heavy line in the center, and the individual differences around this group average are bounded by the 95% confidence limits. An additional confidence limit is included at each time point. These are not connected because these are used to describe error of measurement specific to a particular testing session. Essentially, this representation (1B) appears to be a

visual smoothing of the growth curves of Figure 1A. This is one way to model a single developmental function running through all our data.

It is not immediately obvious how we can model this simple visual analogy within the context of a structural equation model. One possible approach follows a theme adumbrated by Horn (1972):

The central concept of the multivariate meta-theory is that of *functional unity*, as defined by Cattell. . . . A functional unity is indicated by a configuration—a pattern—of processes which are themselves distinct but are integral parts of more general process. To distinguish a functional unity from a mere collection of distinct processes it is necessary to show that the processes work together—that they rise together, fall together, appear together, disappear together, or, in general, covary together. . . . A functional unity is thus a rather high level of abstraction. In operational terms it can be defined in a number of ways. One of the simplest such definitions is that furnished by the methods of factor analysis. According to this definition a functional unity is indicated by the set of variables which go together in the sense of correlating in a way that defines a particular factor. (pp. 161–162.)

In this view, a common factor is a functional relationship. This means we can model a developmental function as a factor of repeated observations over time. One model that can provide such a data analysis tool has been termed a *latent growth model* or *LGM*. This model is drawn as a path diagram in Figure 2 (for more diagram details, see McArdle & Epstein, 1987).

Some researchers have already used these functional ideas in aging research. Among others, Horn and McArdle (1980) examined the use of latent variable means, time-staggered age groups, and age-appropriate constraints in models. In these SEMs we examine age changes in group parameters. Meredith and Tisak (1984, 1989) went one step further by estimating and evaluating the preceding LGM as a SEM. This SEM approach allows age changes in group and individual scores. In other work on this topic, we have used the LGM in path models (McArdle & Epstein, 1987), longitudinal behavioral genetics (McArdle, 1986), missing data convergence models (McArdle, Anderson, & Aber, 1987; McArdle, 1988c), and multivariate models (McArdle, 1988a).

In the rest of this chapter we overview this latent variable structural modeling approach to longitudinal data on aging. We limit these models to data analysis that can be accomplished using traditional data designs and current SEM computer programs (e.g., LISREL, COSAN). We also use these illustrations to highlight some key problems for the design and data analysis of research on aging.

II. Methods for Latent Growth Model Analyses

In this section we describe some mathematical and statistical issues arising from the need to analyze the data of Figure 1. Strictly speaking, we only require available structural modeling techniques such as LISREL or COSAN. But these analyses also require several nonstandard devices, so we try to explain these specific requirements here. This section is not intended to be overly technical, but some readers may wish to turn to the results section first (section III, p. 29).

A. Selected Univariate Cohort-Sequential Data

The data of Figure 1 are based on the design and analyses reported by Botwinick and Siegler (1980). In this research, four age cohorts were selected from the classic Duke Longitudinal Study (DLS). At the initial testing the four groups were aged 60 to 63, 64 to 67, 68 to 71, and 72 to 75. These age groupings were chosen so that the time of measurement and age of testing were approximately *staggered*. By this term we mean the average age of the first group at the second measurement is approximately the average age of second group at the first measurement, and so on. More details on the sampling procedures and the measurement techniques are presented by Botwinick and Siegler (1980).

For the purpose of our analysis, we included four age cohorts with a total N-87 measured over the four longitudinal occasions. To simplify this presentation further we created a single unweighted composite of the 11 WAIS subscales. All raw subscale scores were divided by their maximum possible score to obtain a "percent correct" score, and this score was averaged to form a single composite score henceforth called Total-WAIS. In Figure 1A we present the means and 95% confidence boundaries for each of the four groups measured over four occasions of measurement. Both longitudinal means and cross-sectional means are plotted against the age of testing to demonstrate the design overlap. In Table I we present the means standard deviations, and correlations for all four groups on the single composite score.

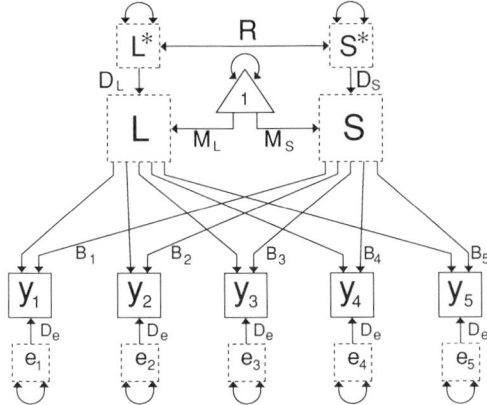

Figure 2 A structural path diagram of a latent growth curve model. Graphic key: (1) solid boxes represent observed variables; (2) dashed boxes (or circles) represent unobserved variables; (3) one-headed arrows are asymmetric regressions; and (4) two-headed arrows are symmetric cross-products (e.g., covariances). Latent growth model key: (1) The variables are $Y(t)$ = observed scores at Time t, L = levels, S = slopes, L^* = standardized levels, S^* = standardized slopes, $E(t)$ = error at Time t, and 1 = constant. (2) The parameters are $B(t)$ = basis loadings at Time t representing constants of proportionality or "shape," Ml = mean of levels, Dl = standard deviation of levels, Ms = mean of slopes, Ds = standard deviation of slopes, R = correlation of levels and slopes, and De = standard deviation of errors at Time t.

B. The Latent Growth Curve Model

The model of Figure 2 is termed a *latent growth curve* because the basic parameters describe a systematic pattern of individual differences in change over time. In the LGM of Figure 2 we assume that n =1 to N individuals have been measured on t=1 to T occasions on one variable termed Y, and we write

$$Y(t,n) = L(n) + B(t)\, S(n) + E(t,n). \quad (1)$$

In this SEM the observed scores $Y(t,n)$ for each individual n at each time point t come from three unobserved sources of individual differences: (1) $L(n)$ are *level* scores that are the same across all occasions t, (2) $S(n)$ are *slope* scores that are

weighted by a set of *basis coefficients* $B(t)$, and (3) $E(t,n)$ are the *error* or disturbance factors. We also make a few additional statistical assumptions about the latent variables (for complete details see McArdle & Epstein, 1987, McArdle, 1988a). The common factors of level L and slope S are allowed means Ml and Ms, deviations Dl and Ds, and correlation, Rls. The error variables have deviations De but are assumed to have mean zero and are uncorrelated with all other factors. The latent variables L and S provide a structure for the time series of the repeated variables $Y(t)$, for t=1 to T.

The parameters of these models describe both the group change and the individual change over time. The curve presented in Figure 1B shows an organization that includes group characteristics, such as the average growth curve, as well as individual characteristics, such as the variation around the average growth curve. The mean of the latent-level variable (termed Ml), the mean of the latent slope variable (termed Ms), and the basis shape (termed $B(t)$), are parameters that reflect the deterministic or group change pattern. Alternatively, the deviations around the means for the latent levels (Dl), and latent slopes (Ds), as well as the correlation of level and slopes (Rls), reflect the stochastic individual differences around this group change pattern. The error variables $E(n)$ are specific to each occasion, uncorrelated over occasions, and have mean zero, so the deviation (De) accounts for individual differences that are independent over time. All parameters of the growth curve are depicted in the path diagram of Figure 2.

Model 1 is a typical confirmatory factor analysis model except for a few important differences. In this model we restrict the loadings of the first factor L to be a value of 1 at all occasions. But we also allow the loadings $B(t)$ of the second factor S to change with time. We usually interpret these $B(t)$ coefficients relative to the age of testing $A(t)$, or the occasion of

Table I
Observed Statistics on WAIS-Total Score from Duke Longitudinal Study[a]

Means for Four Groups

	Age at Testing						
Age Group	62	66	70	74	78	82	86
62 (N = 25)	53.5	54.1	52.5	51.9	*	*	*
66 (N = 28)	*	49.7	49.9	48.7	48.6	*	*
70 (N = 25)	*	*	56.9	56.2	55.2	52.9	*
74 (N = 9)	*	*	*	46.1	45.9	42.8	40.0

Standard Deviations for Four Groups

	Age at Testing						
Age Group	62	66	70	74	78	82	86
62 (N = 25)	18.1	17.5	16.9	17.9	*	*	*
66 (N = 28)	*	16.7	17.1	16.8	17.5	*	*
70 (N = 25)	*	*	12.9	11.8	12.8	13.0	*
74 (N = 9)	*	*	*	18.3	19.2	18.0	17.2

Correlation Matrices for Four Groups

		Age at Testing						
Age Group		62	66	70	74	78	82	86
62 (N = 25)	62	1.000						
	66	.981	1.000					
	70	.973	.985	1.000				
	74	.946	.963	.963	1.000			
	78	*	*	*	*	*		
	82	*	*	*	*	*	*	
	86	*	*	*	*	*	*	*
66 (N = 28)	62	*						
	66	*	1.000					
	70	*	.983	1.000				
	74	*	.983	.981	1.000			
	78	*	.976	.962	.976	1.000		
	82	*	*	*	*	*	*	
	86	*	*	*	*	*	*	*
70 (N = 25)	62	*						
	66	*	*					
	70	*	*	1.000				
	74	*	*	.974	1.000			
	78	*	*	.954	.964	1.000		
	82	*	*	.879	.903	.941	1.000	
	86	*	*	*	*	*	*	*
74 (N = 9)	62	*						
	66	*	*					
	70	*	*	*				
	74	*	*	*	1.000			
	78	*	*	*	.966	1.000		
	82	*	*	*	.957	.985	1.000	
	86	*	*	*	.878	.938	.962	1.000

[a]From Botwinick and Siegler, 1980.
Note: All scores scaled as percentage correct of Maximum Score; asterisk denotes data missing by design structure.

measurement $O(t)$, or to some restrictive combination of both $A(t)$ and $O(t)$. This means the pattern of the loadings of the basis $B(t)$ reflects the shape of the underlying developmental function. The measurements of variables $Y(t)$ do not change over time, so these are not factors of variables—instead, these latent variables are *factors of time*.

C. Latent Growth Model Hypotheses

The LGM model allows one component of variance L for the intercept or level and another one, S, for the time-based slope. These two latent scores for each individual are parameters that combine to form each individual's linear curve. Of course the individual curves may not all be linear, or the collection of curves may not be completely characterized by two components of individual differences organized in this way. This model is restrictive, so it does not automatically fit any set of longitudinal data. This property is important because it allows us to test hypotheses about the underlying pattern of growth and decline.

In order to form hypotheses about the LGM, we need a few more technical details about the model. For any set of longitudinal data we can form the expected values of the means $My(t)$ and covariances $Cy(t,t+d)$ of variable $Y(t)$ over time (for details see McArdle, 1988a). The hypotheses for the standard deviations and correlations among particular time points work precisely the same way as any covariance-based factor model—the variances for any variable are formed by the predictions about the model at each time point t, and the covariances are the product of the loadings between time points t and $t+d$. Also, the means Ml and Ms in this model need to follow the basic pattern of change seen in the correlations and variances. That is, for any set of longitudinal data, we assume the means $My(t)$ and covariances

$Cy(t,t+d)$ of variable $Y(t)$ over time are proportional. The $B(t)$ parameters are included in all the expectations for the means, deviations, and correlations. Without doubt, the most critical parameters of the model are the basis coefficients $B(t)$; these are the *constants of proportionality over time*.

This LGM is equivalent to a two common-factor covariance-based model except here the level and slope factors are assumed to have means Ml and Ms. The inclusion of factor means is an unusual requirement in a factor model, but means are essential here. Indeed, this strict proprotionality relationship between the means and the covariances makes the model substantially different than other factor analysis models. The combination of these assumptions provides statistical expectations for the LGM to be derived using linear algebra representations as expected values of average cross-products, or moments. More technical details are provided by McArdle (1986, 1988a) and also Meredith and Tisak (1989).

D. Additional Statistical Issues

The statistical basis of LGM estimation and testing is developed from well-known structural equation theory. In general, the preceding model expectations are compared to the model observations of Table 1, and we compute a chi-square value based on *likelihood ratio criterion* (LRC). The *degrees of freedom* (DF) for any model come from restrictions placed on the parameters of the model expectations. As usual, values of LRC that are large compared to their associated DF reflect a misfit between the model expectations and the data observations.

A statistical concern arises because our model needs to be fitted to both means and covariances. One popular way to do this is to enter a moment matrix of raw cross-products with an additional unit variable (drawn here as a closed triangle). This implies that *maximum likelihood* estimates (MLE) and goodness-of-fit indexes are based on a likelihood function defined such that the expectations for the means are added onto the usual expectations of the covariances. This is unusual for structural equation models, but it is required to test the assumptions of this model. The fit of the means is defined by the multivariate mean difference usually termed Hotelling's T^2. All indexes of fit need to be evaluated in this context (for more details see Joreskog & Sorbom, 1986; McArdle, 1986, 1988a).

A second statistical issue arises because the data of Table 1 have been collected on four independent age cohorts and the groups are measured at different times. The path diagram in Figure 3 illustrates our solution to this problem. In Figure 3 we assume the same path model in all groups, but each dataset is assumed to have different latent or hidden variables $X(t)$. These hidden variables act as surrogates for the missing data and are simply treated as any other latent variable in any other model. This puts us in a position to test hypotheses about convergence across separate groups by using standard techniques for testing the *invariance of factor loadings across groups.*

The statistical analysis of the multiple group LGM can be accomplished using available computer software, such as LISREL. These basic ideas were used by Horn and McArdle (1980) within an autoregressive context and were also used by Joreskog and Sorbom (1981) with a different structural model (for more details, see McArdle, 1988a; McArdle & Epstein, 1987). Many other researchers have used a similar statistical approach for the estimation of missing data (i.e., Allison, 1987; Little & Rubin, 1987; Muthen, Kaplan, & Hollis, 1987; Rock, 1982), but this presentation most closely follows the models of Meredith and Tisak (1984, 1989).

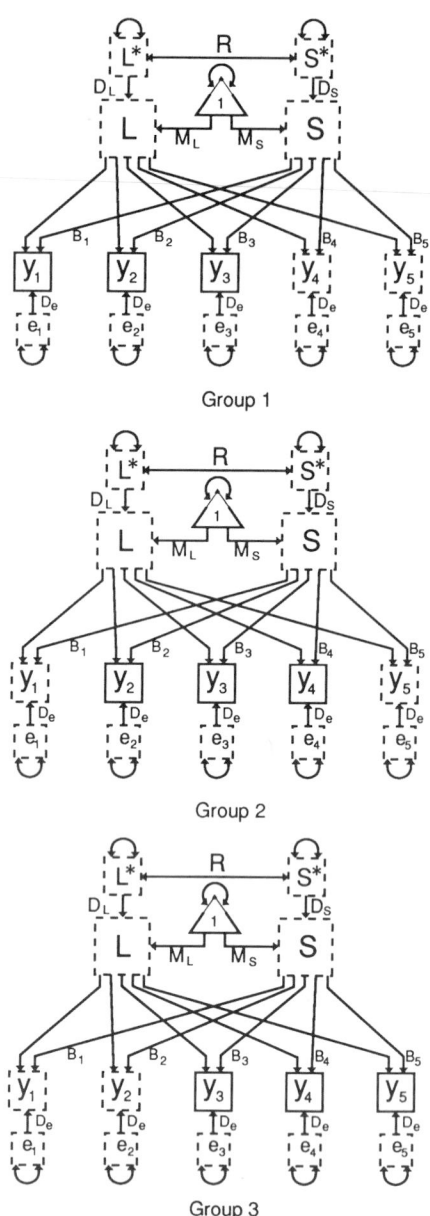

Figure 3 A multiple group convergence model based on missing data patterns. (Notes: All groups drawn here have scores on three time points and are missing data at two time points. Missing data given by dashed boxes around $Y(t)$. For more details see the graphic key and model key of Figure 2.)

III. Results of Latent Growth Models

In Table II we list some numerical results for various latent growth models fitted to the WAIS data of Table I. In Table III we present some additional statistical comparisons of the goodness of fit of these models to the data.

A. Fitting a No-Growth Baseline Model

In the first model, we assume no change occurs over age or time in these data. In this version of the LGM we explicitly assume

$$Y(t,n) = L(n) + E(t,n), \qquad (2)$$

and we only allow one mean Ml, one common deviation Dl, and one error deviation De. This model explicitly requires $Ms=0$, $Ds=0$, and $B(t)=0$, and this simplifies the expectations for the means and covariances of Table I. If the multiple group data conform with this simple model, then no further change models need to be fitted.

The first column of Table II is labeled $\#N$ and gives the numerical results of the no-growth model fitted to the WAIS data of Table II. The only nonzero parameters in this model are the $Ml=51.5$, $Dl=15.9$, and $De=3.4$. These parameters can be interpreted to mean: (a) on the average all groups obtain a mean score of about 52% of the possible WAIS score, (b) individual variation around this group average is relatively large (with a standard deviation of 15.9% points), and (c) the error variance at any one time is small (with a standard deviation of 3.4 percent points). The function is flat or level over age because we have modeled the restriction by forcing the shape $B(t)=0$. The fit of this highly restrictive model to these data obtains an $LRC=134$ on $DF=53$. This statistic has a normal Z-value of $Z=5.66$ that indicates this model is highly unlikely for these data. This model is usually used as a base-line or starting point (see Sobel & Bohrnstedt, 1985).

B. Fitting a Linear Age-Basis Model

Next we consider the more complex model where $B(t)$ bears some relation to chronological age. A restricted version of the LGM can be written as

$$Y(t,n) = L(n) + Ba(t) Sa(n) + E(t,n), \qquad (3)$$

where we define $Ba(t)$ is some function of the age at testing $A(t)$ of the groups.

In a first model, let us assume the shape coefficients $Ba(t)$ are fixed to be proportional $Pa(t)$ of the age at testing $A(t)$. The average ages at testing here are approximately $A(t) = [62, 66, 70, 74, 78, 82, 86]$. This means we can define the differences between all ages and the first time point as $dA(t) = A(t)-A(T) = [0, 4, 8, 12, 16, 20, 24]$. Usually we also scale these differences in ages so they are normalized relative to some specific time point. If we write $Pa(t) = dA(t)/A(T) = [0, .166, .341, .502, .659, .840, 1.00]$, then $Pa(t)$ represents the proportion of the total age scale up to the t-th point in time. This rescaling of age is identical to a fixed contrast coefficient of the traditional linear repeated measures MANOVA model $P(t) = [\%_7, \frac{1}{7}, \frac{2}{7}, \frac{3}{7}, \frac{4}{7}, \frac{5}{7}, \frac{6}{7}]$ (see Bock, 1979). If there were unequal age intervals between testings we would still follow the same plan.

The column labelled $\#Pa$ in Table II gives numerical values for the free parameters. The latent variable means are estimated with mean level $Ml = 54.0$ and mean slope $Ms = -5.5$. So, on the average over all ages, the individuals correctly answer 54% of the maximum possible score, and over this 24-year period the individuals lose about 5.5% of the scores. This is a loss of about ¼ of a WAIS percent point for each year of age.

The latent standard deviations also are estimated, and these show substantial individual differences. The level standard

Table II
Maximum Likelihood Estimates for Multiple Age-Staggered Group Models

Alternative Growth Model

Model Parameters	#N, no growth	#Pa, linear age	#Fa, latent age	#Po, linear occasions	#Fo, latent occasions	#PaPo, linear and linear	#PaFo, linear and latent	#FaPo, latent and linear	#FaFt, latent and latent
Latent Age Loadings									
Sa → Y(62) :=Ba(1)	.0==	.0==	.0==	.0==	.0==	.0==	.0==	.0==	.0==
Sa → Y(66) :=Ba(2)	.0==	.166==	.112*	.0==	.0==	.166==	.166==	.084*	-.163*
Sa → Y(70) :=Ba(3)	.0==	.341==	.151	.0==	.0==	.341==	.341==	.136*	-.097*
Sa → Y(74) :=Ba(4)	.0==	.502==	.288	.0==	.0==	.502==	.502==	.261*	-.008*
Sa → Y(78) :=Ba(5)	.0==	.659==	.390	.0==	.0==	.659==	.659==	.344*	.148*
Sa → Y(82) :=Ba(6)	.0==	.840==	.666	.0==	.0==	.840==	.840==	.632	.519
Sa → Y(86) :=Ba(7)	.0==	1.0==	1.0==	.0==	.0==	1.0==	1.0==	1.0==	1.0==
Latent Occasion Loadings									
So → Y(t1) :=Bo(1)	.0==	.0==	.0==	.0==	.0==	.0==	.0==	.0==	.0==
So → Y(t2) :=Bo(2)	.0==	.0==	.0==	.33==	.121*	.33==	.176*	.33==	-.077*
So → Y(t3) :=Bo(3)	.0==	.0==	.0==	.67==	.449	.67==	.488*	.67==	.300
So → Y(t4) :=Bo(4)	.0==	.0==	.0==	1.0==	1.0==	1.0==	1.0==	1.0==	1.0==
Latent Means									
1 → L :=M1	51.5	54.0	53.6	52.9	51.4	55.1	52.7	53.5	52.1
1 → Sa :=Ma	.0==	-5.5	-6.8	.0==	.0==	-9.0*	-.2*	-8.6*	-4.2*
1 → So :=Mo	.0==	.0==	.0==	-2.7	-2.7	1.8*	-2.7*	.5*	-.7*
Latent Age Deviations									
L* → L :=Dl	15.9	16.4	16.3	16.1	15.3	18.7	-16.6	16.3	16.0
Sa* → Sa :=Da	.0==	8.9	11.1	.0==	.0==	26.5*	14.1*	7.7*	11.8
So* → So :=Do	.0==	.0==	.0==	4.6	4.9	4.5	4.8*	0.0*	-3.1
E* → E :=De	3.4	2.5	2.4	2.5	2.4	2.5	2.2	2.4	2.2
Latent Variable Correlations (bounded between +1 and −1)									
L* ↔ Sa* :=Rla	.0==	-.26	-.21*	.0==	.0==	-.63*	.35*	-.50*	.02*
L* ↔ So* :=Rlo	.0==	.0==	.0==	-.02*	.04*	.91*	-.42*	1.0*	-.06*
Sa* ↔ So* :=Rao	.0==	.0==	.0==	.0==	.0==	-.45*	-.86*	1.0*	-.76
Latent Level Loadings									
L → Y(t) :=Bl(t)	1.0==	1.0==	1.0==	1.0==	1.0==	1.0==	1.0==	1.0==	.0==
Goodness of Fit Indexes									
Likelihood ratio	134	68	46	67	54	65	48	44	37
Degrees of freedom	53	50	45	50	48	46	44	41	39
Normal Z-value	5.7	1.7	.2	1.6	.7	1.8	.5	.4	-.2

Notes: Model fitted to four group data of Table I; mean and deviation parameters have been fully equated over all groups whereas loadings have been partially equated over some groups; asterisk indicates parameter not different from zero by MLE < 2 * SE[MLE].

Table III

Overall Goodness of Fit for Univariate Convergence Hypotheses for WAIS-TOTAL Score

Step-Down Hypotheses Tests about Model Differences (convergent models only)

Model Fitted	Convergent LRC	(DF)	Z	Null Difference LRC	(DF)	Z	First Difference dLRC	(dDF)	Zd
#N: No growth	134	(53)	5.7	0	(0)	0	0	(0)	0
#Pa: Linear age	68	(50)	1.7	66	(3)	6.9	0	(0)	0
#Fa: Latent age	46	(45)	.2	88	(8)	7.5	22	(5)	3.2
#Po: Linear time	67	(50)	1.6	67	(3)	7.0	0	(0)	0
#Fo: Latent time	54	(48)	.7	80	(5)	7.4	13	(2)	2.9
#PaPo: Linear & linear	65	(46)	1.8	69	(7)	6.6	0	(0)	0
#PaFo: Linear & latent	48	(44)	.5	86	(9)	7.3	17	(2)	3.5
#FaPo: Latent & linear	44	(41)	.4	90	(12)	7.2	4	(3)	6.4
#FaFo: Latent & latent	37	(39)	−.2	97	(14)	7.3	7	(2)	1.9

Hypotheses Tests about Group Convergence ("?" indicates identification problem)

Model Fitted	Convergent LRC	(DF)	Z	Not Convergent LRC	(DF)	Z	Difference dLRC	(dDF)	zd
#N: No growth	134	(53)	5.7	108	(44)	4.98	26	(9)	2.9
#Pa: Linear age	68	(50)	1.7	43	(32)	1.33	26	(18)	1.3
#Fa: Latent age	46	(45)	.2	22?	(12)	1.78?	24?	(33)	−1.2?
#Po: Linear time	67	(50)	1.6	42	(32)	1.22	25	(18)	1.2
#Fo: Latent time	54	(48)	.7	22	(24)	−.20	32	(24)	1.1
#PaPo: Linear & linear	65	(46)	1.8	20	(16)	.77	45	(30)	1.8
#PaFo: Linear & latent	48	(44)	.5	15?	(8)	1.57?	33?	(36)	−.3?
#FaPo: Latent & linear	44	(41)	.4	14?	(−4)	?	?	(?)	?
#FaFo: Latent & latent	37	(39)	−.2	6?	(−12)	?	?	(?)	?

Notes: LRC = likelihood ratio criterion; DF = degrees of freedom; Z = normal Z value; dLRC = difference in LRC; Zd = normal Z of difference in LRC.

deviation $Dl = 16.4$, so, on the average over all ages, the individuals vary about 16.4% units in each direction. The standard deviation of slopes is $Da = 8.9$, so, at all occasions, the individuals vary around the shape mean by 8.9 percent units in each direction. The deviation of the errors is $De=2.5$, and this is required to be equal over all time points. The correlation of level and shape scores, $Rla = -.26$, is small.

This model is not exactly a MANOVA model. We have used the principles of the fixed contrast vector from MANOVA logic to make explicit predictions about the means and covariances. However, we also have staggered these expectations so that the $Pa(t)$ are required to be the equal for any group measured at any specific age $A(t)$. These constraints often are hard to parameterize in a simple MANOVA model, and these effects are not equivalent to the full and often arbitrary set age-by-occasion interaction effects (e.g., McCrae, Arenberg, & Costa, 1987, p. 133). This staggered age basis represents a very specific age-by-occasion interaction term. This is the mathematical hypothesis that the function is linear over age while ignoring occasions. This is the visual hypothesis that the data of Figure 1A can be organized with a single set of lines like Figure 1B. The statistical hypothesis test of Table II shows this model obtains a fit of $LRC=68$ on $DF=50$ with a $Z=1.69$. We do not doubt that this model fits these data fairly well. More formally, we cannot detect any departures from this linear age model in these data.

C. Fitting a Latent Age-Basis Model

The previous model used a basis with a fixed parameter restriction. There are many other choices we might consider as alternatives. For example, we could set some of the parameters equal to zero and others equal to one and fit a developmental step function. Other fixed basis parameters $P(t)$ follow the usual rules of contrast analysis in MANOVA. But suppose, instead, we want to find a set of $B(t)$ parameters that reflect an optimal patterning over occasions for the changes in the scores. In this approach we estimate the $B(t)$ like a factor loading from a factor analysis model.

This empirical estimation of $B(t)$ leads to a few more mathematical and statistical identification problems. As in the typical factor analysis case, at least one entry of the $B(t)$ needs to be fixed at, say, $B(1)=0$, and another at, say, $B(T)=1$. This is a somewhat arbitrary choice, but this fixed interval scaling provides a reference point for the estimation of other free parameters $B(t)$. Because the other parameters $B(2)$ to $B(T-1)$ are allowed to be freely estimated, we still end up with an empirically based nonlinear shape for the whole curve.

This latent variable approach we are now suggesting has an interesting interpretation: This is a rubber ruler, as it were, that stretches or reshapes the observed time scale at a new time scale so the new latent slopes $S(n)$ are maximally linear. The freely estimated $B(t)$ reflects a "metameter" or "latent time" scale (see Rao, 1958; Tucker, 1966; McArdle, 1988a). The interpretations of this new latent scale are usually facilitated by a comparison with the observed scale. In substantive terms, the $B(t)$ reflects a

developmental function with maximum fit to our data.

The results of this model are listed under model #Fa of Table 2. The estimated shape parameters $Ba = [0, .11, .15, .29, .39, .67, 1]$ and their first difference, $dBa = [0, .11, .04, .14, .10, .28, .28]$ can be compared to an equal age interval step where $dPa = .14$ (or $\frac{1}{7}$). Here we see relatively small changes between the ages of 62 and 78, but these are followed by relatively dramatic changes between ages 78 and 86. The means in this model show a starting point of $Ml=53.6$ and $Ma=-6.8$. This depicts a curve that averages out at 54% at age 62, and this is followed by a proportional loss of 6.8 percent points over the 24-year period. One crucial substantive aspect of this model is that the changes are not equal across all ages.

The parameters of this model have already been plotted as Figure 1B. This visual display shows this LGM to be a single decline function with a varying influence at each year of age. This latent age-basis model fits these data with $LRC=46$ on $DF=45$ and $Z=.17$, and this is a very good fit once again. Also, the difference between the linear age model and this latent age model is indexed by the difference in fit between the linear model #Pa and this model #Fa. This difference yields a $dLRC=22$ on $dDF=5$, so the move up to a nonlinear shape $Ba(t)$ costs five parameters, but it represents a significant improvement in fit.

The unobserved factor scores $S(n)$ in this model reflect the individual differences in the change over age. These slopes are individual *rates of change* over the entire 12-year testing period. Yet these scores are interpreted in the same way as factor scores from any factor analysis. Because the single factor of shape is estimated from the data, we posit that this shape is the most likely organizing function for all individual curves. The slope scores are themselves latent, but they reflect how much the individuals' curve looks like the group curve. All individual curves will be drawn with the same basic shape defined by $B(t)$, but they will be different by the multiplier or amplitude $S(n)$. If the component score $S(n)$ =1.0 then the individuals curve equals the group curve. Alternatively, if the score $S(n)$ is low, say .25, then the individuals curve is much lower than the group curve. In this model, both of these individuals are assumed to have curves of the same shape. The factor scores also have the same benefits and problems here as in any factor analysis (see Browne, 1987; McDonald, 1985).

D. Fitting Occasion-Basis Models

Next we consider the effect of the structural restriction written as

$$Y(t,n) = L(n) + Bo(t) So(n)$$
$$+ E(t,n), \qquad (4)$$

where $Bo(t)$ reflects a developmental function of the occasion at testing $O(t)$ of the groups. Because all groups were tested four times at 3 years apart, we presume the parameters $Bo(t)$, $Mo(t)$, and $Do(t)$ are precisely equal over all four groups. This model ignores the actual age at testing $A(t)$ and instead tries to account for all changes as an occasion-based or retest phenomenon only.

The first model fit presumes the growth is linear over occasions $O(t)$ by forcing the basis $Bo(t)$ to be a *fixed* linear function of occasions $O(t)$. There are many choices of scaling the basis, but here we force $Bo(t) = Po(t) = \{[O(t)-O(T)]/O(T)\}$ $= [0, \frac{1}{3}, \frac{2}{3}, 1]$. This fixed proportional basis $Po(t)$ reflects the equal 4-year differences between occasions and makes the level component equal to the first occasion of measurement. Again, this model is precisely the linear polynomial model of repeated measures MANOVA (as in Bock, 1979) and all other interpretations follow in the same way.

The results from this linear occasion

model are presented in the #Po column of Table II. These results give the means as Ml=52.9 and Mo=−2.7. This linear change over age starts at 53% at the first occasion followed by a slight decline of 2.7% points over the 12-year testing period. Although this Mo is small, it is statistically significant and because the basis $Po(t)$ is linear, this change is the same for all occasions of measurement. This Mo parameter reflects the same loss of about ¼ points per year of measurement. Because this is a loss over occasions of measurement and not a gain over testings, it is unlikely to be an effect of retesting. The deviations Dl=16.1 and Do=4.6 index the individual differences in these levels and slopes. The correlation index $Rlo^{1/2} = Dlo$ = −.02 and the error deviation De=2.5 are small. The fit of this model obtains LRC =67 on DF=50.

In the occasions model (Equation 4) we also can allow the curve basis $Bo(t)$ to take on a pattern based on the empirical data. The #Fo model of Table II uses the factor analysis model to define a latent time scale for occasions. The main difference between this model and the previous linear model is that here we have estimated some of the shape parameters $Bo(2)$=.12 and $Bo(3)$=.45. These small model changes seems trivial at first, but the new LRC=54 with DF=48; thus these small differences may be worthy of further explanation.

As before, the restriction of $Bo(1)$=0 provides a required starting point. But now the estimated $Bo(2)$=.121 rather than Po (2)=.333. This means the growth between occasions 1 and 2 was about ⅓ as large as expected by a linear change over time. Following a similar logic, the function is approximately linear between Time 2 and Time 3 and shows the most change during the last two occasions. A plot of this pattern over occasions of measurement would show a curve that is flat between the first testing to the second, increases in rate between Occasions 2 and 3, and then rises steeply during Occasions 3 and 4. Again, because the mean *Mo* is negative, this is a decline function. This *Mo* parameter reflects a loss of ¼ points per year, but now this loss is most rapid during the last two times of measurement and is less apparent at the earlier times.

This curve is coincident with occasions of testing so it might reflect the effects of retesting. But these effects are negative, and this decline only begins to appear at the last few occasions. Alternatively, we might interpret this curve as the effect of a date-of-testing cohort: All individuals are steady between the calendar years (1962 to 1966) but then decline in the last few years (1969 to 1973). In this data design the potentially different influences associated with retesting time and calendar time are totally confounded, and there is no way to separate these interpretations. Also, of course, these could simply be age effects obscured by our new occasions basis.

E. Fitting both Occasion-Basis and Age-Basis Models

We have examined models in which change was viewed either as a function of age at testing or as a function of occasion at testing. However, these axes are not strictly confounded in this cohort-sequential dataset so we may be able to examine these functions simultaneously. In these cases we may wish to write a model such as

$$Y(t,n) = L(n) + Ba(t) Sa(n) \\ + Bo(t) So(n) + E(t,n), \quad (5)$$

where both occasions of testing $O(t)$ and age of testing $A(t)$ influences are assumed to create means, variance, and covariance in the observed scores. In this model we have three curve components: The first component is a level L, the second component is a slope Sa based on $Ba(t)$ which is some function of age of testing $A(t)$, and

the third component is a second slope So based on $Bo(t)$ that is some function of occasion of testing $O(t)$. In a single group of data where all subjects were measured on the same number of consecutive occasions, these slopes Sa and So would be perfectly correlated. However, the staggering apparent in the cohort-sequential data design allows these parameters to be separable and the Ba and Bo can be estimated from the same data. This model (Equation 5) parallels part of Cattell's (1970) treatment of multiple curves. This model is drawn as a path diagram in Figure 4. We next fit it to the data of Table I.

The numerical results of model #PaPo of Table II shows a mixed model where the basis $Ba(t)=Pa(t)$ and $Bo(t)=Po(t)$ are both fixed to be linear with their respective time scales. The parameters of this model yield $Ml=55.1$, $Mo=-9.0$, and $Ma=1.8$. The model parameters imply the prediction of any observed mean is based on a linear combination of the starting point average of 55.1 points at age 62 and Time 1, plus a $\%_{24} = .375$ point loss for each additional year since the first age, plus a $1.\%_{12} = .150$ point gain for each additional year since the first occasion. These numerical results also show substantial individual differences, $Dl=18.7$, $Da=26.5$, $Do=4.5$, $De=2.5$, and substantial correlations among these time axes. This model fits these data very well with $LRC=65$ on $DF =46$, but some of these are not significantly different from zero (with asterisks).

This pattern of results is interesting—the WAIS scores go down with age but about half of this decline is counteracted by a slight gain with retesting or calendar year. Unfortunately, several model parameters have large standard errors, and this is primarily a feature of the data design structure. Because age and occasion of measurement are partially correlated design features, these means are estimates of the orthogonal aspects of each dimension of time. Unfortunately, the

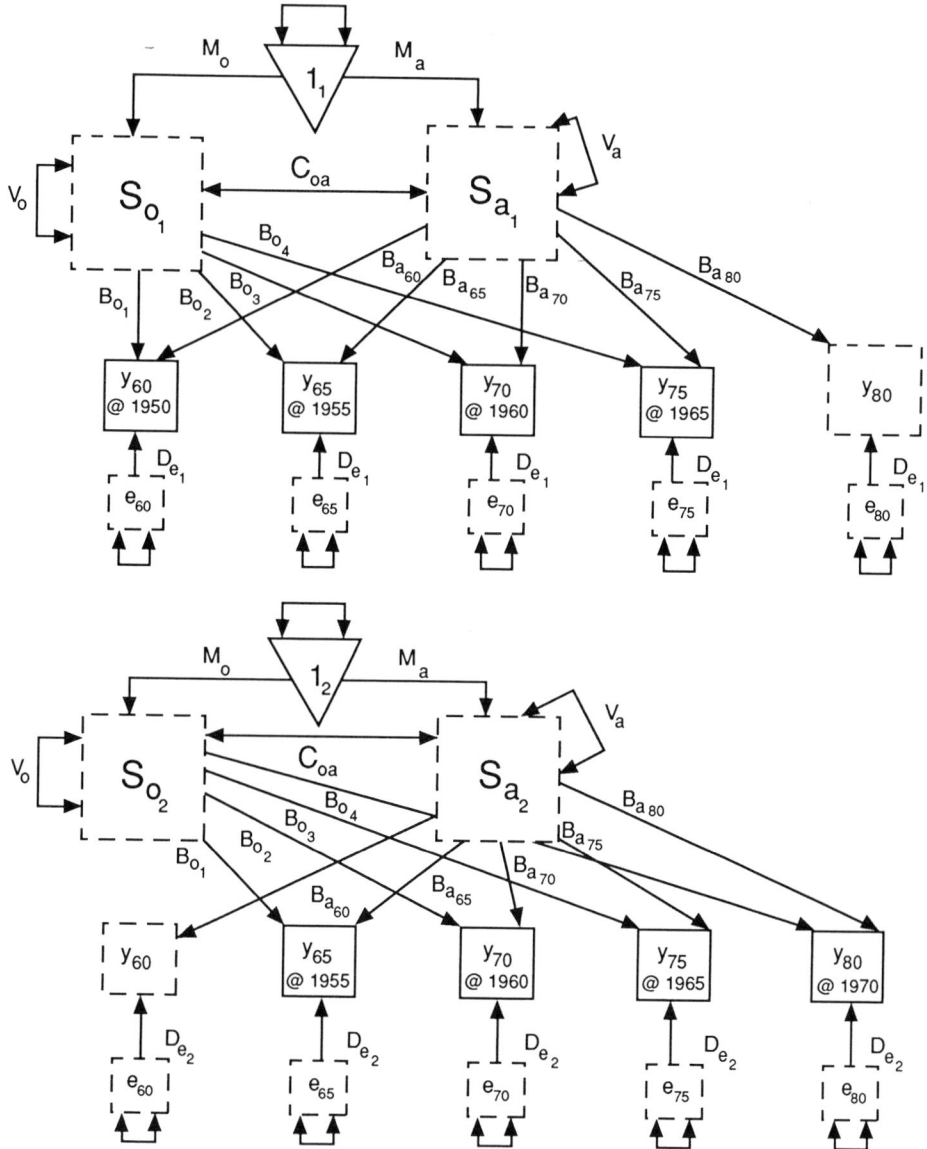

Figure 4   A multiple curve latent growth model for staggered groups. (Notes: All groups drawn here have scores on four time points and are missing data at one time point. The component $Sa(n)$ reflects age effects because the basis $Ba(t)$ is based on age at testing. The component $So(n)$ reflects occasions effects because the basis $Bo(t)$ is based on occasion at testing. The level L component is not drawn here but is fitted in most models of Table III. Missing data given by dashed boxes around $Y(t)$. For more details, see the graphic key and model key of Figure 2).

age groupings and time of measurements are not staggered as far apart as they could be, and this results in high collinearity of age-of-testing and occasion-of-testing dimensions and corresponding poor (i.e., widely ranging) statistical estimates. We do not solve this difficult problem here, but we simply explore a few more relaxed model alternatives.

In the last three models we examined combinations of linear and latent basis functions for both age-based and occasion-based time axes. The model labeled *#PaFo* fits a linear age function *Pa(t)* combined with a latent occasions function *Fo(t)*. The results seem to be linear with respect to age and not significant with respect to occasions. The next model labeled *#FaPo* fits a latent age function *Fa(t)* combined with a linear occasions function *Po(t)*. The results seem to be latent with respect to age, except the shape it is not as steep, and occasions are not significant. In the final model labeled *#FaFo*, we estimate a dual latent function—the latent age function *Fa(t)* is combined with a latent occasions function *Fo(t)*. Here each of the components *Sa(n)* and *So(n)* serve as the location parameter for the other curve. This model obtains estimates for age that are very flat until the last few ages, and the occasions basis seems to be flat until the very end also.

In general, these more complex models fit the data very well, but many key parameters are not significant; these models are probably overparameterized. In many cases, a model such as Figure 4 with both latent *Fa(t)* and *Fo(t)* is *empirically not identified*. In these cases, there is not enough separation of the time axes in the original data collection to estimate both latent functions simultaneously. This kind of experimental design issue usually cannot be overcome by statistical devices.

F. Testing Overall
   Convergence Hypotheses

The models of Table II were all estimated and fit to the data of Table 1 by assuming that some parameters were *invariant* over some groups. This approach combines the cross-sectional and longitudinal information into a single curve, and this makes the model mathematically and substantively interesting. However, the idea of a single curve is a hypothesis that in and of itself can be rejected. We use the term *convergence* (after Bell, 1953) to indicate a model where the longitudinal and cross-sectional data components provide the same information. Because these age groups may be different in many different ways, this analysis can have many substantive implications for later work.

These comparative questions are examined in Table III and the differences in fit can be summarized easily. The restrictive models of limited growth all show a relatively poor convergence over groups, but the relaxed age-based models show almost complete convergence. For example, the no-growth model #N fits over all groups with $LRC=134$ on $DF=53$ but fits each group separately with $LRC=108$ on $DF=44$. The difference in fit due to the additional convergence restrictions is indexed by a $dLRT=26$ on $dDF=9$ with a $dZ =2.9$. This means a flat curve over occasions is probably not the same for each group. Alternatively, the latent age model #Fa fits over all groups with $LRC=46$ on $DF=45$ and fits each group separately with $LRC=22$ on $DF=12$. The differences due to convergence of the latent age model are trivially small with $dLRT=24$ on $DF=33$. This implies all between-group age effects converge with all within-group age-based effects. Although this result can be seen for the means in the plot of Figure 1B, this principle applies to the covariances as well.

This statistical strategy and these kind of modeling results are mainly used to illustrate the basic structural modeling approach to longitudinal data analysis. We conclude here that the developmental function is not flat, not linear, has little occasion-based effects, and is best considered to be latent within these age ranges. Some of these models also demonstrate the obvious complexity in mixing models relating latent variables within the age by occasions matrix. Further technical details on this analysis can be found in the more detailed treatment of Little and Rubin (1987).

IV. Discussion of Latent Growth Models

The previous LGM analyses illustrate some of the strategic uses of the SEM approach for aging research. There are many difficult problems that we need to overcome. The key benefit of this approach comes from its flexible extension to other problems of developmental interest. So, to wrap up, we now discuss a few latent growth modeling problems and extensions.

A. Current Problems in Structural Equation Modeling

There are many problems in contemporary structural modeling that we have not discussed in any detail. The selection of the best model for any set of data is a complex issue without a clear resolution. This problem is often discussed as an issue of statistical power (as in Matsueda & Bielby, 1986) or of the choice of an appropriate goodness-of-fit index (see Marsh, Balla, & McDonald, 1988). If alternative models require only a few parameters, we will not need many replications (e.g., individuals) to examine their differences. Some of the convergence models we illustrated earlier fall into this category, so $N =87$ seemed adequate. However, many LGM extensions require a large number of parameters and, hence, a large numbers of subjects (see Overall, 1987).

The issue of data design complexity is related to this problem as well. Rogosa and Willett (1985) showed how a linear growth process cannot be distinguished from an autoregressive model when the growth parameters are not large enough. In general, the age-by-occasion design structure of the longitudinal and cross-sectional data collection has important implications for our ability to distinguish between models. Many of the problems we faced in the separation of age of test-ing, occasion of testing, and the interpretation of other effects are long-standing problems in research on aging (see Horn & McArdle, 1980; Schaie, 1977, 1986). We have reoriented this old ANOVA problem to be a problem of contemporary factor analysis; here the issues of identification, rotation, and selection effects are active research topics.

Most available structural programs only allow a block-structured approach to the analysis of age groupings, selection effects, and so on. For example, retest effects are often built into data collection designs as random variables, but they are often not treated in this way (McCrae et al., 1987). Our current LISREL-based approach is inadequate for dealing with the full complexity of most developmental data collections. These are concepts of continuous variation so we need to move away from these overly rigid structural techniques toward models for continuous variation in individual trajectories (as in Bock & Thissen, 1980, Vandenberg & Falkner, 1965; Woodbury and Manton, 1983). The availability of post-LISREL computer programs (e.g., Jardine & Martin, 1984; Little & Rubin, 1987; Goldstein, 1986) will no doubt change the way we analyze and think about data.

The techniques we have described require interval level measurement for all the dependent variables. This is often not possible in applied situations where binary or categorical data are more likely. One structural solution is based on a conjoint scaling approach based on canonical regressions (Bagozzi, Fornell, & Larker, 1981). A number of more complete but complex solutions have been proposed for the problem of dynamic analysis for categorical variables (see Featherman & Petersen, 1986; Schoenberg, 1986; Zeger, Liang, & Self, 1985). As in our functional factor analysis models, these dynamic models all bear a formal resemblance to item-level factor analysis models and novel computer programs (see Browne,

1987; Heckman, 1981; McDonald, 1983; Muthen *et al.*, 1987).

These problems all point to the need for high-quality data merged with high-quality models. As always, there is a need to be cautious about new and unreplicated claims of new research findings. But these cautions are not specific to the LGM approach, or any structural modeling, for that matter. To the contrary, these problems apply to ANOVA, regression, and factor analysis with equal force. Often structural equation models use less parameters and overcome measurement and statistical biases that are not at all obvious to the casual user of multiple ANOVAs. Perhaps the main benefit of all new structural models is that they once again raise these old unresolved problems. These cautious comments are simply a reflection of the state of the art in design and data analysis.

B. Extensions for Research on Aging

Can the LGM analysis approach meet the objectives of research on aging? One way to examine this question is to define these objectives and extend the LGM approach to meeting these objectives. Baltes and Nesselroade (1979) outline these issues under five "objectives of longitudinal research":

- Direct identification of intraindividual change
- Direct identification of interindividual differences (similarity) in intraindividual change
- Analysis of interrelationships in behavioral change
- Analysis of causes (determinants) of intraindividual change
- Analysis of causes of interindividual differences in intraindividual change

The first rationale of the longitudinal method identifies an entity-specific analysis of change as *the* foundation of devel-

opmental research. (Baltes & Nesselroade, 1979, p. 23). The LGM illustrations and extensions meet this objective by making a formal description of the individual change patterning. The basis shape $B(t)$ is a group change characteristic but the slope $S(n)$ is an individual change variable. By using this basic model we can examine extensions including more complex growth models and other, more complex data collections. More complex models include exponential, quadratic, autoregressive parameters, and nonlinear factor score distributions have been examined by Bock and Thissen (1980), Browne (1987), Keats (1983), and McArdle (1988b).

"The second rationale of longitudinal research requires the comparison of change processes for the different entities (e.g., individuals) under developmental investigation" (p. 24). The LGM approach meets this objective by combining information from many different data sources, by allowing the structured comparison of different curves for different groups, and by providing for more complete studies of nonrandom subject selection. Models that permit a statistical correction in the shape due to age-related or score-related attrition are complex, but these models are critically important to our understanding of underlying aging processes. More detailed treatments of these and other models may be found in Allison (1987), Berk and Ray (1982), Little and Rubin (1987, see pp. 158–161), Siegler and Botwinick (1979), and Woodbury and Manton (1983).

"The third rationale for longitudinal research is related to the identification of the interrelationships among classes of behavior during development" (p. 25). The LGM approach meets this objective by allowing the addition of a classical factor analytic measurement model as well as the direct multivariate analyses of the slope correlations. The key question of factorial invariance can be a testable hypothesis within the context of repeated measures and factor curves. Details on these models are given by Horn, McArdle, and Mason (1983), Meredith and Tisak (1982), Nesselroade (1983), McArdle (1988a,c), and McArdle and Cattell (1989). Other models based on a simple patterning of the variable curves can be used to define a complex but invariant structure of the multivariate dynamics (in McArdle, 1988a).

The fourth rationale is similar. "Intraindividual development extends over time. Explanation of a phenomenon that extends over time requires establishing linkages between outcome variables (consequents) and determining factors, which also extend over time and which, as antecedent, precede the phenomenon. Thus a time-ordered study of change needs to be supplemented by a time ordered study of explanatory determinants" (p. 26). The LGM approach meets this objective when we examine structural differences between groups and effects on curves, and when we include time-based effects within growth models. The idea that an experiment or an intervention might have an effect on the way individuals change is certainly an interesting substantive hypothesis (as in McArdle & Epstein, 1987; McArdle, 1988c). Behavioral genetic designs offer strong possibilities for the isolation of genetic and nongenetic effects on the latent slopes (see Vandenberg & Falkner, 1965; Loehlin, 1979; McArdle, 1986; McArdle & Goldsmith, 1988). More highly structured developmental questions about amplitude and phase differences require more complex models (see McArdle, 1988c).

"A fifth rationale for longitudinal analysis follows from the possibility that causes for intraindividual change differ for entities (individuals). . . . The need to recognize differential patterns of causation applies both to the extreme situation, where identical intraindividual-change processes are observed for two individuals, and to the more usual situation; that is, the causal analysis of interindividual differences in change" (p. 27). The LGM approach meets this objective when we combine group characteristics to an explicit experimental design structure or time series ordering, and especially when we examine change on many variables and groups.

These LGMs may be used to compare multiple curves within a group. As a crude example here, we might wish to split these individuals on WAIS-Verbal and WAIS-Performance (Botwinick & Siegler, 1980). The two variables may be two measures of intellectual ability, or they may be a psychological variable and a biological marker of health. In either case, we are interested in their interrelationships. Additional restrictions upon these curve patterns allows us to test a variety of important hypotheses. In a first model we might ask, "Do the curves for Y and X look the same?" This can be done by requiring parallel variable parameters to be invariant. That is, we might force $Msy=Msx$ and $By(t)=Bx(t)$, and so on. These are extrinsic hypotheses about the shapes of the curves. In a more complex model, we might ask about amplitude and phase differences. The concept of the same curve in a different phase may be especially important in the timing of a system (McArdle, 1988b).

These multivariate models permit the formation of explicit hypotheses about both extrinsic and intrinsic age changes. Baltes (1987) provides an interesting substantive hypothesis about "gain/loss ratios" in adult development that can be formulated in this way. In many datasets we have two variables X and Y both measured over at least two separable periods of time; for example, childhood and adulthood. Given these data we can examine a more complex variation of causal inference using aspects of the *cross-lagged design* (Cook & Campbell, 1979, Gollob & Reichardt, 1987; Hertzog & Nesselroade, 1987). This classical model of causal inference can be combined within the LGM framework (see McArdle, 1988c). Another multivariate alternative is the *Factor-of-Curves* (FOCUS) model; this model can be used to summarize the correlated features of multivariate developmental processes (for an example, see McArdle, 1988a). The overall advantages of using these kinds of multivariate models of aging processes have been discussed by Nesselroade (1977).

C. Modeling Aging Dynamics with Latent Variables

The LGM approach has many problems and many extensions. We believe it meets the objectives of developmental research because it is a relatively free-form developmental model with lots of potential extensions. In this treatment we have suggested a few possible combinations that can be easily implemented using available computer software.

The use of different SEM techniques reflects a compromise between substantive issues about development and the available aging data. The typical choice between autoregression or difference-score SEM is a good example here. For instance, the autoregressive SEM is a good choice if we are interested in systematic covariation over time where changes randomly bounce back to some central average (e.g., as in "states"). Conversely, the difference SEM is a good choice when we think changes may be correlated with other aspects of growth (e.g., as in "traits"). Both of these models allow "simplex" patterns, albeit of different forms (see McArdle, 1988c; also see Gollob & Reichardt, 1987; Hertzog & Nesselroade, 1987; Horn & McArdle, 1980; Schaie & Hertzog, 1982, 1985). A paper by Arminger (1986) presents an interesting reparameterization of the LISREL autoregressive coefficients into differential equation coefficients.

The LGMs presented in this chapter seem to us to be like the ANOVA of the new generation of aging researchers. They should be regarded with the same applause and criticism as the ANOVA models of any other generation. These LGM are very old—they seem to us to follow the proposals of Bell (1953), Meredith (1964), Schaie (1965, 1977), Wohlwill (1970, 1973), Cattell (1970), Horn (1972), and Nesselroade (1977, 1983). These previously complex theoretical models are now formally clear and simple to apply. We hope researchers can use these techniques to observe aging processes that have previously remained unobserved.

Acknowledgments

The ideas presented here are the direct result of discussions with Mark Aber, Dick Bell, John Horn, John Nesselroade, and Bill Meredith. We also thank Ron Abeles, Paul Baltes, and David Featherman for their support, and Ilene Siegler for the use of the DLS-WAIS data. This research has been funded by the National Institute on Aging (AG07137). Requests for reprints should be sent to either author at the Department of Psychology, University of Virginia, Charlottesville, VA 22903.

References

Allison, P. D. (1987). Estimation of linear models with incomplete data. In C. C. Clogg (Ed.), *Sociological methodology* (pp. 71–103). San Francisco: Jossey-Bass.

Alwin, D. F. (1988). Structural equation modeling in research on human development and aging. In K. W. Schaie, R. T. Campbell, W. Meredith, & S. C. Rawlings (Eds.), *Methodological issues in aging research* (pp. 71–170). New York: Springer.

Arminger, G. (1986). Linear stochastic differential equation models for panel data with unobserved variables. *Sociological Methodology*, **16**, 187–213.

Bagozzi, R. P., Fornell, C., & Larcker, D. F. (1981). Canonical correlation as a special case of structural relations model. *Multivariate Behavioral Research*, **4**, 437–454.

Baltes, P. B. (1987). Theoretical propositions of life-span developmental psychology: On the dynamics between growth and decline. *Developmental Psychology*, **23**, 5, 611–626.

Baltes, P. B., Cornelius, S. W., & Nesselroade, J. R. (1979). Cohort effects in developmental psychology. In J. R. Nesselroade & P. B. Baltes (Eds.), *Longitudinal research in the study of behavior and development* (pp. 61–88). New York: Academic Press.

Baltes, P. B., & Nesselroade, J. R. (1979). History and rationale of longitudinal research. In J. R. Nesselroade & P. B. Baltes (Eds.), *Longitudinal research in the study of behavior and development* (pp. 1–40). New York: Academic Press.

Bell, R. Q. (1953). Convergence: An accelerated longitudinal approach. *Child Development*, **24**, 145–152.

Berk, R. A., & Ray, S. C. (1982). Selection biases in sociological data. *Social Science Research*, **11**, 352–398.

Bock, R. D. (1979). Univariate and multivariate analysis of variance of time-structured data. In J. R. Nesselroade & P. B. Baltes (Eds.), *Longitudinal research in the study of behavior and development* (pp. 199–231). New York: Academic Press.

Bock, R. D., & Thissen, D. (1980). Statistical problems of fitting individual growth curves. In F. E. Johnston, A. F. Roche, & C. Susanne (Eds.), *Human physical growth and maturation: methodologies and factors* (pp. 265–290). New York: Plenum.

Botwinick, J., & Siegler, I. (1980). Intellectual ability among the elderly: Simultaneous cross-sectional and longitudinal comparisons. *Developmental Psychology*, **16**(1), 49–53.

Browne, M. W. (1987). Robustness of statistical inference in factor analysis and related models. *Biometrika*, **74**, 375–384.

Campbell, R. T., & Mutran, E. (1982). Analyzing panel data in studies of aging. *Experimental Aging Research*, **4**(1), 3–41.

Cattell, R. B. (1966). *Handbook of multivariate experimental psychology*. Chicago: Rand McNally.

Cattell, R. B. (1970). Separating endogenous, exogenous, ecogenic, and epogenic component curves in developmental data. *Developmental Psychology*, **3**(2), 151–162.

Cook, T. D., & Campbell, D. T. (1979). *Quasi-experimentation: Design and analysis issues for field settings*. Chicago: Rand McNally.

Featherman, D. L., & Peterson, T. (1986). Markers of aging: Modeling the clocks that time us. *Research on Aging*, **8**(3), 339–365.

Fraser, C., & McDonald, R. P. (1988). COSAN: Covariance structure analysis. *Multivariate Behavioral Research*, **23**, 263–265.

Goldstein, H. (1986). Multilevel mixed linear model analysis using iterative generalized least squares. *Biometrika*, **73**(1), 43–56.

Gollob, H. F., & Reichardt, C. S. (1987). Taking account of time lags in causal models. *Child Development*, **58**, 80–92.

Heckman, J. (1981). Statistical models for discrete panel data. In C. F. Manski & D. McFadden (Eds.), *Structural analysis of discrete data with econometric applications* (pp. 114–178). Cambridge, MA: MIT Press.

Hertzog, C. (1987). Applications of structural equation models in gerontological research. *Annual Review of Gerontology and Geriatrics*, **7**, 265–294.

Hertzog, C., & Nesselroade, J. R. (1987). Beyond autoregressive models: Some implications of the trait-state distinction for structural equation modeling of developmental change. *Child Development*, **58**, 93–109.

Hertzog, C., & Schaie, K. W. (1988). Stability and change in adult intelligence: 2. Simultaneous analysis of longitudinal mean and covariance structures. *Psychology & Aging*, **3**(2), 122–130.

Horn, J. L. (1972). State, trait and change dimensions of intelligence. *The British Journal of Educational Psychology*, **42**(2), 159–185.

Horn, J. L., & McArdle, J. J. (1980). Perspectives on mathematical/statistical model building (MASMOB) in research on aging. In L. W. Poon (Ed.), *Aging in the 1980's: Selected contemporary issues in the psychology of aging* (pp. 503–541). Washington, DC: American Psychological Association.

Horn, J. L., McArdle, J. J., & Mason, R. (1983). When is invariance not invariant: A practical scientist's look at the ethereal concept of factor invariance. *The Southern Psychologist*, **1**(4), 179–188.

Jardine, R., & Martin, N. G. (1984). No evidence for sex-linked or sex-limited gene expression influencing spatial orientation. *Behavior Genetics*, **14**(4), 345–354.

Joreskog, K. G. (1979). Statistical estimation of structural models in longitudinal-developmental investigations. In J. R. Nesselroade & P. B. Baltes (Eds.), *Longitudinal research in the study of behavior and development* (pp. 303–350). New York: Academic Press.

Joreskog, K. G., & Sorbom, D. (1979). *Advances in factor analysis and structural equation models*. Cambridge, MA: Abt.

Joreskog, K. G., & Sorbom, D. (1981). *Simultaneous analysis of longitudinal data from several cohorts*. Research Report 80-5, Dept. of Statistics, University of Uppsala, Sweden.

Joreskog, K. G., & Sorbom, D. (1986). *LISREL-VI program manual*. Chicago: International Educational Services.

Keats, J. A. (1983). Ability measures and theories of cognitive development. In H. Wainer & S. Messick (Eds.), *Principals of modern psychological measurement*. Hillsdale, NJ: Erlbaum.

Little, R. T. A., & Rubin, D. B. (1987). *Statistical analysis with missing data*. New York: Wiley.

Loehlin, J. C. (1979). Combining data from different groups in human behavior genetics. In J. R. Royce & L. P. Mos (Eds.), *Theoretical advances in behavior genetics*. The Hague: Sijthoff & Noordhoff.

Marsh, H. W., Balla, J. R., & McDonald, R. P. (1988). Goodness-of-fit indices in confirmatory factor analysis: The effect of sample size. *Psychological Bulletin*, **103**(3), 391–410.

Matsueda, R. L., & Bielby, W. T. (1986). Statistical power in covariance structure models. In N. B. Tuma (Ed.), *Sociological methodology* (pp. 120–158). San Francisco: Jossey-Bass.

McArdle, J. J. (1986). Latent growth within behavior genetic models. *Behavior Genetics*, **16**(1), 163–200.

McArdle, J. J. (1988a). Dynamic and structural equation modeling with repeated measures data. In J. R. Nesselroade & R. B. Cattell (Eds.), *Handbook of multivariate experimental psychology* (Vol. II). New York: Plenum.

McArdle, J. J. (1988b). Structural models of developmental theory in psychology. *Annals of Theoretical Psychology*, **VI**, Developmental Psychology (in press).

McArdle, J. J. (1988c). Structural modeling experiments using multiple growth functions. In P. Ackerman, R. Kanfer, & R. Cudeck (Eds.), *Learning and individual differences: Abilities, motivation, and methodology* (pp. 71–117) (in press).

McArdle, J. J., Anderson, E., & Aber, M. S. (1987). Convergence hypotheses modeled and tested with linear structural equations. *Proceedings Public Health Conference on Records and Statistics, National Center for Health Statistics, Hyattsville, MD* 347–352.

McArdle, J. J., & Cattell, R. B. (1989). Structural equation modeling applied to confactor and parallel proportional profiles *Multivariate Behavioral Research* (in press).

McArdle, J. J., & Epstein, D. (1987). Latent growth curves within developmental structural equation models. *Child Development*, **58**, 110–133.

McArdle, J. J., & Goldsmith, H. H. (1988). Alternative common factor models for multivariate biometric analyses. *Behavior Genetics* (in press).

McArdle, J. J., & Horn, J. L. (1988). An effective graphic model for linear structural equation models. *Multivariate Behavioral Research* (in press).

McCrae, R. M., Arenberg, D., & Costa, P. T. (1987). Declines in divergent thinking with age: Cross-sectional, longitudinal, and cross-sequential analyses. *Psychology and Aging*, **2**(2), 130–137.

McDonald, R. P. (1983). Linear and nonlinear models in item response theory. *Applied Psychological Measurement*, **6**, 379–396.

McDonald, R. P. (1985). *Factor analysis and related methods*. Hillsdale, NJ: Erlbaum.

Meredith, W. (1964). Notes on factorial invariance. *Psychometrika*, **29**(2), 177–185.

Meredith, W., & Tisak, J. (1982). Canonical analysis of longitudinal and repeated measures data with stationary weights. *Psychometrika*, **47**(1), 47–67.

Meredith, W., & Tisak, J. (1984). *"Tuckerizing" curves*. Paper presented at the annual meeting of the Psychometric Society, Santa Barbara, CA.

Meredith, W., & Tisak, J. (1989). "Tuckerizing" curves. *Psychometrika* (in press).

Muthen, B., Kaplan, D., & Hollis, M. (1987). On structural equation modeling with data that are not missing completely at random. *Psychometrika*, **52**(3), 431–462.

Nesselroade, J. R. (1977). Issues in studying developmental change in adults from a multivariate perspective. In J. E. Birren & K. W. Schaie (Eds.), *Handbook on the psychology of aging* (pp. 59–69). New York: Van Nostrand Reinhold.

Nesselroade, J. R. (1983). Temporal selection and factor invariance in the study of development and change. *Life-Span Development & Behavior*, **5**, 59–87.

Nesselroade, J. R., & Baltes, P. B. (Eds.) (1979). *Longitudinal research in the study of behavior and development*. New York: Academic Press.

Nesselroade, J. R., & Labouvie, E. W. (1985). Experimental design in research on aging. In J. E. Birren & K. W. Schaie (Eds.), *Handbook on the psychology of aging* (Vol. II). New York: Van Nostrand Reinhold.

Overall, J. E. (1987). Estimating sample size for longitudinal studies of age-related cognitive decline. *Journal of Gerontology*, **42**(2), 137–141.

Rao, C. R. (1958). Some statistical methods for the comparison of growth curves. *Biometrics*, **14**, 1–17.

Rock, D. (1982). Equating using the confirmatory factor analysis model. In P. W. Holland & D. B. Rubin (Eds.), *Test equating* (pp. 247–257). New York: Academic Press.

Rogosa, D., & Willett, J. B. (1985). Satisfying a simplex structure is simpler than it should be. *Journal of Educational Statistics*, **10**(2), 99–107.

Schaie, K. W. (1965). A general model for the study of developmental problems. *Psychological Bulletin*, **64**, 91–107.

Schaie, K. W. (1977). Quasi-experimental designs in the psychology of aging. In J. E. Birren & K. W. Schaie (Eds.), *Handbook on the psychology of aging*. New York: Van Nostrand Reinhold.

Schaie, K. W. (1986). Beyond calendar definitions of age, time, and cohort: The general developmental model revisited. *Developmental Review*, **6**, 252–277.

Schaie, K. W., & Hertzog, C. (1982). Longitudinal methods. In B. B. Wolman (Ed.), *Handbook of developmental psychology* (pp. 847–870). Englewood Cliffs, NJ: Prentice-Hall.

Schaie, K. W., & Hertzog, C. (1983). Fourteen year cohort sequential analyses of adult intellectual development. *Developmental Psychology*, **19**(4), 531–543.

Schaie, K. W., & Hertzog, C. (1985). Measurement in the psychology of adulthood and aging. In J. E. Birren & K. W. Schaie (Eds.), *Handbook on the psychology of aging* (Vol. II). New York: Van Nostrand Reinhold.

Schoenberg, R. J. (1986). Maximum likelihood estimation with limited latent variables. In N. Tuma (Ed.), *Sociological methodology* (212–241). San Francisco: Jossey-Bass.

Siegler, I. C., & Botwinick, J. (1979). A long term longitudinal study of intellectual ability of older adults: The matter of selective subject attrition. *Journal of Gerontology*, **34**(2), 242–245.

Sobel, M. E., & Bohrnstedt, G. W. (1985). The use of null models in evaluating the fit of covariance structure models. In N. B. Tuma (Ed.), *Sociological methodology* (pp. 152–178). San Francisco: Jossey-Bass.

Tucker, L. R. (1966). Learning theory and multivariate experiment: Illustration by determination of parameters of generalized learning curves. In R. B. Cattell (Ed.), *The handbook of multivariate experimental psychology* (pp. 476–501). Chicago: Rand McNally.

Vandenberg, S. G., & Falkner, F. (1965). Heredity factors in human growth. *Human Biology*, **37**, 357–365.

Wohlwill, J. F. (1970). The age variable in psychological research. *Psychological Review*, **77**(1), 49–64.

Wohlwill, J. F. (1973). *The study of behavioral development*. New York: Academic Press.

Woodbury, M. A., & Manton, K. G. (1983). A

mathematical model of physiological dynamics of aging and correlated mortality selection. I. Theoretical development and critiques. *Journal of Gerontology*, **38**(4), 398–
405.

Zeger, S. L., Liang, K., & Self, S. G. (1985). The
analysis of binary longitudinal data with
time independent covariates. *Biometrika*,
72(1), 31–38.

Three

Concepts of Time and Aging in Science

Johannes J. F. Schroots and James E. Birren

In the present chapter, major concepts of time are reviewed and distinctions are made between physical, biological, psychological, and social time or age, all of which might be classified as variants of calendar time or calendar age. Also reviewed are developments in gerodynamics, which give rise to the concepts of intrinsic time and intrinsic age, as generated by the dynamics of the system. Finally, we will draw implications of the major concepts of time and age for theory and methods in research on aging.

I. Physical Time

Newton (1642–1727) conceived of time as something *absolute*, an immaterial, fixed property of the universe by which motion or change can be measured. Thus, in classical physics, time is an absolute standard or measuring scale. In this view time is not only *linear*, but also *reversible*, for nothing changes when t is replaced by $-t$ in physical equations. Newton's physical time does not have intrinsic direction; there is no difference between its past orientation $(t-)$ and its future orientation $(t+)$.

This concept of time violates generally accepted natural laws. Natural phenomena are described by the second law of thermodynamics, which states that chaos or disorder will increase irreversibly with energetic process. Thus, the *direction* of physical time is defined by the irreversible destruction of macroscopic order, or the increase of *entropy*. In twentieth-century physics, time is no longer reversible but *irreversible*, at least at the macroscopic level (Reichenbach & Mathers, 1959).

Because the Newtonian concept of time is not a product of the perceiving subject, absolute time is often called *objective* time. This concept of time has become equated more and more with its measure, the mechanical clock; time has become transformed into objective, *mechanical, calendar,* or *clock* time (Hendricks & Hendricks, 1976).

Objective time, as measured by clock or calendar, is basic to three descriptive time variables in research on aging: chronological or calendar age, cohort or time of birth,

Handbook of the Psychology of Aging, Third Edition
Copyright © 1990 Academic Press, Inc. All rights of reproduction in any form reserved.

and period or time of measurement. *Chronological age* or the elapsed time in days, months, and years since birth is "one of the most useful single items of information about an individual if not the *most* useful" (Birren, 1959, p. 8). Schaie (1965) proposed a general developmental model with three interdependent, objective time variables. This model is based on the formula that *Age = Time of measurement − Birth cohort.* It resulted in three two-factorial research designs: (a) cross-sequential, (b) time-sequential, and (c) cohort-sequential. In the cohort-sequential design, several cohorts are observed across the same age interval or levels, although at different times of measurement. The corresponding analytic model is based on the assumption that behavioral variation and change are related to age and cohort but not to time of measurement. The discussion of sequential methods, strategies, and designs in research on aging with regard to three objective time variables is continuing (Schaie, 1988).

Given the equating of time with its measure, this *reification* of time tends to obscure the fact that time is not primarily absolute or objective but *relative* and *subjective.* The relational, subjective nature of time will be discussed in sections to follow. Here, it is important to emphasize that seemingly different time variables, such as historical time, age, (birth) cohort, calendar time, and clock time, can be reduced to the same, basic concept of classical-*physical* time. This physical time model, however, does not correspond with the biological reality of aging processes.

It should be noted that the twentieth-century concept of (macro)physical time as linear and irreversible did *not* change the conception of chronological age as additive, that is, a quantity that can be added, subtracted, multiplied, and divided regardless of the age of the organism. The implication is that all possible calendar ages of the organism are equal. For instance, the first 20 years of life are equal to the middle or last 20 years of life. This however, makes sense only from a purely clock or calendar time perspective.

II. Biological Time

A. Biological Clocks

The reification of the concept of physical time encouraged the search for biological instead of mechanical clocks. Positive evidence of the endogenous nature of 24-hour *circadian* clocks in human organisms was obtained in the early 1960s (see Aschoff, 1981). In an aperiodic environment, as presented in Aschoff's (1984) underground bunker experiment, the organism develops *free running* rhythms with an intrinsic period deviating slightly but significantly from 24 hours; the organism desynchronizes from the earth's rotation cycle of 24 hours. Because the intrinsic period deviates somewhat from 24 hours, it has to be reset daily to retain synchrony with the environment light–dark cycle. This process is called *entrainment* or *synchronization.* As the resetting is done in response to the light–dark cycle, this cycle operates as an exogenous, physical timer or so called *Zeitgeber* for the organism.

Recently, the major anatomical center for numerous physiological (blood pressure, hormones, body temperature) and behavioral (attention, reaction time) processes with synchronous circadian variation has been located in the *suprachiasmatic nucleus* (Daan, 1985; Groos & Daan, 1985). The circadian rhythm of this clock differs slightly from one individual to another. However, individual synchronization is influenced more strongly by *social Zeitgebers* as a well-structured 8-hour working day than by purely *physical* synchronization signals, or *Zeitgebers* of the light and dark types.

There is another class of biological

clocks, characterized by physiological functions and processes, related in frequency to *energy turnover*, and typically dependent on the body mass (M) of the mammal (Daan & Aschoff, 1982). These *metabolic* clocks can be easily inferred from the rhythmic activity of, for example, heart, lungs, and intestines, on the basis of the allometric power law $M^{0.25}$. This law says that the length of time between consecutive heart beats increases as a linear function of about the 0.25 power of body mass (M) in mammals.

The *basal metabolic rate,* or the time needed to process one joule per gram, also increases with $M^{0.25}$. On the basis of weight, all mammals use an equivalent amount of joules per heart beat, per generation, or per life span. This suggests that metabolic clocks, as time measures of numerous periodic phenomena in the human organism, are closely associated with the rate of living (Daan, 1985). Also, positive or negative events influence biological-periodic phenomena, modulate metabolic clock rate (Boxenbaum, 1986), and thereby, increase, or decrease, the rate of living within limits.

It might be said that the human organism can be viewed as a complex of clocks, or *clock shop*, with two master clocks— circadian and metabolic clocks—and many entrained slave clocks (Moore-Ede, Sulzman, & Fuller, 1982). Aging of the organism may involve *desynchronization* of the clock shop, in which the various master and slave clocks that are normally in synchrony are put out of phase; and amplitude and period may be changed as well. Van Gool and Mirmiran (1986) reviewed the extensive literature on the subject of aging and circadian rhythms and, essentially, reached the same conclusion that Samis (1968) and Pittendrigh and Daan (1974) hypothesized earlier: The gradual and progressive deterioration of functional potential with age is the result of the loss of coordination among interdependent oscillating systems.

The brain stem contains the regulating nuclei for vital biological processes of the body. In this sense, the brain stem may present itself as the ultimate master control, or clock, with death resulting from its failure to regulate vital biological processes in relation to the organism's needs.

B. Biological Age

As the variability among individuals of the same chronological age becomes increasingly clear, it becomes evident that the useful, though rough, index of chronological age needs to be replaced by other indexes more sensitive to individual differences. Birren (1959) introduced nonchronological age scales and contrasted them to chronological age. One such scale, *biological age,* can be defined as an estimate of the individual's present position with respect to his or her potential life span. Such a measure of biological age should be able to predict the residual life span of the individual with a smaller error than that based on chronological age alone.

The concept of *biological markers of aging* has enjoyed some popularity (Reff & Schneider, 1982). What is not known is the extent of correlation among biomarkers of aging. If they remained independent, then one would merely be measuring the accumulation of random processes, the effects of which are unique within different cells, tissues, and organ systems of the body. The entrainment of the underlying processes presumably results in higher inner correlations with age, among suspected biomarkers of aging.

Due to its close affinity to biological age, a second age scale needs to be discussed, the functional age scale. Birren (1969) defined *functional age* as a dimension in which individuals could be younger or older than their chronological years in their ability to adapt to their environments. In the 1985 *Handbook*, Birren and Cunningham (1985) present an overview of the various studies of functional age. Recently, Salthouse (1986) reviewed the concept of functional age. He identified the many different meanings of the terms *function* or *functional* as a major factor contributing to confusion since the introduction of the concept (McFarland, 1943).

The concept of functional age was pointedly criticized by Costa and McCrae (1980). In the words of Birren and Cunningham (1985):

The conceptual basis for the commonest empirical approach was severely critiqued. The most common approach is to employ multiple-regression techniques to predict chronological age. If the ultimate criterion is chronological age, why not use that variable to begin with since it is easily obtained, readily verifiable, and simple to use and understand? (p. 20)

This quotation illustrates some of the confusion concerning the functional or biological age concept as a consequence of different criteria or dependent variables against which the functional or biological age measures are to be assessed and validated (Salthouse, 1986). Thus far, two criteria have been put forward: chronological age and length of life (Birren, 1959). With regard to the length of life criterion, it seems necessary to elaborate its rationale.

Underlying biological age are the processes of senescence, *senescing*, or biological aging (Birren & Schroots, 1980), which determine the individual's potential length of life. Biological or functional age research has implicitly concentrated on the goal of attempting to measure *rate of biological aging* (Salthouse, 1986).

Three concluding comments should be made. First, Costa and McCrae (1980) cast considerable doubt on the notion of a unitary rate of biological aging, with the result that measures of functional or biological age were considered to be useless. Second, as Birren (1959) observed: "Chronological age is our best general index to the residual lifespan of apparently healthy individuals" (p. 10). To date, there is no evidence of a better predictor

of length of life, residual life span, time until death, residual longevity, or nearness to death (Nuttall, 1972) than plain chronological age. Third, biological age is scaled on a physical time scale with the result that it is measured in units of chronological time.

This raises the question of the intrinsic nature of biological time. The individual human life might be viewed as governed by a single biological clock or individual life cycle with one period. The length of this period, that is, *length of life* or life span, which reflects the rate of biological aging, is one of the most significant characteristics of biological time. Boxenbaum (1982) defined biological time as a species-dependent unit of chronological time required to complete a species-independent physiological event. As it is virtually impossible to construct a time scale for the measurement of biological time on the basis of a single clock with one period, biologists have looked for an alternative length-of-life variable at the population level and have focused on the *probability of dying*. It should be noted, however, that the probability of dying is not a physiological event but a *statistical* concept.

Van Straalen (1983) formulated the definition of biological time even more explicitly, "a physiological time-scale for a specified biological process is a time-scale obtained by transforming a physical time-scale so that the rate of change of the process becomes time-invariant in physiological time" (p. 350). In other words, biological time must be defined with reference to a specified biological process. Hershey and Wang (1980), Yates (1982b), and Boxenbaum (1986), among others, have pointed out that the metabolism of the organism over the life span might be that biological process.

C. Implications

Measures of the *degree of desynchronization* in the elderly might function as predictors of nearness to death. Remarkably high correlations have been found among the elderly between circadian desynchronization and the prevalence of disorders and disease such as sleeping disorder, reduced thermoregulatory capacity, depression, and Alzheimer's disease. There appears to be a strong relationship between the temporal organization of organisms with age and the occurrence of mortality and morbidity patterns.

As pointed out earlier, senescing or biological aging should be defined in terms of a biological time model. Two important features of this model are that biological time is *unidirectional*, at least at the organismic level and that biological time is *nonlinearly* related to physical time or clock time. A unit of clock time for an old person would be equivalent to many years for a young person. To avoid confusion with the well-defined concept of biological age (Birren, 1959), it is suggested that *metabolic* age be substituted for chronological age, as the metabolism of the organism is in all probability the biological process of reference for the definition of biological time (Hershey & Wang, 1980; Schroots, 1988b; Yates, 1982b).

III. Psychological Time

A. Time Experience and Perspective

Time experience is used here as the generic term for the perception, *subjective* judgment and/or estimation of the duration of events or the amount of elapsed time. Previous authors have sought to quantify the subjective acceleration of time as a function of chronological age. Lemlich (1975) suggested that subjective duration varies inversely with the square root of chronological age; Walker (1977) reached about the same arithmetical conclusion. However, as Doob (1971) and Fraisse (1984) pointed out, in both of these studies there was a high variability between subjects, and not all responses were in the same direction. Generally

speaking, it should be noted that the psychophysical research based on the metaphor of *temporal modality*, implying a sensory receptor system for time (Janet, 1877) did not prove to be very productive.

From the literature on time experience (Doob, 1971; Fraser, 1966), the idea has arisen that the slowing of the hypothetical *internal psychological clock* can occur with advanced age, decreased metabolic activity, lower body temperature, barbiturates, alcohol, and other drugs. Outside clock time by comparison seems to be going faster—time seems to fly like magic—and clock time will be underestimated.

However, time experience is not only a matter of biology and psychophysics, psychological factors also are involved in the estimation of time. Fraisse (1984), for instance, relates the faster passage of time to the fact that with advancing age there are less novel events in life worthy of being stored in memory (Ornstein, 1969). For children, everything is new, whereas old age brings fewer surprises. Fraisse's views relate to the more recent *temporal information-processing* approach in cognitive psychology. Michon (1985a) presented an excellent overview of temporal information-processing models, departing from the *time-is-information* metaphor for the description and analysis of human time experience.

McGrath and Kelly (1986) summarized both long-term and short-term memory research on the subjective experience of time in a model of time judgments. In general, unpleasant emotions are associated with a feeling of time urgency, making clock time by comparison seem to pass slowly. During pleasant emotions there is less time urgency and, therefore, clock time by comparison appears to go quickly.

Lewin (1952) defined *time perspective* as "the totality of the individual's views of his psychological future and his psychological past existing at a given time" (p. 75); in other words, the individual span of awareness extending into the past or future (Frank, 1939).

According to James (1890) the mental *now* has a certain duration, "a saddle-back, with a certain breadth of its own on which we sit perched, and from which we look in two directions into time" (p. 600). The question arises, how broad is this metaphorical saddle back, classically known as the specious present? Some authors report 20 to 200 ms as minimum duration of the mental now, whereas others mention 4 to 7 ms (for a brief overview, see Michon, 1985a).

How the past, present, and future temporal realms interrelate with one another has been stated concisely by Hendricks (1982): "Both past and future are hypothetical reconstructions interpreted from and bound together through the mental *now*" (p. 32). In other words, the psychological past and future are *constructions*, experienced as a series of presents.

Kastenbaum (1983) extensively reviewed research on time perspective in later life and identified several dimensions of significance. Most often dealt with is the dimension of *extension*, which is based on reported life events and their estimated ages of occurrence, which can be defined as the length of past, present, future, or total life time considered by the individual (Rakowski, 1979). The basic dimension of *time orientation* refers to the relative dominance of the past, present, and future in an individual's thinking.

Most research on time perspective is based on explicit reports or implicit expectations of (a) life events, and (b) their estimated ages of occurrence (Rakowski, 1979). This type of operationalization is notorious for methodological problems with the analysis, coding, and interpretation of the data, with the result that the outcomes of time perspective studies are difficult to replicate (Nuttin, 1985).

Kastenbaum (1983) asked the question, "Does future extension diminish with advancing age?" In reviewing the evidence, he came to the conclusion that advancing age does not necessarily lead to a loss of futurity. The empirical studies of time perspective instead point to increasing individual differences with age as well as an increasing complexity of the individual's time perspective (Rakowski, 1984).

B. Psychological Aging

As discussed, the concept of biological age was introduced by Birren in 1959, representing a nonchronological age index of biological aging or senescing. The question now arises whether the concept of *psychological age* could replace the chronological age variable. Psychological age refers to the age-related adaptive capacities of the individual, such as perception, learning, and memory (Birren, 1959). "Just as one may be older or younger than one's chronological age, in both a biological and (biomedical) functional sense, one may also be older or younger psychologically. Presumably, a measure of psychological age would correlate highly with chronological age and also with environment" (p. 20).

By analogy with biological time (Boxenbaum, 1982), psychological time might be defined as the unit of chronological time required to complete a psychological event. However, this definition does not provide much information. The four essential characteristics of psychological time, as formulated by Wallis (1968) and quoted by Boxenbaum (1986), offer much more information, "(1) psychological time may pass in a non-linear fashion; (2) its flow may be perturbed by either internal or external influences; (3) it may become detached from the past, affirming persistence within the present; and (4) it may function in a manner unrelated to causality" (p. 1057).

Fraser's (1966) conception of a psychological time scale as discussed by Michon (1985b, p. 290) comes close to the ideal definition of psychological time "in which each psychological event has its own unique place on the absolute time-scale of personal history, which defines a conscious present, a privileged 'now,' but also 'beginnings and endings.'" As a matter of fact, the concept of personal future should be included in this absolute time scale.

On the basis of the foregoing it might be concluded that psychological time and psychological aging are unique and complex phenomena, which require detailed study and operationalizations when used in research on aging.

C. Implications

The quest for psychological time has made it clear that psychological research on aging should take into account one or more basic features of the psychological time explanations of behavioral and social phenomena.

According to Birren (1959), *social age* refers to acquired social habits and status, to the individual's filling the many social roles or expectancies of a person of his or her age in his or her culture and social group. An individual may be older or younger depending on the extent to which he or she shows the age-graded behavior expected of him or her by a particular society or culture. A social age measure would be a composite index of the individual's performance of social roles and would involve such features as type of dress, language habits, and social deference to other persons in leadership positions. A measure of social age presumably would also be related to chronological age, somewhat to psychological age, and to a lesser degree to biological or functional age. The fundamental criticism of the concepts of biological and psychological age also applies to social age, which is scaled on a physical time scale, and is measured in chronological time.

Research into the structure of social age was conducted by Rose (1972). Rose defined *social age* as a changing composite index of social life-styles, attributes, and attitudes at various points in the life cycle. The results led the investigator to conclude that present status, evaluated in terms of future expectations, was a powerful index of age-related status and that age-related self-evaluations could be made reliably by a respondent (Stafford & Birren, 1986). However, Rose's (1972) definition of social age did not recognize the dynamics of aging from a social perspective.

Birren and Schroots (1980, 1984) developed the new concept of *eldering*, or social aging, defined as the processes of social role change and behavior in mature adults in a direction toward those expected and displayed by older individuals in a society; that is, there are roles that are age-graded and that are typical of this part of the life span. Different patterns of dress and speech are expected of persons of different ages in a society, and the social status accorded to individuals also differs at different ages. Social age is presumed to result from the dynamic process of eldering, which is the individual's course of life through the social institutions of which the individual is a member.

D. Social Clocks

Social time, operationalized in terms of social age or social aging, refers primarily to the social role behavior of aging individuals. In Neugarten and Datan's (1973) definition, however, social time refers to the dimension that underlies the age-grade system of society. Anthropologists were the first to introduce the concept of *age-grading*. Age-graded systems are expressions of the fact that all societies divide time into socially relevant units, thus "transforming" calendar time into social time, although "clustering" rather than transforming calendar time into (*chronological*) *age-grades* would be more to the point of the *physical* time scale that Neugarten and Datan introduced.

In their conceptual model of *age stratification*, Riley, Johnson, and Foner (1972) demonstrated how chronological age strata function as an organizing principle in society. Because age-related roles may change under the influence of history-normative events, society will change as new birth cohorts replace older ones. The age stratification model emphasizes that there are significant variations in older people depending on the characteristics of their birth cohort. A second important feature of the model is its emphasis on the relations of cohorts within the age structure of society; this makes possible the analytical distinction between developmental age changes and cohort historical differences (Passuth & Bengtson, 1988, p. 330).

Neugarten and Datan (1973) discuss a number of studies that illustrate their point that the age-status structure of society, age-group identifications, the internalization of *age norms*, and age norms as a network of social controls are important temporal dimensions of the social and cultural context of the life course. "These concepts point to one way of structuring the passage of time in the life span of the individual; and in delineating a *social time clock* that can be superimposed upon the biological clock, these concepts are helpful in comprehending the life cycle" (Neugarten & Datan, 1973, p. 62, emphasis added).

Neugarten (1968) found widespread consensus regarding the timing of events, that is, the appropriate age when individuals are expected to go to school, to marry, to start a career, and so on. People know whether they are "on time" or "off time"; furthermore, they feel good about themselves when they are on time, but they feel bad if they have been either early or late. The lack of fit between the individual timing of events and social clocks is what Seltzer (1976) refers to as *time-disordered relationships* or desynchronization. In general, the greater the degree of individual temporal desynchronization, the greater will be the sense of stress.

McGrath and Kelly (1986, pp. 83–88) de-

veloped the *social entrainment model,* which emphasizes that "various temporal rhythms underlie a wide range of social behavior and that synchronizations among them (or the lack of such synchronizations) have widespread and crucial implications for human cognition, social interaction, task performance, and role behavior, and therefore for human health and well-being." The basis for the social entrainment model lies in the notion of entrainment as introduced in the present chapter's section on *biological clocks*. Viewed from a social perspective, entraining cycles correspond with Neugarten's social clocks or prescriptive time tables, for example, but they may also refer to conversational behavior, group interaction, or task performance.

McGrath and Kelly's social entrainment model provides a framework for describing the operation of biological, psychological and social clocks, their coupling to one another and potentially to outside pacers (signals or *Zeitgebers*) and the temporal patterns of behavior resulting from these clocks and rhythms of human behavior. Although they present an extensive review of entrainment research with regard to organizational and social behavior, particularly in the area of shift work, the conclusion seems to be justified that almost no work has been done with regard to long-term cycles (such as developmental, aging, and role-change patterns) or even annual or seasonal cycles.

E. Time Confounds

The concepts of social age, social aging, age-grading, age norms, age strata, and social clocks are all aspects of the same time scale, calendar time, or physical time, of which chronological age or calendar age is still the most popular, though much abused, index. Chronological age is usually introduced in developmental and aging research as an *independent* or explanatory variable. However, as Wohlwill (1973) already observed, chronological age does not have much explanatory power by itself, which is not surprising after all, as both independent and dependent variables are expressed in terms of the same calendar time, the source of most *time confounds* (Nydegger, 1981). Precisely because of the problem of confounded time parameters, Schaie (1965) proposed a general developmental model to separate statistically age, period (or time of measurement) and cohort effects. However, regardless of how data are collected, there is a triple confound.

Nydegger (1981) has emphasized that the triangular confound is not unique to developmental or aging studies, but even more important is the observation that a strictly statistical solution to the age–period–cohort problem, or any other triangular confound for that matter, is not possible.

A radical solution to the problem of time confounds is to get rid of time itself. Recently Schaie (1986, 1988) made an attempt to solve the age–cohort–period problem by conceptually separating historical time (time of measurement or period) and cohort effects from calendar time. Essentially, he redefined cohort as a selection variable that characterizes the common point of entry for a group of individuals into a given environment. Period, on the other hand, is translated into a measure of event density. Thus Schaie is able to remove calendar age as a confound for cohort or period. However, there is still the question of the extent to which Schaie has succeeded in this attempt.

In concluding this brief discussion of time confounds, it should be noted that Schaie made a fair attempt to solve the age–cohort–period problem by redefining at least one time parameter (period) in terms other than calendar time. Nevertheless, Schaie (1986) was not really satisfied with this solution as indicated at the end of his paper. It is quite possible that

the answer has been given already by Nydegger (1981):

Perhaps it is time to stop inferring psychological and social phenomena from the calendar. Instead, why not specify just what it is that we are trying to capture when we use time measures? Once identified, perhaps we can measure these phenomena more directly. In the process, some of our confounds should unlock. And it can work. . . . We should make every attempt possible to identify the *meaning* we attribute to time in each of our problems and search for the index which will best measure that meaning. It will not be easy, but the alternative is to remain calendar-bound in our riddle-models—literally caught up in time (pp. 10–11, emphasis added).

F. Implications

The term *social time* is used frequently in the field of aging and the social sciences but refers solely to the calendar time of social phenomena. As such, the concepts of social age, social aging, or eldering, and social clocks are all measured in units of chronological time, instead of social time, as the adjective *social* suggests. Featherman and Petersen (1986) developed this critical line of thought one step further and observed that many attempts to identify the dynamics of *aging* in the behavioral and social sciences ought to be interpreted as pure descriptions of static models and theories of *age* and the *aged*. In other words, not only the term *social aging* is open to question but the term *aging* itself. Featherman and Petersen (1986) suggested an alternative analytical approach that emphasizes the dynamics of state-to-state transitions. Using the concept of *duration dependence*, they differentiate changes in state (exits from a state or from a given quantitative level) that are some function of duration in current state or level from changes that are unsystematically related to time in state (or at a given quantitative level). The former are dynamic processes of change that

Featherman and Petersen recognized, by definition, as aging; the latter are conceived as stationary processes of change but *not* as processes of aging.

The notion of duration dependence means that for any individual, the probability of change or transition at any given instant depends on how long that individual has already been in the state. Analysis of interindividual differences in durations in state or level is called *duration analysis* (Tuma & Hannan, 1984). It should be noted that durations are measured in units of chronological time on a physical time scale.

Featherman and his coworkers differentiated duration-dependent changes from stationary changes that are unsystematically related to time. By definition, and on the basis of problematics in marking "normal aging," (see also Schroots, 1988a) they consider all of duration-dependent change as "aging". For example, in standard survival analysis, a person's age since birth might determine the year-by-year probability of death. If the hazard of dying is a function of time since birth, it is duration dependent; if the hazard is constant, or unsystematically related to time (since birth), "aging" is not taking place. Featherman and his coworkers did not make a distinction between development or life span developmental change (Featherman & Lerner, 1985), on the one hand, and aging (Featherman & Petersen, 1986), on the other; both *development* and *aging* are duration-dependent changes and, thus identical processes of *change*. Apparently, there are *no* separate processes of "aging" or "development"; there is just duration-dependent change.

Featherman *et al.* distinguished conceptually between different types of duration dependent changes, that is, age dependence (biographical time), history dependence (historical time), and duration (in-state) dependence, which relates to the constructs of age, period, and cohort (social time), on the one hand, and Baltes, Re-

ese, and Lipsitt's (1980) classification scheme of age-graded influences, history-graded influences, and nonnormative life events, on the other. However, the various "time scales" with regard to biographical, historical, or social time are all linguistic variants of the same calendar or physical time scale.

The question now arises as to the type of model or metaphor that would be most appropriate to characterize the diversity of conceptions of social time among sociologists and social gerontologists. Obviously, the answer should relate to physical time as all variants of social time, as well as its measures and variables, are measured in units of calendar time and scaled on a physical time scale. The growing number of conceptions of social time is not only confusing but also a demonstration of the lack of reflection on the meaning of time variables in research on aging. There is a need for an unifying concept of time, particularly in the social sciences.

IV. Intrinsic Time

A. Gerodynamics

A unifying concept of time might be found in *general systems theory*, which encompasses a variety of fields, including the physical, biological, psychological, and social sciences. The origin of this theory is generally attributed to Ludwig von Bertalanffy (1968); over the years it has been further explored by many other scientists (Boulding, 1956; Buckley, 1967; Miller, 1978; Wilden, 1980). In general systems theory, the individual is regarded as a living system made up of the same elements as inanimate matter. The elements themselves are not the basic characteristics of life but merely contribute to its structure. Humans are hierarchically organized from many subsystems, such as cells, cell tissues, organs, and so on, according to levels of complexity. As a system, humans can be conceived as part of an even more complex, larger system—for example, the physical and social environments. From a thermodynamic or energetic point of view, a living system of any sort is *open*. A flow of energy starts with the sun as solar energy and gets transformed into chemical energy via plants and animals, which are our food. Metabolism introduces further *transformations*, in which food with a relatively high energy level is converted into waste products, such as carbon dioxide and water, with low energy levels.

According to the second law of thermodynamics, there is an increase of *entropy* (S) in energetic systems; entropy is defined here as the degree to which relationships between the components of any aggregate or system are mixed up, undifferentiated, or random. Change in entropy is symbolized by dS: the second law may be stated as $dS > 0$. Accordingly, each system passes from a highly ordered, less probable state to a less ordered, more probable one. It should be pointed out that equation $dS > 0$ holds for closed systems only. This causes the following dilemma for open systems: If the second law states that entropy (disorder) will increase over time, how can open (biological, psychological, and social) systems clearly increase their degree of order (decrease their entropy) over time? To solve this dilemma, Prigogine (1967) expanded the entropy equation for open systems:

$$dS = d_iS + d_eS$$

where dS equals the total entropy change in the system, d_eS is external entropy production that is imported into the system, and d_iS is internal production of entropy due to irreversible processes in the system. If the open system is in a steady state or near equilibrium, then $dS = 0$. While $d_iS > 0$, according to the second law, d_eS must be negative. That is, to sustain an internal steady state there must be some import of *negentropy* (negative entropy) into the system or an export of entropy production out of the system. Thus, dependent on the terms d_eS and d_iS, overall entropy can decrease. However a steady state cannot be reached by living systems, even though most entropy produced internally is still exported. The result is that

$$d_iS - d_eS > 0$$

According to Yates (1982b), the discrepancy between the two values represents an *entropy accumulation rate* that drives senescence. Generally speaking, then, one might say that each living system moves toward maximum disorder or entropy, in short, toward death. In terms of general systems theory from a thermodynamic perspective, aging can now be defined as the process of increasing entropy with age.

The question arises as to how to measure this aging or entropy accumulation rate in human organisms. Hershey and Wang (1980) tried to answer this question by developing a new age-scale for humans. This scale is based on an entropic analysis of living human systems in which the energy metabolism is measured. Essentially, the analysis stems from the *rate of living* theory (Pearl, 1928; Rubner, 1908) that states simply that the human organism has a programmed amount of energy, entropy, or other property that is used up as a function of life and living. When the organism depletes the life "substance," or if the residual amount drops to some critical level or the rate at which the organism consumes it diminishes to some sensitive mark, the individual is sufficiently weakened and dies. Hershey and Wang pointed to the close inverse relation of metabolic rate to life span for homeothermic mammals (Sacher, 1980) and the fact that *metabolic rate* or aging rate (Cutler, 1983; Daan, 1985) is a fair measure of basal metabolic rate or internal entropy production rate (d_iS) plus external entropy flow rate (d_eS), as calculated from respirational data

(Hershey & Wang, 1980). Departing from the known relationship between total rate of change of entropy (dS) or metabolic rate and chronological age, Hershey and Wang were able to define a *metabolic age* for human subjects. Thus they not only developed a new age scale for humans but also met the definition of biological time, namely that a physiological time scale for a specified biological process (i.e., energy metabolism) is a time scale obtained by transforming a physical time scale (i.e., chronological time) so that the rate of change of the process becomes time invariant in physiological time (Van Straalen, 1983).

Although Hershey and Wang supplied a definition of biological time, a much-needed unifying concept of time still eludes us. Apparently, general systems theory from a purely thermodynamic perspective leaves little room for conceptions of entropy other than the classical energetic one. However, two developments in science are indicative of an extension of the concept of entropy. First, in addition to the thermodynamic, energetic concept (S), a statistical measure of uncertainty (H) has been developed, based on Shannon and Weaver's (1949) information theory (Kramer & De Smit, 1977). In the statistical view, *information* or uncertainty equals negative entropy or negentropy. On the basis of this statistical, informational concept of entropy, Bailey (1983, 1987) developed his *social entropy theory* that has many points in common with previous applications of information theory to psychology (Attneave, 1959) and likewise emphasizes the statistical conception of external negative entropy production or flow $(-d_eS)$. Given this interpretation of entropy, it is easily understood that positive or negative (psychological and/or social) events, expressed in terms of information or negentropy $(-d_eS)$ may modulate metabolic clock rates (Boxenbaum, 1986) and therefore, within limits, increase or de-

crease the rate of living (entropy accumulation rate, metabolic rate, biological aging rate, or senescing).

Living open systems such as the human organism are continuously fluctuating. Large fluctuations of the organism, as might be the case with increased age, do not fit well with the model of near-to-equilibrium systems in far-from-equilibrium thermodynamics, or the *theory of dissipative structures*. This theory postulates that a single fluctuation or combination of many may become so powerful, as a result of *positive feedback* (couplings), that it passes a critical level and shatters the preexisting form, structure, or pattern of organization of the system. At this moment, termed the *bifurcation point*, it is impossible to determine in advance which direction change will take; whether the system will disintegrate into chaos (disorder, entropy) or leap to a new, more differentiated order, that is, a dissipative structure. Systems in far-from equilibrium conditions and subjected to strong constraints show relationships that are no longer linear; accordingly, their behavior displays a multiplicity of stationary states, and a lot of new related dynamical characteristics such as bifurcations, hysteresis, and so on. The essence of Prigogine's theory, however, is that there is an *ordering principle* in entropy itself (Prigogine, 1979, 1985; Prigogine & Stengers, 1984). Entropy is not merely a downward slide toward disorganization. Under far-from-equilibrium conditions certain systems run down, whereas other systems simultaneously evolve and grow more coherent. In summary, it may be said that the creation of structure may occur spontaneously in nonlinear open systems maintained beyond a critical distance from equilibrium. The system evolves to a new regime, an organized state (dissipative structure). These new structures are created and maintained by the dissipative entropy-producing processes inside the system.

Yates (1988) developed the beginning of a dynamic model for dissipative structures and processes in aging organisms, incorporating their progressive loss of dynamic stability and increasing entropy, from which order and disorder emerge. According to Yates, most biological information is structure, acting—via couplings or feedback—as constraints on dynamic processes that create and maintain structure. In terms of the second law, the *total* internal entropy change (d_iS) brought about by the metabolism of an organism is always positive. However, with respect to a particular behavioral mode, or internal physiological function, F, the *local* internal entropy change equals:

$$d_iS_F = d_{ic}S + d_{ia}S + (X)$$

where $d_{ic}S$ refers to catabolic $(c,$ entropy increase of $F)$ effects and $d_{ia}S$ refers to anabolic $(a,$ entropy decrease of $F)$ effects. Local internal entropy change (d_iS_F) can thus be $+$, $-$, or 0, dependent on the constraint of some informational structure (X), via coupling (or feedback) between F and X. Thus, a local decrease of internal entropy change or new, differentiated order may arise from fluctuations or an increase of disorder or entropy in systems beyond a critical distance from equilibrium. In terms of general systems theory and the new interpretation of the second law of thermodynamics, *aging* should now be redefined as the process of increasing entropy with age in organisms, from which both *disorder and order* emerge. However, an increasing trend toward more disorder than order results, in the end, in death. The study of the dynamics of aging, as discussed, is appropriately called *gerodynamics*.

Recent developments in gerodynamics suggest where to find the unifying concept of time (Prigogine & Pahaut, 1984; Richardson & Rosen, 1979; Yates, 1988). Paraphrasing Richardson and Rosen (1979), it may be stated that the dynamics of any system will generate their own

intrinsic time scale. That is, intrinsic time is created by physical, biological, psychological, or social processes as an emergent property of their dynamics. As already indicated, any dynamic process can serve as a clock, time being measured by monitoring one of the state variables undergoing change. The dimensional unit of this intrinsic time is simply the unit of the state variable chosen for observation (for further explanation, see Schroots & Birren, 1988). A question should now be raised about what type of dynamics can serve as a basis for the demanded unifying concept of time, that is, intrinsic time, within the framework of general systems theory? Also, given the general system's dynamics and its constitutive parameters, what time metric should be explored? After the foregoing the answer to the first question is obvious: gerodynamics, conceived here as the dynamics of nonlinear, dissipative processes, is associated with the concept of intrinsic time. From this the answer to the second question follows as a matter of course: Richardson and Rosen (1979) have developed an *entropic time metric* that scales the passage of intrinsic time to standard clock time (i.e., seconds, minutes, hours, and so on). Given this entropic time metric, the intrinsic age of any system might be assessed. *Intrinsic age* as an intrinsic, directed measure of the state of a particular system should be distinguished from calendar age (and calendar, clock or chronological time, which is extrinsic, universal, and reversible). For instance, two systems are in temporal corresponding states, that is, at the same intrinsic age, at equal instants of intrinsic time. However, although they are at the same intrinsic age, they may have traversed different periods of clock time and are, then, of different calendar age.

Following a different route, Schroots (1988b) arrived at a similar concept of time and age when he related Prigogine's theory of dissipative structures to a finite series of transformations of formative behavior in an organism toward a behavioral organization pattern of increasing uniqueness, termed *individuation* or *intrinsic aging*. By means of this very process of individuation, which starts right at the beginning of conception, the individual creates his or her own time. As Prigogine and Pahault (1984) would state, each living system has an intrinsic (internal) age, which is not measured in terms of extrinsic (external) parameters—calendar time, for instance—but depends on the *number of transformations*, intrinsic to the dynamics of the system.

Finally, Yates (1988) suggested that "External time and intrinsic time for an individual are coupled through circadian (and perhaps other) endogenous rhythms that can be entrained by geophysical and social rhythms. This, I believe, is the chief function of many of the so-called biological clocks—to connect intrinsic and extrinsic times. (But not all intrinsic time is entrainable by periodic processes in external time)" (p. 99).

B. Implications and Conclusion

In biological systems the entropic time metric is associated with the metabolism of the organism, which relates to entropy production. Given the known relationship between total rate of change of entropy or metabolic rate of a human subject and his or her chronological age, Hershey and Wang (1980) succeeded in defining a metabolic or *intrinsic biological age* measure for human subjects. The definition of an intrinsic age measure at the psychological system level is less obvious but nevertheless feasible. To start with, all psychological events should be formulated in entropic terms. Generally, psychological events are formulated in informational terms. Given, however, the concept of negentropy, which is a measure of negative entropy or information, it should be possible to compute the *intrinsic psychological age* of human sub-

jects by feeding the external entropy flow rate, as calculated from informational data, into the entropy equation for open systems. Similarly, the *intrinsic social age* of social systems might be computed, based on Bailey's (1983, 1987) social entropy theory. By means of these three intrinsic age measures, it should no longer be difficult to develop an *intrinsic functional age* scale for human individuals.

Further study should result in effects of three sorts. First, the newly formed intrinsic functional age measure must prove to be a better predictor of length of life than calendar age, which was until now the best general index. Second, intrinsic functional age should turn out to have such explanatory power that it supplants calendar age, both as an independent variable in the explanation of other phenomena, as well as a dummy variable that stands for a host of undifferentiated processes, called aging. Last, but not least, intrinsic functional age ought to replace age or aging as a dependent variable.

Birren (1959, p. 35) observed that the subsystems of an organism show remarkable autonomy of function and that this autonomy of subsystem function may decline with age (see also Yates, 1982a). When the boundary conditions of the subsystem are reached—as in the period of terminal decline—the various subsystems will interact increasingly until the self-regulation breaks down. Translated into gerodynamical terms, this means that the loosely coupled subsystems of the human system show progressive, dynamic instability with age, the result being that even moderate internal or external fluctuations can become lethal (Yates, 1988).

It should be noted that there is a remarkable similarity between the concept of progressive, dynamic instability, and the concept of progressive desynchronization of the human system in its environment. Both concepts are related to order and entropy. Also, both concepts are related to health, stress, life crises, critical levels of functioning, and nearness to death. From a practical perspective, it would be worthwhile to develop *dynamic measures* of age-related instability and desynchronization, for example, via tests of the individual's *restitutive capacity* after experimental perturbation of his temporal order, or via tests of the individual's *learning potential* to adjust to new situations under experimentally induced stress. Expectations are that these dynamic measures are highly correlated with intrinsic functional age.

For the purpose of integration of the many findings, there is a need for a conceptual *model of time and aging*. So far, the contours of two different models might be distinguished, that is, (1) McGrath and Kelly's (1986) entrainment model of clocks, mutual entrainment, temporal patterns of behavior, and exogenous *Zeitgebers*; and (2) the gerodynamical model of order, entropy, dissipative structures, fluctuations, transformations, individuation, and intrinsic age. It is necessary to develop the conceptual model of time and aging and to further integrate this model with the "branching tree" model for the description and analysis of growing, aging, and formative change over the individual's life span (Schroots, 1988b).

In conclusion, it is appropriate to end this chapter with a quotation from Newton-Smith (1980): "For time is not just an *abstract* beast but also it is a most *promiscuous* beast who regularly couples with equally elusive partners. *Prima facie* there are links between the concept of time and a host of other concepts including the following: motion, space, causality, change, entropy, human action, consciousness" (p. 3). To which we should add: Aging!

References

Ariotti, P. E. (1975). The concept of time in Western antiquity. In J. T. Fraser & N. Lawrence (Eds.), *The study of time* (Vol. 2, pp. 69–82). Berlin: Springer-Verlag.

Aschoff, J. (Ed.) (1981). *Handbook of behavioral neurobiology* (Vol. 4), Biological rhythms. New York: Plenum.

Aschoff, J. (1984). On the perception of time during prolonged temporal isolation. *Human Neurobiology*, in press.

Aschoff, J., Von Saint-Paul, U., & Wever, R. (1971). Die Lebensdauer von Fliegen unter dem Einfluss von Zeitverschiebungen. *Naturwissenschaften, 58*, 574.

Attneave, F. (1959). *Applications of information theory to psychology*. New York: Holt.

Ayensu, E. S., & Whitfield, P.H. (1982). *The rhythms of life*. New York: Crown.

Bailey, K. D. (1983). Sociological entropy theory: Toward a statistical and verbal congruence. *Quality and Quantity, 18*, 113–133.

Bailey, K. D. (1987). Restoring order: Relating entropy to energy and information. *Systems Research, 4*, 83–92.

Baltes, P. B. (1968). Longitudinal and cross-sectional sequences in the study of age and generation effects. *Human Development, 11*, 145–171.

Baltes, P. B., Reese, H. W., & Lipsitt, L. P. (1980). Life-span developmental psychology. *Annual Review of Psychology, 31*, 65–110.

Benjamin, B., & Haycocks, H. W. (1970). *The analysis of mortality and other actuarial statistics*. London: Cambridge University Press.

Benjamin, H. (1947). Biologic versus chronologic age. *Journal of Gerontology, 2*, 217–222.

Birren, J. E. (1959). Principles of research on aging. In J. E. Birren (Ed.), *Handbook of aging and the individual* (pp. 3–42). Chicago: University of Chicago Press.

Birren, J. E. (1969). The concept of functional age, theoretical background. *Human Development, 12*, 214–215.

Birren, J. E., & Bengtson, V. L. (1988). *Emergent theories of aging*. New York: Springer.

Birren, J. E., & Cunningham, W. R. (1985). Research on the psychology of aging: Principles, concepts and theory. In J. E. Birren & K. W. Schaie (Eds.), *Handbook of the psychology of aging* (2nd ed., pp. 3–34). New York: Van Nostrand Reinhold.

Birren, J. E., & Schroots, J. J. F. (1980). A psychological point of view toward human aging and adaptability. *Proceedings of the*

9th International Conference of Social Gerontology, Quebec, pp. 443–454.

Birren, J. E., & Schroots, J. J. F. (1984). Steps to an ontogenetic psychology. *Academic Psychology Bulletin,* **6,** 177–190.

Boulding, K. (1956). *The image.* Ann Arbor: University of Michigan Press.

Boxenbaum, H. J. (1982). Interspecies scaling, allometry, physiological time, and the ground plan of pharmacokinetics. *Journal of Pharmacokinetics and Biopharmaceutics,* **10,** 201–227.

Boxenbaum, H. J. (1986). Time concepts in physics, biology, and pharmacokinetics. *Journal of Pharmaceutical Sciences,* **75,** 1053–1062.

Buckley, W. (1967). *Sociology and modern systems theory.* Englewood Cliffs, NJ: Prentice-Hall.

Butler, R. N. (1963). The life review: An interpretation of reminiscence in the aged. *Psychiatry,* **26,** 65–76.

Campbell, R. T., & O'Rand, A. M. (1988). Settings and sequences: The heuristics of aging research. In J. E. Birren & V. L. Bengtson (Eds.), *Emergent theories of aging* (pp. 58–79). New York: Springer.

Coleman, P. G. (1986). *Ageing and reminiscence processes: Social and clinical implications.* New York: Wiley.

Cooper, P. A., Thomas, L. E., Stevens, S. J., & Suscovich, D. (1981). Subjective time experience in an intergenerational sample. *International Journal of Aging and Human Development,* **13,** 183–193.

Costa, P. T., & McCrae, R. R. (1980). Functional age: A conceptual and empirical critique. In S. S. Haynes & M. Feinleib (Eds.), *Epidemiology of aging.* Bethesda, MD: National Institutes of Health.

Cumming, E., & Henry, W. E. (1961). *Growing old: The process of disengagement.* New York: Basic Books.

Cutler, R. G. (1983). Species probes, longevity and aging. In W. Regelson & F. M. Sinex (Eds.), *Intervention in the aging process: Part B—Basic research and preclinical screening:* (Vol. 3B, pp. 69–144), *Modern Aging Research.* New York: Liss.

Daan, S. (1985). Time and periodicity in organic life. In B. P. L. Scheurer & G. Debrock (Eds.), *Nature, time and history* (Part 1, pp. 67–76). Nijmegen, The Netherlands:

Faculty of Science, Catholic University of Nijmegen.

Daan, S., & Aschoff, J. (1982). Circadian contributions to survival. In J. Aschoff, S. Daan, & G. Groos (Eds.), *Vertebrate circadian systems* (pp. 305–321). Berlin: Springer-Verlag.

Dirken, J. M. (1972). *Functional age of industrial workers.* Groningen: Wolters-Noordhoff.

Doob, L. W. (1971). *Patterning of time.* New Haven, CT: Yale University Press.

Durkheim, E. (1915). *The elementary forms of the religious life* (J. W. Swain, trans.). New York: Macmillan.

Elchardus, M. (1984). *Het sociale substraat van de tijd* [The social substrate of time]. Brussels: Vrije Universiteit.

Elias, N. (1983). Een essay over tijd [An essay on time]. In J. Grashuis, A. Roskam, & S. Rozendaal (Eds.), *Wat is tijd?* [What is time?] (pp. 83–95). Rotterdam: Rotterdamse Kunststichting.

Featherman, D. L., & Lerner, R. M. (1985). Ontogenesis and sociogenesis: Problematics for theory and research about development and socialization across the lifespan. *American Sociological Review,* **50,** 659–676.

Featherman, D. L., & Petersen, T. (1986). Markers of aging: Modeling the clocks that time us. *Research on Aging,* **8,** 339–365.

Fraisse, P. (1984). Perception and estimation of time. *Annual Review of Psychology,* **35,** 1–36.

Frank, L. K. (1939). Time perspectives. *Journal of Social Philosophy,* **4,** 293–312.

Fraser, J. T. (1966). *The voices of time.* New York: Braziller.

Fraser, J. T. (1978). *Time as a conflict: A scientific and humanistic study.* Basel: Birkhaeuser.

Fraser, J. T. (1982a). Time's rite of passage: From individual to society. In E. H. Mizruchi, B. Glassner, & T. Pastorello (eds.), *Time and aging* (pp. 153–184). New York: General Hall.

Fraser, J. T. (1982b). *The genesis and evolution of time: A critique of interpretation in physics.* Amherst: University of Massachusetts Press.

Friedman, W. J. (1982). *The developmental psychology of time.* New York: Academic Press.

Gould, S. (1987). *Time's arrow; time's cycle.* Cambridge, MA: Harvard University Press.

Groos, G., & Daan, S. (1985). The use of the biological clocks in time perception. In J. A. Michon & J. L. Jackson (Eds.), *Time, mind and behavior* (pp. 65–74). Berlin: Springer-Verlag.

Hagestad, G. O. (1986). *The elementary forms of the religious life* (J. W. Swain, trans). New York: Macmillan.

Hall, E. T. (1983). *The dance of life: The other dimension of time.* New York: Anchor/Doubleday.

Hendricks, C. D., & Hendricks, J. (1976). Concepts of time and temporal construction among the aged, with implications for research. In J. F. Gubrium (Ed.), *Time, roles and self in old age* (pp. 13–49). New York: Human Sciences Press.

Hendricks, J. (1982). Time and social science: History and potential. In E. H. Mizruchi, B. Glassner, & T. Pastorello (Eds.), *Time and aging* (pp. 12–45). New York: General Hall.

Hershey, D., & Wang, H. -H. (1980). *A new age scale for humans.* Toronto: Lexington Books.

Hilgard, E. R. (1980). The trilogy of mind: Cognition, affection, and conation. *Journal of the History of the Behavioral Sciences,* **16,** 107–117.

Hochschild, A. (1975). Disengagement theory: A critique and proposal. *American Sociological Review,* **40,** 553–569.

James, W. (1890). *The principles of psychology* (Vols. 1 & 2, 1905 ed.). New York: Holt.

Janet, P. (1877). Une illusion d'optique interne. *Revue Philosophique,* **1,** 497–502.

Kastenbaum, R. (1983). Time course and time perspective in later life. In C. Eisdorfer (Ed.), *Annual Review of Gerontology and Geriatrics,* **3,** 80–101. New York: Springer.

Kerkhof, G. (1983). De biologische klok [The biological clock]. In J. Grashuis, A. Roskam, & S. Rozendaal (Eds.), *Wat is tijd?* [What is time?] (pp. 97–110). Rotterdam: Rotterdamse Kunstkring.

Kluckhohn, C., & Murray, H. A. (1953). Personality formation: The determinants. In C. Kluckholn, H. Murray, & D. Schneider (Eds.), *Personality in nature, society and culture.* New York: Knopf.

Kramer, N. J. T. A., & De Smit, J. (1977).

Systems thinking: concepts and notions. The Hague: Nijhoff.

Kroes, P. A. (1985). *Time: Its structure and role in physical theories.* Dordrecht: Reidel.

Laborit, H. (1977). *Decoding the human message.* London: Allison & Busby.

Landahl, H. D. (1959). Biological periodicities, mathematical biology, and aging. In J. E. Birren (Ed.), *Handbook of aging and the individual: psychological and biological aspects* (pp. 81–115). Chicago: University of Chicago Press.

Lemlich, R. (1975). Subjective acceleration of time with aging. *Perceptual and Motor Skills,* **41,** 235–238.

Lewin, K. (1952). Field theory and learning. In D. Cartwright (Ed.), *Field theory in social science: Selected theoretical papers by Kurt Lewin.* London: Tavistock.

Lo Gerfo, M. (1981). Three ways to reminiscence in theory and practice. *International Journal of Aging and Human Development,* **12,** 39–48.

Lomranz, J., Friedman, A., Gitter, G., Shmotkin, D., & Medini, G. (1985). The meaning of time-related concepts across the lifespan: An Israeli sample. *International Journal of Aging and Human Development,* **21,** 87–107.

McFarland, R. (1943). The older worker in industry. *Harvard Business Review,* **Summer,** 505–520.

McGrath, J. E., & Kelly, J. R. (1986). *Time and human interaction: Toward a social psychology of time.* New York: Guilford.

McMahon, A. W., & Rhudick, P. J. (1964). Reminiscing: Adaptational significance in the aged. *Archives of General Psychiatry,* **10,** 203–208.

Melges, F. T. (1982). *Time and the inner future: A temporal approach to psychiatric disorders.* New York: Wiley.

Michon, J. A. (1985a). Temporality and metaphor. In J. A. Michon & J. L. Jackson (Eds.), *Time, mind and behavior* (pp. 288–296). Berlin: Springer Verlag.

Michon, J. A. (1985b). The complete time experiencer. In J. A. Michon & J. L. Jackson (Eds.), *Time, mind and behavior* (pp. 20–52). Berlin: Springer Verlag.

Miller, J. G. (1978). *Living systems.* New York: McGraw-Hill.

Molinari, V., & Reichlin, R. E. (1984–1985).

Life review reminiscence in the elderly: A review of the literature. *International Journal of Aging and Human Development*, **20**, 81–92.

Moore-Ede, M. C., Sulzman, F. M., & Fuller, C. A. (1982). *The clocks that time us*. Cambridge, MA: Harvard University Press.

Nesselroade, J. R., & Labouvie, E. W. (1985). Experimental design in research on aging. In J. E. Birren & K. W. Schaie (Eds.), *Handbook of the psychology of aging* (2nd ed., pp. 35–60). New York: Van Nostrand Reinhold.

Neugarten, B. L. (1968). *Middle age and aging: A reader in social psychology*. Chicago: University of Chicago Press.

Neugarten, B. L. (1979). Time, age, and the life cycle. *American Journal of Psychiatry*, **136**, 887–894.

Neugarten, B. L., & Datan, N. (1973). Sociological perspectives on the life cycle. In P. B. Baltes & K. W. Schaie (Eds.), *Lifespan developmental psychology: Personality and socialization* (pp. 53–69). New York: Academic Press.

Newton-Smith, W. H. (1980). *The structure of time*. London: Routledge & Kegan Paul.

Nuttall, R. L. (1972). The strategy of functional age research. *Aging and Human Development*, **3**, 149–152.

Nuttin, J. (1985). *Future time perspective and motivation*. Leuven/Hillsdale, NJ: Leuven University Press/Erlbaum.

Nydegger, C. N. (1981). On being caught up in time. *Human Development*, **24**, 1–12.

Ornstein, R. E. (1969). *On the experience of time*. New York: Penguin.

Passuth, P. M., & Bengtson, V. L. (1988). Sociological theories of aging: Current perspectives and future directions. In J. E. Birren & V. L. Bengtson (Eds.), *Emergent theories of aging* (pp. 333–355). New York: Springer.

Pearl, R. (1928). *The rate of living*. New York: Knopf.

Pittendrigh, C. S., & Daan, S. (1974). Circadian oscillations in rodents: A systematic increase of their frequency with age. *Science*, **186**, 548–550.

Prigogine, I. (1967). *Introduction to thermodynamics of irreversible processes* (3rd ed.). New York: Wiley (Interscience).

Prigogine, I. (1979). *From being to becoming*. San Francisco: Freeman.

Prigogine, I. (1985). *Exploring complexity: From the intemporal world of dynamics to the temporal world of entropy*. Eindhoven: Holst Memorial Lecture, Technische Hogeschool Eindhoven.

Prigogine, I., & Pahaut, S. (1984). De tijd herontdekken. In M. Baudson (Ed.), *Tijd, de vierde dimensie in de kunst* (pp. 23–33). Brussels: Vereniging van Tentoonstellingen van het Paleis voor Schone Kunsten.

Prigogine, I., & Stengers, I. (1984). *Order out of chaos: Man's new dialogue with nature*. Toronto: Bantam.

Rakowski, W. (1979). Future time perspective in later adulthood: Review and research directions. *Experimental Aging Research*, **5**, 43–87.

Rakowski, W. (1984). Methodological considerations for research on late life future temporal perspective. *International Journal of Aging and Human Development*, **19**, 25–40.

Reff, M. E., & Schneider, E. L. (1982). *Biological markers of aging*. Washington, DC: U.S. Department of Health and Human services. NIH Publication No. 82-2221, April.

Reichenbach, M., & Mathers, R. A. (1959). The place of time and aging in the natural sciences and scientific philosophy. In J. E. Birren (Ed.), *Handbook of aging and the individual: psychological and biological aspects* (pp. 43–80). Chicago: University of Chicago Press.

Richardson, I. W., & Rosen, R. (1979). Aging and the matrices of time. *Journal of Theoretical Biology*, **79**, 415–423.

Richelle, M., Lejeune, H., Perikel, J. -J., & Fery, P. (1985). From biotemporality to nootemporality: Toward an integrative and comparative view of time in behavior. In J. A. Michon & J. L. Jackson (Eds.), *Time, mind and behavior* (Chap. 5, pp. 75–99). Berlin: Springer-Verlag.

Riegel, K. F. (1977). The dialects of time. In N. Datan & H. W. Reese (Eds.), *Lifespan developmental psychology: Dialectical perspectives on experimental research* (pp. 3–45). New York: Academic Press.

Rietveld, W. J., Boon, M. E., Korving, J., & Schravendijk, K. (1985). Circadian rhythms in elderly rats. *Journal of Interdisciplinary Cycle Research*, **16**, 154.

Riley, M. W., Johnson, M., & Foner, A. (1972). *Aging and society* (Vol. 3): *A sociology of age stratification*. New York: Russel Sage Foundation.

Rockstein, M., Chesky, J. & Sussman, M. (1977). Imperative biology and evolution of aging. In C. E. Finch & L. Hayflick (Eds.), *Handbook of the biology of aging* (pp. 3–34). New York: Van Nostrand Reinhold.

Rose, C. L. (1972). The measurement of social age. *Aging and Human Development*, **3**, 153–168.

Rosen, R. (1980). General theory of dynamical systems. *Conference on Biological Mechanisms in Aging, Proceedings, June, National Institute on Aging, Bethesda, MD*, Chap. 2.

Rubner, M. (1908). Probleme des Wachstums und der Lebensdauer. *Gesellschaft für Innere Medizin und Kinderheilkunde*, **7**, 58–81.

Sacher, G. A. (1959). Relation of life span to brain weight and body weight in mammals. In G. E. W. Wolstenholme & M. O'Connor (Eds.), *The life span of animals* (Seeber Foundation Colloquia on Aging, Vol. 5, pp. 115–141). Boston: Little, Brown.

Sacher, G. A. (1980). Theory in gerontology: Part I. *Annual Review of Gerontology and Geriatrics*, **1**, 3–25.

Salthouse, T. A. (1986). Functional age, examination of a concept. In J. E. Birren, P. K. Robinson, & J. E. Livingston (Eds.). *Age, health and employment* (pp. 78–92). Englewood Cliffs, NJ: Prentice-Hall.

Samis, H. V., Jr. (1968). Aging: Loss of temporal organization. *Perspect. Biol. Med.*, **3**, 95–102.

Schaie, K. W. (1965). A general model for the study of developmental problems. *Psychological Bulletin*, **64**, 92–107.

Schaie, K. W. (1986). Beyond calendar definitions of age, time and cohort: The general developmental model revisited. *Developmental Review*, **6**, 252–277.

Schaie, K. W. (1988). The impact of research methodology on theory building in the developmental sciences. In J. E. Birren & V. L. Bengtson (Eds.), *Emergent theories of aging* (pp. 41–57). New York: Springer.

Schaie, K. W., & Baltes, P. B. (1975). On sequential strategies in developmental research and the Schaie-Baltes controversy: Description or explanation? *Human Development*, **18**, 384–390.

Schaie, K. W., & Hertzog, C. (1985). Measurement in the psychology of adulthood and aging. In J. E. Birren & K. W. Schaie (Eds.), *Handbook of the psychology of aging* (2nd ed., pp. 61–92). New York: Van Nostrand Reinhold.

Schroots, J. J. F. (1988a). Current perspectives on aging, health and behavior. In J. J. F. Schroots, J. E. Birren, & A. Svanborg (Eds.), *Health and aging: Perspectives and prospects* (pp. 3–24). New York/Lisse: Springer/Swets Publishing Service.

Schroots, J. J. F. (1988b). On growing, formative change and aging. In J. E. Birren & V. L. Bengtson (Eds.), *Emergent theories of aging* (pp. 299–329). New York: Springer.

Schroots, J. J. F. & Birren, J. E. (1988). The nature of time. *Comprehensive Gerontology*, **2**, 1–29.

Seltzer, M. M. (1976). Suggestions for the examination of time-disordered relationships. In J. F. Gubrium (Ed.), *Time, roles, and self in old age* (pp. 111–125). New York: Human Sciences Press.

Serebriakoff, V. (1975). *Brain*. London: David-Poynter.

Shannon, C. E., & Weaver, W. (1949). *The mathematical theory of communication*. Urbana: University of Illinois Press.

Sorokin, P., & Merton, R. (1937). Social time: A methodological and functional analysis. *American Journal of Sociology*, **42**, 615–629.

Stafford, J. L., & Birren, J. E. (1986). Changes in the organization of behavior with age. In J. E. Birren, P. K. Robinson, & J. E. Livingston (Eds.), *Age, health and employment* (pp. 1–26). Englewood Cliffs, NJ: Prentice-Hall.

Sterns, H. L., & Alexander, R. A. (1977). Cohort, age, and time of measurement: Biomorphic considerations. In N. Datan & H. W. Reese (Eds.), *Life-span developmental psychology: Dialectical perspectives on experimental research* (pp. 105–120). New York: Academic Press.

Strehler, B. L. (1977). *Time, cells, and aging*. New York: Academic Press.

Thomas, E. A. C., & Brown, I. B. (1974). Time perception and the filled duration illusion. *Perception and Psychophysics*, **16**, 449–458.

Thomas, E. A. C., & Weaver, W. B. (1975). Cognitive processing and time perception. *Perception and Psychophysics*, **17**, 363–367.

Treas, J., & Passuth, P. (1986). *The three sociologies: Age, aging and the aged*. Paper presented at the annual meeting of the Western Sociological Society, Denver.

Tuma, N., & Hannan, M. (1984). *Social*

dynamics: Models and methods. New York: Academic Press.

Van Gool, W. A., & Mirmiran, M. (1986). Aging and circadian rhythms. In D. F. Swaab, E. Fliers, M. Mirmiran, W. A. Van Gool, & F. Van Haaren (Eds.), *Progress in brain research*, (Vol. 70, pp. 255–277). Amsterdam: Elsevier.

Van Straalen, N. M. (1983). Psychological time and time-invariance. *Journal of Theoretical Biology*, **104**, 349–357.

Von Bertalanffy, L. (1968). *General systems theory.* New York: Braziller.

Von Saint-Paul, U., & Aschoff, J. (1978). Longevity among blowflies *Pharma terraenovae* R. D. kept in non-24-hour light-dark cycles. *Journal of Comparative Physiology*, **127**, 191–195.

Vroon, P. A. (1972). *Enkele psychofysische en cognitieve aspecten van de tijdzin.* Thesis, Utrecht Rijksuniversiteit.

Walker, J. T. (1977). Time estimation and total subjective time. *Percept. Mot. Skills*, **44**, 527–532.

Wallis, R. (1968). *Time: Fourth dimension of the mind* (Engl. trans.). New York: Harcourt.

Wax, T. M., & Goodrick, C. L. (1978). Nearness to death and wheelrunning behavior in mice. *Experimental Gerontology*, **13**, 233–236.

Whitbourne, S. K., & Dannefer, W. D. (1985–1986). The "Life Drawing" as a measure of time perspective in adulthood. *International Journal of Aging and Human Development*, **22**, 147–155.

Wilden, A. (1980). *System and structure: Essays in communication and exchange.* New York: Tavistock.

Winfree, A. T. (1987). *The timing of biological clocks.* New York: Scientific American Library.

Winnubst, J. A. M. (1975). *Het Westerse tijds-syndroom: Conceptuele integratie en eerste aanzet tot construct validatie van een reeks molaire tijdsvariabelen in de psychologie.* Amsterdam: Swets & Zeitlinger.

Withrow, G. J. (1980). *The natural philosophy of time* (2nd ed.). Oxford: Clarendon.

Wohlwill, J. F. (1973). *The study of behavioral development.* New York: Academic Press.

Yates, F. E. (1982a). Outline of a physical theory of physiological systems. *Canadian Journal of Physiology and Pharmacology*, **60**, 217–248.

Yates, F. E. (1982b). Senescence from the aspect of physical stability. Paper presented at the International Research Symposium, *Metaphors in the Study of Aging.* University of British Columbia, June.

Yates, F. E. (1988). The dynamics of aging and time: How physical action implies social action. In J. E. Birren & V. L. Bengtson (Eds.), *Emergent theories of aging* (pp. 90–117). New York: Springer.

Zerubavel, E. (1981). *Hidden rhythms: Schedules and calendars in social life.* Chicago: University of Chicago Press.

Zerubavel, E. (1982). Schedules and social control. In E. H. Mizruchi, B. Glassner, & T. Pastorello (Eds.), *Time and aging: Conceptualization and application in sociological and gerontological research* (pp. 129–144). New York: General Hall.

Part Two

Influences of Behavior and Aging

Four
___

Human Behavioral Genetics of Aging

Robert Plomin and Gerald E. McClearn

I. Introduction

One of the most important questions in the psychology of aging concerns the origins of individual variations on the aging theme. Between successful agers, who maintain robust health and functional capacity to the end of a long life, and unsuccessful agers who experience premature senescence, early death, or incapacity, lies one of the most intriguing continuous distributions to challenge science. Quantitative genetics consists of theory and methods that can be applied to the study of both the genetic and environmental origins of differences among individuals. A substantial amount of quantitative genetic research has been conducted on behavioral phenotypes in childhood, adolescence, and young adulthood, but very little is known about the determinants of individual differences during the last half of the life course, even though a chapter on behavioral genetics was included over 30 years ago in the *Handbook on Aging in the Individual* (Kallmann & Jarvik, 1959).

The present chapter attempts to set the stage for the application of modern genetic strategies to the study of the psychology of aging. Here, the term *aging* is used broadly to refer to age differences and age changes with a focus on individual differences in these phenomena. The chapter begins with a description of the recent history of research on the genetics of human behavioral aging, emphasizing the need for serious consideration of both genetic and environmental sources of individual differences among the elderly. The second section illustrates the evolution of this research beyond simple nature–nurture comparisons, using as an example the newly emerging subdiscipline of developmental behavioral genetics. The third section describes what is known about the genetics of psychological aging, emphasizing early results from the first large-scale behavioral genetic study of aging.

Space does not permit presentation of basic concepts and methods of behavioral genetics nor a discussion of relevant nonhuman research; these were the foci of a chapter in the previous edition of this handbook (McClearn & Foch, 1985; see

Handbook of the Psychology of Aging, Third Edition
Copyright © 1990 Academic Press, Inc. All rights of reproduction in any form reserved.

also Ehrman & Parsons, 1981; Fuller & Thompson, 1978; Hay, 1985; Plomin, De-Fries, & McClearn, 1989).

II. Lessons from Recent History

Because behavioral genetics has just begun to be applied in the psychology of aging, the opportunity exists to avoid problems that hampered earlier applications in other fields. During the past 20 years, behavioral genetics has caromed from neglect to antipathy to acceptance. The field-defining book, *Behavior Genetics* (Fuller & Thompson, 1960), was published in 1960, although behavioral genetic research goes back over 80 years through selective breeding and strain comparisons in animals and twin and adoption studies on human beings to Francis Galton who over a century ago coined the phrase *nature and nurture*. During the 1940s and 1950s and continuing into the 1960s, the social and behavioral sciences were dominated by an enviromentalism that attributed behavioral variation to environmental causes. Studies of inbred strains of mice and artificial selection began to show that genetic effects on animal behavior are ubiquitous. Researchers began to ask about effect size, and it was beginning to be clear that the genetic contribution often not only is detectable but also quite substantial.

Although twin and adoption studies of human behavior had been conducted off and on since the 1920s, their impact on the behavioral sciences had been negligible. In the 1960s, studies of IQ (Erlenmeyer-Kimling & Jarvik, 1963) and schizophrenia (Heston, 1966) began to build some momentum for human behavioral genetics. Indifference to genetic effects was ended by Arthur Jensen's 1969 article that raised the issue of possible genetic sources of racial differences in IQ. This publication released a furious reaction unparalleled in the behavioral sciences. Now, just a decade later, behavioral genetics is widely accepted in many areas of the social and behavioral sciences, and there is, for example, "overwhelming support for a significant within-group heritability for IQ" (Snyderman & Rothman, 1987, p. 137). The shift from antipathy to acceptance is one of the most dramatic and rapid reversals in the recent history of the social and behavioral sciences.

It is important to keep in mind that the demonstration of significant genetic influences does not imply that heredity alone is responsible for behavioral differences among individuals. Indeed, behavioral genetic methods have provided the best available quantitative evidence for the importance of nongenetic influences. Research on cognitive abilities, psychopathology, and personality finds that one-third to one-half of the variance for most behaviors is due to genetic differences (Plomin *et al.*, 1989), indicating that most of the variance is due to nongenetic factors.

History carries two messages for the psychology of aging. The first is that genetic influence is likely to be significant and substantial for many dimensions of behavioral variability later in life. Genetic influence in this sense usually is described in terms of the heritability statistic, which is quantitatively expressed as the proportion of the variability in the measured phenotype that is attributable to genetic factors. Heritability is a probabilistic, descriptive population concept that does not imply biological determinism, immutability, or reductionism. In various populations, with different gene pools or different environmental circumstances, heritability of a phenotype can vary. Although single-gene influences on age-related disorders have been identified, the normal range of behavioral variability is likely to be affected by many genes, each with small effects. Rare, single-gene effects contribute very little to the normal range of variability in behavioral aging.

The second message is that at least as much variance in behavior is environmental as genetic. The essence of behavioral genetic strategies is that they not only can, but they do, consider both polygenic and environmental influences in exploring the etiology of variability among individuals. In the field of the psychology of aging, we hope that the nature–nurture battle will not need to be fought again. Forestalling these battles will make it possible for gerontology to skip to the forefront of behavioral genetics research where more sophisticated questions are being asked.

III. Developmental Behavioral Genetics

The earliest studies in human behavioral genetics were developmental, exploring whether twin resemblance changed as a function of age (Galton, 1875; Merriman, 1924). But for nearly 60 years, this developmental dimension disappeared from human behavioral genetic research (Gottesman, 1974; McClearn, 1970; Schaie, 1975). Contemporary developmental behavioral genetics is an emerging subdiscipline that weds developmental methods and behavioral genetic methods to study the etiology of change as well as continuity during development (Plomin, 1986).

Genetic influences are not static and unchanging. For example, much of the current excitement in molecular genetics comes from research on short-term changes in gene expression and in longer term developmental differentiation (Scarr & Kidd, 1983). Two types of age-related change and continuity can be studied in quantitative genetics. One is the cross-sectional study of the relative magnitude of genetic and environmental components of variance in different age groups. The other is longitudinal: genetic and environmental etiologies of differential age-to-age change and continuity throughout the life course.

A. Age Differences

Age of subjects in behavioral genetic analyses has rarely been given serious attention. However, an examination of results for cognitive abilities, personality and psychopathology in infancy, childhood, adolescence, and adulthood reveals several interesting developmental trends. For example, longitudinal and cross-sectional research in childhood suggests that when heritability changes, it tends to increase (Plomin, 1986). This is surprising because it would seem reasonable to predict the opposite: As children develop, their cumulative experiences and environmental exposures become increasingly differentiated, which could lead to decreased heritability.

As is discussed later, hardly any behavioral genetic research has as yet been conducted that permits comparisons of the same phenotypes throughout the life course. Thus, it is not yet possible to determine whether heritability continues to increase during adolescence and adulthood, although there is some indication that for IQ this might be the case (Plomin, 1986). Nonetheless, one lifespan development theory predicts that the influence of nonnormative life events increases throughout the life span (Baltes, Reese, & Lipsitt, 1980, p. 78). This model would predict that heritability decreases during development. Some preliminary data on this issue are described later. Cross-sectional age comparisons raise a related issue: the possible confounding of cohort differences in behavioral genetic analyses of age differences (Schaie, 1975). Estimates of genetic and environmental components of variance are not constants—they can change as the mix of genetic and environmental influences change in a population (Plomin & Thompson, 1988).

Another example of age-related change in the relative magnitude of components of variance lies in shared and nonshared environmental influences relevant to IQ scores. For personality and psychopathology, children growing up in the same family are no more similar than expected on the basis of heredity alone (Plomin & Daniels, 1987). An exception to this rule is IQ. Young children in the same family are substantially similar for IQ even if the children are adoptees who are genetically unrelated, though the influence of shared environmental influences declines to negligible levels by adolescence (Plomin, 1987). An hypothesis for aging is that if shared environmental influences are unimportant in adolescence and young adulthood, such factors will continue to be unimportant later in life. However, it is not inconceivable that rearing environment contains "sleeper" variables, the impact of which becomes increasingly important later in life. This hypothesis and some pertinent data are discussed later in this chapter.

In summary, heritabilities could be completely different later in life because of changes in genetic or environmental sources of variance. Behaviors studied earlier in the life course need to be studied in later life. In addition, behaviors specific to the last third of the life course, such as those associated with transitions from work to retirement, adjustment to the death of spouses or friends and issues related to successful aging, present special opportunities for genetic research on the psychology of aging.

B. Age Changes

Even more important is the use of behavioral genetic strategies to study the genet-
ic and environmental etiologies of age-to-age changes and continuities. This can inform us about the process of aging rather than merely describe genetic and environmental components of variance as a function of age. Phenotypically, change is at least as important as continuity during development, and genetics can contribute to change as well as continuity. Age-to-age genetic change can occur for many reasons, including molecular reasons such as the turning on and off of different genes and changes in the quantitative expression of genes. Changes in gene–behavior relations can also occur because, as the organism develops, the same behavior involves different psychological processes that are affected by different genes (Plomin & Nesselroade, 1989).

Any behavioral genetic method that can assess the variance of a trait at one age can also be used to assess the covariance of the trait across ages with one critical proviso: longitudinal data are necessary to study the etiology of age-to-age change and continuity. Although space does not permit a detailed description of these analyses (see Plomin, 1986), the essence is the genetic correlation between genetic deviations that affect a trait at one age and those that affect the trait at another age. In other words, the genetic correlation indicates the extent to which genetic effects on individual differences overlap at two ages, regardless of their relative contribution to phenotypic variance at either age. The genetic correlation can be high even when heritabilities at the two ages are low; that is, the genetic role may be small at either age, but the same genes are involved at each age. Further, the genetic correlation can be low even when heritabilities at the two ages are high; at each age, there may be substantial genetic influence, but different genes are involved at the different ages.

Although analyses of age-to-age genetic and environmental correlations will become the hallmark of developmental behavioral genetic analyses in the future, only a few longitudinal behavioral genetic studies have been conducted to date. IQ appears to show substantial age-to-age genetic continuity from childhood to adulthood, although even in the case of IQ there is some evidence for genetic change (DeFries, Plomin, & LaBuda, 1987). IQ shows little change; other traits that show both heritability and change are better candidates for finding genetic change.

For example, one longitudinal twin study of height and weight in individuals from 20 to 45 years of age found evidence for age-to-age genetic change for weight but not for height (Stunkard, Foch, & Hrubec, 1986). Although both traits are highly heritable in a Danish population (about 80% at both 20 and 45 years of age), weight shows lower age-to-age phenotypic correlations than height (.64 versus .80 from 20 to 45 years of age). Results for height suggest a genetic correlation of nearly 1.0 from 20 to 45 years of age, indicating that the genes influencing height in early adulthood are essentially the same ones influencing height in middle adulthood. The genetic correlation for weight, about .75, however, suggests some genetic change. Genetic change—that is, genetic correlations that are less than 1.0—could result if the genes influencing physiological or psychological processes that subserve weight differ with age. For example, genetic effects on individual differences in weight could change from young adulthood to middle age because of changes in exercise and eating habits or because of metabolic changes. Psychological processes such as concern with one's appearance could also differ.

Several other advances will be useful in moving behavioral genetic studies on aging beyond mere demonstrations of the significant influence of heredity. One of these advances is multivariate genetic analysis of the covariance among traits. These methods (e.g., DeFries & Fulker,

1986) will be helpful in three ways. They can be used to (a) break down the heterogeneity that exists within domains such as depression, (b) explore the nexus of associations that exists between behavioral domains such as personality and cognitive functioning and (c) study the etiology of associations between behavior and biology such as personality and coronary heart disease.

Three other advances should be mentioned. One methodological advance involves testing the fit between empirical data and explicit models of environmental and genetic effects (e.g., Jinks & Fulker, 1970; Loehlin, 1987). Analyses of environmental influences within the context of genetic designs represent another important direction for research. Such studies have yielded evidence for the importance of nonshared environmental influence (Plomin & Daniels, 1987) and have demonstrated seemingly paradoxical genetic effects on measures of the environment (Plomin, 1986). The third advance concerns the use of molecular genetic techniques. Harnessing the power of molecular genetic techniques for the complex, polygenic, multifactorial traits of greatest relevance to the psychology of aging will eventually alter the way in which behavioral genetic research is conducted (e.g., Plomin et al., 1989). The brevity of this chapter does not permit discussion of these advances, although some are alluded to in the following review.

IV. The Genetics of Behavioral Aging

Given the power of quantitative genetic analyses and the considerable amount of behavioral genetic research earlier in the life span, it is surprising that hardly any research of this type has been conducted on aging. Genetic research on aging has primarily involved single-gene research and molecular mechanisms of disorders such as progeria, Werner's disease, and Alzheimer's disease (McClearn & Foch, 1985). For example, although Alzheimer's is evidently not a simple single-gene disorder as in the case of Huntington's disease, a gene on chromosome 21 has been implicated in some cases of familially transmitted Alzheimer's (Goldgaber, Lerman, McBride, Saffiotti, & Gajdusek, 1987).

A. New York State Psychiatric Institute Study of Aging Twins

The only behavioral genetic study of the last half of the life course has been the twin study of cognitive abilities initiated by Kallmann 40 years ago. In 1946, Franz Kallmann and Gerhard Sander (1948, 1949) organized a survey of twins in New York over the age of 60. Over 1,000 pairs of twins were studied biennially. Although no twin correlations have been reported for this study, intrapair differences for longevity and diseases were consistently smaller for identical twins than for fraternal twins (Jarvik & Falek, 1963; Kallmann, 1957). For example, the average intrapair difference in life span was 37 months for identical twins and 78 months for fraternal twins (Kallmann & Sander, 1948, 1949). The authors concluded that genetic influences are primarily responsible for individual differences in aging.

Six tests—vocabulary, blocks, digit memory, digit symbol substitution, verbal similarities, and motor coordination—were administered to a subsample of 75 identical and 45 fraternal twin pairs between the ages of 60 and 89 years (Kallmann, Feingold, & Bondy, 1951). Identical twins yielded significantly smaller intrapair differences than did fraternal twins except in the case of digit memory.

Small samples of surviving twins were studied again in 1955 (Jarvik, Kallmann, Falek, & Klaber, 1957) and 1967 (Jarvik, Blum, & Varma, 1972). The longitudinal studies included 26 identical and 10 fraternal twin pairs in 1955 and 13 identical and

6 fraternal pairs in 1967. Intrapair differences remained larger for fraternal than for identical twins, although the differences were no longer significant because of the diminished sample size (see Jarvik & Bank, 1983, for an overview of these results).

B. Swedish Adoption/Twin Study on Aging (SATSA)

Begun in 1979, SATSA provides a powerful design and sample for the study of the genetics of behavior later in life (McClearn, Pedersen, Plomin, Nesselroade, & Friberg, 1988). The design combines the strength of the adoption and twin methods by studying four groups of twins: identical and fraternal twins reared apart and matched twins of both types reared together. The power of this design involves its multiple estimates of genetic influence from the resemblance of twins reared apart (for both identical and fraternal twins) and from comparisons between identical and fraternal twin resemblance (for both twins reared apart and twins reared together). Just as important is the design's estimate of the influence of shared rearing environment via comparisons between both identical and fraternal twins reared together and apart.

The SATSA sample was derived from the Swedish Twin Registry, maintained by the Department of Environmental Hygiene of the Karolinska Institute, Stockholm, which contains information on both members of nearly 25,000 pairs of like-sexed twins (Cederlöf & Lorich, 1978). The average age of the 364 pairs of twins reared apart was 58.6 years in 1984; 72% of the twins were then over 50 years of age. For the twins reared apart, the average age at separation is 2.8 years; about half were separated in the first year of life, 80% by their fifth birthday, and the rest by 10 years of age. Although pairs with the earliest separation are most useful for the adoption design, those separated later permit a parametric assessment of the effects of age at separation. Details of the procedures, sample, and design of SATSA are described by McClearn et al. (1988).

Phase I of the testing includes two mail-out questionnaires sent to all members of the SATSA sample. Questionnaire data are available from 99 pairs of identical twins reared apart, 229 pairs of fraternal twins reared apart, 160 pairs of identical twins reared together, and 212 pairs of fraternal twins reared together. The Phase I questionnaires assess physical and mental health status, numerous personality dimensions, activities of daily living, life satisfaction, health-related behaviors of smoking, alcohol consumption and legal drug use, early rearing environment, and the adult work, family, and social environments. Phase II, in progress, consists of in-person interviews, cognitive tests, and a health examination for a sample of 400 pairs. The SATSA sample will be followed longitudinally at 3-year intervals.

In a preliminary study, 12 cognitive tests were administered to 34 pairs of separated fraternal twins (Pedersen, McClearn, Plomin, & Friberg, 1985). A measure of general cognitive ability, an unrotated first principle component score based on the 12 cognitive tests, yielded a twin correlation of .52 for the fraternal twins reared apart after the effects of age, age at separation, and differences in the twins' degree of separation were partialed out. This correlation is similar to the correlation generally reported for fraternal twins reared together and suggests substantial genetic influence. However, the 95% confidence interval for the correlation is from .19 to .75 for this small sample, which suggests caution in estimating heritability for fraternal twins reared apart. The in-person testing of 400 pairs of twins, nearing completion, includes cognitive measures that systematically sample fluid and crystallized abilities.

Table I summarizes model-fitting estimates for analyses of major personality di-

mensions assessed during Phase I of SATSA. The results summarized in Table I indicate significant genetic influence during the last half of the life course. Genetic variance (additive plus nonadditive as explained later) on average accounts for 29% of the total variance for these self-report personality questionnaire variables. The few exceptions to the rule of significant genetic influences are noteworthy: hostility and assertiveness factors from a measure of Type A behavior, a "luck" factor (beliefs concerning the role of luck in determining people's outcomes) from a locus-of-control measure, and the Agreeableness scale from Costa and Mc-Crae's (1985) NEO measure.

It is interesting to compare these results to those for younger adults. Classical twin studies of young adults typically yield heritability estimates of 40 to 50% (Loehlin, Willerman, & Horn, 1988). The only other study that has employed a twin/adoption design is the Minnesota Study of Twins Reared Apart that reported an average heritability estimate of 47% for personality for young adults whose average weighted age was 25 years (Tellegen, Lykken, Bouchard, Wilcox, Segal, & Rich, 1988). The correlation for identical twins reared apart is the best single estimate of heritability. In SATSA, the average correlation for this group is .28 and in the Minnesota study, the average correlation for 44 pairs is .49. Thus these findings raise the possibility that the heritability of personality may be lower later in life. However, differences between SATSA results and results of studies of younger twins could be due to cohort differences or other sample differences, such as nationalities. It is also possible that results for twins older than those in SATSA will be different. Nonetheless, it is noteworthy that, earlier in life, when heritability shows age differences, it tends to increase. In contrast, this first study of twins in the last half of the life span suggests lower heritability

Table I
Summary of SATSA Model-Fitting Results for Personality

	Additive Genetic Variance	Nonadditive Genetic Variance	Shared Environmental Variance	Nonshared Environmental Variance
Extraversion[a]	0%	41%	7%	52%
Neuroticism[a]	31%	0%	10%	58%
Impulsivity[a]	2%	43%	0%	55%
Monotony Avoidance[a]	23%	0%	5%	72%
Emotionality[b]	36%	3%	6%	55%
Fear[b]	0%	39%	4%	57%
Anger[b]	13%	15%	12%	60%
Activity[b]	0%	23%	12%	65%
Sociability[b]	24%	0%	13%	64%
Type A[c]	27%	0%	11%	62%
Pressure[c]	28%	0%	12%	60%
Hard-driving[c]	0%	43%	0%	57%
Ambitious[c]	0%	37%	0%	63%
Hostility[c]	20%	0%	20%	59%
Assertiveness[c]	0%	12%	19%	69%
Luck[d]	0%	0%	31%	69%
Responsibility[d]	34%	0%	0%	66%
Life Direction[d]	31%	0%	0%	69%
NEO Openness[e]	41%	0%	6%	53%
NEO Conscientious[e]	0%	29%	11%	60%
NEO Agreeableness[e]	0%	12%	21%	67%

[a]Pedersen, Plomin, McClearn, and Friberg (1988).
[b]Plomin, Pedersen, McClearn, Nesselroade, and Bergeman (1988).
[c]Pedersen, Lichtenstein, Plomin, DeFaire, McClearn, and Matthews (1989).
[d]Pedersen, Gatz, Plomin, Nesselroade, and McClearn (1989).
[e]Bergeman, Chipuer, Plomin, Pedersen, McClearn, Nesselroade, and Costa (1988).

for personality than do studies of younger twins. Because SATSA is the only study of older twins and because factors other than age might explain its results, this should be treated merely as a hypothesis to be tested in future research.

Table I also indicates that some of the genetic variance for personality is nonadditive, a result found in the Minnesota study (Tellegen et al., 1988) and other research (reviewed by Plomin, 1986). Nonadditive genetic variance refers to two types of interactive effects of genes, dominance and epistasis. Dominance involves interactive effects of alleles (alternate forms of genes) at a locus (a place on a chromosome). Epistasis refers to interactive effects of alleles across different loci. In contrast, additive genetic effects are those that affect the phenotype in an ad-

ditive manner. The practical importance of this distinction is that nonadditive genetic variance, especially the higher-order interactions of epistasis, does not lead to much resemblance among relatives who are not identical twins. Thus, in the presence of substantial nonadditive genetic variance, identical twins will resemble each other but first-degree relatives will not.

Finally, Table I indicates that shared environmental influence accounts for 10% of the variance on average. This is about twice the amount of shared environmental influence found in personality studies of children, adolescents, and young adults (Loehlin et al., 1988; Plomin & Daniels, 1987). This finding suggests the interesting albeit counterintuitive hypothesis that the influence of rearing environment increases slightly in later life. As in all studies of personality, the SATSA results demonstrate that most of the variance is of the nonshared environmental variety (including error of measurement), environmental influences that do not contribute to the resemblance of family members.

The SATSA design has facilitated two other types of environmental analyses. One type involves genotype–environment interaction, the differential effects of environments as a function of genotype. Although this analysis is too complicated to describe here, analyses of this type using the SATSA identical twins reared apart yielded the first evidence for genotype–environment interaction in human development (Bergeman, Plomin, McClearn, Pedersen, & Friberg, 1989).

A second type of environmental analysis addresses possible genetic influence on measures of individuals' perceptions of their environment. One SATSA analysis assessed the extent to which individual differences in perceptions of one's childhood family environment, viewed retrospectively 50 years later, are affected by heredity (Plomin, McClearn, Pedersen, Nesselroade, & Bergeman, 1988). The results indicate significant genetic influence on each of the eight scales of the Family Environment Scales. Maximum-likelihood model-fitting estimates of heritability suggest that on average 26% of the variance of the scales can be explained by genetic differences among individuals. In accord with previous research, the lowest heritability, .15, occurred for perceptions of control. Another analysis considered twins' perceptions of their current family environment rather than the family in which they were reared (Plomin, McClearn, Pedersen, Nesselroade, & Bergeman, 1989). Again, heritability accounted for about one quarter of the variance of these perceptions of family environment. Reared-together twins are no more similar than reared-apart twins, sug-

gesting that family rearing environment has little effect on parents' perceptions of their own family. In each of these studies, evidence suggests that genetic influence on perceptions of family environment is not mediated by traditional dimensions of personality. This finding suggests that traditional measures of personality do not capture the genetically influenced concomitants of environmental measures in the intense, emotion-laden context of familial relationships.

Finally, a measure of life events indicates substantial genetic influence on perceptions of life events (Plomin, Lichenstein, Pedersen, McClearn, & Nesselroade, 1989). Genetic influence occurs primarily for controllable events in which the individual can play an active role, such as conflicts with spouse and children, rather than for uncontrollable events, such as illness of spouse and children.

V. Summary

The recent history of behavioral genetics indicates the need to consider both genetic and environmental sources of individual differences in the psychology of aging. Behavioral genetics provides a theory and methods that can go beyond simple nature–nurture comparisons to consider age differences, age changes, shared and nonshared environments, and multivariate analyses. Other than the New York State Psychiatric Institute Study of Aging Twins initiated 40 years ago, until recently there have been no behavioral genetic studies of the last half of the life span.

Early reports from the Swedish Adoption/Twin Study on Aging provide a glimpse of the potential usefulness of behavioral genetic research in aging. For personality, its results suggest that there may be less genetic influence later in life. Results also indicate significant genetic influence on perceptions of rearing and current family environment and on life events.

Another twin study of aging has also been launched, the Minnesota Twin Study of Adult Development (McGue & Hirsch, 1987). The study will include 100 identical and 100 fraternal twin pairs over 60 years of age. Behavioral measures include IQ, simple and choice reaction time, personality, depression and life satisfaction; biological functioning including cellular measures such as mitogen responsiveness also will be assessed.

The explosion of information about behavioral aging and its relationships to biological aging suggests the need for much more behavioral genetic research, especially longitudinal research that explores the etiology of age changes in later life. Because there are so few behavioral geneticists who study the psychology of aging, the rate of progress in this area will depend on adding behavioral genetics to traditional studies of the psychology of aging. A reorientation concerning sampling strategies might accelerate this development. Instead of regarding individuals as sampling units, investigators could sample biologically related pairs. For example, twins rather than singletons could be studied: One out of 85 births is a twin birth. Using twins, gerontological researchers could study any variable of interest in the traditional manner by treating the twins as individuals. After completing these primary analyses, the researcher could then add a new dimension to the analysis by comparing identical and fraternal twins. The statistical costs of nonindependent sampling is dramatically offset by the greatly enhanced analytic power provided by a "relations" design.

Because adoption was not common until the 1950s, the adoption design cannot be as immediately useful as the twin design in studies of the psychology of aging. The most practical entrée for gerontological researchers is likely to be the family study. Specifically, there is much to be gained by studying the siblings of subjects in research on the psychology of aging. This approach is especially feasible given the large family sizes typical of the contemporary elderly cohort. Although family studies cannot disentangle genetic and environmental sources of familial resemblance, they are valuable for several reasons. For example, family studies suggest upper-limit estimates of the influence of additive genetic variance and shared environmental influence. That is, additive genetic variance, genetic effects that "breed true" among siblings, can be no greater than twice the phenotypic sibling correlation. Family studies also provide important comparison data for the results of twin studies. Finally, family studies make it possible to study nonshared environments by identifying environmental factors that make siblings different from one another.

One example of this approach is an ongoing extension of the Seattle Longitudinal Study (SLS) to assess familial resemblance by studying children and siblings of SLS participants in order to examine parent–offspring and sibling resemblance for cognitive abilities in later life (Schaie, 1988). The long-term longitudinal nature of the SLS facilitates novel analyses. For example, same-age sibling resemblance can be traced backward by examining sibling resemblance for the index case's test scores when the index case was 7, 14, 21, and 28 years younger. Similarly, by adding the offspring of the probands, parent–offspring similarity can be traced forward. Same-age comparisons between parents and offspring can be calculated using test scores of parents obtained when the parents were approximately the same age as their offspring at the time of testing. Parent–offspring resemblance can then be traced forward when the parent is 7, 14, 21, and 28 years older than the age of the offspring at the time of testing.

It is our hope that some of the behavioral

genetics research agenda can be accomplished "on the side" by gerontological researchers who use behavioral genetic designs in studies aimed at whatever issues the researchers would have studied anyway. Adding a behavioral genetic design in any research on individual differences in aging takes an important first step in the direction of understanding the etiology of individual differences.

Acknowledgments

Preparation of this chapter and the conduct of SATSA was supported in part by a grant from the U.S. National Institute on Aging (AG-04563) and by the MacArthur Foundation Research Program in Successful Aging. SATSA is an ongoing study conducted at the Department of Environmental Hygiene of the Karolinska Institute in Stockholm (Nancy L. Pedersen, Lars Friberg, Ülf deFaire, and Stig Berg) in collaboration with the Research Center for Developmental and Health Genetics at The Pennsylvania State University (Gerald E. McClearn, Robert Plomin, and John R. Nesselroade).

References

Baltes, P. B., Reese, H. W., & Lipsitt, L. P. (1980). *Annual Review of Psychology*, **31**, 65–110.

Bergeman, C. S., Chipuer, H. M., Plomin, R., Pedersen, N. L., McClearn, G. E., Nesselroade, J. R., & Costa, P. T., Jr. (1988). *Openness to experience, agreeableness, and conscientiousness assessed separately by age and gender: An adoption/twin study.* Submitted.

Bergeman, C. S., Plomin, R., McClearn, G. E., Pedersen, N. L., & Friberg, L. T. (1989). *Psychology and Aging*, in press.

Cederlöf, R., & Lorich, U. (1978). The Swedish twin registry. In W. E. Nance, G. Allen, & P. Parisi (Eds.), *Twin research: Part C. Biology and epidemiology* (pp. 189–195). New York: Liss.

Costa, P. T., & McCrae, R. R. (1985). *The NEO personality inventory manual.* Odessa, FL: Psychological Assessment Resources.

DeFries, J. C., & Fulker, D. W. (1986). *Behavior Genetics*, **16**, 1–10.

DeFries, J. C., Plomin, R., & LaBuda, M. C. (1987). *Developmental Psychology*, **23**, 4–12.

Ehrman, L., & Parsons, P. A. (1981). *The genetics of behavior.* Sunderland, MA: Sinauer.

Erlemeyer-Kimling, L., & Jarvik, L. F. (1963). *Science*, **142**, 1477–1479.

Fuller, J. L., & Thompson, W. R. (1960). *Behavior genetics.* New York: Wiley.

Fuller, J. L., & Thompson, W. R. (1978). *Foundations of behavior genetics.* St. Louis: Mosby.

Galton, F. (1875). *Journal of the Anthropological Institute*, **6**, 391–406.

Goldgaber, D., Lerman, M. I., McBride, O. W., Saffiotti, U., & Gajdusek, C. (1987). *Science*, **235**, 877–880.

Gottesman, I. I. (1974). Developmental genetics and ontogenetic psychology: Overdue detente and propositions from a matchmaker. In A. D. Pick (Ed.), *Minnesota Symposia on Child Psychology* (pp. 55–80). Minneapolis: University of Minnesota Press.

Hay, D. A. (1985). *Essentials of behaviour genetics.* Melbourne: Blackwells.

Heston, L. L. (1966). *British Journal of Psychiatry*, **112**, 819–825.

Jarvik, L. F., & Bank, L. (1983). Aging twins: Longitudinal psychometric data. In K. W. Schaie (Ed.), *Longitudinal studies of adult psychological development* (pp. 40–63). New York: Guilford.

Jarvik, L. F., Blum, J. E., & Varma, A. O. (1972). *Behavior Genetics*, **2**, 159–171.

Jarvik, L. F., & Falek, A. (1963). *Journal of Gerontology*, **18**, 289–294.

Jarvik, L. F., Kallmann, F. J., Falek, A., & Klaber, M. M. (1957). *Acta Genetica et Statistica Medica*, **7**, 421–430.

Jensen, A. R. (1969). *Harvard Educational Review*, **39**, 1–123.

Jinks, J. L., & Fulker, D. W. (1970). *Psychological Bulletin*, **73**, 311–349.

Kallmann, F. J. (1957). Twin data on the genetics of aging. In G. E. Wolstenhoime & C. M. O'Connor (Eds.), *Methodology of the study of aging* (pp. 131–143). London: Churchill.

Kallmann, F. J., Feingold, L., & Bondy, E. (1951).

American Journal of Human Genetics, **3**, 65–73.

Kallmann, F. J., & Jarvik, L. (1959). Individual differences in constitution in genetic background. In J. E. Birren (Ed.), *Handbook of aging in the individual* (pp. 216–275). Chicago: University of Chicago Press.

Kallmann, F. J., & Sander, G. (1948). *Journal of Heredity*, **39**, 349–357.

Kallmann, F. J., & Sander, G. (1949). *American Journal of Psychiatry*, **106**, 29–36.

Loehlin, J. C. (1987). *Latent variable models*. Hillsdale, NJ: Erlbaum.

Loehlin, J. C., Willerman, L., & Horn, J. M. (1988). *Annual Review of Psychology*, **39**, 101–133.

McClearn, G. E. (1970). Genetic influences on behavior and development. In P. H. Mussen (Ed.), *Carmichael's manual of child psychology* (pp. 77–156). New York: Wiley.

McClearn, G. E., & Foch, T. T. (1985). Behavioral genetics. In J. E. Birren & K. W. Schaie (Eds.), *Handbook of the psychology of aging* (2nd ed., pp. 113–143). New York: Van Nostrand Reinhold.

McClearn, G. E., Pedersen, N. L., Plomin, R., Nesselroade, J. R., & Friberg, L. (1988). *The Swedish adoption/twin study on aging*. Submitted.

McGue, M., & Hirsch, B. (1987). *Twin study of normal aging*. Research grant (AG-06881) awarded by the National Institute on Aging.

Merriman, C. (1924). *Psychological Monographs*, **33** (whole No.), 152.

Pedersen, N. L., Gatz, M., Plomin, R., Nesselroade, J. R., & McClearn, G. E. (1989). *Journal of Gerontology*, **44**, 100–105.

Pedersen, N. L., Lichtenstein, P., Plomin, R., DeFaire, U., McClearn, G. E., & Matthews, K. (1989). *Psychosomatic Medicine*, in press.

Pedersen, N. L., McClearn, G. E., Plomin, R., & Friberg, L. (1985). *Behavior Genetics*, **15**, 407–419.

Pedersen, N. L., Plomin, R., McClearn, G. E., & Friberg, L. (1988). *Journal of Personality and Social Psychology*, in press.

Plomin, R. (1986). *Development, genetics, and psychology*. Hillsdale, NJ: Erlbaum.

Plomin, R. (1987). The nature and nurture of cognitive abilities. In R. J. Sternberg (Ed.), *Advances in the psychology of human intelligence* (pp. 1–33). Hillsdale, NJ: Erlbaum.

Plomin, R., & Daniels, D. (1987). *Behavioral and Brain Sciences*, **10**, 1–16.

Plomin, R., DeFries, J. C., & McClearn, G. E. (1989). *Behavioral genetics: A primer* (2nd ed.). San Francisco: Freeman (in press).

Plomin, R., Lichtenstein, P., Pedersen, N., McClearn, G. E., & Nesselroade, J. R. (1989). *Psychology and Aging*, in press.

Plomin, R., McClearn, G. E., Pedersen, N. L., Nesselroade, J. R., & Bergeman, C. S. (1988). *Developmental Psychology*, **24**, 738–745.

Plomin, R., McClearn, G. E., Pedersen, N. L., Nesselroade, J. R., & Bergeman, C. S. (1989). *Journal of Marriage and the Family*, in press.

Plomin, R., & Nesselroade, J. R. (1989). *Journal of Personality*, in press.

Plomin, R., Pedersen, N. L. McClearn, G. E., Nesselroade, J. R., & Bergeman, C. S. (1988). *Psychology and Aging*, **3**, 43–50.

Plomin, R., & Thompson, L. (1988). Life-span developmental behavioral genetics. In P. B. Baltes, D. L. Featherman, & R. M. Lerner (Eds.), *Life-span development and behavior* (Vol. 8, pp. 1–31). Hillsdale, NJ: Erlbaum.

Scarr, S., & Kidd, K. K. (1983). Developmental behavior genetics. In P. H. Mussen (Ed.), *Handbook of child psychology* (4th ed.), Vol. 2, pp. 345–433). New York: Wiley.

Schaie, K. W. (1975). Research strategy in developmental human behavior genetics. In K. W. Schaie, V. E. Anderson, G. E. McClearn, & J. Money (Eds.). *Developmental human behavior genetics: Nature-nurture redefined* (pp. 205–219). Lexington, MA: Lexington Books.

Schaie, K. W. (1988). *Longitudinal studies of adult cognitive development*. Pennsylvania State University, College of Human Development. Grant funded by the National Institute of Aging.

Snyderman, M., & Rothman, S. (1987). *American Psychologist*, **42**, 137–144.

Stunkard, A. J., Foch, T. T., & Hrubec, Z. (1986). *Journal of the American Medical Association*, **256**, 51–54.

Tellegen, A., Lykken, D. T., Bouchard, T. J., Jr., Wilcox, K., Segal, N., & Rich, S. (1988). *Journal of Personality and Social Psychology*, **54**, 1031–1039.

Five

Biological and Health Influences on Behavior

Merrill F. Elias, Jeffrey W. Elias, and Penelope K. Elias

The present chapter integrates two topics that were treated in separate chapters in the previous *Handbook of the Psychology of Aging*: biological factors and health. This is not an easy task. The amount of information has exploded since Siegler and Costa published their 1985 *Handbook* chapter on this topic. Further, space restrictions require that the present chapter focus on the issues we consider most important and make good use of previous reviews of the literature, including the Master Lecture, "Developmental Health Psychology," presented by Ilene Siegler at the 1988 meetings of the American Psychological Association. We have attempted to "plow new ground" where possible, although in some cases the literature must be placed in brief historical perspective. We emphasize methodological issues because we believe that developmental health psychology is in a transition period between the study of "disease" and "health" in a general sense and the more current focus on specific diseases and health factors. The present chapter deals with vascular dementias and Parkinson's disease, which have not been part of the previous *Handbook* health chapters but are particularly relevant to biological influences on behavior with advancing age.

Disease and health are viewed as special topics of great pertinence to life span psychologists who work within the broad area of biological factors and adult development. Thus, in the present chapter, health and disease are emphasized, but biology enters in with respect to our initial discussion of distinctions between normal aging and disease. We view both aging and disease as developmental processes; the former begins at conception and the latter, at conception or anytime thereafter. However, for practical purposes, we concentrate on the years from young adulthood to old age and employ Siegler's working definition of young adulthood as beginning in the early 20s, extending through middle age (45 years) to the elderly years (65 years) and into old age (85+ years). The distinctions are arbitrary. Aging progresses at different rates for different people, but this crude categorization may be useful to the reader. As is discussed in the next section,

Handbook of the Psychology of Aging, Third Edition
Copyright © 1990 Academic Press, Inc. All rights of reproduction in any form reserved.

disease is even more difficult to define, and distinctions between disease and aging do not come easily.

I. Biology, Disease, and Aging

The impact of disease on morbidity, mortality, and quality of life in the elderly is readily apparent to those who study the aging process. Cardiovascular disease, diabetes, and cancer are among the leading causes of death in the elderly population (Brody, 1988). Cardiovascular and cerebrovascular disease alone account for over one-half of the deaths in patients over age 65. These and other chronic, though often nonfatal, conditions, such as arthritis, bone disease, gastrointestinal disorders, hearing and visual impairments result in disabilities that contribute to a significantly lower quality of life in the later years. Often the chronic diseases and age-related disabilities are accompanied by truly life-threatening disease.

Space limitations preclude a detailed review of the epidemiology of disease in the elderly or a summary of disabilities and biological changes occurring with age. However, chapters in a recent volume by Brody (1988) and a chapter by Gatz, Pearson, and Weicker (1987), among others, make it clear that disease detracts significantly from quality of life, both financially and functionally. In some cases, disease results in catastrophic financial losses for elderly persons, who see their life savings dwindle to nothing. Ultimately, the health psychology of aging has two major goals: (1) to bring psychological data to bear on the prevention of disease and (2) to improve the quality of life for those who suffer from disease and disability. Research in this important area provides the data base to accomplish these goals.

For investigators focusing on the adult life span, there is a need to make conceptual and empirical distinctions between illness and the aging process per se because of their increasingly close interrela-

tionship during the middle and elderly years (Siegler & Costa, 1985). Yet, the appropriateness of the distinction has been questioned. Those who have been challenged to define each can be sympathetic with J. Grimsley Evans's eloquent statement that "in fact, to draw a distinction between disease and normal aging is to attempt to separate the undefined from the indefinable" (Evans, 1988, p. 40). Evans argues persuasively that the distinction made between *normal aging* and *disease* has arisen from clinical medicine because of its tradition of thinking dichotomously, that is, if one must treat or not treat, it is useful to think in terms of disease and nondisease. Further, he argues that the disease and nondisease model is not appropriate for clinical practice with the elderly because it may preclude interventions that are not of the traditional medical form.

Yet one must make the distinction, at least initially, if one is to challenge traditional notions about inevitable consequences of aging. Moreover, there are clinical and social reasons for treating aging and disease as separate entities. Siegler and Costa (1985) point out that patients and family members may seek out treatment if they do not dismiss changes in behavior or health as inevitable consequences of aging. In fact, in a study by Dye and Sassenrath (1979), health care professionals classified as normal aging any condition with an onset accompanying old age, even though the condition could be treated or reversed.

Busse's (1969) distinction between primary and secondary aging has been useful to investigators who wish to categorize reversible and irreversible age-associated changes. *Primary aging* refers to changes inherent to the aging process that are ultimately irreversible. *Secondary aging* refers to changes caused by illnesses that are correlated with age but are usually reversible.

Hayflick's (1987) theoretical perspective is that normal age changes be considered separate from those related to disease processes. The distinction made by Hayflick is that there are losses of function that do not produce increased vulnerability to death (e.g., menopause, graying of hair), and there are losses of function that do permit vulnerability to pathological (disease) processes (e.g., changes in the immune system), and hence death. Nevertheless, a functional change does not have to be considered *part* of a disease process even if it leads to vulnerability to disease (Hayflick, 1987). This last component of Hayflick's theory is somewhat arguable from the perspective that disease processes often make one vulnerable, particularly in association with advanced age (and consequently with those functional changes correlated with advanced age), and vice versa. Both aging and disease lead to increased vulnerability.

A. Universal, Progressive, and Irreversible Disease Processes

Kohn (1985) offers the following perspective on aging and disease, a biological perspective in which aging occurs in all members of a population: Aging is universal, inevitable, and can occur even under optimal genetic and environmental circumstances. It is distinguished from development because it takes place after growth ceases. Thus *senescence* (growing old) begins on a physical basis as soon as growth stops. All systems, however, do not age from the same point in time or at the same rate. For those who study the biology of aging, documenting the rate at which different systems age and how they interact with each other as they age is of major importance (Finch, 1988).

Kohn (1985) has suggested the following taxonomy that is relevant to the definition of disease in the present chapter.

1. There are diseases that are universal, progressive, and irreversible with age. Atherosclerosis, a chronic vascular system disease, is considered a disease of

this nature. It is universal in that it is seen in all populations, and signs of atherosclerotic deposits can be found at a very young age.

2. There are diseases that are common with age but not universal and not inevitable. Cancer would fit into this category. Age is definitely a risk factor for cancer, but not for all types of cancer, and cancer tends to affect subgroups of the population. Some kinds of cancers, such as lung cancer, decrease in probability with age (after age 70). Other kinds of cancers, such as colon cancer, increase sharply in older age groups.

3. A third class of diseases includes those that are not necessarily related to age but may have more of a negative impact as age progresses. Death rates due to pneumonia increase sharply with age due to the increased vulnerability of the physical system. The degree of normal activity restriction due to acute, temporary illness (e.g., colds, flu) in those age 65 and over is three times that observed in younger individuals (Kohn, 1985).

For a change in a system to represent normal aging, Kohn (1985) suggests the following criteria: The change should have universality, progression, and irreversibility. It should not be secondary to some other process or reversible or modifiable as that process changes. The change should contribute to the vulnerability of the system to debility and disease and not be adapted effectively to or compensated for. Thus, Category 1 diseases (e.g., atherosclerosis) would represent normal aging processes.

B. Pathogeric and Eugeric Aging

The terms *pathogeric* and *eugeric* have been adopted by Finch (1988) in an effort to distinguish between age-related phenomena that are secondary to actual disease processes (pathogeric) and those that are more generally distributed with age (eugeric). The designation of a phenomenon as pathogeric versus "normal," and eugeric, may be a matter of defining a threshold of homeostatic balance. For example, Parkinson's disease is thought to manifest itself when there has been an 80% loss of the dopaminergic cells in the nigrostriatal area that project to the neostriatum. Such a cell loss is hypothesized to begin normally in midlife and progress in proportion to the life span (Finch, 1988). A 20% to 40% loss of striatal dopamine receptors over the life span is considered normal for humans. In most individuals (99%), the rate of such cell loss does not accelerate, with or without a toxic insult, to the point where a disease process is evident within the lifespan.

For disease processes that appear to involve a progressive neuronal loss and subsequent imbalance between neurotransmitters (e.g., Alzheimer's disease, Huntington's disease, Parkinson's disease), Finch has proposed two models. The first model is one where an accelerated loss of neuronal material can lead to a point where a threshold of normal functioning is exceeded. For example, in Huntington's disease, where neuronal cells in the striatum are damaged, a possibly genetically determined accelerated loss could be initiated by contact with toxic substances at any point during the life span, effectively resulting in an accelerated aging loss of striatal dopamine receptors.

The second model proposes a congenital deficit in cell number at birth. A disease process develops when congenital loss summates with normal age changes or any insult that would reduce cell number. A combination of models is possible. A susceptibility to a disease like Parkinson's or Alzheimer's diseases could be the result of fewer cells present from birth in combination with an accelerated loss due to genetics, toxins, or injury.

The conceptualizations of Hayflick (1987), Kohn (1985), and Finch (1988) are representative of the spectrum of thought

regarding what is and what is not normal aging. In consideration of such models, pathologist Horton Johnson (1985) pointed out that degenerative processes can be called normal aging until they proceed to clinically significant levels. Some atrophy of the brain is considered normal with aging, as is some degree of atherosclerotic development. From the pathologist's (rather than the clinician's) perspective, the distinction between normal and pathological aging is an artificial construct of little biological importance (Johnson, 1985).

II. Methodological Implications of Health Psychology Paradigms

The methods we use (and those we choose to criticize) are related to our metaphysical biases or world views. These are beliefs about the nature of the universe that extend all the way down to the characteristics of the phenomena we investigate (Reese & Overton, 1970). How one defines disease and aging and how one decides the issue of separability versus inseparability of the two constructs influence research methods. Evan's (1988) argument that disease and aging are inseparable constructs represents an explicit world view. However, often world views are not made explicit. Even more often, the holder of the view may not be aware of its influence on his or her methodological biases.

We suspect that many researchers who utilize regression designs to study degree of illness (or wellness) view normal and abnormal and healthy and unhealthy as correlated continuous dimensions (the continuous distribution model). In contrast, those who study healthy and unhealthy subjects view health and disease as separate constructs and often further assume that healthy is normal (the discrete entity model).

The discrete entity model has been predominant in the historical progression of the health psychology of aging from studies of normal aging, which screen out ill subjects, to studies comparing ill and healthy subjects broadly defined, and finally, to more fine-grained analyses of disease types and subtypes. In evaluating these studies, one must keep in mind that *healthy* and *normal* are psychological constructs. Numbers of subjects in any age group qualifying as "healthy" decrease as a function of the technological sophistication of the diagnostic tools used for screening. For example, with traditional epidemiologic screening tools, that is, history of angina pectoris or myocardial infarction and abnormal electrocardiogram, only about 50% of the older persons with heart disease were identified among the participants in the Baltimore Longitudinal Study (Lakatta, 1987). The remaining one-half of the patients with heart disease were identified using stress exercise electrocardiogram monitoring and thalium scanning.

Group comparisons within the discrete entity model are not intrinsically flawed, but conclusions must be drawn with the limitations of the design in mind. For example, the predominant explanation of why hypertensive and normotensive groups differ in cognitive function postulates the underlying mechanisms of the disease as causal, for example, autoregulation, metabolic factors, and/or CNS pathology (see Elias, Robbins, & Schultz, 1987). Yet hypertensives and normotensives share different experiences from the moment of diagnosis. One group is aware of a potentially life-threatening disease, and the other is not; one is treated for hypertension, often with multiple drugs, diet, and life-style changes, and the other is not. Undue emphasis on obvious physiological mechanisms of the disease can serve to obscure the array of variables that are affected by inclusion in a disease group.

Investigators in adult developmental psychology typically define cohorts as birth cohorts in emphasizing the special characteristics that can be attributed to membership in a particular group born within a range of years. However, the term *cohort* is far more general than its common application in aging research. In a more general sense, it indicates membership in a class with a common set of characteristics defining that class. Thus for researchers in health psychology, it is helpful to think of disease groups as disease cohorts. Further, once diagnosed, disease cohort members become patient cohort members. Patient cohort status includes variables other than those related to the disease process per se, that is, variables related to being defined as "unhealthy" (for example, anxiety, depression, and anger). Thus the effects of patient cohort status must be taken into consideration in developing or evaluating explanatory constructs to identify the mechanisms linking disease to behavior. This is particularly true for retrospective research where the patient enters the study as a member of a cohort defined by patient status and a disease or disease complex. We will avoid the terms *patient cohort* and *disease cohort* in this chapter given the commonly limited use of the term *cohort* to refer to "birth cohort" in the aging research literature. Yet, the concept is important with respect to interpretation of differences between disease groups and healthy or "normal" groups.

It is clear that prospective studies (in which individuals move from healthy cohort status to disease cohort and patient cohort statuses during the course of the study) allow us to avoid many of the difficulties in interpreting causal links between disease and behavior; yet even here we must remember that there are non-disease-related variables that may contribute to the development of disease. Further, these same variables, quite independently, may contribute to various behavioral outcomes. For example, some studies suggest that cardiovascular responsivity, coping styles, and parental environment may contribute to the development of hypertension and cardiovascular disease (see Chesney & Rosenman, 1985). But they may also be related to lower levels of cognitive performance independently of their linkage to disease.

A. Multiple Patient Groups

The use of designs that include patient groups with different diseases avoids the confounding of patient status and disease *per se.* Such designs are useful when a different pattern of behaviors is predicted for different diseases (see for example, Felton & Revenson, 1987). They also are useful to fine-grained analyses involving subtypes of a single disease such as essential hypertension. The comparison of disease subtypes is particularly important because broad classifications of a disease, for example, cardiovascular disease or hypertension, may obscure findings if subtypes have opposite or different effects.

B. Longitudinal Studies

Longitudinal studies represent one solution to the confounds involved in comparisons between patient and nonpatient groups because the "event course" of a disease can be tracked. For example, tracking change in performance from normotensive to uncomplicated hypertensive status and thence to hypertension with medical complication provides better data with regard to disease subtypes than comparisons of different patient groups with these diagnoses.

Limitations of longitudinal designs, including statistical and interpretive problems related to attrition, are well known. Moreover, designs using multiple patient groups involve very small numbers of subjects because careful subject selection (application of medical, endocrine, and other exclusionary criteria), combined with attrition, reduces sample sizes dramatically. On the other hand, adherence to large sample statistics precludes refined analysis with carefully diagnosed subjects. Small sample analytic approaches and single-case study methods are well known to clinical medicine, epidemiology, neurology, and to the behavioral sciences. Such methods can be employed effectively in many instances. In fact, incorporation of small sample size and single-subject techniques into the mainstream of research on the health psychology of aging is essential if we are to move from the more general finding that diseased patients differ from nondiseased nonpatients to an in-depth understanding of which diseases are associated with behavioral decline and at what rates.

We are not advocating small or single-sample studies as the only approach. Clearly, one often trades generalizability for specificity. Our argument is simply that the representativeness of a sample or the generalizability of the findings must be evaluated in terms of the information sought, information gained, and cost-effectiveness. For example, large sample studies of a class of individuals diagnosed as hypertensive provide us with information about the interaction between membership in this general disease category and birth cohort membership. However, we may learn nothing about the subclasses of hypertension (e.g., high renin hypertension with and without angiotensinogenic hypertension) unless we specifically recruit these patients. Attempting to identify them from a large random sample of hypertensives (postbehavioral testing) may be prohibitively costly. Recruiting small samples of particular hypertensive subtypes may be the only way we can understand the mechanisms by which hypertension per se (rather than common membership in a hypertensive disease group) affects behavior.

C. Regression Analyses with Continuous Distributions

Reevaluation of the conceptual basis of comparisons between disease and healthy groups may be forced by what appears to be the beginning of a paradigm shift within medicine. Evans (1988) summarizes this shift in a few well-chosen words:

We now work to a multifactorial model of such diseases in which specific pathological mechanisms of symptoms and impairments are seen as the final common pathway of a wide variety of possible causal chains. . . . We have also been forced to concede that the distinction between the "diseased" and the "healthy" may be quantitative rather than qualitative. . . . The idea of continuous distributions of physiopathological variables, with associated risk functions, is now one of the basic modes of epidemiological thought, and although introduced into clinical medicine by Pickering has not flourished there. (p. 39)

Practical examples abound, for example, the arbitrary nature of cutting scores for "hypertension" even though it is not a single disease entity with a single cause.

Regression analysis using the full range of continuously distributed indices of pathophysiology is more consistent with this "new" paradigm than comparisons of different diagnostic groups. Further, if the case is to be made that mechanisms associated with a disease are causal with respect to impaired performance, it would seem necessary to demonstrate that severity of the disease is correlated with magnitude of performance decrement. For example, a positive correlation between degree of observed coronary artery stenosis and cognitive performance provides more impressive evidence for the role of coronary artery disease in behavior than the observation that patients with and without clinically significant coronary artery disease differ in behavior (see Elias & Robbins, 1987).

III. Methodological Challenges

A. Medication

The majority of the studies reviewed in this chapter use the intact groups (quasi-experimental) design. A major problem in interpretation of results is introduced by the fact that patients must be treated for diseases and, therefore, treatment and disease are confounded. Drug-disease confounding sometimes can be eliminated in cross-sectional designs, for example, patients may take "drug holidays" prior to data collection. This also is possible in controlled short-term studies, such as are undertaken by pharmaceutical companies or the National Institutes of Health. The major problem is encountered in long-term longitudinal studies where patients cannot be denied treatment for extended periods of time. Drug washout periods during data collection intervals constitute only a partial solution because patients take medications during test–retest interims, often come to the study with a history of medication, and could suffer negative effects on performance due to withdrawal from medication (see Light, 1980). The problem increases with the age of the study participant because multiple drug use increases with advancing age (Turner & Rowe, 1988). Further, doses and types of drugs, as well as compliance, can vary considerably during longitudinal test–retest interims.

In clinical and field studies, careful record keeping and analyses of specific types of medications or classes of medications are solutions. This is easier said than done because drug treatment regimens vary greatly from individual to individual, especially for elderly individuals who may be on several drugs simultaneously or at different dosage levels than younger individuals. It is difficult to find large enough numbers of subjects to constitute meaningful groupings even when general drug classification is employed, for example, diuretics and beta blocking agents, diuretics alone, and so on. Regardless of specific medications, it is usually possible to evaluate the success or failure of treatment based on external criteria, for example, reductions in blood pressure values by a certain absolute amount or percentage. We hope pharmaceutical companies will respond to the need for longer term controlled clinical drug trials with humans. To date, they have largely ignored elderly patients, women, and some minorities in drug trials. The NIH studies of isolated systolic hypertension will provide very useful data regarding the interaction of drug therapy and hypertension in the elderly over short study periods. However, primarily because of ethical considerations, the problem of how to follow unmedicated patients over a 10- to 15-year period will not easily be solved. For ethical reasons, drug trials are terminated when one medication proves to be substantially more effective than another, and often such data are available within 6 months or less.

Problems induced by the confounding of treatment and illness are thus a major challenge to behavior medicine, and the study of effects of medication falls squarely within the province of the health psychology of aging.

B. Age at Disease Onset

Most studies employ age at the time of testing as a major independent variable, but Siegler (1988) reminds us that age at onset of the disease may be equally important from a developmental perspective. For example, no self-respecting developmental neuropsychologist would ignore the age at which a lesion was first sustained when evaluating its behavioral consequences. Buck, Baker, Bass, and Donner (1987) examined hypertension as a risk factor within an older birth cohort by ex-

amining age at onset of hypertension. As would be expected, risk increased for those diagnosed as hypertensive earlier in life. It is important to estimate age at onset of diseases such as hypertension in behavioral studies. But what are the best estimates? The critical variable may be age at which the disease is first diagnosed. But the correlation between first diagnosis and the actual onset of the disease depends on the specific disease (and intensity of its symptoms), the techniques available for diagnosis, and, to some extent, the personality of the patient and his or her beliefs and fears about health care. A good example, from the technological standpoint, is the failure to make a rapid diagnosis of AIDS 10 years ago compared with the current emphasis on this disease. Further, immediate diagnosis does not imply immediate treatment. Often the patient cannot be treated until proper treatment regimens are identified. Treatment regimens themselves vary over time in line with current drug research. Thus we argue that age at diagnosis and age at treatment can be indexed as separate variables; age at onset of the disease cannot be specified with total accuracy.

C. Animal Models

Animal models provide the opportunity to track untreated diseases over substantial periods of the life span and to understand the interactions of variables such as early experience and genetic background (Elias, 1980). Animal models are desirable, but they are not a universal panacea for the study of disease. First, one must establish that the pathological model has validity for the human; second, one can err when inferring causal relationships between disease and behavior with animals as well as humans (see Elias, 1980, for a discussion, as well as the previous section on methodological implications). In our view, the major advantage of animal models is that controlled (e.g., treatment versus non-treatment) and manipulative (e.g., genetic factors) studies can be done.

D. Measurement of Health Status

A survey of research on aging between 1963 and 1964 (Abrahams, Hoyer, Elias, & Bradigan, 1975) indicated that only 12% of studies included some measure of health status. A more recent study (Hoyer, Raskind, & Abrahams, 1984), including the years 1975 to 1982, indicated that 65% reported health status. It is not practical to expect every investigator to assess health via physician examination or to make use of the more extensive and expensive laboratory diagnostic techniques. Further, cost benefit and ethical considerations often preclude refined invasive techniques. Yet the practice of describing subjects as healthy because they were able to reach the testing site is also unacceptable by current standards.

The easiest and least costly solution is to assume that the number of symptoms a subject reports is an indication of the degree of illness and that symptom report subcategories catalogue specific diseases. For example, patients may be placed in a cardiovascular disease group because they endorse related items on the Cornell Medical Index. Costa and McCrae (1985) argue that the use of self-ratings "as proxy measures of objectives status" is quite common and that investigators justify this approach based on significant correlations between patient self-ratings of health and physician-rated health (even though the correlations are modest in magnitude). The issue of validity of self-ratings is complex. They are appropriate where self-assessment is central to the investigation. They can be useful for general screening purposes where the objective is to identify subjects with obvious health problems. However, symptom self-reports are not necessarily veridical and can indicate neu-

roticism as well as physical ill health (Costa & McCrae, 1985). Thus, their validity for studies where the focus is on one or more well-defined disease process is questionable, and cost considerations do not justify their use. The issue of whether illness questionnaires have value for studies of ill health is arguable. In a provocative paper, Zonderman, Heft, and Costa (1985) conclude that using elevated scores on an illness behavior questionnaire as indices of illness without corroborating medical information may be more misleading than simply accepting patients' symptom reports at face value.

Siegler, Nowlin, and Blumenthal (1980) note that where the objective is simply screening for ill health, self-report indices are not the only alternative. Some diagnostic techniques, such as blood pressure measurement, are easily done, and, together with self-reports, represent a better index of ill health. Medical records often are used as an adjunct to symptom self-reports. Obviously they are limited to the extent to which they are current and available to the investigator. Hospital records have been used to classify subjects in longitudinal studies, particularly for patient subgroups. However, there is no substitute for concurrent medical examination procedures where the objective of the study is to explore the effects of a specific disease or eliminate a specific disease as an important control. Siegler and Costa (1985) discuss other points relevant to the measurement of health in which the study of disease is not the central focus of discussion.

Although the need to continue to improve research methods is obvious, we now have a data base that will contribute to meeting a major objective in behavior medicine: decreasing the number of behaviorally dysfunctional years associated with every increase in years lived. The data can be organized by examining two sides of the same coin: the effects of

health on behavior and the effects of behavior on health. We devote more effort
to the former as the latter has received an
extraordinarily comprehensive treatment
in the 1985 *Handbook of the Psychology
of Aging* (Siegler & Costa, 1985). The
Master Lecture on "Developmental
Health Psychology" delivered by Ilene Siegler at the 1988 meetings of the American Psychological Association provides a
virtually complete update of this topic.

Effects of Health on Behavior

We no longer question the fact that poor
health contributes to accelerated decline
in intellectual and social function.
Among others, two very important questions remain: (1) which specific diseases
(and disease subtypes) are responsible for
these changes and (2) what are the underlying causal mechanisms? It is quite obvious from clinical observation and the
terminal drop literature (e.g., Siegler,
1975) that catastrophic diseases result in
a sharp and generalized decline in cognitive function and related social skills.
The real challenge has been presented by
the subtle, progressive diseases, such as
hypertension and cardiovascular diseases.
Indeed, these have received the greatest
attention in the literature, possibly because they are very common age-associated diseases that contribute to high levels of morbidity and mortality. Thus it is
to these diseases that we first turn.

E. Hypertension and
Cardiovascular Disease

Heart and blood vessel diseases account
for one-half of all deaths in the United
States (Blanchard, Martin, & Dubbert,
1988). Blanchard *et al.* (1988) point out
that, despite the decline in deaths due to
heart disease (26%) and stroke (48%) in
the last two decades, these diseases ac-

count for more hospitalized days than any
other conditions.

Perhaps this is why cardiovascular disease and hypertension have received more
attention than other diseases. A clear
summary of work in the previous
Handbook chapter (Siegler & Costa,
1985) and a text dealing with these topics
(Elias & Marshall, 1987) make it possible
to discuss major conclusions and to update the summary of work in this area.

As a result of pioneering studies by Birren, Spieth, and others (e.g., Abrahams,
1976; Light, 1978), we know that the more
severe forms of vascular disease, cerebrovascular disease and atherosclerosis,
are associated with lower levels of performance. In fact, when cardiovascular disease has been broadly defined (i.e., the cardiovascular cohort includes multiple
types of vascular disease including hypertension), groups with cardiovascular disease show more accelerated decline over
time than those who are free from disease,
and psychomotor speed is one of the primary measures affected (e.g., Hertzog,
Schaie, & Gribbin, 1978). Recent studies
by Schaie's group (reported by Siegler,
1988) have indicated that those who
showed cognitive decline over time in a
longitudinal study (beginning at age 50
and extending for 7 years) showed twice as
many cardiovascular symptoms, related
physician visits, and cardiovascular incidents. These studies and studies with
twins (e.g., Jarvik, Vineta, & Matsuyama,
1980) have contributed to a research climate in which explanations of decline in
terms of primary CNS aging are no longer
accepted carte blanche.

The next challenge is to determine
which specific diseases, and even more
specifically, which subtypes of specific
diseases, are associated with decline. Hypertension is a disease worthy of this effort
given its dramatically increasing incidence with advancing age and the fact that
primary (essential) hypertension leads to
cardiovascular, renal, and cerebrovascular

diseases. In studies with very elderly persons, it is difficult to separate hypertension-associated pathology from hypertension per se (e.g., Wilkie & Eisdorfer, 1971). Recent studies in which uncomplicated (no functionally significant end organ changes) essential hypertensives have been studied longitudinally indicate the following. Compared to normotensive birth cohorts, significant decline in intellectual, motor, and psychomotor functioning is either not observed (Costa & Shock, 1980) or is trivial and clearly not clinically significant (e.g., Schultz, Elias, Robbins, Streeten, & Blakeman, 1986, 1989; Elias, Schultz, Robbins, & Streeten, 1986; Elias, Schultz, Robbins, & Elias, 1989; Elias, Robbins, Schultz, Streeten, & Elias, 1987). On balance, recent studies suggest that when one controls for hypertension related diseases, hypertensives show lower mean levels of performance than normotensives, but the rate of change over time is similar. However, hypertensive patients participating in the studies supporting this generalization (Costa & Shock, 1980; Elias *et al.*, 1986, 1989; Schultz *et al.*, 1989) were carefully medicated throughout the studies and highly educated.

Every longitudinal study dealing with the behavioral consequences of moderate to severe hypertension has been unavoidably confounded by medications. Recent evidence indicates that medications used in younger persons and with moderate hypertension, for example, beta blocking agents (Miller, Shapiro, King, Ginchereau, & Hosutt, 19840, can improve performance, at least over short time intervals (15 months). However, some forms of medication used when first and second choice medications fail can affect performance negatively (Larsson, Kukull, Buchner, & Reifler, 1987; Light, 1980). This is particularly true for elderly persons who may not respond to first line treatments and are often on multiple medications (Turner & Rowe, 1988).

There are partial solutions to the disease–drug confound. Costa and Shock (1980) have performed regression and longitudinal analyses of the cognitive performance of borderline hypertensives free of medication (with no significant results). For more severe hypertension and other diseases demanding sustained treatment, we suggest an approach in which those responding successfully to treatment (by clinically relevant criteria) are compared with those who do not.

In a recent study (Farmer, White, Abbott, Kittner, Kaplan, Wolz, Brody, & Wolf, 1987), self-report of medication status (*on* versus *off*) was unrelated to test performance. Two variables often uncontrolled in studies of hypertension were controlled statistically: alcohol consumption and smoking. Blood pressure was only measured once or twice but concurrent with testing. A single outcome measure (an education adjusted composite of eight neuropsychological test scores based on a 20- to 25-minute battery) was unrelated to blood pressure. Given the impressively large sample ($n=2123$) and the fact that the investigators "found no consistent relation between blood pressure and cognitive performance" (p. 1103), the study has attracted considerable attention. However, there were positive findings for individual test measures, that is, better or poorer performance for hypertensives as compared to normotensives depending on age and the neuropsychological measure employed. For example,

Both isolated systolic hypertension as well as diastolic hypertension were associated ($p <0.05$) with Number of Digits Forward with the direction dependent on age. . . . Again, the cognitive performance of those aged 75 and older improved if they had either isolated systolic hypertension or diastolic hypertension. Diastolic hypertension, interestingly, was associated in a protective way with Similarities; performance on this test improved if a person had diastolic hypertension. (p. 1108)

These are interesting findings in view of Wilkie and Eisdorfer's (1971) finding of improved performance for elderly patients with mild hypertension. The cut scores for hypertension in the Farmer *et al.* study were > 160 mmHg systolic and 95 mm Hg diastolic (mild hypertension for persons over 75 years of age).

It is important to note that the Farmer *et al.* study does not deal with specific subtypes of hypertension in relationship to specific performance measures. Rather it is descriptive of a broad class of patients defined as hypertensive (excluding only those who had experienced stroke).

A fundamental problem with single-outcome measures is that some individual tests discriminate between hypertensives and normotensives better than others, and some not at all. Clinical measures of memory (e.g., Wilkie, Eisdorfer, & Nowlin, 1976; Elias *et al.*, 1989) seem to be particularly sensitive to differences between hypertensives and normotensives, yet clinical tests confound memory functions with other dimensions of information processing. Studies with information-processing paradigms (e.g., Madden & Blumenthal, 1989) will be most useful in identifying specific memory processes affected by membership in hypertensive groups.

One must not accept, uncritically, explanations of disease–behavior relationships that postulate pathophysiological mechanisms as the intervening variable, compelling though they may be. Wilkie and Eisdorfer (1971) explained improvement in performance over time for mildly hypertensive elders (60 to 69 years at baseline) in terms of facilitation of cerebrovascular perfusion in a system where blood flow was already compromised by arterio- and atherosclerotic disease and impaired autoregulatory processes. These same pathophysiological mechanisms were employed to explain a decline in performance for an older group of moderately severe hypertensives (70 to 79 years at

baseline). The argument was that cerebrovascular lesions had now developed to the point where the advantages of increased pressure were offset by the negative effects of cerebrovascular pathology. The hypothesis is consistent with the fact that moderately severe hypertension was associated with subsequent intellectual decline for the 70- to 79-year-old group, and none of the severely hypertensive subjects in the 70- to 79-year-old group survived the 10-year retest interval. The hypothesis, as applied to this elderly sample of complicated hypertensives (end organ changes such as cardiovascular disease), is consistent with data from cardiovascular physiology (Berne & Levy, 1986) and provided a very useful model for studies in this area. Yet, as the investigators themselves emphasized, the model has not been demonstrated to have validity in an experimental context and remains hypothetical in nature.

The present authors (e.g., Elias *et al.*, 1987) urge the development of explanatory constructs based on mood state and social psychological variables, for example, anxiety and depression, although we are inclined toward a model in which non-pathophysiological mechanisms contribute more to hypertension and behavior relationships in young adults, whereas pathophysiological processes play an increasingly significant role with advancing age. This is a complex research area because hypertension is a multifactoral disease with many causes, some known and many yet unknown. We urge investigators who would become involved in this exciting area of research first to become familiar with the issues as discussed in the literature cited.

F. Diabetes

Studies of non-insulin dependent diabetes mellitus (NIDDM) are among the most important future efforts in the health psychology of aging. Perlmuter, Tun, Sizer,

McGlinchey, and Nathan's (1987) summary of the literature indicates that diabetes is associated with cognitive deficits greater than those seen in normal aging, although studies by Perlmuter *et al.* (1987) and Tun, Perlmuter, Russo, and Nathan (1987) indicate main effects for age and diabetes, rather than disease × age interactions. These investigators have examined a variety of components of performance including various measures of memory, verbal fluency, and serial learning. The importance of controlling for emotional variables, such as depression (Geringer, Permuter, Stern, & Nathan, 1988), when studying diabetes is emphasized by the finding (Tun *et al.*, 1987) that diabetes ceased to be a predictor of memory complaints when depression levels were controlled.

Given the methodological problems encountered in comparing patients and nonpatients (discussed earlier in this chapter), manipulative studies in which behavior is compared before and after glycemic control are very important, as are studies of the effects of acute increases in blood glucose levels. The notion that diabetes represents a form of accelerated aging (Kent, 1976) underscores the conceptual difficulties encountered in treating disease and aging as orthogonal constructs.

G. Other Diseases

Space limitations do not permit review of the scattered literature on other chronic diseases. The health psychology of aging has just begun to scratch the surface of a vast, potentially available, knowledge base. Examples include toxin exposure, liver disease, renal disease, disorders of the pancreas, pituitary abnormalities, normal and abnormal variations in sex hormones, thyroid disorders, cancer, nutritional deficiencies, irritable bowel syndrome, periodontal disease, and many diseases and syndromes subsumed under these major classifications.

We turn now to one of the most feared illnesses in old age, that is, functional decline to the extent known as dementia.

H. The Dementias

By one estimate, 15% of those over age 65 can be considered demented. In raw numbers, this includes 4.28 million out of an estimated 28.53 million aged 65 and older in the United States in 1985 (Huang, Cartwright, & Hu, 1988) It is estimated that there are some 60 disorders that can result in dementia syndromes (Hutton, 1987), with some 10% to 20% of these having an underlying medical disorder that is treatable. The dementia syndromes that are the most commonly treatable are those related to metabolism, toxins, endocrine disorders, space occupying lesions, functional psychiatric problems, and occult hydrocephalus (Hutton, 1981, 1987).

Dementia is a syndrome, not a disease per se (Hutton, 1987; Marsden, 1984). The prominent clinical signs of dementia include a global impairment of higher cortical functions such that memory, judgment, initiation of action, social functioning, control of emotions, and the ability to carry out everyday tasks may all be affected (Hutton, 1987; Marsden, 1984). In diagnosing dementia, it is important to note the global nature of cognition impairment so as to distinguish progressive and irreversible dementia from other types of more specific intellectual impairments.

1. Alzheimer's Disease

Despite the fact that there are a number of disease processes that can lead to dementia, some reversible and treatable, by far the dominent pathology leading to dementia is Alzheimer's disease (AD). It is estimated that about 50% of those with progressive and irreversible dementia have AD, another 20% have a combination of AD and multi-infarct disease, and 20% have multi-infarct dementia without AD involvement (Marsden, 1984). Because of its catastrophic impact on the lives of elderly persons, Alzheimer's disease is dealt with in a separate chapter in this volume (Chapter 26) and thus will not be discussed further here. It is, however, an important research problem that falls within the domain of behavioral medicine and aging.

2. Vascular Dementias

Because the incidence of cerebral atherosclerosis and mental deterioration increases with age, it was not uncommon in years past to diagnose mental deterioration as a consequence of cerebral atherosclerosis (Marsden, 1984). Actually atherosclerosis affects the larger arteries and tends to spare the smaller cerebral blood vessels that contribute most to cerebral vascular resistance (Marsden, 1984). The result is that cerebral blood flow tends to be maintained even in the presence of advanced atheroma. Dementia due to cerebrovascular involvement most commonly occurs as a result of multiple infarctions. The term *multi-infarct dementia* (MID) is commonly used to refer to all forms of vascular dementias (Roman, 1987). Roman (1987) reports that many patients with a clinical diagnosis of vascular dementia do not show evidence of extensive cerebral infarcts via computed tomography. With high-resolution-computed tomography or magnetic resonance imaging, such patients do show low density lesions of the periventricular white matter, ventricular dilation, and lacunes (small deep cerebral infarcts). The lacunar strokes are most often found in the basal ganglia. Thus Roman (1987) has suggested that the vascular dementias be classified into two major categories: (1) multi-infarct dementia (cortical dementia with large artery involvement mainly from atherosclerosis or embolisms) resulting in a loss of brain volume exceeding 50 ml and (2) lacunar dementia (LD) or Binswanger's disease (small artery disease) with basal ganglia and periventricular white matter involvement.

The clinical picture of LD is one involving gait difficulty, urinary incontinence, pseudobulbar palsy, emotional lability and dementia. Onset would be expected between ages 50 to 65 years, with features of frontal lobe involvement, a history of hypertension, diabetes, and/or discrete strokes. The multi-infarct dementia syndrome (including LD) is distinguished clinically from AD by virtue of its more acute onset, fluctuating course, focal neurological symptoms, and stepwise deterioration (Marsden, 1984). Hashinski, Iliff, Zilkha, DuBoulay, McAllister, Mashall, Russell, and Symon (1975) have developed a scale as an initial means by which to identify possible MID.

3. Parkinson's Disease

Dementia associated with Parkinson's disease (PD) has received a great deal of attention recently, but few behavioral studies have been done to date. PD affects one-half to 1 million individuals in the United States (Rajput, Offord, Beard, & Kurland, 1984). Eighty-five percent is considered to be idiopathic parkinsonism (Rajput, Vitti, Stern, & Laverty, 1986). PD is rarely diagnosed before the age of 40 but shows an increasing prevalence from ages 50 to 79. There are four characteristic signs: tremor, akinesia or bradykinesia, rigidity of movement, and loss of normal postural reflexes (Birkmayer, Danielczyk, & Riederer, 1983). The prominence of these symptoms varies and as many as one-third of those with PD may initially show a lack of tremor (Perlmutter, 1988). The development of PD has been related primarily to the degeneration of neurons in the substantia nigra that project to the striatum and a subsequent loss of dopamine content to the striatum. Receptors in the striatum, however, remain intact, permitting treatment of PD by use of l-dopa (Hutton, Morris, Roman, Imke, & Elias, 1988). L-dopa crosses the blood–brain barrier and is converted to dopamine.

Dopamine initially relieves the symptoms but is not thought to slow the progression of the disease. After several years many receiving l-dopa therapy may develop marked symptomatic fluctuations in response to therapy. Progression through the disease is characterized typically by use of a scale developed by Hoehn and Yahr (1967) that classifies the disease process according to stages: Stage 1 = unilateral disease involvement; Stage 2 = bilaterial disease involvement with no balance impairment; Stage 3 = bilateral impairment and balance impairment; Stage 4 = independent mobility markedly incapacitated; and Stage 5 = confinement to bed or wheelchair unless aided.

Not all parkinsonians develop dementia. It is difficult to estimate the actual numbers of those who do, but reasonable estimates range from 20% to 30% (Marsden, 1984). Our review of the studies most often cited as evidence of dementia in PD shows that the same level of caution in diagnosis of dementia associated with AD is not observed for PD. In fact, some studies of cognitive functioning in PD have defined demented groups solely on the basis of a mental status screening exam or the results of a battery of cognitive tests that have not been related to dementia specifically. Such exams usually are designed for screening purposes only and have arbitrary cutoff points for designation of dementia specifically. The level of cognitive testing that should be considered just a starting point in the diagnosis of AD is often used as a diagnostic end point for designating dementia in PD. Because cognitive performance is neither considered an initial symptom of PD nor of importance in plotting the progression of the disease, great care is not given to the degree of cognitive impairment shown. The clinical stages of the disease have been found to correlate only modestly with cognitive performance (Mortimer & Webster, 1982; Netherton, Elias, Albrecht, Acosta, Hutton, & Albrecht, 1989). Nevertheless,

some parkinsonians do develop a dementia. It is not known if this is the same type of dementia as that seen in AD, if the progression is the same, or if the end point is the same.

Even among those with PD who do not show signs of dementia, most will show poorer cognitive performance as a group compared to age-matched comparison groups. Differences between those with PD and comparison groups on generalized tests of general intellectual function are slight (Albrecht, Elias, Netherton, Hutton, & Albrecht, 1986; Elias, Netherton, Albrecht, Hutton, & Albrecht, 1988; Netherton *et al.*, 1989). Perceptual motor or visual spatial performance in PD are the areas most often cited as consistently different between parkinsonians and comparison groups (Netherton *et al.*, 1989; Passafiume, Boller, & Keefe, 1986; Stern & Mayeux, 1986; Taylor, Saint-Cyr, & Lang, 1987). Much of the recent attention focused on PD has been due to the discovery of the "MPTP" neurotoxin-induced form of PD (Langston, Ballard, Tetrud, & Irwin, 1983). The neurotoxin is a meperidine derivative (1-methyl-4-phenyl-1,2,3,6-tetrahydro-pyridine (MPTP). The victims of this drug were cocaine and demerol users who had received a badly prepared synthesized demerol derivative (MPP+). Stern and Mayeux (1986) studied perceptual motor performance in those with MPP+ toxin-induced parkinsonism and found that construction, Stroop Color-Word performance, and category naming were impaired relative to performance of a comparison group. Measures of attention, memory, digit span, calculation, and language performance were comparable. The unique aspect of testing the MPTP parkinsonians was that the toxin selectively affects lesions in the dopaminergic system. Levels of other neurotransmitters (e.g., noradrenalin, acetylcholine, serotonin) are affected only acutely and then return to normal levels. Thus, it may be that the most prominent cognitive change noted in

PD, perceptual-motor/visual-spatial performance, is mostly influenced by dopaminergic changes. The study employed only a small sample of six parkinsonians, so more subtle changes in the remaining areas of performance might not have been detected. Despite this possibility, the sensitivity of the tasks to dopaminergic systems was clearly demonstrated. Recently, attention has been focused on the role of other toxins in PD. The reader may consult Lux and Kurtzke (1987) among others for reviews, including the role of pesticides (as cited in Barbeau, Roy, Cloutier, Plasse, & Paris, 1986).

At one time, bradyphrenia, or slowness of thought, was taken to be a sign of cognitive dysfunction in PD, but with the advent of l-dopa treatment this was not clinically apparent. A recent study of this phenomenon by Elias, Netherton, Albrecht, Hutton, and Albrecht (1988) found no relationship between indices of cognitive slowing and the motor slowing that accompanies PD. A question may be raised as to whether early onset of PD, like early onset of AD, is associated with greater cognitive deficits. To the contrary, Netherton et al. (1989) found that patients who experienced later onset of PD were more likely to show poorer cognitive performance, particularly on visual-spatial tasks, than those who experienced earlier onset.

IV. The Impact of Behavior on Health

The impact of behavior on health has been addressed in considerable depth in the chapter by Siegler and Costa (1985) in the previous *Handbook* and by Siegler (1988). Thus we will restrict our discussion to some of the more pressing research areas.

A. Behavior Pathogens

Matarazazo (1984) coined the term *behavioral pathogen* to express the fact that per-

sonal habits and life-styles can contribute to mortality and morbidity. The reader is directed to a series of conferences dealing with the role of behavior in the development of disease (Hamburg, Elliot, & Parron, 1982). Siegler (1988) has identified age, sex, and family history as prominent biological risk factors and smoking, excessive alcohol consumption, Type A behavior pattern, hostility, job strain, psychosocial stress, and sexual malfunctioning as major behavioral risk factors. Risk-reducing behaviors include reduced fat and increased fiber intake, exercise, use of aspirin under prescribed circumstances, moderate alcohol consumption, social supports, and regular medical care. It is obvious that these are not specific to any single disease. The reader working in this area may wish to consult the table in the Siegler (1988) article. It summarizes the major, known, primary links between habits and disease.

Although some studies indicate that the probability of changing health practices over substantial periods of time is low (Rakowski, 1987), older persons respond to intervention at least as well as younger persons (Siegler, 1988). The question of what is a successful intervention for all age groups remains a challenge for health psychologists. Rakowski (1987) found that the best predictor of health habits over a year was the previous year's habits. Siegler and Costa (1985) caution against overinterpreting data on habits as predictors of health outcomes until the roles of personality and other factors are understood more clearly.

B. Personality

Personality has been treated extensively in the previous *Handbook* chapter by Siegler and Costa (1985). Recently there have been some exciting papers and volumes dealing with the topic (e.g., Chesney & Rosenman, 1985; Costa, McCrae & Arenberg, 1983; Williams & Anderson, 1987). In particular, Type A behavior has received very thoughtful attention (Dembroski & Costa, 1987; Haynes & Matthews, 1988). Authors of two previous *Handbook* chapters (Eisdorfer & Wilkie, 1977; Siegler & Costa, 1985) conclude that global Type A behavior per se has been a poor predictor of coronary heart disease among older persons, and Siegler (1988) reports data from the Second Duke Longitudinal Study indicating that the top distribution of Type A scores is not found in nonclinical samples of older subjects. This is consistent with earlier data from the Framingham Study indicating that Type A behavior pattern predicts coronary heart disease for men and women 45 to 65 years of age but not beyond. The obvious thought is that persons with Type A behaviors do not survive. On the other hand, the predictive value of Type A at any age has been challenged (Costa, Krantz, Blumenthal, Furberg, Rosenman, & Shekelle, 1987; Haynes & Matthews, 1988), and extreme Type A behavior itself may be subject to social shaping by life-style changes such as retirement.

Siegler and Costa (1985) argue that evidence does not support the generalization that premorbid personalities predict disease but rather that the Type A construct may be useful if one carefully evaluates the specific behaviors included as predictors. Two potentially important areas of research on cardiovascular disease in aging emerge from this strategy: (1) the examination of physiological, specifically endocrine, differences between Type A and non-Type A individuals (Williams, Lane, Kuhn, Melosh, White, & Schanberg, 1982) and (2) the study of "toxic" behaviors such as cynical hostility (Costa, Zonderman, McCrae, & Williams, 1986; Dembroski & Costa, 1987).

One major methodological problem is that investigators often use self-report of somatic symptoms, for example, angina, as criteria for cardiovascular disease. These are not objective indicators. Work by Costa, Fleg, McCrae, and Lakatta (1982) and Elias, Robbins, Blow, Rice, and Edge-comb (1982) indicates that the number of somatic symptoms reported (including cardiovascular symptoms) is inversely related to degree of coronary artery stenosis and positively related to indices of neuroticism. Further, elderly persons may fail to report symptoms that they attribute to "normal" aging (Kart, 1981), and self-report of symptoms interacts with other birth cohort phenomena, such as educational level (Cockerman, Sharp, & Wilcox, 1983).

The study of personality factors in self-perceptions of health can contribute to development of models of health behavior. These, in turn, are important for models of health service utilization by the elderly (e.g., Krause, 1988). One important question is the extent to which older persons report symptoms that do not exist. An important paper by Costa and McCrae (1985) dispells the popular myth that older persons are hypochondriacs. Three findings are relevant: (1) there is an increase in real physical diseases in the areas reported by older individuals; (2) older people tend to underreport symptoms; (3) there are enduring individual differences in neuroticism that are much better predictors of somatic complaints than age. However, the literature reviewed by Costa and McCrae (1987a) does not indicate that high levels of neuroticism are related to disease. In fact, neuroticism may protect against disease because neurotic individuals are more likely to seek out health care.

Research in the area of personality as it relates to health psychology and aging is compromised by large numbers of tests, scales, and constructs in the absence of accurate knowledge about how they relate to each other and to fundamental dimensions of personality and cognitive function. Costa and McCrae (1987b) point out that we would benefit greatly from a systematic taxonomy of personality dimensions that would allow the grouping together of related personality traits and constructs. For example, the five-factor model of Norman (1963) may be used in this way. Thus, as is illustrated by the work of Costa and McCrae (1987a), one may use this model to identify scales that have the same name but that measure different personality constructs, and, conversely, to identify scales that have different names but measure the same constructs. If investigators make better use of this "taxometric" approach, it will facilitate the task of relating current and future research findings in a meaningful way.

C. Stress and Coping

Response to stress is an important intervening variable between personality characteristics and health (e.g., Williams 1979). Perception of ill health is itself a stressor (Parron, Solomon, & Rodin, 1981). Stress has been related to the development of cancer (e.g., Sklar & Anisman, 1981) and to decreased immune system functioning (see Weksler, 1981, for a review). Even though the *Handbook* chapter by Eisdorfer and Wilkie (1977) was written some time ago, it is well worth reading as these authors build a model of health, behavior, and aging around the construct of stress.

The term *stress* often is used in such a general way that its power as an explanatory construct is questionable. Studies typically involve a self-report measure of coping, personality, or physical symptom report as an index of response to what the researchers consider a stressful event. The intervening physiological or psychological construct is rarely specified. Nonetheless, several models of stress prove to be important, for example, those linking psychosocial stressors and cardiovascular disease (Williams, 1979), the relationship between neuroendocrines and the immune system (Su, London, & Jaffey, 1988; Weksler, 1981), and the impact of stressful life events (Radkin & Struening, 1976). Recent reviews and discussions of the stressful life events instruments and paradigms

have been provided by Chiriboga (1984) and Schroeder and Costa (1984).

The emergence of a body of literature focusing on the coping responses to stress is not new, but current expansion is rapid. We direct the reader to a review of the literature by Felton and Revenson (1989) and the chapter by Schooler in this *Handbook*. Siegler and Costa (1985) point out that a particularly pertinent research question is the extent to which coping with illness actually requires different coping mechanisms than coping with other stressful life events.

D. Locus of Control

The locus of control literature has become very important to the health psychology of the elderly given the loss of control represented by age-associated decrements in homeostasis and health (Rodin, 1986). Among the potentially important areas for future research are (a) the links between controllable and noncontrollable life situations and changes in the immune system and (b) the notion of psychological "hardiness" developed by Kobasa (1979). Research by Elias, Weinstein, Hutton, and Brat (1987) with Alzheimer's caregivers indicates that internal locus of control and a higher degree of mental toughness (desensitization) produces consistently lower estimates of depression, higher self-esteem, and fewer reports of physical symptoms of aging.

V. Health-Related Behaviors and Interventions

There are many topics relevant to health that we could not cover in the space available. Two of the most important are the topics of intervention and issues of health in women. Much of the work on intervention has been summarized in a book by Engel (1983). Gatz *et al.* (1987) discuss intervention and compliance in the context of an applied adult developmental psychology designed to utilize psychological interventions with the physically (rather than mentally) ill. See also the chapter by Smyer in this *Handbook*.

The *Handbook of Behavioral Medicine for Women* (1988) covers an extensive literature dealing with health psychology and women. Chapters on adulthood (Diamond & Levy, 1988), menopause (Strickland, 1988), and later life (Wisocki & Keuthen, 1988) fall into this category and should be read by those who wish current information on this issue. We will summarize their more important points.

According to Wisocki and Keuthen (1988), women over the age of 65 years are the fastest growing segment of the population in the United States. The authors emphasize the need to study diseases of special importance to women such as osteoporosis, arthritis, and urinary incontinence. Further, they challenge traditional beliefs that women are more hypochondriacal, less healthy, and/or report their health less positively than men. Strickland (1988) takes issue with the "almost exclusive reliance on drug therapy for the treatment of menopausal symptoms" (p. 42) and points out that the sole reliance on estrogen therapy places large numbers of women at risk for health disorders. Diamond and Levy (1988) suggest that, throughout life, women's physiology differs from that of men's, not only in obvious ways, but also as it interacts with disease and the sequence of life events and stressors related to disease. They state that what we think we know about women "has been conceived in a man-made world with man-made methods that conceptualize women's lives in ways that are inconsistent with how women experience them" (p. 28). We agree with these authors that a major challenge is to develop a health psychology with appropriate interventions more relevant to aging women. This effort

must begin at the fundamental level of measurement instruments. Strickland (1988) argues against the common assumption that identical instruments yield comparable information for women and men. She cites papers indicating that the two sexes differ in their perceptions of illness and even in their perceptions of the same illness- and health-related words, primarily because they exist in different social milieus and, in most cases, have done so since early childhood. In this context, the concepts of "sex cohort" and "disease cohort" must be combined with that of "birth cohort" to yield an historical as well as concurrent perspective. It further suggests that, in our development of models for a health psychology of aging, we must examine carefully new variables (e.g., sex-related perceptions of illness) and carefully reevaluate old variables (e.g., physiological determinants of psychological performance), which were perhaps too readily assumed to provide causal links between disease and behavior.

VI. Conclusions

We began this chapter with a review of the various conceptualizations that have been developed to distinguish "disease" and "normal aging." It is primarily in a research environment where this distinction must be made. From a broader intervention perspective, it may be wiser to focus on a healthy–unhealthy dimension, thereby decreasing the likelihood that many physical changes will be attributed solely to advanced age. The measurement of ill health, itself, is very much deserving of attention because physician reports and self-reports are not always isomorphic with disease. Further, the discrete entity paradigm, which forces categorization into "disease" and "healthy" groups presents obvious problems of interpretation when the goal of research is to find linkages between pathological mechanisms and behavior. We have suggested various solutions to these problems including longitudinal study of disease subtypes, utilizing small-sample statistics, and regression models based upon a conceptualization of continuous distributions of pathophysiological variables with associated risk functions (see for example, Evans, 1988). Current models in health psychology must recognize the importance of social and emotional constructs, and it is in this regard that we urge caution in interpreting differences between disease groups as solely and causally linked to the disease process itself.

Acknowledgments

The authors would like to express thanks to Paul Costa and Ilene Siegler for reviewing a draft of this paper and providing helpful suggestions. Thanks is also expressed to Carol L. Phillips for patiently word processing many drafts of this manuscript.

References

Abrahams, J. P. (1976). Psychological correlates of cardiovascular disease. In M. F. Elias, B. F. Eleftheriou, & P. K. Elias (Eds.), *Special review of experimental aging research* (pp. 330–349). Bar Harbor, ME: EAR.

Abrahams, J. P., Hoyer, W. J., Elias, M. F., & Bradigan, B. (1975). Gerontological research in psychology published in the *Journal of Gerontology*, 1963–1974: Prospectives and progress. *Journal of Gerontology*, **30**, 668–673.

Albrecht, N. N., Elias, J. W., Netherton, S. D., Hutton, J. T., & Albrecht, J. W. (1986). *Intellectual deficits in Parkinson's disease.* Paper presented at the 37th annual meeting of the Gerontological Society of America, Washington, DC.

Barbeau, A., Roy, M., Cloutier, T., Plasse, L., & Paris, S. (1986). Environmental and genetic factors in the etiology of Parkinson's disease. In M. D. Yahr & K. J. Bergman (Eds.), *Advances in neurology* (pp. 299–306). New York: Raven.

Berne, R. M., & Levy, M. N. (1986). *Cardiovascular physiology.* St. Louis: Mosby.

Birkmayer, W., Danielczyk, W., & Riederer, P. (1983). Symptoms and side effects in the course of Parkinson's disease. *Journal of Neural Transmission* (Suppl. 19), 185–189.

Blanchard, E. B., Martin, J. E., & Dubbert, P. M. (1988). *Non-drug treatments for essential hypertension* (p. 1). New York: Pergamon.

Brody, J. A. (1988). Changing health needs of the aging population. In D. Evered & J. Whelan (Eds.), *Research in the aging population* (pp. 208–215). New York: Wiley.

Buck, C., Baker, P., Bass, M., & Donner, A. (1987). The prognosis of hypertension according to age at onset. *Hypertension*, **9**, 204–208.

Busse, E. W. (1969). Theories of aging. In E. W. Busse & E. Pfeiffer (Eds.), *Behavior and adaptation in later life* (pp. 11–32). Boston: Little, Brown.

Chesney, M. A., & Rosenman, R. H. (1985). *Anger and hostility in cardiovascular and behavioral disorders.* Washington, DC: Hemisphere.

Chiriboga, D. A. (1984). Social stressors as antecedents of change. *Journal of Gerontology*, **39**, 468–477.

Cockerman, W. C., Sharp, K., & Wilcox, J. A. (1983). Aging and perceived health status. *Journal of Gerontology*, **38**, 349–355.

Costa, P. T., Jr., Fleg, J. L., McCrae, R. R., & Lakatta, E. G. (1982). Neuroticism, coronary artery disease, and chest pain complaints: Cross-sectional and longitudinal studies. *Experimental Aging Research*, **8**, 37–44.

Costa, P. T., Jr., Krantz, D. S., Blumenthal, J. A., Furberg, C. D., Rosenman, R. H., & Shekelle, R. B. (1987). Task Force 2: Psychological risk factors in coronary artery disease. *Circulation*, **76** (Suppl. 1), 145–149.

Costa, P. T., Jr., & McCrae, R. R. (1985). Hypochondriasis, neuroticism and aging: When are somatic complaints unfounded? *American Psychologist*, **40**, 19–28.

Costa, P. T., Jr., & McCrae, R. R. (1987a). Personality assessment in psychosomatic medicine: Value of a trait taxonomy. *Advances in Psychosomatic Medicine*, **17**, 71–82.

Costa, P. T., Jr., & McCrae, R. R. (1987b). Neuroticism, somatic complaints, and disease: Is the bark worse than the bite? *Journal of Personality*, **55**(2), 299–316.

Costa, P. T., Jr., McCrae, R. R., & Arenberg, D.

(1983). Recent longitudinal research on personality and aging. In K. W. Schaie (Eds.), *Longitudinal studies of adult psychological development* (pp. 222–265). New York: Guilford.

Costa, P. T., Jr., & Shock, N. W. (1980). New longitudinal data on the question of whether hypertension influences cognitive performance. In M. F. Elias & D. H. P. Streeten (Eds.), *Hypertension and cognitive processes* (pp. 83–93). Mt. Desert, ME: Beech Hill.

Costa, P. T., Jr., Zonderman, A. B., McCrae, R. R., & Williams, R. B., Jr. (1986). Cynicism and paranoid alienation in the Cook and Medley HO scale. *Psychosomatic Medicine*, **48**, 283–285.

Dembroski, T. M., & Costa, P. T., Jr. (1987). Coronary prone behavior: Components of the Type A pattern and hostility. *Journal of Personality*, **55**, 211–235.

Diamond, T., & Levy, J. A. (1988). Adulthood. In E. A. Blechman & K. D. Brownell (Eds.), *Handbook of behavioral medicine for women* (pp. 28–40). Oxford: Pergamon.

Dye, C., & Sassenrath, D. (1979). Identification of normal aging and disease-related processes by health care professionals. *Journal of the American Geriatrics Society*, **27**, 472–475.

Eisdorfer, C., & Wilkie, F. (1977). Stress, disease, aging and behavior. In J. E. Birren & K. W. Schaie (Eds.), *Handbook of the psychology of aging* (pp. 251–275). New York: Van Nostrand Reinhold.

Elias, J. W., & Marshall, P. H. (Eds.) (1987). *Cardiovascular disease and behavior*. Washington, DC: Hemisphere.

Elias, J. W., Netherton, S. D., Albrecht, J. W., Hutton, J. T., & Albrecht, N. N. (1988). *Cognitive slowing in Parkinson's disease.* Paper presented at the 38th annual meeting of the Gerontolgical Society of America, San Francisco.

Elias, J. W., Weinstein, L., Hutton, J. T., & Brat, A. (1987). Global internal-external attributions of control as a predictor of coping in Alzheimer's caregivers. *The Southwestern*, **4**, 83–84 (Abstract).

Elias, M. F. (1980). A behavior genetic approach to the study of age, hypertension, and behavior: Testing the non-causality hypothesis. In R. L. Sprott (Ed.), *Age, learning ability, and intelligence* (pp. 114–138). New York: Van Nostrand Reinhold.

Elias, M. F., & Robbins, M. A. (1987). Use of cinearteriography in behavioral studies of patients with chest pain in the absence of clinically significant coronary artery disease. In J. W. Elias & P. H. Marshall (Eds.), *Cardiovascular disease and behavior* (pp. 67–193). Washington, DC: Hemisphere.

Elias, M. F., Robbins, M. A., Blow, F. C., Rice, A. P., & Edgecomb, J. L. (1982). A behavioral study of middle-aged chest pain patients: Physical symptom reporting, anxiety and depression in arteriographically classified middle-aged chest pain patients. *Experimental Aging Research*, **8**, 45–52.

Elias, M. F., Robbins, M. A., & Schultz, N. R., Jr. (1987). Influence of hypertension on intellectual performance: Causation or speculation? In J. W. Elias & P. H. Marshall (Eds.), *Cardiovascular disease and behavior* (pp. 107–149). Washington, DC: Hemisphere.

Elias, M. F., Robbins, M. A., Schultz, N. R., Jr., Streeten, D. H. P., & Elias, P. K. (1987). Clinical significance of cognitive performance in hypertensive patients. *Hypertension*, **9**, 192–197.

Elias, M. F., Schultz, N. R., Jr., Robbins, M. A., & Elias, P. K. (1989). A longitudinal study of neuropsychological performance by hypertensives and normotensives: A third measurement point. *Journal of Gerontology: Psychological Sciences*, **41**, 25–28.

Elias, M. F., Schultz, N. R., Jr., Robbins, M. A., & Streeten, D. H. P. (1986). A longitudinal study of neuropsychological test performance for hypertensive and normotensive adults: Initial findings. *Journal of Gerontology*, **41**, 503–505.

Engel, B. T. (1983). Behavioral medicine. In X. F. Walker & R. L. Cooper (Eds.), *Experimental and clinical interventions in aging*. New York: Dekker.

Evans, J. G. (1988). Aging and disease. In D. Evered & J. Whelan (Eds.), *Research and the aging population* (pp. 38–57). New York: Wiley.

Farmer, M. E., White, L. R., Abbott, R. D., Kittner, S. J., Kaplan, E., Wolz, M. M., Brody, J. A., & Wolf, P. A. (1987). Blood pressure and cognitive performance: The Framingham study. *American Journal of Epidemiology*, **126**, 1103–1114.

Felton, B. J., & Revenson, T. A. (1987). Age differences in coping with chronic illness. *Psychology and aging*, **2**, 164–170.

Felton, B. J., & Revenson, T. A. (1989). The psychology of health: Issues in the field with special focus on the older person. In I. A. Parham, L. W. Poon, & I. C. Siegler (Eds.), *Access*. New York: Springer (in press).

Finch, C. E. (1988). Neuronal and endocrine approaches to the resolution of time as a dependent variable in the aging process of mammals. *Gerontologist*, **28**, 29–42.

Gatz, M., Pearson, C., & Weicker, W. (1987). Older persons and health psychology. In G. C. Stone, S. M. Weiss, J. D. Matarazzo, N. E. Miller, J. Rodin, G. E. Schwartz, C. D. Belar, M. J. Follick, & J. E. Singer (Eds.), *Health psychology: A discipline and a profession*. Chicago: University of Chicago Press.

Geringer, E. S., Perlmuter, L. C., Stern, T. A., & Nathan, D. M. (1988). Age and diabetes related changes in verbal fluency. *Journal of Geriatric Psychiatry and Neurology*, **1**, 11–15.

Hamburg, D. A., Elliot, G. R., & Parron, D. L. (Eds.) (1982). *Health and behavior: Frontiers of research in the biobehavioral sciences*. Washington, DC: National Academy Press.

Hashinski, V. C., Iliff, L. D., Zilkha, E., DuBoulay, G. H., McAllister, V. L., Marshall, J., Russell, R. W., & Symon, L. (1975). Cerebral blood flow in dementia. *Archives of Neurology*, **32**, 632–637.

Hayflick, L. (1987). The cell biology and theoretical basis of human aging. In L. Carstensen & B. Edelstein (Eds.), *Handbook of clinical gerontology* (pp. 3–17). New York: Pergamon.

Haynes, S. G., & Matthews, K. A. (1988). Review and methologic critique of recent studies on Type A behavior and cardiovascular disease. *Annals of Behavior Medicine*, **10**, 47–59.

Hertzog, C., Schaie, K. W., & Gribbin, K. (1978). Cardiovascular diseases and changes in intellectual functioning from middle to old age. *Journal of Gerontology*, **33**, 872–883.

Hoehn, M. M., & Yahr, M. D. (1967). Parkinsonism: Onset, progression, and mortality. *Neurology*, **17**, 427–442.

Hoyer, W. J., Raskind, C. L., & Abrahams, J. P. (1984). Research practices in the psychology of aging: A survey of research published in the *Journal of Gerontology*, 1975–1982. *Journal of Gerontology*, **39**, 44–48.

Huang, L., Cartwright, W. S., & Hu, T. (1988). The economic cost of senile dementia in the United States, 1985. *Public Health Reports*, **103**, 3–7.

Hutton, J. T. (1981). Results of clinical assessment for the dementia syndrome: Implications for epidemiologic studies. In J. A. Mortimer & L. M. Schuman (Eds.), *The epidemiology of dementia* (pp. 62–69). New York: Oxford University Press.

Hutton, J. T. (1987). Evaluation and treatment of dementia. *Texas Medicine*, **83**, 20–24.

Hutton, J. T., & Kenny, A. D. (Eds.) (1985). *Senile dementia of the Alzheimer's type*. New York: Liss.

Hutton, J. T., Morris, J. L., Roman, G. C., Imke, S. C., & Elias, J. W. (1988). Treatment of chronic Parkinson's disease with controlled-release carbidopa/levodopa. *Archives of Neurology*, **45**, 861–864.

Jarvik, L. F., Vineta, R., & Matsuyama, S. S. (1980). Organic brain syndrome and aging. *Archives of General Psychiatry*, **37**, 280–286.

Johnson, H. A. (1985). Is aging physiological or pathological? In H. A. Johnson (Eds.), *Relation between normal aging and disease* (pp. 239–247). New York: Raven.

Kart, C. (1981). Experiencing symptoms: Attribution and misattribution of illness among the aged. In M. R. Haug (Ed.), *Elderly patients and their doctors* (pp. 70–78). New York: Springer.

Kent, S. (1976). Is diabetes a form of accelerated aging? *Geriatrics*, **31**, 140, 145, 149–151.

Kobasa, S. C. (1979). Stressful life events, personality and health: An inquiry into hardiness. *Journal of Personality and Social Psychology*, **37**, 1–11.

Kohn, R. R. (1985). Aging and age-related diseases: Normal processes. In H. A. Johnson (Ed.), *Relations between normal aging and disease* (pp. 1–43). New York: Raven.

Krause, N. (1988). Stressful life events and physician utilization. *Journal of Gerontology*, **43**, 553–561.

Lakatta, E. G. (1987). The aging heart: Myth and realities. In J. W. Elias & P. H. Marshall (Eds.), *Cardiovascular disease and behavior* (pp. 179–193). Washington, DC: Hemisphere.

Langston, J. W., Ballard, P., Tetrud, J. W., & Irwin, I. (1983). Chronic parkinsonism in humans due to a product of merperidine-analogy synthesis. *Science*, **219**, 979–980.

Larsson, E. B., Kukull, W. A., Buchner, D., & Reifler, B. V. (1987). Adverse drug reactions associated with global cognitive impairment in elderly persons. *Annals of Internal Medicine*, **107**, 169–173.

Light, K. C. (1978). Effects of mild cardiovascular and cerebrovascular disorders on serial reaction time performance. *Experimental Aging Research*, **4**, 3–22.

Light, K. C. (1980). Antihypertensive drugs and behavioral performance. In M. F. Elias & D. H. P. Streeten (Eds.), *Hypertension and cognitive processes* (pp. 119–136). Mt. Desert, ME: Beech Hill.

Madden, D. J., & Blumenthal, J. A. (1989). Slowing of memory-search performance in men with mild hypertension. *Health Psychology*, **8**, 131–142.

Marsden, C. D. (1984). Neurological causes of dementia other than Alzheimer's disease. In D. W. K. Kay & G. D. Burrows (Eds.), *Handbook of studies on psychiatry and old age* (pp. 145–167). Amsterdam: Elsevier.

Matarazzo, J. D. (1984). Behavioral health: A 1990 challenge for the health sciences professions. In J. D. Matarazzo, S. M. Weiss, A. Herd, N. E. Miller, & S. M. Weiss (Eds.), *Behavioral health: A handbook of health enhancement and disease prevention* (pp. 3–39). New York: Wiley.

Miller, R. E., Shapiro, A. P., King, E., Ginchereau, E. H., & Hosutt, J. A. (1984). Effect of antihypertensive treatment on the behavioral consequences of elevated blood pressure. *Hypertension*, **6**, 202–208.

Mortimer, J. A., & Webster, D. D. (1982). A comparison of extrapyramidal motor function in normal aging and Parkinson's disease. In F. J. Pirozzolo & G. J. Maletta (Eds.), *The aging motor system: Advances in neurogerontology* (pp. 217–241). New York: Praeger.

Netherton, S. D., Elias, J. W., Albrecht, N. N., Acosta, C., Hutton, J. T., & Albrecht, J. (1989). Changes in the performance of Parkinsonian patients and normal aged on the Benton Visual Retention Test. *Experimental Aging Research*, in press.

Norman, W. T. (1963). Toward an adequate taxonomy of personality attributes. Replicated factor structure in peer nomination personality ratings. *Journal of Abnormal Social Psychology*, **17**, 265–276.

Parron, D. L., Solomon, F., & Rodin, J. (Eds.) (1981). *Health behavior and aging: A research agenda*. (Interim Report No. 5). Washington, DC: National Academy Press.

Passafiume, D., Boller, F., & Keefe, N. C. (1986). Neuropsychological impairment in patients with Parkinson's disease. In I. Grant & K. M. Adams (Eds.), *Neuropsychological assessment of neuropsychiatric disorders* (pp. 374–383). New York: Oxford University Press.

Perlmuter, L. C., Tun, P., Sizer, N., McGlinchey, R. E., & Nathan, D. M. (1987). Age and diabetes related changes in verbal fluency. *Experimental Aging Research*, **13**, 9–14.

Perlmutter, J. S. (1988). New insights into the pathophysiology of Parkinson's disease: The challenge of positron emission tomography. *Trends in Neuroscience*, **11**, 203–208.

Radkin, J. G., & Struening, E. L. (1976). Life events, stress and illness. *Science*, **194**, 1013–1020.

Rajput, A. H., Offord, K. P., Beard, C. M., & Kurland, L. T. (1984). Epidemiology of parkinsonism: Incidence, classification, and mortality. *Annals of Neurology*, **16**, 278–282.

Rajput, A. H., Vitti, R. J., Stern, W., & Laverty, W. (1986). Early onset Parkinson's disease and childhood environment. In M. D. Yahr & K. J. Bergmann (Eds.), *Advances in Neurology* (pp. 295–297). New York: Raven.

Rakowski, W. (1987). Persistence of personal health practices over a one year period. *Public Health Reports*, **102**, 483–493.

Reese, H. W., & Overton, J. W. (1970). Models of development and theories of development. In L. R. Goulet & P. B. Baltes (Eds.), *Life span developmental psychology: Research and theory*. New York: Academic Press.

Rodin, J. (1986). Aging and health: Effects of the sense of control. *Science*, **223**, 1271–1276.

Roman, G. C. (1987). Senile dementia of the Binswanger type: A vascular form of dementia in the elderly. *Journal of the American Medical Association*, **258**, 1782–1788.

Schroeder, D. H., & Costa, P. T., Jr. (1984). The influences of life stress on physical illness: Substantive effects of methodological flows? *Journal of Personality and Social Psychology*, **46**, 853–863.

Schultz, N. R., Jr., Elias, M. F., Robbins, M. A., Streeten, D. H. P., & Blakeman, N. (1986). Longitudinal comparison of hypertensives and normotensives on the Wechsler Adult Intelligence Scale: Initial finding. *Journal of Gerontology*, **41**, 169–175.

Schultz, N. R., Jr., Elias, M. F., Robbins, M. A.,

Streeten, D. H. P., & Blakeman, N. A. (1989). A longitudinal study of the performance of hypertensive and normotensive subjects on the Wechsler Adult Intelligence Scale. *Psychology and Aging*, in press.

Siegler, I. C. (1975). The terminal drop hypothesis: Fact or artifact? *Experimental Aging Research*, **1**, 169–185.

Siegler, I. C. (1988). *Developmental health psychology*. Master lecture presented as part of the series on the adult years: Continuity and change. Annual meeting of the American Psychological Association.

Siegler, I. C., & Costa, P. T., Jr. (1985). Health behavior relationships. In J. E. Birren & K. W. Schaie (Eds.), *Handbook of the psychology of aging* (pp. 144–166). New York: Van Nostrand Reinhold.

Siegler, I. C., Nowlin, J. B., & Blumenthal, J. A. (1980). Health and behavior: Methodological considerations for adult development and aging. In L. W. Poon (Ed.), *Aging in the 1980's Selected contemporary issues* (pp. 599–612). Washington, DC: American Psychological Association.

Sklar, L. S., & Anisman, X. X. (1981). Stress and cancer. *Psychological Bulletin*, **89**, 369–406.

Stern, Y., & Mayeux, R. (1986). Possible dopaminergic basis for perceptual motor dysfunction. In A. Fisher, I. Hanin, & C. Lachman (Eds.), *Alzheimers and Parkinson's diseases* (pp. 185–190). New York: Springfield.

Strickland, B. R. (1988). Menopause. In E. A. Blechman & K. D. Brownell (Eds.), *Handbook of behavioral medicine for women* (pp. 41–47). New York: Pergamon.

Su, T., London, E. F., & Jaffey, J. H. (1988). Steroid binding at sigma receptors suggests a link between endocrine, nervous, and immune systems. *Science*, **240**, 219–221.

Taylor, A. E., Saint-Cyr, J. W., & Lang, A. E. (1987). Parkinson's disease. *Brain*, **110**, 35–51.

Tun, P. A., Perlmuter, L. C., Russo, P., & Nathan, D. M. (1987). Memory self-assessment and performance in aged diabetics and non-diabetics. *Experimental Aging Research* **13**, 151–157.

Turner, F. G., & Rowe, J. (1988). Are we making progress in the treatment of hypertension in the elderly? *Geriatric Cardiovascular Medicine*, **1**, 29–33.

Weksler, M. E. (1981). Three great networks: The central nervous system, endocrine system, immune system and aging. In D. L. Parron, F. Solomon, & J. Rodin (Eds.), *Health behavior and aging: A research agenda* (Interim Report No. 5) (pp. 57–64). Washington, DC: Division of Mental Health and Behavioral Medicine, National Academy Press.

Wilkie, F. L., & Eisdorfer, C. (1971). Intelligence and blood pressure in the aged. *Science*, **172**, 959–962.

Wilkie, F. L., Eisdorfer, C., & Nowlin, J. B. (1976). Memory and blood pressure in the aged. *Experimental Aging Research*, **2**, 3–16.

Williams, R. B. (1979). Psychological mechanisms underlying the association between psychosocial factors and coronary disease. In W. D. Gentry & R. B. Williams (Eds.), *Psychosocial aspects of myocardial infarction and coronary care* (pp. 50–64). St. Louis: Mosby.

Williams, R. B., & Anderson, N. B. (1987). Hostility and coronary heart disease. J. W. Elias & P. H. Marshall (Eds.), *Cardiovascular disease and behavior*. Washington, DC: Hemisphere.

Williams, R. B., Lane, J. D., Kuhn, C. M., Melosh, W., White, A. C., & Schanberg, S. M. (1982). Physiological and neuroendocrine response pattern during different behavioral challenges: Differential hyperresponsivity of young Type A men. *Science*, **218**, 483–485.

Wisocki, P. A., & Keuthen, N. K. (1988). Later life. In E. A. Blechman & K. D. Brownell (Eds.), *Handbook of behavioral medicine for women* (pp. 48–58). New York: Pergamon.

Zonderman, A. B., Heft, M. W., & Costa, P. T., Jr. (1985). Does the illness behavior questionnaire measure abnormal illness behavior? *Health Psychology*, **4**, 425–436.

Six

Cultural, Racial, and Ethnic Minority Influences on Aging

James S. Jackson, Toni C. Antonucci, and Rose C. Gibson

I. Overview

The purpose of this chapter is to explore the influences of racial, ethnic, and cultural factors on biological/health, social, and psychological aging processes. Literature related to selected indicators of these interrelated aging processes will be critically reviewed. A life-span perspective, the consideration of historical and cohort factors that affect the life situations of ethnic racial minority group individuals, provides the context for this review. The development of universal models of aging is best accomplished by first understanding the ways in which ethnicity, culture, and race contribute to the aging process. This can facilitate the formulation of more general models of aging (Fry, 1988; Ikels, Keith, & Fry, 1987). Although these issues are explored generically, sensitivity to the issues under consideration leads us to acknowledge that all cultural, racial, and ethnic minority influences are not the same.

In this chapter we focus not on all ethnic or cultural groups but rather on racial and ethnic minority groups (Kobata, Lockery, & Moriwaki, 1980) whose "language and physical and cultural characteristics make them visible and identifiable—the people of color" (p. 449). It is the relative deprivation of these groups, in comparison to other groups, that might differentially shape their aging and makes them an important focus of study. Ethnicity, national origin, and culture, in fact, all play important roles in aging-related processes (Gelfand & Barresi, 1987; J. J. Jackson, 1985; Rosenthal, 1986). Other social group memberships also contribute significantly to aging processes, for example, gender, sexual preference, or physically stigmatized status; these topics are worthy of more thorough coverage than possible here. Much of the research considered in this chapter is taken from work on the black elderly; we recognize that the findings presented may not always generalize to other cultural, racial, and ethnic minority groups. It is well known, for example, that there are differences in the life span and older age experiences of black, Native American, Hispanic, and Asian-American groups. Comparable research findings on

Handbook of the Psychology of Aging, Third Edition
Copyright © 1990 Academic Press, Inc. All rights of reproduction in any form reserved.

topics of interest in the field of aging are rarely available across all ethnic minority groups. We hope that this review will help to stimulate such new research.

A. Ethnicity, Race, and Culture Defined

Swidler (1986) proposed a definition of culture as a symbolic vehicle of meaning, including beliefs, ritual practices, art forms and ceremonies, as well as informal practices such as language, gossip, stories, and rituals of daily life. Key to this definition is the role of culture in providing strategies of action, continuity in the ordering of these actions through time, and a template for constructing action (Roberts, 1987). This perspective is consistent with formulations of the role of culture in understanding aging and aging-related processes (Fry, 1988; Sokolovsky, 1989).

Ethnic group is defined within the larger cultural context (Holzberg, 1982a; Rosenthal, 1986). Modern theories of ethnicity (Yinger, 1985) postulate that the development and persistence of ethnicity—the crystallization of solidarity and identification—are dependent upon structural conditions in society (Taylor, 1979). In contrast, pluralist notions of ethnicity hold that cultural heritage is the major basis for ascriptive group identity. Yancey, Erickson, and Juliani (1976) suggest that ethnicity, defined in terms of frequent patterns of association and identification with common origins, occurs under conditions that reinforce the maintenance of kinship and friendship networks.

Several researchers have taken a self-identifying approach to the definition of ethnicity (Roberts, 1987; Sokolovsky, 1989). This view emphasizes the dynamic interactions among cultural traits, socialized patterns of social behavior, and environmental influences. Processes of aging related to the self–other defining characteristics, the nature and basis of contact, attitudes, values and action both on behalf of and against oppressed minor-

ity groups of color are the focus of this chapter.

Race also should be defined within the larger cultural context. We concur with Cooper (1984) that the biologic concept of race has no scientific meaning and that social definitions of race and ethnicity should be viewed simply as clues for seeking environmental causes of observed differences between groups. Work in illness behavior and behavioral medicine, for example, support the view that cultural and life-style differences among racial and ethnic groups account for differences in behavioral and health outcomes (Wilkinson & King, 1987). "There is now widespread, if not universal, agreement that racial differences derive social significance from cultural diversity" (Yinger, 1985, p. 159).

Ethnicity and culture are resources for the group and the aging individual. For example, tangible goods and services may ensue from positions of power and reverence held by elders in particular racial and ethnic cultural groups. Similarly, psychological and social rewards may be derived by the aging individual from the shared identities and social supports made available by racial and ethnic cultural group memberships (Bengtson & Morgan, 1983). Further, ethnic and racial group memberships and identities can affect role transitions, perceptions of life events, and the nature and perceptions of old age and aging (Barresi, 1987). In this chapter, an integration of resource-base and life-span continuity perspectives provides the framework for the examination of the biological, social, and psychological consequences and sequelae of aging in ethnic and racial minority groups.

B. Ethnicity, Race, and the Life-Span Perspective

Examining the issue of aging within racial and ethnic minority groups from a life-course perspective implies that the events and changes over the life span for those cohorts already born and aging lay the foundation for their health and role statuses in old age. Among members of oppressed racial and ethnic minority groups, these events and changes include problems of single parenthood, infant morbidity, childhood diseases, poor diets, lack of preventive health care, deteriorating neighborhoods, poverty, adolescent violence, un- and underemployment, teen pregnancy, drug and alcohol abuse, and broken marriages. Although significant improvements in the life situation of many racial and ethnic minorities, particularly health, have occurred over the last 40 years, recent literature (Farley, 1987) describes life events and structural conditions, particularly for poor racial and ethnic minorities in major northeastern and midwestern cities, similar to the list presented above. Although the exact causal relationships are not known, it is clear that these are predisposing factors for high morbidity and mortality and diminished life quality at later points in the life span (Hamburg, Elliott, & Parron, 1982).

The life-span perspective highlights the importance of cumulative individual and social strengths and deficits in the life experience of racial and ethnic minorities; the importance of birth cohort experiences; and the lasting effects of aging and period events, for example, the Asiatic Exclusion Act of 1924, *Brown vs. Board of Education*, Medicare, Older Americans Act, and Medicaid. These sociohistorical events have reshaped and are reshaping the future of existing cohorts of early- and late-middle-aged racial and ethnic groups.

The changing demography of the older population will have important effects on the health and well-being of older racial and ethnic minorities. Among other changes, the imbalanced sex ratio; changes in the gerontic (number of persons 65 years of age and over per 100 persons of prime working age) and neontic (the number of persons under age 20 per 100 persons 20 to 64 years of age) dependency

ratios (Siegel & Taeuber, 1986); geographic distributions; and the proportions in poverty will have profound influences upon the status of older racial and ethnic groups over the next forty years.

Life circumstances in earlier stages of the life course have significant influences upon the quality (and quantity) of life in the latter stages. Negative environmental, social, and economic conditions early in the life course of racial and ethnic minorities have deleterious effects on later social, psychological, and biological growth (Jackson, 1985). These damaging experiences accumulate over the individual life span, and, when combined with the negative consequences of old age itself, eventuate in serious morbidity and mortality in older racial and ethnic minorities. This life-span conception is related to the multiple jeopardy hypothesis, which holds that negative experiences related to ethnic and racial group memberships combine with negative consequences of aging to yield larger disparities between majority and minority group members in old age (Dowd & Bengtson, 1978). Little empirical support has been found for the double jeopardy hypothesis. For example, a growing disparity with increasing age among minority groups and the majority is not found (Jackson, 1985), and some research even suggests a narrowing on some social and psychological variables (Gibson, 1989). As discussed later, however, differential early mortality and the continued disparities that do exist between racial and ethnic minorities and the general population support a particularly important role of early negative social, economic, and environmental influences on later poor biological, social, and psychological functioning of racial and ethnic minorities.

The data on one racial ethnic minority group, blacks, support the need for a life-span conception. Blacks, in comparison to the general population, have a shortened life expectancy at birth, and at every point in the life span have greater disability and morbidity (Jackson, 1981). In infancy, this is marked by higher mortality figures as well as higher accident and disease rates. Adolescence, young adulthood, and even older ages in blacks are characterized by comparatively higher homicide deaths than in the general population. Middle age and early old age show more disability, earlier retirement, and ultimately higher death rates. Similar trends are also found in Hispanic (Lacayo, 1984) and Native American groups (National Indian Council on Aging, 1984). It is only after about the age of 80 that blacks, for example, tend to show increased longevity in comparison to the general population (Manton, 1982; Markides, 1982).

II. Biological, Social, and Psychological Processes in the Aging of Racial and Ethnic Minorities

Definitions of Aging

Individual aging is generally defined in biological, psychological, and social terms. Biological aging refers to basic processes from cell physiology to whole organism physical health status. Social aging refers to changes in role positions and social functioning with increasing chronological age. Psychological aging generally refers to changes in cognitive and mental functioning. The major point is that chronological age as a marker of organism growth and development is at best imprecise (Brody & Brock, 1985; Schroots & Birren, this volume).

Ryder (1965) suggested that old age be arbitrarily defined as the point in a group's life span when the expected remaining years of life is 10 (Siegel & Taeuber, 1986). Neugarten (1975) proposed that older age should be at least divided into the young-old and the old-old because the service delivery needs, health, and functional limitations of these groups diverge widely. Although the exact age for this boundary

differs among investigators (Neugarten prefers a functional definition), the old-old have often been defined as 75 years of age and above (Soldo, 1980); although more recent writings on the "oldest-old" have placed this age at 80 or 85 years (Suzman & Riley, 1985).

In sum, there is no generally agreed upon definition of age aside from a chronological one (Siegel & Davidson, 1984). Chronological age, however, is an arbitrary measure of aging, perhaps particularly so among older racial and ethnic minority adults. For example, some research suggests that events in the early years may simultaneously accelerate aging processes and contribute to hardier oldest-old survivors among racial and ethnic minority populations (Gibson, 1986).

III. Biological and Health Processes in the Aging of Racial and Ethnic Minorities

In this section we review the little that is known about biological and health functioning and how life-span health influences might affect the overall biological process of aging in racial and ethnic minorities (Berkman, 1988). One example is the long-term effects of poor health care over the life span on the biological processes of aging in the later years. Unfortunately, comparable quality and quantity of data on mortality and morbidity are unavailable across all ethnic and racial minority groups. National data are largely available on blacks, whereas some local and regional estimates are available for Hispanic, Native American, and Asian-American groups. These data are noted where appropriate.

A. Mortality in Older Racial and Ethnic Minorities

Although all Americans have made gains in life expectancy, there have been persistent lags in the gains for some groups, notably blacks. Bradshaw, Frisbie, and Eifler (1985) reported systematic differences in cause-specific mortality between Hispanics and the general population. In some categories, older Mexican-Americans, like blacks, demonstrated disadvantaged status (diabetes mellitus, pneumonia, influenza, and homicide), whereas in other categories, unlike blacks, Mexican-Americans enjoyed a significant advantage over the general population (malignant neoplasms and circulatory diseases).

A crossover in expected remaining years of life between blacks and whites occurs at the oldest ages (Manton, Poss, & Wing, 1979). At about age 80, black males and females can expect to outlive their white counterparts. It has been suggested that this crossover in expected years of life is due to the effects of socioeconomic status, other social, economic, and cultural factors and possible specific gene-linked diseases that are overrepresented in certain ethnic and racial groups (Siegel & Davidson, 1984). Bradshaw *et al.* (1985) reported that in their Mexican-American sample the mortality crossover occurs much earlier in life, in fact during early adulthood. On the other hand, some racial ethnic minority groups do not show a crossover. Native Americans have age-adjusted death rates comparable to those of the general population, whereas Asian-American groups have age-adjusted rates that are lower than the general population (Yu, Chang, Liu, & Kan, 1985a). Cultural differences in smoking, drinking, and other life-style risk behaviors are proposed to account for the relative advantage demonstrated by Asian groups (Yu *et al.*, 1985a).

Work on the racial crossover phenomenon among blacks (see Jackson, 1985, for a review) suggests that it is unrelated to changes in age-specific causes of death because there is a black/white crossover for each of the major causes of death (Manton, 1982); age misreporting (Siegel & Davidson, 1984), population enumeration problems, or inappropriate analyses.

Nor is it unique to the United States (Manton, 1982). In a recent 20-year longitudinal analysis of the Evans County Study data, Wing, Manton, Stallard, Hames, and Tyroler (1985) found a black/white mortality crossover for both men (at age 73) and women (at age 85). Wing *et al.* (1985) concluded that socioeconomic factors and selection mechanisms cannot fully account for the observed crossover. Thus, black/white differences in risk and protective factors must also play a role, "different age patterns of blood pressure changes in Blacks and whites may reduce white advantages at the oldest ages where protective factors in Blacks become more important" (p. 83). Similar factors, operating at younger ages, may account for the possible earlier crossover in Hispanics (Bradshaw *et al.*, 1985) and the relative advantages that Asians enjoy at every age in the life span (Yu *et al.*, 1985a).

B. Morbidity in Older Racial and Ethnic Minorities

Trends in health self-assessments, reports on restrictions in minor and major activities, workdays lost, and other measures of morbidity are consistent with survey reports indicating that most minority elderly have greater morbidity than whites (Gibson, 1986; Siegel & Davidson, 1984). Although good trend data comparing ethnic and racial minorities and whites are not available, the sparse data reveal diminishing but continuing differentials in the major morbidity indicators (Kii, 1984; Lacayo, 1984: NICA, 1984; Taplin & Carlson, 1985; Yu, Liu, & Kyrzeja, 1985b). Demonstrating the heterogeneity among minority groups, Yu *et al.* (1985b) found that Asian-American and Pacific Islander elderly reported lower rates of activity limitations and better perceptions of health status than those reported in the general population.

Minority older adults are at higher risk than the general population for a number of chronic diseases that negatively affect health status and effective functioning (Siegel & Taeuber, 1986). Trend data document spectacular improvements in some indicators of health among minority groups; the reduction in hypertension among blacks is one excellent example (Cooper, Steinhauer, Schatzkin, & Miller, 1981). Heart disease also has declined as a killer of older people but remains much more prevalent in black and Hispanic than in white groups of older adults (Kumanyika & Savage, 1985).

Low social economic level (SEL) has been proposed as a major risk factor in mortality and morbidity, both alone and in combination with other risk factors (Haan & Kaplan, 1985). The weight of the evidence suggests that higher SEL is associated with better health and lowered morbidity and mortality. For both individual and aggregate measures of SEL, these relationships have been found with blood pressure, cancer, coronary heart disease, cerebrovascular disease, diabetes, obesity, and crude mortality rates. Hispanic and black lower socioeconomic status groups in old age, however, are still relatively worse off than comparable low socioeconomic status nonminorities in terms of perceived health status, restrictions of activities, work loss and bed disability days. How SEL status, ethnicity, and race interact to affect these health outcomes has not yet been demonstrated (James, 1985).

Manton and Soldo's (1985) research on health changes in the oldest-old provides a model that can usefully identify health/age differences among different groups and is illustrative of the life-span perspective taken in this chapter. They examined health changes by age, plotting the proportion of each cohort that survives to a specific age without the occurrence of a negative health event (morbidity, disability, or mortality).

Two points are relevant from Manton and Soldo's work. The first is the examination of health events by age. This permits the comparison of both health status differences among different age groups across different birth cohorts and different majority/minority groups of the same age. Also important is their functional criteria of health status, which are more extensive, and perhaps, for minority groups, more relevant, than the usual criteria. They consider absence of a critical negative health event to be important in the assessment of health among the oldest-old. This type of research exposes what has already been demonstrated to some degree among some elderly minorities, that is, the disproportionately high level of disability among the young-old and the contrasting disproportionately low level of functional disability among the oldest-old.

C. Life-Span Health Influences

Siegel and Taeuber (1986) note that there has been a significant shift in the principal causes of ill health from the parasitic and infectious diseases of the early 1900s to the chronic diseases, accidents, and stress of today (Omran, 1977). Of the factors thought to contribute most to morbidity and mortality in older adults, elevated blood pressure, smoking, alcohol use, and obesity have been the most frequently studied (Brody & Brock, 1985). These factors are related to mortality and morbidity in most minority older adults, but demonstrating the heterogeneity among minority groups, Yu et al. (1985b) reported culturally determined lower smoking and alcohol consumption patterns among Asian/Pacific Islanders than among other American population groups.

Sociocultural factors, particularly socioeconomic ones, are also proposed as major contributors to morbidity and mortality (Haan & Kaplan, 1985). Ethnicity, race, and national origin are generally considered part of a long list of sociocultural factors related to morbidity and mortality.

This simplistic view of race and ethnicity has contributed to the emphasis on minority/nonminority group comparisons, rather than intraminority group assessments of factors that might contribute to the heterogeneity of health behaviors and health statuses within and between minority populations (Cooper, 1984; Jackson, 1981).

Issues related to comorbidity in the elderly and blacks and other ethnic and racial groups are only recently beginning to emerge (Hamburg *et al.*, 1982; Rowe, 1985). A burden of illness rests upon the shoulders of ethnic and racial minorities in this society from cradle to grave (Hamburg *et al.*, 1982). When combined with the adverse physiologic changes associated with aging itself (Rowe, 1985), the capability of successfully coping is a difficult task for the older minority adult (Gibson, 1986). A review of the health, mortality, morbidity, and risk factors literatures reveals that the examination of minority health status of aging adults has been conducted in a relative vacuum. Although several authors suggest the need for life-course models (e.g., Barresi, 1987; Manton & Soldo, 1985) that include aging, cohort, and period effects on racial and ethnic biological and health processes, few have collected the type of data needed to test such models. The fault lies in both poor conceptual frameworks and the lack of quality data on large representative samples of racial and ethnic Americans.

Cohorts of racial and ethnic minorities born today are still at considerable risk. Large numbers are likely to spend childhoods in low-income, single female-headed households. Children in these families will undoubtedly have inadequate diets and be exposed to inadequate educational opportunities. Job prospects will be poor in young adulthood, and a large proportion will not reach middle adulthood. A relatively small number will receive meaningful intergenerational economic transfers from parental sources, including those born into middle-class homes, because middle-class status is often transient for racial and ethnic minorities. Thus there will be few legacies for children in these families, such as support for a college education. Dental visits, preventive health maintenance, well-baby examinations, sensory adjustments for poor hearing and vision, among other health-promoting tasks, will be largely unavailable to these children.

While this characterization of risk holds for the most deprived of minority groups (blacks and Hispanics), Yu *et al.*, (1985b) reported that on some measures of preventive health-promoting activities (e.g., well-baby examinations and early physician visits), Asian/Pacific Islander rates exceed those of the general population. Kii (1984) notes, however, that Asian-Americans tend to underutilize services and that the negative consequences of such underutilization differ among specific Asian groups. Yu *et al.* (1985b) found that cultural factors related to family ties and health beliefs (e.g., use of herbal prescriptions, balance of hot and cold elements of the body, etc.) play a significant role in the health status of the elderly in these groups. Among Native Americans several indices of health prevention and promotion approximate those of the general population. The lack of sensitivity to cultural differences, however, lowers the quality of service delivery and utilization by Native Americans (NICA, 1984).

The early morbidity, disability, and excess mortality in most groups of racial and ethnic American older adults are understandable when viewed within a framework of lifetime barriers to educational and occupational mobility and high probabilities of exposure to environmental risk factors. Older age among minorities, as in the general population, however, is not a time of inevitable decline (Rowe & Kahn, 1987). Survey data (e.g., Gibson & Jackson, 1987; Yu *et al.*, 1985b) show that many older minorities suffer little from functional disability and limitations of activity due to chronic illness and disease. In fact, after the age of 65 racial and ethnic minorities (particularly blacks and Hispanics) and whites, within sex groups, show relatively small differences, compared to birth and earlier ages, in years of expected remaining life. The lack of contemporary differences in older age may be due to the greater mortality of certain racial and ethnic groups at younger ages. However, it also is due to improved health care for older minority adults (largely through Medicare and Medicaid benefits) and the existence of cohorts of racial and ethnic older adults who are better educated and better able to take advantage of available opportunities.

Research by Gibson and Jackson (1987) on a national sample of black elderly suggests that the racial and ethnic elderly are a heterogeneous group. Approximately 40% of older black elderly, for example, reported no or only mild functional limitations. Physical limitations were more concentrated in the younger-old groups (age 65 to 74) rather than being a linear function of age (Gibson & Jackson, 1987). The data also suggest that the oldest groups of blacks may be psychologically more able than younger-old blacks as well and are more likely to have effective and helpful informal networks to depend upon. These survey data on the black oldest-old are consistent with Manton's (1982) conclusions that view black survivors in older ages as somehow aging differently than their white counterparts. Although the same level of analysis has not been applied to other racial and ethnic minorities, the morbidity and mortality data reviewed earlier, particularly on Hispanics and Asians, suggest that these findings may generalize to other groups as well. Given the critical life-span link to biological/health-related aging factors, future older cohorts may or may not be as well off as current cohorts of older racial and ethnic minorities.

The issues of morbidity and mortality in the biological aging of racial and ethnic minority elderly are related to social and psychological aging dimensions addressed in the remainder of the chapter.

IV. Social Processes of Aging in Racial and Ethnic Minorities

Social processes of aging refer to the age-related losses and changes in informal and formal roles and changes in participation and involvement in informal and formal organizations (George, 1988). In our view, these social structures and social processes provide resources for older racial and ethnic minorities in maintaining and improving life quality (Jackson, Chatters, & Taylor, in press) and good physical and mental health. In addition to these important dimensions, George (1988) notes that political participation, voluntary organization memberships, religious participation, and living arrangements are major sources of formal social participation; and friendship networks and family support systems are important arenas for informal participation that may be related to life quality and physical and mental well-being. Evidence regarding racial and ethnic participation, however, is scant (George, 1988).

Recent research offers some guidance. For example, data have been accumulating on the role of social support in the health and well-being of the elderly. Research focusing largely on blacks and Hispanics has shown that much of what is known about family and friend social support among whites applies to these groups as well (e.g., Cantor, 1979). But other culturally related factors, for example, religion among blacks (Taylor & Chatters, 1986), family structures among Asian/Pacific Islanders and Hispanics (Kii, 1984; Lacayo, 1984), household composition and tribal customs among Native Indians (Driedger & Chappell, 1988; NICA, 1984) all can play a special role in understanding the nature of social aging processes among racial and ethnic minorities. In this section, we focus our attention (as the data permit) on sociostructural and economic resources, social participation in formal and informal organizations, and the nature and role of family and social supports among racial and ethnic minority elderly.

A. Population Structure of Older Racial and Ethnic Adults

The sex ratio in the total population shows a decided disadvantage for males relative to females for middle aged and older adults. In 1985, there were 67 males for every 100 females aged 65 and older. At the ages 75 and over, there were 54 males for every 100 females. The ratios among different racial and ethnic minority groups are decidedly different. For example, in 1980 the overall sex ratios for Asian/Pacific Islanders stood at 96 men to 100 women (Kii, 1984). In fact, among some Asian subgroups (Chinese, for example), the ratios are even reversed, primarily due to patterns of immigration early in the century. This is in contrast to the figures for blacks in 1985, which show 64 males for every 100 females aged 65 and over, and 56 males for every 100 females in the 75-year-old and older category. The sex ratio is much more favorable for blacks than whites after age 100.

When combined with the higher mortality and morbidity figures for black males at each age, the prospects for marriage and family support are bleak for the women who are increasingly larger proportions of successively older age groups of black adults. The presence of fewer men per women up to about age 100 and growing sex differentials in educational and occupational attainment are major sources of marital strain and dissolution. These effects might be even more pronounced if the geographical distributions of older minority males and females were considered.

Among Hispanic populations, the sex ratios are distinctly different than those among blacks. Among Cuban-Americans there are 80 males for each 100 females 55 years of age and older. Among Puerto Ricans, however, there are only 67 males per 100 females. This is in contrast to Mexican-Americans where there are 94 males for each 100 females, a number that Becerra and Shaw (1984) indicated changes very little among advanced aged cohorts.

The sex ratios noted have direct consequences on marital status differences in late life among racial and ethnic minorities and the larger white population. For whites, approximately 50% of the females over age 65 are married, in comparison to 83% of the males. This is approximately twice as high as the figures for blacks. Patterns of marital status vary among Asian-American groups, largely due to historical patterns of immigration (Kii, 1984). Japanese-Americans, for example, exhibit patterns of marital status close to those of whites, whereas Chinese and Filipino elderly men are much more likely to live alone.

Living arrangements among Hispanic and Asian-Americans also are influenced by patterns of immigration. Generally, all racial and ethnic minorities are more likely than whites to live in multigenerational households, particularly Native Americans. Though socioeconomic differences are often suggested to account for multigenerational households (e.g., George, 1988), cultural preferences, values, and feelings of filial piety have been proposed as underlying reasons for the maintenance of these households.

B. Resources for Social Participation

The social resources mentioned earlier—education, occupation, marital status, and income—provide structural and tangible resources for social, formal, and informal organization, participation, and role changes in late life. Although racial and ethnic groups vary widely, it is clear that all are deprived on most or some of these resource dimensions. Some groups, like blacks and Native Americans, tend to be disadvantaged on all dimensions. Others, like Asian-Americans, tend to be relatively well off on some indicators but deprived on others.

In 1980 among the general population, approximately 58% of adults over the age of 65 had completed high school and 9% had attained 4 or more years of college. In 1980, approximately 27% of blacks over the age of 65 had attained a high-school degree (Jackson, 1985) and 2.5% had 4 or more years of college. Among Hispanics, Valle (1983) reported that only 18% had graduated from high school and only 59% had five years or more of schooling in contrast to the 82% figure in the general population. Among Native American elders, only 18% are high-school graduates, whereas 63% have not attended high school at all (Edwards, 1983).

Racial and ethnic minorities over the age of 65 are also relatively worse off financially compared to the general population. Overall, since 1950, families (and individuals) over the age of 65 have enjoyed an increase in unadjusted median income, rising to $12,882 in 1980. The black total median family income has risen to $8382, reflecting the increase in relatively more affluent older cohorts. In 1980 approximately 65% of all older Hispanic men had median incomes below $5000; 90% of older Hispanic women fell below $5000. Native American median family incomes are even lower. Asian groups are relatively better off than other groups; median family incomes range from near parity for Japanese to approximately $1000 less on average than the general population for Chinese elderly (Kii, 1984).

The figures for poverty status among racial and ethnic minorities indicate significant hardships in comparison to the general elderly population. These numbers, more so than the median income data, reveal the financial straits of older racial and ethnic populations. In 1980, the poverty rate among the general older population hovered at about 14%. Among older Hispanics, the number stood at 31% (Lacayo, 1984). Among blacks, 38% were reported to be in poverty in 1980 (Watson, 1983). If slightly more generous criteria for poverty (Chen, 1985) are employed, approximately 52% of blacks 65 years of age and older in 1980 were below 125% of the poverty level. Among female-headed households, some 68.5% of blacks over the age of 65 were below 125% of the poverty level. Among Hispanics, 42% are poor or near poor using the 125% criteria. Edwards (1983) reported that among Native Americans approximately 50% of the elderly population was in poverty in 1978. Although relatively advantaged in comparison to other minority groups, Pacific and Asian elderly still show an overall 20% poverty figure (Kim, 1983).

C. Sources of Social Participation

Reflecting the problems noted in income and poverty, occupational status, and labor force participation, other important resources and sources of social participation among racial and ethnic groups also show significant differences in comparison to the general population. Blacks, Hispanics, and Native Americans tend to hold life-time jobs that are significantly lower in quality on status, income, security, and benefit dimensions than whites (Kim, 1983; Lacayo, 1984; Valle, 1983; Watson, 1983). In some cases (Jackson & Gibson, 1985), members of these groups have to work past what would be normal retirement ages (and often in poor health) because of minimum social security benefits and lack of adequate private retirement incomes (Jackson & Gibson, 1985). A similar argument has been made for many Asian-American groups (Kii, 1984), though because of early immigration patterns, some Asian elderly have enjoyed considerably higher status positions than other racial and ethnic groups. Generally, minority groups have worked at poorer jobs (Kii, 1984), tend to retire earlier because of poor health (George, 1988), and have access to less opportunity and face greater discrimination than elderly in the general population. Thus, like other economic and social resources, occupation and labor force participation have been less viable sources of social participation for members of racial and ethnic minority populations than for individuals in the general population.

Another important source of participation is in the electoral arena (Torres-Gil, 1983). George (1988) reported that older blacks are less likely to vote than older people in the general population. Some data, however, suggest that if socioeconomic status is taken into account, then older blacks may be even more likely to vote than older people at comparable socioeconomic levels in the general population. In fact, among racial and ethnic groups, particularly in comparison to Hispanics, blacks are the most likely to vote (George, 1988). Although data are not available about other areas of political participation (George, 1988), black political participation in older ages may be at least partly a function of belonging to politically active religious institutions.

Among all the formal participation areas, religion seems to be the one institutional form whose importance crosses all racial and ethnic groups. Although actual religion and religious denomination vary widely among Hispanics, blacks, Asians, and Native Americans, in all groups high formal and informal religious involvement is present. Although it is not clear that institutional religious attendance differs substantially among groups, and from that of the general population, the reported significance of religious customs, rituals, and practices seems to be of more lifetime significance to racial and ethnic minorities, particularly in older age (Becerra & Shaw, 1984; Edwards, 1983; Kii, 1984; Lacayo, 1984; Taylor & Chatters, 1986).

Very little data exist on differences and similarities in voluntary association memberships among racial and ethnic minority populations and whites. George (1988), who reviewed data on black/white differences in voluntary associations, indicated that there seemed to be little differences but that no definitive conclusions could be reached. Recent national survey data indicated little or no differences between blacks and whites in number of associations but that blacks may spend less hours than whites in participation; these latter differences may be due to differences in socioeconomic status.

D. Family and Friend Support

A great deal of research has focused on family and friends as sources of tangible and emotional social support. In this section we highlight those issues of special relevance or distinction with respect to research findings on minority groups. More general findings are covered in other review chapters within the handbooks on aging. Familism is one of the basic distinguishing factors in the lives of racial and ethnic minorities. Although Asian-Americans show some demographic subgroup differences (Kii, 1984), other racial and ethnic groups, in comparison to the general population, have larger household sizes, are more likely to live in intergenerational households, and seem to have closer and more frequent family contact (Becerra & Shaw, 1984). Perhaps even more importantly, within each of the major racial and ethnic groups, dimensions of filial piety, importance of family bonds, and family support exchanges stand out as major characteristics. While the American family is undergoing major transformations, families from many minority groups appear to be maintaining close associational bonds (Kii, 1984; Layaco, 1984; Tate, 1983; Taylor, Jackson, & Quick, 1982; Taylor, 1985, 1986).

Basic descriptive studies of social support suggest that a life-course perspective is particularly useful for understanding specific events or behaviors. To understand current social participation and supportive exchanges, it is best to view the present within the context of past experiences and exchanges. In addition, research has shown that demographic factors, such as socioeconomic status, sex, marital status, and age, also affect supportive behaviors. These are issues of particular relevance for ethnic and racial group minorities. For example, a lifetime of limited economic resources does not provide the same capability of building a tangible "support reserve," that is, a history of having provided tangible resources to others so that they might provide the same or similar resources to you in some future time of need (Antonucci, 1985). However, the research does suggest that exchanges occur among racial and ethnic minorities (e.g., Stack, 1974), utilizing the more limited tangible and more bountiful emotional and affective resources that are available, creating special mutually supportive, intergenerational, though not necessarily linear exchanges (Mutran, 1985; Stevens, 1988).

Similarly, because structural position affects socially supportive arrangements, it is important to note that racial and ethnic minorities evidence deficits in socioeconomic level, marital status, and education. The effects on support networks and social support are relatively direct. People of lower socioeconomic status, education, and income are more likely to have exclusively family linked networks and to have multiple relations with fewer people. Because spouses are important support resources, especially for men, the decreased availability of a spouse, for example, among Filipino older men, has deleterious effects on support relationships. Interestingly, sex differences in social support—women have more complex and qualitatively superior relations—seem to hold across ethnic and racial minority groups. Thus both minority and nonminority widows are better able than men

without spouses to develop substitute or compensatory support relationships.

On the other hand, minority groups, although showing deficits in comparisons to majority groups in some areas, have developed alternative sources of support. For example, for many blacks the church is an important alternative source of support from that of family and friends (Ortega, Crutchfield, & Rushing, 1983). (Religion as social support should not be confused with religiosity—the intrinsic value of religion.) Thus, social support research on blacks and the limited research available on other ethnic and racial minority groups (Cantor, 1979; Mahard, 1988), suggest some effects of deficits on social networks but also highlights some compensatory effects of cultural factors, such as religion.

Another major area of investigation has been the function of social network and social support in alleviating the effects of stress, promoting effective health behaviors and influencing health outcomes (Berkman, 1988). Unfortunately, little of this research has been devoted to racial and ethnic minority groups, particularly in the older ages (Berkman, 1988). That social support is important for racial and ethnic minorities in stress, health, and functioning is suggested by the important role of extended families (Mutran, 1985). Only a few studies, however, have examined among ethnic and racial minorities the effects of social support on health outcomes. These studies have been poorly controlled and largely atheoretical (James, 1985) but do suggest that (1) social disorganization is related to elevated stroke mortality rates; (2) individuals within strong families are at reduced risk for elevated blood pressure; and (3) there is a positive role of social ties and support in reducing elevated blood pressure.

In summary, it seems indisputable that social networks and social support have etiologic and buffering roles in the health and well-being of racial and ethnic minorities (Berkman, 1988; Mahard, 1987). The precise role, as well as the processes and mechanisms through which they have an effect, is unknown in the general population (Antonucci & Jackson, 1987; Berkman, 1988), as well as within racial and ethnic minority groups (Chatters, Taylor, & Jackson, 1985).

V. Psychological Processes of Aging in Racial and Ethnic Minorities

A. Intellectual Functioning and Cognitive Potential

A great deal of research has been conducted in this area on minority children, youth, and young adults but not on older individuals. This research has consistently shown blacks to score lower than whites on standardized measures of intellectual functioning and achievement. Hispanics have normally scored at intermediate levels in comparison to blacks and whites, whereas Asian-Americans generally outperform whites, particularly on standardized achievement tests. Much of this research points to an important contributory role of social class and family norms among blacks and some Hispanic and Asian groups. Because long-term longitudinal data are not available, as is the case for whites (Schaie, 1983), the trajectory of intellectual functioning over the life course in ethnic and racial minorities is not clear.

Recent theorizing in this area by Perlmutter (1988) suggests that a decline view of cognitive potential in late life is even less defensible than a view of inevitable decline in intellectual abilities with age (Baltes, 1987; Schaie, 1983). As has been suggested by an impressive body of empirical work (e.g., Schaie, 1983; Baltes, 1987), some abilities decline, some remain the same, and some improve with chronological age. The direction of change depends on the specific ability under investigation and the prevalence of risk factors,

such as low educational level and decline in the ability of the spouse. The fact that ethnic and racial minorities show such marked differences on standardized measures of cognitive ability among the young may make for an enlightening comparison to patterns of lifelong changes in these abilities found in whites. It remains to be seen if there is lifelong continuity or a crossover effect in the intellectual functioning, as indicated in standardized measures, of racial and ethnic minorities in comparison to whites.

The work of Labouvie-Vief (1985) stresses the importance of cultural evolution in considering adult cognitive development, suggesting a critical role of opportunity structures and the definition of adaptive roles by elders within these structures. This view of adult cognitive development seems compatible with perspectives on racial and ethnic minority behaviors that stress their coping capacities and adaptive skills in the face of real systemic constraints (Jackson, 1988).

We are unaware of quality studies on cognitive deficits among black and other racial and ethnic groups. In a recent review of dementing illnesses among blacks, Baker (1988) suggested that little could be concluded on the basis of available data. The Established Populations for Epidemiologic Studies of the Elderly (EPESE) and Epidemiologic Catchment Area Program (ECA) data, however, are beginning to provide large-scale survey data on depressive symptomatology among the black and white elderly (George, 1988).

B. Memory and Learning

The learning and memory literature is even more devoid of content relevant to understanding the role of ethnicity and race in psychological aging processes. Recent advances in experimental work designed to explicate the role of retrieval, encoding, and decoding processes in the learning of meaningful material (Perlmutter,

1988) show promise for studying possible factors related to race and ethnicity. At present we know of no experimental work in this area that has demonstrated understandable differences among older groups due to racial and ethnic group membership. This may be due to an emphasis on biological substrates and neural mechanisms in learning and memory rather than consideration of perceptual and motivational factors (Poon, 1985). We believe that investigation of cultural and ethnic factors (contexual factors) related to changes in learning and memory over the life span could be a very fruitful area of study.

C. Personality and Motivation

The construct of control is becoming increasingly important as a basic organizing framework in aging research (Rodin, 1986). In a review, Rodin (1986) suggested that the relations between health and control may strengthen with increased age. She speculated that this may occur through an increase in control experiences with age, the association between control and health may be altered by aging, and age may influence the association between control and health-related behaviors.

Generally the sparse research on racial and ethnic groups suggests a significantly greater degree of external control (fatalism is often used interchangeably) among blacks, Native Americans, and Hispanics than whites (Varghese & Medinger, 1979). It is proposed that this fatalistic orientation is important in providing an adaptive response to real systemic constraints to mobility among minority older persons. Little empirical research, however, exists that documents the distribution of control perceptions, their etiology and relationship to health, and mental health outcomes among racial and ethnic groups.

Personality and motivational research has shown that a distinction between personal and general control beliefs is necessary and leads to different behavioral predictions. In particular, externality, defined in terms of sensitivity to social system determinants, predicts greater, rather than less, effectiveness (Gurin, Gurin, Lao, & Beattie, 1969; Jackson, Tucker, & Bowman, 1982). This reconceptualization of the original construct is the direct result of analyses of the special meaning of internal and external control in groups deprived of power in our society, notably blacks. This new concept made explicit a set of implicit assumptions in the traditional concept and resulted in the development of a generally more meaningful and richer construct and methods of assessment in all groups (Jackson, Tucker, & Bowman, 1982).

The multidimensionality of the I-E construct is now well established within the social science literature (Levenson, 1974). Although researchers ultimately may have arrived at the multidimensional nature of the control construct through research on whites, in fact, it was the pioneering study of Gurin et al. (1969) on black college students that laid the basis for the reformulation of I-E as a universally multidimensional construct (Levenson, 1974). Enhanced control, shown experimentally under certain conditions to have positive relationships to health and well-being in white elderly (Rodin, 1986), may not be as effective, and in fact may be detrimental to the adjustment of minority elderly. The I-E example demonstrates the problematic nature of many social science personality constructs in aging and their usefulness in cross-ethnic and racial group comparisons.

Another area that appears likely for a similar reconceptualization is age-related changes in self-conceptions, particularly self-esteem (Bengtson, Reedy, & Gordon, 1985). Numerous articles, books, and studies over several decades have tended to document that whites have higher self-esteem than blacks or that blacks have higher self-esteem than whites, particularly in young adult and adolescent samples. Data are sparse in older adult samples, particularly in racial and ethnic groups, and rarely has the nature and meaningfulness of the concept been raised. Similar to findings in white samples (Bengtson *et al.*, 1985), in analyses of national data on blacks, self-esteem has been found to be positively correlated with age. Similarly, positive racial group conceptions are also positively correlated with age, though a complex interaction with region and education also is present (Broman, Neighbors, & Jackson, 1988).

D. Psychopathology, Social Pathology, and Mental Health

Epidemiological research shows little difference in the distribution of the major mental disorders among the full age populations of racial and ethnic groups (Roberts, 1987). Work of comparable quality, although underway, has not been completed yet on older groups (George, 1988). Some work suggests race and ethnic differences in paranoia, suicide, and depression. The only conclusion to be drawn at this time, however, is that age makes a difference in the epidemiology of mental disorders. Alcoholism, neuroses, and schizophrenia decrease, for example, whereas depressive and organically based psychiatric disorders may increase in successively older age groups (LaRue, Desseonville, & Jarvik, 1985). Some recent survey data, however, suggest that depression may be actually lower in successively older age groups. A given disease, in fact, can manifest itself differently among the young and old (Minaker & Rowe, 1985), and individuals at midlife, in contrast to those at older ages, are at higher risk for stress reactions and perhaps depression due to major life losses like divorce.

Stress events, responses, consequent adaptation, and ways in which these factors are interrelated also differ across age (Schaie, 1981). The personal resources of the white elderly, for example, appear to insulate against or buffer stress in ways that may be different from the young (Kasl & Berkman, 1981; Rodin & Langer, 1980; Satariano & Syme, 1981). Age also changes relationships between mental health constructs and certain variables. For example, risks for nervous and mental disorders are greater for black than white men aged 24 to 64 but less for black than white women aged 65 to 69—young black men are at greater risk for certain mental disorders than older black women (Manton, Patrick, & Johnson, 1987). These findings suggest complex interactions among age, race, gender and the risk for developing mental disorders. Heterogeneity in physical and mental health and functioning increases in successively older age groups (Rowe & Kahn, 1987). For example, Manton *et al.* (1987) identify three distinct groups of black women aged 65 and over with contrasting prevalence of mental illness diagnoses and conditions. Group 1 (aged 80 to 89) was characterized by the greatest prevalence of dementia, psychoses, neuroses, and conditions such as wandering, agitation, confusion, withdrawal, and anxiety; Group 2 (aged 75 to 70) was the healthiest and exhibited a striking absence of disorders and maladaptive behaviors; and Group 3 (aged 90 and over) resembled the younger, healthier group and surpassed them in independent behaviors. These findings suggest that the relationship between age, mental illness diagnoses and conditions is nonlinear in older age groups of black women. If true, caution must be taken in extrapolating the psychiatric epidemiology of one age group of racial and ethnic minorities to another.

Based upon this discussion, it might be tentatively concluded that age group, aging, or cohort membership have special effects on the mental health epidemiology of blacks; age is clearly pivotal in the interpretation of any model of stress and adaptation. The model, in fact, could vary at different ages or points in the life span, among different cohorts and in different sociohistorical periods. This makes it clear that the mental illness of ethnic and racial minorities should be examined within a theoretical model that takes a life-span perspective (Baresi, 1987). A great deal of research on Americans of different racial and ethnic backgrounds point to important cultural distinctions that make the assessment and treatment of mental disorders difficult (Jackson, Chatters, & Neighbors, 1982). Differences in cultural expression, distribution of disorders, differential reactions to environmental exigencies, and differential responsiveness to treatment modality, all have been found to be related to ethnic and racial backgrounds.

VI. Summary and Conclusions: Toward a Life-Span Perspective on Cultural, Racial, and Ethnic Influences on Aging

In this chapter we speculated on the possibility of extending life-span theory to develop an integrated model of development and aging that includes historical, cohort, and cultural influences on successful biological/health, psychological, and social aging among racial and ethnic minorities. In most demographic categories, older minority adults show relatively poorer status. On the other hand, over the age of 65, populations have grown and will continue to do so, based upon current estimates of mortality and life expectancies.

Survey data indicate that some minority populations of advanced ages, for example blacks, may be more robust in comparison to whites, reflecting the outcome of different aging processes and selection over time for hardier individuals

(Manton, 1982). Whatever the cause of the racial (and ethnic in the case of Hispanics) survival age crossover, it is quite clear from available data that at every point earlier in the life span most racial and ethnic minority groups are at greater mortality and morbidity risk than whites. The burden of illness arising from mortality, morbidity, and disability early in the family life course, however, can have important implications not only for the individual but also for the nature and constitution of the family and others in minority social and economic networks. When mortality and morbidity occurrences are combined, not only are individual minority group members at increased risk for death and illness, but these losses along with the added burdens of health care may require levels of familial economic and social network resources that are simply unavailable.

There is a need for a greater infusion of racial and ethnic minority content and cross-cultural issues in research on aging (Fry, 1988; Gelfand & Barresi, 1987). We continue to run the risk of developing theories, research paradigms, and service delivery models that are not sensitive to large portions of the populations that make up the United States. Culture and life-style differences may be of fundamental importance in the constructs, theories, and interventions that are employed (Holzberg, 1982a; Jackson, 1985; Rosenthal, 1986). Some studies have shown how recognition and inclusion of cultural and racial considerations in service delivery programs can increase the effectiveness and reduce the cost of delivering services to racial and ethnic populations. It also has been suggested that the infusion of racial minority and ethnic content has positive effects on the health of the nation more broadly, regardless of whether the direct focus of that work is on racial and ethnic minorities (Cooper et al., 1981).

We also have underscored the need to separate the constructs of minority group, race, ethnicity, and culture (Holzberg, 1982a; Rosenthal, 1986). Ethnicity and culture were viewed as mutable and changeable over the life course for different cohorts, while retaining potency and continuity over time and generations (Holzberg, 1982a; Rosenthal, 1986). Race, ethnicity, and cultural distinctiveness were viewed as more than stratification variables (Bengtson, 1979). They were instead considered to be resources, providing psychological, social, and personal identity and group connectedness and more tangible sources of family and friend networks. In the assessment of the psychological literature related to race and ethnicity in old age, we noted the poor research and sparse empirical literature on the topic.

Although there is a convergence of thought toward a resource, life-span model of ethnicity that transcends notions of traditional culture and assimilation, the empirical literature has not kept pace. The data that we reviewed suggest directions that new research might take. Cultural differences in illness expression (Manton *et al.*, 1987), personality differences (Bastida, 1987), patterns of family and friend interaction (Kii, 1984), coping and adaptation (Gibson & Jackson, 1987), among other findings, all point to the existence of distinct, measurable, ethnic and racial dimensions that influence, and are influenced by, biological/health, social, and psychological aging processes. We believe that theory is beginning to emerge (Barresi, 1987; Fry, 1988; Holzberg, 1982a; Rosenthal, 1986) that will lead to more and better empirical studies. What is clear is that race, ethnicity, and cultural effects on the multidimensional nature of aging are not reducible to social class, theories of stratification, modernization, age leveling, minority status, disengagement, activity, or a host of other models proposed as general conceptualizations of the aging process. The life-span framework holds great promise for discovering midrange theo-

ries that may help to organize the few available, but hopefully burgeoning, empirical results in this area.

Acknowledgments

We would like to thank Sally Oswald and Keith Hirsh for their assistance in preparing this manuscript.

References

Antonucci, T. C. (1985). Personal characteristics, social networks, and social behavior. In B. H. Binstock & E. Shanas (Eds.), *Handbook of aging and the social sciences.* New York: Van Nostrand Reinhold.

Antonucci, T. C., & Jackson, J. S. (1987) Social support, interpersonal efficacy and health. In L. L. Carstensen & B. A. Edelstein (Eds.), *Handbook of clinical gerontology.* New York: Pergamon.

Baker, F. M. (1988). Dementing illness and black Americans. In J. S. Jackson (Ed.), *The black American elderly: Research on physical and psychosocial health.* New York: Springer.

Baltes, P. B. (1987). Theoretical propositions of life-span developmental psychology: On the dynamics between growth and decline. *Developmental Psychology,* **23,** 61–626.

Barresi, C. M. (1987). Ethnic aging and the life course. In D. E. Gelfand & C. M. Barresi (Eds.), *Ethnic dimensions of aging.* New York: Springer.

Bastida, E. (1987). Issues of conceptual discourse in ethnic research and practice. In D. E. Gelfand & C. M. Barresi (Eds.), *Ethnic dimensions of aging.* New York: Springer.

Becerra, R. M., & Shaw, D. (1984). *The hispanic elderly.* New York: University Press of America.

Bengtson, V. L. (1979). Ethnicity and aging: Problems and issues in current social science inquiry. In D. E. Gelfand & A. J. Kutzik (Eds.), *Ethnicity and aging: Theory, research and policy.* New York: Springer.

Bengtson, V. L., & Morgan, L. A. (1983). Ethnicity and aging: A comparison of three ethnic groups. In J. Sokolovsky (Ed.), *Growing old in different societies* (pp. 157–167). Belmont, CA: Wadsworth.

Bengtson, V. L., Reedy, M. N., & Gordon, C. (1985). Aging and self-conceptions: Personality processes and social contexts. In J. E. Birren & K. W. Schaie (Eds.), *Handbook of the psychology of aging*. New York: Van Nostrand Reinhold.

Berkman, L. F. (1988). *The changing and heterogenous nature of aging and longevity: A social and biomedical perspective*. Unpublished manuscript. New Haven, CT: Yale University.

Bradshaw, B. S., Frisbie, A. P., & Eifler, C. W. (1985). Excess and deficit mortality due to selected causes of death and their contribution to differences in life expectancy of Spanish-surnamed and other white males—1970 and 1980. In *Black and minority health*. (Vol. II), *Cross-cutting issues in minority health*. Washington, DC: U.S. Department of Health and Human Services.

Brody, J. A., & Brock, D. B. (1985). Epidemiologic and statistical characteristics of the United States elderly population. In C. E. Finch & E. L. Schneider (Eds.), *Handbook of the biology of aging* (2nd ed.). New York: Van Nostrand Reinhold.

Broman, C. L., Neighbors, H. W., & Jackson, J. S. (1988). Racial group identification among Black adults. *Social Forces*, **67**(1), 146–158.

Cantor, M. H. (1979). The informal support system of New York's inner city elderly: Is ethnicity a factor. In D. E. Gelfand & A. J. Kutzik (Eds.), *Ethnicity and aging: Theory, research and policy*. New York: Springer.

Chatters, L. M., Taylor, R. J., & Jackson, J. S. (1985). Aged blacks' choices for an informal helper network. *Journal of Gerontology*, **41**, 94–100.

Chen, Y. (1985). Economic status of the elderly. In B. H. Binstock & E. Shanas (Eds.), *Handbook of aging and the social sciences*. New York: Van Nostrand Reinhold.

Cooper, R. (1984). A note on the biologic concept of race and its application in epidemiologic research. *American Heart Journal*, **108**, 715–723.

Cooper, R., Steinhauer, M., Schatzkin, A., & Miller (1981). Improved mortality among U.S. blacks, 1968–1978: The role of antiracist struggle. *International Journal of Health Services*, **11**, 511–522.

Dowd, J. J., & Bengtson, V. L. (1978). Aging in minority populations: An examination of the double jeopardy hypothesis. *Journal of Gerontology*, **33**, 427–436.

Driedger, L., & Chappell, N. (1988). *Aging and ethnicity: Toward an interface*. London: Butterworths.

Edwards, E. D. (1983). Native American elders: Current issues and social policy implications. In J. N. Colen & R. L. McNeely (Eds.), *Aging in minority groups*. Beverly Hills, CA: Sage.

Farley, R. (1987). Who are black Americans? The quality of life for black Americans twenty years after the civil rights revolution. *The Milbank Quarterly*, **65** (Suppl. 1), 9–34.

Fry, C. (1988). Theories of aging and culture. In J. E. Birren & V. L. Bengtson (Eds.), *Emergent theories of aging*. New York: Springer.

Gelfand, D. E., & Barresi, C. M. (1987). Current perspectives in ethnicity and aging. In D. E. Gelfand & C. M. Barresi (Eds.), *Ethnic dimensions of aging*. New York: Springer.

George, L. K. (1988). Social participation in later life: Black-white differences. In J. S. Jackson (Ed.), *The black American elderly: Research on physical and psychosocial health*. New York: Springer.

Gibson, R. (1986). Blacks in an aging society. *Daedalus*, **115**, 349–372.

Gibson, R. C. (1989). Guest editorial: Minority aging research: Opportunity and challenge. *The Journal of Gerontology: Social Sciences*, **44**, 2–3.

Gibson, R. C., & Jackson, J. S. (1987). The black aged. *The Milbank Quarterly*, **65**, (Suppl. 2), 421–454.

Gibson, R., & Jackson, J. S. (1989). The black oldest old: Informal support, physical, psychological and social functioning. In R. Suzman & D. Willis (Eds.), *The oldest old*. New York: Oxford Press.

Gurin, P., Gurin, G., Lao, R. C., & Beattie, M. (1969). Internal-external control in the motivational dynamics of Negro youth. *Journal of Social Issues*, **25**, 29–53.

Haan, M. N., & Kaplan, G. A. (1985). The contribution of socioeconomic position to minority health. (Vol. II), Crosscutting issues in minority health. *Report of the Secretary's Task Force on Black and Minority Health*. Washington, DC: U.S. Department of Health and Human services.

Hamburg, D. A., Elliott, G. R., & Parron, D. L. (1982). *Health and behavior: Frontiers of re-*

search in the biobehavioral sciences. Washington, DC: National Academy Press.

Holzberg, C. S. (1982a). Ethnicity and aging: Anthropological perspectives on more than just the minority elderly. *Gerontologist*, **22**, 249–257.

Holzberg, C. S. (1982b). Ethnicity and aging: Rejoiner to a comment by Kyriakos S. Markides. *Gerontologist*, **22**, 471–472.

Ikels, C., Keith, J., & Fry, C. L. (1987). The use of qualitative methodologies in cross-cultural research. In G. D. Rowles & S. Reinharz (Eds.), *Qualitative gerontology.* New York: Springer.

Jackson, J. J. (1981). Urban black Americans. In A. Harwood (Ed.), *Ethnicity and medical care.* Cambridge, MA: Harvard University Press.

Jackson, J. J. (1985). Race, national origin, ethnicity, and aging. In R. B. Binstock & E. Shanas (Eds.), *Handbook of aging and the social sciences.* New York: Van Nostrand Reinhold.

Jackson, J. S. (Ed.) (1988). *The black American elderly:Research on physical and psychosocial health.* New York: Springer.

Jackson, J. S., Chatters, L. M., & Taylor, R. (in press). *Roles and resources of the black elderly.* Westview, CA: Sage.

Jackson, J. S., Chatters, L. C., & Neighbors, H. W. (1982). The mental health status of older black Americans: A national study. *Black Scholar*, **13**, 21–35.

Jackson, J. S., Chatters, L. M., & Neighbors, H. W. (1986). The subjective life quality of black Americans. In F. W. Andrews (Ed.), *Research on the quality of life.* Ann Arbor, MI: Institute for Social Research.

Jackson, J. S., & Gibson, R. (1985). Work and retirement among black elderly. In Z. Blau (Ed.), *Work, leisure, retirement and social policy.* New York: JAI Press.

Jackson, J. S., Tucker, M. B., & Bowman, P. J. (1982). Conceptual and methodological problems in survey research on black Americans. In W. Liu (Ed.), *Methodological problems in minority research.* Chicago: Pacific/Asian American Mental Health Center.

James, S. A. (1985). Coronary heart disease in black Americans: Suggestions for future research on psychosocial factors. In A. M. Ostfield (Ed.), *Measuring psychosocial variables in epidemiologic studies of cardiovascular disease.* Washington, DC: NIH Publication No. 85-2270, Public Health Service, U.S. Department of Health and Human services.

Kasl, S. V., & Berkman, L. (1981). Psychosocial influences on health status of the elderly: The perspective of social epidemiology. In J. L. McGaugh & S. B. Kiesler (Eds.), *Aging: Biology and health.* New York: Academic Press.

Kii, T. (1984). Asians. In E. B. Palmore (Ed.), *Handbook on the aged in the United States,* (pp. 201–218). Westport, CT.: Greenwood Press.

Kim, P. K. H. (1983). Demography of the Asian-Pacific elderly: Selected problems and implications. In J. N. Colen & R. L. McNeely (Eds.), *Aging in minority groups.* Beverly Hills, CA: Sage.

Kobata, F. S., Lockery, S. A., & Moriwaki, S. Y. (1980). Minority issues in mental health. In J. E. Birren & R. B. Sloane (Eds.), *Handbook of mental health and aging.* Englewood Cliffs, NJ: Prentice-Hall.

Kumanyika, S. K., & Savage, D. D. (1985). Ischemic heart disease risk factors in black Americans. In *Report of the Secretary's Task Force on Black and Minority Health* (Vol. IV), *Cardiovascular and Cerebrovascular Diseases.* Washington, DC: U.S. Department of Health and Human Services.

Labouvie-Vief, G. (1985). Intelligence and cognition. In J. E. Birren & K. W. Schaie (Eds.), *Handbook of the psychology of aging.* New York: Van Nostrand Reinhold.

Lacayo, B. J. (1984). Hispanics. In E. B. Palmore (Ed.), *Handbook on the aged in the United States* (pp. 253–268). Westport, CT: Greenwood Press.

LaRue, A., Dessonville, C., & Jarvik, L. F. (1985). Aging and mental disorders. In J. E. Birren & K. W. Schaie (Eds.), *Handbook of the psychology of aging.* New York: Van Nostrand Reinhold.

Levenson, H. (1974). Activism and powerful others: Distinctions within the concept of internal-external control. *Journal of Personality Assessment*, **38**, 377–383.

Mahard, R. E. (1987). *Functional status, social support and distress among elderly Puerto Ricans.* Paper prepared for San Diego State University Center on Aging Conference, June.

Mahard, R. E. (1988). *Research needs and gaps: Hispanic Americans.* Paper prepared for Conference, "Minority Aging: Geriatric Education Curriculum for Selected Health Professionals," Rockville, MD, February.

Manton, K. G. (1982). Differential life expectancy: Possible explanations during the later years. In R. C. Manual (Ed.), *Minority aging: Sociological and psychological issues.* Westport, CT: Greenwood Press.

Manton, K. G., Patrick, C. H., & Johnson, K. W. (1987). Health differentials between blacks and whites: Recent trends in mortality and morbidity. *The Milbank Quarterly,* **65** (Suppl. 1), 129–199.

Manton, K., Poss, S. S., & Wing, S. (1979). The black/white mortality crossover: Investigation from the perspective of the components of aging. *Gerontologist,* **19,** 291–300.

Manton, K. G., & Soldo, B. J. (1985). Dynamics of health changes in the oldest old: New perspective and evidence. *Milbank Memorial Fund Quarterly,* **63,** 177–186.

Markides, K. S. (1982). Ethnicity and aging. *Gerontologist,* **22,** 467–470.

Minaker, K. L., & Rowe, J. W. (1985). Health and disease among the oldest old: A clinical perspective. *Milbank Memorial Fund Quarterly,* **63,** 324–349.

Mutran, E. (1985). Intergenerational family support among blacks and whites: Responses to culture or to socioeconomic differences. *Journal of Gerontology,* **40,** 382–389.

National Indian Council on Aging (NICA) (1984). Indian and Alaskan natives. In E. B. Palmore (Ed.), *Handbook on the aged in the United States* (pp. 269–278). Westport, CT: Greenwood Press.

Neugarten, B. L. (1975). The future and the young-old. *Gerontologist,* **15,** 4–9.

Omran, A. R. (1977). Epidemiologic transition in the U.S. *The Population Bulletin,* **32,** 3–42.

Ortega, S. T., Crutchfield, R. D., & Rushing, W. A. (1983). Race differences in elderly personal well-being. *Research on Aging,* **5,** 101–118.

Perlmutter, M. (1988). Cognitive potential throughout life. In J. E. Birren & V. L. Bengtson (Eds.), *Emergent theories of aging.* New York: Springer.

Poon, L. W. (1985). Differences in human memory with aging: Nature, causes, and clinical implications. In J. E. Birren & K. W. Schaie (Eds.), *Handbook of the psychology of aging.* New York: Van Nostrand Reinhold.

Roberts, R. E. (1987, December). *Depression among black and Hispanic Americans.* Paper presented at the NIMH Workshop on Depression and Suicide in Minorities, Bethesda, MD.

Rodin, J. (1986). Aging and health: Effects of the sense of control. *Science,* **233,** 1271–1276.

Rodin, J., & Langer, S. (1980). Aging labels: The decline of control and the fall of self-esteem. *Journal of Social Issues,* **36,** 12–29.

Rosenthal, C. J. (1986). Family supports in later life: Does ethnicity make a difference? *Gerontologist,* **26,** 19–24.

Rowe, J. W. (1985). Health care of the elderly. *New England Journal of Medicine,* **312,** 827–835.

Rowe, J. W., & Kahn, R. L. (1987). Human aging: Useful and successful. *Science,* **237,** 143–149.

Ryder, N. B. (1965). The cohort as a concept in the study of social change. *American Sociological Review,* **30,** 843–861.

Satariano, W., & Syme, S. L. (1981). Life changes and disease in elderly populations. In J. L. McGaugh & S. B. Kiesler (Eds.), *Aging: Biology and Health.* New York: Academic Press.

Schaie, K. W. (1981). Psychological changes from midlife to early old age: Implications for the maintenance of mental health. *American Journal of Orthopsychiatry,* **51,** 199–218.

Schaie, K. W. (Ed.) (1983). *Longitudinal studies of adult psychological development.* New York: Guilford.

Siegel, J. S., & Davidson, M. (1984). *Demographic and socioeconomic aspects of aging in the United States.* Washington, DC: U.S. Bureau of the Census, Current Population Reports, Series P-23, No. 138. U.S. Government Printing Office.

Siegel, J. S., & Taeuber, C. M. (1986). Demographic perspectives on the longlived society. *Daedalus,* **115,** 77–118.

Sokolovsky, J. (Ed.) (1989). Bringing culture back home: Ethnicity, aging and family support. *The cultural context of aging.* New York: Bergin & Garvey.

Soldo, B. (1980). America's elderly in the 1980's. *Population Bulletin,* **35,** 3–47.

Stack, C. (1974). *All our kin.* New York: Harper & Row.

Stevens, J. H. (1988). Social support, locus of control, and parenting in three low-income groups of mothers: Black teenagers, black adults, and white mothers. *Child Development, 59,* 635–642.

Suzman, R., & Riley, M. W. (1985). Introducing the "oldest old." *Milbank Memorial Fund Quarterly, 63,* 177–186.

Swidler, A. (1986). Culture in action: Symbols and strategies. *American Sociological Review, 51,* 273–286.

Taplin, C., & Carlson, R. H. (1985). Minority access to health care in the mid-1980's. *Report of the Secretary's Task Force on Black and Minority Health* (Vol. II), *Cross-cutting Issues in Minority Health.* Washington, DC: U.S. Department of Health and Human Services.

Tate, N. (1983). The black aging experience. In J. N. Colen & R. L. McNeely (Eds.), *Aging in minority groups.* Beverly Hills, CA: Sage.

Taylor, R. J. (1985). The extended family as a source of support to elderly blacks. *Gerontologist, 25,* 488–495.

Taylor, R. J., & Chatters, L. M. (1986). Patterns of informal support to elderly black adults: Family, friends, and church members. *Social Work, 31,* 432–438.

Taylor, R. J., Jackson, J. S., & Quick, A. D. (1982). The frequency of social support among black Americans: Preliminary findings from the National Surveys of Black Americans. *Urban Research Review, 8,* 1–4.

Taylor, R. L. (1979). Black ethnicity and the persistence of ethnogenesis. *American Journal of Sociology, 84*(6), 1401–1423.

Taylor, R. J. (1986). Receipt of support from family among black Americans: Demographic and familial differences. *Journal of Marriage and the Family, 48,* 67–77.

Torres-Gil, F. (1983). Political involvement among older members of national minority groups: Problems and prospects. In J. N. Col-en & R. L. McNeely (Eds.), *Aging in minority groups.* Beverly Hills, CA: Sage.

Valle, R. (1983). The demography of Mexican-American aging. In J. N. Colen & R. L. McNeely (Eds.), *Aging in minority groups.* Beverly Hills, CA: Sage.

Vargheses, R., & Medinger, F. (1979). Fatalism in response to stress among the minority aged. In D. E. Gelfand & A. J. Kutzik (Eds.), *Ethnicity and aging: Theory, research and policy.* New York: Springer.

Watson, W. H. (1983). Selected demographic and social aspects of older blacks: An analysis with policy implications. In J. N. Colen & R. L. McNeely (Eds.), *Aging in minority groups.* Beverly Hills, CA: Sage.

Wilkinson, D. T., & King, G. (1987). Conceptual and methodological issues in the use of race as a variable: Policy implications. *The Milbank Quarterly, 65,* (Suppl. 1), 56–71.

Wing, S., Manton, K. G., Stallard, E., Hames, C. G., & Tyroler, H. A. (1985). The black/white mortality crossover: Investigation in a community based study. *Journal of Gerontology, 40,* 78–84.

Yancey, W., Ericksen, E., & Juliani, R. (1976). Emergent ethnicity: A review and reformulation. *American Sociological Review, 41,* 391–403.

Yinger, J. M. (1985). Ethnicity. *Annual Review of Sociology, 11,* 151–180.

Yu, E. S. H., Chang, C., Liu, W. T., & Kan, S. H. (1985a). Asian-white mortality differences: Are there excess deaths? In D. H. H. S. (Ed.), *Black and minority health* (Vol. II), *Cross-cutting issues in minority health.* Washington, DC: U.S. Department of Health and Human services.

Yu, E. S. H., Liu, W. T., & Kyrzeja (1985b). Physical and mental health status indicators for Asian-American communities. In D. H. H. S. (Ed.), *Black and minority health* (Vol. II), *Cross-cutting issues in minority health.* Washington, DC: U.S. Department of Health and Human Services.

Seven

Gender Differences in Aging

Margaret Hellie Huyck

This chapter is intended as a guide to understanding how sex and gender may organize experience and functioning in later life. It is important to bring together the more "mainstream" literature on sex and gender with the gerontological literature concerning behavior in the second half of life. This overview will examine several key questions. (1) How have sex and gender been conceptualized and used as research variables in psychology and aging? (2) How different are older women and men in the functions of greatest interest to psychologists? (3) What models are useful in understanding gender differences over the life course? (4) What should researchers do to advance the study of gender differences in later life?

I. Approaches to the Study of Gender

This chapter will follow the emerging consensus in differentiating aspects of sex and gender. *Sex* is used to indicate physiological differentiation between males and females. *Gender role* includes the social prescriptions or stereotypes associated with each sex, to which an individual may or may not conform; and *gender identity* includes the introspective part of gender role, such as the gender-linked qualities that one sees as part of the self (Money, 1987). Readers should be aware that the use of these and related terms (e.g., sex role, sex role identity) is variable across historical time and researcher; the only reasonable stance is to note carefully the definition of these basic terms for each researcher, theorist, or advocate.

Deaux (1984) distinguished three approaches used in recent research on sex and gender. Sex is often used as a subject variable, to make categorical distinctions. Individual differences in masculinity, femininity, and androgyny have been assessed as presumed traits. Researchers have also focused on the ways individuals use sex as a social category, a cue to form judgments and choose actions.

Psychologists have become sensitized to the ways in which research on gender and age often have involved biased as-

Handbook of the Psychology of Aging, Third Edition
Copyright © 1990 Academic Press, Inc. All rights of reproduction in any form reserved.

sumptions and methods (Denmark, Russo, Frieze, & Sechzer, 1988; Schaie, 1988). Thus, any summary assessment of the kinds of gender differences evident in later adulthood must be viewed cautiously. The patterns of differences described below are selective and suggestive; a major challenge is to enhance the research base to assess the extent and importance of age-gender interactions in the areas summarized: health, mental health, cognition, personality, social stereotypes, and social role behavior in later life.

II. Gender and Psychological Functioning

A. Longevity, Health, and Morbidity

Increasingly, it appears that females are hardier. Their life expectancy is greater, particularly if they survive female infanticide and childbirth (Olson & Seager, 1986; U.S. Census, 1987), and the differences seem to be increasing rather than decreasing with advances in health care and changes in social roles. Table I shows the life expectancy for males and females in the United States at birth, age 50, and age 65, in 1959–1961 and 1983, for whites and nonwhites separately. The gender gap consistently favors females. At birth, the gender gap is 7 years for whites and 7.7 for nonwhites; by age 50, the gap is reduced to

5 to 6 years; and among those who survive to age 65, the gap is 4.2 years for whites and 3.8 for nonwhites. Although there has been a secular trend toward increased life expectancy, the gender gap has increased from the 1959–1961 period.

Morbidity patterns also show gender differences. The gender gap in chronic health problems is shown in Table II. The rate for most problems is higher among women; the gap is measured by indicating the female rate as a percentage of the male rate. (If there were no gender gap, the percentage would be 100%.) The largest gender differences are for varicose veins of the lower extremities, diseases of the urinary system, migraines, and arthritis; the least gender differences are for deformities or orthopedic impairments, hay fever, hemorrhoids, and heart conditions. Men are more vulnerable than women to visual and hearing impairments.

There are minimal sex differences in the percentage of persons reporting activity limitations: 13.9% of males and 14.6% of females (U.S. Census, 1987, Table 167).

There is also evidence of gender patterns in the cause of death. The age-adjusted death rates show the largest gender gap in deaths from suicide, accidents, and pulmonary obstruction, and the smallest gap in diabetes melitus, cardiovascular diseases, and cancer. Heart diseases are the most common cause of death; in which case the rate for women is half that for

Table I
Life Expectancy by Sex, Age, and Race: 1960 and 1983

		White		Nonwhite	
		1959–1961	1983	1959–1961	1983
At Birth:	Male	67.6	71.7	61.5	67.2
	Female	74.2	78.7	66.5	74.9
Age 50:	Male	73.2	75.7	71.3	73.5
	Female	78.1	81.2	74.3	79.0
Age 65:	Male	78.0	79.5	77.8	79.1
	Female	80.9	83.7	80.1	82.9

Source: U.S. Bureau of the Census, *Statistical Abstract of the United States: 1987* (107th Ed.). Adapted from Table No. 106, p. 70.

Table II
The Gender Gap in Chronic Health Problems: 1983

Chronic Condition	Female Rate as Percentage of Male Rate	Male Rate	Female Rate
Varicose veins, lower	403.4	11.6	46.8
Urinary system diseases	330.1	14.4	46.1
Migraines	294.3	15.8	46.5
Arthritis	174.2	94.9	165.3
Visual impairments	66.0	42.7	28.2
Hypertension	132.0	104.1	137.4
Hearing impairments	69.6	107.1	74.5
Diabetes	129.1	21.3	27.5
Chronic bronchitis	124.7	119.0	148.4
Heart conditions	108.4	79.3	86.0
Hemorrhoids	106.5	46.1	49.1
Hay fever, rhinitis	105.9	83.7	88.6
Deformities, orthopedic impairments	105.6	93.8	99.2

Source: U.S. Bureau of the Census, *Statistical Abstract of the United States: 1987* (107th Edition). Calculated from Table 166, p. 104.
Note: Rates per 1000 persons of selected chronic health problems, arranged from most to least difference between males and females.

men. Since 1960 the gender gap in death rates has increased for some important diseases; men now are even more likely than women to die of cancer, pneumonia, or heart disease. Thus, whereas death rates from cancer have changed little for women, men are now more likely to die of cancer; death rates from heart disease and pneumonia have declined for both sexes, but the decline has been more marked for women than for men (U.S. Census, 1987, Table 115).

The causes and implications of such patterns of gender differences are complex. Efforts to reduce the gender gaps in life expectancy must focus on identifying the biogenetic and life-style factors that operate all along the life course. Verbrugge (1988) observed that five critical facets of women's lives increase their morbidity relative to men: their lower labor force participation, higher levels of emotional stress, stronger feelings of vulnerability to illness, fewer time constraints, and less strenuous physical activity each week. Men are at higher risk of morbidity from smoking and job hazards. However, Ver-

brugge (1988) also suggested that if women and men were similar in social attitudinal characteristics, their health profiles would be much more similar—except that men would still be likely to die earlier than women.

B. Mental Health

The relationships between gender and mental health, and changes in later life, remain controversial (Cleary, 1987; Walsh, 1987). Although women have higher rates of psychiatric treatment for narrowly defined mental illnesses (that is, neuroses or functional psychoses but excluding brain syndromes and personality disorders), men are more likely than women to show antisocial personality disorders and alcohol and drug abuse. If these latter disorders are included, there are no gender differences in rates of psychiatric impairment (Cleary, 1987). A review of 15 U.S. community mental health studies showed no consistent pattern of sex differences in reported symptoms (Feinson, 1987). Gender patterns for depression are complex and depend partly upon the definition used. Women are more likely to be diagnosed with depression, and younger women are more vulnerable to depression than older women. Older men are more likely than younger men or older women to commit suicide, which is one index of depression (Cleary, 1987). Overall, the data suggest that sex differences in mental health are more evident in earlier adult years than in later life (e.g., after age 65) (Feinson, 1987).

Relatively few studies have assessed directly the relationship between gender (as contrasted to sex) and mental illness, or mental health, in the later years. A great deal of research has compared the well-being of gender-typed (masculine or feminine) and androgynous styles; and some of this research has focused on older adults (Frank, Towell, & Huyck, 1985; Sinnott, 1986). Having a gender identity that includes the "masculine" agentic attributes seems to be a better predictor of well-being than feminine expressivity or nurturance, or an equal balance of masculine and feminine traits (Puglisi & Jackson, 1980–1981; Sinnott, 1986; Taylor & Hall, 1982).

Some clinical research indicates that vulnerability to late-onset affective disorders in middle or later life is linked to gender identity, with men or women with a more fragile sense of gender identity feeling more threatened by normal changes in gender-linked style in themselves or in a spouse (Gutmann, Grunes, Griffin, & Jacobowitz, 1987).

C. Cognitive Functioning

The assessment of gender differences in cognitive functioning involves questions about overall intelligence, components of intelligence and information processing, changes in functioning over time, and susceptibility of declines to remediation.

Thus far, there is no evidence that men and women differ systematically on global intelligence or the extent of intellectual decline with age (Halpern, 1986; Schaie & Hertzog, 1986). However, there are some reliable gender differences in performance on some of the standard subscales.

The most consistent difference is the superior performance of males in *spatial ability*, though the difference is small in magnitude (Halpern, 1986; Willis & Schaie, 1988). Data from the Seattle Longitudinal Study (Schaie & Hertzog, 1986) revealed that men scored higher on spatial ability over a 14-year period. Although there were no gender differences in the amount of decline, men declined more in speed of processing, and women declined somewhat more in accuracy. The consistency of reported differences and the fact that superiority is linked both to sex and handedness suggest some kind of biogenetic coding for spatial abilities. However, sex differences between children are greatly modified with training in spatial orientation (Halpern, 1986), and the gender differences were reduced when the older women in the SLS responded more positively than did men to training in mental rotation ability (Willis & Schaie, 1988).

Girls and women typically show superior performance on tests of verbal abilities, and men show superiority on mathematical tests. However, gender differences are decreasing as girls and young women show gains in mathematics and spatial abilities (Halpern, 1986). Such historical trends, and the intervention research with older adults, indicate that cognitive abilities are and will remain somewhat plastic.

D. Personality

The difficulties in summarizing what constitutes "personality" are familiar to gerontologists (Kogan, this volume), particularly because gender-linked aspects are often summarized as sex/gender role or sex/gender identity. The size, consistency, and meaning of gender differences in personality remain controversial matters (Deaux & Kites, 1987). Many personality measures do not reveal consistent sex differences (Deaux & Kites, 1987; Turner, 1981).

In terms of characteristics presumed to assess masculinity and femininity, at covert, dispositional levels and often in social behavioral and self-attribution levels, men and women seem most divergent in late adolescence and young adulthood and become more similar in the later middle years (Feldman, Biringen, & Nash, 1981; Gutmann, 1987; Lowenthal, Thurnher, & Chiriboga, 1975; Sinnott, 1986). Changes at the covert level (as assessed by projective tests or other fantasy material) seem to precede, and predict, later changes in social behavior (Gutmann, 1987; Shanan, 1985).

There is substantial controversy about the nature (and consequences) of such reduced differentials. Some theorists argue that the modifications are statistically small and do not constitute an appreciable shift in personality (Costa & McCrae, 1980). At the other extreme, some have hypothesized that men and women become essentially "gender free" in later life, moving away from a gender-typed self-concept into a genuinely androgynous identity (Sinnott, 1986). Others feel that gender identity is so crucial that even statistically small changes may be personally significant (Gutmann, 1987).

E. Social Stereotypes

Cross-cultural stereotypes reflect shared conceptions of what are considered prototypically "masculine" and "feminine" styles (Williams & Best, 1982). Females are typically described as weaker, less active, and more concerned with affiliation, nurturance, and deference than are men, and men are regarded as stronger, more active, and higher on autonomy, achievement, and aggression. However, as Gut-

mann has pointed out (1977, 1987), there are also widespread stereotypes that reflect gender–age differences. Old men are seen as less "masculine" and less the "warrior"; they may become powerful elders negotiating peace. Old women may be stereotyped as "matriarchs," managing extended family systems, or as "witches," using power malevolently. Some cultures seem to define older people (like children) as "genderless," having lost the gender-differentiated qualities associated with the reproductive, parenting years (Gailey, 1987).

F. Gender Role Behavior

Some sex differences in social roles and social status are evident cross-culturally. Younger women generally are held responsible for caring for small children and contraception (Olson & Seager, 1986); older women are responsible for ensuring smooth family functioning (Lopata, 1987). Females are generally socialized into these responsibilities. Whatever work men do is more valued by the culture (Olson & Seager, 1986). Worldwide, poverty is associated with having (or being) a female head of household, particularly for mothers and older women (Hess, 1985; Olson & Seager, 1986). Poverty is one outcome of differential access to education, employment, or pensions that accompany official or unofficially acknowledged gender differences in social status. On the other hand, men are more likely to face active combat and disability or death in warfare as one aspect of their masculine protector/provider role (Gutmann, 1987), and most males are socialized into these potential realities.

III. Models of Gender Differentiation

There are a diverse array of models that have been proposed to account for the kinds of gender differences summarized here. Ideally, models would be available to account for the patterns of stability and change over the life course, as well as differences between cultures and historical periods. There is no single model that accounts adequately for group-level sex differences and for individual variability within each sex group. Readers and researchers should look for the model used, implicitly or explicitly, and assess its appropriateness for the phenomena considered.

A. Biogenetic Models

Biogenetic models assume that differential structures and functions resulting from genetic coding carried on the 23rd chromosomal pair are implicated in complex expressions of sex-dimorphic behavior. Coding for internal and external reproductive structure and function differences, overall body appearance, and some immunities are carried on these chromosomes.

B. Socioevolutionary Models

Most socioevolutionary models assume that the sexually dimorphic behaviors observed in any society (or species) reflect the outcome of cumulative adaptive strategies by the group as a whole. The most ambitious and comprehensive model of gender diffentiation across the life span has been proposed by Gutmann (1977, 1987). He suggests that the core qualities stereotypically associated with males and females have evolved in response to the demands of parenting. The observed shifts toward less sexually differentiated, or more androgynous behaviors are tied to a sense of release from the "parental imperatives" associated with caring for vulnerable offspring. Elders also have gender-specific contributions to the survival of the culture, as (female) "kin tenders" and (male) "culture tenders."

C. Early Cognitive-Emotional Differentiation

According to cognitive developmental models, the child learns early to categorize others and the self as male or female. This basic information is used as a filter through which subsequent information is processed, and the child learns which other attributes are gender congruent or gender relevant (Bem, 1985). Beliefs about what is congruent, as well as actual behaviors, may change substantially after the early years but are biased by that early perspective (Money, 1987).

Recent research on the cognitive processing involved in adult thinking about gender indicates that gender categorizing seems to be processed automatically, triggered by physical attributes (Deaux & Kites, 1985; Smith & Midlarsky, 1985). Gender constitutes a "fuzzy" cognitive schema; each individual identifies characteristics that she or he thinks define each gender and those that are optional. Although initial perceptions may be analyzed more rationally and revised with experience with the particular persons who have been categorized, a cognitive-processing model suggests one way in which very early learning persists and one of the reasons why individuals are seldom (if ever) regarded by others as gender neutral.

Some models link observed gender differences in adult relationship style to the early processes of differentiation, particularly from the mother or other primary caregiver (Dinnerstein, 1977). It is not clear, in fact, to what extent early, prerational gender schemata continue to act as a cognitive/emotional "filter" through which subsequent, more rational experiences are organized.

D. Social Learning and Social Structure Models

Social learning theories postulate that males and females learn gender behaviors by imitation, observation, and reinforcement. The larger social structure shapes experiences and meaning, locates people in the social world, and defines and allocates economic and social rewards; gender is regarded, then, as a "property of systems, not people" (Hess & Ferrea, 1987, p. 17). As such, gender is malleable by revising social structure and learning contingencies. Gender-linked behaviors may also change, nonintentionally, as a correlate of historic shifts, such as those presumed to be linked to the ratio of men to women in the culture (Secord, 1983).

IV. Implications for Aging Research and Practice

Researchers and practitioners are caught between the perils of either over- or underestimating the separate and interacting effects of gender and age (Hare-Mustin, 1988). Gender and age, as well as ethnicity and social class, constitute important status characteristics that shape experiences and life chances and that often seem to invoke unfortunate biases. At the most general level, researchers must develop a sensitivity to issues of gender in doing fieldwork and reporting results (Schaie, 1988; Warren, 1988). Minimally, this means moving from sex- and age-differences research to trying to conceptualize and measure directly the gender and age dimensions that would help account for the behavior of interest. It means accepting the possibility that men and women have substantially different basic experiences and that one cannot assume "equivalence" of gestalt experience on the basis of equivalence in particular responses. On the other hand, it also means guarding against the assumption that statistically significant differences are necessarily meaningful in individual or social terms. Given the evidence regarding the increased diversity of functioning among

older adults (compared with younger adults and children), researchers should look for and report evidence of variability within gender-age groups, as well as reporting mean trends between status groups. Efforts must be directed toward identifying variables that may correlate with gender and/or age and that are the "real" determinants of the phenomena under question.

Perhaps the strongest need at this point is for research that takes the experiences of elders, particularly women as the starting point, describing their experiences in terms of the relevance for their lives. There is no good model describing and accounting for variability in the experiences of being an older woman.

Designing and delivering supportive services that help men and women to function more effectively means that one must be sensitive to the age- and gender-linked patterns of need and potential utility of the services. Many public policies have been framed in terms of the life course and concerns of men, with the result that the longer life expectancy of women often means a lower quality of life (Hess, 1985). It will be a challenge for planners to develop policies that are gender-sensitive, that is, appropriate to the life-stage needs of the variety of males and females in the society.

References

Bem, S. L. (1985). Androgyny and gender schema theory: A conceptual and empirical integration. In T. B. Sonderegger (Ed.), *Nebraska symposium on motivation 1984:Psychology and gender* (Vol. 32). Lincoln: University of Nebraska Press.

Cleary, P. D. (1987). Gender differences in stress-related disorders. In R. C. Barnett, L. Bierer, & G. K. Baruch (Eds.), *Gender and stress* (pp. 39–72). New York: Free Press.

Costa, P. T., & McCrae, R. R. (1980). Still stable after all these years: Personality as a key to some issues in aging. In P. B. Baltes & O.

G. Brim (Eds.), *Life-span development and behavior* (Vol. 3). New York: Academic Press.

Deaux, K. (1984). From individual differences to social categories: Analysis of a decade's research on gender. *American Psychologist,* **39**(2), 105–116.

Deaux, K., & Kites, M. E. (1985). Gender stereotypes: Some thoughts on the cognitive organization of gender-related information. *Academic Psychology Bulletin,* **7**(2), 123–144.

Deaux, K., & Kites, M. E. (1987). Thinking about gender. In B. B. Hess & M. M. Feree (Eds.), *Analyzing gender* (pp. 92–117). Beverly Hills, CA: Sage.

Denmark, F., Russo, N., Frieze, I., & Sechzer, I. (1988). Guidelines for avoiding sexism in psychological research. *American Psychologist,* **43**, 582–585.

Dinnerstein, D. (1977). *The mermaid and the minotaur: Sexual arrangements and human malaise.* New York: Harper.

Feinson, M. (1987). Mental health and aging: Are there gender differences? *Gerontologist,* **27**(7), 703–711.

Feldman, S. S., Biringen, Z. C., & Nash, S. C. (1981). Fluctuations of sex-related self-attributions as a function of stage of family life cycle. *Developmental Psychology,* **17**(1), 24–35.

Frank, S., Towell, P., & Huyck, M. (1985). The effects of sex role traits on three aspects of psychological well-being in a sample of middle aged women. *Sex Roles,* **12**(9–10), 1073–1082.

Gailey, C. W. (1987). Evolutionary perspectives on gender hierarchy. In B. B. Hess & M. M. Feree (Eds.), *Analyzing gender* (pp. 32–67). Beverly Hills, CA: Sage.

Gutmann, D. L. (1977). The cross-cultural perspective: Notes toward a comparative psychology of aging. In J. E. Birren & K. W. Schaie (Eds.), *Handbook of the psychology of aging* (pp. 302–326). New York: Van Nostrand Reinhold.

Gutmann, D. L. (1987). *Reclaimed powers: Toward a new psychology of men and women in later life.* New York: Basic Books.

Gutmann, D. L., Grunes, J., Griffin, B., & Jacobowitz, J. J. (1987). *A model of late-onset psychopathology.* Paper presented at 40th annual scientific meetings, Gerontological Society of America, Washington, DC.

Halpern, D. (1986). *Sex differences in cognitive abilities.* Hillsdale, NJ: Erlbaum.

Hare-Mustin, R. (1988). Family change and gender differences: Implications for theory and practice. *Family Relations,* **37**(1), 36–41.

Hess, B. B. (1985). Aging policies and old women: The hidden agenda. In A. S. Rossi (Ed.), *Gender and the life course* (pp. 319–331). New York: Aldine.

Hess, B. B., & Ferrea, M. M. (Eds.) (1987). *Analyzing gender: A handbook of social science research.* Beverly Hills, CA: Sage.

Lopata, H. Z. (1987). Women's family roles in life course perspective. In B. B. Hess & M. M. Feree (Eds.), *Analyzing gender* (pp. 381–407). Beverly Hills, CA: Sage.

Lowenthal, M. F., Thurnher, M., & Chiriboga, D. (1975). *Four stages of life.* San Francisco: Jossey-Bass.

Money, J. (1987). Propaedeutics of diecious G-I/R: Theoretical foundations for understanding dimorphic gender identity roles. In J. M. Reinisch, L. A. Rosenblum, & S. A. Sanders (Eds.), *Masculinity/femininity: Basic perspectives* (pp. 13–28). New York: Oxford University Press.

Olson, A., & Seager, J. (1986). *Women in the world: An international atlas.* New York: Touchstone/Simon & Schuster.

Puglisi, J. T., & Jackson, D. (1980–1981). Sex role identity and self esteem in adulthood. *International Journal of Aging and Human Development,* **12**(2), 129–138.

Schaie, K. W. (1988). Ageism in psychological research. *American Psychologist,* **43**(3), 179–183.

Schaie, K. W., & Hertzog, C. (1986). Toward a comprehensive model of adult intellectual development: Contributions of the Seattle longitudinal study. In R. J. Sternberg (Ed.), *Advances in human intelligence* (Vol. 3, pp. 79–118). Hillsdale, NJ: Erlbaum.

Secord, P. F. (1983). Imbalanced sex ratios: The social consequences. *Personality and Social Psychology Bulletin,* **4**, 525–543.

Shanan, J. (1985). Personality types and culture in later adulthood. *Contributions to human development,* (Vol. 12). New York: Karger.

Sinnott, J. D. (1986). Sex roles and aging: Theory and research from a systems perspective. *Contributions to human development* (Vol. 15). New York: Karger.

Smith, P. A., & Midlarsky, E. (1985). Empirically derived conceptions of femaleness and maleness: A current view. *Sex Roles,* **12** (3/4), 313–328.

Taylor, M. C., & Hall, J. A. (1982). Psychological androgyny: Theories, methods, and conclusions. *Psychological Bulletin,* **92**(2), 347–66.

Turner, B. F. (1981). Sex-related differences in aging. In B. B. Wolman & G. Stricker (Eds.), *Handbook of developmental psychology.* Englewood Cliffs, NJ: Prentice-Hall.

U.S. Bureau of the Census (1987). *Statistical Abstracts of the United States: 1987* (107th ed.). Washington, DC.

Verbrugge, L. M. (1988). Unveiling higher morbidity for men. In M. W. Riley (Ed.), *Social structures and human lives* (pp. 138–160). Beverly Hills, CA: Sage.

Walsh, M. W. (Ed.) (1987). *The psychology of women: Ongoing debates.* New Haven, CT: Yale University Press.

Warren, C. A. (1988). *Gender issues in field research.* Beverly Hills, CA: Sage.

Williams, J. E., & Best, D. L. (1982). *Measuring sex stereotypes: A thirty-nation study.* Beverly Hills, CA: Sage.

Willis, S., & Schaie, K. W. (1988). Gender differences in spatial ability in old age: Longitudinal and intervention findings. *Sex Roles,* **18**(3/4), 189–213.

Part Three

Behavioral Processes in Aging

Eight

Electrophysiology and Aging

Patricia N. Prinz, Robert E. Dustman, and Rita Emmerson

The spontaneous EEG contains an abundant variety of dynamic waveforms. The most dramatic waveform changes occur in response to fluctuating states of wakefulness, drowsiness, sleep, coma, or death. Significant EEG changes also occur in a variety of brain diseases, drug, or metabolic states, and with life-span developmental stages and aging. The purpose of this chapter is to provide an updated overview of electrophysiological changes associated with "normal" aging along with a discussion of possible underlying mechanisms. The possibility that physical fitness modulates electrophysiologic age differences also will be discussed.

I. Electrophysiologic Age Differences

A. Age Differences and the Clinical EEG during Relaxed Wakefulness

The most consistent differences in the clinical EEG on "normal" older populations (comprehensively reviewed by Obrist, 1976; Prinz, 1976; Marsh & Thompson, 1977; Miller, Bashore, Farwell, & Donchin, 1987; Niedermeyer & Lopes da Silva, 1987; Woodruff, 1985) include decreased frequency and abundance of the alpha rhythm along with a pattern of increased slower (delta and theta) activities, both diffuse and focal. Increased higher frequency (beta) activities are often observed, particularly in older women. With the exception of the beta increase, these changes are in the direction of a shift toward lower frequency activities and parallel the EEG changes typically seen in disease states that compromise brain functioning, such as cardio- and cerebrovascular diseases. Studies that rigorously screen for disease have observed smaller or minimal age differences in these parameters. Thus, in spite of its rich complexity, the clinical EEG does not contain identifiable features that reflect normal aging not confounded by age-related disease states. To complicate matters further, all of these age differences (including the increased beta activity) are quantitatively similar to EEG changes associated with alert/drowsy transition states

Handbook of the Psychology of Aging, Third Edition
Copyright © 1990 Academic Press, Inc. All rights of reproduction in any form reserved.

(Low, 1987; Santamaria & Chiappa, 1987). Studies of EEG features during carefully controlled behavioral states, such as cognitively defined alertness or various stages of sleep, are not in complete agreement with clinical EEG studies.

B. Age Differences in the Quantitative EEG during Cognitive Effort

There are now a limited number of studies that have employed computer analysis methods to quantitate age-related differences in EEG. Unlike visual analyses that focus on more organized rhythmic waves or spike episodes that transiently "stand out" from the background EEG, the quantitative EEG assesses the more abundant polymorphic background waves. Using a computerized frequency analysis of EEGs of healthy subjects actively engaged in cognitive testing, several labs have documented age-related decreases in the amount of slower frequency activity (delta and theta) along with an increased amount of higher frequency (beta) activity (Duffy, Albert, McAnulty, Garvey, 1984; Roubicek, 1977; Tucker, Penland, & Heck, 1988). These changes are in a direction of a shift toward higher rather than lower frequencies, an age trend opposite to that observed in clinical EEG studies. A similar age shift toward increased high frequency activity has been observed in earlier life-span studies of the quantitative EEG; as children mature to adolescence and beyond, a gradual shift toward higher EEG frequencies (less delta and theta, more beta) is generally observed (John, Ahn, Prichep, Trepetin, Brown, & Kaye, 1980; Gasser, Verleger, Bacher, & Sroka, 1988; Niedermeyer & Lopes da Silva, 1987). The quantitative EEG data suggest that this trend may continue into healthy old age.

It is puzzling that quantitative EEG and clinical EEG studies have resulted in opposite conclusions about the nature of the age effect on EEG frequencies (overall shifts towards higher and lower frequencies, respectively). The discrepancy may result from the small number of quantitative EEG studies reported in the literature. Additional studies clearly are needed. The discrepancy also may reflect the different emphasis on background EEG activity or the differing behavioral conditions employed in quantitative and visual methods. Clinical EEG studies are generally conducted during relaxed waking states free of cognitive load, whereas quantitative studies have generally utilized tasks to control subject alertness during EEG recording. There is considerable evidence to suggest that under relaxed, low demand states, dynamic shifts in vigilance are more likely to occur (Schultz & Lavie, 1985), a phenomenon that may be more operative during clinical EEG studies than during effortful task performance.

C. The Sleep EEG and Age Differences in Sleep Quality

Age effects on sleep are well documented (see reviews by Dement, Richardson, Prinz, Carskadon, Kripke, & Czeisler, 1985; Miles & Dement, 1980; Woodruff, 1985). The quality of sleep is impaired in older subjects. In particular, "slow wave" stages of sleep are reduced while wakefulness is increased. The stages of sleep and wakefulness are defined on behavioral as well as polygraphic (including EEG) grounds, as summarized in Prinz (1976) and Pivik (1986).

1. Age Differences in the Sleep EEG

The most prominent age difference in the sleep EEG is reduced amplitude and amount of the high voltage delta waves that characterize slow wave (S3 and S4) sleep (Feinberg, Koresko, & Hellner, 1967; Kahn & Fisher, 1969; Prinz, 1976). These changes also are found in the all-night computer quantitated EEG (Dijk,

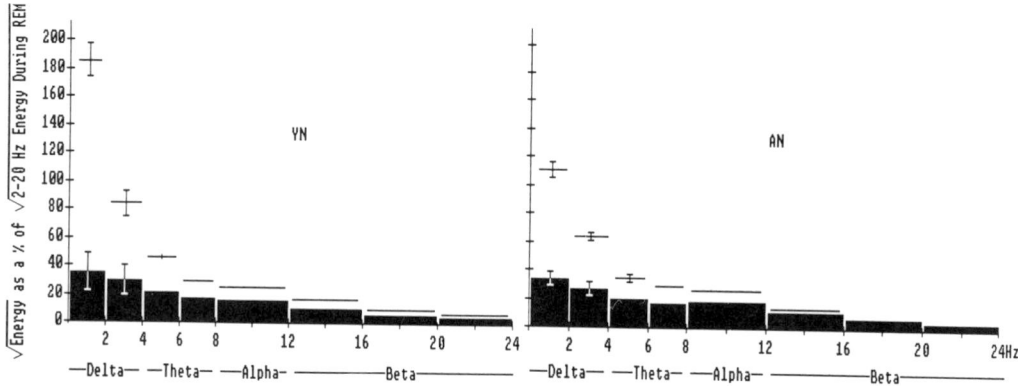

Figure 1 Quantitative EEG measure of amplitude [square root of mean energy (power spectral) (+SEM)] in each EEG (C4 vs. A1) frequency band as a percentage of the 2 to 20 Hz total "amplitude" during REM sleep for 7 young (YN) and 20 aged normal (AN) men during REM (shaded bar graph) and during slow wave sleep (SWS) (upper lines). Age effects are greatest for delta waves during SWS. Age effects during REM are minimal except for alpha. Similarly, age effects during wakefulness (W) (not shown) are minimal with values similar to those during REM (within 10%) except for alpha, which is more prominent during W. From Prinz (unpublished observations).

Beersma, & Van den Hoofdakker, 1989; Feinberg, Fein, Floyd, & Aminoff, 1983; Smith, Karacan, & Yang, 1977) (Figure 1). This age difference is particularly striking for the higher amplitude (>50µV), lower frequency waveforms, which are apparently reduced in both amplitude and amount (Smith *et al.*, 1977). Decreased delta amplitude and abundance is found even in healthy elderly people screened to be free of sleep disorders or diseases affecting brain function (Feinberg, 1976; Prinz, 1976). Preliminary data indicate that delta, theta, and beta activity during REM sleep are less affected by age (Dijk, *et al.*, 1989; Smith, Karacan, & Yang, 1978) (Figure 1). Age differences in spindle activity during sleep have been observed. Senescent sleep spindles are often poorly formed, of lower amplitude and less abundant (Guazzelli, Feinberg, Aminoff, Fein, Floyd, & Maggini, 1986; Smith, Karacan, & Yang, 1979). Senescent spindle frequencies were reported to be higher in visual but not in quantitative EEG analysis (Guazzelli *et al.*, 1986). Overall, the abundance of activities in the various frequency bands in the senescent sleep EEG are

unchanged or less abundant at all frequencies except alpha (Smith *et al.*, 1979) (Figure 1).

2. Age Differences in Sleep Stages and Daytime Sleepiness

Coincident with altered EEG characteristics during sleep, there are also age differences in the amount and patterning of the various stages of sleep and wakefulness (reviewed in Miles & Dement, 1980) (Figure 2). The most striking changes include a reduction in slow wave sleep, particularly Stage 4 sleep along with increased nighttime wakefulness and increased fragmentation of sleep by periods of wakefulness. Age reductions in REM sleep and total nighttime sleep are of much lesser magnitude and are nonsignificant in many studies (Miles & Dement, 1980; Williams, Karacan, & Hursch, 1974) (Figure 2). Taken together, these age differences in sleep and wakefulness are in the direction of impaired sleep maintenance and depth, a conclusion that is further supported by observations that older subjects are more

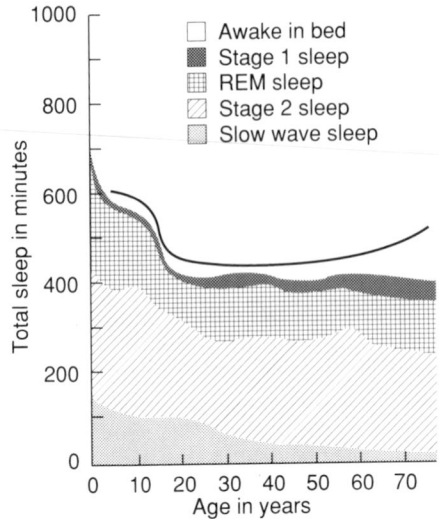

Figure 2 Nocturnal sleep in humans from birth to old age shows a characteristic pattern of declining total sleep and slow wave (Stages 3 and 4) sleep and increased time awake in bed with advanced age. Reproduced with permission from Dement, Richardson, Prinz, Carskadon, Kripke, and Czeisler (1985).

easily aroused from nighttime sleep by auditory stimuli (Zepelin, McDonald, & Zammit, 1984).

Sleep quality is known to be adversely affected by diseases that compromise brain functioning, such as various drug states, cerebrovascular or cardiovascular disease, and dementing disorders (Prinz, Poceta, & Vitiello, 1989). Additional factors that impair sleep quality include other medical and psychiatric disorders, circadian rhythm disturbances, and sleep-related apnea and myoclonus (Association of Sleep Disorders Center, 1979). Many of these sleep-impairing conditions become more prevalent with advancing age (Miles & Dement, 1980; Shepard, 1988; Vitiello & Prinz, 1988). Because sleep disorders may confound normative aging assessments, efforts to screen for pathological disorders that compromise sleep are well justified.

The age differences described (increased

fragmentation of nighttime sleep with wakefulness and decreased slow wave sleep) appear to reflect a "normal" aging process, because they can still be observed in older adults carefully screened for good health and absence of sleep disorders. Although not well documented, daytime sequelae of this "normal" age difference may include decreased ability to maintain alert or effortful vigilant states across long time periods, fatigue, and performance impairments, as have been documented for sleep deprived young adults (Schultz & Lavie, 1985). Daytime sequelae of nighttime sleep loss would seem to have great relevance for improved quality of life and for theories of the psychology of aging. Possible biological implications of chronic sleep loss have been reviewed elsewhere (Dement *et al.*, 1985; Prinz, Halter, Raskind, Cunningham, & Karacan, 1981). The short- and long-term consequences of age-related sleep impairment remains poorly understood and deserving of further study.

D. EEG Responsivity: Event-Related Potentials in Aging

Event-related potentials (ERPs) offer another approach for assessing brain–behavior relationships in aging. ERPs are characterized by a series of polarity shifts (components) that can be measured for latency, polarity, and amplitude. It is assumed that component latencies and amplitudes are modulated by underlying neurobiological processes and that changes in CNS structure and function, such as might occur during normal aging, are reflected in altered ERP characteristics.

A variety of ERPs have been used in aging studies. These include early latency brain stem auditory and somatosensory evoked potentials (BAEPs and BSEPs) that provide information regarding neural transmission from lower brain stem to cortex. Middle latency components (roughly 20 to 80 msec) reflect the arrival and initial processing of sensory volleys within primary sensory receiving areas (Beck, 1975), and long latency components (80 to 300 msec) are sensitive to arousal, attention, and habituation (Beck, 1975; Regan, 1972). These components are termed *exogenous* as their latencies and amplitudes are coupled to characteristics of eliciting stimuli (Donchin, Ritter, & McCallum, 1978); they are relatively resistant to subject variables of a psychological nature. Endogenous components are sensitive to the information-processing qualities of stimuli such as stimulus relevance and task difficulty (Donchin *et al.*, 1978). The most widely studied endogenous component is the P300 that occurs 300 to 600 msec after stimulus presentation.

Not surprisingly, ERP components provide evidence of age-related slowing at all functional levels of the brain. Almost all investigations of BAEPs indicate age-related transmission delays attributable to changes in peripheral auditory structures (Simpson, Knight, Brailowsky, Prospero-Garcia, & Scabini, 1985). At least half of available studies also report significant age-related slowing within the auditory brain stem (e.g., Allison, Wood, & Goff, 1983; Chu, 1985). BSEP studies show that sensory nerve conduction velocities slow with age (Allison *et al.*, 1983; MacKenzie & Phillips, 1981; Strenge & Hedderich, 1982) and that the rate of slowing accelerates after about 45 to 50 years of age (Simpson & Erwin, 1983). Conduction time from brain stem to cortex for auditory and somatosensory stimulation also appears to slow with advancing age (Allison *et al.*, 1983; MacKenzie & Phillips, 1981; Strenge & Hedderich, 1982), although a recent study reported that central conduction time within the somatosensory system was not affected by age (Zegers de Beyl, Delberghe, & Brunko, 1988). Age-re-

lated increases in middle latency components have been demonstrated, suggesting delayed transmission and slowed processing of sensory volleys arriving at auditory, somatosensory, and visual cortical receiving areas of elderly subjects (Drechsler, 1978; Dustman & Beck, 1969; Kelly-Ballweber & Dobie, 1984; Schenkenberg, 1970; Shagass, 1972). Although the consensus has been that long-latency exogenous components are slowed in ERPs of elderly individuals (see Klorman, Thompson, & Ellingson, 1978), age-related delays were not found for long-latency VEP components, when stimulation was adjusted to compensate for age-related visual loss (Dustman, Shearer, & Snyder, 1982; Dustman & Snyder, 1981). Finally, P300 studies consistently show that P300 latency slows at a rate of about 1 to 2 msec/year from early age to adulthood (e.g., Beck, Swanson, & Dustman, 1980; Goodin, Squires, Henderson, & Starr, 1978).

II. Theoretical Implications of Electrophysiologic Changes in Aging

A. The Arousal Hypothesis of Aging

The arousal hypothesis of aging contends that older adults may be less aroused (more drowsy) across daytime waking hours, with consequent effects on psychophysiologic measurements. The senescent clinical EEG contains many EEG features that are common to less vigilant waking states, including increased beta, slower, more diffuse alpha frequency, and left anterior temporal sharp waves (Santamaria & Chiappa, 1987). The arousal hypothesis of aging would suggest that clinical EEG findings commonly attributed to age may reflect, in part, age differences in maintenance of alert states during EEG monitoring. The hypothesis also suggests that correlations between EEG and cognitive performance may result from the common influence of alert/drowsy states.

The concept that changes in arousal may contribute to psychophysiological age differences is not new. Recent reviews by Woodruff (1985) and Empson (1986) have emphasized the theoretical importance of arousal measures in understanding normal age differences. Although arousal is a major model of geropsychology, studies involving arousal have resulted in interesting but often conflicting results (Marsh & Thompson, 1977; Woodruff, 1985), possibly because it is extremely difficult to define operationally arousal states in a manner applicable to all individuals (Belyavin & Wright, 1987). Lacking a comprehensive index of arousal level, most investigators focus on selected EEG or behavioral correlates of arousal. More comprehensive relationships among these factors have been worked out for young than for old adults. Correlations of EEG features with performance and reaction time are not uniformly observed in young adults (Kripke, Mullaney, & Fleck, 1985; Low, 1987; Townsend & Johnson, 1979). However, when drowsiness or fatigue is present during longer term repetitive vigilance testing, a clear relationship between these variables emerges (Belyavin & Wright, 1987; Schacter, 1977; Schultz & Lavie, 1985; Williams, Kearney, & Lubin, 1965). In sleep-deprived young subjects, resting EEG patterns appear more drowsy (more theta, less alpha) during error than during correct trials (Townsend and Johnson, 1979; Williams, Granda, Jones, Lubin, & Armington, 1962). Even in correct trials, sleep-deprived subjects perform more slowly, and clear EEG differences can be detected (as reviewed in Empson, 1986). Townsend and Johnson (1979) summed up much of this work in their conclusion that "changes in the frequency content of the EEG predict performance only when they are secondary to changes in arousal, which in turn predict performance" (p. 278). Arousal levels are known to decline in mid-afternoon, as indexed by both performance and EEG changes. This phenomenon is apparently tied to a midafternoon dip in circadian temperature rhythm (Campbell & Zulley, 1985) and may reflect brain mechanisms generating sleepiness rather than those responsible for arousal. Alert/drowsy states are influenced by circadian (24-hour) and ultradian (less than 24-hour) rhythms such that drowsier EEG patterns (e.g., slower alpha and appearance of theta rhythm) correlate with circadian and ultradian temperature rhythm minima (Gundel & Hilbig, 1983; Okawa, Matousek, & Petersen, 1984; Takii, 1986). The circadian and ultradian temperature minima are highly correlated with a sense of fatigue and with poorer test performance (Gundel & Hilbig, 1983; Takii, 1986) and may be exaggerated by sleep deprivation (Schultz & Lavie, 1985). The ultradian EEG and performance decrements are relatively impervious to normal daytime activities (Okawa et al., 1984) but may be minimized during brief periods of cognitive demand (Aschoff & Gerkema, 1985; Schultz & Lavie, 1985). Taken together, these phenomena suggest that spontaneously fluctuating arousal levels may have a significant impact on psychophysiological measures of interest to gerontologists. It is not clear whether older adults are more susceptible to these phenomena than young adults. One way to address this question is to track multiple measures of arousal in a circadian or ultradian time frame in both young and old subjects. Such studies are now feasible due to advances in ambulatory monitoring techniques for temperature, behavior, & EEG. Of course, the researcher also can bypass the arousal issue and minimize potential age differences in arousal level by focusing on brief periods of cognitive effort. Both approaches have an important role in future aging research.

B. Central Inhibitory Deficits in Aging

1. CNS Excitation-Inhibition

The importance of inhibition is eloquently described by McGeer, Eccles, and McGeer (1978). "We can think that inhibition is a sculpturing process. The inhibition, as it were, chisels away at the diffuse and rather amorphous mass of excitatory action and gives a more specific form to the neuronal performance at every stage of synaptic delay" (p. 133). The role of inhibition in behavior changes across the life span. Central inhibition is relatively weak in infancy but assumes an ever increasing importance during childhood development (Diamond, Balvin, & Diamond, 1963; Fishbein, 1976; White, 1965). A reverse trend is believed to occur during adult aging; inhibitory control weakens with approaching senescence (Dustman & Shearer, 1987; Roberts, 1972; Shagass, 1972). Optimum balance between excitation and inhibition reportedly occurs during late adolescent and early adult years when the capacity for coordinated movement and mental productivity is greatest (Roberts, 1972).

An electrochemical bias toward relatively greater excitation might be expected to influence behavior in subtle to more obvious ways depending on the magnitude of the inhibitory deficit. For example, a relative inability to inhibit external and internal stimuli might result in distractibility and impaired attention and concentration. Difficulty in suppressing ongoing motoric and mental activity might contribute to impulsiveness, behavioral rigidity, or a relative inability to quickly shift from one cognitive activity to another (mental inflexibility). These kinds of cognitive problems have been reported for children and the elderly (Botwinick, 1973; Hoyer & Plude, 1980; Schaie, 1958; Strommen, 1973; White, 1965). As reviewed later, age-related changes in EEG and ERPs suggest that in-

hibitory control may be progressively weakened during adult aging (see also Woodruff, 1985).

2. Amplitude of Exogenous Middle-Latency Components

Nearly 25 years ago it was observed that amplitude of middle-latency SEP and VEP components recorded from areas overlying the respective cortical sensory receiving areas was larger for old than for young adults (Shagass, 1972). These findings for SEPs and VEPs have been replicated since (Dustman & Beck, 1969; Dustman, Shearer, & Emmerson, 1989; Luders, 1970; Man'kovskii, Belong, & Gorbach, 1978; Schenkenberg, 1970), and similar results have been shown for ERPs to auditory stimulation (Woods & Clayworth, 1986). The larger middle-latency components for older individuals have been commonly interpreted as reflecting weakened central inhibitory modulation of stimulus effects at sensory end organs and/or at sensory way stations.

3. Inhibition and the Visual System

Another line of evidence regarding central inhibition derives from short duration flashes that project a checkerboard pattern. These evoke VEPs at occipital scalp that differ from VEPs elicited by unpatterned flashes (Regan, 1972). The difference in waveforms of "patterned" and "unpatterned" VEPs is believed to be related to inhibition within the visual system as the detection of lines and contours is dependent upon inhibitory processes (Bloom, Lazerson, & Hofstadter, 1985). Dustman, Snyder, and Schlehuber (1981) speculated that waveforms of the two kinds of VEPs should be more similar for normal subjects believed to have reduced inhibitory efficiency, children and the elderly, than for subjects of intermediate age. The latter, because of a more efficient

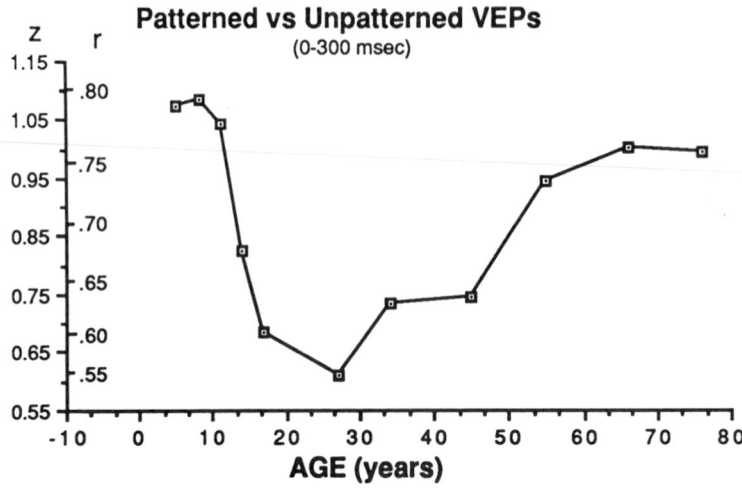

Figure 3 Life-span changes in similarity of VEP waveforms from occipital scalp elicited by patterned and unpatterned flashes. Similarity was determined by correlating the digital values comprising the 0 to 300 msec of patterned VEPs with corresponding values for unpatterned VEPs. Each data point represents the mean correlation (r) and Fisher z-coefficient (z) for 20 males. Statistical analyses were done on z-coefficients that have a normal sampling distribution. Data with permission from Dustman, Snyder, and Schlehuber (1981).

inhibitory system, would produce a more differentiated VEP response to patterns. Waveform similarity was determined by correlating the digital representation of the two VEP types. Figure 3 illustrates that the patterned-unpatterned VEP correlations portrayed a U-shaped function across age, that similarity was significantly greater for individuals at the age extremes than for subjects of late adolescent to young adult age, and that age-related changes were noticeable by the mid-40s.

4. VEP Augmenting and Reducing

For many individuals (*augmenters*), an increase in stimulus intensity is accompanied by larger ERPs. For others (*reducers*), amplitude may remain stable or become smaller (Buchsbaum, 1976; von Knorring, Monakhov, & Perris, 1978). A predisposition toward augmenting and reducing is presumably related to inhibitory functioning, with individuals who are reducers having stronger inhibitory

systems than augmenters. For example, individuals thought to have cortical inhibitory deficits, for example, withdrawing alcoholics and subjects with Down's syndrome, are VEP augmenters. Both groups reportedly have compromised frontal cortical function and reduced availability of neurotransmitters that are predominantly inhibitory (Coleman & Mahanand, 1973; Gliddon, Busk, & Galbraith, 1975; von Knorring & Oreland, 1978).

If a reduction in central inhibitory control is a concomitant of normal aging, elderly subjects should show stronger augmenting responses than young adults to increasing stimulus intensity. This has been confirmed for VEPs elicited by dim, medium, and bright flashes and recorded from 220 healthy males aged 4 to 90 years (Dustman & Snyder, 1981). Regression of amplitude on intensity, amplitude/intensity (A/I) slope, provided a measure of each subject's propensity to augment or reduce amplitude of late VEP components re-

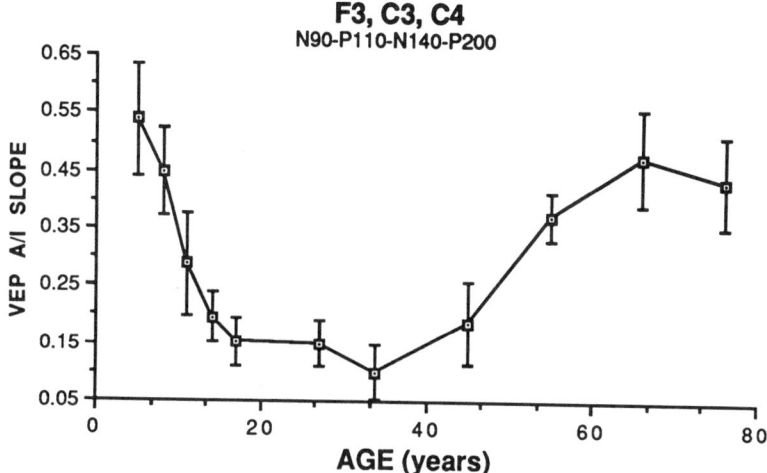

Figure 4 Mean VEP amplitude-intensity (A/I) slope for 11 groups of 20 males. Note the U-shaped curve for A/I slope across age, values being larger for children and old adults than for subjects of intermediate age. A/I slope was based on the mean of the amplitudes of nine components: N90-P110, P110-N140, and N140-P200 in VEPs recorded from F3, C3, and C4 scalp sites. Vertical bars show standard errors of the mean. Reproduced with permission from Dustman, Shearer, and Emmerson (1989).

corded from frontal-central scalp areas. Figure 4 shows a U-shaped function of A/I slope across the life span. Augmentation was strongest for the young and the elderly, ages during which central inhibition is speculated to be weakest. Aging effects were apparent by middle age.

5. Topographic Homogeneity of EEG and ERPs

Gaches (1960) reported that EEG alpha activity showed an age-related accelerating spread into central and frontal areas from parieto-occipital sites where alpha is typically found. A similar phenomenon was noted for somatosensory ERPs. Liberson (1976) and Drechsler (1978) observed that SEPs, usually restricted to fronto-central areas, were found in parietal and occipital recordings of elderly subjects. Drechsler (1978) suggested the age-related spread of SEPs over the hemisphere was related to a decreasing strength of inhibition.

Cortical coupling procedures that pro-vide a measure of time-dependent similarity of EEGs across recording sites were employed with 40 young (25 to 35 years) and 40 old (55 to 70 years) community volunteers (Dustman, LaMarche, Cohn, Shearer, & Talone, 1985). As shown in Table I, EEGs across recording sites were more homogeneous for the old than for the young subjects. The EEG of these subjects was also evaluated by power spectral analysis. PSA, which shows abundance of EEG activity, was computed for EEG from Fz, Cz, Pz, and Oz scalp electrodes for four frequency bands that spanned 5 to 13 Hz. Although mean EEG power failed to distinguish old from young subjects for all frequency-electrode combinations, the groups were significantly different with respect to variability of power loadings across electrode sites.

Recent reports regarding interarea amplitudes of the P300 component in recordings of young and old subjects appear to agree quite well with these findings. A number of investigators found that P300

Table I
Cortical Coupling Values of Young and Old Individuals

Electrode Pair	Young[a] Mean	SD	Old[b] Mean	SD	F[c]	p[d]
Fz-Cz	0.627	0.120	0.736	0.153	12.6	<0.001
Fz-C3	0.390	0.108	0.415	0.128	0.9	NS*
Fz-Pz	0.239	0.082	0.340	0.120	19.5	<0.001
Fz-Oz	0.087	0.036	0.160	0.083	26.3	<0.001
Cz-C3	0.544	0.127	0.584	0.147	1.7	NS
Cz-Pz	0.509	0.104	0.651	0.125	31.8	<0.001
Cz-Oz	0.159	0.065	0.279	0.097	41.9	<0.001
C3-Pz	0.403	0.094	0.524	0.106	29.8	<0.001
C3-Oz	0.150	0.048	0.290	0.121	46.6	<0.001
Pz-Oz	0.422	0.120	0.630	0.138	53.7	<0.001

Source: Reproduced with permission from Dustman, LaMarche, Cohn, Shearer, and Talone (1985).
[a]Forty individuals, 25 to 35 years of age.
[b]Forty individuals, 55 to 70 years of age.
[c]ANOVA F value.
[d](1, 76) degrees of freedom.
*Not significant.

amplitude was distributed in a more equipotential manner across midline recording sites for old as compared to young subjects (e.g., Goodin *et al.*, 1978; Mullis, Holcomb, Diner, & Dykman, 1985; Polich, Howard, & Starr, 1985).

Together these neurophysiologic findings suggest that aging is accompanied by a diminution of inhibitory strength. Neuropsychological observations of reduced mental flexibility (ability to quickly shift perceptual set) and impaired attention and concentration (Craik, 1977; Lizak, 1983) in the elderly indicate that this interpretation may be meaningful at a behavioral level. Further testing of the inherent prediction of the inhibitory hypothesis will determine its efficacy as a behavior model of aging.

III. Modulation of CNS Age Differences with Physical Fitness

Age Differences in the EEG

Are the changes in EEG and ERPs that occur during normal aging, or at least the rate of change, an inevitable consequence of the passage of time? Earlier we indicated that disease may exacerbate CNS deterioration. It is possible that an increased emphasis on maintaining good physical health will have an opposite effect and slow the rate at which CNS deterioration occurs during aging (see also chapter by Spirduso in the present volume). Recent findings for ERPs indicate that aerobically trained individuals process visual information more rapidly than people who are sedentary. VEP late component and P300 latencies of 30 young and 30 older adult males whose fitness levels were either high or low were compared. The results indicated that high fitness was associated with earlier VEP latencies for both the young and old. P300 showed an expected slowing with age but only for the sedentary older men. Despite a 30-year difference in age, P300 latency for the aerobically fit older adults was not different from latencies for the young subjects (Dustman, Emmerson, Ruhling, Shearer, Steinhaus, Johnson, Bonekat, & Shigeoka, 1989).

IV. Summary and Conclusions

Age differences typically seen in clinical EEG studies include increased abundance of lower relative to higher frequency activities during relaxed (unchallenged) wakefulness. Age differences reported in a limited number of quantitative EEG studies are opposite in direction, with a decreased abundance of lower relative to higher frequencies during cognitive effort. This discrepancy may partially be explained by the arousal hypothesis of aging, which states that older adults may be less aroused (more prone to drowsiness) across unchallenged daytime hours with consequent effects on psychophysiological measurements. There are now numerous studies documenting an age impairment in sleep quality, but comprehensive studies of daytime psychophysiological sequelae of this phenomenon of aging are lacking. EEG and ERP studies document that adult aging is associated with a generalized slowing of nervous system functioning that is observed at peripheral, brain stem, sensory receiving, and cognitive-integrative levels.

Some EEG and ERP findings also suggest that central inhibition weakens during normal aging and that these changes are evident by middle age. Finally, recent studies indicate that a life-style that includes the practice of strenuous physical activity may contribute to healthier CNS functioning in old age.

References

Allison, T., Wood, C. C., & Goff, W. R. (1983). Brain stem auditory, pattern-reversal visual, and short-latency somatosensory evoked potentials: Latencies in relation to age, sex, and brain and body size. *Electroencephalography and Clinical Neurophysiology, 55*, 619–636.

Aschoff, J., & Gerkema, M. (1985). On diversity and uniformity of ultradian rhythms. In H. Schulz & P. Lavie (Eds.), *Ultradian rhythms in physiology and behavior* (pp. 321–334). Berlin and New York: Springer.

Association of Sleep Disorders Center (1979). Nosology of sleep disorders. *Sleep, 2*(1), 1–137.

Beck, E. C. (1975). Electrophysiology and behavior. *Annual Review of Psychology, 26,* 233–262.

Beck, E. C., Swanson, C., & Dustman, R. E. (1980). Long latency components of the visually evoked potential in man: Effects of aging. *Experimental Aging Research, 6,* 523–545.

Belyavin, A., & Wright, N. A. (1987). Changes in electrical activity of the brain with vigilance. *Electroencephalography and Clinical Neurophysiology, 66,* 137–144.

Bloom, F. E., Lazerson, A., & Hofstadter, L. (1985). *Brain, mind and behavior.* San Francisco: Freeman.

Botwinick, J. (1973). *Aging and behavior.* New York: Springer.

Buchsbaum, M. S. (1976). Self regulation of stimulus intensity: Augmenting/reducing and the averaged evoked response. In G. E. Schwartz & D. Shapiro (Eds.), *Consciousness and self-regulation* (Vol. 1, pp. 101–135). New York: Plenum.

Campbell, S. S., & Zulley, J. (1985). Ultradian components of human sleep/wake patterns during disentrainment. *Experimental Brain Research*: *Ultradian Rhythms in Physiology and Behavior, Suppl. 12,* 234–255.

Chu, N. S. (1985). Age-related latency changes in the brain-stem auditory evoked potentials. *Electroencephalography Clinical Neurophysiology, 62,* 431–436.

Coleman, M., & Mahanand, D. (1973). Baseline serotonin levels in Down's syndrome patients. In M. Coleman (Ed.), *Serotonin in Down's syndrome* (pp. 5–24). New York: American Elsevier.

Craik, F. M. (1977). Age differences in human memory. In J. E. Birren & K. W. Schaie (Eds.), *Handbook of the psychology of aging* (pp. 384–420). New York: Van Nostrand Reinhold.

Dement, W., Richardson, G., Prinz, P., Carskadon, M., Kripke, D., & Czeisler, C. (1985). Changes of sleep and wakefulness with age. In C. E. Finch & E. L. Schneider (Eds.), *Handbook of the biology of aging* (pp. 692–717). New York: Van Nostrand Reinhold.

Diamond, S., Balvin, R. S., & Diamond, F. R. (1963). *Inhibition and choice.* New York: Harper.

Dijk, D. J., Beersma, D. G. M., & Van den Hoofdakker, R. H. (1989). All night spectral analysis of EEG sleep in young adult and middle aged male subjects. *Neurobiology of Aging,* in press.

Donchin, E., Ritter, W., & McCallum, W. C. (1978). Cognitive psychophysiology: The endogenous components of the ERP. In C. Callaway, P. Tueting, & S. H. Koslow (Eds.), *Event-related brain potentials in man* (pp. 349–411). New York: Academic Press.

Drechsler, F. (1978). Quantitative analysis of neurophysiological processes of the aging CNS. *Journal of Neurology, 218,* 197–213.

Duffy, F. H., Albert, M. S., McAnulty, G., & Garvey, A. (1984). Age-related differences in brain electrical activity of healthy subjects. *Annals of Neurology, 16,* 430–438.

Dustman, R. E., & Beck, E. C. (1969). The effect of maturation and aging on the wave form of visually evoked potentials. *Electroencephalography and Clinical Neurophysiology, 26,* 2–11.

Dustman, R. E., Emmerson, R. Y., Ruhling, R. O., Shearer, D. E., Steinhaus, L. A., Johnson, S. C., Bonekat, W. H., & Shigeoka, J. W. (1989). *The effects of aerobic fitness on human aging and brain electrical activity.* Submitted.

Dustman, R. E., LaMarche, J. A., Cohn, N. B., Shearer, D. E., & Talone, J. M. (1985). Power spectral analysis and cortical coupling of EEG for young and normal adults. *Neurobiology of Aging, 6,* 193–198.

Dustman, R. E., & Shearer, D. E. (1987). Electrophysiological evidence for central inhibitory deficits in old age. In R. J. Ellingson, N. M. F. Murray, & A. M. Halliday (Eds.), *The London symposia* (pp. 408–412). Amsterdam: Elsevier.

Dustman, R. E., Shearer, D. E., & Emmerson, R. Y. (1989). Evoked potentials and EEG suggest inhibitory deficits in aging. In D. Armstrong, J. M Ordy, M. F. Marmor, & M. D. Benedetto (Eds.), *The effects of age and environment on vision.* New York: Plenum (in press).

Dustman, R. E., Shearer, D. W., & Snyder, E. W. (1982). Age differences in augmenting/reducing of occipital visually evoked potentials. *Electroencephalography and Clinical Neurophysiology, 54,* 99–110.

Dustman, R. E., & Snyder, E. W. (1981). Lifespan changes in visually evoked potentials at central scalp. *Neurobiology of Aging, 2,* 303–308.

Dustman, R. E., Snyder, E. W., & Schlehuber, C. V. (1981). Life-span alterations in visually evoked potentials and inhibitory function. *Neurobiology of Aging, 2,* 187–192.

Empson, J. (1986). *Human brainwaves: The psychological significance of the electroencephalogram.* New York: Stockton.

Feinberg, I. (1976). Functional implications of changes in sleep physiology with age. In R. D. Terry & S. Gershon (Eds.), *Neurobiology of aging* (pp. 23–41). New York: Raven.

Feinberg, I., Fein, G., Floyd, T. C., & Aminoff, M. J. (1983). Delta (.5-3 Hz) EEG waveforms during sleep in young and elderly normal subjects. In M. H. Chase & E. D. Weitzman (Eds.), *Sleep disorders: Basic and clinical research* (pp. 449–462). New York: Spectrum.

Feinberg, I., Koresko, R., & Hellner, N. (1967). EEG sleep patterns as a function of normal and pathological aging in man. *Journal of Psychiatric Research, 5,* 107–144.

Fishbein, H. D. (1976). *Evolution, development and children's learning.* Pacific Palisades, CA: Goodyear.

Gaches, J. (1960). Etude statistique sur les traces "alpha largement développé" en fonction de l'âge. *La Presse Medicale, 68,* 1619–1622.

Gasser, T., Verleger, R., Bacher, P., & Sroka, L. (1988). Development of the EEG of school-age children and adolescents. I. Analysis of band power. *Electroencephalography and Clinical Neurophysiology, 69,* 91–99.

Gliddon, J. B., Busk, J., & Galbraith, G. C. (1975). Visual evoked responses as a function to light intensity in Down's syndrome and nonretarded subjects. *Psychophysiology, 12,* 416–422.

Goodin, D. S., Squires, K. C., Henderson, B. H., & Starr, A. (1978). Age-related variations in evoked potentials to auditory stimuli in normal human subjects. *Electroencephalography and Clinical Neurophysiology, 44,* 447–458.

Guazzelli, M., Feinberg, I., Aminoff, M., Fein, G., Floyd, T. C., & Maggini, C. (1986). Sleep spindles in normal elderly: Comparison with young adult patterns and relation to nocturnal awakening, cognitive function and brain atrophy. *Electroencephalography and Clinical Neurophysiology, 63,* 526–539.

Gundel, A., & Hilbig, A. (1983). Circadian acrophases of powers and frequencies in the waking EEG. *International Journal of Neuroscience, 22*, 25–33.

Horne, J. A., & Moore, V. J. (1985). Sleep EEG effects of exercise with and without additional body cooling. *Electroencephalography and Clinical Neurophysiology,* 60, 33–38.

Hoyer, W. J., & Plude, D. J. (1980). Attentional and perceptual processes in the study of cognitive aging. In L. W. Poon (Ed.), *Aging in the 1980s* (pp. 227–238). Washington, DC: American Psychological Association.

John, E., Ahn, H., Princhep, L., Trepetin, M., Brown, D., & Kaye, H. (1980). Developmental equations for the electroencephalogram. *Science, 210*, 1255–1258.

Kahn, E., & Fisher, C. (1969). The sleep characteristics of the normal aged male. *Journal of Nervous and Mental Diseases, 148*, 477–494.

Kelly-Ballweber, D., & Dobie, R. A. (1984). Binaural interaction measured behaviorally and electrophysiologically in young and old adults. *Audiology, 23*, 181–194.

Klorman, R., Thompson, L. W., & Ellingson, R. J. (1978). Event-related brain potentials across the life span. In E. Callaway, P. Tueting, & S. H. Koslow (Eds.), *Event-related brain potentials in man* (pp. 511–570). New York: Academic Press.

Kripke, D. F. K., Mullaney, D. J., & Fleck, P. A. (1985). Ultradian rhythms during sustained performance. *Experimental Brain Research: Ultradian Rhythms in Physiology and Behavior, 12*, 201–216.

Liberson, W. T. (1976). Scalp distribution of somato-sensory evoked potentials and aging. *Electromyography and Clinical Neurophysiology, 15*, 221–224.

Lizak, M. D. (1983). *Neuropsychological assessment* (2nd ed.). New York: Oxford University Press.

Low, M. D. (1987). Psychology, psychophysiology, and the EEG. In E. Niedermeyer & F. Lopes da Silva (Eds.), *Electroencephalography: Basic principles, clinical applications and related fields* (pp. 455–460). Munich: Urban & Schwarzenberg.

Luders, H. (1970). The effects of aging on the wave form of the somatosensory cortical evoked potential. *Electroencephalography and Clinical Neurophysiology, 29*, 450–460.

Mackenzie, R. A., & Phillips, L. H. (1981). Changes in peripheral and central nerve conduction with aging. *Clinical and Experimental Neurology, 18*, 109–116.

Man'kovskii, N. B., Belong, R. P., & Gorbach, L. N. (1978). Evoked potentials to light during aging. *Human Physiology, 4*, 499–506.

Marsh, G. R., & Thompson, L. W. (1977). Psychophysiology of aging. In J. E. Birren & K. W. Schaie (Eds.), *Handbook of the psychology of aging* (pp. 219–248). New York: Van Nostrand Reinhold.

McGeer, P. L., Eccles, J. C., & McGeer, E. G. (1978). *Molecular neurobiology of the mammalian brain* (pp. 133). New York: Plenum.

Miles, L. E., & Dement, W. C. (1980). Sleep and aging. *Sleep, 3*, 119–220.

Miller, G. A., Bashore, T. R., Farwell, L. A., & Donchin, E. (1987). Research in geriatric psychophysiology. *Annual Review of Gerontology and Geriatrics, 7*, 1–27.

Mullis, R. J., Holcomb, P. H., Diner, B. C., & Dykman, R. A. (1985). The effects of aging on the P3 component of the visual event-related potential. *Electroencephalography and Clinical Neurophysiology, 62*, 141–149.

Niedermeyer, E., & Lopes da Silva, F. (Eds.) (1987). *Electroencephalography: Basic principles, clinical applications and related fields*. Munich: Urban & Schwarzenberg.

Obrist, W. D. (1976). Problems of aging. In A. Remond (Ed.), *Handbook of Electroencephalography and Clinical Neurophysiology* (Vol. 6, Part A, pp. 275–292). Amsterdam: Elsevier.

Okawa, M., Matousek, M., & Petersen, I. (1984). Spontaneous vigilance fluctuations in the daytime. *Psychophysiology, 21*, 207–211.

Pivik, R. T. (1986). Sleep: Physiology and psychophysiology. In M. G. H. Coles, E. Donchin, & S. W. Porges (Eds.), *Psychophysiology: Systems, processes, and applications* (pp. 378–406). New York: Guilford.

Polich, J., Howard, L., & Starr, A. (1985). Effects of age on the P300 component of the event-related potential from auditory stimuli: Peak definition, variation, and measurement. *Journal of Gerontology, 40*, 721–726.

Prinz, P. N. (1976). EEG during sleep and waking states. *Experimental Aging Research, 1*, 135–163.

Prinz, P. N., Halter, J., Raskind, M., Cunningham, G., & Karacan, I. (1981). Aging, sleep and diurnally varying hormones in man. *Proceedings of the NIA Conference of Biological Mechanisms in Aging*, 618–628.

Prinz, P. N., Poceta, S., & Vitiello, M. V. (1989). Sleep in the dementing disorders. In F. Boller & J. Grafman (Eds.), *Handbook of neuropsychology*. Amsterdam: Elsevier (in press).

Regan, D. (1972). *Evoked potentials in psychology, sensory physiology and clinical medicine*. London: Chapman & Hill.

Roberts, E. (1972). Coordination between excitation and inhibition: Development of the GABA system. In C. D. Clemente, D. P. Purpura, & F. E. Mayer (Eds.), *Sleep and the maturing nervous system* (pp. 79–98). New York: Academic Press.

Roubicek, J. (1977). The electroencephalogram in the middle-aged and elderly. *Journal of the American Geriatrics Society*, 25, 145–152.

Santamaria, J., & Chiappa, K. H. (1987). The EEG drowsiness in normal adults. *Journal of Clinical Neurophysiology*, 4, 327–382.

Schacter, D. L. (1977). EEG theta waves and psychological phenomena: A review and analysis. *Biological Psychology*, 5, 47–82.

Schaie, K. W. (1958). Rigidity-flexibility and intelligence: A cross-sectional study of the adult life span from 20 to 70 years. *Psychological Monographs*, 72, 1–26.

Schenkenberg, T. (1970). *Visual, auditory and somatosensory evoked responses of normal subjects from childhood to sensescence*. Unpublished doctoral dissertation, University of Utah.

Schultz, H., & Lavie, P. (1985). *Ultradian rhythms in physiology and behavior*. Berlin and New York: Springer-Verlag.

Shagass, C. (1972). *Evoked potentials in psychiatry*. New York: Plenum.

Shepard, J. W. (1988). Aging and sleep apnea. In R. Strong, W. G. Wood, & W. J. Burke (Eds.), *Central nervous system disorders of aging: Clinical intervention and research* (pp. 127–148). New York: Raven.

Simpson, D. M., & Erwin, C. W. (1983). Evoked potential latency change with age suggests differential aging of primary somatosensory cortex. *Neurobiology of Aging*, 4, 59–63.

Simpson, G. V., Knight, R. T., Brailowsky, S., Prospero-Garcia, O., & Scabini, D. (1985).

Altered peripheral and brainstem auditory function in aged rats. *Brain Research*, 348, 28–35.

Smith, J. R., Karacan, I., & Yang, M. (1977). Ontogeny of delta activity during human sleep. *Electroencephalography and Clinical Neurophysiology*, 43, 229–237.

Smith, J. R., Karacan, I., & Yang, M. (1978). Automated analysis of the human sleep EEG. *Waking and Sleeping*, 2, 75–82.

Smith, J. R., Karacan, I., & Yang, M. (1979). Automated measurement of alpha, beta, sigma, and theta burst characteristics. *Sleep*, 1, 435–443.

Strenge, H., & Hedderich, J. (1982). Age-dependent changes in central somatosensory conduction time. *European Neurology*, 21, 270–276.

Strommen, E. A. (1973). Verbal self-regulation in a children's game: Impulsive errors on "Simon Says." *Child Development*, 44, 849–853.

Takii, O. (1986). Diurnal rhythm in appearance of frontal midline theta activity. *The Japanese Journal of Psychiatry and Neurology*, 40, 609–615.

Townsend, R. E., & Johnson, L. C. (1979). Relation of frequency-analyzed EEG to monitoring behavior. *Electroencephalography and Clinical Neurophysiology*, 47, 272–279.

Tucker, D. M., Penland, J. G., & Heck, D. G. *Life span developmental changes in the electroencephalogram*. (Unpublished manuscript available on request.)

Vitiello, M. V., & Prinz, P. N. (1988). Aging and sleep disorders. In R. L. Williams, I. Karacan, & C. A. Moore (Eds.), *Sleep disorders: Diagnosis and treatment* (pp. 293–312). New York: Wiley.

Vitiello, M. V., Smallwood, R. G., Avery, D. H., Pascualy, R. A., & Prinz, P. N. (1986). Circadian temperature rhythms in young and aged men. *Neurobiology of Aging*, 7, 97–100.

von Knorring, L., Monakhov, K., & Perris, C. (1978). Augmenting/reducing: An adaptive switch mechanism to cope with incoming signals in healthy subjects and psychiatric patients. *Neuropsychobiology*, 4, 150–179.

von Knorring, L., & Oreland, L. (1978). Visual averaged evoked responses and platelet monoamine oxidase activity as an aid to identify a risk group for alcoholic abuse: A preliminary study. *Progress in Neuropharmacology and Biological Psychiatry,* **2,** 385–392.

White, S. H. (1965). Evidence for a hierarchical arrangement of learning processes. In L. P. Lipsitt & C. C. Spiker (Eds.), *Advances in child development and behavior* (pp. 187–220). New York: Academic Press.

Williams, H., Kearney, O. F., & Lubin, A. (1965). Signal uncertainty and sleep loss. *Journal of Experimental Psychology,* **69,** 401–407.

Williams, H. L., Granda, A. M., Jones, R. C., Lubin, A., & Armington, J. C. (1962). EEG frequency and finger pulse volume as predictors of reaction time during sleep loss. *Electroencephalography and Clinical Neurophsyiology,* **14,** 64–70.

Williams, R., Karacan, I., & Hursch, C. (1974). *Electroencephalography of human sleep: Clinical applications* (pp. 1–169). New York: Wiley.

Woodruff, D. (1985). Arousal, sleep and aging. In J. E. Birren & K. W. Schaie (Eds.), *Handbook of the psychology of aging* (pp. 261–295). New York: Van Nostrand Reinhold.

Woods, D. L., & Clayworth, C. C. (1986). Age-related changes in human middle latency auditory evoked potentials. *Electroencephalography and Clinical Neurophysiology,* **65,** 297–303.

Zegers de Beyl, D., Delberghe, X., & Brunko, E. (1988). The somatosensory central conduction time: Physiological considerations and normative data. *Electroencephalography and Clinical Neurophysiology,* **71,** 17–26.

Zepelin, H., McDonald, C. S., & Zammit, G. K. (1984). Effects of age on auditory awakening thresholds. *Journal of Gerontology,* **39,** 294–300.

Nine

Vision and Hearing in Aging

James L. Fozard

I. Introduction

This review of vision and hearing is combined in the present edition of the *Handbook*, whereas it was covered in separate chapters in the first two editions. Accordingly, the present discussion is not as tutorial and self-contained as the earlier ones, and it emphasizes material published since the last edition of the *Handbook* or the other recent reviews cited.

II. Vision

Most surveys of visual function describe acuity and the prevalence of blindness and ocular pathologies (Corso, 1987; Kline & Schieber, 1985). Such surveys provide a limited view of many significant practical and research issues relative to the visual functioning of older persons. Kosnik, Winslow, Kline, Rasinski, and Sekuler (1988), surveying adults 18 to 100 years of age, found that five dimensions of visual function are relatively more problematic for older persons: visual processing speed,

for example, reading speed; light sensitivity, for example, seeing in twilight or dark; dynamic vision, for example, reading scrolling TV displays or other externally paced displays; near vision, for example, reading small print; and visual search, for example, locating a sign. Although the prevalence of ocular pathologies in the respondents were typical of national surveys, their greater wealth and use of medical care suggests that survey results may underestimate the difficulties in visual functioning in older adults. Note that acuity is a major component of the fourth dimension, near vision. Many problems identified are amenable to environmental interventions (Fozard, 1981; Fozard & Popkin, 1978).

Johnson and Choy (1987) reviewed age differences in acuity, stereopsis, perimetric fields, threshold sensitivity, and visual evoked potentials. They suggested that 50 years is the typical age at which age-related differences in these visual functions begin to change noticeably. Yet there are few visual biomarkers (Sekuler, Wilson, & Owsley, 1984) that are continu-

Handbook of the Psychology of Aging, Third Edition
Copyright © 1990 Academic Press, Inc. All rights of reproduction in any form reserved.

ous across age, and cross-sectional information on different visual functions from the same individuals shows great variability (Eisner, Fleming, Klein, & Mauldin, 1987).

Age differences in the anatomy and physiology of the visual system are reviewed by Corso (1981, 1987), Keunen, van Norren, and van Meel (1987), and Weale (1984, 1986a,b). Weale (1986b, p. 53), commenting on the complexity of age changes in the retina, stated: "The human retina . . . is likely to manifest stochastic events or random cell death . . . it will probably be affected vicariously by aging processes occurring elsewhere . . . [and] is exposed to environmental influences such as light."

The lens acts as a image-forming device and a filter of light. Weale (1988) studied the transmissiveness of excised human lenses and found age-related increases in absorbance for all wave lengths measured. The strongest correlations were in the 450 to 500-nm range. Weale (1986c) and Pokorny, Smith, and Lutze (1987), reviewing different evidence, agreed that responses to shorter wave lengths are mostly affected by aging.

Many studies try to equate various aspects of the retinal image of young and old observers by using artificial pupils, refracting all observers to the test distance of the stimulus material under study, and/or adjusting the effective target illumination or luminance for one age group to equal that of another. One of the most important technical requirements for future psychophysical studies of age differences in visual function is to standardize the procedure for the description of the amount of light reaching the retinas of observers of different ages.

A. Light Sensitivity

Domey and MacFarland's (1961) data on dark adaptation, interpreted by them to re-

flect age differences in oxygen uptake, continue to be reinterpreted. The researchers controlled for age differences in pupil diameter and used a test light (405 nm) supposedly maximally sensitive to rods. Because the ability of the lens to transmit light decreases with age, particularly at the short wavelengths, Weale (1984) suggested that the original data exaggerated the age effect reported. Unknown to MacFarland, the retina and the lens accumulate a flurogen sensitive to violet light that fluoresces with blue–green light (Lerman & Borkman, 1978), implying that the cones of the older observers of Domey and MacFarland's study responded more to the test light than those of the younger ones. Finally, the white adapting light did not bring young and old observers to the same level of adaptation prior to dark adaptation. The conservative conclusion from all this is that the age differences in final level of adaptation are underestimated.

Following work by Eisner (1986), Eisner et al. (1987) studied dark adaptation of the foveal receptors and found that thresholds increased between 60 and 88 years by about 0.09 log unit per decade in men and women with 20/20 acuity. The rate of adaptation did not differ with age, a finding similar to that of Birren and Shock (1950).

Pupil diameter and lens opacity influence light sensitivity. Pupil diameter in the dark decreases by a third from age 20 to 80 with wide variation at all ages (Lowenfeld, 1979). Owsley (1987), using data of Woodhouse (1975), demonstrated that with increasing illumination, the effect of smaller pupil diameter becomes a relatively less important determinant of contrast sensitivity.

The practical significance of such information was demonstrated by Sivak, Olson, and Pastalan (1981) who studied nighttime legibility of highway signs for adults under age 25 and over age 60 driving a test course. The distance from the observer to the sign that was readable by older adults was 65 to 75% that of younger ones.

Practical research on age differences in response to temporary high levels of illumination (glare) shows that the older drivers require a target to be brighter to be seen at night. They are much more adversely affected by glare than younger persons both with respect to required target illumination in the presence of glare and also in the time required to recover from it (Olson & Sivak, 1984).

At higher levels of illumination (11.7 trolands), Sturr, Kelly, Kobus, and Taub (1982) found age differences in the threshold for seeing momentary increases in light with adaptation periods less than 0.5 seconds. The increase in illumination required to see the target declined monotonically with longer periods of adaption in 27-year-old subjects but not 47-year-old ones. Because the time course of adaptation was less for the older group, the investigators concluded that their results were consistent with the age-related loss in transient visual channels (Kline & Schieber, 1981). Sturr, Church, and Taub (1985) confirmed their earlier findings in young, middle-aged, and old adults. Then, Sturr, Church, Nuding, Van Orden, and Taub (1986) extended their studies to include several levels of illumination of the adapting field. The results showed no age difference when it was on continuously (steady state) but an age-related loss when the target was presented for only 1,000 msec with an onset coinciding with that of the test field. The conclusion that neural factors explain the age difference was based partly on the findings of an auxiliary experiment in which the old subjects were tested at levels of retinal illumination thought to be equivalent to those of younger observers.

B. Color Vision

A 10-year longitudinal study of color vision in 577 males ranging in age from 20 to 95 years indicated very little change in color vision (Gittings, Fozard, & Shock, 1987). Accuracy remained above 90% for all but men in their 80s at the beginning of the observation period. Cross-sectional age differences for women volunteers in the Baltimore Longitudinal Study of Aging were similar.

Similar inconclusive results from studies of age differences in color vision reported over the years (See Kline & Schieber, 1985, for a review) suggested that the reported results are quite specific to the test materials and conditions used, a conclusion supported directly by data from two studies. Stanford and Pollack (1984) observed age declines in performance on a color vision test with test patterns consisting of dots that differ in hue from background dots of equal brightness. The results indicated that color vision tests in which hue is used as a camouflage are sensitive to age-related determiners of performance beyond those that the tests were designed to measure.

Knoblauch, Saunders, Kusada, Hynes, Podgor, Higgins, and de Monasterio (1987) reported age differences in performance on the Farnsworth–Munsell 100 hue test at five levels of illumination from 5.7 to 1,800 lux. Mean errors increased with decreasing illumination, indicating that some, but certainly not all, of the age difference could be accounted for by less overall illumination.

Eisner et al. (1987) measured age differences (60 to 88 years) in color matching achieved by varying intensities of a 588-nm half field probe to varying red/green mixtures and found small but statistically significant declines of about 0.01 log unit per decade in sensitivity, supposedly reflecting losses in functioning receptors as well as age differences in pupil size.

Finally, Weale (1986c) analyzed the trichromatic equation for a color match and its application to the 100-hue test and concluded that data on age differences in color vision have two aspects: one related to changes in the selective absorption of the lens with age, particularly shorter wavelengths and a second related to changes in discrimination of colors associated with changes in the nervous system with age. Although there have been advances in research on color vision, we still do not have information about age-specific losses in different kinds of photoreceptors.

C. Spatial Resolution

Classical perimetry and derived tasks have documented age declines in the total area within which a target can be detected (Haas, Flammer, & Schneider, 1986; Jaffe, Alvarado, & Juster, 1986; Wolf, 1967). Recent studies of visual tasks that depend on acuity as well as sensitivity to light show that age differences cannot be defined independently of the task demands, context, and distractor effects, and illumination levels of target and background.

Scialfa, Kline, and Lyman (1987) required 22- and 66-year-old adults to identify one of two briefly presented target letters located 0 to 10.5 deg from fixation. The letter was presented alone, or with one or 19 distractors. Elderly adults were at a relative disadvantage in cluttered visual "environments"; errors for 1 versus 19 distractors increased more rapidly for elderly than for young adults. The disadvantage reflects both a slower rate of scanning the display and a constriction of the useful field of view.

Cerella (1985) measured the time required to identify letters presented in isolation or embedded in other letters and found that time was greater for older versus younger adults and that the age difference was relatively larger when the target was embedded in other letters. Cerella also demonstrated that the observed age difference depended on the visibility of the target as defined by its size and contrast and on the context of the target as defined by its juxtaposition with congruous versus incongruous distractors. Cerella concluded that poorer performance by older adults resulted from reduced visibility of relatively peripheral stimuli.

Sekuler and Ball (1986) and Ball, Beard, Roenker, Miller, and Griggs (1987) studied age differences in the size of the useful field of view by requiring young and elderly adults to localize briefly presented targets in a display extending up to 30 deg and filled with 23 to 47 distractors. They found that both young and old adults improved performance with practice but that the older adults never increased their useful field of view more than about 20 deg, considerably less than young adults.

When fixation is allowed to vary, age differences in the ability to change fixation and track moving targets become important in determining visual performance. Age differences in the ability to maintain fixation over 12 sec does not vary much with age (Kosnik, Fikre, & Sekuler, 1986; Kosnik, Kline, Fikre, & Sekuler, 1987). About 95% of the fixation falls within an area 20% of the size of the fovea, about one deg.

Age differences in the time required for a saccad are relatively small unless the older person has a presumed diagnosis of dementia (Pirozzolo & Hansch, 1981), in which case the time required to change regard from a central fixation point to a target located 2 to 15 deg from fixation can as much as double depending on the severity of the disease. The major consequence of such increases in time required for a saccad is getting less information from the visual environment by persons with Alzheimer's disease (Fozard, 1985).

Hutton, Nagel, and Loewenson (1983) studied age differences in continuous eye movements and saccads while tracking horizontally moving targets across a 23 deg trajectory at velocities of 9 and 18 deg/sec. In comparison to adults in their 20s, men and women in their 60s and 70s lagged farther behind the target and, at the higher velocity, made 2 to 12 times as many "catchup" saccads. Hutton, Nagel, and Loewenson (1984) found that the number of required "catchup" saccads in a group of elderly persons with clinically defined dementia increased even more rapidly with target velocity than in the normal elderly.

1. Acuity

Cross-sectional descriptions of age differences in visual acuity exhibit consider-

able consistency in showing that presenting distance acuity declines after age 45. A different story is told by longitudinal data describing age-related changes in presenting and uncorrected distance and near acuity for 577 males ranging in age from the 20s to the 80s. The results summarized in Figure 1 are based on an average of seven repeated observations spaced approximately 2 years apart. The functions shown in the figure are the best fit linear changes for each group taken from the means and slopes shown in Table 2 of Gittings and Fozard (1986). Uncorrected dis-

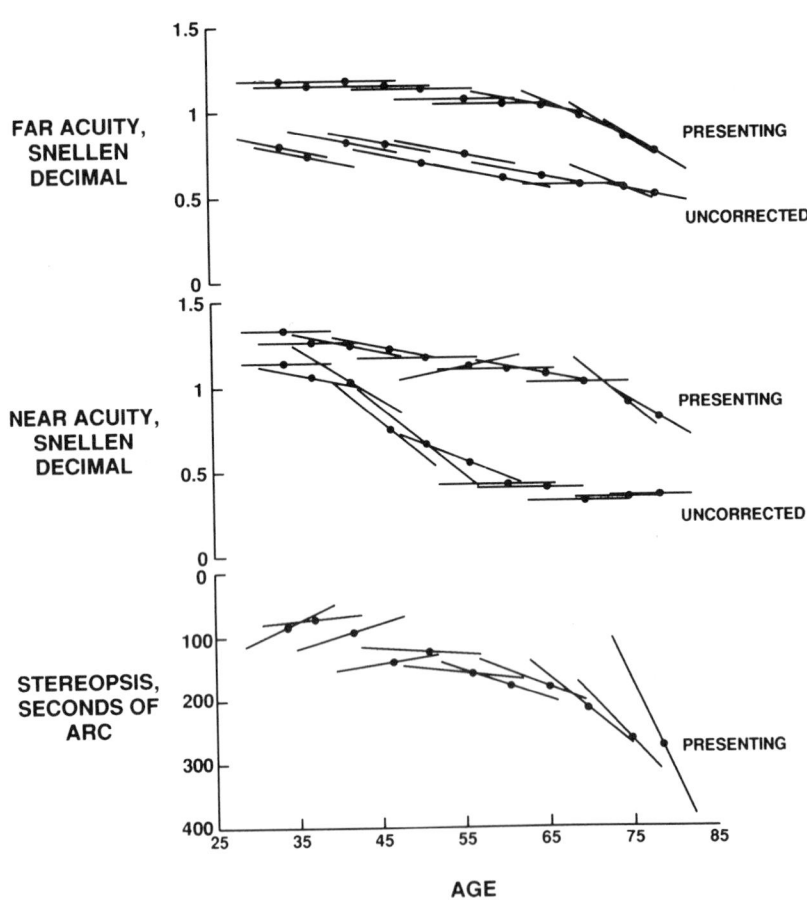

Figure 1 Longitudinal changes in visual binocular acuity as measured by Sloan letters and depth perception in 577 males. The Snellen decimal is the reciprocal of the Snellen fraction, for example, 20/20 = 1.0. Each point is located at the mean age for men in a particular group; the length of line represents the number of years followed. The slope of the line represents the best fit linear regression on age. Figure constructed from acuity data by Gittings and Fozard (1986) and depth perception data by Gittings, Fozard, and Shock (1987).

tance acuity declines over the age range from 30 through 80, although the fall in presenting acuities is not apparent until the 70s. The fall in presenting acuities for near distance is similar. Auxiliary analyses indicated that the relation of acuity to age is independent of the effects of various ocular pathologies on acuity. There was no evidence that the age changes in acuity observed differed over generations or time of measurement. The cross-sectional data of both men and women were very close to those from other published studies.

Age differences in acuity beyond the fovea were measured by Scialfa, Leibowitz, and Gish (1989) who found that adults in their 60s had greater amounts of spherical error than those in their 20s. Spherical error increased with greater distance from the fovea for both groups.

As expected from the data on tracking described, dynamic visual acuity is relatively poorer in older persons. Scialfa, Garvey, Goebel, Gish, Deering, and Leibowitz (1989) measured contrast sensitivity for static [1.5 to 18 cycles/degree^2 (c/deg^2)] and moving targets (.93 to 3.72 c/deg^2), static acuity to a traditional target, and the ability to detect a moving face. Both dynamic and static sensitivity declined across age, dynamic more than static. The results showed that the same factors that influence static acuity, for example, illumination levels, contrast, and so on, similarly affect dynamic acuity but that the detection of detail in moving objects cannot adequately be predicted from measures of static acuity and so should be measured independently.

2. Contrast Sensitivity

A contrast sensitivity function is the brightness required to differentiate between alternating light and dark bars of a test pattern, the widths of which vary. Sensitivity, the reciprocal of the threshold contrast, is determined for light–dark bar pairs that vary in width defined as c/deg of visual angle. Poor sensitivity, that is, high

contrast required to identify pattern, occurs for adults of all ages at 0.5 c/deg and 22 c/deg with best sensitivity at 3 to 6 c/deg. For frequencies around 3 c/deg and above, sensitivity is poorer for older adults. Part, but not all, of the difference at the intermediate and high frequencies is attributable to lowered retinal illumination (Owsley, Sekuler, & Siemsen, 1983) in subjects who were refracted individually to the test distance.

Morrison and McGrath (1985) used laser interferometry to present grating (10 to 50 c/deg) images at the level of the retina in addition to the conventional display. Except for the scattering of light in the lens, the technique hopefully assessed the contrast sensitivity of the retina and visual nervous system without complications from preretinal factors. Contrast sensitivity with both displays declined with older age particularly at intermediate and high frequencies. The relationship between the two measures was stable over age and spatial frequency, indicating that the visual nervous system is a limiting factor in performance. The age trends observed could not be explained by reduced retinal illumination. Taken in conjunction with the results of Owlsey et al. (1983), the study by Morrison and McGrath, and the later one by Elliott (1987) make the most convincing case for the involvement of the retina and postretina nervous system in age differences in spatial vision available at this time.

The question of how many visual channels underlie contrast sensitivity was studied by Sekuler et al. (1984) using a mathematical model. They concluded that three spatially tuned channels, 0.5 to 1.0, 2.0 to 8.0, and 16 c/deg, accounted for existing data. Age and acuity were negatively correlated with the two higher frequency channels. The model required an additional channel to account for very low frequencies, for example, 0.25 c/deg.

With respect to practical implications of age differences in contrast sensitivity, Sekuler, Owsley, and Hukman (1982) showed that older persons have greater difficulty in detecting and discriminating faces presented under low contrast, a finding predictable from age differences in contrast sensitivity but not acuity. Owsley and Sloane (1987) demonstrated that contrast sensitivity for middle and low frequency targets were the best predictors of age differences in the ability to detect faces, signs, and objects. Kline, Schieber, Abusamra, and Coyne (1983) found that the times required for the detection of spatial frequencies were longer for adults in their 60s than those in their teens. The slower response times of older persons to the high frequency targets were attributable largely to age differences in target visibility, whereas those at lower frequencies were attributed to poorer responsiveness to transient neural channels.

The theoretical significance of contrast sensitivity research includes the distinctions made between the contribution of neural and optical factors and the establishment of the involvement of the nervous system as a limiting factor in spatial resolution throughout the frequency range (Kline & Schieber, 1981). As a development to the latter, Kline (1987) described research in which young and old observers were adapted to a 1 c/deg grating after which sensitivity for low frequency targets was determined. In contrast to the young, whose exposure increased their thresholds only for frequencies similar to the adaptation stimulus, the older adults experienced adaptation over frequencies an octave below the adaptation stimulus, showing that older persons experience difficulty in identification and detection of large objects, either moving or stationary.

3. Depth Perception

The role of retinal disparity in age differences in binocular depth perception is unclear (Corso, 1987; Kline & Schieber, 1985) partly because the method of determining the threshold for depth perception itself requires the target to be at varying distances from the observer, thereby adding visual cues for acuity to those required for retinal disparity of right and left images. Gittings et al. (1987) reported 10-year age changes in 577 men using varying retinal disparities while holding target illumination (a cue for acuity) and distance to the target constant. The results, summarized in the bottom panel of Figure 1, show that retinal disparity required for depth perception increased over time particularly in the six older age groups. The results offer support for Corso's (1987) hypothesis that age changes, at least up to the level where the optic nerve fibers cross, are responsible for the loss in depth perception with age. The age differences in stereopsis and the relation of stereopsis to acuity was also found by Greene and Madden (1987). In contrast to the modest amount of work on age differences in binocular cues to depth, research on the monocular cues for depth perception and related phenomena such as size constancy continues to be neglected.

D. Temporal Resolution

Kline and Schieber (1985) argued that age-related increases in stimulus persistence and temporal summation (e.g., Kline & Orme-Rogers, 1978), greater times required for escape from masking, and poorer dynamic acuity are all phenomena consistent with the idea that there are two visual channels that are differentially affected by age. Specifically, they posited that contrast sensitivity to targets with low frequency gratings are mediated by transient channels. Increasing stimulus presentation time for low frequency targets should only improve sensitivity up to a maximum duration that is shorter than if the target is a high frequency grating. For the latter, contrast sensitivity, mediated by sustained channels, should continue over a greater range of presentation times. Building on Legge's (1978) research, Sturr, Church, and Taub (1989) reasoned that contrast sensitivity for a target with low spatial frequency should improve over a greater range of target presentation times in older than in younger adults. The investigators confirmed Legge's findings that increasing target presentation time beyond 100 msec did not improve sensitivity for the low frequency target, whereas sensitivity for the high frequency target increased through presentation times of 1,000 msec. Contrary to hypothesis, there were no age differences between the shapes of the sensitivity-target duration functions for the low spatial frequency target. The results, confirmed in a second study using shorter target presentation times, did not support the idea of age differences in sustained and transient channels.

Masking

In a study of forward masking, Coyne (1981) found that older adults required three to four times longer presentation times to identify letters shown after the mask than younger subjects. Practice effects were the same in both groups; the older adults never reached the same absolute level of performance of the younger.

Gilmore, Allan, and Royer (1986), noting the backward masking research of Walsh and Thompson (1978) that found that most elderly persons could not perform the Averbach and Coriell (1961) procedure, used an auditory rather than a visual cue to identify the portion of the display to be reported. They demonstrated that elderly adults could respond to the task demands. Later, Coyne, Burger, Berry, and Botwinick (1987) found that the time required to translate an auditory cue into a recall instruction and the time needed to escape from masking without the partial report procedure overlapped. Moreover, the contribution of longer reaction times of the older persons to the observed age difference in iconic readout time was not significant.

Cerella, Poon, and Fozard (1982), using Sperling's (1963) procedure, found that

the two-stage function relating the number of letters identified to stimulus duration was the same in young and old adults and that the number of letters identified by older adults was less by a constant amount in both segments of the function. The conclusion is that less information is taken in per unit time by older adults at this stage of information processing. The slower rate of processing in normal aging is trivial in comparison to that observed in persons with clinically diagnosed dementia (Coyne, Liss, & Geckler, 1984; Fozard, 1985).

E. Visual Information Processing

Recent research has focused on the effects of context, both beneficial and deleterious, on the ease of identifying letters and words. Cerella and Fozard (1984) found that semantic priming improved by equal amounts the ability of young and elderly adults to distinguish letter strings that were words from those that were not words both when the target letter strings were degraded and when they were not. Madden (1988) later concluded from a long series of studies by himself and others that old and young adults benefit equally well from appropriate priming and that both age groups require extra time to overcome the effects of inappropriate priming information.

1. Search

Rabbitt (1965) hypothesized that older persons are poorer in visual search because they have greater difficulty in ignoring irrelevant stimuli. But what is irrelevant? Madden (1984) found that when letters that had been positive during practice became distractors in a subsequent test, correct responses to the newly designated targets were markedly slowed in both young and old. Wright and Elias (1979) and Plude and Hoyer (1985) showed that under some circumstances old adults are no more susceptible to distractors than young ones and that they can benefit equally well from context information that aids rather than hinders search (Madden, 1986, 1987; Thomas, Waugh, & Fozard, 1978). The effects are similar when the search is focused by information in the visual display or by memorized items (Madden, 1984). Currently, considerable research effort is being devoted to the question of the timing of information used to facilitate visual search (Fisk, McGee, & Giambra, 1989; Hoyer & Familitant, 1987).

Current research interest also emphasizes possible age differences in target localization versus target identification in visual search. Plude and Hoyer (1985) argued that identification and localization are independent processes in young but not in old adults so that poorer search in older adults may be attributed to their poorer localization. Scialfa and Kline (1988) required adults in their 20s and 60s to localize a briefly presented letter located 2 to 7 deg on either side of fixation either when the letter was presented alone or in a string of eight other letters that were either very confusable with the target or very dissimilar. Older subjects were relatively slower than younger ones moving a cursor to where they thought the target had been, but they made relatively fewer errors when the distractors were similar to the target than young adults. The researchers concluded that identification and location are correlated in both young and elderly adults. Further research is needed to identify the conditions under which the hypothesis of Plude and Hoyer (1985) holds.

At present, the area of age differences in visual search is receiving much research attention, the examples here representing a narrowly selected subset. (See the chapter by McDowd and Birren, this volume, for the literature on divided attention both within and across modalities.) Research on visual search overlaps with that on temporal resolution and iconic memo-

ry. It is differentiated from research on other complex perceptual processes in that the stimuli are not camouflaged, distorted, or incomplete. Above all, research on visual search brings together visual and cognitive research more dramatically than most areas discussed in the chapter, for example, Hoyer and Clancy (1987).

2. Mental Rotation

Previous research on age differences in mental rotation has consistently found age differences in response time (e.g., Cerella, Poon, & Fozard, 1981). Puglisi and Morrell (1986), using three-dimensional mental rotation, confirmed and extended earlier findings (e.g., Gaylord & Marsh, 1975). Sharps and Gollin (1987), noting inconsistencies in age differences in accuracy, studied age differences in mental rotation of three-dimensional objects under instructional sets emphasizing speed, accuracy, or both. In the speed condition, older adults, on average, were as fast as the young but were less accurate. In the accuracy and speed/accuracy conditions, however, the older adults were as accurate as the young, although they were slower, indicating that accuracy was poorer in older adults only when the instructions emphasized speed.

F. Complex Perceptual Judgments

Age differences in the ability to identify incomplete or distorted visual stimuli are being studied both as a function of providing clues to the identification of the item or by an examination of the way in which the stimuli are altered. Cerella and Fozard (1984) found that speed of recognition of a target word was facilitated for both young and elderly adults when its presentation was preceded by a semantically related primer both when the target word was intact or when visually degraded. The primer as a semantic clue compensated for the longer time required to extract information from the degraded stimulus. Madden (1986) reached a similar conclusion. Madden (1988) degraded words by separating successive letters of a word by asterisks and used plausible, neutral, or implausible priming sentences for context. As in earlier studies, speed of word recognition was relatively greater when the target word was degraded, but unlike earlier studies, the benefit of the plausible sentence context on the speed of naming degraded targets was relatively greater for older adults. Together, the results are consistent with the idea that plausible semantic cues can improve speed of recognition of degraded words equally in all age groups.

Research by Danziger and Salthouse (1978) found no support for three possible explanations of age differences in identification of incomplete figures (closure), namely that old adults in comparison to younger ones were more reluctant to guess, less familiar with the stimuli, or less likely to distinguish important and unimportant parts of the figures. Salthouse and Prill (1989) found age declines in closure using computer-generated dot drawings of objects and ambiguous counterparts from which 94% of the picture dots were removed. Young and elderly adults were instructed to identify features of the objects on the basis of a prompt about what it was, to determine if a designated part of an ambiguous figure was part of a particular figure that was complete, and for comparison, to determine if parts of intact drawings were part of a complete drawing. Auxiliary experiments evaluated practice and transfer effects. The results failed to identify components of the task that were uniquely associated with the observed age decline in closure.

Cremer and Zeef (1987), using the same materials as Salthouse and Prill, varied the rules used to make incomplete representations of the figures. In a random noise condition, the incomplete pictures were embedded in a noisy background made by adding 6% additional dots or pixels to the picture outline that was itself unaltered. As predicted, this type of distortion lowered the level of recognition at all levels of completeness. In a proximal noise condition, the elements of the picture were altered in both horizontal and vertical positions so that the incomplete pictures were made from versions of the pictures with elements that were themselves perturbed in the complete version. As predicted, the slopes relating correct recognition to completeness were lower than for incomplete pictures without the perturbations, and the levels of performance were about the same in the most incomplete versions of the pictures. The relationships just described were established using young adults. The age comparison involved showing adults with average ages of 23 and 70 years the incomplete pictures without either form of noise. The function relating recognition to picture completeness for the older group had a lower intercept but a slope equal to that of the younger groups, a finding compatible with the hypothesis that the performance of older persons is similar to that of younger ones who have had random noise added to the incomplete pictures.

III. Hearing

The U.S. Congress, Office of Technology Assessment's (1986, p. 6) report on hearing impairment and the elderly precedes its discussion: "Most hearing research has been focused on very severe impairments. . . . Hearing impairment in the elderly is often mild or moderate, but it is widespread . . . . A significant, but as yet undefined, number of elderly people have decreased ability to tune out background noise and thus have more difficulty hearing in noisy settings than younger people with comparable hearing ability."

Since the review of hearing in the

second edition of the *Handbook* (Olsho, Harkins, & Lenhardt, 1985) and Corso's (1987) review, the Office of Technology Assessment report cited here and the Working Group on Speech Understanding and Aging (1988) have provided current reviews of the research on hearing and aging. To avoid duplication, the present review will focus on recent research that emphasizes longitudinal studies of hearing thresholds and experimental studies that manipulate the characteristics of the speech signal that are responsible for the difficulties older persons have understanding speech.

A. Hearing Thresholds for Tones and Speech

Pure tone audiograms for continuous and pulsed tones were obtained from 813 male volunteers in the Baltimore Longitudinal Study of Aging (Shock, Greulich, Andres, Arenberg, Costa, Lakatta, & Tobin, 1984) using a Bekesy audiometer. Thresholds for 11 frequencies ranging from 0.125 to 8 kHz were obtained from both ears (Brant & Fozard, 1990). The number of observations per subject ranged from two to six with an average intertest interval of 3 years. The data, collected between 1968 and 1987, were organized into the seven age groups shown in Figure 2, according to age at first measurement. The six functions shown in each panel represent the typical frequency-intensity function for the designated group at 3-year intervals between the bottom and top functions displayed in the panel. Each function represents a nonlinear equation fit to the data from each group and was utilized to simplify the presentation of data and to provide a useful characterization of the frequency intensity function (Brant & Fozard, 1987). The correlations of the idealized functions in the figure and the observed data ranged from 0.59 to 0.81. The figure shows that changes in hearing thresholds occur con-

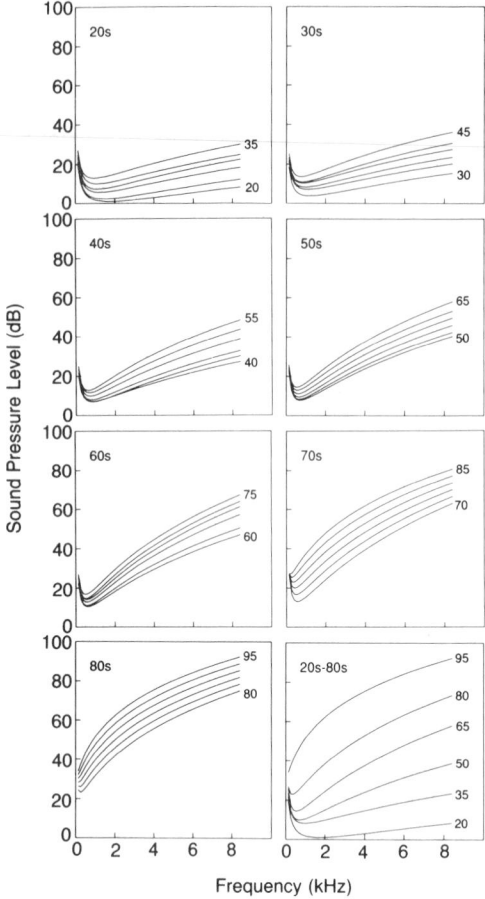

Figure 2 Longitudinal changes in thresholds for continuously presented pure tones ranging from 0.125 to 8.0 kHz in 813 males. The six idealized functions in each panel characterize the thresholds for men in each age group measured at 3-year intervals from the youngest to the oldest age represented in the panel. The right-hand panel at the bottom of the figure is a composite of the other data. Figure constructed from data by Brant and Fozard (1987).

tinuously throughout adulthood. The average change per year at 8 kHz was 1 dB. For the speech frequencies of 0.5, 1.0, and 2.0 kHz, the change was lower, about 0.3 to 0.4/year through age 60 but much greater after that, reaching a level of 1.2 to 1.4 dB/year in the age range from 80 to 95.

The findings extended cross-sectional results (Robinson & Sutton, 1979) in several important ways. First, they showed that age changes are not simply an artifact of mixing persons in different ways across cohorts, a frequent criticism of previously published studies. Indeed, there were significant individual differences among persons across the frequencies studied within all age groups including the oldest. Second, the data do not appear to be artifacts of specific otological diseases or subjective complaints of hearing difficulties identified on the medical histories. However, no detailed histories of noise exposure were available (Corso, 1980). Third, there were no statistically significant differences in thresholds measured in different persons who were the same age at different points in time over the 20-year period of data collection, thereby indicating that the age trends are not artifacts of general changes in the environment that might affect hearing. Fourth, the longitudinal findings may be a good extension of cross-sectional findings. Comparison of the cross-sectional data to those of Corso's (1963) representative sample indicated that over 86% of Corso's means fell within one standard deviation of the lowermost function in each panel of Figure 2. Fifth, the findings showed that in old age there is a disproportionate spread of hearing loss to lower frequencies. Stability of the shape of the audiogram (Dayal & Nussbaum, 1971) during aging is not the typical pattern as previously believed (Dayal, Kane, & Mendolsohn, 1971).

The findings of Bergman, Blumenfeld, Cascardo, Dash, Levitt, and Margulis (1976) on age-related changes in perception of altered speech, reviewed in earlier editions of the *Handbook*, received strong confirmation from the longitudinal study on pure tone hearing thresholds already summarized. A major finding of Brant and Fozard (1990) was that the rate of change in thresholds for the speech frequencies rose at an accelerating rate between the 50s and the 90s. Bergman and colleagues, using subjects whose pure tone hearing loss did not exceed 35 dB in the speech frequen-

cies, found significant declines over a 7-year follow-up period for variations in speech for the group originally in their 60s at the time of first test. Although the group originally in their 50s did not decline in unaltered or overlapping speech, they did in all other conditions, and the group originally in their 40s showed a decline in understanding of interrupted speech. The alterations in speech signal most strongly associated with age differences were interrupted speech, reverberated speech, selective listening, and speeded speech, whereas interrupted and speeded speech showed the largest age changes. On the basis of the two sets of longitudinal findings, it is clear that both age differences and age changes occur in pure tone thresholds within the speech frequency range and in direct measures of speech perception starting around age 50 and that the changes in speech perception are greatest for signals that are temporally distorted. What is less clear is the relative contributions of peripheral and central processes to the age changes observed. In the work of Bergman *et al.* (1976), and in some but not all studies to be discussed later in this chapter, subjects of different ages who are matched on the basis of pure tone audiometry are found to have difficulties in speech perception that cannot be accounted for by differences in peripheral or sensorineural hearing deficits presumed to be measured by the pure tone audiogram. The longitudinal findings on changes in pure tone thresholds in the speech frequency range indicate that these change dramatically with age as well.

B. Speech Perception in Noise

After reviewing recent research on age differences in speech recognition, Gordon-Salant (1987) concluded that controversial findings on speech recognition in quiet and in noise could be explained by procedural differences in subject selection, presentation level, presence and type of background noise, response format (open versus closed), and test paradigm. Using groups of young and elderly adults who had either no hearing loss or a progressive (sensorineural) loss, she attempted to determine the minimal conditions necessary to identify age differences in speech recognition independently of hearing loss. Monosyllabic words from two different tests were presented in quiet or in a babble at either 80 or 95 dB SPL. Performance was measured in the quiet, when the Signal/Babble ratio was 10 dB, and when the babble was adjusted to bring performance to the 50% level. Age effects were task specific. Signal/Babble ratios were higher for both normal hearing and hearing impaired older listeners than for younger ones. Materials presented in quiet or in fixed noise did not uniformly show age effects. The sufficient condition for establishing age effects was the adaptation of noise levels to a common threshold across individuals. Her findings are consistent with those of Dubno, Dirk, and Morgan (1984) with the Speech Perception in Noise Test (Kalikow, Stevens, & Elliott, 1977) and indicate that the critical variable is the adaptive noise procedure common to both studies rather than the stimulus materials, which were different.

C. Changing Intensity and Duration of Speech Components

Because consonants typically have less energy in the total speech signal than vowels, the loudness appropriate for their understanding defines a lower limit for understanding speech. Gelfand, Piper, and Silman (1985) presented syllables in quiet using each listener's most comfortable listening levels as well as 8 dB above and below that level. Adults representing age decades from the 20s through the 60s chose loudness levels typical of conversational speech. For adults selected to have normal audiograms, there was a significant age decline in percent recognition of

consonants mostly at the −8 dB presentation level. The confusion matrices were similar across age.

Consonant intelligibility in aging was further studied by Gordon-Salant (1986) who altered nonsense syllables either by increasing consonant duration by 100%, increasing the consonant vowel intensity ratio by 10 dB, or both. Adults from 21 to 33 or 65 to 72 years of age were selected to have normal hearing. The nonsense syllables were presented at 75 or 90 dB SPL, 6 dB above the level of a background babble. No quiet condition was used. Younger adults performed better in all conditions; age did not interact with any of the other variables. Increasing the relative intensity of the consonant had the most beneficial effect on recognition. The effects of increasing consonant duration varied, as would be expected, with the consonant vowel combinations.

Guelke (1987) studied effects of increasing the energy of the consonants p, t, k, b, d, g, presented in noise. As intensity increased from 9 to 17 dB, correct responses increased from 50% to over 90%. For example, the enhancement reduced confusion between p and t by about two thirds.

The significance of the experiments discussed is the demonstration that both the relative temporal and intensity characteristics of consonants and vowel consonant combinations are the basis for proper speech recognition and can be altered to improve speech intelligibility of normal hearing elderly persons. At a practical level, when the overall intensity of the consonants is brought up to an acceptable level, is the loudness uncomfortable? Montgomery, Prosek, Walden, and Cord (1987) varied the relative consonant–vowel intensities from −20 to 9 dB in four words (*gave, seen, robe, their*). The resulting variations were matched to subjectively equal loudness to a 90 dB SPL recording of the word *laugh*. A comparable task was constructed with noise stimuli. The results for subjects with mild to moderate hearing loss, high frequency hearing loss, and normal hearing were that the overall judgments of loudness did not change as a result of increasing the relative consonant intensity. This result has practical implications for the design of digital hearing aids because such devices can selectively enhance elements of the speech signal (see Levitt, 1987, and Neuman, 1987, for reviews of digital hearing aids).

D. Context and Speech Compression

Holtzman, Familitant, Deptula, and Hoyer (1986) presented word strings at the individual speech reception thresholds for adults with average ages of 35 or 74 years. Word recognition was better for both groups when words were in a sentence as opposed to random order. Although the young adults recognized more words than the older ones, the findings did not result in the elimination of any of four hypotheses that could be used to explain the age difference: memory, high frequency hearing loss, response bias, or better application of linguistic rules by younger adults.

The facilitation effect of good context in speech understanding of the elderly is better understood as a result of studies of compressed speech. Wingfield, Poon, Lombardi, and Lowe (1985) compressed five and eight word strings to rates of presentation ranging from 275 to 424 words/minute and presented them to young and elderly adults as normal sentences, word sequences devoid of meaning but with intact syntax, and random strings. The effect of speech compression and number of words was almost totally dictated by variations in the context. As shown in Figure 3, a small but statistically significant decline was found for normal sentences as words/minute increased. With random strings, the effects of faster rates on declines in recall were five times greater in the elderly than in the younger group. The syntactic condition yielded intermittent results. No independent assessment of hearing loss for speech was made in this or the other studies in the series.

Stine, Wingfield, and Poon (1986) measured recall for sentences containing 4 to 10 propositions presented at 200 to 400

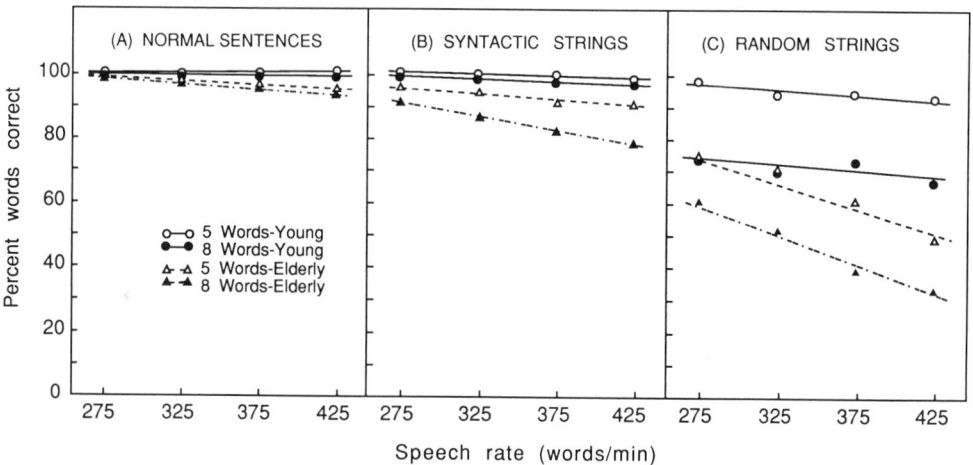

Figure 3 Mean percentage of words correctly reported by elderly (triangles) and young (circles) adults presented in speech strings of 5 or 8 words presented at speech rates ranging from 275 to 425 words per minute. Left panel: Normal sentences. Center panel: Meaningless strings of the same words presented with the formal syntax of sentences. Right panel: Meaningless strings of the same words presented in random sequence. Reproduced with permission from Wingfield, Poon, Lombardi, and Lowe (1985).

words/minute. Recall fell with increasing rates of presentation relatively more rapidly for older adults. Increasing the number of propositions decreased recall for both groups by about the same amount at all presentation rates, so that the greater decline in performance with faster presentation rate for the elderly was attributed to the removal of processing time. A subsequent study by Wingfield and Stine (1986) using different methods provided further support for this hypothesis. They found that the recall strategies of the young and elderly adults were the same at conventional and fast rates of presentation, but the loss of time for processing had a more deleterious effect for the elderly.

Finally, Stine and Wingfield (1987) manipulated the degree of linguistic and prosidic cueing on the recall of sentences presented as compressed speech. The most striking finding was the relatively greater loss in recall by older adults when normal intonation and other prosodic cues were removed. Together, these results reveal how strikingly the effects of slower processing speeds of older adults are mitigated by context effects and, conversely, how dependent older adults are on context for comprehension relative to young adults.

E. Methodological Issues in Speech Research

As in the case of vision, there is considerable difficulty in hearing in specifying the characteristics of the stimulus that yield equivalent and different experiences for young and old listeners whether normal hearing or hearing impaired. The Working Group on Speech Understanding and Aging (1988) addressed the issue with respect to speech understanding by asking if listeners of different ages should be matched on the basis of equal sensation levels or equal intensity levels? The difficulty of the former is that context or back-

ground noise relative to the signal may be very different for persons so matched. The group recommends that both bases for matching young and old listeners be used for now. In addition, how is the contribution of noise to hearing impairment measured in normal hearing and hearing-impaired adults of different ages? The Signal/Noise ratio required for equal intelligibility in the presence of various contexts that improve performance across age may not be the same. At present there is little choice but to systematically vary the level of background as well as signal intensity in psychophysical research.

IV. Summary and Conclusions

The vigorous scientific activity in vision and hearing in relation to age provides an impressive report card with respect to both quantity and quality of research. In vision, major advances revolve around the studies generated by the idea that different visual channels respond differently to age; the studies of age differences in photoreceptors as related to color vision and adaptation; the ever more successful efforts to distinguish between optical and neural contributions to age differences in visual function; and the extensions of research to include considerations of cognitive aspects of visual functioning as in the case of search.

In hearing research, one advance in knowledge is that there are two kinds of changes in thresholds, a continuous increase with age for high frequency stimuli and a second discontinuous change in thresholds for frequencies from 0.5 to 2.0 kHz after the 50s. Significant information is accumulating on the sufficient conditions for reducing age differences in understanding speech. The manipulation of the relative intensity and duration of consonants and vowels in speech both in quiet and in noise have markedly increased our knowledge of the factors in the speech signal that contribute to poorer understanding of speech in older age.

A general feature of the numerous studies of context effects and the quality of auditory and visual information on stimulus recognition is that older persons suffer relatively more than younger ones from stimulus impoverishment whether achieved by altering the temporal or the spatial aspects of the signal. Conversely the elderly appear to benefit as much as or more than younger adults from good context or stimulus familiarity. Perhaps by necessity, resulting from poorer sensory functioning, older persons are forced to become relatively greater experts at inferring the meaning of stimulus events. Many interventions based on this principle have been proposed and require research evaluation.

With respect to practical application in vision, the research identifies more clearly than before age-related difficulties identifying moving objects and poorly lighted objects. Research on visual search identifies many human factor approaches to improve the ease of identifying targets in cluttered visual environments. Yet the relatively straightforward possibilities for increasing visual performance of older adults in static environments by improvements in illumination have not yet occurred nor have there been significant improvements in the assessment of visual problems in driving and related tasks that are most salient to older persons.

The practical significance of much of the research in manipulating the intensity and duration of consonants in the speech signal is that it sets the stage for development of digital hearing aids and related devices. The continuously developing distinctions between "top-down and bottom-up" factors that contribute to speech intelligibility reveal the very important role that context effects play in understanding speech. The role of training and rehabilitative interventions that

take such information into account in improving speech understanding can hardly be overemphasized.

In both vision and hearing, there have been advances in the efforts made to match young and elderly adults on factors that can complicate the interpretation of age differences in psychophysical measurements. It is becoming routine to see visual research in which subjects of all ages are refracted to the test distance used in the research and in which the effects of presumed age differences in retinal illumination of stimulus material are assessed by some method. In hearing, it is becoming more common to see research planned so that various steps are taken to equate the level of the signal and the background for young and elderly listeners.

The big story of current research on age differences in vision and audition is that the nervous system at and beyond the level of the end organ is implicated in age differences in seeing and hearing. The need for histopathological studies of the auditory and visual nervous system in persons with documented measures of hearing and vision takes on a new urgency, as does the need for noninvasive studies of nervous system function in living subjects. We can anticipate an increase in such activity as well as a greater emphasis of the use of animal models to elucidate age-related changes in the nervous system as well as the end organ (see Livingstone & Hubel, 1988, for exciting possibilities in vision).

The increasing awareness of the importance of the nervous system in age differences in auditory and visual functioning encourages speculation about the degree to which age-related losses in different sensory and perceptual functioning are interrelated. Existing evidence is indirect and scattered. One possible approach to the issue would be to use cross-modality matching of stimulus intensity. This is commonly done in assessments of taste sensitivity. Equal sensation functions are common within vision and hearing but surprisingly little has been done with these in relation to age, and I know of no such studies that ask persons of different ages to subjectively match or make magnitude estimates of stimuli across vision and audition. Such research might provide a basis for investigating the notion that "sensory underload" is a characteristic of the elderly's responsiveness to environmental information.

A second aspect of sensory and perceptual processes that cuts across modalities is slowing of assimilation and processing of information. Studies of age differences in visual masking, eye tracking movements, and speeded speech, as well as response times to visual and auditory signals suggest that relatively less information per unit time is available to older persons and that the effects cannot be explained on the basis of peripheral factors. The research performed to date provides an excellent basis for further cross-modality studies.

Acknowledgments

Thanks are due to Frank Schieber who provided several suggestions and critiques of the vision material while it was being written. James Birren made several excellent suggestions for relating the materials on vision and hearing that were used in preparing the text. Much of the organization of this chapter was influenced by the extensive writings of John L. Corso and Robert A. Weale, who have contributed much to the critical review of current research information on perception and aging as well as to its content. Eloise Acord prepared the manuscript and references. The Gerontology Research Library Staff provided excellent help in tracking down literature reviewed.

References

Averbach, E., & Coriell, A. S. (1961). Short-term memory in vision. *Bell System Technical Journal*, **70**, 419–425.

Ball, K. K., Beard, B. L., Roenker, D. L., Miller, R. L., & Griggs, D. S. (1987). *Age and visual search: Expanding the useful field of view*. Paper presented at the annual meeting of the Gerontological Society of America, Washington, DC, November.

Bergman, M., Blumenfeld, V. G., Cascardo, D., Dash, B., Levitt, H., & Margulis, M. K. (1976). Age related decrement in hearing for speech. *Journal of Gerontology*, **31**, 533–538.

Birren, J. E., & Shock, N. W. (1950). Age changes in rate and level of visual dark adaptation. *Journal of Applied Physiology*, **2**, 407–411.

Brant, L. J., & Fozard, J. L. (1987). A model for examining longitudinal and cross-sectional changes in a study of human aging. *Proceedings of the 1987 Social Statistics Section of the American Statistical Association*, pp. 300–305.

Brant, L. J., & Fozard, J. L. (1990). Age changes in pure tone thresholds in a longitudinal study of normal aging. *Journal of the Acoustical Society of America*, in press.

Cerella, J. (1985). Age-related decline in extrafoveal letter perception. *Journal of Gerontology*, **40**, 727–736.

Cerella, J., & Fozard, J. L. (1984). Lexical access and age. *Developmental Psychology*, **20**, 235–243.

Cerella, J., Poon, L. W., & Fozard, J. L. (1981). Mental rotation and age reconsidered. *Journal of Gerontology*, **36**, 620–624.

Cerella, J., Poon, L. W., & Fozard, J. L. (1982). Age and iconic read-out. *Journal of Gerontology*, **37**, 197–202.

Corso, J. F. (1963). Age and sex differences in pure tone thresholds. *Archives of Otolaryngology*, **77**, 385–405.

Corso, J. F. (1980). Age correction factor in noise-induced hearing loss: A quantitative model. *Audiology*, **19**, 221–232.

Corso, J. F. (1981). *Aging sensory systems and perception*. New York: Praeger.

Corso, J. F. (1987). Sensory-perceptual processes and aging. *Annual Review of Gerontology and Geriatrics*, **7**, 29–55.

Coyne, A. C. (1981). Age difference and practice in forward visual masking. *Journal of Gerontology*, **36**, 730–732.

Coyne, A. C., Burger, M. C., Berry, M. J., & Botwinick, J. (1987). Adult age, information processing and partial report processing. *Journal of Genetic Psychology*, **148**, 219–224.

Coyne, A. C., Liss, L., & Geckler, C. (1984). The

relationship between cognitive status and visual information processing. *Journal of Gerontology*, **39**, 711–717.

Cremer, R., & Zeef, E. J. (1987). What kind of noise increases with age? *Journal of Gerontology*, **42**, 515–518.

Danziger, W. L., & Salthouse, T. A. (1978). Age and the perception of incomplete figures. *Experimental Aging Research*, **4**, 67–80.

Dayal, V. S., Kane, N., & Mendelsohn, M. (1971). Patterns of puretone loss in presbycusis. *Acta Otolaryngology*, **71**, 382–384.

Dayal, V. S., & Nussbaum, M. A. (1971). Pattern of puretone hearing loss. *Acta Otolaryngology*, **69**, 329–332.

Domey, R. G., & McFarland, R. A. (1961). Dark adaptation as a function of age: Individual prediction. *American Journal of Ophthalmology*, **51**, 1262–1268.

Dubno, J. R., Dirk, D. D., & Morgan, D. E. (1984). Effects of age and mild hearing loss on speech recognition in noise. *Journal of the Acoustical Society of America*, **76**, 87–96.

Eisner, A. (1986). Multiple components in photopic dark adaptation. *Journal of the Optical Society of America*, **3**, 655–666.

Eisner, A., Fleming, S. A., Klein, M. L., & Mauldin, W. M. (1987). Sensitivities in older eyes with good acuity: Cross-sectional norms. *Investigative Ophthalmology and Visual Science*, **28**, 1824–1831.

Elliott, D. B. (1987). Contrast sensitivity decline with aging: A neural or optical phenomenon? *Ophthalmic and Physiological Optics*, **7**, 415–419.

Fisk, A. D., McGee, N. D., & Giambra, L. M. (1989). The influence of age on consistent and varied semantic category search performance. *Psychology and Aging*, in press.

Fozard, J. L. (1981). Changing person-environment relations in adulthood. *Human Factors*, **23**, 7–27.

Fozard, J. L. (1985). Psychology of aging: Normal and pathological age differences in memory. In J. C. Brocklehurst (Ed.), *Textbook of geriatric medicine and gerontology* (3rd ed., pp. 122–142). London: Churchill Livingstone.

Fozard, J. L., & Popkin, S. J. (1978). Changing person-environment relationships over the adult years: Optimizing adult development. *American Psychologist*, **33**, 711–717.

Gaylord, S. A., & Marsh, G. R. (1975). Age differences in the speed of a spatial cognitive process. *Journal of Gerontology*, **30**, 674–678.

Gelfand, S. A., Piper N., & Silman, S. (1985). Consonant recognition in quiet as a function of aging among normal hearing subjects. *Journal of the Acoustical Society of America*, **78**, 1198–1206.

Gilmore, G. C., Allan, T. M., & Royer, F. L. (1986). Iconic memory and aging. *Journal of Gerontology*, **41**, 183–190.

Gittings, N. S., & Fozard, J. L. (1986). Age changes in visual acuity. *Experimental Gerontology*, **21**, 423–434.

Gittings, N. S., Fozard, J. L., & Shock, N. W. (1987). *Age changes in stereopsis, visual acuity, and color vision.* Paper presented at the annual meeting of the Gerontological Society of America, Washington, DC, November.

Gordon-Salant, S. (1986). Recognition of natural and time/intensity altered CVs by young and elderly subjects with normal hearing. *Journal of the Acoustical Society of America*, **80**, 1599–1607.

Gordon-Salant, S. (1987). Age-related differences in speech recognition performance as a function of test format and paradigm. *Ear and Hearing*, **8**, 277–282.

Greene, H. A., & Madden, D. J. (1987). Adult age differences in visual acuity, stereopsis, and contrast sensitivity. *American Journal of Optometry and Physiological Optics*, **64**, 749–753.

Guelke, R. W. (1987). Consonant burst enhancement: A possible means to improve intelligibility for the hard of hearing. *Journal of Rehabilitation Research and Development*, **24**(4), 217–220.

Haas, A., Flammer, J., & Schneider, U. (1986). Influence of age on visual fields of normal subjects. *American Journal of Ophthalmology*, **101**, 199–203.

Holtzman, R. E., Familitant, M. E., Deptula, P., & Hoyer, W. J. (1986). Aging and the use of sentential structure to facilitate word recognition. *Experimental Aging Research*, **12**, 85–88.

Hoyer, W. J., & Clancy, S. M. (1987). Age and skill in visual search: Dual task effects. *Proceedings of the 31st annual meeting of the Human Factors Society, Santa Monica, CA*, **1**, 21.

Hoyer, W. J., & Familitant, M. E. (1987). Adult age differences in the rate of processing expectancy information. *Cognitive Development*, **2**, 59–70.

Hutton, J. T., Nagel, J. A., & Loewenson, R. B. (1983). Variable affecting eye tracking performance. *Electroencephalography and Clinical Neurophysiology*, **56**, 414–419.

Hutton, J. T., Nagel, J. A., & Loewenson, R. B. (1984). Eye tracking dysfunction in Alzheimer-type dementia. *Neurology*, **34**, 99–102.

Jaffe, G. J., Alvarado, J. A., & Juster, R. P. (1986). Age-related changes of the normal visual field. *Archives of Ophthalmology*, **104**, 1021–1025.

Johnson, M. A., & Choy, D. (1987). On the definition of age-related norms for visual function testing. *Applied Optics*, **26**, 1449–1454.

Kalikow, D. N., Stevens, K. N., & Elliott, L. L. (1977). Development of a test of speech intelligibility in noise using sentence materials with controlled word predictability. *Journal of the Acoustical Society of America*, **61**, 1337–1351.

Keunen, J. E. E., van Norren, D., & van Meel, G. J. (1987). Density of foveal cone pigments at older age. *Investigative Ophthalmology and Visual Science*, **28**, 985–991.

Kline, D. W. (1987). Aging and the spatiotemporal discrimination performance of the visual system. *Eye*, **1**, 323–329.

Kline, D. W., & Orme-Rogers, C. (1978). Examination of stimulus persistence as a basis for superior visual identification among older adults. *Journal of Gerontology*, **33**, 76–81.

Kline, D. W., & Schieber, F. (1981). Visual aging: A transient/sustained shift? *Perception and Psychophysics*, **29**, 181–182.

Kline, D. W., & Schieber, F. (1985). Vision and aging. In J. E. Birren & K. W. Schaie (Eds.), *Handbook of the psychology of aging* (2nd ed., pp. 296–331). New York: Van Nostrand Reinhold.

Kline, D. W., Schieber, F., Abusamra, L. C., & Coyne, A. C. (1983). Age, the eye, and the visual channels: Contrast sensitivity and response speed. *Journal of Gerontology*, **38**, 211–216.

Knoblauch, K., Saunders, F., Kusada, M., Hynes, R., Podgor, M., Higgins, K. E., & de Monasterio, F. M. (1987). Age and luminance effects in the Farnsworth-Munsell 100-hue test. *Applied Optics*, **26**, 1441–1448.

Kosnik, W., Fikre, J., & Sekuler, R. (1986). Visu-

al fixation stability in older adults. *Investigative Ophthalmology and Visual Science*, **27**, 1720–1725.

Kosnik, W., Kline, D., Fikre, J., & Sekuler (1987). Ocular fixation control as a function of age and exposure duration. *Psychology and Aging*, **2**, 302–305.

Kosnik, W., Winslow, L., Kline, D., Rasinski, K., & Sekuler, R. (1988). Visual changes in daily life throughout adulthood. *Journal of Gerontology*, **43**, P63–P70.

Legge, G. E. (1978). Substained and transient mechanisms in human vision: Temporal and spatial properties. *Vision Research*, **18**, 69–81.

Lerman, S., & Borkman, R. (1978). Ultraviolet radiation in the aging and cataractous lens: A survey. *Acta Ophthamologica*, **56**, 139–149.

Levitt, H. (1987). Digital hearing aids: A tutorial review. *Journal of Rehabilitation Research and Development*, **24**(4), 7–20.

Livingstone, M., & Hubel, D. (1988). Segregation of form, color, movement, and depth: Anatomy, physiology, and perception. *Science*, **240**, 740–749.

Lowenfeld, I. E. (1979). Pupillary changes related to age. In G. S. Thompson (Ed.), *Topics in neuro-ophthalmology* (pp. 124–150). Baltimore: Williams & Wilkins.

Madden, D. J. (1984). Data-driven and memory-driven selection attention in visual search. *Journal of Gerontology*, **39**, 72–78.

Madden, D. J. (1986). Adult age differences in visual word recognition: Semantic encoding and episodic retention. *Experimental Aging Research*, **12**, 71–78.

Madden, D. J. (1987). Aging, attention, and the use of meaning during visual search. *Cognitive Development*, **2**, 201–216.

Madden, D. J. (1988). Adult age differences in the effects of sentence context and stimulus degradation during visual work recognition. *Psychology and Aging*, **3**, 167–172.

Montgomery, A. A., Prosek, R. A., Walden, B. E., & Cord, M. T. (1987). The effects of increasing consonant/vowel intensity ratio on speech loudness. *Journal of Rehabilitation Research and Development*, **24**(4), 221–228.

Morrison, J. D., & McGrath, C. (1985). Assessment of the optical contributions to the age-related deterioration in vision. *Quarterly Journal of Experimental Physiology*, **70**, 249–269.

Neuman, A. C. (1987). Digital technology and clinical practice: The outlook for the future. *Journal of Rehabilitation Research and Development*, **24**(4), 1–6.

Olsho, L. W., Harkins, S. W., & Lenhardt, M. L. (1985). Aging and the auditory system. In J. E. Birren & K. W. Schaie (Eds.). *Handbook of the psychology of aging* (2nd ed., pp. 332–377). New York: Van Nostrand Reinhold.

Olson, P. L., & Sivak, M. (1984). Glare from automobile rear-vision mirrors. *Human Factors*, **26**, 269–282.

Owsley, C. (1987). Aging and night vision. In Committee on Vision. *Night vision, current research and future directions* (pp. 275–287). Washington, DC: National Academy Press.

Owsley, C., Sekuler, R., & Siemson, D. (1983). Contrast sensitivity throughout adulthood. *Vision Research*, **23**, 689–699.

Owsley, C., & Sloane, M. E. (1987). Contrast sensitivity, acuity, and the perception of "real-world" targets. *British Journal of Ophthalmology*, **71**, 791–796.

Pirozzolo, F. J., & Hansch, E. C. (1981). Oculomotor reaction in dementia reflects degree of cerebral dysfunction. *Science*, **214**, 349–350.

Plude, D. J., & Hoyer, W. J. (1985). Attention and performance: Identifying and localizing age defects. In N. Charness (Ed.), *Aging and human performance* (pp. 97–99). New York: Wiley.

Pokorny, J., Smith, V. C., & Lutze, M. (1987). Aging of the human lens. *Applied Optics*, **26**, 1437–1440.

Puglisi, J. T., & Morrell, R. W. (1986). Age-related slowing in mental rotation of three-dimensional objects. *Experimental Aging Research*, **12**, 217–220.

Rabbitt, P. M. A. (1965). An age-decrement in the ability to ignore irrelevant information. *Journal of Gerontology*, **20**, 233–238.

Robinson, D. W., & Sutton, G. J. (1979). Age effect in hearing—A comparative analysis of published threshold data. *Audiology*, **18**, 320–334.

Salthouse, T. A., & Prill, K. A. (1989). Effects on aging on perceptual closures. *American Journal of Psychology*, in press.

Scialfa, C. T., Garvey, P. M., Goebel, C. C., Gish, K. W., Deering, L. M., & Leibowitz, H. W. (1989). Relationships among measures of static and dynamic sensitivity. *Human Factors*, in press.

Scialfa, C. T., & Kline, D. W. (1988). Effects of noise type and retinal eccentricity on age differences in identification and localization. *Journal of Gerontology*, **43**, P91–P99.

Scialfa, C. T., Kline, D. W., and Lyman, B. J. (1987). Age differences in target identification as a function of retinal location and noise level: Examination of the useful field of view. *Psychology and Aging*, **2**, 14–19.

Scialfa, C. T., Leibowitz, H. W., & Gish, K. W. (1989). Age differences in peripheral refractive error. *Psychology and Aging*, in press.

Sekuler, R., & Ball, K. (1986). Visual localization: Age and practice. *Journal of the Optical Society of America (Section A)*, **3**, 864–867.

Sekuler, R., Owsley, C., & Hukman, L. (1982). Assessing spatial vision of older people. *American Journal of Optometry and Physiological Optics*, **59**, 961–968.

Sekuler, R., Wilson, H. R., & Owsley, C. (1984). Structural modeling of spatial vision. *Vision Research*, **24**, 689–700.

Sharps, M. J., & Gollin, E. S. (1987). Speed and accuracy of mental image rotation in young and elderly adults. *Journal of Gerontology*, **42**, 342–34.

Shock, N. W., Greulich, R. C., Andres, R., Arenberg, D., Costa, P. T., Jr., Lakatta, E. G., & Tobin, J. D. (1984). *Normal human aging: The Baltimore longitudinal study of aging* (NIH Publication No. 84-2450). Washington, DC: U.S. Government Printing Office.

Sivak, M., Olson, P. L., & Pastalan, L. A. (1981). Effect of driver's age on nighttime legibility of highway signs. *Human Factors*, **23**, 59–64.

Sperling, G. A. (1963). A model for visual memory tasks. *Human Factors*, **5**, 19–21.

Stanford, T., & Pollack, R. H. (1984). Configuration color vision tests: The interaction between aging and the complexity of figure-ground segregation. *Journal of Gerontology*, **39**, 568–571.

Stine, E. L., & Wingfield, A. (1987). Process and strategy in memory for speech among younger and older adults. *Psychology and Aging*, **2**, 272–279.

Stine, E. L., Wingfield, A., & Poon, L. W. (1986). How much and how fast: Rapid processing of spoken language in later adulthood. *Psychology and Aging*, **1**, 303–311.

Sturr, J. F., Church, K. L., Nuding, S. C., Van Orden, K., & Taub, H. A. (1986). Older observers have attenuated increment thresholds upon transient backgrounds. *Journal of Gerontology*, **41**, 743–747.

Sturr, J. F., Church, K. L., & Taub, H. A. (1985). Early light adaptation in young, middle-aged, and older observers. *Perception and Psychophysics*, **37**, 455–458.

Sturr, J. F., Church, K. L., & Taub, H. A. (1989). Temporal summation functions for detection of sine-wave gratings in young and older adults. *Vision Research*, in press.

Sturr, J. F., Kelly, S. A., Kobus, D. A., & Taub, H. A. (1982). Age-dependent magnitudes and time course of early light adaptation. *Perception and Psychophysics*, **31**, 402–404.

Thomas, J. C., Waugh, N. C., & Fozard, J. L. (1978). Age and familiarity in memory scanning. *Journal of Gerontology*, **33**, 528–533.

U.S. Congress, Office of Technology (1986). *Hearing impairment and elderly people—A background paper* (OTA-BP-BA-30). Washington, DC: U.S. Government Printing Office.

Walsh, D. H., & Thompson, L. W. (1978). Age differences in visual sensory memory. *Journal of Gerontology*, **33**, 383–387.

Weale, R. A. (1984). The aging retina. In D. Platt (Ed.), *Geriatrics* (Vol. III, pp. 425–450). Berlin: Springer-Verlag.

Weale, R. A. (1986a). Aging and vision. *Vision Research*, **26**, 1507–1512.

Weale, R. A. (1986b). Retinal senescence. In N. Osborne & J. Chader (Eds.), *Progress in retinal research* (Vol. 5, pp. 53–73). New York: Pergamon.

Weale, R. A. (1986c). Senescence and color vision. *Journal of Gerontology*, **41**, 635–640.

Weale, R. A. (1988). Age and the transmittance of the human crystalline lens. *Journal of Physiology*, **395**, 577–587.

Wingfield, A., Poon, L. W., Lombardi, L., & Lowe, D. (1985). Speed of processing in normal aging: Effects of speech rate, linguistic structure, and processing time. *Journal of Gerontology*, **40**, 579–585.

Wingfield, A., & Stine, E. L. (1986). Organizational strategies in immediate recall of rapid speeds by young and elderly adults. *Experimental Aging Research*, **12**, 79–83.

Wolf, E. (1967). Studies in the shrinkage of the visual field with age. *Highway Research Record*, **167**, 1–7.

Woodhouse, J. M. (1975). The effect of pupil size on grating detection at various contrast levels. *Vision Research*, **15**, 645–648.

Working Group on Speech Understanding and Aging (1988). Speech understanding and aging. *Journal of the Acoustical Society of America*, **83**, 859–895.

Wright, L. L., & Elias, J. W. (1979). Age differences in the effects of perceptual noise. *Journal of Gerontology*, **34**, 704–708.

Ten

Motivation, Human Aging, and Cognitive Performance

Donald H. Kausler

Individual differences in human performance on most cognitive tasks, including those of learning, memory, problem solving, and intelligence, are the products of complex interactions between ability and motivational factors. These interactions enter prominently into a long-standing issue in cognitive aging research: the extent to which age-related decrements in performance on many cognitive tasks reflect adult age differences in ability or motivational processes (Jakubczak, 1973; Kausler, 1982).

In principle, elderly adults may be comparable in ability to young adults on a given task, but they may, nevertheless, perform at a lower level if their motivational processes are less efficacious than those of younger adults. For example, the distribution of anxiety may differ markedly between younger and older adults. If so, then representative groups of young and elderly subjects, unselected for motivational status, are likely to differ in the degree to which the debilitating effects of anxiety adversely affect cognitive performance. Individual differences in such intrinsic motives as anxiety and need achievement have been assessed psychometrically in young adults for many years. Groups of young adults selected on the basis of being high or low scorers on these tests have been found to differ greatly in their performances on many cognitive tasks (Geen, Beatty, & Arkin, 1984; Mook, 1987). Comparable assessments of older adults were unavailable for many years, but, fortunately, a number of such assessments have been conducted since the last review of motivation in the second edition of this *Handbook* (Elias & Elias, 1977). One of the primary objectives of the present review is to summarize and evaluate the results of these assessments.

A second objective is to review the research of the past decade on the effects of age on motivation–performance relationships. The nature of these relationships has been a topic of great interest for many years (Eysenck, 1982; Geen *et al.*, 1984), but the extent of their generalizability to older adults has received relatively little attention in the experimental psychology of human aging. Here, too,

Handbook of the Psychology of Aging, Third Edition
Copyright © 1990 Academic Press, Inc. All rights of reproduction in any form reserved.

there has been a moderate flurry of activity since the review by Elias and Elias. The final objective is to evaluate models or theories of motivation in terms of their capacities to incorporate aging's effects on motivation–performance relationships.

I. Assessments of Intrinsic Motivation

Intrinsic motivation is commonly defined as having its origin within the organism, rather than from external stimulation (i.e., extrinsic motivation). Thus one may read a complex article on astronomy because of a high "need for cognition" (intrinsic motivation) or because a grade in a course requires doing so (extrinsic motivation). Thus intrinsic motivation is a state of the organism that is likely to affect behavior in some way. The concept has been broadened in motivational research to include both negative and positive states and both psychological and physiological components. Negative states refer to forms of motivation that, when activated to a high degree, interfere with ongoing performance; positive states refer to forms that, when present to a high degree, facilitate performance. Cognitive psychologists have been interested primarily in anxiety and need achievement as psychological states, and arousal as a physiological state. The present review will focus largely on anxiety and need achievement. Age differences in arousal were reviewed recently by Woodruff-Pak (1985, 1988).

A. Anxiety

Research on anxiety has been greatly influenced by Spielberger's (Spielberger, Gorsuch, & Lushene, 1970) distinction between trait and state anxiety. *Trait anxiety* is defined as "relatively stable individual differences in anxiety proneness" and *state anxiety* as "characterized by subjective consciously perceived feelings

of tension and apprehension, and heightened autonomic nervous system activity" (Spielberger et al., 1970, p. 3). It is state anxiety that affects cognitive performance directly, but the degree of state anxiety depends on the amount of trait anxiety possessed by the performer and by the degree of environmental stress presented by the to-be-performed task.

It is unclear whether or not there are systematic changes in trait anxiety over the course of the adult life span. Himmelfarb and Murrell (1984) examined age differences on trait anxiety scores for Spielberger et al.'s (1970) State Trait Anxiety Inventory (STAI). Although a large sample of men and women (over 2000) was tested, interpretation of the results is made difficult by the exclusion of subjects younger than 55 years. Within the age range sampled, the researchers found a peculiar curvilinear relationship between age and trait anxiety test scores. Scores were found to decrease from the 55 to 59 age range to the 65 to 69 age range, increase to the 75 to 79 age range, decrease again in the 80 to 84 age range, and increase once more at ages 85 to 89. A similar problem occurred in a smaller scale study by La Rue and D'Elia (1985). Only 60 middle-aged (40 to 59 years) and 60 elder (60 to 79 years) subjects were tested. The age difference in mean test scores (also on the STAI) was found to be slight and statistically nonsignificant. Only 100 young adults (mean age = 19.5 years) and 100 elderly adults (mean age = 64.0 years) were compared by Hoyer and Kaye (1980) for mean trait anxiety scores on the Bendig Anxiety Scale. Surprisingly, young adults averaged significantly higher in test scores than did elderly adults.

Much more comprehensive studies were conducted by Kata (1975), Hutto and Smith (1980), and Costa (e.g., Costa, McCrae, Zonderman, Barbano, Lebowitz, & Larson, 1986) but with conflicting outcomes. In Kata's study (1975), large samples of subjects spanning the entire age range from 15 to 64 years were tested. Progressive increments in scores on a brief (nine items) inventory were found from the youngest age level (15 to 19 years) to the highest age level (60 to 64 years) tested. Moreover, this pattern of progressive increments in trait anxiety was replicated in separate samples of subjects from Denmark, Finland, Norway, and Sweden. A large number of subjects (employees at a large federal facility), ranging in age from 25 to 69 years, were tested by Hutto and Smith (1980). Test scores (STAI) were found to *decrease* with increasing age, with the lowest mean score being for subjects age 60 and older.

In many respects, Costa's studies are the most informative ones. In the Costa *et al.* (1986) study, thousands of participants in a national survey, ranging in age from 32 to 88 years, were tested on Costa and McCrae's (1986) NEO (Neuroticism, Extraversion, Openness) Inventory. Of particular interest are scores on the Neuroticism factor, a broad factor that includes trait anxiety among the traits it encompasses. As in Hutto and Smith's study, with increasing age a statistically significant linear *decrement* in Neuroticism was found, but the overall correlation between age and test scores was only $-.12$. This basic cross-sectional pattern of a modest decrement in test scores with increasing age was replicated on the anxiety component of Neuroticism in different large samples by Costa and McCrae (1988) and also by Hoyer and Kaye (1980). These results, combined with comparable longitudinal results obtained in the Baltimore Longitudinal Study with the Guilford–Zimmerman Temperament Survey (Costa, McCrae, & Arenberg, 1983) and with the NEO Inventory (Costa & McCrae, 1988a), indicate that trait anxiety is a stable trait over the course of adult development.

The magnitude of an individual's state anxiety response is viewed as being dependent on that person's perception of a particular test situation as being personally threatening. Consequently, high test anxiety persons tend to perceive examinations as being more threatening than do low test anxiety persons. Performances in the laboratory on difficult cognitive tasks do seem to be comparable to performances on examinations. However, why individual differences in test anxiety level should affect individual differences in performance level on cognitive tasks is complicated by many theorists' postulation that the activation of state anxiety may have both facilitating and debilitating effects on performance. For example, in classical Hullian drive theory, situational anxiety is viewed as contributing to an individual's drive, or energization, level (Spence, 1958). Heightened drive via anxiety's contribution should be facilitating for simple tasks where there are few, if any, competing responses (e.g., classical eyeblink conditioning) but debilitating for complex tasks with many interfering responses (e.g., a serial learning task with high interitem similarity).

Others (e.g., Alpert & Haber, 1960; Mandler & Sarason, 1952) have analyzed anxiety from the perspective of its cue or stimulus properties. From this perspective, state anxiety may be facilitating if it elicits task-relevant responses (e.g., concentration on component processes needed to perform the task) or debilitating if it elicits task-irrelevant responses (e.g., concentration on one's inability to do well on that task). Understanding the nature of adult age differences for each component is obviously important.

The picture regarding adult age differences in test (state) anxiety is as confusing as that of trait anxiety. A particular problem in the few studies comparing young and elderly subjects' mean test anxiety scores is the small sample sizes (usually ranging from 12 to 60 per age group). Martin (1984) employed a self-rating of perceived arousal while performing on a card sorting task as an index of test anxiety and found elderly subjects to score significantly *lower* than young adult subjects. In an exception to the small sample problem, Hutto and Smith (1980) also found decreasing test anxiety scores with increasing age (STAI; the same pattern they found for trait anxiety). For the Debilitating Scale of Alpert and Haber's (1960) Achievement Anxiety Test, Whitbourne (1976) found the exact opposite (i.e., elderly subjects scored significantly higher than young subjects), whereas Mueller, Kausler, and Faherty (1980) found no age effect. A null effect for a middle-aged group/elderly group comparison was also reported by La Rue and D'Elia (1985) for subjects tested on Spielberger *et al.*'s STAI. Either a null effect for age variation or modestly *lower* scores for elderly than for young subjects have also been reported on Buss's (1980) social anxiety test (Mueller & Johnson, 1987; Mueller, Wonderlich, & Dugan, 1986; Wells & Rankin, 1987). The questions included on this test (e.g., "Do you have trouble working when observed?") seem to make scores comparable to those obtained on tests of test anxiety. In addition, young versus old group differences on the facilitating effects of test anxiety as measured by Alpert and Haber's Anxiety Achievement Test were examined in Whitbourne's (1976) and Mueller *et al.*'s (1980) studies. In neither study was a significant difference found in mean scores.

Overall, our conclusion is that if age differences exist in either trait or state anxiety, the difference is too negligible to be of importance as a causative factor for age-related deficits in performance on most cognitive tasks. It should be noted, however, that there are many problems associated with the use of self-reports to evaluate age differences for any component of anxiety. Assessed age differences on the trait being evaluated—or the *absence* of assessed age differences—may reflect age differences in such characteristics as social desirability and response bias, rather than in the trait per se. Fortunately, these

attributes have been thoroughly investigated by Costa *et al.* (1983) with respect to their potential effects on age differences in scores obtained on Neuroticism and are found to contribute little variance to age differences obtained on the factor itself. Comparable studies with other tests of anxiety are clearly needed. Interestingly, Costa and McCrae (Costa & McCrae, 1988a; McCrae & Costa, 1987) have found substantial correlations between self-report scores on the anxiety component of Neuroticism (and also on the broader factor) and assessments made by peers and spouses of the individuals providing the self-reports. Social desirability and response bias attributes are less likely to influence the ratings given by others, thus adding further to the probable validity of the results on age differences in Neuroticism. Peer/spouse evaluations of older adults may prove to be more closely related to performance on many cognitive tasks than are self-evaluations. It seems unlikely that these measurement problems should alter our conclusion about the absence of pronounced age differences in anxiety.

B. Need Achievement

Need achievement is a postulated predisposition that, when activated, yields a motivational state, in this case, achievement motivation (McClelland, Atkinson, Clark, & Lowell, 1953). When successful performance is important to self-esteem, individuals high in need achievement are expected to be more highly motivated than individuals low in need achievement. For many years, individual differences in need achievement have been assessed largely by a projective test derived from the Thematic Apperception Test (McClelland *et al.*, 1953). Veroff, Reuman, and Feld (1984) examined adult age differences in need achievement using this projective test with national representative samples of 1,363 individuals in 1957 and an additional 1,208 individuals in 1976. Ages of the participants ranged from the early 20s to the 80s and older. Fairly linear declines in need achievement scores with increasing age were found for both men and women, with decline being more pronounced for women. Other cross-sectional data, with smaller groups using self-report tests of need achievement rather than a projective test, have been reported by Mellinger and Erdwins (1989) and Costa and McCrae (1988b). In Mellinger and Erdwins's study, the Edwards Personal Preference Schedule (Edwards, 1959) was administered to groups of women in the age ranges of 29 to 39, 40 to 55, and 60 and over years. As in the Veroff et al. study, a decline in need achievement scores was found from early to late adulthood, but the magnitude of the decline was greater for both married career women and homemakers than for single career women. A very different outcome was reported by Costa and McCrae using Jackson's (1984) Personality Research Form. The correlation between age and need achievement scores was slight and statistically nonsignificant (.09). Thus, stability, rather than change, was demonstrated, as in the same investigators' demonstration of stability in Neuroticism. Although educational level does seem to covary positively with need achievement scores (e.g., the correlation was .19 in Costa & McCrae's study), it cannot be argued reasonably that the disparity in outcomes between Mellinger and Erdwins's study and Costa and McCrae's study resulted from disparities in educational levels of their subjects. In both studies, the subjects were fairly well educated.

A recent longitudinal study (Stevens & Truss, 1985) also has been reported for need achievement test scores (Edwards Personal Preference Test). College students tested originally in the late 1950s and in 1965 were retested in 1978 when they were in their 40s and 30s, respectively. In addition, a new group of college students was tested in 1978. Significant increases in test scores were found for both of the retested groups. In addition, college students in 1978 had lower scores than subjects in either their 30s or 40s, but they also had higher scores than these same individuals when tested as college students in either the late 1950s or in 1965. These results imply the presence of both a positive maturational effect and a negative cohort effect on need achievement, at least as measured in this study. Of course, the positive maturational effect extends only through the 40s. However, even then, it conflicts with the cross-sectional results reported by Veroff et al. This is especially true for the women in Veroff et al.'s study. Their scores showed progressive decrements from the 20s through the 40s. Hopefully, Stevens and Truss will extend their longitudinal analyses through late adulthood. Such an extension would serve to resolve the current ambiguities about the reality of adult age differences in need achievement. For the present, it seems unlikely that investigators comparing young and old subjects selected without reference to scores on tests of need achievement should be concerned about their age groups differing markedly in such scores. However, the cautionary note sounded by Maehr and Kleiber (1981) should be heeded. They observed that tests designed to measure individual differences in need achievement were designed only with young adults in mind. Even projective tests of need achievement may be less informative for elderly than for young adults, given the propensity of older adults to be less responsive on these tests than younger adults. Moreover, they cautioned that the traditional view of need achievement in terms of striving for success in competitive situations is less appropriate for elderly adults than for young adults.

C. Other Needs

Adult age differences in a plethora of other needs were examined in the studies by

Costa and McCrae (1988b), Mellinger and Erdwins (1989), Stevens and Truss (1985), and Veroff *et al.* (1985). The lengthy list includes needs for affiliation, succorance, nurturance, dominance, and so on. Obviously, knowledge about age differences in such needs is of great value to investigators in many areas of gerontology. However, with the possible exception of need affiliation, these other needs are probably of little relevance to research in cognitive aging. Need affiliation is of potential interest because age differences in the "need to please the experimenter" could yield age differences in motivational level during cognitive performance and because the effects of variation in affiliation motivation on level of cognitive performance have been demonstrated in a number of basic research studies (e.g., Horner, 1974). Here, too, however, the results of the different studies lead to conflicting conclusions. Costa and McCrae found stability in need affiliation scores over the full course of the life span. Mellinger and Erdwins found an increment in test scores from early to late adulthood, especially for single and married career women. Stevens and Truss found decreases in test scores from the 20s through the 40s, and especially so for women. Finally, Veroff *et al.* reported largely stable scores with increasing age for men but markedly decreasing scores for women.

There is one other intrinsic need that should be of particular interest to cognitive aging researchers. It is the need for cognition, defined as an individual's need for cognitive stimulation. A measure of this need (Cacioppo & Petty, 1982) was included in Salthouse, Kausler, and Saults's (1988) large-scale assessment of individual differences in performances on many cognitive tasks for noncollege subjects ranging in age from 20 to 79 years. Although a negative correlation was found between age and need for cognition, the magnitude was small and attained significance ($r = -.18$) for only one of the samples of sub-

jects included in this study. In smaller samples, Mueller and Johnson (1987) also found a modest, and statistically nonsignificant, decline with age in mean need for cognition scores.

II. Age and Motivation–Performance Relationships

A. Intrinsic Motivation: Anxiety and Need Achievement

Level of intrinsic motivation has been varied factorially with age in only a few studies involving anxiety as the motivational variable. For trait anxiety, Hoyer and Kaye (1980) found neither an anxiety main effect nor an Age × Anxiety Level interaction effect for performance scores on several tests of both spontaneous flexibility (e.g., Hidden Pictures) and intelligence (e.g., Digit Symbol). La Rue and D'Elia (1985) found a moderate interaction between age and trait anxiety for performance scores on several problem-solving tasks. However, the direction of the interaction was opposite of that expected if the debilitating effects of anxiety are especially pronounced for elderly subjects. That is, the negative correlation between anxiety level and performance level was greater for middle-aged than for elderly subjects. For test anxiety, La Rue and D'Elia found the same pattern as for trait anxiety. No significant interaction between age (young and old) and test anxiety level (low and high) was observed by Martin (1984) for scores on a card sorting task involving varying numbers of nontarget items. Hoyer and Kaye's conclusion that "age-related declines in either spontaneous flexibility or intelligence cannot be explained by increased anxiety" (1980, p. 290) seems to apply to age-related declines in other cognitive activities as well. Moreover, the results obtained in interesting studies by Bäckman and Molander (1986a,b) suggest that this conclusion may generalize to age-related declines on physical skills tasks. They found an age-related deficit on a precision sport (miniature golf) despite equivalent increments in arousal during competition for their younger and older (47 to 58 years) subjects.

Other studies have also been concerned with the relationship between anxiety and performance but only as it involves elderly adults. For example, West, Boatwright, and Schleser (1984) discovered state anxiety scores to be negatively correlated with performance scores on laboratory memory tasks (e.g., free recall). This is not a surprising finding in that a negative relationship between anxiety and memory performance is a frequent finding with young adults (Mueller, 1980). A more interesting finding by West *et al.* is the negative relationship between anxiety and self-assessment of everyday memory proficiency. Memory complaints are commonly associated with elderly adults. Training programs involving anxiety reduction, if successful, could serve to improve both memory self-evaluation and actual memory proficiency. There is some evidence indicating that performance scores on various cognitive tasks do increase following such training (e.g., Hayslip, 1989; Yesavage, Rose, & Spiegel, 1982). Unfortunately, the absence of young subjects in these studies makes it impossible to determine the extent to which age differences in performance are affected by training. Nevertheless, it is important to explore further the degree to which the everyday cognitive proficiency of elderly people may be enhanced by effective training programs.

The relationships between levels of need achievement and performance on various cognitive tasks have been well established for young adults (Geen *et al.*, 1984). Greater persistence was found on a task for subjects scoring high in need achievement than for those scoring low, as well as greater likelihood of selecting tasks of intermediate difficulty when

given the opportunity to select from within tasks varying in level of difficulty. One possible direction would be to extend Okun's studies (e.g., Okun & DiVesta, 1976) comparing young and elderly subjects on their selection of which vocabulary test to receive from a series of tests ranging in difficulty. The extension would require both young and elderly subjects to be preselected at each age level to represent high and low scores on a need achievement test and eliminating differential incentives for the various levels of difficulty.

B. Intrinsic Motivation: Activity

Level of intrinsic motivation should be related to activity level on those behaviors that seemingly lead to gratification of the motivational state. For example, individuals high in the need for cognition are expected to pursue more intellectual activities than individuals low in that need. Potential age differences in such pursuits have received little investigation, however. Salthouse *et al.* (1988) did find a modest positive correlation (.20) between age and the time spent per week reading books and magazines, despite the fact that they also found little relationship between age and need for cognition scores. They also reported a significant positive correlation (.24) between age (20 to 79 years) and hours per week spent participating in clubs and other types of organizations. This outcome is suggestive of increased affiliation motivation with increasing age, but, as noted earlier, age-related increases in the need for affiliation as assessed psychometrically are questionable.

C. Extrinsic Motivation

A guiding theme in research on extrinsic motivation is that elderly individuals are underaroused when confronted by a laboratory task and therefore perform at a level well below their true competence. By offering external stimulation, for example, through incentives for proficient performance, task involvement and motivational level increase, and task performance improves accordingly. This principle guided the study by Hartley and Walsh (1980) who hypothesized that "monetary incentive would increase the degree of task involvement for older subjects and result in a noticeable reduction in the magnitude of age-related performance differences" (p. 899). Their choice of a free recall memory task as the medium for testing this hypothesis is especially important in that past research with this task apparently revealed little effect of incentives on the performance of young adult subjects. Surprisingly, Hartley and Walsh found little effect for the incentive variable at either age level, with, consequently, no effect of incentive variation on the magnitude of the age-related decrement in recall scores.

Comparable outcomes have been found when incentives are offered for faster performance on a given task, such as a digit symbol task (Grant, Storandt, & Botwinick, 1978) or a letter cancellation task (Hoyer, Hoyer, Treat, & Baltes, 1978). In an interesting study by Warren, Butler, Katholi, and Halsey (1985) the underarousal–incentive hypothesis was given a more direct test by employing measures of cerebral blood flow as an index of cortical arousal. Blood flow was assessed for young and older subjects as they performed on mental arithmetic tasks with and without monetary incentives. Although the incentive increased arousal, it did so equally for all age levels, in agreement with results obtained with more molar performance measures of increased arousal.

It is tempting to conclude that functional relationships between variation in extrinsic motivation and performance scores show little, if any, age differences. Both young and old individuals frequently perform below their true ability levels. Inducing higher motivation externally serves to make performance approximate

more closely that permitted by one's competence level but equally so for adults of all ages. The net effect is that age-related differences in performance as determined by age-related differences in abilities persist regardless of the amount of induced motivation. There is, however, one important source of potential variation in extrinsic motivation that apparently has not received the attention it deserves in aging research. The variable is that of control versus noncontrol over the task subjects are asked to perform. Perlmuter's research (see Perlmuter, 1987, for a review) has revealed that young adults perform at a higher level when they have control over the content of the task to be performed. Conceivably, such control is even more motivating for elderly adults. The typical laboratory task, of course, offers no opportunity for control. Studies directed at potential variation in age differences as affected by the presence or absence of control would certainly be a welcomed addition to the motivation literature.

III. Aging and Models of Motivation

Given the lack of evidence regarding potent age differences in motivation–performance relationships, it may appear needless to discuss the appropriateness of existing models of motivation in terms of their fit to age effects on such relationships. However, a fair assessment is that what little evidence there is has been gathered with little effort to test hypotheses derived from a motivational model/theory or a theory of aging. Perhaps we have been ignoring potential age differences attributable to motivation simply because we have not been asking the right questions and therefore we have not been conducting the right kinds of experiments.

Asking the right questions based on an appropriate model of motivation/performance has not proved to be easy, however.

For example, the classical Hull–Spence model of H (habit) $\times$ D (drive) translates poorly to aging issues. Ideally H should be equivalent for subjects performing under different drive levels if we wish to examine the effects of variation in drive on performance. Such equivalence between young and old subjects is unlikely to be the case for most tasks. However, there are methodological paradigms involving aversive motivation that may circumvent this problem. For example, in Spence's paradigm for eyeblink conditioning (e.g., Trapold & Spence, 1960), intensity of motivation (via intensity of the UCS, a puff of air) is varied as a separate determiner of H and D by employing both CS-UCS and UCS-alone trials. Cognitive models of motivation/performance relationships have their own problems to overcome. This may be seen in models relating anxiety to performance, such as that of Eysenck (1979). Heightened anxiety is viewed as reducing the functional capacity of working memory. The problem in employing this concept is the common postulate that the structural capacity of working memory decreases in late adulthood. The means of separating functional (i.e., temporary) and structural (i.e., permanent) components of capacity reduction awaits an appropriate methodological paradigm.

Application of other contemporary models of motivation is limited by the fact that they usually are directed at relationships with affect and self-esteem, rather than with performance (e.g., Dweck & Leggett, 1988). There are, however, intriguing models (e.g., Mook, 1987) focusing on goal-seeking behavior that do have potential applicability to aging research. Actions are planned and executed in terms of their utility in attaining a goal. For example, when the goal is to memorize a list of words in the laboratory, goal-seeking behaviors of accessing task-relevant information in semantic memory and then rehearsing that information are activated. Effective performance, however, requires another important mechanism, namely the *inhibition* of non-goal-oriented behaviors. As noted by Mook, "Behaving effectively . . . is at least as much a matter of *not* doing wrong or irrelevant things as of doing right things" (1987, p. 319). In fact, Hasher and Zacks (1989) have postulated an inhibitory deficit as being a major determiner of age-related decrements in prose memory. As a result of this deficit, elderly adults are seen as "wasting" valuable cognitive resources in the pursuit of processing task-irrelevant information. The validity of this conceptualization is questioned, however, by evidence indicating that, if anything, elderly adults engage in less "mindwandering" than younger adults (Giambra, 1989). Nevertheless, efforts to incorporate motivational concepts into theories of cognitive aging are to be commended. Hopefully, the future will bring many more such efforts.

IV. Summary

A number of recent studies have indicated that adult age differences in intrinsic motivation as assessed by standard tests of anxiety and need achievement are too negligible to be of importance as a causative factor for age-related deficits in performance on most cognitive tasks. In addition, the relation between variation in extrinsic motivation (e.g., reward versus no reward) shows little age difference. More promising areas for future studies relating motivation to adult age differences in performance on cognitive task may be those concerned with the needs for cognitive and physical activities and with the inhibition of non-goal-oriented behaviors during performance on a cognitive task.

Acknowledgment

I would like to thank John H. Mueller for his valuable comments on an early draft of this chapter.

References

Alpert, R., & Haber, R. N. (1960). Anxiety in academic achievement situations. *Journal of Abnormal and Social Psychology*, **51**, 207–215.

Bäckman, L., & Molander, B. (1986a). Adult age differences in the ability to cope with situations of high arousal in a precision sport. *Psychology and Aging*, **1**, 133–139.

Bäckman, L., & Molander, B. (1986b). Effects of adult age and level of skill on the ability to cope with high-stress conditions in a precision sport. *Psychology and Aging*, **1**, 334–336.

Buss, A. H. (1980). *Self consciousness and social anxiety.* San Francisco: Freeman

Cacioppo, J. T., & Petty, R. (1982). The need for cognition. *Journal of Personality and Social Psychology*, **42**, 116–131.

Costa, P. T., Jr., & McCrae, R. R. (1986). Cross-sectional studies of personality in a national sample: 1. Development and validation of survey measures. *Psychology and Aging*, **1**, 140–143.

Costa, P. T., Jr., & McCrae, R. R. (1988a). Personality in adulthood: A six-year longitudinal study of self-reports and spouse ratings on the NEO Personality Inventory. *Journal of Personality and Social Psychology*, **54**, 853–863.

Costa, P. T., Jr., & McCrae, R. R. (1988b). From catalog to classification: Murray's needs and the five factor model. *Journal of Personality and Social Psychology*, **55,** 258–265.

Costa, P. T., Jr., McCrae, R. R., & Arenberg, D. (1983). Recent longitudinal research on personality and aging. In K. W. Schaie (Ed.), *Longitudinal studies of adult psychological development* (pp. 222–265). New York: Guilford.

Costa, P. T., Jr., McCrae, R. R., Zonderman, A. B., Barbano, H. E., Lebowitz, B., & Larson, D. M. (1986). Cross-sectional studies of personality in a national sample: 2. Stability in neuroticism, extraversion, and openness. *Psychology and Aging*, **1**, 144–149.

Dweck, C. S., & Leggett, E. L. (1988). A social-cognitive approach to motivation and personality. *Psychological Review*, **95**, 256–273.

Edwards, A. L. (1959). *Edwards Personal Preference Schedule.* New York: The Psychological Corporation.

Elias, M. F., & Elias, P. K. (1977). Motivation and activity. In J. E. Birren & K. W. Schaie (Eds.), *Handbook of the psychology of aging.* New York: Van Nostrand Reinhold.

Eysenck, M. W. (1979). Anxiety, learning, and memory: A reconceptualization. *Journal of Research in Personality*, **13**, 363–385.

Eysenck, M. W. (1982). *Attention and arousal.* Berlin: Springer-Verlag.

Geen, R. G., Beatty, W. W., & Arkin, R. M. (1984). *Human motivation: Physiological, behavioral, and social approaches.* Boston: Allyn & Bacon.

Giambra, L. M. (1989). Task-unrelated-thought frequency as a function of age: A laboratory study. *Psychology and Aging*, 136–143.

Grant, E. A., Storandt, M., & Botwinick, J. (1978). *Journal of Gerontology*, **33,**413–415.

Hartley, J. T., & Walsh, D. A. (1980). The effect of monetary incentive on amount and rate of free recall in older and younger adults. *Journal of Gerontology*, **35**, 899–905.

Hasher, L., & Zacks, R. T. (1989). Working memory, comprehension, and aging: A review and a new view. In G. H. Bower (Ed.), *The psychology of learning and motivation.* San Diego: Academic Press, in press.

Hayslip, B., Jr. (1989). Alternative mechanisms for improvements in fluid ability performances among the aged. *Psychology and Aging*, 122–124.

Himmelfarb, S., & Murrell, S. S. (1984). The prevalence and correlates of anxiety symptoms in older adults. *Journal of Psychology*, **116**, 159–167.

Horner, M. (1974). In J. W. Atkinson & J. O. Raynor (Eds.), *Motivation and achievement.* New York: Holt.

Hoyer, F. W., Hoyer, W. J., Treat, N. J., & Baltes, P. B. (1978). Training response speed in young and elderly women. *International Journal of Aging and Human Development*, **9**, 247–253.

Hoyer, W. J., Kaye, D. B. (1980). Trait anxiety, spontaneous flexibility, and intelligence in young and elderly adults. *Journal of Consulting and Clinical Psychology*, **48**, 289–291.

Hutto, G. L., & Smith, R. C. (1980). *The self-report of anxiety in adults: The effects of age and other variables on STAI scores.* Paper presented at the annual meeting of the Southwestern Psychological Association, Oklahoma City, OK, April.

Jackson, D. N. (1984). *Personality research*

form manual (3rd ed.). Port Huron, MI: Research Psychologists Press.

Jakubczak, L. F. (1973). Age and animal behavior. In C. E. Eisdorfer & M. P. Lawton (Eds.), *The psychology of adult development and aging*. Washington, DC: American Psychological Association.

Kata, K. (1975). Anxiety in the Scandinavian countries. In C. D. Spielberger & I. G. Sarason (Eds.), *Stress and anxiety*: (Vol. II, pp. 275–302). Washington, DC: Hemisphere/Wiley.

Kausler, D. H. (1982). *Experimental psychology and human aging*. New York: Wiley.

La Rue, A., & D'Elia, L. F. (1985). Anxiety and problem solving in middle-aged and elderly adults. *Experimental Aging Reseasrch*, **11**, 215–220.

Maehr, M. L., & Kleiber, D. A. (1981). The graying of achievement motivation. *American Psychologist*, **36**, 787–793.

Mandler, G., & Sarason, S. B. (1952). A study of anxiety and learning. *Journal of Abnormal and Social Psychology*, **47**, 166–173.

Martin, G. A. (1984). Selective attention deficits associated with aging: Anxiety in experimental subjects? Unpublished doctoral dissertation, Ohio University, 1983. *Dissertation Abstracts International*, **44**, 2900-B.

McClelland, D. C., Atkinson, J. W., Clark, R. A., & Lowell, E. L. (1953). *The achievement motive*. New York: Appleton.

McCrae, R. R., & Costa, P. T., Jr. (1987). Validation of the five-factor model of personality across instruments and observers. *Journal of Personality and Social Psychology*, **52**, 81–90.

Mellinger, J. C., & Erdwins, C. J. (1989). Personality correlates of age and life roles in adult women. *Psychology of Women Quarterly*, in press.

Mook, D. G. (1987). *Motivation: The organization of action*. New York: Norton.

Mueller, J. H. (1980). Test anxiety and the encoding and retrieval of information. In I. G. Sarason (Ed.), *Test anxiety: Theory, research, and applications*. Hillsdale, NJ: Erlbaum.

Mueller, J. H., & Johnson, W. C. (1987). *Training distinctiveness and age specificity in self-referent information processing*. Paper presented at the annual meeting of the Midwestern Psychological Association, Chicago, May.

Mueller, J. H., Kausler, D. H., & Faherty, A. (1980). Age and access time for different memory codes. *Experimental Aging Research*, **6**, 445–449.

Mueller, J. H., Wonderlich, S., & Dugan, K. (1986). Self-referent processing of age specific material. *Psychology and Aging*, **1**, 293–299.

Okun, M. A., & DiVesta, F. J. (1976). Cautiousness in adulthood as a function of age and instructions. *Journal of Gerontology*, **31**, 571–576.

Perlmuter, L. C. (1987). Motivation: Theory/human models. In G. L. Maddox, Atchley, R. C., Poon, L. W., Roth, G. S., Siegler, I. C., & Steinberg, R. M., (Eds.), *The encyclopedia of aging*. New York: Springer.

Salthouse, T. A., Kausler, D. H., & Saults, J. S. (1988). Investigation of student status, background variables, and feasibility of standard tasks on cognitive aging research. *Psychology and Aging*, **3**, 29–37.

Spence, K. W. (1958). A theory of emotionally based drive (D) and its relation to performance in simple learning situations. *American Psychologist*, **13**, 131–141.

Spielberger, C. D. (1972). Conceptual and methodological issues in anxiety research. In C. D. Spielberger (Ed.), *Anxiety: Current trends in theory and research* (Vol. 2). New York: Academic Press.

Spielberger, C. D., Gorsuch, R., & Lushene, R. (1970). *The State Trait Anxiety Inventory (STAI) test manual*. Palo Alto, CA: Consulting Psychologists Press.

Stevens, D. P., & Truss, C. V. (1985). Stability and change in adult personality over 12 and 20 years. *Developmental Psychology*, **21**, 568–584.

Trapold, M. A., & Spence, K. W. (1960). Performance changes in eyelid conditioning as related to the motivational and reinforcing properties of the UCS. *Journal of Experimental Psychology*, **59**, 209–213.

Veroff, J., Reuman, D., & Feld, S. (1984). Motives in American men and women across the adult life span. *Developmental Psychology*, **20**, 1142–1158.

Warren, L. R., Butler, R. W., Katholi, C. R., & Halsey, J. H., Jr. (1985). Age differences in cerebral blood flow during rest and during mental activation measurements with and without monetary incentive. *Journal of Gerontology*, **40**, 53–59.

Wells, P. D., & Rankin, J. L. (1987). *Age, selfconsciousness, and sympathy for stigmatized others*. Paper presented at the annual meeting of the Midwestern Psychological Association, Chicago, May.

West, R. L., Boatwright, L. K., & Schleser, R. (1984). The link between memory performance, self-assessment, and affective status. *Experimental Aging Research*, **10**, 197–200.

Whitbourne, S. K. (1976). Test anxiety in elderly and young adults. *International Journal of Aging and Human Development*, **7**, 201–210.

Woodruff-Pak, D. S. (1985). Arousal, sleep, and aging. In J. E. Birren & K. W. Schaie (Eds.), *Handbook of the psychology of aging* (pp. 261–295). New York: Van Nostrand Reinhold.

Woodruff-Pak, D. S. (1988). *Psychology and aging*. Englewood Cliffs, NJ: Prentice-Hall.

Yesavage, J. A., Rose, T. L., & Spiegel, D. (1982). Relaxation training and memory improvement in elderly normals: Correlation of anxiety ratings and recall improvement. *Experimental Aging Research*, **8**, 195–198.

Eleven

Motor Performance and Aging

Waneen W. Spirduso and Priscilla Gilliam MacRae

In this chapter intrinsic factors of motor performance such as work capacity, muscular strength, and psychomotor speed in relation to the performance of average older adults is addressed. The effectiveness of different interventions, such as exercise and practice, in enhancing motor performance with increasing age will be discussed as well as the ultimate capacities and limits of performance as expressed by exceptional older adults. The chapter will conclude with a discussion of the specificity of the aging effects and the importance of understanding motor function, both to the individual and to society.

Motor performance, the execution of tasks that require coordinated muscle activity, is of primary concern to aging adults because it is the basis for activities of daily living, such as walking, eating, bathing, and dressing; job-related tasks such as typing, writing, lifting, and reaching; and participation in sport and recreational pursuits. The prevailing stereotype, and consequently the expectation, for human performance across the life span is that physical ability and efficiency im-

prove through the early years, peak in the third decade, then linearly decline until death. However, each person is born a unique individual, and the interaction of aging and life experiences increases the intraindividual and interindividual variability in many variables across the life span (Sprott, 1988). Motor performance variability, particularly in the aging adult, grows with each increasing decade. The variability in motor performance ranges from the frail older adult living in a care facility, who experiences severe difficulty walking, bathing, and dressing, to an 80-year old living independently, who occasionally runs a 26.2 mile marathon race in a masters' track meet. Evidence that interindividual variability in motor performance increases dramatically with increasing age is abundant. Therefore, descriptions of "average" behavior for specific age groups grow less and less accurate for an individual's performance as the age of the group increases. Physiological changes occur with age and these changes eventually limit motor performance. However, it is difficult to distinguish

Handbook of the Psychology of Aging, Third Edition
Copyright © 1990 Academic Press, Inc. All rights of reproduction in any form reserved.

183

physiological changes due to aging per se from those due to declining physical activity, decreases in motivation, lower societal expectations, and the occurrence of disease.

I. Work Capacity

A. Job Skills

Interest in the impact of age upon motor performance has been greatly stimulated by the increasing number of litigations over physical criteria for job performance, which serve as the basis for decisions regarding employee appointment, termination, and compulsory retirement. Human performance criteria are of particular interest in jobs related to public safety. Compulsory retirement at the age of 70 is prohibited by the Age Discrimination in Employment Act unless based on a "bona fide occupational qualification." Before age may be used exclusively as a criterion for compulsory retirement, it must be shown to represent the only valid criterion by which inference on the ability to perform the job could be made. Because individuals age at different rates, motor performance testing has been suggested as an alternative basis for establishing occupational qualification criteria for hiring, promoting, and retiring personnel (for review, see *Medicine and Science in Sports and Exercise*, 1987).

How physically capable are older individuals to perform certain tasks associated with work? The National Center for Health Statistics surveyed the ability of 38.3 million individuals to perform work-related activities (Kovar & LaCroix, 1987). The population sampled included individuals from 55 to 74 years of age who had worked at some time since they were age 45. The 10 work-related activities covered a wide range of abilities such as:

- Mobility (walking one-quarter of a mile and walking up 10 stairs without resting)
- Endurance for confined activities (standing and sitting for 2 hours)
- Lower and upper body strength (stooping, crouching, or kneeling, and lifting or carrying 25 or 10 pounds)
- Freedom of movement (reaching up over head and reaching out to shake hands)
- Fine motor skills (grasping with fingers)

Of the activities studied, the ones depending upon lower body strength caused people the greatest difficulty (Table I; Kovar & LaCroix, 1987). In general, a greater proportion of women than men had difficulty performing the work-associated activities, particularly in the tasks of lifting or carrying 25 pounds (31% versus 15%). However, this sex difference may be confounded with body size and weight since 25 pounds is a larger proportion of body weight for women than for men. The results also indicated that as age increased from 55 to 74 years, there was a doubling in the percentage of the population that had difficulty performing activities related to mobility, endurance, and lower body strength, whereas those activities related to freedom of movement and fine motor skills were much less affected by age. Overall, 58% of this population had no difficulty with any of the work-related activities. Potentially, many of the people who had retired for reasons other than their health could have remained in the work force.

B. Physical Work Capacity

Jobs require a variety of work capacities from almost no physical work to very heavy physical labor. Activities of daily living tax the physical work capacity of the employed, younger, sedentary adult very little, but the physical work capacity required in these activities of daily living can become major challenges to some older adults, particularly those who suffer additional incapacitation due to chronic

Table I
Percentage of People 55 to 74 Years of Age Who Have Worked since Age 45 with Difficulty or Are Unable to Perform Specified Activities: United States, 1984

Activity	Both Sexes					Men					Women				
	Total	55–59[a]	60–64	65–69	70–74	Total	55–59	60–64	65–69	70–74	Total	55–59	60–64	65–69	70–74
Number															
Sample	9.805	2.000	1.968	3.285	2.552	5.100	1.036	1.067	1.731	1.266	4.705	.964	.901	1.554	1.266
Number in Thousands															
Estimated population	32.305	9.645	9.235	7.561	5.864	16.936	5.023	5.037	3.969	2.907	15.368	4.622	4.197	3.592	2.957
Percent of Population															
Walking 1/4 mile															
Difficulty	17.6	12.4	16.5	20.0	25.0	17.4	12.3	17.0	20.1	23.3	17.9	12.6	15.8	19.9	26.6
Unable	7.6	5.4	8.0	8.7	9.5	7.6	5.0	7.9	9.4	8.7	7.7	5.8	8.0	7.9	10.2
Walking up 10 steps															
Difficulty	15.2	10.9	14.5	16.9	21.4	12.8	9.5	12.1	14.2	17.9	17.9	12.4	17.4	19.7	24.8
Unable	6.9	5.2	6.9	7.4	9.5	5.6	3.8	5.3	6.0	8.7	8.4	6.7	8.8	8.8	10.2
Standing on feet for 2 hours															
Difficulty	22.0	15.1	20.7	26.1	30.1	20.6	13.5	18.9	25.5	28.9	23.5	16.8	22.8	26.7	31.2
Unable	9.0	6.5	8.3	10.9	11.6	8.1	5.2	7.2	10.6	11.5	9.9	7.8	9.7	11.3	11.6
Sitting for 2 hours															
Difficulty	9.7	8.3	10.6	10.4	9.7	8.4	7.0	8.9	9.9	7.9	11.2	9.8	12.7	10.9	11.6
Unable	5.9	5.3	6.5	6.4	5.5	4.9	4.2	5.4	5.7	4.1	7.1	6.4	7.9	7.2	6.9
Stooping, crouching, or kneeling															
Difficulty	27.8	20.1	27.0	30.9	37.8	24.6	18.0	23.4	27.7	33.7	31.4	22.4	31.3	34.3	41.7
Unable	12.6	9.4	12.5	13.7	16.5	11.4	8.3	11.1	12.5	15.9	13.9	10.7	14.2	15.0	17.2
Reaching up over head															
Difficulty	11.5	9.0	11.2	13.1	14.2	10.5	9.0	9.9	12.4	11.6	12.7	9.1	12.8	13.8	16.6
Unable	6.4	4.6	6.7	7.3	7.7	5.7	3.9	6.3	6.9	6.0	7.2	5.4	7.1	7.7	9.5
Reaching out to shake hands															
Difficulty	1.8	1.8	1.6	1.8	2.0	1.6	1.5	1.3	1.8	2.0	2.0	2.2	1.9	1.8	2.0
Unable	1.0	1.0	1.1	1.0	1.2	1.0	0.8	0.9	1.1	1.0	1.1	1.2	1.2	0.8	1.4
Grasping with fingers															
Difficulty	7.8	6.4	7.4	8.7	9.5	6.3	4.5	6.0	7.1	8.8	9.4	8.5	9.0	10.5	10.2
Unable	5.0	4.2	5.0	5.2	5.9	4.0	2.6	4.0	4.5	5.4	6.1	5.8	6.2	6.1	6.3
Lifting or carrying 25 pounds															
Difficulty	23.1	17.0	22.5	24.8	32.0	15.9	11.6	15.4	16.6	23.1	31.1	22.9	31.0	33.8	40.8
Unable	6.9	6.2	6.0	7.3	9.1	4.8	3.5	3.8	5.6	7.5	9.3	9.1	6.7	9.3	10.7
Lifting or carrying 10 pounds															
Difficulty	7.3	5.0	6.9	8.2	10.5	5.3	3.7	5.4	6.6	6.3	9.4	6.4	6.7	9.9	14.6
Unable	2.6	2.2	2.5	2.7	3.0	1.9	1.6	1.9	2.2	1.7	3.3	2.6	3.3	3.3	4.3

[a] Ranges denote age in years.

disease (Shephard, 1978). Fortunately, substantial data exist to support the hypothesis that a life-style of systematic physical activity may maintain a person's physical work capacity and thereby delay the age at which environmental demands exceed physical capabilities. Clearly, the maintenance of a high physical work capacity has implications for the quality of life of the older person.

The best single measurement of a person's physical work capacity, or a person's cardiorespiratory fitness, is maximal oxygen uptake (VO_2 max), also known as aerobic capacity (McArdle, Katch, & Katch, 1986). Maximal oxygen uptake is the largest amount of oxygen that one can utilize under the most strenuous exercise conditions. It is one of the more important factors determining an individual's ability to sustain moderate to high intensity work for longer than 4 or 5 minutes. The relationship of age to VO_2 max was studied as early as the 1930s by Robinson (1938), who demonstrated that VO_2 max in men declined steadily between 25 and 75 years of age. Others have confirmed these findings in men and women who vary in their physical activity patterns (Astrand, Astrand, Hallback, & Kilbom, 1973; Dehn & Bruce, 1972). In healthy men, VO_2 max declines approximately 1% per year after the age of 25, but if the amount of physical activity and body composition remain constant, deterioration resulting from the aging process may be less than 0.5% per year (Heath, Hagberg, Ehsani, & Holloszy, 1981). These results were based on cross-sectional samples; the impact of lifelong training on VO_2 max levels has only recently been examined in longitudinal samples.

Kasch, Wallace, and Van Camp (1985) measured the VO_2 max of 13 men, 50 to 74 years of age. These men remained physically active across an 18-year period by participating in swimming, walking, running, and cycling for an average of 3.3 days per week using approximately 700 kcal per session. VO_2 max remained relatively constant over the 18-year period (44.6 ml per kg per minute^{-1} to 43.1 ml per kg per minute^{-1}), but the maximum heart rate declined 17 beats per minute over the 18-year period. A second longitudinal study examined 24 male track athletes, between 50 and 82 years of age, to evaluate the effect of age and training on VO_2 max over a 10-year period (Pollock, Foster, Knapp, Rod, & Schmidt, 1987). During that period, only 11 of the athletes remained highly competitive and continued to train at the same intensity. The other 13 participants in the study became noncompetitive and reduced their training intensity. The competitive individuals maintained their VO_2 max (54.2 to 53.3 ml per kg × minute^{-1}), whereas the noncompetitive subjects declined significantly in VO_2 max (52.5 to 45.9 ml per kg × minute^{-1}). Maximum heart rate was unaffected by training, declining similarly in both groups (seven beats per minute). These data support the contention that the decline in VO_2 max with age, demonstrated in some studies, is not strictly a function of age but also is affected by other factors such as present level of training, age of onset of training, disease, and genetic profile.

II. Muscular Strength

Muscular strength is a necessary component of athletic activities such as weight lifting, shot putting, high jumping, and sprinting during running, swimming, and bicycling. In addition, muscular strength is required for daily activities such as walking, stair climbing, and carrying. It also plays a role in preventing falls and accidents particularly in the older adult. Muscular strength is defined as the maximum force or tension generated by a muscle in a single maximal contraction (McArdle et al., 1986). Strength may be assessed statically with dynamometers, such as a handgrip dynamometer that measures handgrip strength, or dynamically as one-repetition maximum (1-RM), the maximal amount of weight an individual can lift at one time. Newer computer-assisted isokinetic strength measuring devices allow for peak torque (rotary force), work, and power output to be determined while movement velocity is held constant.

Many investigators have shown that peak values for maximal strength are achieved during the 20s or 30s and then decline with age (Fisher & Birren, 1947; Larsson, 1978; Norris & Shock, 1960). The magnitude of the decline with age remains unclear. Age changes in handgrip strength from 0 to 20% have been reported. Montoye and Lamphiear (1977) reported declines of 10 to 20% in handgrip and arm strength of men and women 20 to 69 years of age. Muscles of the lower body exhibit greater declines with age than do the muscles of the upper body (Larsson, 1978; Larsson, Grimby, & Karlsson, 1979; Murray, Gardner, Mollinger, & Sepic, 1980). Larsson (1978) reported losses in both static and dynamic strength of 26 to 38% in the quadriceps of men, 20 to 65 years of age, with most of the loss occurring after the fourth decade. Similar losses for women have been found (Murray, Duthie, Gambert, Sepic, & Mollinger, 1985). For example, Young, Stokes, and Crowe, (1984) found that the voluntary, static quadriceps strength of 70-year-old women was 35% less than that of twenty-year-old women.

For the most part, the age-related decline in muscle strength can be accounted for by a deterioration in muscle mass that occurs with aging. This decline in muscle mass is due to a decrement in the size and number of muscle fibers, which are particularly evident after 70 years of age (Green, 1986). It was previously thought that the aged human muscle experienced selective loss of Type II fibers (fast twitch) rather than Type I (slow twitch). However, the most recent evidence suggests that with aging a loss of muscle fiber is not fiber-type-specific (Green, 1986). No definite conclusions are possible at this time regarding other alterations in the structure and function of muscle with age. There is evidence that the changes in muscle structure and function are substantially smaller in active older adults, suggesting that the age-related decrements in muscle strength are a function of type of activity and degree of muscle involvement (Aniansson, Sperling, Rundgren, & Lehnberg, 1983; Cunningham, Morrison, Rice, & Cooke, 1987; Dummer, Clark, Vaccaro, Vander Velden, Goldfare, & Sockler, 1985; Frontera, Meredith, O'Reilly, Knuttgen, & Evans, 1988; Petrofsky & Lind, 1975).

It is well established that strength can be increased through resistive exercises in young and older adults (Frontera et al., 1988; Moritani & deVries, 1980; Tomanek & Wood, 1970) and in aged animals (Goldspink & Howells, 1974). Old subjects increased their maximal arm strength the same percentage (20%) as young subjects after 8 weeks of progressive strength training (Moritani & de Vries, 1980). Frontera and his colleagues (1988) examined the effects of a 12-week strength training program on the strength and hypertrophy of knee flexors and extensors in older men (age range 60 to 72 years). They reported significant improvements in strength that were accompanied by significant hypertrophy of the muscles as measured by computerized tomographic scans and girth measurements. Muscle biopsies revealed similar increases in Type I and II fiber sizes in these trained older men. These results show that the neural and muscular plasticity of the older adults is such that they can increase muscular strength with physical activity of sufficient intensity, duration, and frequency.

III. Muscular Endurance

Muscular endurance, the capacity of the muscle to perform continuous submaximal contractions, should be differentiated from muscular strength. Muscular endurance is measured by determining the length of time an individual can hold a certain percentage of his or her maximal force until fatigued or by recording the number of times an individual can repeatedly lift a percentage of maximal weight. Age-related declines in muscular endurance are less than the losses seen in muscular strength (Aniansson et al., 1983; Burke, Tuttle, Thompson, Janney, & Weber, 1953; Dummer et al., 1985; Petrofsky & Lind, 1975). In fact, Petrofsky and Lind (1975) reported no age changes in muscular strength or muscular endurance of the handgrip muscles when measured in a group of men ($N = 100$) employed in a machine shop, who ranged from 22 to 62 years of age. Dummer and colleagues (1985) examined age-related differences in muscular strength and muscular endurance among 73 female swimmers aged 24 to 71 years of age. Though the number of training sessions ($X = 4.13$ sessions per week) and the length of each session ($X = 64$ minutes per session) was similar across age groups, the oldest group swam only half the distance that the youngest group swam. Swimming training did result in higher strength values for swimmers than for less active women, though there was still an age-related decline in muscular strength of the shoulder and knee. However, no significant declines in muscular endurance were found. The fact that muscular endurance can be maintained rather successfully in active older adults is probably the reason that many track, swimming, and cyclist competitors move from sprint and short distance races to longer races as they age.

IV. Upper Limits of Performance

The limits of motor performance over the life span are no better expressed than in the documentation of world records for age groups in athletic events. Age-related changes in masters athletic records are important to the study of aging and motor performance for several reasons. First, records in track and field, swimming, and weight lifting are highly reliable, having been collected under conditions standardized as rigorously as those prevailing among better controlled field experiments. Second, world record holders of all ages undoubtedly are highly motivated individuals in extremely good physical condition with similar goals. Consequently, athletic performance trends are probably less contaminated by extraneous sources of variation such as diet, differential levels of activity, health status, or variations in motivation than most field studies. Third, the variety of athletic events showcases different attributes of performance (i.e., aerobic capacity, strength, and speed).

All the world records for running distances from the 100-meter sprint to the marathon are held by individuals younger than 35 years of age except for the men's marathon record that until very recently, was held by Carlos Lopes, who was 37 years of age when he set the record. The oldest male who broke a world track and field record was John J. Flanagan who set a world record in the hammer throw in 1909 at the age of 41 years, 196 days (World Almanac, 1987). The oldest female record is held by Dana Zatopkova, of Czechoslovakia, who broke the women's javelin record in 1958 at the age of 35 years, 255 days (World Almanac, 1987).

It is not surprising that an examination of trends in athletic records of all ages reveals that for sports such as running, race walking, and swimming, the average speed (meters/second) decreases as the distance of the event increases in the mile-to-marathon distances (Moore, 1975; Riegel, 1981). Riegel compared world record holders of varying ages and found that the running speed of men over 40 years of age declined less with increasingly longer distance races than that of younger men. In other words, at the shorter distances, such as 1500 meters, the fastest 40-year-old could run at 88% of the speed of the younger world record holder. At the longer marathon distance, however, the speed (meters per second) of the fastest 40-year old was virtually the same as that of a world-class runner. The running speed of older runners deteriorates more slowly at longer distances than at shorter ones. The relatively slower performance of the older men at the shorter distances (1,500 to 10,000 meters) may be due to age-related neurophysiological and structural changes, but it may also be attributable to differential training regimes. Older men may be less likely to adhere to the rigorous, intense, and painful interval training protocols that young athletes employ.

In addition to examining the peak motor performance at various ages, it is instructive to examine the percentage of change across age groups. Moore (1975) reported world age-group records as percentages of world records for events such as the shot put, discus, 200 meters, and marathon. The age effects, for men 30 to 60 years of age, were much greater in events that require explosive strength (power), such as the shot put and discus, than in the running events. The shot-put age group record for a 60-year-old was only 49% of the world record, whereas in the marathon the 60-year-old age group record was 76% of the world record. These performance data corroborate the laboratory conclusions mentioned earlier that strength losses are greater than endurance losses with advancing age.

In examining the 1987 world track and field records for a sprint (100 meter), middle distance (800 meter), and long distance (10,000 meter) by expressing age group records as a percentage of the world record for the various events, it appears that the lines of regression of age on percentage of world record are virtually identical up to age 70. After age 70, the sprint distance appears to be slightly less affected by age than the middle and long distances. However, the greatest age effects across the life span occur in the jumping events (high, long, triple jump). These age differences between track and field events are probably due to the fact that explosive strength

is a more significant performance variable in the jumping events. Also, the skill required for the jumping events is greater than that required for the running events. Another factor that contributes to age differences in jumping events may be that the greater incidence of injuries (bone, tendon, and muscle) with age in the jumping events than in the running events discourages many older athletically talented individuals from continuing competition (Schulz & Curnow, 1988). This decreases the overall number of competitors in jumping events, which in turn decreases the possibility of outstanding performance in these events.

Although athletic records suggest substantial age-related decreases in motor performance with advancing decades, the magnitude of decline in athletic record performance across age groups is exaggerated by the cross-sectional analysis technique that is generally used. The decline obtained by cross-sectional analysis was approximately twice that of the decline determined by a longitudinal analysis in both athletic performance and laboratory measures of VO_2 max (Stones & Kozma, 1982; Heath et al., 1981). Athletic records are continually broken, but when longitudinal records of individual athletes were examined for the years 1973 to 1979, the world record running times for the younger men, age 40 to 49, were relatively stable (0 to 2%). The records in the older age group, 50 to 59 and 60 to 69, improved 6 to 24% over this same time period. The improvements seen in the athletes aged 50+ may be related to an improvement in the amount and quality of training, an improvement in the frequency and quality of competitive experience, or a decrease in injuries.

A. Psychomotor Performance

Motor behavior in which a rapid response, with one or more limbs or digits, is made to an environmental stimulus is described as a *psychomotor behavior.* When the response is a single or coordinated movement made as rapidly as possible to the onset of a signal, the initiation and execution control mechanisms have been described by information-processing models (Schmidt, 1981). In these models, the initiation and execution of movements are described as being controlled by sequential and/or parallel stages of mental function, such as stimulus perception, encoding and memory functions, decision making, motor programming, and initiation and execution of movement. The relative role of the stages depends on whether the task has heavy stimulus-related processing or motor programming demands. Psychomotor behaviors vary in the amount of verbal manipulation required (Hale, Myerson, & Wagstaff, 1987), the degree of decision making required, and the relative proportion of decision making and motor programming to sensorimotor function that occurs. Verbal abilities generally decline with aging much more slowly than motor capacities, suggesting that performance changes on nonverbal tasks may be qualitatively different from performance changes on verbal tasks (Hale *et al.,* 1987).

Because the information processing involved in psychomotor behaviors is dependent upon the integrity of the central nervous system, an integrity that erodes with chronological aging, speeded psychomotor performance such as is required in reaction time tasks has been used for many years as an age marker (Borkan & Norris, 1980). From their analysis of nine studies utilizing reactivity as a dependent variable, Hale *et al.* (1987) proposed that the reaction latencies of old subjects were disproportionately slower than the young as task difficulty increased. Their results strongly support earlier hypotheses (Birren, 1965; Cerella, Poon, & Williams, 1980; Salthouse & Somberg, 1982a) that the effect of aging is a general effect that influences similarly all types of nonverbal information processing.

B. Factors that Affect Reaction Time

1. Verbal–Nonverbal Task Requirements

The extent to which psychomotor behavior is slowed with aging depends upon the extent to which the behavior is loaded for motor response preparation and execution versus verbal or lexical decision making. Speed of lexical decisions is the same in old and young subjects, and factors such as stimulus degradation, word frequency, and semantic priming that affect primarily these decisions, equally affect old and young subjects (Chiarello, Church, & Hoyers, 1985). However, in tasks where the processing is focused on mapping a nonverbal stimulus onto a specific motor response, age differences appear as early as the fifth decade. Identification of stimulus characteristics and the encoding process, when they are associated with a specific movement to be made, are slower in older adults (Hines, Poon, Cerella, & Fozard, 1982; Salthouse & Somberg, 1982b). Indeed, all stages of nonverbal information processing are similarly affected by age (Birren, Woods, & Williams, 1980; Botwinick, 1984; Cerella *et al.,* 1980; Salthouse & Somberg, 1982a,b).

2. Complexity

Complexity, of both the stimulus display and the movements to be made in response to the stimulus, influences the extent of age-related behavioral slowing. Simple reaction time, which requires only the programming of a single movement to the activation of a single light, can be maintained well into older ages. If experimental factors such as novelty, practice, stimulus quality, and performance expectations are held constant, age differences in simple reaction time can be reduced to almost zero (Gottsdanker, 1982). Rabbitt (1980) has claimed that with extraordinary practice age differences in choice reaction time can be substantially reduced. There is, however, a lag constant that remains in CRT, even after extensive practice, that is probably the age difference in basic reactivity in the central nervous system. However, changing the stimulus display by manipulating the clarity and quantity of stimuli increases the latency of response for most individuals, and disproportionately increases the latencies of older persons. As stimulus discriminations and choices to be made increase (Simon & Pouraghabagher, 1978), so do age differences (Birren, 1965; Cerella et al., 1980; Hale et al., 1987; Welford, 1977).

Response complexity refers to difficulty of the motor response to be performed after receiving the stimulus. More complex movements require more time to program and initiate than simple movements (Henry & Rogers, 1960), even in a simple reaction time paradigm. In fact, increasing the complexity of the movement to be made in a simple reaction time paradigm can produce age differences in simple reaction time that were not apparent when a simple movement was performed (Griew, 1959; Osborne, 1986). A movement requiring a coordinated bilateral response of the limbs is more difficult to program and initiate than a movement requiring only the unilateral activation of a single digit (Light, 1989a). Older individuals program responses more slowly than do young individuals (Larish & Stelmach, 1982). The more complex the movement to be made, the greater the age disparity in response latency (Cerella et al., 1980; Jordan & Rabbitt, 1977; Plude, Hoyer, & Lazar, 1982; Tolin & Simon, 1968; Welford, 1965). In fact, individuals over 60 years of age took as long to respond with a unilateral response as 20-year olds took to respond with a bilateral response (Lowe & Spirduso, 1988). Light (1989a) found that the response programming capability of older subjects was more sensitive to small changes in response complexity and less consistent than that of younger women. Griew (1959) proposed that younger individuals may be capable of preparing the response simultaneously with receiving the stimulus, whereas in old individuals the processing of stimulus interpretation and response preparation occurs in discrete stages.

3. Compatibility

Stimulus–response (S-R) compatibility refers to the extent to which the response to be made to a stimulus seems natural and logical. For example, a right-hand response to a stimulus located on the right side of a display would be a S-R compatible response. A left-hand response to that same stimulus would be less compatible. It has long been known that S-R incompatibility lengthens reaction time (Welford, 1968, 1977) and increases the differences between young and old reaction times. Less well known is that response–response compatibility also lengthens RT. Response–response compatibility refers to the ease with which two responses can be performed either simultaneously (Fitts, 1959), or singly when paired as the two alternatives in a two-choice situation (Kornblum, 1965). For example, it is easier to react with both index fingers simultaneously than with a simultaneous response of one index finger and thumb in a "pinch" type movement (Light, 1989b). Incompatible movements may be programmed serially in the response determination and program selection stages of processing, thus producing a longer response latency, whereas compatible movements may be programmed in parallel or as one unit.

Response–response incompatibility exacerbates age differences in reaction time by making the movement selection process more difficult. (Light, 1989b) and Lowe and Spirduso (1988) ranked 12 combinations of four movements from most compatible to least compatible on the basis of response latencies. Sixty-year-olds were significantly slower in programming all movement combinations than 20- and 40-year-olds, but as response–response compatibility decreased, age differences increased. The middle-aged subjects were not significantly slower than young subjects in programming except in movement combinations of moderate or low compatibility. Because both response complexity and response compatibility increase response programming time and age interacts with complexity and compatibility, age differences in programming time increase linearly as response complexity increases and response compatibility decreases. Thus the exponential model of age-related increasing latencies with increasing task difficulty (Hale *et al.*, 1987) seems also to apply to task difficulty that is increased by manipulations of compatibility and complexity.

4. Motor System Response Type

Curiously, several researchers have found that when decisions regarding nonverbal stimuli were mapped onto the vocal apparatus, their old subjects were not slower than young ones (Nebes, 1978; Salthouse & Somberg, 1982a; Thomas, Waugh, & Fozard, 1978). Older subjects who indicated the location of a stimulus light by saying "left" or "right" rather than by pressing a button with the right or left hand appeared to have simple and choice reaction times that were similar to those of young subjects. Osborne (1986), after providing ample practice and controlling for task complexity, also reported that old and young men were not different in vocal reaction time. He found that when two levels of complexity were provided in both the vocal and manual response modes, the old were disproportionately slower only when reacting with the complex manual response. The number of well-controlled studies in which age appeared to have no effect on vocal reaction time is not inconsequential, yet other investigators have reported age differences in vocal responses.

These age differences were reported when perceptual judgments, memory scanning, or higher order cognitive functions were under investigation (see Salthouse, 1985, for a review), and the reaction times were long. The investigators who reported that vocal reactions appeared to be resistant to age effects utilized experimental procedures that produced reactions of less than 400 msec. (Nebes, 1978; Osborn, 1986; Salthouse & Somberg, 1982a).

When either the manual or vocal response to be made is very simple, such as uttering a one-syllable word or lifting an index finger from a key, a long response time can be interpreted as a period in which substantial central nervous system coding, retrieving, and processing is occurring. The hypothesis that aging results in a general slowing of all functions of the central nervous system (Birren, 1965) suggests that the longer the time required to initiate a response, the more probable it is that age differences are seen. Apparent similarities of old and young vocal response times may be attributable more to the length of the responses used in these experiments rather than the motor response type. When simple reaction time is reduced by experimental manipulation, extensive practice, and/or careful subject selection to extremely short reactions, age differences can be greatly minimized in manual reaction time (Gottsdanker, 1982). In the short reactions used in vocal response experiments, both the minimal central nervous system processing required and the lifelong practice provided by daily speech may account for what appears to be differential age effects on the two different motor systems. The general slowing hypothesis (Birren, 1965), which is based on a model of neurochemical changes that are diffuse in the brain, provides no basis on which to propose that the vocal motor system might be spared the effects of this general mechanism. Nevertheless, the issue should be further studied. Vocal responses may be the most highly practiced motor responses that individuals ever make, and as is discussed next, extensive practice can substantially reduce age differences. Within this perspective, vocal reaction time experiments could play an important role in clarifying the interaction of aging and practice on motor responses.

C. Factors that Minimize Age Differences in Psychomotor Speed

1. Practice Effects

In laboratory tests of psychomotor speed, subjects of all ages improve dramatically with practice. Practice reduces novelty, and novelty is well known to have a more negative impact on the performance of older rather than younger subjects. Murrell's (1970) analysis of the effects of huge numbers of trials (20,000) on the reaction time of three secretaries, two 17 to 18 years old and one 57 years old, indicated that at least in one subject's case, although it took the 57-year-old 300 trials of practice, she eliminated the differences in her reaction time from that of the two younger females. Most investigators, however, have not been successful in completely deleting age differences in psychomotor speed with practice. Hertzog, Williams, and Walsh (1976) reported that age differences remained stable throughout practice over a 5-day period. Salthouse (1985) reviewed six other studies, including his own, that failed to eliminate significant age differences through extensive practice. Lowe and Spirduso (1988) found that young subjects, unlike old subjects, were able, with 1 day of practice, to program a more complex response as quickly as the simple response. In fact, after two additional days of practice, the old continued to respond significantly slower on the complex task. They hypothesized that one of the functions of practice that is lost to older subjects is the ability to bypass a stage of processing. One effect of extended

practice may be to reduce the age-by-complexity interaction so that the disproportionately longer response times of older individuals in tasks requiring more complex processing are shortened. This effect has not been extensively studied in response time literature but has been suggested by the research results of Falduto and Baron (1986).

The effects of laboratory practice are, however, totally unlike the effects of practice in daily activities. Salthouse (1984) correctly emphasized that the effects of years of practice cannot be overestimated. He calculated that an experienced typist would produce as many keystrokes in 17 minutes of 60-wpm typing on the job as he or she would in 5,000 choice reaction time trials in a research study. Previewing letters and words in advance, which he described as an anticipatory processing phenomenon (Salthouse, 1988), enabled the older individuals in his studies to perform as fast as young individuals. Although these old individuals were 80 to 150 milliseconds slower than young subjects in choice reaction time laboratory tests, the analogous interkey reaction times that occur in the typing of experienced typists was nearly identical to that of 20-year-olds. In their 1982a paper, Salthouse and Somberg found that even though they provided older individuals 50 hours of practice over a 10-week period on a variety of perceptual motor laboratory tasks, age differences remained. His admonition deserves repeating: "A dramatic discrepancy therefore clearly exists between the results of traditional laboratory tasks and the performance of the real-life activity of typing" (Salthouse, 1984, p. 369).

Several investigators have observed that the overpractice that occurs in activities of daily living appears to retard age-related deterioration of physical performance. Years ago, Murrell, Powesland, and Forsaith (1962) showed that older middle-aged men (44 to 60 years) with years of work experience in a motor skill can perform as well as young experienced men (20 to 33) and better than naive young men on an occupational motor skill with light physical demands. Men whose occupations included skills similar to copying digits maintained higher speeds of copying performance into the seventh decade than those whose jobs called for little or no copying skills (LaRiviere & Simonson, 1965). In spite of several experimental design problems in both of these studies, the results suggest that as individuals age, with practice a multitude of compensatory mechanisms can be developed that result in little observable difference in some types of skilled performance of older and younger individuals. Stones and Kozma (1989) provided stronger evidence that the overpracticing of daily activity retards aging effects on psychomotor performance. They compared young and old subjects on a psychomotor task that is highly related to aging (number of taps that can be made in 30 seconds), requiring task performance by using hands or feet. Tapping with the feet incorporated movements not unlike those made during normal locomotion, whereas tapping with the hands was an unfamilar task. The familar age effects were observed to be robust in the data from hand tapping, but no age effects were evident in the foot-tapping data. They concluded that "overpracticed movement is more resistant to deleterious aging effects than its less familiar forms" (Stones & Kozma, 1989, p. 314).

2. Predictability

Uncertainty in testing situations increases the difference between young and old performances. Choice reaction time paradigms produce slower reactions than simple reaction time tests partly because choice adds the element of uncertainty. Plude et al. (1982) reported that uncertainty contributes more to differential age-related slowing of responses than does the complexity of the movement to be made.

Old subjects were tested for 2 days under conditions where the target set was predictable. They were not significantly slower than the young subjects in initiating either a simple or a complex movement. The age difference in movement complexity did not disappear with practice, however, when the target sets were unpredictable.

3. Physical Fitness Level

The strong negative relationship between age and speed of reactive response in adults has, with few exceptions, been established with randomly sampled, average men and women. The health and physical fitness of a random sample of average individuals, however, is generally moderate to low (Adams & deVries, 1970, 1973; Shephard, 1978). More importantly, just as the proportion of vigorously physically active 70-year-old individuals is dramatically smaller than the proportion of active 20-year-olds (Ostrow, 1984), the proportion of healthy and physically fit individuals within each sample decade grows smaller with each increasing decade (Speith, 1964). Consequently, a comparison of the psychomotor speed of 20-year-olds with 70-year-olds is not just a comparison of young and old individuals, it is also a comparison of individuals who have drastically different levels of health, physical fitness, nutrition, and a host of other factors. In 1975, Spirduso reported that a subject group of men older than 60 years who had maintained their physical fitness by adhering to a life-style of aerobic training (jogging), were not significantly slower in simple and choice reaction time than college sophomores. Since that time, many investigators have replicated her findings (see Spirduso, 1987, for review) and extended them to female samples (Rikli & Busch, 1986; Spirduso, MacRae, MacRae, Prewitt, & Osborne, 1988). Although a few investigators failed to find improved reactivity with an exercise intervention design

(Barry, Steinmetz, Page, & Rodahl, 1966), many have found that older individuals who complete at least a 4-month exercise program and achieve significant increases in their aerobic endurance also improve their performance on psychomotor behaviors (Dustman, Ruhling, Russell, Shearer, Bonekat, Shigeoka, Woods, & Bradford, 1984).

The relationship of physical fitness to faster response has been found in all components of the psychomotor response. The premotor latencies of older physically fit men and women are shorter than those of sedentary individuals (Baylor & Spirduso, 1988; Clarkson, 1978; Hart, 1981; MacRae, Crum, Giessman, Greene, & Ugolini, 1988). Contractile times, however, are only significantly shorter in physically fit individuals if the limb used to react is also the limb primarily involved in the exercise used to develop fitness. That is, Baylor and Spirduso (1988), who employed a kicking motion as the reacting limb, found that contractile time of older women runners was significantly faster than that of their sedentary counterparts. MacRae *et al.* (1988) found that the contractile time in an elbow flexion/extension task in older women runners was not significantly faster than that in older sedentary women.

4. General versus Moderator Effects of Physical Activity

Although the relationship between physical fitness and speed of response is quite robust in older individuals, the interaction between age, fitness, and reactive speed remains unclear. Stones and Kozma (1988) proposed two models to explain the putative effect of exercise on reaction time. The first model they described as a "tonic and overpractice effect" model (TOPE), in which exercise has an age-invariant, invigorating, tonic effect, coupled with the overpractice effect that occurs with daily physical activity that is generalized across physical and psychological domains. In this model, putative exercise effects would affect individuals similarly at all ages. The model would be valid if age-by-exercise interaction terms in research studies were nonsignificant.

Mechanisms by which this model might operate would be exercise-induced regional blood flow changes, trophic influences of neuromuscular activity, biochemical modulations, and morphological changes that are seen in both young and old and in both cross-sectional and longitudinal research designs (see MacRae, 1989; Spirduso, 1975; Spirduso *et al.*, 1988, for review). Several researchers have reported nonsignificant age-by-exercise results (Dustman *et al.*, 1984; Stacey, Kozma, & Stones, 1985; Stones & Kozma, 1989; Vanfraechem & Vanfraechem, 1977). If this model is valid, it might also be expected that researchers would find more robust tonic effects in dependent variables that more discretely measure central nervous system integrity than in choice reaction time or other psychomotor tasks where more complex processing is required and more additional factors act upon the dependent variable.

The second model described by Stones and Kozma (1989) is the "moderator effects" model, which states that exercise moderates the rate of aging. If this model is valid, exercise programs would affect old people more than young, and age-by-exercise interaction terms seen in the literature would be statistically significant. This model presupposes that functional deterioration with age is postponed by exercise. It is known that physical inactivity contributes approximately 50% to the functional deterioration of physical work capacity. This model suggests that physical inactivity contributes substantially to the deterioration of central nervous system processing as well. In their meta-analysis of studies of age, physical fitness, and reaction time, Stones and Kozma found that only 5 of the 15 studies reported a significant interaction between age and exercise. At the moment, the weight of the evidence seems to support the TOPE model, which predicts that exercise effects probably occur for all ages. However, because older individuals are operating at a lower functional level, they may have more to gain by exercise-related improvements in central nervous system processing than do young individuals. That is, similar proportional improvements in reaction time may have more functional significance for older people because older people are operating at a much slower speed than young.

A third possibility cannot be completely ruled out—the selection factor that holds that people who exercise throughout their lives are inherently healthier and/or physically superior to those who do not exercise. These individuals may have been faster in reactivity all their lives, and the observation that they are faster as 60- and 70-year-olds should be attributed to some more indirect factors that may be related only indirectly to physical fitness. Intervention studies (e.g., Dustman et al., 1984) provide some evidence to refute this possibility, and the animal intervention experiment reported by Spirduso and Farrar (1981) also argues against the subject selection hypothesis.

V. Conclusion

It is important when discussing aging effects on performance to remember that the effects are different for different systems of the body, for different individuals, and for different tasks. It is known that at least one component of the cardiovascular system (maximum heart rate) declines in the active older adult, whereas another (stroke volume) does not. Muscle mass decreases, but there is little evidence that significant changes occur in the muscle fibers of older active adults. Some aspects of psychomotor function, such as long-term memory are maintained, whereas others, such as

encoding and response selection deteriorate. Though many motor task performances decline with aging, some (e.g., typing speed) can be performed just as effectively by 60-year-olds as by 20-year-olds.

Because relatively few studies of muscular strength have been conducted on old subjects, the amount of neural and muscular plasticity that can occur with training, as well as the stimulus parameters necessary to produce it, is not fully characterized. In almost all studies, the number of subjects in the oldest decades is very small, the subjects are generally not randomly selected, and the way they are treated by the experimenter is somewhat different than the way 20-year-olds are treated. Similarly, so few old individuals participate in strength and power athletic events that the records must surely underestimate the upper limits of human strength and power in the seventh, eighth, and ninth decades. Consequently, much research remains to be done to document and understand human strength and power capabilities in the older decades, Not only would it be informative and utilitarian from a health and physical fitness perspective to know the upper limits, but it would be extremely useful to know the contribution that different levels of muscular strength and power might make toward the prevention of injuries, accidents, and fatalities in the very old. One might envision a time when a taxonomy of strength, endurance, and power effects on work skills in the 40-, 50-, and 60-year-olds, and on the health, fitness, and well being of 70-, 80-, and 90-year-olds, might be available.

The extant research on compatibility and complexity of stimuli and appropriate motor responses in older individuals suggests that these parameters interact substantially with aging, but present knowledge of the extent and nature of this interaction is rudimentary. These factors not only affect response speed, but they can affect coordination, which is known to deteriorate with aging. Future research is needed not only on how compatibility and complexity interact to impact motor skill in older individuals but on how factors such as stimulus quality, compatibility, performance expectations, and practice can be utilized to maintain and upgrade the psychomotor performance of late-middle-aged and older persons.

Exercise and physical activity play an important role in the maintenance of physical strength, endurance, and work capacity of older individuals and also appear to have a beneficial relationship to some types of mental functions. Because some type of exercise and physical activity is accessible to almost everyone, and many of the ways to exercise are inexpensive, research regarding the characteristics of the exercise–psychomotor–mental relationships and the mechanisms by which exercise contributes to these relationships should have a high priority.

The motor performance of aging adults is of substantial importance, not only to the psychological and physical well-being of individuals, but to the society to which they contribute and upon which they depend. Knowledge of motor performance capabilities of the older adult influences many aspects of life; for example, health insurance policies, age discrimination considerations, work site regulations, and architectural design of living and working environments. A greater understanding of normal and maximal physical and psychomotor capabilities of different aged individuals will enable society to develop reasonable expectations for performance and to provide guidelines for achieving these expectations.

References

Adams, G. M., & deVries, H. A. (1970). Physiological effects of an exercise training regimen upon men aged 52–88. *Journal of Gerontology*, **25**, 325–336.

Adams, G. M., & deVries, H. A. (1973). Physiological effects of an exercise training regimen upon women aged 52–79. *Journal of Gerontology*, **28**, 50–55.

Aniansson, A., Sperling, L., Rundgren, A., & Lehnberg, E. (1983). Muscle function in 75-year-old men and women, a longitudinal study. *Scandinavian Journal of Rehabilitation Medicine* (Suppl.), **193**, 92–102.

Astrand, I., Astrand, P. O., Hallback, I., & Kilbom, A. (1973). Reduction in maximal oxygen uptake with age. *Journal of Applied Physiology*, **35**, 649–654.

Barry, A. J., Steinmetz, J. R., Page, H. F., & Rodahl, K. (1966). The effects of physical conditioning on older individuals. II. Motor performance and cognitive function. *Journal of Gerontology*, **21**, 182–191.

Baylor, A. M., & Spirduso, W. W. (1988). Systematic aerobic exercise and components of reaction time in older women. *Journal of Gerontology*, **43**, P121–126.

Birren, J. E. (1965). Age changes in speeded behavior: Its central nature and physiological correlates. In A. T. Welford & J. E. Birren (Eds.), *Behavior, aging, and the nervous system*. Springfield, IL: Thomas.

Birren, J. E., Woods, A. M., & Williams, M. V. (1980). Behavioral slowing with age: Causes, organization and consequences. In L. W. Poon (Ed.), *Aging in the 1980s: Psychological issues*. Washington, DC: American Psychological Association.

Borkan, G. A., & Norris, A. H. (1980). Assessment of biological age using a profile of physical parameters. *Journal of Experimental Psychology*, **35**, 177–184.

Botwinick, J. (1984). *Aging and behavior* (3rd ed.). New York: Springer.

Burke, W. E., Tuttle, W. W., Thompson, C. W., Janney, C. D., & Weber, R. J. (1953). Relation of grip strength and grip-strength endurance to age. *Journal of Applied Physiology*, **5**, 628–630.

Cerella, J., Poon, L. W., & Williams, D. M. (1980). Age and the complexity hypothesis. In L. W. Poon (Ed.), *Aging in the 1980s: Psychological issues*. Washington, DC: American Psychological Association.

Chiarello, C., Church, K. L., & Hoyers, W. J. (1985). Automatic and controlled semantic priming: Accuracy, response, bias, and aging. *Journal of Gerontology*, **40**, 593–600.

Clarkson, P. (1978). The effect of age and activity level on simple and choice fractionated response time. *European Journal of Applied Physiology, 40,* 17–25.

Cunningham, D. A., Morrison, D., Rice, C. L., & Cooke, C. (1987). Ageing and isokinetic plantar flexion. *European Journal of Applied Physiology, 56,* 24–29.

Dehn, M. M., & Bruce, R. A. (1972). Longitudinal variations in maximal oxygen intake with age and activity. *Journal of Applied Physiology, 33,* 805–807.

Dummer, G. M., Clark, D. H., Vaccaro, P., Vander Velden, L., Goldfare, A. H., & Sockler, J. M. (1985). Age-related differences in muscular strength and muscular endurance among female masters swimmers. *Research Quarterly for Exercise and Sport, 56,* 97–110.

Dustman, R. E., Ruhling, R. O., Russell, E. M., Shearer, D. E., Bonekat, W., Shigeoka, J. W., Wood, J. S., & Bradford, D. C. (1984). Aerobic exercise training and improved neuropsychological function of older individuals. *Neurobiology of Aging, 5,* 35–42.

Falduto, L. L., & Baron, A. (1986). Age-related effects of practice and task complexity on card sorting. *Journal of Gerontology, 41,* 659–661.

Fisher, M. B., & Birren, J. E. (1947). Age and strength. *Journal of Applied Psychology, 31,* 490–497.

Fitts, P. M. (1959). Human information handling in speeded tasks. *IBM Research Report,* RC-109, 29.

Frontera, W. R., Meredith, C. N., O'Reilly, K. P., Knuttgen, H. G., & Evans, W. J. (1988). Strength conditioning in older men: Skeletal muscle hypertrophy and improved function. *Journal of Applied Physiology, 64,* 1038–1044.

Goldspink, G., & Howells, K. F. (1974). Work-induced hypertrophy in exercised normal muscles of different ages and the reversibility of hypertrophy after cessation of exercise. *Journal of Physiology, 239,* 179–193.

Gottsdanker, R. (1982). Age and simple reaction time. *Journal of Gerontology, 37,* 342–348.

Green, H. J. (1986). Characteristics of aging human skeletal muscles. In J. R. Sutton & R. M. Brock (Eds.), *Sports medicine for the mature athlete* (pp. 17–26). Indianapolis: Benchmark Press.

Griew, S. (1959). Complexity of response and time of initiating responses in relation to age. *American Journal of Psychology, 72,* 83–88.

Hale, S., Myerson, J., & Wagstaff, D. (1987). General slowing of nonverbal information processing: Evidence for a power law. *Journal of Gerontology, 42,* 131–136.

Hart, B. A. (1981). The effect of age and habitual activity on the fractionated components of resisted and unresisted response time. *Medicine and Science in Sports and Exercise, 13,* 78.

Heath, G. W., Hagberg, J. M., Ehsani, A. A., & Holloszy, J. O. (1981). A physiological comparison of young and older endurance athletes. *Journal of Applied Physiology, 51,* 634–640.

Henry, F. M., & Rogers, D. E. (1960). Increased response latency for complicated movements and a "memory drum" theory of neuromotor reaction. *Research Quarterly, 31,* 448–458.

Hertzog, C., Williams, M., & Walsh, D. (1976). The effect of practice on age differences in central perceptual processing. *Journal of Gerontology, 31,* 428–433.

Hines, T., Poon, L. N., Cerella, J., & Fozard, J. L. (1982). Age related differences in the time course of encoding. *Experimental Aging Research, 8,* 175–178.

Jordan, T. C., & Rabbitt, P. M. A. (1977). Response times to stimuli of increasing complexity as a function of ageing. *British Journal of Psychology, 68,* 189–201.

Kasch, F. W., Wallace, J. P., & Van Camp, S. P. (1985). Effects of 18 years of endurance exercise on the physical work capacity of older men. *Journal of Cardiopulmonary Rehabilitation, 5,* 308–312.

Kornblum, S. (1965). Response competition and/or inhibition in two choice reaction time. *Psychonomic Science, 2,* 55–56.

Kovar, M. G., & LaCroix, A. Z. (1987). Aging in the eighties, ability to perform work-related activities. *National Center for Health Statistics Advance Data, 136,* 1–12.

Larish, D. D., & Stelmach, G. E. (1982). Preprogramming, programming, and reprogramming of aimed hand movements as a function of age. *Journal of Motor Behavior, 14,* 322–340.

LaRiviere, J. E., & Simonson, E. (1965). The effect of age and occupation on speed of writing. *Journal of Gerontology, 20,* 415–416.

Larsson, L. (1978). Morphological and functional characteristics of the ageing skeletal muscle in man. *Acta Physiologica Scandinavia* (Suppl.), **457**, 1–29.

Larsson, L., Grimby, G., & Karlsson, J. (1979). Muscle strength and speed of movement in relation to age and muscle morphology. *Journal of Applied Physiology*, **46**, 451–456.

Larsson, L., & Karlsson, J. (1978). Isometric and dynamic endurance as a function of age and skeletal muscle characteristics. *Acta Physiologica Scandinavica*, **104**, 129–136.

Light, K. (1989a). Effects of adult aging on the movement complexity factor of response programming. *Journal of Gerontology*, submitted.

Light, K. (1989b). Effects of adult aging on response-response compatibility. *Journal of Gerontology*, submitted.

Lowe, D., & Spirduso, W. W. (unpublished data). *Differences in short and long term memory for response selection and programming in young and elderly women.*

MacRae, P. G. (1989). Physical activity and central nervous system integrity. In H. M. Eckert & W. W. Spirduso (Eds.), *Physical activity and the older adult*. Champaign, IL: Human Kinetics Publishers (in press).

MacRae, P., Crum, K., Giessman, D., Greene, J., & Ugolini, J. (unpublished). *Fractionated reaction time responses in women as a function of age and fitness.*

McArdle, W. D., Katch, F. I., & Katch, V. L. (1986). *Exercise physiology*, Philadelphia: Lea & Febiger.

Medicine and Science in Sports and Exercise (1987). Age as a criterion for work performance. **19**, 157–185.

Montoye, H. J., & Lamphiear, D. E. (1977). Grip and arm strength in males and females, ages 10–69. *Research Quarterly*, **48**, 109–120.

Moore, D. H. (1975). A study of age group track and field records to relate age and running speed. *Nature (London)* **253**, 264–265.

Moritani, T., & deVries, H. A. (1980). Potential for gross muscle hypertrophy in older men. *Journal of Gerontology*, **35**, 672–682.

Murray, M. P., Duthie, E. H., Gambert, S. R., Sepic, S. B., & Mollinger, L. A. (1985). Age-related differences in knee muscle strength in normal women. *Journal of Gerontology*, **40**, 275–280.

Murray, M. P., Gardner, G. M., Mollinger, L. A., & Sepic, S. B. (1980). Strength of isometric and isokinetic contractions. *Physical Therapy*, **60**, 412–419.

Murrell, F. H. (1970). The effect of extensive practice on age differences in reaction time. *Journal of Gerontology*, **25**, 268–274.

Murrell, K. F. H., Powesland, P. F., & Forsaith, B. (1962). A study of pillar-drilling in relation to age. *Occupational Psychology*, **36**, 45–52.

Nebes, R. D. (1978). Vocal versus manual response as a determinant of age difference in simple reaction time. *Journal of Gerontology*, **33**, 884–889.

Norris, A. H., & Shock, N. W. (1960). Exercise in the adult years—with special reference to the advanced years. In W. R. Johnson & E. R. Buskirk (Eds.), *Science and medicine of exercise and sports* (pp. 466–492). New York: Harper.

Osborne, L. (1986). *The effects of age, modality and complexity of response, and practice on reaction time*. Unpublished master's thesis, University of Texas, Austin.

Ostrow, A. (1984). *Physical activity in the older adult*. Princeton, NJ: Princeton Book Company.

Petrofsky, J. S., & Lind, A. R. (1975). Aging, isometric strength and endurance, and cardiovascular responses to static effort. *Journal of Applied Physiology*, **38**, 91–95.

Plude, D. J., Hoyer, W. J., & Lazar, J. (1982). Age, response complexity, and target consistency in visual search. *Experimental Aging Research*, **8**, 99–102.

Pollock, M. L., Foster, C., Knapp, E., Rod, J. L., & Schmidt, D. H. (1987). Effect of age and training on aerobic capacity and body composition of master athletes. *Journal of Applied Physiology*, **62**, 725–731.

Rabbitt, P. M. A. (1980). A fresh look at changes in reaction time in old age. In D. G. Stein (Ed.), *The psychobiology of aging: Problems and perspectives* (pp. 425–445). New York: Elsevier.

Riegel, P. S. (1981). Athletic records and human endurance. *American Scientist*, **69**, 285–290.

Rikli, R., & Busch, S. (1986). Motor performance of women as a function of age and physical activity level. *Journal of Gerontology*, **41**, 645–649.

Robinson, S. (1938). Experimental studies of physical fitness in relation to age. *Arbeitsphysiologie*, **10**, 251–323.

Salthouse, T. A. (1984). Effects of age and skill

in typing. *Journal of Gerontology*, **113**, 345–371.

Salthouse, T. A. (1985). Speed of behavior and its implications for cognition. In J. E. Birren & K. W. Schaie (Eds.). *Handbook of the psychology of aging* (pp. 400–426). New York: Van Nostrand Reinhold.

Salthouse, T. A. (1988). Cognitive aspects of motor functioning. In J. A. Joseph (Ed.), *Central determinants of age-related declines in motor function* (pp. 33–41). New York: New York Academy of Sciences.

Salthouse, T. A., & Somberg, B. L. (1982a). Skill performance: Effects of adult age and experience on elementary processes. *Journal of Experimental Psychology: General*, **111**, 176–207.

Salthouse, T. A., & Somberg, B. L. (1982b). Isolating the age deficit in speeded performance. *Journal of Gerontology*, **37**, 59–63.

Schmidt, R. A. (1981). *Motor control and learning*. Champaign-Urbana, IL: Human Kinetics.

Schulz, R., & Curnow, C. (1988). Peak performance and age among superathletes: Track and field, swimming, baseball, tennis, and golf. *Journal of Gerontology*, **43**, 113–120.

Shephard, R. J. (1978). *Physical activity and aging*. London: Croom Helm.

Simon, J. R., & Pouraghabagher, A. R. (1978). The effect of aging on the stages of processing in a choice reaction time task. *Journal of Gerontology*, **33**, 553–561.

Speith, W. (1964). Cardiovascular health status, age, and psychological performance. *Journal of Gerontology*, **19**, 277–284.

Spirduso, W. W. (1975). Reaction and movement time as a function of age and physical activity level. *Journal of Gerontology*, **30**, 435–440.

Spirduso, W. W. (1987). Physical activity and the prevention of premature aging. In V. Seefeldt (Ed.), *Physical activity and well-being* (pp. 142–160). Reston, VA: American Association for Health, Physical Education, Recreation and Dance.

Spirduso, W. W., & Farrar, R. P. (1981). Effects of aerobic training on reactive capacity: An animal model. *Journal of Gerontology*, **35**, 654–662.

Spirduso, W. W., MacRae, H., MacRae, P. G., Prewitt, J., & Osborne, L. (1988). Exercise effects on aged motor function. *Annals of the New York Academy of Sciences*, **515**, 363–375.

Sprott, R. L. (1988). Age-related variability. In J. A. Joseph (Ed.), *Central determinants of age-related declines in motor function* (Vol. 515, pp. 42–51). New York: New York Academy of Sciences.

Stacey, C., Kozma, A., & Stones, M. J. (1985). Simple cognitive and behavioral changes resulting from improved physical fitness in persons over 50 years of age. *Canadian Journal of Aging*, **4**, 67–73.

Stones, M. J., & Kozma, A. (1982). Cross-sectional, longitudinal, and secular age trends in athletic performance. *Experimental Aging Research*, **8**, 185–188.

Stones, M. J., & Kozma, A. (1989). Physical activity, age and cognitive/motor performance. In M. L. Howe & C. J. Brainerd (Eds.), *Cognitive development in adulthood: Progress in cognitive development research*. New York: Springer.

Thomas, J. C., Waugh, N. C., & Fozard, J. L. (1978). Age and familiarity in memory scanning. *Journal of Gerontology*, **33**, 528–533.

Tolin, P., & Simon, J. R. (1968). Effect of task complexity and stimulus duration on perceptual motor performance of two desparate age groups. *Ergonomics*, **11**, 283–290.

Tomanek, R. J., & Wood, Y. K. (1970). Compensatory hypertrophy of the plantaris muscle in relation to age. *Journal of Gerontology*, **25**, 23–29.

Vanfraechem, A., & Vanfraechem, R. (1977). Studies of the effect of a short training period on aged subjects. *Journal of Sports Medicine and Physical Fitness*, **17**, 373–380.

Welford, A. T. (1965). Performance, biological mechanisms and age: A theoretical sketch. In A. T. Welford & J. E. Birren (Eds.), *Behavior, aging and the nervous system*. (1–23) Springfield, IL: Thomas.

Welford, A. T. (1968). *Fundamentals of skill*. London: Methuen.

Welford, A. T. (1977). Motor performance. In J. E. Birren & K. W. Schaie (Eds.), *Handbook of the psychology of aging*. New York: Van Nostrand Reinhold.

World Alamanac (1987). New York: Newspaper Enterprises Association.

Young, A., Stokes, M., & Crowe, M. (1984). Size and strength of the quadriceps muscles of old and young women. *European Journal of Clinical Investigation*, **14**, 282–287.

Twelve

Aging and Information-Processing Rate

John Cerella

Like as the waves make towards the pebbled shore,
So do our minutes hasten to their end,
Each changing place with that which goes before,
In sequent toil all forwards do contend.

SHAKESPEARE, SONNET 60

I. Introduction

A handbook chapter typically attempts to convey the recent theory and data in its area. This charge is only half met in the present case. A body of recent theory is covered, so recent that many citations are to manuscripts and proceedings. The data, however, are not so recent. The new theories have been applied to old data; upwards of 1,000 observations culled from published studies dating back several decades. Each of these observations has the same format, the mean latency of some information-processing task performed by adult subjects of several ages.

Accompanying the data in the original literature are countless "focused" accounts of the age deficits they harbor, tied to the particular information-processing stages engaged by the tasks. The achievement of the new theoretical work has been the characterization of the entire spectrum of age effects in a few broad strokes, replacing the piecemeal explanations of the past. The work sprang from two key ideas. One was the realization, given its fullest form by Salthouse's massive 1985 compendium, that age deficits could be interpreted as being distributed throughout the information-processing system rather than being localized in particular stages. References to task content could thereby be eliminated; deficits were tied to the amount, not the type, of the information processing. The *generalized slowing hypothesis*, as this interpretation was called, represented the data fairly well but was limited in its theoretical productiveness. The one "model" it suggested was of a

Handbook of the Psychology of Aging, Third Edition
Copyright © 1990 Academic Press, Inc. All rights of reproduction in any form reserved.

microcomputer whose cycle time was increasing. This recurrent metaphor simply did not lead to new insights.

The second key idea is in the process of reshaping cognitive psychology. It is the attempt, given its fullest form by the two volumes of McClelland and Rumelhart (1986) to interpret cognition as a computation on a neural network, rather than as a succession of information-processing stages. This idea combines with the preceding idea in a natural way: *The new aging theories view age deficits as defects of some sort distributed throughout a neural network of some sort.*

In the work to be surveyed, this barebones recipe will be fleshed out in a variety of ways. We will begin with what was chronologically the first of these variations, a model of striking simplicity that describes with great economy some of the classic effects of age on information-processing latencies. The model will be developed and its successes noted. At the same time, many of its descriptions will be shown to be only approximately correct. We will go on to outline a second generation of models spawned by the failures of the first. Gains in accuracy will be noted, as well as some loss in coherency.

II. Aging in a Neural Network

The reference model (Cerella & Poon, 1983; Greene, 1983) represents the brain as a neural network composed of links and nodes. A cognitive process is represented by the propagation of a signal from the input end of the network to the output end (the intervening logic is left for the connection theorists to elaborate). Each step through the network takes a fixed quantum of time (μ). Given that a stimulus has been impressed on the input nodes, the "reaction time" or latency (L) of the network is simply the time required for the signal to reach an output node. This time is given by the number of links (N) that

must be traversed times the delay per link, or in equation form, $L = \mu N$.

Aging is defined as a destructive process that breaks links at random with a constant probability (k) over time. A signal must step around broken links in its path, as illustrated in Figure 1. Each detour increases the path length by exactly one step, adding μ time to the final latency. For now we assume that alternate routes are always available when needed.

From this simple formulation, two classic patterns of data can be derived. First, consider the performance of the network at a fixed point in time, such as age 70. A fixed portion of links (p) will be intact, and the complimentary portion $1 - p$ will be broken. Signal transmission will require N direct steps plus $(1 - p)N$ detour steps. A portion $1 - p$ of the detour steps will themselves have to be rerouted because the desired links are not in place, adding $(1 - p)((1 - p)N)$ additional detour steps. A similar fraction of these second order detours will necessitate third order detours, and so on, leading to an overall latency in the aged network:

$$L_{\text{aged}} = \mu N + (1 - p)\mu N$$
$$+ (1 - p)(1 - p)\mu N$$
$$+ (1 - p)(1 - p)(1 - p)\mu N \ldots .$$

The series sums to:

$$L_{\text{aged}} = (1/p)\mu N = (1/p)L_{\text{intact}}, \quad (1)$$

where L_{intact} refers to the latency of the network with all links intact—what we will call the *young* latency.

Equation 1 asserts that the latencies of a degraded network will be a constant multiple of those of an intact network, regardless of the cognitive processes involved. Supposing, for example, $p = 2/3$ of the links are preserved at age 70, Equation 1 shows old latencies equal to $1/p = 3/2$, or 1.5 times, young latencies. This coincides with the prediction of the generalized slowing hypothesis, a generalization widely supported by the data (Salthouse, 1985).

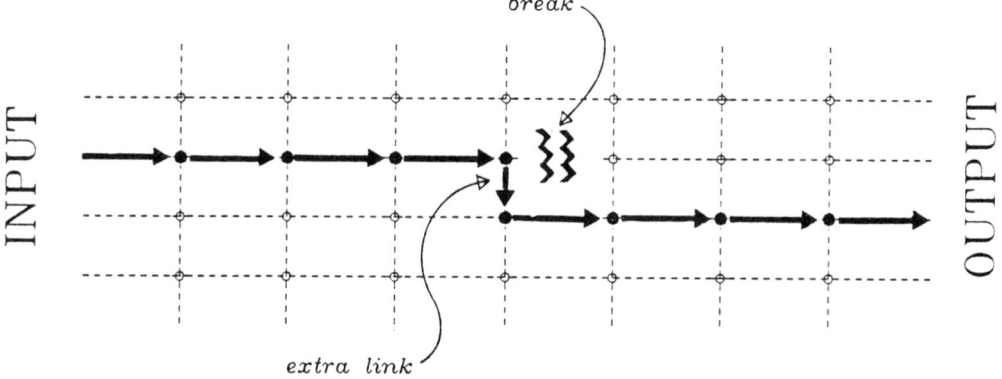

Figure 1 Schematic neural network; nodes represent neurons and dotted lines axon connections between neurons. The illustrated network performs no computation, merely transmits signal from left to right. Latency is determined by the number of links, eight in the "intact" network. However one link on the optimal route is broken, forcing the signal to detour and adding one more link to the path for a total of nine. Progressive loss of connectivity in a schematic network matches quantitatively the increase in information-processing latencies observed in elderly subjects.

Consider now how the latency of the network changes as it ages. The hazard rate k is constant over the life span, but the defects it gives rise to accumulate. As a consequence, the proportion of unaltered links p is a negatively accelerated function of network age (a) given by $p(a) = exp(-ka)$, the same equation that governs the decay of atoms in a radioactive sample. Substituting for p in Equation 1 gives the second classical result:

$$L(a) = exp(ka)L_{intact}, \qquad (2)$$

an exponential decline of functionality with age, characteristic of the data on sensory functions collected many decades ago and surveyed by Weiss (1959).

Equation 2 has extraordinary scope; it describes the processing time of the network for any task and for any age, based on a single parameter, the neural decay rate k. These processing times are illustrated in the two-dimensional surface of Figure 6. In the next two sections, we will consider the goodness of fit of the model to the data along each dimension of Figure 6 separately: latency as a function of age (with task fixed) and latency as a function of task (with age fixed).

III. Latency as a Function of Age

Exponential declines have been called "classical," but the actual data take many forms. The full function relating mental competence to age, say from age 5 to age 95, is rarely seen and is invariably U-shaped, reflecting processes of maturation at one end and senescence at the other. Gerontological research has focused on the second leg, starting at age 20 or so, and in an unpublished survey 40 such data sets were abstracted from the literature, requiring only that at least four age groups be represented so that second order polynomial fits could be assessed. The data sets all measured cognitive functioning, as opposed to sensory or motor functioning, but only 23 reported processing times. Fortunately this subset illustrates the varieties of the whole and is presented in Figure 2. Each data set derives from a different information-processing task, but each has been normalized by dividing by the young adult latency, thereby eliminating task duration as a factor in the analysis. Data sets have all been shifted to start the young adults at age zero and have been offset vertically in the figure for clarity.

Our approach to these data will be casu-

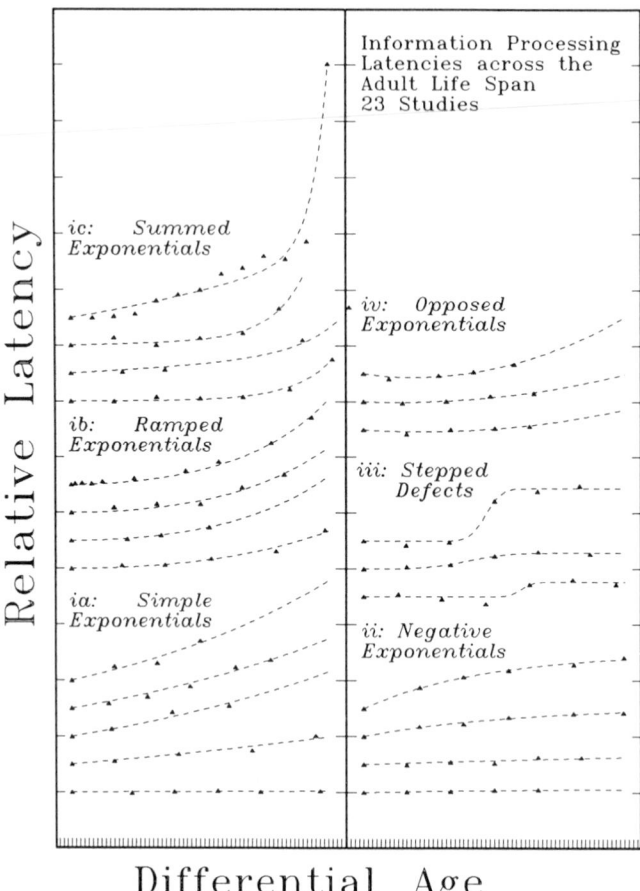

Figure 2 Information-processing latencies as a function of age. Data from 23 published studies on a variety of information-processing tasks. Each point is the mean of a group of same-aged subjects. Data have been normalized on the abscissa by subtracting the age of the youngest subject group in a study (typically 20 years old) from the age of every subject group in the study (20-year-olds show as zero, 80-year-olds show as 60). Tics are in units of years. Data have been normalized on the ordinate twice, first by dividing the latency of every subject group in a study by the latency of the youngest subject group in the study (20-year-olds show a latency of 1.0, 80-year-olds would show a latency of 1.5 if they were 50% slower), and second by offsetting every study an arbitrary amount for clarity. Tics are in units of 100% slowing. Studies were divided into six sets, each set was fitted by a different theoretical equation (dotted curves). Sets *ia* and *ib* instance the network model of Figure 1.

al, each set being fitted to a one-, two-, or three-parameter equation whose form struck the present author as characteristic of the data. Given this latitude, good fits are to be expected; the mean variance ac- counted for over the 23 data sets was 92%. The traces are a heterogeneous lot, and a variety of theoretical notions will be needed to make sense of this or that in the context of network models.

A. Positively Accelerated Functions

Figure 2 is divided into six zones according to the equation chosen for one or another data set. The curves of zones *ia*, *ib*, and *ic* are positively accelerated, the only form allowed by the basic model. Zones *ii*, *iii*, and *iv* obviously challenge the adequacy of the basic model. The situation is worse; the variation in curvature within zone *i* also challenges the model. Only the shallow curves of zone *ia* are simple exponentials, $L(a) = exp(ka)$ [the L_{intact} term in Equation 2 no longer appears because we have divided through by this value, expressing $L(a)$ relative to the young latency rather than absolutely in msecs]. The rapidly rising data of zones *ib* and *ic* can only be fit by more rapidly accelerating equations.

One such equation follows from a natural extension of the basic model. The basic model makes the conservative assumption that the rate of neural degeneration k is constant over the life span. It may be physiologically more realistic (Cutler, 1982) to assume that the rate intensifies with age. The simplest embodiment of the latter assumption is a proportionality, $k(a) = k'a$. The term k' is a conversion factor that ties the breakage rate to the age of the network. Substituting the "ramp" $k'a$ for k in Equation 2 gives:

$$L(a) = exp[(k'a)a] = exp(k'a^2), \quad (3)$$

the equation used in zone *ib*. As expected, Equation 3 accelerates faster than Equation 2; simple exponentials cannot match the curvature of ramped exponentials.

Ramped exponentials fail in zone *ic* for the same reason that simple exponentials fail in zone *ib*; the data are too precipitous. The zone *ic* data increase gradually through middle age and turn sharply upward thereafter (around age 60 or 70). Confronted with data that do not conform to a one-process model, the standard approach of the physiologist is to attempt to fit a two-process model. The zone *ic* data yield gracefully to a two-process model:

$$L(a) = zexp(ra) + (1 - z)exp(sa), z<1 \quad (4)$$

Equation 4 represents $L(a)$ as the sum of two weighted exponentials. As fitted to the data, the first component has a small rate constant r and a large weight z; it dominates the sum through the middle decades. The second component has a large rate constant s and a small weight $1 - z$. Its effect is hardly felt in the middle decades but eventually overwhelms its weight to govern the whole in later decades.

Equation 4 suggests Cerella's (1985) description of a large number of middle and old-aged subject groups. A modest level of sensory motor slowing was observed in both middle-aged and old-aged samples (small r and large z), whereas an extreme level of cognitive slowing was observed in the old-aged samples alone (large s and small $1 - z$). This pattern cannot be modeled on the homogeneous network of Figure 1. A network differentiated into two regions, a cognitive core and a sensory motor fringe each with its own decay constant, does accommodate both Cerella's (1985) observations and Equation 4.

The data of zone *iv* are positively accelerated without being monotonic. They return us to the U-shaped functions we sought to sidestep by skipping over children and adolescents. One assumes at this stage that biological maturation is complete. Horn (1979) and Charness (1983) have suggested that we are witnessing, instead, psychological maturation, the acquisition of skill in early adulthood. Skill acquisition may be delineated, at least approximately (Mazur & Hastie, 1978), by a negative exponential function of time on the task, $exp(-ha)$. Horn and Charness also acknowledge biological decline, which we have represented by a positive exponential, $exp(ka)$. The observed latency might be determined by the algebraic sum of the two influences, one positive and the other negative:

$$L(a) = exp(ka) - exp(-ha) + 1. \quad (5)$$

This is the zone *iv* equation—it is indeed U-shaped: Early skill acquisition leads to improved performance through the third or fourth decade; in the decades beyond, skill level is overshadowed by the declining substrate.

Can skill be modeled on a simple network? Myerson (1987) has done just this by supposing that skill acts on the path length N of a network. As the computation is optimized, the number of steps involved diminishes; at the same time missing links add to the steps required. Zone *iv* may bear witness to the resulting interaction.

B. Negatively Accelerated Functions

Zone *ii* draws our attention to the curvature of the aging function, the difference between a deficit that grows frighteningly larger from decade to decade (positive curvature), or comfortingly smaller (negative curvature). The difference was pointed out by Talland (1965) who suggested that the curvature changed from positive to negative as task complexity was reduced.

A slight modification of the network model leads to a negatively accelerated aging function. We suppose that instead of breaking the link between two nodes, the aging process merely attenuates the link. The signal is not interrupted, but transit time on an attenuated link increases from μ time units to $h\mu$ time units, where the attenuation factor (h) is a constant somewhat greater than unity.

Network latency overall will be a mixture of μ-delays and $h\mu$-delays. At age a, a proportion $exp(-ka)$ of the links are intact and will each contribute a delay of μ, and the complimentary proportion $1 - exp(-ka)$ of links are attenuated and will each contribute a delay of $h\mu$. Total latency will be

$$L(a) = exp(-ka)\mu N + (1 - exp(-ka))h\mu N \text{ (absolute)},$$

$$L(a) = h + (1 - h)exp(-ka) \text{ (relative)}. \quad (6)$$

This was the equation used to fit zone *ii*. It describes a negatively accelerated curve that asymptotes at h—the deficit is bounded by this value. If aging involves a gradual conversion of fast neurons to slow neurons, then performance will decline as the neural population matures but will remain stable thereafter.

C. Inflected Functions

We are left with the most exotic zone, *iii*. The functional form is sigmoidal (I used a three parameter cumulative normal), such as relates sensory thresholds to stimulus intensity. Pursuing the psychophysical analogy, aging would be conceptualized as a step function, a single catastrophic event permanently altering brain function. Prior to the episode, a computation might involve process P; after the episode, process P would no longer be attainable; a less efficient process Q must be substituted. The sigmoid results from averaging over individuals with slightly different transition ages.

Two of the curves in zone *iii* derive from a figure–ground segmentation task. The network model blithely assumes that alternate routes are always available to circumvent broken links. Resnikoff (1989) argues that the brain is sparsely, not densely, connected. The figure–ground segmentation problem is one of the few known not to be computable on a locally connected network; the support set must be global (Minsky & Papert, 1988). In zone *iv*, we may be witnessing a more drastic consequence of a breakdown in connectivity than increased latencies; the computation may fail altogether (in its initial efficient form) because essential links are missing.

D. In Toto

Zones *ia*, *ib*, *ic*, *ii*, *iii*, and *iv* encompass many notions. Looking back, two impressions emerge. First, schematic neural networks are a rich modeling medium. Figure 1 has been cut and stretched in many directions; the perturbations have been more plausible than strained, and their issue has been a variety of useful behaviors. The next section introduces still further network modifications, again with plausible premises and gratifying conclusions.

A second impression is that a "complete" aging equation will be an intricate object. We have been offered not one equation but half a dozen equations, with no indication of which applies where. What is wanting at this stage is not more data, but further consideration of the existing data. Such consideration might take the form of a task analysis of the Figure 2 and other data sets, motivated by the stage-theoretic assumption that age effects vary with information processes. More in the spirit of this chapter would be a reanalysis of Figure 2 in absolute rather than relative latency units, motivated by the distributed-deficit assumption that age effects vary with the amount but not the kind of information processes.

IV. Latency as a Function of Task

Documenting the decade-by-decade change in a cognitive process is a major research effort. Most gerontological studies focus more modestly on two points of the function, describing performance at age 20 and at age 65 or 75. The body of data available in this format is so substantial that aging theory has more and more assumed the same focus. This development is due to Brinley (1965). He suggested that an "aging theory" could be regarded as a function (f) that captures numerically the relation between L_{yng} and L_{old},

$$L_{old} = f(T, L_{yng}),$$

given a collection of information-processing tasks $\{T\}$ for which latencies at age 20 $(L_{intact}$ or $L_{yng})$ and age 70 $(L_{aged}$ or $L_{old})$ were known. The theoretical goal is a

function that correctly describes the performance of the elderly subject given the performance of a young subject and/or the requirements of the task.

Brinley portrayed data in the latency space $L_{yng} \times L_{old}$. The actual measurements from a task appear as a point (L_{yng}, L_{old}) in this space, and the locus of points from a collection of tasks may serve to characterize f. Salthouse (1978) was the first to assemble an extensive set of data in these coordinates, followed by Cerella, Poon, and Williams (1980); the latter set comprised 94 information-processing conditions drawn from 14 published studies and is reproduced in Figure 3a. Both data sets were well described by a multiplicative function:

$$L_{old} = mL_{yng}. \qquad (7)$$

Task type does not enter the function, although the supporting data derive from mixed conditions. The singular regularity of the age outcome is independent of every aspect of task content except for task duration, indexed by L_{yng}. This striking phenomenon is known as *generalized slowing*, and its potential importance has long been recognized (Birren, 1965; Welford, 1965).

The descriptive Equation 7 is of course identical to the theoretical Equation 1; the latter provides one framework from which generalized slowing may be understood. The slowing factor $m = 1.43$ derived from Figure 3a may be interpreted as the increase in computation time on a neural network in which only $1/m = 1/1.43 = 70\%$ of the connecting links are preserved.

A. Multilayered Slowing

I term generalized slowing *classical*, but once again it is more the beginning than the end of a story. In 1985, Cerella, and in 1987, Hale, Myerson, and Wagstaff, advanced data sets for which Equation 7 did not hold. Curiously both authors started with data that were simpler than those of

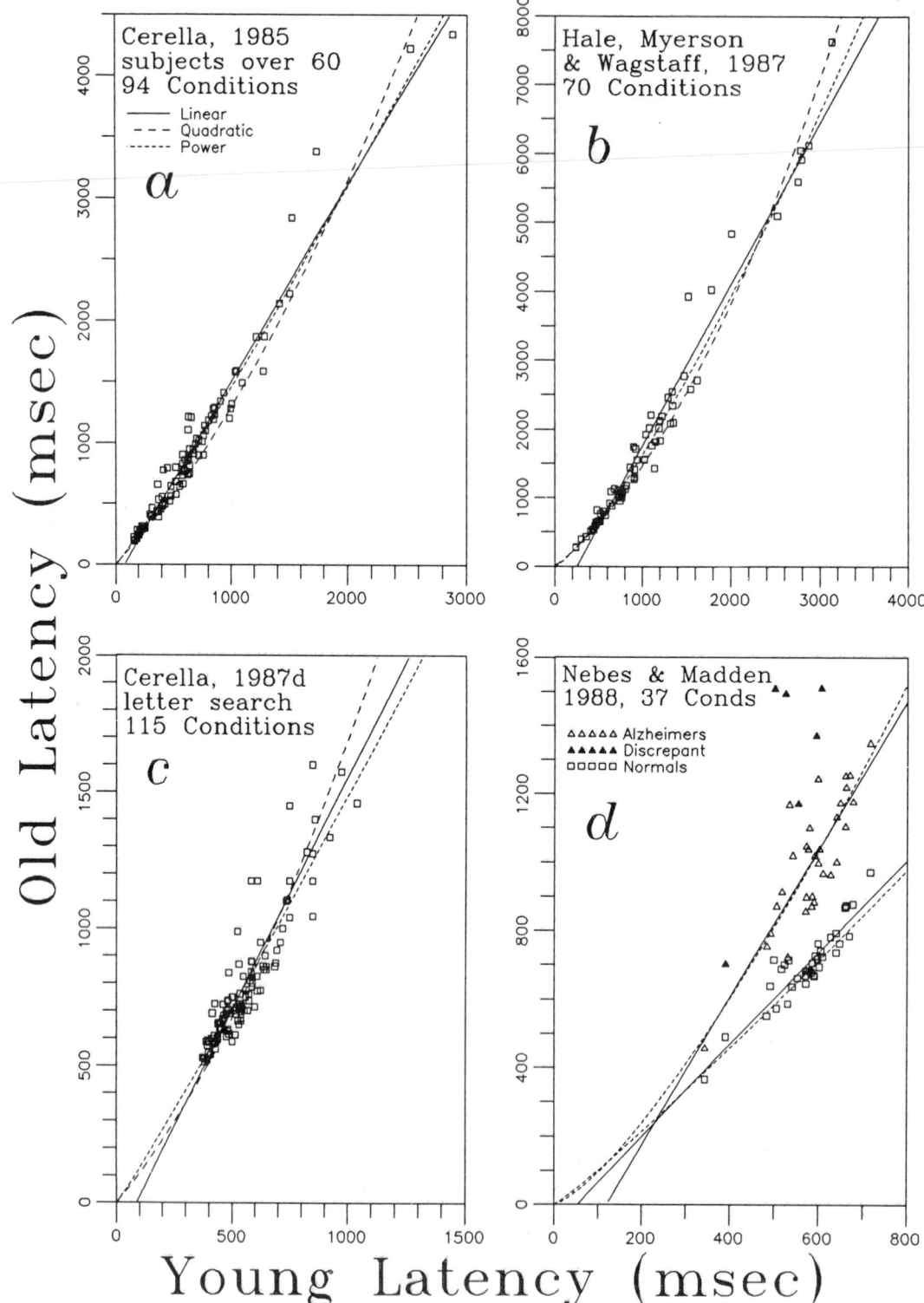

Figure 3 Information-processing latencies as a function of task complexity, as indexed by the magnitude of the "standard" 20-year-old latency. Data from four surveys of about a dozen published studies each. Each point pairs the mean latency of a group of 60- or 70-year-old subjects on some information-processing task (ordinate) with the mean latency of a group of 20-year-old subjects on the same task (abscissa). Data are well fit (see Table 1) by each of three theoretical functions (superimposed curves).

the 1978 and 1980 analyses, and both ended with theories that were more complicated. Cerella began by analyzing each of the fourteen 1980 studies separately (each contributed six or seven conditions to the total of 94). Rather than a fan of 14 lines radiating from the origin $(L_{yng}, L_{old}) = (0, 0)$, each reflecting a slightly different m, the analysis generated a fan of lines radiating from the point $(L_{yng}, L_{old}) = (464, 568)$. The fan is given by:

$$(L_{old} - 568) = m_s(L_{yng} - 464),   (8)$$

where the slowing factor m_s is subscripted to indicate that it varied from study to study (the median value was 1.82)

Cerella (1985) pointed out that Equation 8 could be accounted for by means of two, rather than one, slowing factors. The young latency is viewed as the sum of two processing stages, a perceptual-motor stage of duration P and a computational stage of duration C, $L_{yng} = P + C$. The perceptual-motor stage is taken to be constant (ideally every condition of every study involves the receipt of a visual stimulus and the press of a button), allowing C to be expressed as $L_{yng} - P$. Each stage is stipulated to be slowed with age by a different factor, m_P and m_C. The old latency is thereby given by:

$$L_{old} = m_P P + m_C C$$
$$= m_P P + m_C(L_{yng} - P)$$
$$(L_{old} - m_P P) = m_C(L_{yng} - P).   (9)$$

Equation 9 has the form of Equation 8, with 464 ms identified as the young perceptual-motor time, $568/464 = 1.22$ as the perceptual-motor slowing factor, and m_s as the computational slowing factor specific to a study.

This two-layered logic has already been introduced to account for the aging functions of Figure 2 zone ic. Equation 9 describes the processing times of a network with a deeply defective cognitive core surrounded by a marginally defective input/output shell.

B. Curvilinear Slowing

Hale et al. (1987) compiled a set of nine studies with more uniform input–output requirements. The studies spanned 70 information-processing conditions and are illustrated in Figure 3b. These data are strikingly curvilinear and were fitted to a power function:

$$L_{old} = bL_{yng}{}^m.   (10)$$

Welford (1962) has put linear (7) and nonlinear (10) equations in a common context. Equation 10 may be rewritten as a product of two factors:

$$L_{old} = (bL_{yng})(L_{yng}{}^{m-1}).$$

The first factor evokes generalized slowing, a "proportionate age deficit" in Welford's terms. The proportionate deficit is increased by the second factor, by an amount that grows larger with the task duration, leading to a final "disproportionate deficit."

Because of the sliding factor, differences between proportionate and disproportionate slowing should be more apparent at larger task durations. Figure 3a fits into the lower left quadrant of Figure 3b. The simple multiplicative function derived from Figure 3a fairly well describes the lower quadrant of Figure 3b. Disproportionate slowing emerges in the upper right quadrant, a consequence of the one study that generated latencies in this range.

1. Overhead Model

Two age theories have combined Welford's idea of a cumulative deficit with the geometry of a neural network in a way that accommodates disproportionate slowing. The two theories have a similar flavor but were developed independently (Cerella, 1987b; Myerson, Hale, & Wagstaff, 1985; Myerson, 1987). Both construe L_{yng} as the sum of a large number of brief steps or microprocesses. Cerella's version is the simpler; the microprocesses all have unit duration μ (assigned a value of 1ms for convenience as in Townsend & Ashby, 1983). L_{yng} can therefore be thought of as simple transit time on a network,

$$L_{yng} = \sum_i^N \mu. \qquad (11)$$

In an aged network, the microprocess duration is given by $\mu + d$: Age adds an "overhead" penalty (d) to the duration of each processing step. The model thus appeals to a form of attenuation rather than loss of connectivity as the aging mechanism. The attenuation factor is not a constant as it was in the zone ii model. Instead, the overhead penalty is assumed to grow with each step: at step 1, $d = 1c$; at step 2, $d = 2c$; at step 3, $d = 3c$; and so on, where the attenuation factor (c) is a small constant >0. This sliding penalty leads to the summation:

$$L_{old} = (\mu + 1c) + (\mu + 2c) + \ldots + (\mu + Nc) = (1 + c/2)L_{yng} + (c/2)L_{yng}^2.$$

Empirically this equation can be approximated by the simpler:

$$L_{old} = L_{yng} + dL_{yng}^2 \qquad (12)$$

(letting $d = c/2$), the defining equation of what Cerella calls the $overhead$ $model$. Age has a novel effect here. Elementary processes (unit steps) are unimpaired. Deficits arise when many steps must be organized into an information-processing sequence; the longer the sequence the more time a given step takes.

2. Information Loss Model

The starting point of Myerson's version of the theory is the supposition that task complexity retards the process times of young subjects as well as old subjects. Myerson proposed an alternative to Equation 11 that embodies this effect. Rather than a constant μ, the microprocess duration of the young subject grows with the step

number, i. The source of the slowing is conceptualized differently—it is due not to organizational overhead but to information loss. At each step of a computation, a constant fraction (p) of the stimulus information is lost. At step 0 the information quotient is 1, at step 1 the quotient is reduced to $(1 - p)1$, at step 2 to $(1 - p)(1 - p)1$, and at step i to $(1 - p)^i$. The actual duration of a step is assumed to be inversely proportional to the information available; processes performed with reduced information take longer. The inverse proportion is written $\mu_i = \mu_0/(1 - p)^i$, where μ_0 is the standard, uninflated duration. Myerson's counterpart to Equation 11 follows directly:

$$L_{yng} = \sum_i^N \mu_i = \mu_0 \sum_i^N (1 - p)^i = \mu_0 \sum_i^N exp(pi).$$

The summation can be approximated by

$$L_{yng} = \mu_0(exp(p)/(exp(p)-1))exp(pN). \qquad (13)$$

Where Equation 11 depicts young latencies as increasing multiplicatively with task complexity N, Equation 13 depicts young latencies as increasing exponentially with N.

Old latencies are governed by the same equation. The effect of age is elegantly focused in a single parameter, p: The rate of information loss is assumed to be greater in the old than in the young, $p_{old} > p_{yng}$.

Our analysis requires L_{old} to be expressed as a function of L_{yng}. Equation 13 may be solved for N once for the young and once for the old, and the two solutions equated. The exercise leads to:

$$L_{old} = cL_{yng}^{p_{old}/p_{yng}} \qquad (14)$$

(as applied by Myerson, c is a constant dependent only on p_{old} and p_{yng}), the defining equation of the Information Loss model. The theoretical Equation 14 is identical to the descriptive Equation 10, with the empirical exponent m identified as the ratio of the old and young decay rates.

Table I
Percentage of the Variance of the Latencies of 60- to 80-Year-Old Subjects[a]

Survey	Conditions	Models			
		Generalized Slowing $L_{old} = mL_{yng}$	Multilayered Slowing $L_{old} = mL_{yng} + b$	Overhead $L_{old} = L_{yng} + dL_{yng}^2$	Information Loss $L_{old} = bL_{yng}^m$
Cerella (1985)	94	95	96	93	97
Hale *et al.* (1987)	70	91	97	96	97
Cerella (1987d)	115	82	84	85	84
Nebes and Madden (1988)					
Normals	37	83	84	84	84
Alzheimers	37	67	70	70	70
Totals	353	86	88	88	88

[a]Variance accounted for by four models of cognitive aging fitted to five collections of information-processing tasks.

C. Support for the Models

Power functions (via the Information Loss Equation 14), linear functions (via the Multilayered Slowing Equation 9), and quadratic functions (via the Overhead Equation 12) have all arisen as successors to multiplicative functions (via the Generalized Slowing Equation 7). Table I shows the fit of each, applied to the four large collections of data depicted in Figure 3a–d. The fits are strikingly high; in terms of their ability to predict age outcomes over a wide variety of information-processing conditions, the three models must all be taken seriously.

The equations also have been applied to more restricted data sets chosen by their proponents to illustrate underlying theory. Vis à vis two factor slowing, Cerella (1985) focused on procedures that measure information processing rates directly. The rate of "iconic readout," "short-term memory scanning," and "mental rotation" have been measured in pure form, for old as well as young subject groups. Published rate measures agree on a 1.25 to 1.35 slowing factor for iconic readout (a perceptual process) and a 1.8 to 2.0 slowing factor for both memory scanning and mental rotation (postperceptual, computational

processes). These factors correspond nicely with those extracted from his mixed data, $m_P = 1.22$ on the one hand, and $m_C = 1.82$ on the other (cf. Equations 8 and 9). Cerella (1987a) measured both a perceptual rate and a cognitive rate using the same subjects and the same process, letter rotation. Again two levels of slowing emerged. Where the rotation was given perceptually in an apparent motion paradigm, 1.40 slowing was recorded; where the rotation was achieved cognitively in a mental rotation paradigm, 1.93 slowing was recorded.

Myerson's group has shown that the step count parameter N of the Information Loss Model can account for several sources of variability in performance above and beyond task complexity. Random trial-to-trial fluctuations of a subject, as well as systematic trial-by-trial improvements, can both be modeled by changes in N, random *ups* and *downs* in the first case (Smith, Poon, Hale, & Myerson, 1989) and systematic *downs* in the second (Myerson, 1987).

Cerella (1987b) established mathematically that the family of Overhead Functions (12) is coincident with a subset of power functions. He returned to the 14 studies of the 1980/1985 survey and fit power functions to these data. The power functions determined by the data fell strikingly on the Overhead constraint.

We noted that all three models describe aggregate data well (Table I). We now see that each also describes significant details. It is not clear at this stage whether one of the models will prove to be definitive, or if this second generation of theory will be replaced by a third. Either way, the framework of analysis sketched by Brinley (1965) will have proved fruitful.

V. Contrary Views

The theories we have surveyed assume that L_{aged} directly reflects the status of the neural substrate and that the limits of performance are given biologically, in some sense. This assumption has been challenged by several poorly documented but influential alternatives, whose status will be examined here.

A. Increased Cautiousness

In one alternative, increased latencies have been attributed to a decreased tolerance of error. The implication is that young and old subjects may be operating at different points of a common speed–accuracy trade-off function, in which case there would be no difference in underlying information-processing capacity, only a difference in the speed–accuracy setpoint.

Typical L_{yng} and L_{old} appear as vertical bars in the latency × accuracy space illustrated in Figure 4a, where L_{yng} is assumed to derive from trade-off function A. If L_{old} were associated with an increased accuracy, it could have originated from the same function A; it is even possible that L_{old} originated from a higher capacity function B. These are the cases alleged by the "speed-accuracy shift hypothesis." We, on the other hand, have implicitly assumed a third case, L_{old} originated from a lesser capacity function C, which would

obtain if L_{old} were associated with an equal or diminished accuracy.

Plude, Cerella, and Raskind (1984) assembled data from 201 information-processing conditions reporting both latencies and accuracies for young and old subject groups. For each condition, the age difference in latency and in accuracy was computed and entered as a point in the latency × accuracy "difference" space depicted in Figure 4b. For example, L_{yng} and L_{old} for one condition might be 400 msec and 600 msec, respectively, a difference of $(600 - 400)/400 = 50\%$; young and old accuracies for the same condition might be 95% correct and 90% correct, respectively, a difference of $(90 - 95)/95 = -5\%$. The condition would be represented by a point at $(50, -5)$ in the lower right quadrant of Figure 4b.

The speed–accuracy shift hypothesis predicts that points will cluster in the upper right quadrant; increased latencies will be associated with increased accuracies. The actual data leave the upper right quadrant virtually empty. Instead, points are clustered along the abscissa, that is, young and old accuracies were about equal. When they differed, it was at the expense of the old—overall, elderly subjects showed a slight -6% decline in accuracy. At the same time, consistent increases in processing speeds are seen; the average increase of 52% (a slowing factor of 1.52) is not too far from the 1.43 slowing seen in the 1980 survey, Figure 3a. We conclude that elderly subject latencies indeed originate from lower capacity trade-off functions, as has been found consistently by the few studies that have traced the full functions (the earliest are from Salthouse, 1988; Strayer, Wickens, & Braune, 1987, Figure 4, is a fine late example).

B. Decreased Use

In another alternative, increased latencies have been attributed to a lack of exercise of mental functions. The implication is that

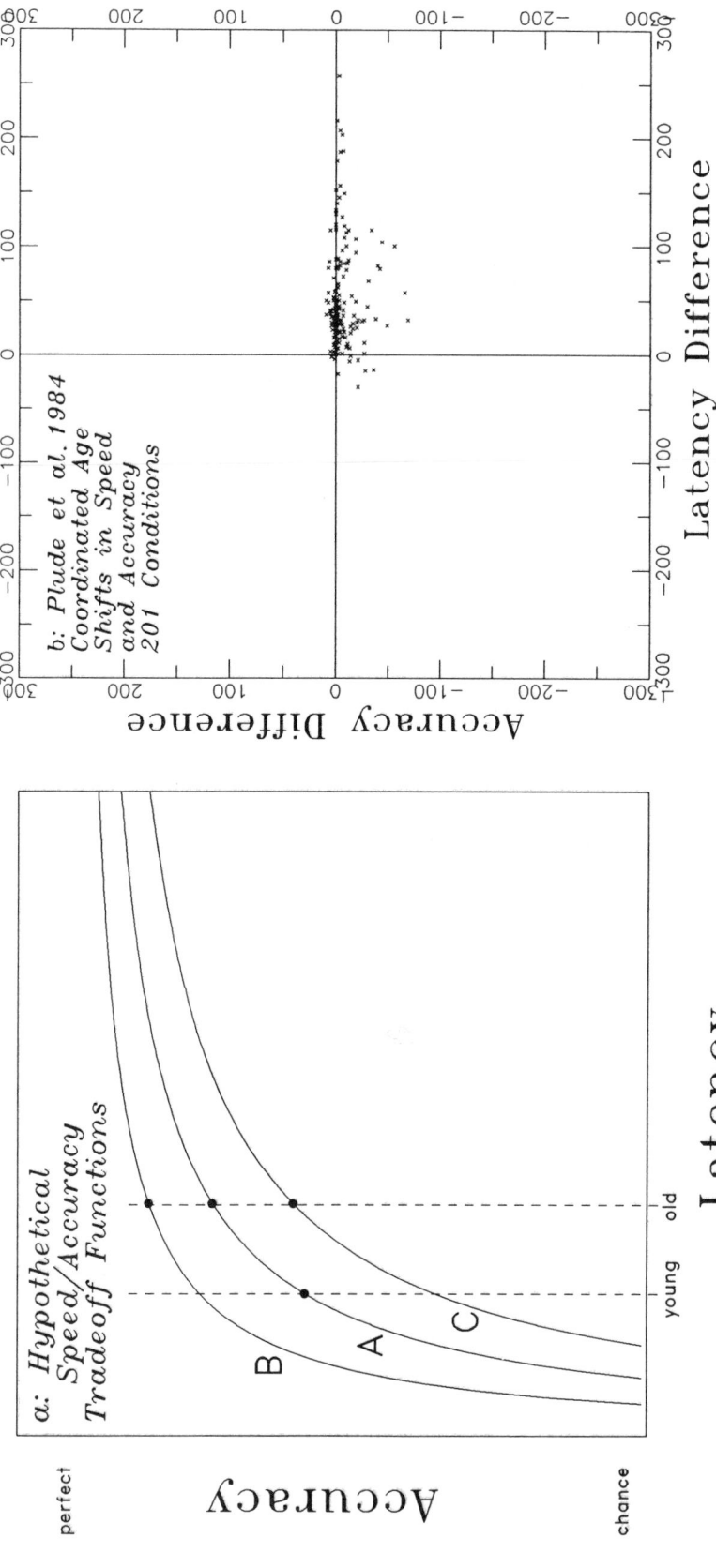

Figure 4 a: Ambiguity of pure latency comparisons: Old latency may derive from a speed–accuracy trade-off function reflecting capacity equal to (curve A) or greater than (B) the young (A), rather than a lower capacity function (C). Ambiguity can only be resolved by concurrent comparison of accuracy. b: Survey of coordinated speed–accuracy data (each point reflects the mean latency and accuracy of a group of young and of old subjects taken from a published study). Points clustered in lower right quadrant show that old latencies overwhelmingly derive from lower capacity trade-off functions, rather than equal or higher capacity functions (points in upper right quadrant).

with sufficient practice on a task, the initial deficit of an elderly subject will be reduced or disappear, and parity with the young subject will be achieved.

The decline in latency as a function of time (t) on a task can best be described by a negatively accelerated hyperbolic function (Mazur & Hastie, 1978):

$$L(t) = [k(t + m)/(t + m + r)]^{-1},$$

where the parameter m determines the initial latency level, k determines the final latency level, and r, the rate at which the performance level improves from m to k. A typical "young" acquisition curve, A, is illustrated in Figure 5a. Curve B depicts an elderly subject who shows a typical latency deficit at the start of an experiment (the left end of the time axis), given mathematically by the condition $m_{old} > m_{yng}$, but whose performance improves disproportionately over the course of the experiment so that the latency lag is eventually eliminated, given mathematically by the condition $k_{old} = k_{yng}$. This is the case alleged by the "disuse hypothesis." We, on the other hand, have implicitly assumed Case C, in which young and old

improve by proportional amounts, and the latency lag is uncompensated by practice, $k_{old} > k_{yng}$.

Cerella (1987c) extracted from the pre-1983 literature 20 studies that tracked performance across at least four levels of practice and fitted hyperbolic functions to the old and young data from each. Half of the studies reported accuracies and half reported latencies; the latter are presented here and do not differ in outcome from the former. The 10 latency studies were large, averaging 13 levels of practice each and were well described by the hyperbolas, an average of 93% of the variance in $\{L_{yng}\}$ and 97% of the variance in $\{L_{old}\}$ was accounted for per study. Age effects were assessed from the fitted parameters. The age difference in starting level $(m_{old} - m_{yng})/m_{yng}$ and in final level $(k_{old} - k_{yng})/k_{yng}$ was calculated for each study, and entered as a point in the $m \times k$ difference space depicted in Figure 5b. The disuse hypothesis predicts points clustered along the abscissa of this space: A range of initial deficits is expected, but final deficits should be uniformly near zero. The "biological limits" prediction is of points clustered along

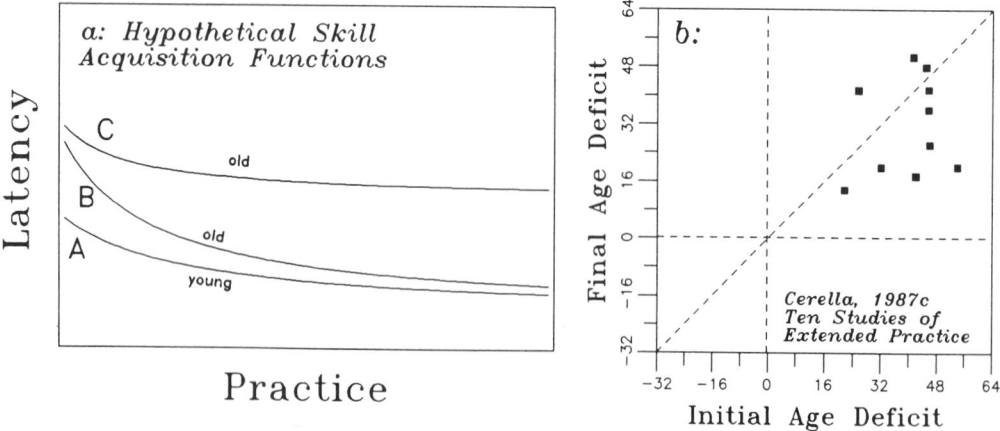

Figure 5 a: Ambiguity of single-session latency comparisons: Old subjects may be sampled in the early phase of an acquisition function (curve B) that would eventually bring them to parity with young subjects (A) if the experiment were continued for additional sessions, rather than on an acquisition function (C) that would leave the age deficit unchanged with practice. b: Survey of 10 studies that tracked the performance of young and old subject groups over multiple sessions shows that the final age deficit matched the initial age deficit fairly closely (perfect matches would fall on the horizontal axis).

the diagonal: Final deficits should be equal to initial deficits.

The actual data fall somewhere between these two extremes. Overall, elderly subjects were slowed initially by a factor of 1.66 (averaging along the abscissa of Figure 5b) and finally by a factor of 1.47 (averaging along the ordinate). Thus $(1.66 - 1.47)/1.66 = 11\%$ of the initial deficit was eliminated over the course of training; this portion of the deficit may be ascribed to the relative inexperience of the elderly subject. By the same token, 89% of the initial deficit proved irreversible; perhaps here we contact a biological limit. Notice once again that the final deficit recorded from these studies, 1.47, is not too far from the 1.43 deficit found in the 1980 studies (Figure 3a). Indeed the closeness of the two values suggests that the earlier experiments provided sufficient exposure to the task to overcome the inexperience of the old.

C. Strategy Shift

In a third alternative, increased latencies have been interpreted as reflecting shifts in "software strategies" rather than defects in the component "hardware." The alternative highlights a key assumption of the models of the chapter, *the correspondence axiom*: Young and old are assumed to be performing the same computation, which is to say that age operates solely on the integrity and not the logic of a network. How might this assumption be tested? Except for a few exhaustively modeled tasks in the literature on individual differences, it probably cannot be tested rigorously. Less rigorously, a minimal condition may be set: The data from any set of tasks taken from the same subjects should be monotonic-increasing when plotted in young × old latency space; that is, old subjects should experience the same rank order of task difficulty as young subjects. This condition is overwhelmingly satisfied in the data of the chapter. The

models herein are disputing the form of this monotonic-increasing function; a precondition of the dispute is satisfaction of the correspondence axiom.

Some procedures involving multiple stimuli may violate the correspondence axiom perforce. Salthouse (1985) develops an example: A lexical decision task that displays a prime too briefly to allow it to be processed might record semantic facilitation in the young but not in the old. The "content-free" networks of this chapter cannot model such situations. Salthouse (1988) explores the use of content-laden networks in these cases.

VI. Recapitulation

The chapter began with a picture (Figure 1) of a neural network at "time zero"; a single link was broken, and the resulting step-around incremented the passage time of a signal over the network by a microscopic amount. We are now in a position to follow the network through the remainder of its life. Figure 6 pictures not the network but the passage times it gives rise to. The depiction is two dimensional. On one axis network age is plotted, traversing a 60-year range. The accumulation of broken links and the detours they precipitate lead to latencies that increase exponentially over the lifespan.

The other axis plots what might be called the computational requirement, which is simply the duration of a task when performed on the intact network. It anchors the cross-section function at age zero to the positive diagonal, shown for a typical laboratory range of 300 to 1500 ms. With the network age fixed anywhere greater than zero, the cross-section function is still linear but has a slope greater than unity, reflecting the proportional increase in latencies incurred by a signal that must circumvent a fixed portion of defects as it attempts to negotiate the computational requirement.

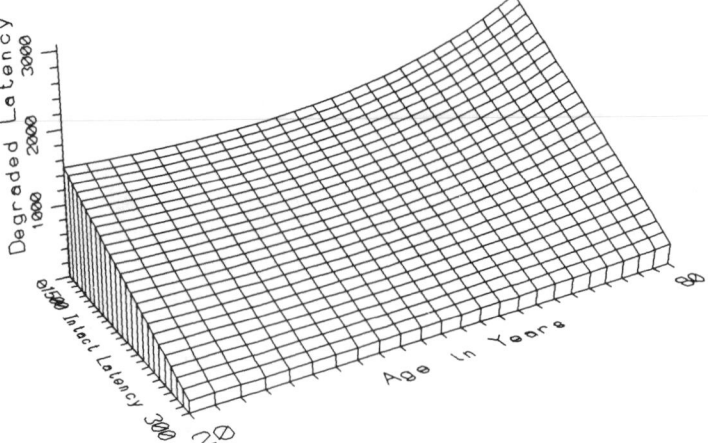

Figure 6 Full ramification of the network model presented in Figure 1. Loss of connectivity leads in the short term to a proportional increase in the execution time of every information process and in the long term to an exponential increase in the proportionality factor. The entire response surface is generated by a single constant, the rate at which interneuron links are broken.

The final product is a curvilinear surface that depicts the response time of the network to any task at any age. The entire response surface is generated by a single free parameter, the hazard rate k in Equation 2. Despite this simplicity, the surface of Figure 6 represents to a first approximation a vast amount of data, the majority of the latencies compiled in Figures 2, 3, 4, and 5.

Modifications of the basic model were introduced to improve its approximation to the data; they can be visualized as deformations of the Figure 6 surface on one or the other axis. Most of the deformations had the effect of increasing its tilt or curl, which is to say that the basic model failed to adequately represent the increase in deficit as age advanced or as task durations grew. For example, as age advanced some of the predictive gap could be closed by assuming that the hazard rate k increased with age rather than remained constant. The resulting surface curls upward at a greater than exponential rate along the age axis. As task durations grew, the gap could

be closed by assuming that the magnitude (as opposed to the frequency) of the defects increased as the computation evolved. The resulting cross-section functions have a quadratic as well as a linear component. These modifications involved no more than one or two additional parameters and captured what was clearly systematic variance not reached by the original model.

Although the model is two dimensional, the analyses of this chapter were one dimensional. Task durations were factored out of Figure 2 (by normalizing on the young latencies) while we focused on the form of the deficit as a function of age. Age variation was eliminated in Figure 3 (and Figures 4 and 5) by admitting only 60- to 70-year-old subject samples while we considered the effects of task duration. A two-dimensional analysis is clearly called for, attempting to fit the data of Figures 2 and 3 simultaneously on a single set of model parameters. It is my suspicion that two- or three-parameter models will represent the joint data quite well, leaving little but noise in the residuals.

VII. The Theoretical Gain

What do these models buy us? There are at least two gains. The first is descriptive economy; a large accumulation of data on cognition and age is predicted by a few parameters. Second and more important is theoretical coherence: A few notions about degeneration in the central nervous system replace the myriad task-specific explanations of age effects that have proliferated in the literature. In the process, cognitive aging reemerges as a subfield of neurophysiology rather than cognitive psychology.

Researchers who feel that references to cognitive psychology are essential ought at least to demonstrate that their data exhibit more than generalized slowing. Cerella et al. (1980) elaborated the logic of this assessment. The usual age-by-task ANOVA is performed not on latencies but on log latencies. If an interaction remains, then something more than the simplest of the models presented here is needed to account for the data. The success of even the simplest model (Table I, Column 1) indicates that more often than not, nothing more is needed. Cerella et al. (1980) proceeded by this means to eliminate the "cognitive content" of a small study by Arnold and Farkas (1978) on target detection as an illustration. I offer a few more elaborate examples.

Figure 7a shows simple reaction time to a square wave grating as a function of grating frequency (Kline, Schieber, Abusamra, & Coyne, 1983). Figure 7c shows detection latency for letter features in visually presented and/or imagined letters (Weber, Hochhaus, & Brown, 1981). Because neither set of curves were parallel, both sets of authors concluded that age acted differentially on the various task conditions. The data are replotted in semilog coordinates in Figures 7b and 7d, and the age interactions disappear. Generalized slowing (that is, constant L_{old}/L_{yng} ratios) is sufficient to account for age effects in all the task conditions.

The next example (Figure 3d) shows how generalized slowing can be used as a lever to extricate exceptional conditions that require more elaborate explanation. The data are from 37 verbal tasks assembled by Nebes and Madden (1988). The lower set of points pairs young subjects with healthy old subjects and is nicely fit by all the network models (Table I, about 83% variance explained). The upper set of points pairs the same young subjects with demented subjects; these data cannot be fit by any of the models (about 30% variance explained).

The authors identified six conditions on the basis of task content that were responsible for the lack of fit of the demented data. When they were removed, the remaining points could be described by "normal" aging models, albeit with more extreme parameter values (about 70% variance explained—these are the smooth curves drawn through the upper data set). Nebes and Madden concluded that the discrepant conditions reflected disabilities specific to senile dementia over and above the elevated levels of normal aging that accompanied the senility.

A final example is taken from Cerella (1987d). Ten "Schneider and Shiffrin-type" letter search studies were drawn from the literature (Figure 3c). Again the aggregate data (115 conditions) were well fit by the network models (Table I, about 94% variance explained). A two-level slowing model (Equation 9) was also fit to the individual studies. The equation:

$$(L_{old} - 548) = m_s(L_{yng} - 398), \quad (15)$$

with m_s specific to a study, described the 11 or so conditions of each experiment well. The similarity both in form and in value to Equation 8, which describes the 14 experiments of Cerella's 1985 survey, is striking. The same pattern emerged once more in a survey of five "Posner-type"

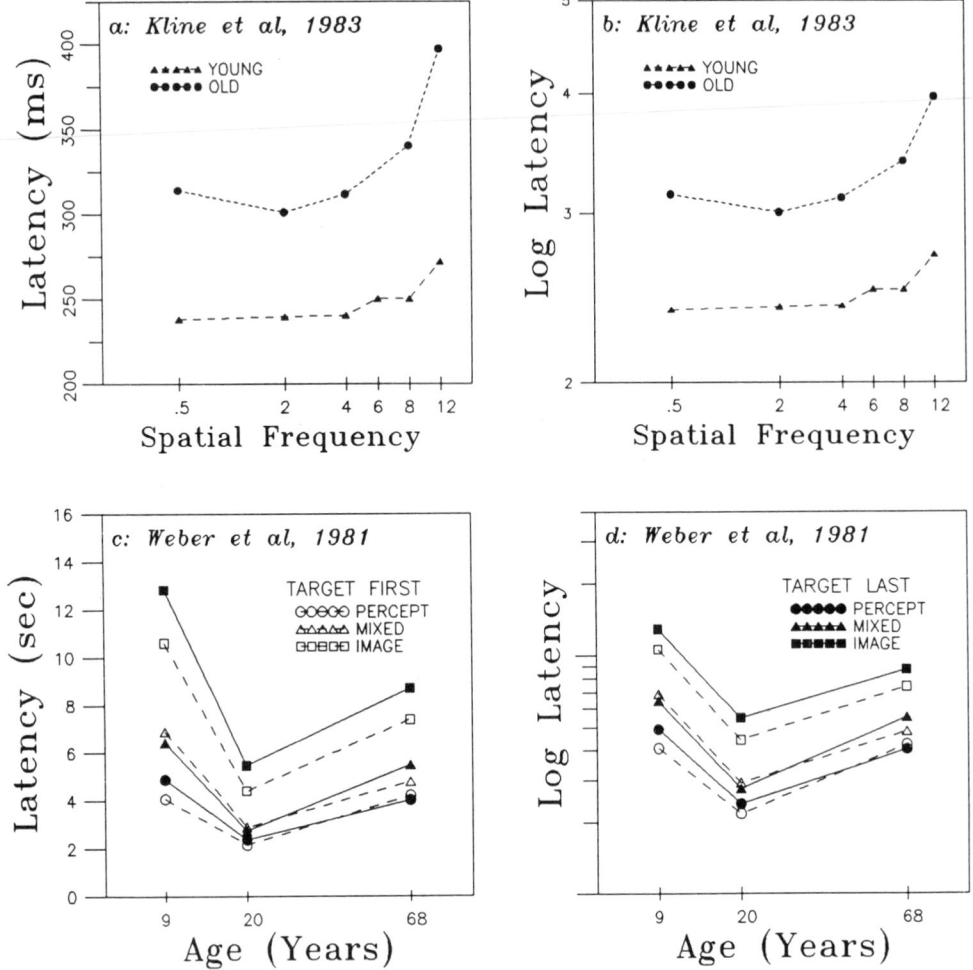

Figure 7 Possible misinterpretation of slowing effects as task effects. a,c: An analysis of untransformed latencies showed an age-by-task interaction and led to conclusions that age acted differentially on spatial frequency channels or on imagined vs. perceived targets. b,d: Reanalysis of log latencies eliminates age-by-task interactions—older subjects are slowed by a constant factor in all conditions.

dual task studies (55 conditions). Cerella (1987d) concluded that no more appeal to "attentional deficits" was necessary to explain the age effects in these 15 studies of attention than was necessary to explain the age effects in the earlier nonattentional studies.

VIII. Conclusions

A vast body of data describes the information-processing latencies of elderly adults.

These data have been approached here at a more primitive level than usual. References have been to neural notions of axonal degeneration and attenuation, rather than to psychological notions of attentional capacity, working memory, and the like. The low level of the aging mechanisms allowed them to be applied to the data in a general way, irrespective of task content. The success of the approach was striking—upwards of 1,000 points abstracted from the aging literature are illustrated, clustered tightly around the theoretical predictions of the neural models. The conclusion is inescapable: *The data are orderly at this low level.* In closing, we will consider some implications of this result.

On the positive side, we are encouraged to take seriously the processes of brain deterioration described in ever-increasing detail by the neurophysiologist and neuroanatomist. Information-processing latencies taken from elderly subjects match exactly, qualitatively and quantitively, those that would be expected from a brain whose interconnections were systematically disrupted or attenuated.

On the negative side, we are discouraged from elaborating higher level accounts of the same latencies. Case by case, we saw that appeals to disuse, cautiousness, attentional deficits, software shifts (and a host of more specific psychological notions attached to the data as originally published), were simply not needed—the data were adequately predicted by the declines in the neural substrate. This does not mean that skill acquisition, speed–accuracy trade-offs, attentional capacity, strategy differences, and other phenomena on which our understanding of young subject latencies are based do not pertain to elderly adults. The implication is rather that they operate in the old as they do in the young, so that their particular effects do not influence the age deficits.

Such sweeping claims ought to be set in perspective. The analyses herein dealt exclusively with group means; there was no treatment of individual means nor of trial-by-trial distributions. Extension of the work in these directions may not be too difficult, following, for example, Waugh, Fozard, Talland, and Erwin's early example (1973) (but see McClelland's, 1979, discussion of the indeterminacy of gamma models). Model parameters such as the connectivity constant, or the signal loss rate, may emerge as powerful predictors of individual differences.

More serious is the limitation of the analyses herein to latency measures. The development of models that treat accuracy together with latency is a great challenge, although here too early work may show the way (Birren, Allen, & Landau, 1954). Right now, we are far from spanning the gap between neural connectivities and, say, abstract intelligence. Given the very loose connection between latency-only measures and IQ scores (Cerella, DiCara, Williams, & Bowles, 1986), probably only a joint speed–accuracy platform will carry us in that direction.

Acknowledgment

This work was supported by the Veterans Administration Medical Research Service.

References

Arnold, S., & Farkas, M. (1978). Age differences in speed and strategies of perceptual search. *Gerontologist*, **18**, 45.

Birren, J. E. (1965). Age changes in speed of behavior: Its central nature and physiological correlates. In A. T. Welford & J. E. Birren (Eds.), *Behavior, aging and the nervous system* (pp. 191–216). Springfield, IL: Thomas.

Birren, J. E., Allen, W. R., & Landau, H. G. (1954). The relation of problem length in simple addition to time required, probability of success, and age. *Journal of Gerontology*, **9**, 150–161.

Brinley, J. F. (1965). Cognitive sets, speed and accuracy of performance in the elderly. In A. T. Welford and J. E. Birren (Eds.), *Behavior, aging and the nervous system*. Springfield, Ill.: Charles C. Thomas.

Cerella, J. (1985). Information processing rates in the elderly. *Psychological Bulletin*, **98**, 67–83.

Cerella, J. (1987a). *Aging: Fast perceptual processes and slow cognitive processes.* Paper presented at the Cognitive Aging Conference, Atlanta.

Cerella, J. (1987b). *Overhead models of mental slowing: Preliminary investigations.* Paper presented at the Cognitive Aging Conference, Atlanta.

Cerella, J. (1987c). *Are age deficits disuse only?*

Paper presented at the Human Factors Society annual meeting, New York.

Cerella, J. (1987d). *Attention deficits as processing rate reductions.* Paper presented at the Conference on Attention and Aging, National Institute of Aging, Bethesda, MD.

Cerella, J., DiCara, R., Williams, D., & Bowles, N. (1986). Relations between information processing and intelligence in elderly adults. *Intelligence,* **10**, 75–91.

Cerella, J., Poon, L. W., & Williams, D. (1980). Age and the complexity hypothesis. In L. W. Poon (Ed.), *Aging in the 1980's* (pp. 332–340). Washington, DC: American Psychological Association.

Cerella, J. C., & Poon, L. W. (1983). *Life cycles: How grim the reaper?* Paper presented at the annual meeting of the Gerontological Society of America, San Francisco.

Charness, N. (Ed.) (1983). Aging and problem solving performance. *Aging and human performance.* New York: Wiley.

Cutler, R. G. (1982). Longevity is determined by specific genes: Testing the hypothesis. In R. C. Adelman & G. S. Roth (Eds.), *Testing the theories of aging* (pp. 25–114). Boca Raton, FL: CRC Press.

Greene, V. L. (1983). Age dynamic models of information-processing task latency: A theoretical note. *Journal of Gerontology,* **38**, 46–50.

Hale, S., Myerson, J., & Wagstaff, D. (1987). General slowing of nonverbal information processing: Evidence for a power law. *Journal of Gerontology,* **42**, 131–136.

Horn, J. L. (1979). The rise and fall of human abilities. *Journal of Research and Development in Education,* **12**, 59–77.

Kline, D. W., Schieber, F., Abusamra, L. C., & Coyne, A. C. (1983). Age, the eye, and the visual channels: Contrast sensitivity and response speed. *Journal of Gerontology,* **38**, 211–216.

Mazur, J. E., & Hastie, R. (1978). Learning as accumulation: A reexamination of the learning curve. *Psychological Bulletin,* **85**, 1256–1274.

McClelland, J. L. (1979). On the time relations of mental processes: An examination of systems of processes in cascade. *Psychological Review,* **86**, 287–330.

McClelland, J. L., Rumelhart, D. E., & the PDP Research Group (1986). *Parallel distributed processing: explorations in the microstructure of cognition.* Cambridge, MA: MIT Press.

Minsky, M. L., & Papert, S. A. (1988). *Perceptrons.* Cambridge, MA: M.I.T. Press.

Myerson, J. (1987). *The search for regularities in cognitive aging.* Paper presented at the annual meeting of the Gerontological Society of America, Washington, DC.

Myerson, J., Hale, S., & Wagstaff, D. (1985). *Changes in response latency with age: An allometric analysis.* Paper presented at the annual meeting of the American Psychological Association, Los Angeles.

Nebes, R. D., & Madden, D. J. (1988). Different patterns of cognitive slowing produced by Alzheimer's disease and normal aging. *Psychology and Aging,* **3**, 102–104.

Plude, D. J., Cerella, J., & Raskind, C. L. (1984). *Speed-accuracy tradeoffs in cognitive aging research.* Paper presented at the annual meeting of the Gerontological Society of America, San Antonio, TX.

Resnikoff, H. L. (1989). *The illusion of reality.* New York: Springer.

Riggs, D. S. (1963). *The mathematical approach to physiological problems.* Cambridge, MA: M.I.T. Press.

Salthouse, T. A. (1978). *Age and speed: The nature of the relationship.* Unpublished manuscript, Department of Psychology, University of Missouri, Columbia.

Salthouse, T. A. (1985). *A theory of cognitive aging.* Amsterdam: North-Holland Publ.

Salthouse, T. A. (1988). Initiating the formalization of theories of cognitive aging. *Psychology and Aging,* **3**, 3–16.

Smith, G. A., Poon, L. W., Hale, S., & Myerson, J. (1989). A regular relationship between old and young adults' latencies on their best, average and worst trials. *Australian Journal of Psychology,* in press.

Strayer, D. L., Wickens, C. D., & Braune, R. (1987). Adult age differences in the speed and capacity of information processing: 2. An electrophysiological approach. *Psychology and Aging,* **2**, 99–110.

Talland, G. A. (1965). Response and reaction time in aging and with brain damage. In A. T. Welford & J. E. Birren (Eds.), *Behavior, aging and the nervous system.* Springfield, IL: Thomas.

Townsend, J. T., & Ashby, F. G. (1983).

Stochastic modeling of elementary psychological processes. London: Cambridge University Press.

Waugh, N. C., Fozard, J. L., Talland, G. A., & Erwin, D. E. (1973). Effects of age and stimulus repetition on two-choice reaction time. *Journal of Gerontology, 28,* 466–470.

Weber, R. J., Hochhaus, L., & Brown, W. D. (1981). Equivalence of perceptual and imaginal representation: Developmental changes. In J. Long & A. Baddeley (Eds.), *Attention and performance IX* (pp. 295–309). Hillsdale, NJ: Erlbaum.

Weiss, A. D. (1959). Sensory functions. In J. E. Birren (Ed.), *Handbook of aging and the individual* (pp. 503–542). Chicago, IL: University of Chicago Press.

Welford, A. T. (1962). Changes of performance time with age: A correction and methodological note. *Ergonomics, 5,* 581–582.

Welford, A. T. (1965). Performance, biological mechanisms and age: A theoretical sketch. In A. T. Welford & J. E. Birren (Eds.), *Behavior, aging and the nervous system* (pp. 3–20). Springfield, IL: Thomas.

Thirteen

Aging and Attentional Processes

Joan M. McDowd and James E. Birren

This chapter reviews research on aging and attention, comments on research trends, and draws implications for future research. The topic of attention occupied a major place in research and theory from the beginning of experimental psychology in the last century, for example, James (1890), Pillsbury (1908), Ribot (1890). In 1914, Whipple devoted 86 pages of his *Manual of Physical and Mental Tests* to the measurement of attention in children and adolescents. It is only recently, however, that psychologists have begun to examine the course of attention over the life span. The lag in initiative in research in older adults is somewhat surprising in light of the fundamental nature of attention as a precondition for cognition and its importance for effective behavior and survival.

I. Definitions

For Yerkes (1911), *attention* determined the level of sensory clarity. The spirit of Yerkes's view persists today. The indi-
vidual is continually bombarded with stimuli from the environment and from within the organism itself, and attention governs which of the many impinging stimuli we process. The 1987 *Handbook of Physiology* examined the neurophysiological basis of attention and defined attention as "the mechanisms by which we prepare to process stimuli, focus on what to process, and determine how far it will be processed and whether it should call us to action" (Heilman, Watson, Valenstein, & Goldberg, 1987, p. 461).

Attention also has been viewed as "the capacity or energy to support cognitive processing" (Plude & Hoyer, 1985, p. 49). This capacity view posits attention as a limited commodity or resource, necessary to support information processing. Out of this view comes a picture of cognitive aging that holds that older adults experience a global reduction in attentional resources that in turn reduces the efficiency with which cognitive processes can be executed (e.g., Craik & Byrd, 1982; Craik & McDowd, 1987; Craik & Simon, 1980; Hasher & Zacks, 1979; Wright, 1981).

Handbook of the Psychology of Aging, Third Edition

Copyright © 1990 Academic Press, Inc. All rights of reproduction in any form reserved.

However, this view has been notoriously difficult to substantiate empirically (e.g., Navon, 1984; Salthouse, 1985) and remains a focus of some controversy (e.g., see Madden, 1987b).

II. Aging and Attention

For organizational convenience, the present chapter discusses research on aging and attention under four commonly used categories: *divided, switching, sustained,* and *selective* attention. We do not wish to argue that these four aspects of attention are completely independent; rather we make the distinction to provide a framework around which to discuss the relevant literature.

A. Divided Attention

For the purposes of this review, *divided attention* refers to the process by which attention is controlled to successfully perform two simultaneous tasks. Craik (1977) reviewed the literature on divided attention and aging in the context of age changes in memory and concluded that an age-related deficit in divided attention was a reliable finding. Subsequently, it seemed that the book was closed on the topic. However, the study of aging and divided attention has enjoyed something of a resurgence with the work of Salthouse and colleagues (Salthouse, Rogan, & Prill, 1984; Somberg & Salthouse, 1982). Surprisingly, a paper by Somberg and Salthouse (1982) reported no age differences in divided attention performance. The tasks involved were simple perceptual search tasks, requiring subjects to indicate the presence or absence of a target in a visual display or pair of displays. When single-task, baseline performance accuracy was equated in young and old age groups, no age-related decrement in divided attention performance was observed. Somberg and Salthouse concluded that previously observed age differences in divided attention

performance were artifacts of initial single-task performance differences and once these initial differences were controlled, the age deficit would disappear.

A later paper by Salthouse *et al.* (1984) forced a qualification of the earlier conclusion. The Salthouse *et al.* (1984) study involved tasks more complex than those used in the previous work, requiring memory for simultaneously presented letter series. In this case, despite statistical control for age differences in single-task baseline performance, age-related deficits in divided attention performance were observed. Thus with the more complex tasks, age differences in performance were evident. In light of this body of research, Plude and Hoyer (1985) and Madden (1987b) have pointed out the necessity of a closer look at the conditions under which dual tasks do and do not produce age differences in performance. Such an elaboration on existing data is made all the more important by the work of Wickens, Braune, and Stokes (1987) who found no age differences in divided attention performance on a memory-search task not unlike that of Salthouse *et al.* (1984).

McDowd and Craik (1988) reported on a set of studies designed to examine the effects of task complexity on age differences in divided attention performance. The outcome of the McDowd and Craik (1988) and the Salthouse *et al.* (1984) papers is that an age-related divided attention deficit appears to be a robust phenomenon in all but the simplest of tasks (e.g., Somberg & Salthouse, 1982), even when the most conservative measures of performance are employed. Further work on this phenomenon must begin to consider the roles of skill, practice, and expertise in divided attention performance (e.g., McDowd, 1986).

B. Attention Switching

Attention switching is the process of alternately monitoring two or more sources of input. Until recently, there has been little work done on this aspect of attentional functioning. A related literature, however, comes from early work showing age-related increases in cognitive rigidity (e.g., Chown, 1961; Kounin, 1941; Schaie, 1958) and perseveration (Talland, 1968) in the context of perception (Botwinick, 1961, 1965) and problem solving (Hartley, 1981; Hayslip & Sterns, 1979; Jerome, 1959; Talland, 1968).

The role of short-term memory in attention switching has been enumerated by Welford (1964) and McGhie (1969). Welford (1964) concluded that short-term memory capacity was reduced by any switch of attention between taking in and responding to various bits of information and that this reduction was especially pronounced in older adults. If the switching per se requires more time in the elderly, there will be an embarrassment or extra load on short-term working memory (Birren, Woods, & Williams, 1980). A somewhat different view of the relationship between short-term memory and attention switching was given by McGhie (1969) who suggested that the problems older adults have with tasks that require attention switching stem from an impairment in short-term memory. The elderly adult is unable to maintain in memory one set of information while responding to another set of information. Schonfield (1981) further suggested that switching attention is limited because of difficulties in retrieval. Switching attention implies that there is the awareness of separate trains of thought and that, although one is the focus of attention, the others must be maintained for later retrieval. Schonfield proposed that this retrieval is more difficult and takes longer for older adults to accomplish. An example of everyday problems is the phenomenon of going into a room but forgetting why; the intention of retrieving some item is lost while attending to the goal of going to another room.

In the realm of visual attention, Hartley, Kieley, and McKenzie (1987) carried out a series of studies designed to measure age differences in the ability to switch from a narrow to a broad focus of attention. The attention switching task involved a condition in which attention was required to be focused on the center character of a five-character string (NARROW condition) and on occasional trials, broadened to encompass all five characters in order to detect a peripheral target. For both old and young adults, reaction times to target stimuli increased as a function of target eccentricity relative to the central focus. This increase contrasts with a flat function obtained when attention was initially broadened to encompass all five characters and so did not have to be shifted to detect a peripheral target (BROAD condition). In both conditions, older adults were slower overall in responding to the target stimulus. However, in the condition requiring a shift of attention from a narrow to a broad focus, slopes of reaction times against target eccentricity were equivalent for old and young adults. The basic finding of age similarities in the rate at which individuals can reallocate attention replicated earlier work by Hartley and Kieley (1986) and also was replicated in two further experiments reported by Hartley et al. (1987) that varied peripheral target eccentricity and instructions regarding the focus of attention as ways of controlling the contribution of sensory factors in accounting for age differences in performance.

Cerella (1985) has argued that search RT is simply a function of retinal eccentricity and that age differences in visual search reflect peripheral sensory processes. However, Hartley et al. (1987) concluded that the slope differences between the NARROW and BROAD conditions indicated that there are attentional processes which contribute to search reaction time (RT). Even so, Hartley's results suggested that there are no age differences in the speed of switching the focus of attention.

Taken together, these results on visual attention seem to indicate that attention switching does not change much with age, at least as it has been measured to date. This conclusion is somewhat surprising in light of existing behavioral data on perseveration and rigidity and in light of data from tasks requiring attention switching in the auditory modality, which have shown age differences (e.g., Barrett, Mihal, Panek, Sterns, & Alexander, 1977; Braun & Wickens, 1985). Given these results, it is unclear what the relevant task dimensions are for producing age differences. The Hartley et al. (1987) task required switching the "aperture" of visual attention rather than switching between tasks or trains of thought. Perhaps these issues are relevant to understanding the apparently contradictory findings.

C. Sustained Attention

The activity of maintaining performance on a task over extended time requires sustained attention. The notion of vigilance is related to sustained attention, and the vigilance paradigm is most often used to assess sustained attention.

Parasuraman (1985) reviewed the literature on aging and vigilance performance and concluded that evidence regarding age changes in sustained attention was sparse and mixed. One well-known study is that by Surwillo and Quilter (1964) in which young and old adults performed the Mackworth Clock vigilance task. Surwillo and Quilter reported an overall effect of reduced detection accuracy on the part of older adults and also an age-related increase in the rate of decline in detection accuracy over time. In a replication attempt, Giambra and Quilter (1985) found the overall effect of reduced detection accuracy in older adults but failed to find an age difference in the rate of decline over

time. The more recent study had a substantially larger sample size than the earlier study and involved a longitudinal component that also failed to demonstrate an age-related increase in the rate of decline of detection accuracy. Although there seem to be reliable age differences in overall detection accuracy, there is little evidence for age-related changes in the rate of decline in vigilance during extended performance.

Another method for assessing sustained attention is to use tasks that involve the continuous and rapid presentation of sometimes degraded stimuli, requiring a constant and concerted focus of attention in order to maximize performance. In using a continuous paradigm, Parasuraman (1987) found that older adults were less accurate in detecting the target stimulus than were young adults, but d-prime measures of sensitivity indicated a comparable decline in performance across time for young and older adults. Thus, again, overall levels of performance in sustained attention or vigilance tasks appear to be reduced with age, but the vigilance decrement that normally occurs during an extended task does not seem to be greater for older than for young adults.

The mechanism accounting for the main effect of age on detection accuracy in vigilance performance remains unknown. One possibility is that of lower arousal or alertness levels among older adults relative to young adults. There are a number of physiological studies to indicate reduced CNS arousal as measured by EEG slowing (e.g., Thompson & Marsh, 1973; Woodruff, 1975), sensory evoked potential slowing (e.g., Dustman & Beck, 1965; Dustman, Snyder, & Schlehuber, 1981), and slowing of event-related potentials (e.g., Duncan-Johnson & Donchin, 1977; Goodin, Squires, Henderson, & Starr, 1978). However, others have postulated that *overarousal* on the part of older adults accounts for observed age differences in performance (e.g., Eisdorfer, 1968; Powell, Eisdorfer, & Bogdonoff, 1964). Thus the nature and role of arousal in sustained attention performance needs to be more carefully specified.

Distractibility would seem to be another possible candidate to account for the age differences observed in vigilance performance. Perhaps older adults are more distracted during often boring vigilance tasks and so are more likely to miss the occurrence of targets. Giambra (1989) has investigated this hypothesis. He reported five experiments in which young and old adults were engaged in boring vigilance tasks and were asked to indicate the frequency with which they experienced task-unrelated thoughts (TUTs). In a visual detection task lasting 62.3 minutes, subjects were to press a key each time a task-unrelated thought ended. Under these conditions, older adults reported *fewer* TUTs than did young adults.

Because the requirement to report TUTs might itself inhibit them, in a second study subjects were probed every 25 seconds during the 62.3 minutes as to whether a TUT had occurred in the last 25-second interval. In Experiments 3 and 4, Giambra controlled the preexperimental activities of his research participants for a period of 2 hours in an attempt to control for the availability of task-unrelated thoughts. With both the TUT-end and TUT-probe methods, older adults still reported fewer TUTs than did young adults. Experiment 5 manipulated the level of intellectual stimulation provided by the pretask activity and also the information-processing demand made by the vigilance task itself. In all cases, accuracy rates for the vigilance task exceeded 93%, so it can not be argued that the demands of the vigilance task exceeded the capacity of the older adults, yet older adults continued to report significantly fewer TUTs than did young adults.

Giambra interpreted his data as indicating that, with age, there is reduced non-conscious processing of thoughts that might surface in boring situations like a vigilance task and that older adults therefore have less potent or productive information processing systems than do young adults.

Giambra's data and interpretation are not consistent with the data of other investigators (e.g., Birren, 1959; Jerome, 1959), suggesting that older adults have an overflow of task-unrelated thoughts, nor are these findings consistent with other anecdotal evidence (e.g., Obler, 1980) or evidence such as increased intrusion errors on the part of older adults in free recall (Stine & Wingfield, 1987). In fact, Hasher and Zacks (1989) have recently cited an age-related decline in the efficiency of inhibitory processes and a concomitant increase in the intrusion of thoughts, opinions, experiences and daydreams, as central to their theoretical framework designed to account for age differences in working memory capacity. One possibility for reconciling these conflicting sets of data is to consider the issue of *rate* of occurrence of thoughts versus *task-relatedness* of thoughts that occur. Perhaps older adults have fewer thoughts overall, but a greater proportion of them are irrelevant to the task. Testing this possibility, however, poses difficult measurement problems of the sort faced by Giambra.

Whatever the cause of age differences in detection accuracy, vigilance and sustained attention performance are worthy of continued investigation. There are a number of practical implications for age-related changes in vigilance performance. For example, there are increasing numbers of older drivers on the roads, and more older workers remaining in the workplace.

D. Selective Attention

The filtering, or selective, function of attention is perhaps the most basic function. For behavior to be efficiently goal-directed, an individual must filter out irrelevant information available in the environment and select or focus on information that is goal relevant. One hypothesis investigated in the literature for at least 20 years (e.g., Rabbitt, 1965) is that older adults are less able to select and focus on a single input in the face of competing inputs, that competing inputs draw attention away from relevant inputs. There exists a variety of evidence to support notions of an age-related increase in distractibility or reduction in inhibitory processes. This evidence came first from observations such as those made by Birren (1959), Jerome (1959), and Luria (1973) that older adults show a reduction in inhibitory control over behavior.

In more direct tests of the distractibility hypothesis, older adults have continued to show more susceptibility to the negative effects of the presence of irrelevant information in the context of a memory task (Kausler & Kleim, 1978), a frequency judgment task (Kausler & Hakami, 1982), and a problem-solving task (Hoyer, Rebok, & Sved, 1979). Studies of electrical and chemical activity in the brain also have indicated reduced inhibitory function in older adults (Dustman & Snyder, 1981; Prinz et al., this volume). Instead of remaining confined to specific areas of the brain, event-related electrical activity appears to spread across cortical areas. The result may be increased cross-talk between processing components of the older brain, a result consistent with Layton's (1975) perceptual noise hypothesis.

Another approach to the study of aging and selective attention involves visual search, a paradigm pioneered in this context by Rabbitt (1965). Rabbitt had young and old adults sort decks of cards based on information on the cards. Sorting times of older adults were more slowed by the presence of irrelevant information than were those of young adults and became increasingly slowed as the number of irrelevant items increased. He concluded that older adults were more distracted by irrel-

evant information than were the young adults (Rabbitt, 1965).

The role of age-related distractibility in visual search has continued to be a topic for investigation (e.g., Cerella, 1985; Hoyer & Plude, 1980; Madden, 1982, 1984, 1986; Plude & Hoyer, 1985). This work has resulted in a number of qualifications being placed on Rabbitt's original conclusion that the presence of irrelevant items distracts and slows the performance of older adults more than that of young adults. For example, there is evidence to suggest that older adults have difficulty with irrelevant information only when those items must be processed along with the relevant information in the course of performing the task (e.g., Kausler, 1982; Mergler, Dusek, & Hoyer, 1977; Wright & Elias, 1979). Other research has indicated that the source of the problem experienced by older adults is difficulty in *discriminating* relevant from irrelevant information (e.g., Farkas & Hoyer, 1980; Ford, Hink, Hopkins, Roth, Pfefferbaum, & Kopell, 1979; Hoyer & Plude, 1982; Nebes & Madden, 1983; Plude & Doussard-Roosevelt, 1989; Plude & Hoyer, 1985). Finally, the argument has been made that irrelevant items have their detrimental effects on older adults only when the search task is particularly effortful or demanding (e.g., Kausler, 1982; Madden, 1982, 1986, 1987a; Nebes & Madden, 1983). Thus older adults are not merely passive victims of indiscriminate stimuli impinging on them from the environment, but there do seem to be situations in which they are at a disadvantage relative to young adults in selecting and processing only task-relevant information.

Plude and Hoyer (1985) reviewed the evidence relevant to visual selective attention and described a framework within which to begin to organize the data on age differences in visual search: the spatial localization hypothesis. The spatial localization hypothesis posits that age decrements in selective attention are due to a decline in the ability to locate task-relevant information in the visual field. Plude and Hoyer (1985) postulated that the operation of the selective attention mechanism is more capacity demanding for older adults than for young adults. In this view, because the capacity available for information processing is an inverse function of the amount of capacity required by the selective attention mechanism, older adults are slowed significantly in situations in which task-relevant information is not easily located. On the other hand, if information processing is slowed, then capacity for searching for relevant information would be limited.

Plude and Hoyer (1985) cite a variety of evidence to support the spatial localization hypothesis. In most studies, subjects are required to search a visual array of items for the presence or absence of a predetermined target item. When targets are easily discriminable from distractors, as when target and distractor items differ in color (e.g., Nebes & Madden, 1983) or when targets and distractors differ in physical form (e.g., Madden, 1982) or when target locations are specified a priori (e.g., Plude & Hoyer, 1986), age differences in search performance are slight or nonexistent. Thus, when the demands on the selective attention mechanism to locate task-relevant information are slight, the older individual is quicker to process that information and is not subject to distraction or interference from nonrelevant information. In the context of spatial localization processes, Hoyer (1987; Hoyer & Plude, 1982) has recently looked at the role of expertise in visual search. Knowing what to look for can speed search, and experts in particular domains can compensate for sensory acuity problems by knowing which features of a search field are relevant and which are not.

Plude and Doussard-Roosevelt (1989) have extended the work on visual search using the feature-integration theory of Treisman and Gelade (1980). In this context, visual search is comprised of two stages: an initial stage of parallel feature extraction that goes on unlimited by selective attention limits, and a second, serial stage in which features are integrated or conjoined to represent multidimensional objects. Young and older adults perform equivalently on the initial stage in a search task where a single distinguishing feature identifies the target stimulus. However, age differences in search performance are significant when the target item is represented by a conjunction of features that are shared individually with distractor items. Plude and Doussard-Roosevelt (1989) suggested that selective attention is the glue that holds together the visual features of complex objects and that age-related slowing in this function of selective attention exacerbates age-related slowing of spatial localization abilities.

Plude and Doussard-Roosevelt (1989) also took some pains to argue that their findings implicate central attentional processes in accounting for age differences in performance and are not simply due to age-related sensory changes in extrafoveal acuity. Plude and Hoyer (1986) made the same argument based on their experimental control of acuity differences. These arguments are made in response to those put forth by Cerella and colleagues (e.g., Cerella, 1985; Cerella, Poon, & Fozard, 1982) and by Madden (1985), which hold that age effects in visual letter search tasks can be explained by a general slowing hypothesis (Salthouse, 1982) without having to introduce the concept of attention. Madden (1985) stated that "visual search . . . appear[s] to be a cognitive task in which age differences are determined primarily by quantitative changes in the speed of information processing rather than by qualitative changes in the ability to attend" (p. 664–665). Cerella again makes the same argument in his chapter in this volume. This controversy continues to rage, perhaps representing a healthy attempt to keep parsimony in theories of cognitive aging.

III. New Directions in Research on Aging and Attention

Luria (1973) pointed to the hierarchical organization of attention in the brain at three levels, the brain stem, the thalmic nuclei, and the frontal lobes. Presumably, this reflects the evolution of the mammalian brain in which the reptilian, equine, and primate brains show a rerepresentation of functions at the different levels. It is thus not surprising that one can modify attention by verbal instructions, with selectivity in attention controlled by the frontal lobes, and the selective attention to incoming stimuli controlled at the thalamic level in gating of input, and at the level of brain stem in alerting or orienting responses. The concept of a hierarchically organized attentional system also may fit new evidence of the role of attention in intellectual functions.

Stankov (1988) carried out a factor analytic study of age and measures of attention, intelligence, and speed of search. A total of 19 psychometric measures of intelligence and 17 measures of attentional processes were given to 100 subjects between the ages of 20 and 70. The attentional factors appeared to explain the differences with age in fluid intelligence. Of interest to students of attention is the fact that no separate factor appeared for divided and selective attention. Stankov's research is a contribution to our knowledge about the organization of intelligence, attention, and aging and opens the way to further studies that link psychometric and experimental approaches to the study of behavior (see Willis, Blow, Cornelius, & Baltes, 1983; Cornelius, Willis, Nesselroade, & Baltes, 1983). Studies are now called for which incorporate, in the same

design, measures of fluid and crystallized intelligence, attention, speed of behavior, and age, and modification conditions such as practice, effects of disease, alcohol, and drugs.

The research of Stankov (1988) and that reviewed in this chapter suggests that it is now possible to plan research that will link some of the islands of knowledge about aging. These islands include those of psychometrically defined intelligence (see Schaie, this volume), speed of behavior (see Cerella, this volume), behaviorally defined attention, and the neurophysiological substrate of attention (Prinz, Dustman, & Emmerson, this volume). For too long these areas of research have stood independent as though there were separate underlying processes within the organism.

IV. Conclusions

The subject of attention is alive and vigorous in research on aging despite its long eclipse during the dominance of psychology by behaviorism. The focus of this research is on prescribing the normal course of attention over the life span and the nature of deficits that appear as a consequence of disease and altered states of the organism. The fact that attentional states can now be observed physiologically and that specific brain nuclei can be identified that participate in attentional processes suggests that new explanations of altered attentional states are in the offing (e.g., Freed, Corkin, Growdon, & Nissen, 1988; Vitaliano, Breen, Albert, Russo, & Prinz, 1984). In particular, we have the promise of multilevel explanations of variations of attentional behavior in normal aging and dementia, in which factors of arousal, intention, and motivation can be distinguished.

In this nexus of scientific interest, research on the psychology of attention and aging has a role to play in providing methods, findings, concepts, and theoretical explanations to other scientific disciplines. It is hoped, however, that psychology will continue to look both ways to its scientific neighbors to generate ideas and to make contributions. On the one hand, there are the "hardware sciences," the neurosciences, to which psychology can contribute, and, on the other hand, there are the "software sciences," the social sciences that examine the influences on preoccupations and attention. Those interested in understanding human attention might do well to look also at animal studies. If attention is an evolved pattern of behavior, it would seem productive to encourage an ethology of attention.

Future research might be directed toward a better understanding of the variety of attentional processes and their hierarchical organization, how these processes might be quantified, how attention relates to everyday complex tasks, and the impact of such variables as aging, clinical illness, and life-style on attentional functioning. Implications of this research include improved diagnostic tools, identification of both adverse and optimum conditions for attention and the modifiability of these conditions, and potential contributions to lifelong well-being.

References

Barrett, G. V., Mihal, W. L., Panek, P. E., Sterns, H. L., & Alexander, R. A. (1977). Information processing skills predictive of accident involvement for younger and older commercial drivers. *Industrial Gerontology*, **4**, 173–182.

Birren, J. E. (Ed.) (1959). *Handbook of aging and the individual.* Chicago: University of Chicago Press.

Birren, J. E., Woods, A. M., & Williams, M. V. (1980). Behavioral slowing with age: Causes, organization and consequences. In L. Poon (Ed.), *Aging in the 1980s* (pp. 293–308). Washington, DC: American Psychological Association.

Botwinick, J. (1961). Husband and father-in-law—a reversible figure. *American Journal of Psychology*, **74**, 312–313.

Botwinick, J. (1965). Perceptual reorganization in relation to age and sex. *Journal of Gerontology*, **20**, 224–227.

Braun, R., & Wickens, C. D. (1985). The functional age profile: An objective decision criterion for the assessment of pilot performance capacities and capabilities. *Human Factors*, **27**, 681–693.

Cerella, J. (1985). Age-related decline in extrafoveal letter perception. *Journal of Gerontology*, **40**, 727–736.

Cerella, J., Poon, L. W., & Fozard, J. L. (1982). Age and iconic read-out. *Journal of Gerontology*, **37**, 197–202.

Chown, S. M. (1961). Age and the rigidities. *Journal of Gerontology*, **16**, 353–362.

Cornelius, S. W., Willis, S. L., Nesselroade, J. R., & Baltes, P. B. (1983). Convergence between attention variables and factors of psychometric intelligence in older adults. *Intelligence*, **7**, 253–269.

Craik, F. I. M. (1977). Age differences in human memory. In J. E. Birren & K. W. Schaie (Eds.), *Handbook of the psychology of aging.* New York: Van Nostrand Reinhold.

Craik, F. I. M., & Byrd, M. (1982). Aging and cognitive deficits: The role of attentional resources. In F. I. M. Craik & S. Trehub (Eds.), *Aging and cognitive processes.* New York: Plenum.

Craik, F. I. M., & McDowd, J. M. (1987). Age differences in recall and recognition. *Journal of Experimental Psychology: Learning, Memory and Cognition*, **13**, 474–479.

Craik, F. I. M., & Simon, E. (1980). Age differences in memory: The role of attention and depth of processing. In L. W. Poon, J. L. Fozard, L. S. Cermak, D. Arenberg, & L. W. Thompson (Eds.), *New directions in memory and aging* (pp. 95–112). Hillsdale, NJ: Erlbaum.

Duncan-Johnson, C., & Donchin, E. (1977). On quantifying surprise: The variation of event-related potentials with subjective probability. *Psychophysiology*, **14**, 456–467.

Dustman, R. E., & Beck, E. C. (1965). Phase of alpha brain waves, reaction time, and visually evoked potentials. *Electroencephalography and Clinical Neurophysiology*, **18**, 433–440.

Dustman, R. E., & Snyder, E. W. (1981). Lifespan changes in visually evoked potentials at central scalp. *Neurobiology of Aging*, **2**, 303–308.

Dustman, R. E., Snyder, E. W., & Schlehuber, C. J. (1981). Lifespan alterations in visually evoked potentials and inhibitory function. *Neurobiology of Aging*, **2**, 187–192.

Eisdorfer, C. (1968). Arousal and performance: Experiments in verbal learning and a tentative theory. In G. A. Talland (Ed.), *Human aging and behavior* (pp. 189–216). New York: Academic Press.

Farkas, M. S., & Hoyer, W. J. (1980). Processing consequences of perceptual grouping in selective attention. *Journal of Gerontology*, **35**, 207–216.

Ford, J. M., Hink, R. F., Hopkins, W. A., III, Roth, W. T., Pfefferbaum, A., & Kopell, B. S. (1979). Age effects on event-related potentials in a selective attention task. *Journal of Gerontology*, **35**, 207–216.

Freed, D., Corkin, S., Growdon, J., & Nissen, S. (1988). Selective attention in Alzheimer's disease: CSF correlates of behavioral impairments. *Neuropsychologia*, **26**, 895–902.

Giambra, L. M. (1989). Task-unrelated-thought frequency as a function of age: A laboratory study. *Psychology and Aging*, **4**, 136–143.

Giambra, L. M., & Quilter, R. E. (1985). *Sustained attention during adulthood: A longitudinal and multicohort analysis using the Mackworth clock test.* Paper presented at the annual meeting of the Gerontological Society of America, New Orleans.

Goodin, D., Squires, K., Henderson, B., & Starr, A. (1978). Age-related variations in evoked potentials to auditory stimuli in normal human subjects. *Electroencephalography and Clinical Neurophysiology*, **44**, 447–458.

Hartley, A. A. (1981). Adult age differences in deductive reasoning processes. *Journal of Gerontology*, **36**, 700–706.

Hartley, A. A., & Kieley, J. (1986). *Aging and the time course of attention shifts.* Paper presented at the annual meeting of the Psychonomic Society, New Orleans.

Hartley, A. A., Kieley, J. M., & McKenzie, C. A. (1987). *Aging and the allocation of visual attention.* Paper presented at the National Institute on Aging Conference on Aging and Attention. Washington, D.C., November.

Hasher, L., & Zacks, R. T. (1979). Automatic and effortful processes in memory. *Journal of Experimental Psychology: General*, **108**, 350–388.

Hasher, L., & Zacks, R. T. (1989). Working memory, comprehension, and aging: A review and a new view. In G. H. Bower (Ed.), *The Psychology of Learning and Motivation*, **22**, 193–225.

Hayslip, B., & Sterns, H. L. (1979). Age differences in relationships between crystallized and fluid intelligence and problem solving. *Journal of Gerontology*, **34**, 404–414.

Heilman, K. M., Watson, R. T., Valenstein, E., and Goldberg, M. E. (1987). Attention: Behavior and neural mechanisms. In V. B. Mountcastle (Ed.), *Handbook of physiology. Section 1: The nervous system* (pp. 461–481). Bethesda, MD: American Physiological Society.

Hoyer, W. (1987). *Domains of attention.* Paper presented at the National Institute on Aging Conference on Aging and Attention, Washington, DC, November.

Hoyer, W. J., & Plude, D. J. (1980). Attentional and perceptual processes in the study of cognitive aging. In L. W. Poon (Ed.), *Aging in the 1980'sR: Psychological issues.* Washington, DC: American Psychological Association.

Hoyer, W. J., & Plude, D. J. (1982). Aging and the allocation of attentional resources in visual information processing. In R. Sekuler, D. Kline, & K. Dismukes (Eds.), *Aging and human visual function* (pp. 245–263). New York: Liss.

Hoyer, W. J., Rebok, G. W., & Sved, S. M. (1979). Irrelevant information and problem-solving. *Journal of Gerontology*, **34**, 553–560.

James, W. (1890). *Principles of psychology.* New York: Holt.

Jerome, E. A. (1959). Age and learning—experimental studies. In J. E. Birren (Ed.), *Handbook of aging and the individual* (pp. 655–699). Chicago: University of Chicago Press.

Kausler, D. H. (1982). *Experimental psychology and human aging.* New York: Wiley.

Kausler, D. H., & Hakami, M. K. (1982). Frequency judgments by young and elderly adults for relevant stimuli with simultaneously presented irrelevant stimuli. *Journal of Gerontology*, **37**, 438–442.

Kausler, D., & Kleim, D. M. (1978). Age differences in processing relevant versus irrelevant stimuli in multiple-item recognition learning. *Journal of Gerontology*, **33**, 87–93.

Kounin, J. S. (1941). Experimental studies of rigidity. *Character and Personality*, 251–282.

Layton, B. (1975). Perceptual noise and aging. *Psychological Bulletin*, **82**, 875–883.

Luria, A. R. (1973). *The working brain*. London: Penguin.

Madden, D. J. (1982). Age differences and similarities in the improvement of controlled search. *Experimental Aging Research*, **8**, 91–98.

Madden, D. J. (1984). Data-driven and memory-driven selective attention in visual search. *Journal of Gerontology*, **39**, 72–78.

Madden, D. J. (1985). Adult age differences in memory-driven selective attention. *Developmental Psychology*, **21**, 655–665.

Madden, D. J. (1986). Adult age differences in the attentional capacity demands of visual search. *Cognitive Development*, **1**, 335–363.

Madden, D. J. (1987a). Aging, attention, and the use of meaning during visual search. *Cognitive Development*, **2**, 201–216.

Madden, D. J. (1987b). *Divided attention and aging*. Paper presented at the National Institute on Aging Conference on Aging and Attention, Washington, DC, November.

McDowd, J. M. (1986). The effects of age and extended practice on divided attention performance. *Journal of Gerontology*, **41**, 764–769.

McDowd, J. M., & Craik, F. I. M. (1988). Effects of aging and task difficulty on divided attention performance. *Journal of Experimental Psychology: Human Perception and Performance*, **14**, 267–280.

McGhie, A. (1969). *Pathology of attention*. London: Penguin.

Mergler, N. L., Dusek, J. B., & Hoyer, W. J. (1977). Central/incidental recall and selective attention in young and elderly adults. *Experimental Aging Research*, **3**, 49–60.

Navon, D. (1984). Resources—A theoretical soupstone? *Psychological Review*, **86**, 214–255.

Nebes, R. D., & Madden, D. J. (1983). The use of focused attention in visual search by young and old adults. *Experimental Aging Research*, **9**, 139–143.

Obler, L. (1980). Narrative discourse style in the elderly. In L. Obler & M. Albert (Eds.), *Language and communication in the elderly*. Lexington, MA: Heath.

Parasuraman, R. (1985). *A literature review of the study of the relation between aging and sustained attention*. Paper presented at the annual meeting of the Gerontological Society, New Orleans.

Pillsbury, W. (1908). *Attention*. London: Allen & Unwin.

Plude, D. J., & Doussard-Roosevelt, J. A. (1989). Aging, selective attention, and feature integration. *Psychology and Aging*, **4**, 98–105.

Plude, D. J., & Hoyer, W. J. (1985). Attention and performance: Identifying and localizing age deficits. In N. Charness (Ed.), *Aging and performance* (pp. 47–99). New York: Wiley.

Plude, D. J., & Hoyer, W. J. (1986). Age and the selectivity of visual information processing. *Journal of Gerontology*, **1**, 4–10.

Powell, A. H., Eisdorfer, C., & Bogdonoff, M. D. (1964). Physiologic response patterns observed in a learning task. *Archives of General Psychiatry*, **10**, 192–195.

Rabbitt, P. (1965). An age-decrement in the ability to ignore irrelevant information. *Journal of Gerontology*, **20**, 233–238.

Ribot, T. A., (1890). *The psychology of attention*. Chicago: Open Court Press.

Salthouse, T. A. (1982). *Adult Cognition*. New York: Springer-Verlag.

Salthouse, T. A. (1985). *A theory of cognitive aging*. Amsterdam: Elsevier.

Salthouse, T. A., Rogan, J. D., & Prill, K. (1984). Division of attention: Age differences on a visually presented memory task. *Memory and Cognition*, **12**, 613–620.

Schaie, K. W. (1958). Rigidity-flexibility and intelligence. *Psychological Monographs*, **72** (462).

Schonfield, D. H. (1981). Attention switching in higher mental processes. In F. I. M. Craik & S. Trehub (Eds.), *Aging and cognitive processes*. New York: Plenum.

Somberg, B. L., & Salthouse, T. A. (1982). Divided attention abilities in young and old adults. *Journal of Experimental Psychology: Human Perception and Performance*, **8**, 651–663.

Stankov, L. (1988). Aging, attention and intelligence. *Psychology and Aging*, **3**(1), 59–74.

Stine, E. L., & Wingfield, A. (1987). Process and strategy in memory for speech among younger and older adults. *Psychology and Aging, 2,* 272–279.

Surwillo, W. W., & Quilter, R. E. (1964). Vigilance, age, and response time. *The American Journal of Psychology, 77,* 614–620.

Talland, G. A. (1968). *Disorders of memory and learning.* Baltimore: Penguin.

Thompson, L. W., & Marsh, G. R. (1973). Psychophysiological studies of aging. In C. Eisdorfer & M. P. Lawton (Eds.), *The psychology of adult development and aging.* Washington, DC: American Psychological Association Press.

Treisman, A., & Gelade, G. (1980). A feature-integration theory of attention. *Cognitive Psychology, 12,* 97–136.

Vitaliano, P., Breen, A., Russo, J., & Prinz, P. (1984). Memory, attention and functional status in community residing Alzheimer type dementia patients and optimally healthy aged. *Journal of Gerontology, 39,* 58–64.

Welford, A. T. (1964). Experimental psychology in the study of aging. *British Medical Bulletin, 20,* 65–69.

Whipple, G. M. (1914, 1915). *Manual of mental and physical tests. Part I: Simpler processes. Part II: Complex processes.* Baltimore: Warwick & York.

Wickens, C. D., Braune, R., & Stokes, A. (1987). Age differences in the speed and capacity of information processing. 1: A dual-task approach. *Psychology and Aging, 2,* 70–78.

Willis, S. L., Blow, F. C., Cornelius, S. W., & Baltes, P. B. (1983). Training research in aging: Attentional processes. *Journal of Educational Psychology, 75*(2), 257–270.

Woodruff, D. (1975). Relationships between EEG alpha frequency, reaction time, and age: A biofeedback study. *Psychophysiology, 12,* 673–681.

Wright, L. L., & Elias, J. W. (1979). Age differences in the effects of perceptual noise. *Journal of Gerontology, 34,* 704–708.

Wright, R. E. (1981). Aging, divided attention, and processing capacity. *Journal of Gerontology, 36,* 605–614.

Yerkes, R. M. (1911). *Introduction to psychology.* New York: Holt.

Fourteen

Mammalian Models of Learning, Memory, and Aging

Diana S. Woodruff-Pak

The purpose of this chapter is to provide an overview of the available mammalian models of learning, memory, and aging and to highlight the power of these models in elucidating processes of behavioral aging in humans and their amelioration. Although each animal model has limitations, the value of animal models for research on learning, memory, and aging is immeasurable. Our progress in establishing a knowledge base about learning, memory, and aging would be slowed, and in some cases prevented, without animal models.

One means for examining the significance of animal models for the study of learning, memory, and aging is to try to imagine what the state of our knowledge would be in the absence of such models. If we were unable to examine the brains of young and older animals during learning and memory tasks, we would know very little about the neurobiological substrates of these behaviors. It is only with animal models that we can record neural activity from inside the brain while observing behavior. Drugs are tested first in animals.

Although pharmacological trials eventually involve humans, they begin with animals, and in many cases drug trials never reach the human level because of the deleterious side effects observed in animals. Drug intervention is one of the most promising treatments for memory loss in aging and dementia, and it could not be undertaken without animal models.

There are two obvious features of animal models that make them of invaluable assistance in research on learning, memory, and aging. First, the life spans of most animals are considerably shorter than the human life span, compressing the time required to observe processes of aging. For the rapid advancement of knowledge about learning, memory, and aging, animal models are practical and expedient. Second, invasive and/or high-risk observations and experimental manipulations are feasible with animals but not with humans. In many cases, experiments can be performed on animals to demonstrate causal relationships between aging and behavior that simply cannot be undertaken in humans. Legal and ethical constraints

Handbook of the Psychology of Aging, Third Edition
Copyright © 1990 Academic Press, Inc. All rights of reproduction in any form reserved.

on human experimentation lead us to use animals as surrogates. Animal models are an essential tool for the understanding of processes of aging.

A number of the mammalian models of learning, memory, and aging will be presented in this chapter. However, space limitations preclude an exhaustive description of the manifold mammalian models, let alone description of invertebrate models. Coverage in this chapter is focused on mammalian models due to their ready application to human aging. Discussion is limited to laboratory learning and memory tasks and will not extend to ethological perspectives and mammalian learning in natural environments. In this regard, it should be noted that laboratory animals caged throughout their life spans are likely to be limited in neurobiological development compared to animals living in natural or enriched laboratory environments. Although environmental enrichment for aging animals is beginning to be explored (e.g., Diamond, Johnson, Protti, Ott, & Kajisa, 1985; Greenough, 1986), this expanding literature cannot be discussed in the present chapter.

One chapter cannot begin to cover all of the facets of research using animal models of aging. Fortunately, there are several excellent publications entirely devoted to this topic. Additional effective animal models for the study of learning, memory, and aging are presented in a volume published by the New York Academy of Sciences (Olton, Gamzu, & Corkin, 1985) and in a special issue of the *Neurobiology of Aging* (Ingram, Bartus, Olton, & Khachaturian, 1988).

The Committee on Animals Models for Research on Aging (1981) identified three broad roles for animals in research on aging: (a) models for the study of normal aging; (b) models for the study of and pathology in aging; and (c) sources of cells, tissues, organs, and fluids for in vitro studies of normal and pathological aging. All

three are significant and will be demonstrated in the examples included in this chapter. What follows are some of the many applications in which animal models are of demonstrated usefulness and long-range potential in expanding knowledge about learning, memory, and aging.

I. Animal Models in Gerontology

Throughout most of the twentieth century, animal models have been used to study processes of aging. However, the utilization of animal models for the study of learning and memory in aging is more recent. Mammalian models in learning, memory, and aging are linked to the post-World War II surge of research in psychology and aging and to the even more recent advent of neuroscience research. The major portion of the animal model research on learning, memory, and aging has been published in the 1980s. This is a relatively new area of research; it is making rapid progress; and it holds promise for optimizing learning and memory capacities in aging humans.

A. Parallels in the Life Span of Humans and Other Mammals

If our goal is to use mammalian models to understand and improve learning and memory in aging humans, it is important to be able to compare ages in humans and other mammals. Table I compares human life expectancy to life expectancy in some of the mammalian models that have been used for research on learning, memory, and aging.

Although life expectancy of many mammalian species has been established, approximating human age from animal age is a more formidable problem. There are difficulties in paralleling human and animal life expectancy. Different physiological systems age at different rates in different species. Using the aging brain to compare

Table I

Life Expectancies of Species Used as Animal Models in Research on Learning, Memory, and Aging

Species	Life Expectancy
Rodents	
Mice	
C57BL	26.8 months
DBA/2	23.7
Rats	
Fischer 344	23.1 months
Sprague-Dawley	24.0
Long Evans	27.5 (median)
Wistar	24.0
Lagomorphs	
Rabbits	8 years
Carnivores	
Cats	Life expectancy not established; life span in excess of 20 years
Dogs	
Beagles	12 to 13 years
Nonhuman primates	
Apes	
Chimpanzee	Life span of 49 years
Monkeys	
Old World	
macaque	Life span of 33 years
baboon	Life span of 31 years
New World	
capuchin (*Cebus*)	Life span of 43 years
squirrel monkey	Life span of 18 years

Source: Data from Committee on Animal Models for Research on Aging (1981).

aging across species, Flood and Coleman (1988) surveyed neuron numbers and sizes in aging humans, monkeys, and rodents. They found that the number of brain regions that have been studied in more than one species is surprisingly limited. Regions showing the greatest correspondence of age-related changes between humans and selected mammals were primary visual cortex and CA1 of the hippocampus. For the majority of regions of the brain, the data are conflicting, sometimes even within species. Flood and Coleman concluded that neuron numbers and sizes may show similar age-related changes in human and animal brains only

for sharply defined brain regions, animal species and/or strains, and age ranges.

In addition to the problems created by the differential aging of tissue in different species, it is difficult to equate phases of the life span in different species. Puberty is a useful marker for young adulthood, but it is difficult to identify middle and old age in various mammalian species. Identification of comparable points in the adult life span in humans and other mammals is a serious problem in animal model research (Woodruff-Pak, 1988b).

B. Criteria to Evaluate Animal Models of Aging

The attempts to create animal models of learning, memory, and aging are so numerous and diverse that it is helpful to provide criteria to evaluate these models. Bartus, Flicker, and Dean (1983) created logical criteria for developing behavioral animal models of aging. These criteria are presented in Table II and have been slightly modified to expand them beyond the pharmacological applications for which they were initially intended. These criteria will be

Table II

Logical Criteria for Developing Animal Models of Learning, Memory, and Aging

1. Behavior measured should display natural age-related deficits in the species used.
2. Conceptual or operational similarities should exist between that behavior and relevant behavioral changes in aged humans.
3. Species selected should share age-related neurobiological changes with some of those observed in humans, especially those that correlate with the behavioral deficit measured.
4. If a behavioral deficit is artificially induced in younger subjects, concomitant changes in the central nervous system function should mimic some of those known to exist in aged subjects.
5. Some of the drugs known to improve behavior in the aged in clinical trials should also produce positive neurobiological and behavioral effects in the animal model.

Source: Adapted from Bartus, Flicker, and Dean (1983).

used to assess the animal models of learning, memory, and aging examined in this chapter.

II. Mammalian Models of Learning and Memory in Normal Aging

On average, older adults take longer to learn a task to criterion, they have greater difficulty retrieving recently learned material, and they are particularly handicapped at recall as opposed to simply recognizing what they have learned (Arenberg & Robertson-Tchabo, 1977). Mammalian models are useful in providing similar deficits in organisms that age in a shorter time than humans and can be studied invasively. Learning and memory tasks such as classical conditioning, operant conditioning, instrumental learning, spatial learning and memory, and problem solving are within the capacity of various species of mammals. Processes of aging often affect these behaviors in animals in a fashion similar to the way they affect human behavior. According to the criteria identified in Table II, species with behavioral and neurobiological characteristics exhibiting natural age-related changes that parallel human aging are logical candidates for animal models of aging.

A. Classical Conditioning of the NM/Eyeblink Response in Rabbits

Classical conditioning of the nictitating membrane (NM)/eyeblink response in rabbits is promising as a model system for the study of learning, memory, and aging. There are striking parallels in classical conditioning and aging in rabbits and humans, and the neurobiological substrates for this simple form of learning is quite well understood in rabbits. We are at a point where we may be able to identify with a great degree of specificity the neu-

robiological changes resulting in the age changes in this type of classical conditioning. For these reasons, Thompson (1988) has suggested that classical conditioning of the eyelid response may be the Rosetta stone for brain substrates of age-related deficits in learning and memory. Thompson views this model system as among the most promising animal models of the human condition in which to analyze brain mechanisms of normally occurring aging effects on learning and memory.

Figure 1 identifies techniques for eyelid classical conditioning in rabbits and humans. For this simple kind of learning to occur, a tone (or light) conditioned stimulus (CS) is presented first, followed about half a second later by a corneal airpuff unconditioned stimulus (US). The US always causes the organism to blink. The repeated pairing of the CS and US results in a conditioned response (CR): The organism blinks to the CS before the onset of the US. The "third eyelid" or NM of the rabbit and the rabbit eyeblink response are highly correlated and show similar patterns of response to classical conditioning and to cerebellar lesions (Lavond, Logan, Sohn, Garner, & Thompson, 1988; McCormick, Lavond, & Thompson, 1982). We will refer to the response as the eyeblink response in this discussion of rabbits, cats, and humans.

Using this model system, it may now be possible to identify and characterize the critical age-related changes in the brain involved in aging of the learning and memory processes for eyeblink classical conditioning (Thompson & Woodruff-Pak, 1987; Woodruff-Pak & Thompson, 1985, 1988b). Age differences in the classically conditioned eyeblink response are large and have been demonstrated in rabbits, cats, and humans (Braun & Geiselhart, 1959; Graves & Solomon, 1985; Harrison & Buchwald, 1983; Kimble & Pennypacker, 1963; Powell, Buchanan, & Hernandez, 1981; Solomon, Pomerleau, Bennett, James, & Morse, 1989; Woodruff-Pak,

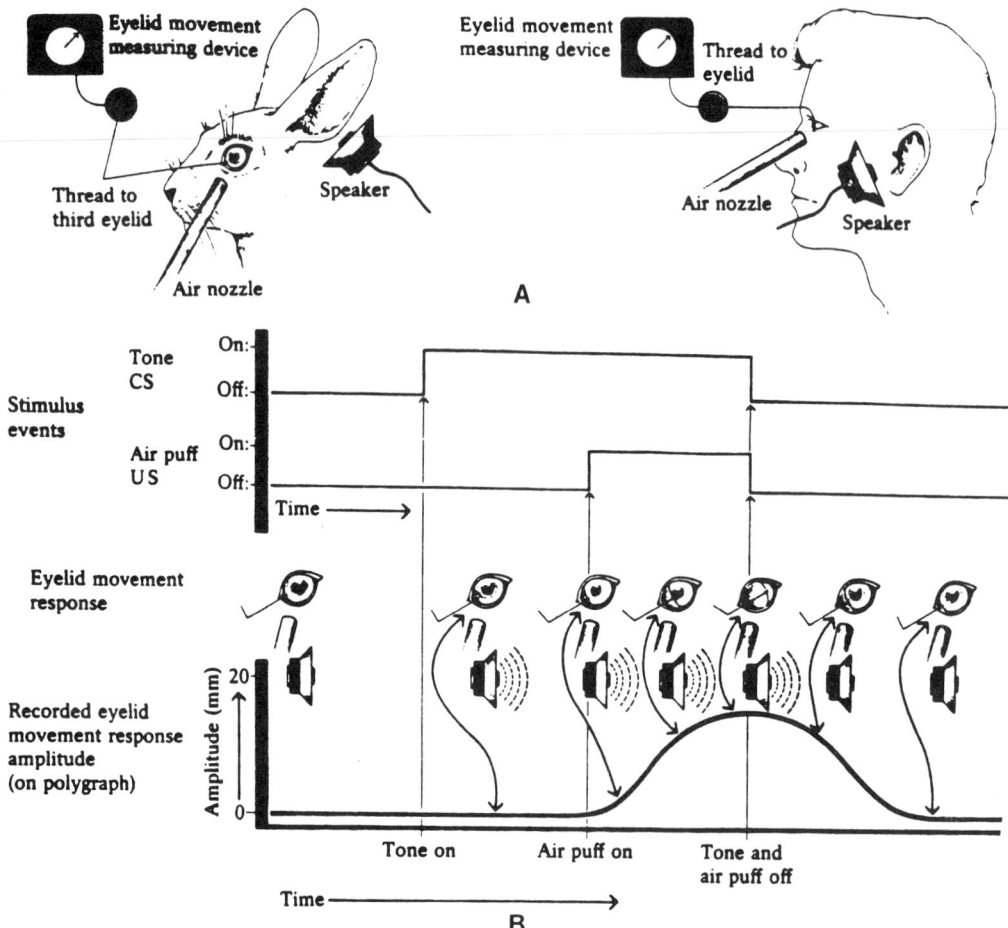

Figure 1 Classical conditioning of the eyelid response in rabbits and humans. A. Experimental setup. The rabbit's third eyelid and the human's eyelid are used. A thin wire is attached to the eyelid and connected to a transducer—a device that measures movement of the thread and hence the eyelid. Air puffed from a nozzle near the eye serves as the unconditioned stimulus (US). A tone from a speaker is the conditioned stimulus (CS). B. The transducer measures movement of the rabbit's third eyelid. This movement is displayed on a computer screen. The example shown here occurs early in training before conditioning has developed. Note that the tone does not elicit an eyelid response. Shortly after the air puff is turned on, the eyelid begins to close; this is recorded as an upward movement of the time line. After the air puff is turned off, the eyelid opens again. Closing the eyelid to an air puff is an unconditioned response (UR), also called a reflex response. After learning has taken place, eyelid closure will have become a conditioned response (CR). It will occur in the time period between onset of the CS (the tone) and onset of the US (the air puff). (From *Psychology* (3rd Ed.) by Lindzey, Thompson, and Spring. Worth Publishers, New York (1988).

Lavond, Logan, & Thompson, 1987; Woodruff-Pak & Thompson, 1988a). Parallels between rabbits and humans (cats have not been tested extensively) exist in the age function over the adult life span when deficits in eyeblink conditioning appear. Some of the neurobiological age changes that could account for the behavioral deficits occur in all three species.

Using the criteria for an animal model presented in Table II, classical conditioning of the eyeblink response in rabbits has met requirements stated in the first three. First, eyeblink conditioning displays natural age-related deficits in rabbits and cats. Second, the similarities in age differences in classical conditioning in rabbits and humans are striking. Third, neurobiological age-related changes that are likely to be involved with the behavioral changes occur in humans as well as in rabbits (i.e., Purkinje cell loss). With regard to the fourth criterion involving artificial inducement of behavioral and neurobiological aging changes in young animals, Lavond, Steinmetz, and Thompson (1987) demonstrated that aspiration of area HVI in the cerebellar cortex delayed but did not prevent acquisition in young rabbits. That lesion removes Purkinje cells in HVI, and it simulates behavioral aging. Criterion 5, involving pharmacological manipulation to ameliorate age-related deficits in classical conditioning, is beginning to be tested in this model system. Devo, Straube, and Disterhoft (1988) demonstrated more rapid acquisition in old rabbits in the trace classical conditioning paradigm using the drug nimodipine (NIM). These preliminary data do not test the mechanism by which NIM facilitates associative learning, but they do indicate the promise of this model system for understanding neurobiological mechanisms through pharmacological manipulation.

1. Control of Peripheral Aging Processes

Using animal models to study learning, memory, and aging requires rigorous controls. In the case of classical conditioning, as in the case of other behavioral measures of learning and memory processes, peripheral sensory and motor aging can interfere with stimulus input and response presentation making it appear that learning and memory are affected. In all of the animal models of learning, memory, and aging, controls are essential. We will present the controls used in studies of classical conditioning as examples of some of the types of controls required in all animal model research on learning, memory, and

aging. Sensory or motor impairment are subject to age change and must be ruled out as contributing to age differences in eyeblink classical conditioning if associative learning factors are to be implicated. Graves and Solomon (1985) found no age differences in sensory thresholds to the tone CS in the same rabbits (ranging in age from 3 to 60 months) in which there were large age differences in acquisition in the trace classical conditioning paradigm. Corneal sensitivity declines with age. Thus older rabbits might find the airpuff less aversive. In this sense, age differences in motivation would not be equated. However, the oldest rabbits and humans still blink vigorously in response to an airpuff. The latency and amplitude of the unconditioned response (UR), reflecting measures of the motor response system, are similar in young and old rabbits and young and old humans (Woodruff-Pak et al., 1987; Woodruff-Pak & Thompson, 1988a). We also have ruled out age differences in eyeblink rate and in voluntary responses as causes of age differences in eyeblink classical conditioning in humans (Woodruff-Pak & Thompson, 1988a).

2. Neurobiological Correlates of Classical Conditioning

The two brain structures with major involvement in classical conditioning of the eyeblink response are structures clearly affected by processes of aging: the cerebellum and the hippocampus. The hippocampus plays a modulatory role in classical conditioning (Thompson & Woodruff-Pak, 1987). We have demonstrated that hippocampal multiple unit modeling of the behavioral unconditioned and conditioned response is delayed in older rabbits (Woodruff-Pak et al., 1987). However, hippocampal theta frequency that predicts rate of acquisition in young rabbits was close to identical in 3-, 30-, and 45-month-old rabbits (Woodruff-Pak & Logan, 1988). It is important to continue to explore the role of aging in the hippocampus in age changes in classical conditioning as well as in age changes in short- and long-term memory, rate of forgetting, effects of interference, memory for precise information, and general skills. Winocur (1984, 1986, 1988, 1989) examined all of these types of learning and memory (except for classical conditioning) in rodents and humans and argued that memory loss with age is related in large part to progressive hippocampal dysfunction. Landfield and his associates have made a strong case for the significance of the hippocampus in the study of learning, memory, and aging (Landfield, 1988; Landfield, Pitler, & Applegate, 1986).

In classical conditioning of the eyeblink response, aging in the cerebellum may be more significant than aging in the hippocampus. There has been success in defining a substantial portion of the essential memory trace circuit underlying classical conditioning of the eyeblink response in rabbits (McCormick & Thompson, 1984a,b; Thompson, 1986; Thompson, McCormick, & Lavond, 1986). Data from stimulating, recording, and lesion studies suggest that the ipsilateral cerebellum is the site of the primary memory trace for the classically conditioned eyeblink response. To date, evidence is most consistent with storage of the memory traces in localized regions of cerebellar cortex and interpositus nucleus. We have found some contribution to age changes in conditionability in the cerebellar circuit (Woodruff-Pak & Thompson, 1988b). For example, stimulation of mossy fibers in the pons to input the conditioned stimulus (CS) directly into the cerebellum (avoiding the peripheral auditory circuit) results in significantly delayed acquisition in older rabbits (Woodruff-Pak, Steinmetz, & Thompson, 1988). Measuring the cerebellum more directly, one finds that the loss of Purkinje cells in cerebellar cortex (areas HVI and vermis) is highly correlated

with delayed acquisition in older rabbits (Woodruff-Pak & Sheffield, 1987).

3. Parallels in Eyeblink Classical Conditioning in Humans and Animals

In young adult rabbits, cats, and humans, classical conditioning of the eyeblink response in the delay paradigm is quite similar. Rabbits condition best at shorter CS-US intervals (250 to 500 msec) than humans whose maximal conditionability ranges from approximately 400 to 1200 msec. Cats condition well at 400 to 500 msec. Rabbits take about 110 trials to attain criterion, which is similar to the acquisition curve for cats (Patterson, Olah, & Clement, 1977). Young humans attain a similar criterion in 40 trials (Woodruff-Pak & Thompson, 1988a).

Very apparent age differences in conditioning in the delay paradigm (which involves an overlapping of the CS and US) appear in humans (Braun & Geiselhart, 1959; Kimble & Pennypacker, 1963; Solomon et al., 1989; Woodruff-Pak & Thompson, 1988a). Harrison and Buchwald (1983) have demonstrated age differences in the delay paradigm in cats, and Powell et al. (1981) and Woodruff-Pak (1988a) have demonstrated age differences in delay conditioning in rabbits. Age differences in delay classical conditioning begin to appear at about the same point in the adult life span in rabbits and humans (Woodruff-Pak, 1988b).

There are parallels between humans, rabbits, and cats in the age effects on acquisition and retention of the classically conditioned eyeblink response (Woodruff-Pak, 1988b). There are striking similarities in several mammalian species, including humans, rabbits, and cats, in the loss of Purkinje cells with age. Neurobiological and behavioral data in rats and rabbits also converge to implicate age changes in the mossy fiber-granule cell-parallel fiber system as a source of aging deficits. These parallels in neurobiological and behavioral aging hold the promise that knowledge gained with the rabbit model system will generalize to aging in many mammalian species, including humans. Because we understand and can explore the neural circuit underlying classical conditioning of the eyeblink response in rabbits, this model system has significant potential to enhance understanding of the neurobiology of aging on both an animal and human level.

B. Classical Conditioning in Rats

The rabbit has some major advantages as an animal model in classical conditioning research due to its size and, especially, its docile nature. Rabbits tolerate well the restraint required in classical conditioning studies. However, a major disadvantage of the rabbit related to research on aging is its relatively long life expectancy of 8 years. Old rabbits are seldom, if ever, obtainable from breeders. National Institute on Aging (NIA) barrier-reared colonies of rabbits do not exist, and the health history of older rabbits used in the published studies is unspecified and presumably unknown. In this regard, mice and rats are a much more useful species for gerontological research. Mice and rats have the advantage of small space requirements and short life spans. Neither the genetic controls nor the breeding environments currently available for rabbits equal those in place for mice and rats provided by breeding colonies established by the NIA.

These advantages were undoubtedly among the incentives that induced Powell and Buchanan and their associates who had published the first eyeblink classical conditioning studies on aging rabbits to explore classical conditioning of the cardiac and leg flexion responses in aging Fischer 344 rats (Buchanan & Ginn, 1988; Prescott, Buchanan, & Powell, 1989). As

Buchanan and Powell (1988) pointed out, the biology as well as functional changes associated with aging in the rat are much better known than in the rabbit. However, because rats are so totally intolerant of restraint, they were not good candidates for classical conditioning. An attempt to surmount this problem was made by instituting a period of 5 days of daily gentling by the experimenters followed by a 1-week period of adaptation to the restraint apparatus and electrodes. Although this long period of gentling and adaptation reduced the movement of the rats, movement was still considerably greater in rats than in rabbits, even though rabbits require only one day of adaptation. Furthermore, the rat data were still problematic due to the strong inclination of this species, and especially of young male rats, to attempt to free themselves from any restraint. At present, age differences in the behavioral classical conditioning data of the leg flexion response in rats are somewhat difficult to interpret due to these problems. There appear to be age differences in this type of classical conditioning between 12- and 24-month-old rats, and older males show greater deficits than older females. Because of the well-defined biological and behavioral parameters in rats, their short life expectancy, and their small space requirements, continued efforts to develop the rat as an animal model for the study of aging and classical conditioning is worthwhile.

C. Operant Conditioning

Operant conditioning refers to the type of learning in which the probability of a response is altered by a change in the consequences for that response. When a rat presses a lever and receives a food pellet, the probability that the rat will press the lever again is increased. Relatively few attempts have been made to create animal models of learning, memory, and aging using operant conditioning. In his survey of the research literature on this topic, Kausler (1982) pointed out that there was a paucity of human and animal research on aging and operant conditioning. One reason for this scarcity of research is that age is not a variable of interest to operant psychologists.

1. Positive Reinforcement

A deterrent to the creation of animal models using operant conditioning is that age differences in operant conditioning in humans are small or nonexistent. Kausler cited studies of elderly psychotic patients, senile dementia patients, and nursing home residents that indicate that even these elderly subjects are amenable to behavior modification through the use of positive reinforcers. This has led some investigators to promote operant conditioning as a useful tool for gerontological intervention (e.g., Baltes & Baron, 1977; Baltes & Lerner, 1980).

From the perspective of the logical criteria identified in Table II for creating animal models, there is no need to create an animal model using operant conditioning, at least using positive reinforcement. Furthermore, the animal studies that have been undertaken provide contradictory results. Goodrick, noted for his careful behavioral studies of rodents, reported greater bar pressing in young rats in one study (1965), greater bar pressing in older rats in a second study (1969), and equal bar pressing in young and older rats in a third study (1970). Reliable behavioral aging phenomena have been assessed in so many other domains of learning and memory that animal models of behavioral aging using operant conditioning appear among the least promising.

2. Avoidance Conditioning

The type of operant conditioning for which there appear to be the largest age differences is avoidance conditioning. In this kind of learning, a response is emitted that enables the organism to avoid receipt of a noxious stimulus event. Early avoidance conditioning studies were conducted by Doty (1966a,b; Doty & Doty, 1964; Doty & Johnson, 1966). More recently, deficits in passive avoidance retention in different strains of aged mice and rats have been reported by Brizzee and Ordy (1979), Dean, Scozzafava, Goaf, Regan, Beer, and Bartus (1981), Gold and McGaugh (1975), Kubanis, Gobbel, and Zornetzer (1981), Lippa, Pelham, Beer, Critchett, Dean, and Bartus (1980), and Zornetzer, Thompson, and Rogers (1982).

The passive avoidance task is illustrated along with other behavioral tasks for rodents in Figure 2. The passive avoidance task reinforces rodents for remaining on one side of a chamber. The active nature of rodents results in their inclination to explore the entire chamber. As soon as they cross to the opposite side of the chamber, they receive a paw shock. To avoid shock to the paws, the rodent must remain on one side of the chamber and avoid exploring the other side. Retention of this passive response over a 4-hour period shows moderate age differences, and retention over a 24-hour period shows robust age differences. No age differences in retention were observed after 1 hour (Lippa et al., 1980).

Dean et al. compared the performance of C57 mice on retention of passive avoidance to performance on a number of other tasks and concluded that the performance of the aged mice reflected an impairment in the ability to remember the aversive event for sufficiently long periods of time. Bartus, Flicker, and Dean (1983) pointed out that certain operational similarities existed between the passive avoidance retention deficit and impairment of recent memory observed in aged human and nonhuman primates. The event to be remembered is brief and discrete, there is little or no practice or rehearsal, and retention de-

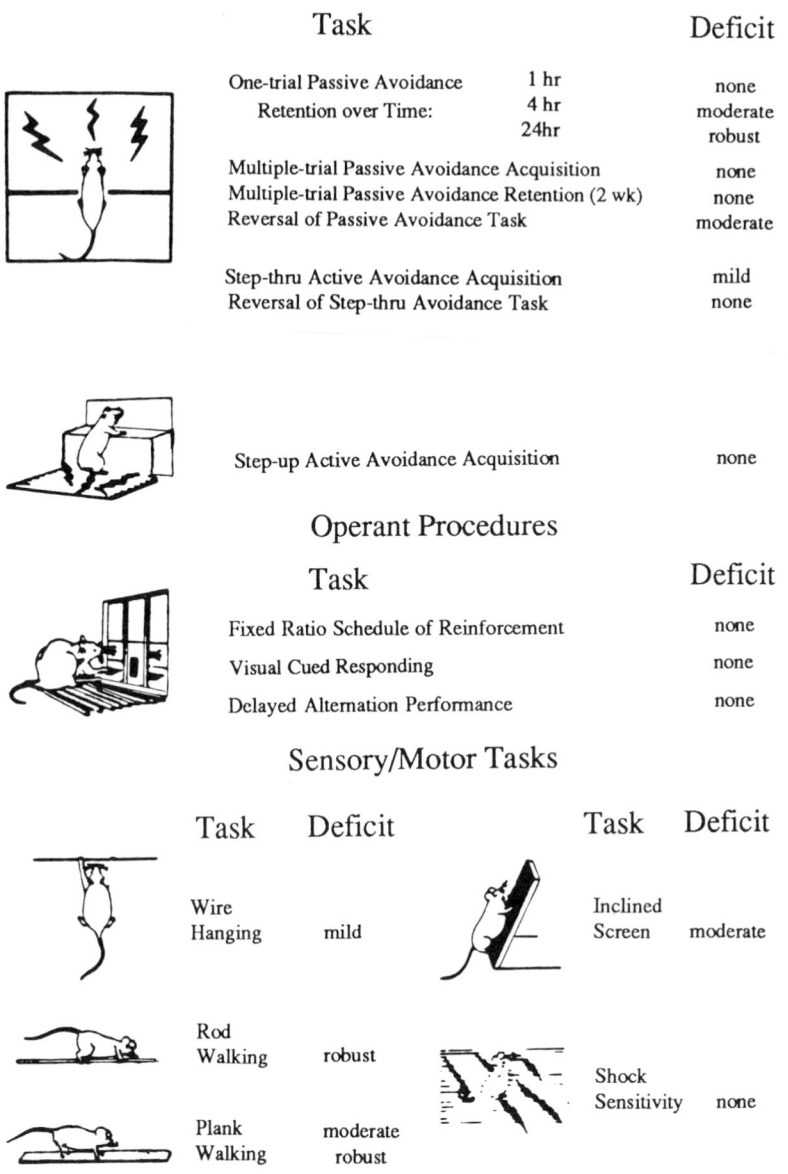

Learning/Memory Paradigms

Task		Deficit
One-trial Passive Avoidance	1 hr	none
Retention over Time:	4 hr	moderate
	24hr	robust
Multiple-trial Passive Avoidance Acquisition		none
Multiple-trial Passive Avoidance Retention (2 wk)		none
Reversal of Passive Avoidance Task		moderate
Step-thru Active Avoidance Acquisition		mild
Reversal of Step-thru Avoidance Task		none
Step-up Active Avoidance Acquisition		none

Operant Procedures

Task	Deficit
Fixed Ratio Schedule of Reinforcement	none
Visual Cued Responding	none
Delayed Alternation Performance	none

Sensory/Motor Tasks

Task	Deficit	Task	Deficit
Wire Hanging	mild	Inclined Screen	moderate
Rod Walking	robust	Shock Sensitivity	none
Plank Walking	moderate robust		

Figure 2 Summary of behavioral procedures used and the results obtained in comparisons between aged versus young F-344 rats. From Dean, Scozzafava, Goaf, Regan, Beer, and Bartus (1981). By permission of the authors and editors. © 1981 by Beech Hill Enterprises, Inc.

cays rapidly, usually within hours after the event. Because this task met the first three logical criteria for developing animal behavioral models of aging, Bartus, Dean, Sherman, Friedman, and Beer (1981) used pharmacological agents to determine if the memory deficit could be ameliorated. Cholinergic and nootropic agents only caused subtle improvements of the memory deficit. Striking improvement on the task was caused by combining choline and piracetam. The synergistic action of the two agents supports the hypothesis that multiple, interactive neurochemical dysfunctions or deficient metabolic pathways may be involved in age-related memory impairment (Bartus et al., 1981). This rodent study resulted in several applications of these synergistic agents to human demented patients with significant improvement resulting in some of the human patients (Bartus, Dean, & Beer, 1983).

D. Instrumental Learning

A multiple choice point maze is the typical apparatus for studying instrumental learning. The task of the animal is to learn the shortest path to the end of the maze where it is rewarded. The behavior of the animal is instrumental in achieving the goal, and this is why the term, *instrumental learning*, is used.

The problems with restraining rats in studies of classical conditioning are avoided in paradigms such as instrumental learning because the animals can run freely. In this sense, instrumental learning has a tremendous advantage over classical conditioning for research on aging. Mammals such as mice and rats with a relatively short life span about which we know the most in terms of neurobiological aging are the ideal subjects. On the other hand, there are also drawbacks to animal models using instrumental learning to study aging.

In behavioral studies of aging, it is the overt behavior or performance of the organism that we measure, and from this performance we evaluate the competence of the aging organism. We assume that the competence has deteriorated if the performance is poor. Botwinick (1978) has discussed this issue at length. In instrumental learning, there is only one assessment of the competence of the organism, the response that it gives. Motor impairment causing the animal to be unable to respond

could be interpreted as a learning or memory deficit because learning or memory and motor components are combined in the instrumental response. In classical conditioning, a measure of the motor performance is the UR, and a measure of learning is the CR. An investigator can always separate performance effects occurring with aging from the learned response. This cannot be done with instrumental learning or with most other behavioral assessments.

Another difference between classical and instrumental learning is that the neurobiological substrates for instrumental learning are not clearly delineated. It has been pointed out that the neural circuitry underlying classical conditioning of the eyeblink response in rabbits is well described (Thompson, 1986, 1988). Progress is being made with instrumental learning models, but advances proceed more slowly. Precision in understanding and control over the stimulation and response parameters are not as easily attainable with animal models of instrumental learning as with classical conditioning.

Ingram (1988) has used both the strategy of describing the age-related behavioral impairment and the strategy of age simulation with the animal model of complex maze learning in rodents to examine age-related memory impairment. An attribute of this approach is that rats (Wistar, C57BL/6, F-344) and mice (A/J, C3B10RF$_1$) of several strains have been used at a number of points in the life span to generalize the age-related changes over ages, strains, and species. Thus Ingram has established the complex maze paradigm as one showing generalizable natural aging effects.

The use of complex mazes for the assessment of learning and memory in rodents has a long history, beginning with Stone (1929) after whom the maze is named. Goodrick (e.g., 1973, 1984) was among those who elaborated complex maze learning as an animal model for the study of aging, but he, like previous researchers, used food motivation to elicit performance in the maze. Ingram (1985) initiated shock motivation to reduce the pretraining and maze training time while preserving the age-related performance impairment.

Of the behavioral phenomena he observed, Ingram (1988, p. 479) concluded that "data from this and other laboratories would suggest that the age-related impairment observed in Stone maze learning is a robust phenomenon in rodents. It has been observed in several strains of rats and mice, tested in physically different apparatuses, under a variety of training schedules and motivational manipulations."

Because they felt that cholinergic mechanisms might be involved in memory impairment in older rodents, Ingram and his colleagues used several approaches to explore the effects of disrupting cholinergic neurotransmission on Stone maze performance. The effects of cholinergic blockade were explored in young F-344 rats with the muscarinic antagonist, scopolamine hydrochloride (Spangler, Rigby, & Ingram, 1986). Learning was impaired, and further experimentation suggested that scopolamine primarily affects acquisition in this task (Spangler, Chachich, & Ingram, 1989). Comparing scopolamine effects on young and older rats, Spangler, Chachich, Curtis, and Ingram (1987) observed age and scopolamine effects, but the age and scopolamine interaction was not statistically significant. These results suggested to the investigators that age differences in receptor concentration probably do not account for the scopolamine-induced impairment or the age impairment. It is not clear what neurobiological mechanisms are involved in Stone maze performance.

In a search for the synaptic loci of the age-related impairment, Ingram and his associates continued to examine the cholinergic system using lesion techniques. Bilateral electrolytic lesions of the fimbria–fornix input to the hippocampus

in young F-344 rats was made (Bresnahan, Kametani, Spangler, Chachich, Wiser, & Ingram, 1989). Performance of the lesioned rats was poorer than performance of sham-operated or unoperated animals. Deficits in maze learning were similar to scopolamine-treated young rats or aged rats.

In an effort to improve Stone maze performance in acute preparations, Ingram and his colleagues used direct and indirect cholinergic agonists and a nootropic agent, but these agents were not successful. They are currently using chronic pharmacological applications as well as fetal neural tissue grafts in attempts to improve Stone maze performance.

From the perspective of the logical criteria for the development of animal models, the rodent Stone maze model shows a robust effect of aging (Criterion 1), it uses species demonstrating neurobiological age changes shared with humans (Criterion 3) and age simulation in young rodents mimics aging effects (Criterion 4). Criterion 2, involving the parallels between the behavioral changes in humans on a task similar to the Stone maze in rodents, is not met by this animal model because very few human aging studies of maze learning have been conducted. Ingram (1988) commented on this point and suggested that when successful animal models of aging are identified, perhaps it would be useful to run humans in similar paradigms to capitalize on the animal models. Although Criterion 5, involving pharmacological agents producing ameliorative effects, has not been met, drug studies attempting to ameliorate learning in this animal model were attempted.

This animal model of learning, memory, and aging has many virtues. It uses rodents that are an ideal animal species with a short life span and with well-defined neurobiological age changes. It employs a task that requires no restraint and suits rodents well, running through a maze. However, Stone maze learning provides an example of an animal model with robust aging effects replicated across several species that has thus far provided little insight about neurobiological mechanisms of aging. This is because the neurobiology of the behavior is not defined in young rodents. Investigators have not yet been able to focus on the likely loci of neural aging effects resulting in Stone maze deficits. In addition to the cholinergic studies, Ingram and associates are exploring noradrenergic, dopaminergic, and opioid involvement in learning in the Stone maze task. They are creating deficits in these neurotransmitter systems in young rodents to simulate aging effects. The difficulty with this approach is that there is no information to guide the investigators in their search for which neurobiological circuits and systems are involved in Stone maze learning. In this regard, animal models for which the underlying neurobiological mechanisms are known or at least partially established may result in more rapid progress in research on learning, memory, and aging.

E. Learning and Memory for Spatial Relations

Spatial memory has been operationally defined as the ability of an organism to know or to have a representation of where it is and thus to be able to navigate effectively in its environment (Barnes, 1988). In old age, spatial memory is less efficient in humans (e.g., Evans, Brennan, Skorpanich, & Held, 1984; Light & Zelinski, 1983; Ohta & Kirasic, 1983; Perlmutter, Metzger, Nezworski, & Miller, 1981; Shaps & Gollin, 1987). Old rats also demonstrate deficits on tasks requiring spatial information processing (reviewed in Barnes, 1988). The intact functioning of the hippocampus is necessary for learning and remembering spatial tasks in rats and humans. Thus, spatial memory in rats is a useful animal model of learning, memory, and aging because it parallels human behavioral and neurobiological aging, and its brain sub-

strates have been identified, at least in part.

There are several kinds of spatial tasks on which older rats perform more poorly. Compared to 12-month-old rats, 24- to 30-month-old rats do not remember the location of a dark goal tunnel in which they can escape the high illumination they experience on a circular platform that is aversive to them (Barnes, 1979). Older rats rarely solve a two-choice discrimination in a T-maze using a spatial strategy, but younger rats use such a strategy a significant proportion of the time (Barnes, Nadel, & Honig, 1980). On the radial 8-arm maze in which the animal must locate each of eight rewards without repeating entries into arms into which it has received a reward, older rats are worse at remembering where they have been (Barnes et al., 1980; Beatty, Bierley, & Boyd, 1985; Davis, Idowu, & Gibson, 1983; de Toledo-Morrell & Morrell, 1985; Gallagher, Bostock, & King, 1985; Geinisman, de Toledo-Morrell, & Morrell, 1986; Ingram, London, & Goodrick, 1981; Wallace, Krauter, & Campbell, 1980).

The radial maze task requires memory of past navigations and is classified as a spatial working memory task. The circular platform task involves the use of distal cues in the environment and is called a spatial reference memory task. Barnes, Green, Baldwin, and Johnson (1987) tested young and older rats on nonspatial versions of working and reference memory to determine if deficits observed in older animals were in working or reference memory in general or were related to spatial information processing. Although the nonspatial tasks were judged to be more difficult, older animals performed as well as younger animals on both working and reference memory. What appears problematic for older rats is the spatial aspect of the tasks.

Young rats with bilateral hippocampal lesions have spatial deficits similar to intact old rats (e.g., O'Keefe & Nadel, 1979).

Normal environmental navigation in humans requires the hippocampus (Corkin, 1984). Senile dementia of the Alzheimer's type (SDAT) results in severe degeneration of the hippocampus (Hyman, Van Hoesen, Damasio, & Barnes, 1984; Whitehouse, Price, Struble, Clark, Coyle, & DeLong, 1982), and SDAT patients characteristically get lost, even in very familiar surroundings such as their neighborhood of 50 years.

Barnes (1988) summarized several electrophysiological parameters in the older rat hippocampus that appear to be involved with spatial deficits in older rats. The first is a change in the ability to maintain long-term enhancement (LTE) that is a long-lasting plasticity induced by high-frequency stimulation of hippocampal afferents (Barnes, 1979; Landfield & Lynch, 1977; Landfield, McGaugh, & Lynch, 1978). This phenomenon is thought to be a mechanism of information storage in the mammalian central nervous system. Landfield et al. (1986) reported that the deficit in LTE may be due to a relative elevation of calcium in certain hippocampal neurons. The change in the ability to maintain LTE in older rats may represent a change in the physical substrate of memory itself.

The second electrophysiological change related to spatial ability deficiencies is a reduction of afferent input and an increase in the excitability of hippocampal cells (Barnes & McNaughton, 1980; Barnes, Rao, & McNaughton, 1987). These changes result in less precision in information processing—the accuracy of information-processing ability of older hippocampal neurons declines.

Precise identification of the cause of age-related deficits in animal models can lead to interventions to ameliorate the loss. In the case of the deficiency in LTE, de Toledo-Morrell, Morrell, Fleming, and Cohen (1984) found that drug treatment with pentoxifylline improves spatial memory and extends the decay time con-

stant of LTE in old animals. Although there is no treatment to facilitate afferent input to the hippocampus at present, the identification of the problem should focus research on its solution.

Measuring hippocampal functioning as a rat performed the Morris water maze, Decker, Pelleymounter, and Gallagher (1989) observed that a selective marker for the function of hippocampal cholinergic neurons showed changes during learning. This effect was diminished in aged rats. Gallagher and Pelleymounter (1988) suggested that the results in Gallagher's laboratory in North Carolina along with work from the laboratories of Barnes in Colorado and Bartus in New York implicated the hippocampus and the basal forebrain cholinergic system as being involved in age-related deficits in spatial working memory in rodents. They also pointed out that evidence for cholinergic system involvement in this kind of deficit in aging animals was consistent with reports that transplants of fetal brain tissue rich in cholinergic neurons ameliorate the memory deficit (Gage & Bjorklund, 1986; Gage, Bjorklund, Stenevi, Dunnett, & Kelly, 1984).

A behavioral means to ameliorate spatial working memory as assessed on the eight arm radial maze was discovered by Beatty et al. (1985). These investigators observed that rats trained on the radial maze task when they are young (3 months old) will not show performance deficits at the age of 22 months or even 26 months. Naive 24-month-old rats show large deficits in acquisition and retention on the task. Beatty (1988) discussed the possibility that early experience might preserve the capacity for accurate spatial working memory in humans as well as rats.

From the perspective of criteria listed in Table II for successful animal models of learning, memory, and aging, the rodent model for spatial memory is more useful. Normal older rats have deficits in spatial information processing, and these deficits are similar to poorer performance of older humans on spatial tasks. Age-related neurobiological changes in the hippocampus occur in rats and humans, and in both species the neurobiological changes appear to be responsible for the behavioral deficits. Hippocampal damage in young humans and rats mimics the behavioral results in older humans and rats. Drugs affecting hippocampal efficiency in older rats improve their spatial behavior. Thus this animal model has been useful in the description, explanation, and amelioration of spatial memory deficits in old age.

F. Tasks Assessing Short-Term Memory in Nonhuman Primates

The animal models that are the most similar genetically, anatomically, physiologically, and behaviorally to humans are nonhuman primates. It is with monkeys and apes that we can most easily make generalizations from animal models to humans, particularly in the realm of behavior. With regard to neurobiological processes of aging, nonhuman primates are among the few species that develop senile plaques similar to the senile plaques observed in the brains of aged humans and in greater numbers in patients with SDAT (Walker, Kitt, Cord, Struble, Dellovade, & Price, 1988; Walker, Kitt, Schwam, Buckwald, Garcia, Sepinwall, & Price, 1987).

However, in addition to their obvious advantages, nonhuman primates also have serious drawbacks as animal models for the study of learning, memory, and aging. Aged nonhuman primates can be prohibitively expensive. They are often difficult to obtain, and once obtained, they present special problems for housing and care. As presented in Table I, they also have rather long life expectancies. Given their expense and relatively long life expectancies, investigators are often reluctant to perform invasive studies that might involve terminating the animal. Thus, a major advantage of animal models may be partially

thwarted in the case of nonhuman primates.

Monkeys have been used in several laboratories to study aging and short-term memory. Figure 3 illustrates a monkey in an automated testing apparatus used by Bartus and associates (Bartus, 1979a,b; Bartus & Dean, 1981; Dean, Loullis, & Bartus, 1983). A number of tasks can be programmed into the apparatus, but the task discussed here is called the delayed reponse task. It involved the monkey remembering which of the nine panels in the matrix had lit up. The monkey had to press the correct panel to get a food reward. Aged monkeys suffered deficits in retention on this task. At short retention intervals (2 to 5 sec) the deficit was relatively small, but at longer intervals (20 sec) the deficit increased dramatically. These results were replicated in New World (Bartus, Dean, & Beer, 1980) and Old World (Marriott & Abelson, 1980) monkeys.

Bartus, Flicker, Dean, Fisher, Pontecorvo, and Figueiredo (1986) argued that the short-term memory dysfunction in aged monkeys bears a strong resemblance to short-term memory loss observed in aged humans. Empirical support for this assertion was provided by Flicker, Bartus, Crook, and Ferris (1984) using a human test procedure designed to share as many of the operational characteristics of the monkey task as possible. Subjects were asked to remember which of several windows of a house displayed on a screen had been illuminated. As in the monkey task, various intervals of retention were tested. Delays of 15 and 30 seconds differentiated young and older normal adults. Moderately impaired and severely impaired older adults clinically suspected of having Alzheimer's disease performed significantly more poorly than the normal older adults. Bartus and his colleagues concluded that because of the parallels between the performance of aged monkeys and aged normal and demented humans, the aged monkeys are useful animal models. They

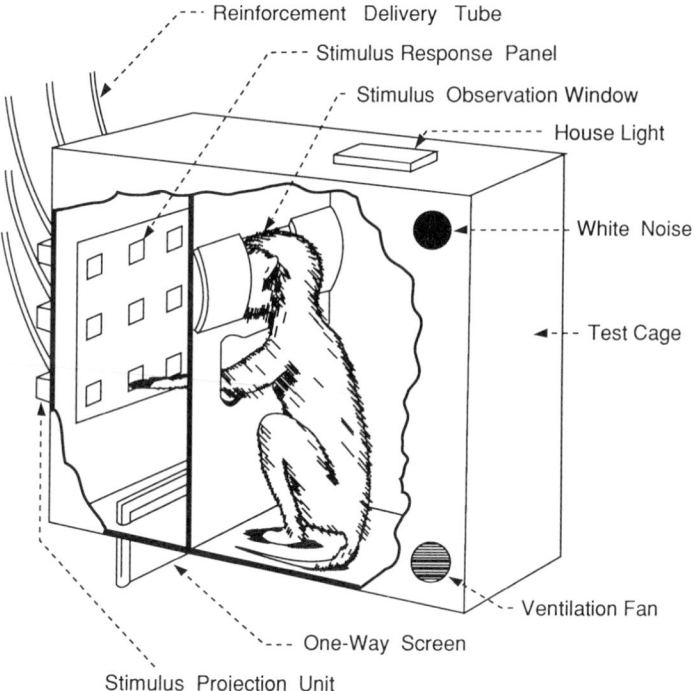

Reinforcement Delivery Tube
Stimulus Response Panel
Stimulus Observation Window
House Light
White Noise
Test Cage
Ventilation Fan
One-Way Screen
Stimulus Projection Unit

Figure 3 Illustration of monkey making choice response in the auto-mated apparatus used in nonhuman primate studies. The most important features of the apparatus are labeled, with the exception of a reinforcement feeder and router mechanism (not shown) and the photocell-detecting unit located on either side of the stimulus observation window (not visible). In the delayed response task, the monkeys are required to remember the stimulus location. (Bartus, Flicker, and Dean, 1983).

can be used to study memory dysfunction in aging, and they are useful in evaluating experimental drugs intended to treat geri-atric memory problems.

Much of the drug testing with memory-deficient older monkeys undertaken by Bartus and his colleagues has involved the cholinergic neurotransmitter system that involves nuclei in the basal forebrain that provide the major source of cholinergic in-put to the hippocampus, cortex, and olfac-tory bulb. This system is seriously im-paired in Alzheimer's patients (Coyle, Price, & DeLong, 1983). Modeling deficits in this system have been a major preoc-cupation of researchers devising animal models of learning and memory loss in Alzheimer's disease.

A brain structure affected by aging pro-cesses in humans (Albert & Kaplan, 1980) that is likely to be involved in short-term memory loss in aged monkeys is the pre-frontal cortex (Arnsten & Goldman-Rakic, 1985b). Goldman-Rakic (1987) has de-scribed the basic neural circuitry underly-ing delayed-response function in non-human primates and has suggested that the developmental increase in synaptic density in the principal sulcus of the front-al lobe coincides with the development of the ability to perform the delayed response task at short delays. Arnsten and Gold-man-Rakic (1985a) have demonstrated that age-related changes in the prefrontal cortex of older monkeys are likely to be responsible for the difficulties these ani-mals have on delayed response tasks.

In the delayed response task, one of two

wells is baited while the animal watches. Then the wells are covered with identical cardboard plaques, and a screen is lowered to remove them from the animal's view. After a prescribed delay, the screen is raised, and the animal is allowed to choose one of the two wells. Delayed alternation is a variation of this task in which the animal does not see the wells baited. Instead, it must remember which side it chose correctly on the last trial and alternate the response. What is common in the tasks used in laboratories of Bartus and Goldman-Rakic is that the monkey must retain what was learned on the previous trial for some prescribed number of seconds.

The catecholamine, dopamine, is found in the highest levels in the monkey cortex in the prefrontal region. Most areas of the frontal lobe are innervated in a dense manner with norepinephrine as well (Levitt, Rakic, & Goldman-Rakic, 1984). The presence of catecholamines, particularly dopamine, appears to be essential for the prefrontal cortex to function properly (Brozoski, Brown, Rosvold, & Goldman, 1979). Biochemical analysis of neurotransmitter levels in the brains of "young-old" rhesus monkeys (age 10 to 18 years) revealed substantial depletions in cortical catecholamine levels (Goldman-Rakic & Brown, 1981). Of the many regions studied, only the prefrontal and temporal cortices showed large depletions of dopamine of 50% or more. The older the animal, the greater were the dopamine depletions. Bartus, Dean, and Beer (1983) did not observe any cognitive improvement in Cebus monkeys over 18 years of age when they administered various doses of the dopamine-enhancing drug, clonidine. On the other hand, more recent research by Arnsten and Goldman-Rakic (1985a,b) demonstrated that 18- to 30-year-old rhesus monkeys, which were impaired on spatial delayed alternation and delayed response, benefitted from treatment with clonidine. Robust improvements in delayed response performance were observed

in a dose-related manner. At the most effective dose level, a majority of the monkeys were able to achieve near perfect performance. Although the neurochemical mechanisms underlying the ability of the drug to ameliorate performance are not understood, the dose-reponse curves are consonant with clonidine having actions at postsynaptic receptors.

The animal model of nonhuman primates for short-term memory loss in aging meets all of the criteria for developing animal behavioral models listed in Table II. The memory deficit occurs naturally, and it parallels extremely well the short-term memory deficit observed in normal aging and exacerbated in Alzheimer's disease. Neurobiological changes occurring in aging nonhuman primates resemble human neurobiological aging phenomena more closely than any nonprimate animal models. Inducing the aging effects in young nonhuman primates with anatomical and/or neurochemical lesions mimic aging processes, and drug facilitation is parallel in the animal model and humans. This is an excellent animal model for human aging, and it is limited only by expense, by the long life spans of nonhuman primates, and by the scarcity of aged nonhuman primates.

G. Mammalian Models in Pathological Aging

The major portion of this chapter has been devoted to animal models of learning and memory in normal aging reflecting the fact that the vast majority of older adults experience aging without dementia. However, there is a sizable number of older adults, currently estimated by NIA to number around 2 million, who experience severe memory loss and eventual death resulting from senile dementia of the Alzheimer's type (SDAT). It is imperative to find treatments to ameliorate the memory loss and suffering of the victims of SDAT. In this regard, animal models hold great promise. However, animal models for SDAT are beyond the scope of this chapter.

III. Summary and Conclusions

Mammalian models provide a means to observe behavioral and neurobiological aging in organisms with shorter life spans that can be experimentally manipulated and invasively examined. The use of animal models in neurobiological research on learning, memory, and aging increased dramatically in the 1980s. The following are some general conclusions documented in this chapter:

1. Most behavioral research involves rats or mice—species that have relatively short life spans and identified genetic and neurobiological characteristics.
2. Avoidance conditioning is the type of operant conditioning for which the largest age differences appear in rats.
3. Instrumental conditioning has been examined extensively using the Stone maze, and age-related deficits on this task have been replicated in many strains of rats and mice.
4. Older rats are impaired on a number of spatial learning tasks, and age-related changes in the hippocampus are related to these behavioral changes.
5. A model system that has considerable promise to accelerate progress in the understanding of neurobiological mechanisms of learning, memory, and aging is classical conditioning of the eyeblink response. There are dramatic parallels between aging effects on eyelid classical conditioning in rabbits and humans, and most of the essential circuitry for this form of learning and memory has now been identified in the animal model.
6. Primate models provide the greatest similarities to human behavior and neurobiology, and there are great strengths and large drawbacks in using

them. Old primates are rare and extremely expensive, making scientists reluctant to undertake invasive studies. On the other hand, only primates can perform a range of learning and memory tasks that begin to simulate human capacity. Studies using primate models have identified striking similarities in neurobiological aging in these mammals and humans.

The 1990s hold the promise of being a remarkable era of progress in the domain of learning, memory, and aging. Using the mammalian models now in place, a basic knowledge base is being laid down that is permitting identification and experimentation with means to ameliorate age-related deficits. Pharmacological agents to reverse memory loss in normal and pathological aging are in various stages of testing in mammalian models. Some have advanced to human trials. Brain grafting and research on the factors that facilitate integration of the graft into existing tissue is one of the most dynamic areas of neuroscience. Because of recent advances in research on mammalian models of learning and memory, there is in the next decade the prospect of providing drugs to older adults to help their learning and memory processes. There is also some probability that grafting techniques using nervous system tissue will advance to the stage of providing certain improvement in learning and memory function in older adults. Without mammalian models, the state of our knowledge would never have reached the point where we are now—in the early, beginning stages of identifying agents and techniques that can improve learning and memory in aging humans.

References

Albert, M. S., & Kaplan, E. F. (1980). Organic implications of neuropsychological deficits in the elderly. In L. W. Poon, J. Fozard, L. Cermak, D. Arenberg, & L. W. Thompson

(Eds.), *New directions in memory and aging: Proceedings of the George A. Talland memorial conference*. Hillsdale, NJ: Erlbaum.

Arenberg, D., & Robertson-Tchabo, E. A. (1977). Learning and aging. In J. E. Birren & K. W. Schaie (Eds.), *Handbook of the psychology of aging*. New York: Van Nostrand Reinhold.

Arnsten, A. F. T., & Goldman-Rakic, P. S. (1985a). Alpha 2-adrenergic mechanisms in prefrontal cortex associated with cognitive decline in aged nonhuman primates. *Science*, **230**, 1273–1276.

Arnsten, A. F. T., & Goldman-Rakic, P. S. (1985b). Catecholamines and cognitive decline in aged nonhuman primates. *Annals of the New York Academy of Sciences*, **444**, 218–234.

Baltes, M. M., & Baron, E. M. (1977). New approaches toward aging: A case for the operant model. *Educational Gerontology: An International Quarterly*, **2**, 383–405.

Baltes, M. M., & Lerner, R. M. (1980). Roles of the operant model and its methods in the life span approach to human development. *Human Development*, **23**, 362–367.

Barnes, C. A. (1979). Memory deficits associated with senescence: A neurophysiological and behavioral study in the rat. *Journal of Comparative and Physiological Psychology*, **93**, 74–104.

Barnes, C. A. (1988). Aging and the physiology of spatial memory. *Neurobiology of Aging*, **9**, 563–568.

Barnes, C. A., Green, E. J., Baldwin, J., & Johnson, W. E. (1987). Behavioral and neurophysiological examples of functional sparing in senescent rat. *Canadian Journal of Psychology*, **41**, 131–140.

Barnes, C. A., & McNaughton, B. L. (1980). Physiological compensation for loss of afferent synapses in rat hippocampal granule cells during senescence. *Journal of Physiology (London)*, **309**, 473–485.

Barnes, C. A., Nadel, L., & Honig, W. K. (1980). Spatial memory deficit in senescent rats. *Canadian Journal of Psychology*, **34**, 29–39.

Barnes, C. A., Rao, G., & McNaughton, B. L. (1987). Increased electrotonic coupling in aged rat hippocampus: A possible mechanism for cellular excitability changes. *Journal of Comparative Neurology*, **259**, 549–558.

Bartus, R. T. (1979a). Effects of aging on visual memory, sensory processing and discrimination learning in the non-human primate. In J. M. Ordy & K. Brizzee (Eds.). *Aging* (Vol. 10, pp. 85–114). New York: Raven.

Bartus, R. T. (1979b). Physostigmine and recent memory: Effects in young and aged nonhuman primates. *Science*, **206**, 1087–1089.

Bartus, R. T., & Dean, R. L. (1981). Age-related memory loss and drug therapy: Possible directions based on animal models. In S. J. Enna, T. Samorajski, & B. Beer (Eds.), *Aging* (Vol. 17, pp. 209–223). New York: Raven.

Bartus, R. T., Dean, R. L., & Beer, B. (1980). Memory deficits in aged Cebus monkeys and facilitation with central cholinomimetics. *Neurobiology of Aging*, **1**, 145–152.

Bartus, R. T., Dean, R. L., & Beer, B. (1983). An evaluation of drugs for improving memory in aged monkeys: Implications for clinical trials in humans. *Psychopharmacology Bulletin*, **19**, 169–194.

Bartus, R. T., Dean, R. L., Sherman, K. A., Friedman, E., & Beer, B. (1981). Profound effects of combining choline and piracetam on memory enhancement and cholinergic function in aged rats. *Neurobiology of Aging*, **2**, 105–111.

Bartus, R. T., Flicker, C., & Dean, R. L. (1983). Logical principles for the development of animal models of age-related memory impairments. In T. Crook, S. Ferris, & R. T. Bartus (Eds.), *Assessment in geriatric psychopharmacology* (pp. 263–300). Madison, CT: Powley Associates.

Bartus, R. T., Flicker, C., Dean, R. L., Fisher, S., Pontecorvo, & Figueiredo, J. (1986). Behavioral and biochemical effects of nucleus basalis magnocellularis lesions: Implications and possible relevance to understanding or treating Alzheimer's disease. In D. F. Swaab, E. Fliers, M. Mirmiran, W. A. Van Gool, & F. Van Haaren (Eds.), *Progress in brain research* (Vol. 70, pp. 345–361). New York: Elsevier.

Beatty, W. W. (1988). Preservation and loss of spatial memory in aged rats and humans: Implications for the analysis of memory dysfunction in dementia. *Neurobiology of Aging*, **9**, 557–561.

Beatty, W. W., Bierley, R. A., & Boyd, J. G. (1985). Preservation of accurate spatial memory in aged rats. *Neurobiology of Aging*, **6**, 219–225.

Botwinick, J. (1978). *Aging and behavior*. New York: Springer.

Braun, H. W., & Geiselhart, R. (1959). Age differences in the acquisition and extinction of the conditioned eyelid response. *Journal of Experimental Psychology*, **57**, 386–388.

Bresnahan, E. Kametani, H., Spangler, E., Chachich, M., Wiser, P., & Ingram, D. (1989). Fimbria-fornix lesions impair acquisition performance in a 14-unit T-maze similar to prior observed performance deficits in aged rats. *Psychobiology*, in press.

Brizzee, K. R., & Ordy, J. M. (1979). Age pigments, cell loss and hippocampal function. *Mechanisms of Aging and Development*, **9**, 143–162.

Brozoski, T. J., Brown, R. M., Rosvold, H. E., & Goldman, P. S. (1979). Cognitive deficit caused by depletion of dopamine in prefrontal cortex of rhesus monkey. *Science*, **205**, 929–931.

Buchanan, S. L., & Ginn, S. R. (1988). Classically conditioned cardiac responses in "old" and "young" Fischer 344 rats. *Psychology and Aging*, **3**, 51–58.

Buchanan, S. L., & Powell, D. A. (1988). Age-related changes in associative learning: Studies in rabbits and rats. *Neurobiology of Aging*, **9**, 523–534.

Committee on Animal Models for Research on Aging (1981). *Mammalian models for research on aging*. Washington, DC: National Academy Press.

Corkin, S. (1984). Lasting consequences of bilateral medial temporal lobectomy: Clinical course and experimental findings in *Seminar in Neurology*, **4**, 249–259.

Coyle, J. T., Price, D. L., & DeLong, M. R. (1983). Alzheimer's disease: A disorder of cortical cholinergic innervation. *Science*, **219**, 1184–1190.

Davis, H. P., Idowu, A. A., & Gibson, G. E. (1983). Improvement of 8-arm maze performance in aged Fischer 344 rats with 3,4-diaminopyridine. *Experimental Aging Research*, **9**, 211–214.

Dean, R. L., Loullis, C., & Bartus, R. T. (1983). Drug effects in an animal model of memory deficits in the aged: Implications for future clinical trials. In R. F. Walker, & R. L. Cooper (Eds.), *Experimental and clinical interventions in aging*. New York: Dekker.

Dean, R. L., Scozzafava, J., Goaf, J. A., Regan, B., Beer, B., and Bartus, R. T. (1981). Age-related

differences in behavior across the life span of the C57BL/6J mouse. *Experimental Aging Research*, **7**, 427–451.

Decker, M. W., Pelleymounter, M. A., & Gallagher, M. (1989). The effects of training on a spatial memory task on high affinity choline uptake in hippocampus and cortex in young adult and aged rats. *Journal of Neuroscience*, in press.

de Toledo-Morrell, L., & Morrell, F. (1985). Electrophysiological markers of aging and memory loss in rats. *Annals of the New York Academy of Sciences*, **444**, 296–311.

de Toledo-Morrell, L., Morrell, F., Fleming, S., & Cohen, M. (1984). Pentoxifylline reverses age related deficits in spatial memory. *Behavioral and Neural Biology*, **42**, 1–8.

Devo, R. A., Straube, K. T., & Disterhoft, J. F. (1988). Nimodipine facilitates trace conditioning of the eye-blink response in aging rabbits. *Abstracts of the Society for Neuroscience*, **14**, 579.

Diamond, M. C., Johnson, R. E., Protti, A. M., Ott, C., & Kajisa, L. (1985). Plasticity in the 904-day-old male rate cerebral cortex. *Experimental Neurology*, **87**, 309–317.

Doty, B. A. (1966a). Age and avoidance conditioning in rats. *Journal of Gerontology*, **21**, 287–290.

Doty, B. A. (1966b). Age differences in avoidance conditioning as a function of distribution of trials and task difficulty. *Journal of Genetic Psychology*, **109**, 249–254.

Doty, B. A., & Doty, L. A. (1964). Effect of age and cholorpromazine on memory consolidation. *Journal of Comparative and Physiological Psychology*, **57**, 331–334.

Doty, B. A., & Johnson, M. M. (1966). Effects of post-trial eserine administration, age and task difficulty on avoidance conditioning in rats. *Psychonomic Science*, **6**, 101–102.

Evans, G., Brennan, P., Skorpanich, M. A., & Held, D. (1984). Cognitive mapping and elderly adults: Verbal and location memory for urban landmarks. *Journal of Gerontology*, **39**, 452–457.

Flicker, C., Bartus, R. T., Crook, T., & Ferris, S. H. (1984). Effects of aging and dementia upon recent visuospatial memory. *Neurobiology of Aging*, **5**, 75–83.

Flood, D., & Coleman, P. (1988). Neuron numbers and sizes in human, monkey and rodent data. *Neurobiology of Aging*, **9**, 453–463.

Gage, F. H., & Bjorklund, A. (1986). Cholinergic

septal grafts in the hippocampal formation improve spatial learning and memory in aged rats by an atropine-sensitive mechanism. *Journal of Neuroscience*, **6**, 2837–2847.

Gage, F. H., Bjorklund, A., Stenevi, U., Dunnett, S. B., & Kelly, P. A. T. (1984). Intrahippocampal septal grafts ameliorate learning impairments in aged rats. *Science*, **225**, 533–536.

Gallagher, M., Bostock, E., & King, R. (1985). Effects of opiate antagonists on spatial memory in young and aged rats. *Behavioral and Neural Biology*, **44**, 374–385.

Gallagher, M., & Pelleymounter, M. A. (1988). Spatial learning deficits in old rats: A model for memory decline in the aged. *Neurobiology of Aging*, **9**, 549–556.

Geinisman, Y., de Toledo-Morrell, L., & Morrell, F. (1986). Loss of perforated synapses in the dentate gyrus: Morphological substrate of memory deficit in aged rats. *Proceedings of the National Academy of Sciences, U.S.A.* **83**, 3027–3031.

Gold, P. E., & McGaugh, J. L. (1975). Changes in learning and memory during aging. In J. M. Ordy & K. R. Brizzee (Eds.), *Neurobiology of aging* (145–148). New York: Plenum.

Goldman-Rakic, P. S. (1987). Development of cortical circuitry and cognitive function. *Child Development*, **58**, 601–622.

Goldman-Rakic, P. S., & Brown, R. M. (1981). Regional changes of monoamines in cerebral cortex and subcortical structures of aging rhesus monkeys. *Neuroscience*, **6**, 177–187.

Goodrick, C. L. (1965). Operant level and light-contingent bar presses as a function of age and deprivation. *Psychological Reports*, **17**, 283–288.

Goodrick, C. L. (1969). Operant responding of nondeprived young and senescent male albino rats. *Journal of Genetic Psychology*, **114**, 29–40.

Goodrick, C. L. (1970). Light- and dark-contingent bar pressing in the rat as a function of age and motivation. *Journal of Comparative and Physiological Psychology*, **73**, 100–104.

Goodrick, C. L. (1973). Maze learning of mature-young and aged rats as a function of distribution of practice. *Journal of Experimental Psychology*, **98**, 344–349.

Goodrick, C. L. (1984). Effects of lifelong restricted feeding on complex maze performance in rats. *Age*, **7**, 1–2.

Graves, C. A., & Solomon, P. R. (1985). Age related disruption of trace but not delay classical conditioning of the rabbit's nictitating membrane response. *Behavioral Neuroscience*, **99**, 88–96.

Greenough, W. T. (1986). What's special about development? Thoughts on the bases of experience-sensitive synaptic plasticity. In W. T. Greenough & J. M. Juraska (Eds.), *Developmental neuropsychobiology*. New York: Academic Press.

Harrison, J., & Buchwald, J. (1983). Eyeblink conditioning deficits in the old cat. *Neurobiology of Aging*, **4**, 45–51.

Hyman, B. T., Van Hoesen, G. W., Damasio, A. R., & Barnes, C. L. (1984). Alzheimer's disease: Cell-specific pathology isolates the hippocampal formation. *Science*, **225**, 1168–1170.

Ingram, D. K. (1985). Analysis of age-related impairments in learning and memory in rodent models. *Annals of the New York Academy of Sciences*, **444**, 312–331.

Ingram, D. K. (1988). Complex maze learning in rodents as a model of age related memory impairment. *Neurobiology of Aging*, **9**, 475–485.

Ingram, D. K., Bartus, R. T., Olton, D. S., & Khachaturian, Z. S. (Eds.) (1988). Special issue: Experimental models of age-related memory dysfunction and neurodegeneration. *Neurobiology of Aging*, **9**, 443–765.

Ingram, D. K., London, E. D., & Goodrick, C. L. (1981). Age and neurochemical correlates of radial maze performance in rats. *Neurobiology of Aging*, **2**, 41–47.

Kausler, D. H. (1982). *Experimental psychology and human aging*. New York: Wiley.

Kimble, G. A., & Pennypacker, H. S. (1963). Eyelid conditioning in young and aged subjects. *Journal of Genetic Psychology*, **103**, 283–289.

Kubanis, P., Gobbel, G., & Zornetzer, S. F. (1981). Age-related memory deficits in Swiss mice. *Behavioral and Neural Biology*, **32**, 241–247.

Landfield, P. W. (1988). Hippocampal neurobiological mechanisms of age-related memory dysfunction. *Neurobiology of Aging*, **9**, 571–579.

Landfield, P. W., & Lynch, G. (1977). Impaired monosynaptic potentiation in *in vitro* hippocampal slices from aged, memory-deficient rats. *Journal of Gerontology, 32*, 523–533.

Landfield, P. W., McGaugh, J. L., & Lynch, G. (1978). Impaired sysnaptic potentiation processes in the hippocampus of aged, memory-deficient rats. *Brain Research, 150*, 85–101.

Landfield, P. W., Pitler, T. A., & Applegate, M. D. (1986). The aged hippocampus: A model system for studies on mechanisms of behavioral plasticity and brain aging. In R. L. Isaacson & K. H. Pribram (Eds.), *The hippocampus* (Vol. 3, pp. 323–367). New York: Plenum.

Lavond, D. G., Logan, C. G., Sohn, J. H., Garner, W. D. A., & Thompson, R. F. (1988). Lesion of the cerebellar interpositus nucleus abolishes both nictitating membrane and eyelid EMG conditioned responses. *Society for Neuroscience Abstracts, 14*, 783.

Lavond, D. G., Steinmetz, J. E., & Thompson, R. F. (1987). Learning of a classically conditioned nictitating membrane/eyelid response without cerebellar cortex. *Society for Neuroscience Abstracts, 13*, 642.

Levitt, P., Rakic, P., & Goldman-Rakic, P. S. (1984). Region-specific distribution of catecholamine afferents in primate cerebral cortex: A florescence histochemical analysis. *Journal of Comparative Neurology, 31*, 533–538.

Light, L. L., & Zelinski, E. M. (1983). Memory for spatial information in young and old adults. *Developmental Psychology, 19*, 901–906.

Lindzey, G., Thompson, R. F., & Spring, B. (1988). *Psychology*. New York: Worth.

Lippa, A. S., Pelham, R. W., Beer, B., Critchett, D. J., Dean, R. L., & Bartus, R. T. (1980). Brain cholinergic dysfunction and memory in aged rats. *Neurobiology of Aging, 1*, 13–19.

Marriott, J. G., & Abelson, J. S. (1980). Age differences in short-term memory in test-sophisticated rhesus monkeys. *Age, 3*, 7–9.

McCormick, D. A., Lavond, D. G., & Thompson, R. F. (1982). Concomitant classical conditioning of the rabbit nictitating membrane and eyelid responses: Correlations and implications. *Physiology and Behavior, 28*, 769–775.

McCormick, D. A., & Thompson, R. F. (1984a). Cerebellum: Essential involvement in the classically conditioned eyelid response. *Science, 223*, 296–299.

McCormick, D. S., & Thompson, R. F. (1984b). Neuronal responses of the rabbit cerebellum during acquisition and performance of a classically conditioned nictitating membrane/eyelid response. *Journal of Neuroscience, 4*, 2811–2822.

Ohta, R. J., & Kirasic, K. C. (1983). The investigation of environmental learning in the elderly. In G. D. Rowles & R. J. Ohta (Eds.), *Aging and milieu* (pp. 83–95). New York: Academic Press.

O'Keefe, J., & Nadel, L. (1979). Precis of O'Keefe & Nadel's The hippocampus as a cognitive map. *The Behavioral and Brain Sciences, 2*, 487–533.

Olton, D. S., Gamzu, E., & Corkin, S. (Eds.) (1985). *Memory dysfunctions: An integration of animal and human research from preclinical and clinical perspectives*. New York: New York Academy of Sciences.

Patterson, M. M., Olah, J., & Clement, J. (1977). Classical nictitating membrane conditioning in the awake, normal, restrained cat. *Science, 196*, 1124–1126.

Perlmutter, M., Metzger, R., Nezworski, T., & Miller, K. (1981). Spatial and temporal memory in 20 and 60 year olds. *Journal of Gerontology, 36*, 59–65.

Powell, D. A., Buchanan, S. L., & Hernandez, L. L. (1981). Age related changes in classical (Pavlovian) conditioning in the New Zealand albino rabbit. *Experimental Aging Research, 7*, 453–465.

Prescott, L., Buchanan, S. L., & Powell, D. A. (1989). Leg flexion conditioning in the rat: Its advantages and disadvantages as a model system of age-related changes in associative learning. *Neurobiology of Aging*, in press.

Shaps, M. J., & Gollin, E. S. (1987). Memory for object locations in young and elderly adults. *Journal of Gerontology, 42*, 336–341.

Solomon, P. R., Beal, M. F., & Pendlebury, W. W. (1988). Age-related disruption of classical conditioning: A model systems approach to memory disorders. *Neurobiology of Aging, 9*, 535–546.

Solomon, P. R., Pomerleau, D., Bennett, L., James, J., & Morse, D. L. (1989). Acquisition of the classically conditioned eyeblink response in humans over the life span. *Psychology and Aging*, in press.

Spangler, E. L., Chachich, M., Curtis, N., & Ingram, D. K. (1987). Effects of scopolamine on complex maze learning in young and aged rats. *Gerontologist*, **27**, 192A–193A.

Spangler, E. L., Chachich, M., & Ingram, D. K. (1989). Scopolamine in rats impairs acquisition but not retention in a 14-unit T-maze. *Pharmacology Biochemistry & Behavior*, in press.

Spangler, E. L., Rigby, P., & Ingram, D. K. (1986). Scopolamine impairs learning performance in rats in a 14-unit T-maze. *Pharmacology Biochemistry & Behavior*, **25**, 673–679.

Stone, C. (1929). The age factor in animal learning: 1. Rats in the problem box and the maze. *Genetic Psychology Monographs*, **5**, 1–130.

Thompson, R. F. (1986). The neurobiology of learning and memory. *Science*, **233**, 941–947.

Thompson, R. F. (1988). Classical conditioning: The Rosetta stone for brain substrates of age-related deficits in learning and memory? *Neurobiology of Aging*, **9**, 547–548.

Thompson, R. F., McCormick, D. A., & Lavond, D. G. (1986). Localization of the essential memory trace system for a basic form of associative learning in the mammalian brain. In S. Hulse (Ed.), *One hundred years of psychological research in America* (pp. 125–171). Baltimore: Johns Hopkins University Press.

Thompson, R. F., & Woodruff-Pak, D. S. (1987). A model system approach to age and the neuronal bases of learning and memory. In M. W. Riley, J. D. Matarazzo, & A. Baum (Eds.), *The aging dimension* (pp. 49–76). Hillsdale, NJ: Erlbaum.

Walker, L. C., Kitt, C. A., Cork, L. C., Struble, R. G., Dellovade, T. L., & Price, D. L. (1988). Multiple transmitter systems contribute neurites to individual senile plaques. *Journal of Neuropathology and Experimental Neurology*, **47**, 370–381.

Walker, L. C., Kitt, C. A., Schwam, E., Buckwald, B., Garcia, F., Sepinwall, J., & Price, D. L. (1987). Senile plaques in aged squirrel monkeys. *Neurobiology of Aging*, **8**, 291–296.

Wallace, J. E., Krauter, E. E., & Campbell, B. A. (1980). Animal models of declining memory in the aged: Short-term and spatial memory in the old rat. *Journal of Gerontology*, **35**, 355–363.

Whitehouse, P. J., Price, D. L., Struble, R. G.,

Clark, A. W., Coyle, J. T., & DeLong, M. R. (1982). Alzheimer's disease and senile dementia: Loss of neurons in the basal forebrain. *Science*, **215**, 1237–1239.

Winocur, G. (1984). The effects of retroactive and proactive interference on learning and memory in old and young rats. *Developmental Psychobiology*, **17**, 537–545.

Winocur, G. (1986). Memory decline in aged rats: A neuropsychological interpretation. *Journal of Gerontology*, **41**, 758–763.

Winocur, G. (1988). A neuropsychological analysis of memory loss with age. *Neurobiology of Aging*, **9**, 487–494.

Winocur, G. (1989). Long-term memory loss in senescent rats: A neuropsychological analysis of interference and context effects. *Psychology and Aging*, in press.

Woodruff-Pak, D. S. (1988a). Age differences in classical conditioning of the NM/eyeblink response in rabbits in the delay paradigm. *Society for Neuroscience Abstracts*, **14**, 392.

Woodruff-Pak, D. S. (1988b). Aging and classical conditioning: Parallel studies in rabbits and humans, *Neurobiology of Aging*, **9**, 511–522.

Woodruff-Pak, D. S., Lavond, D. G., Logan, C. G., & Thompson, R. F. (1987). Classical conditioning in 3-, 30-, and 45-month-old rabbits: Behavioral learning and hippocampal unit activity. *Neurobiology of Aging*, **8**, 101–108.

Woodruff-Pak, D. S., & Logan, C. G. (1988). No apparent age differences in hippocampal theta frequency in rabbits aged 3–50 months. *Comprehensive Gerontology*, **2**, 24–28.

Woodruff-Pak, D. S., & Sheffield, J. B. (1987). Age differences in Purkinje cells and rate of classical conditioning in young and older rabbits. *Society for Neuroscience Abstracts*, **13**, 441.

Woodruff-Pak, D. S., Steinmetz, J. E., & Thompson, R. F.(1988). Classical conditioning of rabbits 2-1/2 years old using mossy fiber stimulation as a CS. *Neurobiology of Aging*, **9**, 187–193.

Woodruff-Pak, D. S., & Thompson, R. F. (1985). Classical conditioning of the eyelid response in rabbits as a model system for the study of brain mechanisms of learning and memory in aging. *Experimental Aging Research*, **11**, 109–122.

Woodruff-Pak, D. S., & Thompson, R. F.

(1988a). Classical conditioning of the eye-blink response in the delay paradigm in adults aged 18–83 years. *Psychology and Aging*, **3**, 219–229.

Woodruff-Pak, D. S., & Thompson, R. F. (1988b). Cerebellar correlates of classical conditioning across the life span. In P. B. Bal-tes, D. M. Featherman, & R. M. Lerner, (Eds.), *Lifespan development and behavior* (Vol. 9, pp. 1–37). Hillsdale, NJ: Erlbaum.

Zornetzer, S. F., Thompson, R., & Rogers, J. (1982). Rapid forgetting in aged rats. *Behavioral and Neural Biology*, **36**, 49–60.

Fifteen

Learning and Memory in Aging

David F. Hultsch and Roger A. Dixon

Research on learning and memory has been a central focus of psychologists interested in adult development and aging for both theoretical and practical reasons. Major reviews of work in this area (e.g., Craik, 1977; Poon, 1985) have documented an increasing amount of research activity as well as changes in paradigmatic emphasis. The years since the last edition of this *Handbook* again have seen continued high levels of research activity in learning and memory in aging. New emphases and approaches are changing the way researchers conceptualize and investigate these processes in later life. Given space restrictions, the goal for the present chapter is to provide an overview of selected research themes and results. The chapter concentrates on work published during the past 5 years, citing comprehensive reviews where possible.

Research in the area of memory and aging appears to reflect several general trends. Some trends are related to a conceptualization of life-span development that emphasizes multiple trajectories of change produced by complex interactions between the individual and his or her context. As in the past, other trends reflect the application of paradigms developed in cognitive psychology to questions of development in later life. In selecting topics to highlight in the present overview, we (1) examined prominent books and journals published in the past 5 years, (2) requested recent publications from numerous researchers in the field of cognitive aging, and (3) conducted an informal poll of selected scientists, asking them to indicate what issues or developments they saw as significant for the field at the present time. Our review and requests generated over 400 recently published works pertinent to learning and memory in adulthood and old age. We classified these papers into approximately 11 research themes. Our initial selection of themes was confirmed by the results of our poll of experts. Prominent themes included (1) those memory systems that show changes with age and those that are spared; (2) the role of context and environmental support in determining age differences in performance; (3) the influence of processing resources and abil-

Handbook of the Psychology of Aging, Third Edition
Copyright © 1990 Academic Press, Inc. All rights of reproduction in any form reserved.

ity components on complex memory tasks; (4) the differentiation of normal from pathological memory changes; (5) the influence of knowledge-based skills and expertise on memory; (6) memory for real world events; (7) how memory functions in the service of other cognitive or social processes; (8) how other processes such as intelligence, personality, and affect are related to memory performance; (9) individual differences as predictors of memory in later life; (10) the role of meta-knowledge and beliefs in memory functioning; and (11) the plasticity of memory and memory training.

In this chapter, we attend briefly to several of these topics. We begin by examining the differential age-related decline exhibited by different memory systems, focusing in particular on the recent distinction between implicit and explicit memory and on working memory. We then summarize some recent work on memory for meaningful materials and events such as memory for discourse and activities. The next section considers the issue of skill and expertise in memory performance in later life and reviews recent evidence for the plasticity of memory through training. Finally, in the last section, we present an individual differences perspective on memory and aging. We focus on the role of individual differences in processing resources and ability components in performance on complex tasks and the ways in which metamemorial knowledge and beliefs may relate to memory functioning in later life.

I. Differential Decline in Memory Systems

Much of the focus of research in memory and aging has been on the question of which tasks show decline and which are spared. This issue is typified in the well-known distinction between primary and secondary memory, indicating greater age-

related decline in the latter system than in the former (e.g., Craik, 1977). Earlier work examining this question also had suggested that episodic tasks typically show decline, whereas semantic tasks typically do not. This simple conclusion no longer appears justified, as recent studies have found a number of age-related decrements in various types of semantic memory tasks (Light & Burke, 1988). The same issue has recently emerged with respect to the distinction between explicit and implicit memory (Schacter, 1987). Generally, the present evidence suggests that age-related differences that are frequent and pronounced on many explicit memory tasks are absent or attenuated on implicit memory tasks (see Howard, 1988; Light, 1988, for reviews). Working memory has also been distinguished as a critical memory system (Baddeley, 1986) that may show substantial age-related decrements with increasing age.

A. Learning and Memory without Awareness

Explicit memory requires an intention to remember and, thus, yields an awareness of having done so. In contrast, implicit memory does not involve conscious recollection of remembering. Operationally, then, explicit and implicit memory tasks are distinguished by the instructions given to the subject at the time of test; whereas explicit tasks ask for remembering, implicit tasks do not. Implicit memory is shown by the influence of prior experience on performance even in the absence of conscious recollection of its occurrence.

Two types of implicit memory may be distinguished (Schacter, 1987). Implicit item memory involves memory for the occurrence of an item already known to the individual. This type of implicit memory is illustrated by repetition priming tasks (e.g., word fragment completion, perceptual identification of degraded words or pictures) in which prior exposure to a stimulus increases the probability of responding with that item, or speed of responding to that item, even in the absence of intention and awareness of memory. In contrast, implicit associative memory refers to memory for new associations between previously unrelated items. In these tasks, prior exposure to new information (e.g., pairs of unrelated words) influences the nature or speed of later responses on tasks that do not ask for remembering.

Explicit and implicit memory tasks appear to show different patterns of age-related deficits. Performance on explicit memory tasks is often impaired, whereas the current evidence, although incomplete, suggests that implicit memory is largely spared (e.g., Howard, 1988; Light, 1988). Several recent studies have examined implicit item memory and find little evidence for age-related decline, even though on explicit tasks the same older subjects perform more poorly than younger subjects (e.g., Light & Singh, 1987). This has been shown on various repetition priming tasks (e.g., word stem completion, identification of degraded words), lexical decision tasks, and spelling bias tasks. There are a few exceptions to these findings. For example, a recent study by Chiarello and Hoyer (1988) found that younger adults outperformed older adults on both implicit (stem completion) and explicit (cued recall) tasks. They suggest that age differences on implicit tasks, although consistent, may be small thus requiring high power to detect them. Indeed, Light and Burke (1988) also caution that although their studies do not show significant age effects, in all cases the young performed slightly better than the old on the implicit tasks. Such differences may reflect true age differences, or the operation of some aspects of explicit memory in the presumed implicit tasks.

The conclusions that may be drawn for implicit associative memory are less clear. For one thing, less work has been done on this type of implicit memory. Some recent studies also find that age differences are absent (Howard, 1988; Moscovitch, Winocur, & McLachlan, 1986). For example, Howard reports the results of a series of studies using a word stem completion paradigm. In this task, people are exposed to new associations among unrelated word pairs. Following a delay interval, implicit memory is tapped by a word stem completion task in which people are given a stimulus word followed by a word stem and are asked to complete the stem with the first word that comes to mind. Varying the nature of the stimulus word and word stem permits assessment of both implicit item and associative memory, as well as tests of explicit associative memory. In most instances, younger adults outperformed the older adults on the explicit tests, but there were no significant age differences on either type of implicit memory. However, Howard's data also suggest that implicit associative memory does show age effects under certain conditions. In particular, when conditions of study of the new associations are less than optimal, older adults show less implicit associative memory than younger adults.

In sum, age differences on implicit item memory are substantially reduced in comparison to those observed with explicit item memory. As well, age differences for implicit associative memory also appear to be reduced compared to explicit tests. However, under certain conditions of difficult study, there do appear to be reliable age differences in associative implicit memory.

B. Working Memory

Tasks tapping primary or short-term memory generally show little age-related decrement unless they require active manipulation of information or division of attention (Craik, 1977). This characteristic of older adults' performance has recently achieved heightened importance with the specification of the concept of working memory in cognitive psychology and the increasing emphasis on resource theory in cognitive aging.

Working memory generally is seen as a limited capacity system consisting of representation codes for the temporary storage of information and a central executive capable of attention, selection, and manipulation (Baddeley, 1986). Tasks tapping working memory demand simultaneous storage of recently presented material and processing of additional information. Research has suggested that there are substantial age differences on such tasks in favor of the young (e.g., Light & Anderson, 1985; Wingfield, Stine, Lahar, & Aberdeen, 1988). Recent studies by Craik and his colleagues (see Craik, Morris, & Gick, 1989 for review) confirm this age deficit. In addition, their studies suggest that the older adult's difficulty lies primarily in the processing aspects of working memory rather than in the storage aspects.

Working memory is particularly significant to aging research because of its potential link to resource theory (Salthouse, 1985, 1988). In this view, working memory is seen as an important component that contributes to multiple cognitive tasks. If aging is associated with diminished working memory capacity, then a substantial portion of the observed age differences in performance may be related to a reduction of this resource. However, recent work suggests that this view may be too simplistic (Salthouse, 1988). First, it has become increasingly clear that working memory is not a unitary construct and, therefore, working memory measures are not measuring some generalized pool of resources. Rather, working memory appears to be at least domain specific, and perhaps task specific (Daneman, 1987). Similarly, it has become clear that a simple processing resource model does not adequately account for all age-related performance differences (Salthouse, Kausler, & Saults, 1988). Nevertheless, the concept of working memory may prove to be a useful construct for understanding adult cognition. For example, Hasher and Zacks (1988) offer an alternative view to the general processing resource conception based on age-related decrements in the inhibitory control mechanisms of cognition that allow irrelevant information to enter working and secondary memory and thus compromise retrieval.

II. Memory for Meaningful Materials and Events

Much recent research has been devoted to examining adult age differences in memory for meaningful stimulus materials and events. In part, this work has been premised on arguments in cognitive psychology regarding the importance of conducting research on practical or everyday cognition (e.g., Neisser, 1985). These arguments have been motivated by several theoretical and methodological issues (e.g., ecological validity) discussed in various volumes in cognitive psychology (e.g., Gruneberg, Morris, & Sykes, 1988; Neisser & Winograd, 1988) and cognitive aging (e.g., Poon, Rubin, & Wilson, 1989).

There are at least two important caveats that can be derived from these reviews and the literature they cover. First, there are still no optimal resolutions to the many conceptual and methodological problems associated with meaningfulness and ecological validity. Specifically, the criteria for these constructs are difficult to derive and stipulate. Second, the age-related expectations of putatively ecologically valid cognitive work may not be firmly grounded; the assumption seems to be that familiarity breeds success and success is indicated by attenuation of age differences in performance levels. However, no uniform pattern of such attenuation has been observed.

In this section, we review briefly research on general aging (i.e., with samples unselected on skill) and memory for selected categories of meaningful materials, tasks, activities, and events. The categories we have selected for further discussion are memory for discourse (e.g., prose passages) and memory for events (e.g., subject-performed tasks). Because the amount of research conducted on practical memory and aging has grown markedly in recent years, we omit further discussion of such topics as (1) prospective memory (e.g., Meacham, 1988; Sinnott, 1986, 1989; West, 1988); (2) autobiographical memory (e.g., Rubin, 1986); (3) spatial memory (e.g., Sharps & Gollin, 1987; Zelinski & Light, 1988); (4) memory for names and faces (e.g., Cohen & Faulkner, 1986); (5) memory for pictures (e.g., Park, Puglisi, & Smith, 1986; Park, Royal, Dudley, & Morrell, 1988); (6) the tip-of-the-tongue (e.g., Burke, Worthley, & Martin, 1988) and feeling-of-knowing (e.g., Butterfield, Nelson, & Peck, 1988) experience; and (7) memory for source information (e.g., Cohen & Faulkner, 1989; McIntyre & Craik, 1987). Recent reviews of some of these topics may be found in Gruneberg et al. (1988), Poon et al. (1989), and West (1986). We turn now to a brief overview of recent research on memory for discourse.

A. Memory for Discourse

This category of research includes such topics as comprehension and recall of spoken language and written passages ranging in length from sentences through multiple-paragraph texts. Several recent review chapters have considered one or more of these topics from a variety of perspectives (e.g., Cohen, 1988; Hultsch & Dixon, 1984; Meyer, 1987; Spilich, 1985; Zelinski & Gilewski, 1988). Other topics in language processing are discussed by Light (Chapter 16, this volume).

Hultsch and Dixon (1984) organized the research accumulated to that time in terms of Jenkins's (1979) tetrahedral classification system. The four nodes—or classes of variables related to text recall performance—of the tetrahedron were subjects variables (e.g., skills, prior knowledge), criterial tasks (e.g., free recall, recognition), materials variables (e.g., text structure, sensory modality), and orienting tasks (e.g., instructions, activities). Other reviews (e.g., Meyer & Rice, 1989) have used similar organizational schemes. Several conclusions and recommendations of these reviews are worthy of note. First, recent research on memory for text has benefitted from considerable attention to both cognitive and linguistic theories of discourse structure and processing (e.g., van Dijk & Kintsch, 1983). Attention to such theories has suggested numerous new avenues of investigation for aging research. Second, the growing body of cross-sectional research (to about 1983) showed that age differences in favor of young adults were regularly observed. However, multiple factors and interactions (or combinations of factors) appeared to either accentuate or attenuate these observed age differences. Several reviews suggested that further research in this area would benefit from a more theoretical consideration of the apparent exceptions to the rule of negative age differences in performance. This effort would include careful attention to the selection of subjects, criterial tasks, materials, and instructions. It also would include further examination of theories and research questions adapted from nondevelopmental research in cognitive psychology. Some later chapters addressed to topics in aging and discourse processing (e.g., Dixon & Bäckman, 1989; Spilich, 1985; Zelinski, 1988) evince this influence.

The subjects factor of the tetrahedron of influences is one example of a class of variables related to text recall performance for which it may be especially useful to adapt theoretical advances in cognitive psychology to theories and research questions in cognitive aging. Recent research on the influence of knowledge (both generic and domain specific) on text recall performance of young and old adults reflects these advances. For example, reading and understanding a prose passage involves integrating prior knowledge with the information presented in the text. It is conceivable that, to some degree, observed age differences (in favor of young adults) may be accounted for by: (1) age-related differences in activities associated with world knowledge or schemata, (2) age-related differences in ability to integrate or activate such knowledge systems, or (3) age-related biases in the match between topic and content of the text and the domain-specific knowledge of the reader. Several studies are relevant to these issues. Light and Anderson (1983) investigated memory for scripts—which are stereotypical representations of roles, expectations, and actions associated with real-world activities—and found some age differences in accuracy (in recall of actions from scripts) but no age differences in other indicators of integration of real-world knowledge with stimulus scripts (see also Zelinski & Miura, 1988). Hess (1985), however, reported results indicating that older adults were disadvantaged as compared to younger adults in accuracy of some indicators of such integration.

Using a different approach, Hultsch and Dixon (1983) examined the relationship between domain-specific knowledge of cohort-specific entertainment figures and recall of biographical sketches of those figures. They found equivalence in the recall rates of young and old adults for two passages about a figure known equally well by adults of all ages and a figure known best by older adults. Young adults were superior in their recall of information from the passages about a figure known best by young adults. Similarly, Byrd (1986–1987) reported that young and old adults performed well in an immediate condition in recalling the theme of passages about topics for which they had substantial prior

knowledge. In a delayed condition, however, old adults were less able than young adults to differentiate new information from prior knowledge.

The reviews cited describe other related areas of research in the field of text recall and aging. Research on such subject variables as student status (Ratner, Schell, Crimmins, Mittelman, & Baldinelli, 1987), language experience (Dixon & Bäckman, 1989), style of recall (e.g., Adams, Labouvie-Vief, Hobart & Dorosz, in press), and everyday activities (Rice, 1986a,b) point to promising avenues for future research. Research on the effects of strategy training in learning prose (e.g., Meyer, Young, & Bartlett, 1989) has suggested that some age effects may be eliminated by specific instruction. Finally, the issue of text structure—especially age-related differences in sensitivity to structural characteristics—remains an important concern (e.g., Rubin, 1985; Stine & Wingfield, 1988).

B. Memory for Activities

Aging and memory for activities and events is a growing area of research. Kausler and Lichty (1988) suggest that, if queried, one easily remembers having performed numerous daily activities. Memory for everyday activities is persistent despite the fact that performing them is rarely accompanied by a deliberate intention to remember; that is, they are remembered incidentally and automatically. It was, in part, this characteristic of memory for activities—which Kausler and Lichty (1988) called rehearsal-independent—that led to the expectation that adult age differences would be minimized for such stimulus materials. This expectation is in contrast to much research employing tasks that require rehearsal-dependent forms of memory (e.g., free recall of words, sentences, and texts) in which age-related performance differences in favor of young adults are observed regularly. In the case of activity memory, *meaningfulness* refers both to the content of the materials (activities) and to the omnipresent process of rehearsal-independent memory. As with much other research on practical cognition and aging, however, recent studies on activity memory do not reveal a consistent pattern of results across laboratories (partly because of variations in experimental procedures such as activity or item type, list length, and organizability of items). Specifically, there is mixed evidence pertaining to the presence or absence of age-related performance differences.

In a series of studies, Kausler and colleagues (e.g., Kausler & Hakami, 1983; Kausler & Lichty, 1988, for review) demonstrated that memory for performed activities appeared to be a rehearsal-independent form of episodic memory. In both recognition and recall tasks, however, young adults performed better than old adults. Kausler and Lichty (1988) discussed possible explanations for this pattern of results, including the notion that, although activities may be encoded automatically by older adults, the retrieval of such information from long-term episodic store may require effortful processes, including a well-functioning working memory capacity. In contrast to this pattern of results, in another series of studies, Bäckman and colleagues (e.g., Bäckman, 1985; see Bäckman, 1989, for review) found that, although young adults performed better than old adults on free recall of verbal materials (imperative sentences such as "lift the spoon"), the old adults performed as well as young adults on recall of such sentences when accompanied by performance of the indicated activity. Thus, unlike the Kausler studies, age differences in recall were attenuated in the case of activities but not in the case of verbal-only materials.

Recent research has investigated possible moderating factors such as encoding modality (e.g., Lichty, Kausler, & Mar-

tinez, 1986), list length (Cohen, Sandler, & Schroeder, 1987), imagined versus performed actions (Guttentag & Hunt, 1988), and, in the context of more complex actions, instructions (Ratner, Padgett, & Bushey, 1988). As with other areas of research in memory for meaningful materials, no simple conclusions regarding memory for actions and events are forthcoming. Numerous factors, variables indicating those factors, and interactions among factors continue to be investigated.

III. Experience and Plasticity of Memory

Considerable recent research in cognitive aging has focused on the role of experience in the maintenance (and possible improvement) of cognitive performance levels through late adulthood (e.g., Charness, 1989; Salthouse, 1987). Experience (and practice) in a particular domain of cognitively demanding activity (e.g., chess, typing, reading, mental squaring) may be associated with continued high levels of performance on cognitive tasks (e.g., memory or problem solving) related to that domain of activity. Such expertise effects are relatively domain specific; that is, adults who are experienced (especially, experts) in a particular domain may perform well on tasks related to that domain but no better than same-age novices on other complex, laboratory tasks (e.g., Hoyer, 1985). In addition, a given group of young adults may perform better than a group of old adults on given complex cognitive tasks, but when the tasks match the experience (expertise) of the old adults, attenuation of age differences may be expected.

Such expectations regarding the effects of age and expertise derive from several theoretical treatments of the development, mechanisms, and effects of experience and skill (e.g., Anderson, 1985; Charness, 1989; Ericsson, 1985; Salthouse,

1987). Memory skills are characterized by rapid, fluid, virtually error-free performance. They involve several features (e.g., Ericsson, 1985): (1) meaningful encoding and rapid storage in long term memory (LTM); (2) explicit association of to-be-remembered (TBR) information with retrieval structures; (3) durable storage of information; (4) with practice and motivation, increasingly rapid encoding and retrieval of information; and (5) domain specificity. In the field of memory and aging, most research on the effects of experience has dealt with training or practice in the use of mnemonic devices.

How may the memory performance of older adults be improved or maintained? Much recent memory training research has been based on earlier research on the effects of practice, organization, and imagery. Numerous recent studies have indicated that training in a given mnemonic skill (e.g., semantic associations, interactive imagery) or in a package of such skills, often produces domain-specific improvement in memory performance (e.g., Kliegl, Smith, Heckhausen, & Baltes, 1987; West, 1989, see Yesavage & Sheikh, 1989, for review). In one set of studies, Kliegl and Baltes (1987) trained individual young and old adults to memorize and reproduce strings of digits and nouns. The training program was complex and varied, but a typical program for digit recall consisted of three components: (1) acquisition of a mnemonic system (e.g., learning historical dates with which triplets of digits could be recorded); (2) acquisition of a long-term memory retrieval structure (e.g., using the method of loci); and (3) varying the presentation rate of TBR items from self-paced through speeded conditions. Among the noteworthy results are the following: the pretraining baseline was similar for young and old adults; both young and old adults were able to employ the mnemonic system to reach high levels of performance (e.g., one older woman was able to recall a string of 120 digits); and the adaptivity of

the mnemonic system could be tested by varying the presentation rate. Stressing the system (or testing the limits) in this way resulted in a magnification of individual differences (and age differences) in performance levels. Not only does experience (in this case, engineered memory training) reveal substantial plasticity on the part of young and old adults, but there may be some indication that there are age-related differences in the limits of reserve capacity.

An important consideration in some memory training programs is the maintenance and generalization (or transfer) of the skill to selected domains of everyday memory performance (e.g., Yesavage & Sheikh, 1989). The range of generalizability (across domains of TBR information) of mnemonic systems is not known. Similarly, there is very little research addressed to comparisons of "internal" mnemonic systems, "internal" mnemonic devices versus "external" memory aids, and a variety of training procedures. The procedures and systems that are most functional (effective, easy to learn, generalizable) for older adults is a topic of some current and future research (e.g, Wilson, 1989). Other topics include pharmacological interventions and training in pathological aging (see Poon, 1986, for reviews)

Other topics of current and future research include naturally occurring expertise, or memory skill that is acquired through diligent and long-term practice or experience in a given domain. Usually, such skill is a product of extensive leisure (e.g., hobbies) or professional activities (see Charness, 1989, for review). The influence of other skills in the maintenance of memory performance also has been investigated. Thus, expertise in a related, substitutable domain may act as a compensatory mechanism in the maintenance of high levels of memory skill (Charness, 1989). Charness applies similar logic in investigations of the involvement of memory in skill performance. Dixon and Bäckman (1989) discuss issues of expertise and compensation in prose reading and recall. Despite the absence of total control over the development and mechanisms of such skills (and compensatory mechanisms), continued research on naturally occurring memory expertise (or compensation) is likely to be productive.

IV. Individual Differences in Learning and Memory in Aging

As noted, cognitive psychologists have increasingly begun to view cognitive performance as a product of complex interactions among characteristics of both the task and the subjects performing it. Inclusion of subject characteristics focuses fundamentally on the issue of individual differences, or more specifically, on the question of why subjects exhibit substantial variation in performance given identical task conditions. In addition to the notion that subject characteristics may mediate task performance, an individual differences perspective suggests the possibility that the nature or relative contribution of these variables may change with age (Hertzog, 1985). Thus examination of such differences may be an important source of explanation for developmental change (e.g., Horn, 1987; Weinert, Schneider, & Knopf, 1988).

A. Abilities

Considerable recent attention has been directed toward the possibility that variability in performance between age groups and variability among individuals within age groups are a product of individual differences in abilities relevant to the complex tasks typically used to measure learning and memory. In particular, attention has been focused on information-processing components or processing resources (e.g., working memory) that may underlie

performance, as well as on more complex abilities that may be indicative of accumulated knowledge (e.g., verbal comprehension). In the first category of research in this area, for example, several theorists have suggested that working memory should be a critical component or resource for processing complex materials such as texts (van Dijk & Kintsch, 1983). However, the findings in this area have been inconclusive. For example, Light and Anderson (1985) and Hartley (1986) did not find working memory to be a significant predictor of text recall. In contrast, Spilich's (1983) analysis of van Dijk and Kintsch's leading edge model and a study by Stine and Wingfield (1987) suggest that a significant portion of the age-related decrement in performance can be accounted for by individual differences in working memory. In part, these inconsistencies may be related to the methodological difficulties in the measurement of working memory noted earlier. Evidence for the potential role of verbal speed as an individual difference predictor of memory is more persuasive, with several analyses suggesting that individual differences in this variable may account for a significant portion of the age differences in both text memory and word memory (e.g., Hartley, 1986, 1988).

In general, these studies have shown that multiple abilities are predictive of performance on a variety of memory tasks, and age-related effects are substantially reduced, although not eliminated, when component abilities such as verbal speed and working memory are partialled. It is important to stress, however, that age effects are not completely accounted for by individual differences in component abilities. In a recent analysis of processing resource models, Salthouse et al. (1988) found little support for strong processing resource models in which all or none of the effects of age on cognitive performance were mediated by processing resources related to space and time. Support was obtained for a weaker model in which there was a contribution of age to performance independent of individual differences in processing resources. Salthouse (1988) argued that although it is plausible that age-related decrements in processing resources are responsible for at least some of the observed age differences in cognitive performance, the processing resource hypothesis cannot be considered truly explanatory until we have specified the nature of these variables more fully and developed process models that specify when and how such resources determine performance.

Whereas the research summarized here has focused on components or resources, other studies have focused on more complex abilities. In this category, the role of verbal ability has been prominent among the topics of investigation. Within this context, it has frequently been suggested that age differences in performance may be attenuated in high verbal ability samples (e.g., Zelinski & Gilewski, 1988). For example, Meyer and Rice (1989) report that high-verbal-ability older adults performed as well as a randomly sampled group of young adults on some recall measures. Other studies paint a different picture. Dixon, Hultsch, Simon, and von Eye (1984), for instance, found that high-verbal older adults did not recall prose passages overall as well as younger adults but were able to identify the main ideas of the passages as well as high-verbal young adults. Regardless of whether age-related group differences are eliminated with highly verbal subjects, there is strong evidence to suggest that verbal ability is an important predictor of performance and "absorbs" variance that would otherwise be related to age (e.g., Hartley, 1986; Hultsch, Hertzog, & Dixon, 1984).

Recent research also has focused on individual differences in more global experiences as potential predictors of cognitive performance. In particular, research suggests that participation in a range of every-day activities may be related to the maintenance of cognitive performance in later life (e.g., Arbuckle, Gold, & Andres, 1986; Craik, Byrd, & Swanson, 1987; Winocur, Moscovitch, & Freeman, 1987).

B. Self-Knowledge and Self-Evaluation

It has become increasingly clear that cognitive processes do not operate in isolation from personality and social processes. Of course, this realization is not new, but satisfactory paradigms have been in short supply, and the issue keeps reemerging. The fundamental assumption of all of these efforts is that there is a distinction between competence and performance. At least three clusters of variables have been considered to be important determinants of performance (Salomon & Globerson, 1987): (1) metacognitive factors such as knowledge of what the task requires and knowledge of strategies that may be applied; (2) motivational factors such as expectations, sense of self-efficacy, and attribution about outcomes; and (3) personality variables such as traits, states, and stylistic modes of perceiving and responding.

In recent years, aspects of the first two of these domains related to cognitive self-knowledge and self-evaluation have received considerable attention, and we focus on these. These phenomena have been studied under various guises including metamemory, memory complaints, memory monitoring, memory awareness, and cognitive self-efficacy. Research has focused on both general as well as task-specific knowledge and evaluations. This domain is multidimensional and more precise distinctions among different constructs have begun to emerge (e.g., Cavanaugh, 1989; Hultsch, Hertzog, Dixon, & Davidson, 1988). Similarly, a number of questionnaire (Dixon, 1989; Gilewski & Zelinski, 1986) and experimental (Cavanaugh, 1989) methods have been developed.

Research suggests substantial age differences in some areas but not in others. Age differences in various aspects of self-knowledge appear to be relatively minimal. For example, there appear to be few age differences in the domain of general knowledge about cognitive processes such as memory (e.g., Hultsch, *et al.*, 1988). Similarly, there appear to be few age differences in what Cavanaugh (1989) calls epistemic awareness—judgments of what is known with respect to specific items (e.g., Shaw & Craik, 1989). However, it appears that older adults are less likely than younger adults to know the source of previous information (McIntyre & Craik, 1987). There also may be some age differences in certain aspects of what Cavanaugh (1989) refers to as on-line awareness or executive processes occurring during remembering (e.g., Murphy, Schmitt, Caruso, & Sanders, 1987).

In contrast to the area of self-knowledge, age differences in the area of self-evaluation of cognition appear to be substantial. In particular, older adults tend to perceive themselves as less efficacious on many cognitive tasks as compared to younger adults or themselves when they were younger (e.g., Cornelius & Caspi, 1986). Such evaluations appear to be related to expectations of adult cognitive functioning and need to be distinguished from complaints that may be related to personality states such as depression (Niederehe & Yoder, 1989). Related to lower feelings of cognitive efficacy is the finding that older adults report lower feeling of control (e.g., Hultsch *et al.*, 1988; Lachman, 1986). The importance of this variable is heightened by findings that demonstrate that procedures that increase the individual's sense of control, such as providing choices, lead to increments in performance (Perlmuter, Monty, & Chan, 1986). Finally, there is evidence of some age differences in attributions about performance that are consistent with expectations about performance. For example,

older adults' poor performance is more likely to be attributed to ability than younger adults' poor performance, although this unflattering comparison varies across domain, age of target, and age of individual making the attribution (Lachman & McArthur, 1986).

A major remaining issue concerns the significance of these variables either as determinants of age-group differences or as sources of individual variation within age groups. In particular, concern has been directed toward the issue of whether metamemory is related to actual performance on memory tasks (e.g., Dixon, Hertzog, & Hultsch, 1986; Sunderland, Watts, Baddeley, & Harris, 1986). Much of the work has been framed within two relatively straightforward hypotheses. One suggests that deficiencies in self-knowledge (e.g., of task demands, of strategy selection, of monitoring performance) might be a major source of production deficiencies on many cognitive tasks. With some exceptions (Murphy *et al.*, 1987), this view has not been supported, suggesting that the contribution of age-related metacognitive deficiencies may be very task specific. The other hypothesis suggests that poor self-evaluations (low sense of self-efficacy, lack of sense of control, inappropriate performance attributions) result in lowered effort and consequent poor performance. This view has received more support (e.g., Lachman, Steinberg, & Trotter, 1987). However, it is increasingly apparent that the interface between cognitive and social processes is a complex one. What is needed at present are specific models (e.g., Cavanaugh, 1989) that will permit the development and testing of specific hypotheses.

V. Conclusion

Our brief review of recent work in the area of learning and memory and aging has identified several key themes that have received considerable attention in the past five years. It has become apparent that learning and memory processes are embedded within a wide range of contexts that range from relatively narrow (e.g., irrelevant stimulus components) to relatively broad (e.g., culturally based knowledge). This realization has led to greater emphasis on topics such as memory for real-life events and consideration of the ways in which individual differences in abilities and social processes may mediate age-related changes in memory performance. Such approaches provide us with an increasingly rich, although complex, view of learning and memory in adulthood and old age.

One implication of this more complex view of adult cognition is that both traditional and recent conceptual and methodological approaches must be continually examined and compared. For example, the shift from traditional laboratory tasks to presumably ecologically valid tasks has not resulted in consistent attenuation of age differences. The relationships among age, familiarity of task, and performance appear complex, with familiarity perhaps best defined individually and interactively, that is, as the fit between the knowledge, experience, and skills of the learner and the specific demands of the task. Furthermore, criteria for differentiating ecologically valid from invalid tasks remain unclear. It is important to examine (1) the extent to which deriving general principles of learning and memory is still a suitable goal of cognitive research, (2) the extent to which general principles of traditional memory research with young adults apply to older adults, and (3) the extent to which general principles derived from one area of memory and aging research apply to other areas (e.g., Kausler, 1982; Neisser, 1985). Our review has indicated that further attention to the interaction of multiple sources of influence in change in adult memory performance in all varieties of tasks is required. Atheoretical conceptions such as

Jenkins's (1979) tetrahedron have been useful in drawing our attention to the various classes of variables that might be important. However, future work must move beyond such atheoretical perspectives to focus on theoretically based task and process analyses that will permit (1) prediction of when and how age changes or differences will appear, and (2) interpretation of observed age-related improvement, maintenance, or decrement. Conceptually, such an effort may benefit from recent advances in the cognitive sciences. Methodologically, such work requires the use of complex designs and multivariate data analytic strategies. In particular, the importance of intraindividual designs cannot be overlooked. Such designs may range from intensive single-subject training studies (e.g., Kliegl & Baltes, 1987) or replicated single-subject multiple occasion designs (e.g., p-technique), to large-scale single- or multiple-cohort longitudinal work (e.g., Schaie, 1983). The continuing process of comparing and contrasting traditional and recent approaches, as well as simple and complex designs, may result in a higher level of integrative theoretical work (e.g., Salthouse, 1985).

Acknowledgments

The authors wish to thank those individuals who provided us with copies of their recent publications. Although space limitations prevented us from citing many of these articles, we found them invaluable in developing the themes of the chapter. We particularly wish to thank those scientists who responded to our poll concerning recent developments in the field. Finally, we wish to acknowledge that preparation of this chapter was, in part, supported by individual operating grants to each of us from the Natural Sciences and Engineering Research Council of Canada.

References

Adams, C., Labouvie-Vief, G., Hobart, C. J., & Dorosz, M. (in press). Adult age group differences in story recall style. *Journal of Gerontology: Psychological Sciences.*

Anderson, J. R. (1985). *Cognitive psychology and its implications.* San Francisco: Freeman.

Arbuckle, T. Y., Gold, D., & Andres, D. (1986). Cognitive functioning of older people in relation to social and personality variables. *Psychology and Aging,* **1,** 55–62.

Bäckman, L. (1985). Further evidence for the lack of adult age differences on free recall of subject performed tasks: The importance of motor action. *Human Learning,* **4,** 79–87.

Bäckman, L. (1989). Varieties of memory compensation of older adults in episodic remembering. In L. W. Poon, D. C. Rubin, & B. A. Wilson (Eds.), *Everyday cognition in adulthood and old age.* New York: Cambridge University Press (in press).

Baddeley, A. (1986). *Working memory.* Oxford: Clarendon.

Burke, D., Worthley, J., & Martin, J. (1988). I'll never forget what's-her-name: Aging and tip of the tongue experiences in everyday life. In M. M. Gruneberg, P. E. Morris, & R. N. Sykes (Eds.), *Practical aspects of memory: Current research and issues* (Vol. 2, pp. 113–118). New York: Wiley.

Butterfield, E. C., Nelson, T. O., & Peck, V. (1988). Developmental aspects of the feeling of knowing. *Developmental Psychology,* **24,** 654–663.

Byrd, M. (1986–1987). The effects of previously acquired knowledge on memory for textual information. *International Journal of Aging and Human Development,* **24,** 231–240.

Cavanaugh, J. C. (1989). The importance of awareness in memory aging. In L. W. Poon, D. C. Rubin, & B. A. Wilson (Eds.), *Everyday cognition in adulthood and old age.* New York: Cambridge University Press (in press).

Charness, N. (1989). Age and expertise: Responding to Talland's challenge. In L. W. Poon, D. C. Rubin, & B. A. Wilson (Eds.), *Everyday cognition in adulthood and old age.* New York: Cambridge University Press (in press).

Chiarello, C., & Hoyer, W. J. (1988). Adult age differences in implicit and explicit memory: Time course and encoding effects. *Psychology and Aging,* **3,** 358–366.

Cohen, G. (1988). Age differences in memory for texts: Production deficiency or processing limitations? In L. L. Light & D. M. Burke (Eds.), *Language, memory, and aging* (pp. 171–190). New York: Cambridge University Press.

Cohen, G., & Faulkner, D. (1986). Memory for proper names: Age differences in retrieval. *British Journal of Developmental Psychology,* **4,** 187–197.

Cohen, G., & Faulkner, D. (1989). Age differences in source forgetting: Effects on reality monitoring and on eyewitness testimony. *Psychology and Aging,* **4,** 10–17.

Cohen, R. L., Sandler, S. P., & Schroeder, K. (1987). Aging and memory for words and action events. The effects of item repetition and list length. *Psychology and Aging,* **2,** 280–285.

Cornelius, S. W., & Caspi, A. (1986). Self-perceptions of intellectual control and aging. *Educational Gerontology,* **12,** 345–357.

Craik, F. I. M. (1977). Age differences in human memory. In J. E. Birren & K. W. Schaie (Eds.), *Handbook of the psychology of aging* (pp. 384–420). New York: Van Nostrand Reinhold.

Craik, F. I. M., Byrd, M., & Swanson, J. M. (1987). Patterns of memory loss in three elderly samples. *Psychology and Aging,* **2,** 79–86.

Craik, F. I. M., Morris, R. G., & Gick, M. L. (1989). Adult age differences in working memory. In G. Vallar & T. Shallice (Eds.), *Neuropsychological impairments of short-term memory.* New York: Cambridge University Press (in press).

Daneman, M. (1987). Reading and working memory. In J. R. Beech & A. M. Colley (Eds.), *Cognitive approaches to reading* (pp. 57–86). New York: Wiley.

Dixon, R. A. (1989). Questionnaire research on metamemory and aging: Issues of structure and function. In L. W. Poon, D. C. Rubin, & B. A. Wilson (Eds.), *Everyday cognition in adulthood and old age.* New York: Cambridge University Press (in press).

Dixon, R. A., & Bäckman, L. (1989). Reading and memory for prose in adulthood: Issues of expertise and compensation. In S. R. Yussen & M. C. Smith (Eds.), *Reading across the life span.* New York: Springer-Verlag (in press).

Dixon, R. A., Hertzog, C., & Hultsch, D. F. (1986). The multiple relationships among

Metamemory in Adulthood (MIA) scales and cognitive abilities in adulthood. *Human Learning, 5,* 165–177.

Dixon, R. A., Hultsch, D. F., Simon, E. W., & von Eye, A. (1984). Verbal ability and text structure effects on adult age differences in text recall. *Journal of Verbal Learning and Verbal Behavior, 23,* 569–578.

Ericsson, K. A. (1985). Memory skill. *Canadian Journal of Psychology, 39,* 188–231.

Gilewski, M. J., & Zelinski, E. M. (1986). Questionnaire assessment of memory complaints. In L. W. Poon (Ed.), *Handbook for clinical memory assessment of older adults* (pp. 93–107). Washington, DC: American Psychological Association.

Gruneberg, M. M., Morris, P. E., & Sykes, R. N. (Eds.) (1988). *Practical aspects of memory: Current research and issues* (Vol. 2). New York: Wiley.

Guttentag, R. E., & Hunt, R. R. (1988). Adult age differences in memory for imagined and performed actions. *Journal of Gerontology: Psychological Sciences, 43,* 107–108.

Hartley, J. T. (1986). Reader and text variables as determinants of discourse memory in adulthood. *Psychology and Aging, 1,* 150–158.

Hartley, J. T. (1988). Individual differences in memory for written discourse. In L. L. Light & D. M. Burke (Eds.), *Language, memory, and aging* (pp. 36–57). New York: Cambridge University Press.

Hasher, L., & Zacks, R. T. (1988). Working memory, comprehension, and aging: A review and a new view. In G. H. Bower (Ed.), *The psychology of learning and motivation,* (Vol. 22, pp. 193–225). New York: Academic Press.

Hertzog, C. (1985). An individual differences perspective: Implications for cognitive research in gerontology. *Research on Aging, 7,* 7–45.

Hess, T. M. (1985). Aging and context influences on recognition memory for typical and atypical script actions. *Developmental Psychology, 21,* 1139–1151.

Horn, J. (1987). A context for understanding information processing studies of human abilities. In P. E. Vernon (Ed.), *Age-related changes in intelligence and speed of infor-*mation processing (pp. 201–238). Norwood, NJ: Ablex.

Howard, D. V. (1988). Implicit and explicit assessment of cognitive aging. In M. L. Howe & C. J. Brainerd (Eds.), *Cognitive development in adulthood: Progress in cognitive development research* (pp. 3–37). New York: Springer-Verlag.

Hoyer, W. J. (1985). Aging and the development of expert cognition. In T. M. Schlecter & M. P. Toglia (Eds.), *New directions in cognitive science* (pp. 69–87). Norwood, NJ: Ablex.

Hultsch, D. F., & Dixon, R. A. (1983). The role of pre-experimental knowledge in text processing in adulthood. *Experimental Aging Research, 9,* 7–22.

Hultsch, D. F., & Dixon, R. A. (1984). Memory for text materials in adulthood. In P. B. Baltes & O. G. Brim, Jr. (Eds.), *Life-span development and behavior* (Vol. 6, pp. 77–108). New York: Academic Press.

Hultsch, D. F., Hertzog, C., & Dixon, R. A. (1984). Text recall in adulthood: The role of intellectual abilities. *Developmental Psychology, 20,* 1193–1209.

Hultsch, D. F., Hertzog, C., Dixon, R. A., & Davidson, H. A. (1988). Memory self-knowledge and self-efficacy in the aged. In M. L. Howe & C. J. Brainerd (Eds.), *Cognitive development in adulthood: Progress in cognitive development research* (pp. 65–92). New York: Springer-Verlag.

Jenkins, J. J. (1979). Four points to remember: A tetrahedral model of memory experiments. In L. S. Cermak & F. I. M. Craik (Eds.), *Levels of processing in human memory* (pp. 429–446). Hillsdale, NJ: Erlbaum.

Kausler, D. H. (1982). *Experimental psychology and human aging.* New York: Wiley.

Kausler, D. H., & Hakami, M. K. (1983). Memory for activities: Adult age differences and intentionality. *Developmental Psychology, 19,* 889–894.

Kausler, D. H., & Lichty, W. (1988). Memory for activities: Rehearsal-independence and aging. In M. L. Howe & C. J. Brainerd (Eds.), *Cognitive development in adulthood: Progress in cognitive development research* (pp. 93–131). New York: Springer-Verlag.

Kliegl, R., & Baltes, P. B. (1987). Theory-guided analysis of mechanisms of development and aging through testing-the-limits and research on expertise. In C. Schooler & K. W. Schaie (Eds.), *Cognitive functioning and social structure over the life course* (pp. 95–119). Norwood, NJ: Ablex.

Kliegl, R., Smith, J., Heckhausen, J., & Baltes, P. B. (1987). Mnemonic training for the acquisition of skilled digit memory. *Cognition and Instruction*, **4**, 203–223.

Lachman, M. E. (1986). Locus of control in aging research: A case for multidimensional and domain-specific assessment. *Psychology and Aging*, **1**, 34–40.

Lachman, M. E., & McArthur, L. Z. (1986). Adult age differences in causal attributions for cognitive, physical, and social performance. *Psychology and Aging*, **1**, 127–132.

Lachman, M. E., Steinberg, E. S., & Trotter, S. D. (1987). Effects of control beliefs and attributions on memory self-assessments and performance. *Psychology and Aging*, **2**, 266–271.

Lichty, W., Kausler, D. H., & Martinez, D. R. (1986). Adult age differences in memory for motor versus cognitive activities. *Experimental Aging Research*, **12**, 227–230.

Light, L. L. (1988). Preserved implicit memory in old age. In M. M. Gruneberg, P. E. Morris, & R. N. Sykes (Eds.), *Practical aspects of memory: Current research and issues* (Vol. 2, pp. 90–95). New York: Wiley.

Light, L. L., & Anderson, P. A. (1983). Memory for scripts in young and older adults. *Memory and Cognition*, **11**, 435–444.

Light, L. L., & Anderson, P. A. (1985). Working-memory capacity, age, and memory for discourse. *Journal of Gerontology*, **40**, 737–747.

Light, L. L., & Burke, D. M. (1988). Patterns of language and memory in old age. In L. L. Light & D. M. Burke (Eds.), *Language, memory, and aging* (pp. 244–271). New York: Cambridge University Press.

Light, L. L., & Singh, A. (1987). Implicit and explicit memory in young and older adults. *Journal of Experimental Psychology: Learning, Memory, and Cognition*, **13**, 531–541.

McIntyre, J. S., & Craik, F. I. M. (1987). Age differences in memory for item and source information. *Canadian Journal of Psychology*, **41**, 175–192.

Meacham, J. A. (1988). Interpersonal relations and prospective remembering. In M. M. Gru-

neberg, P. E. Morris, & R. N. Sykes (Eds.), *Practical aspects of memory: Current research and issues* (Vol. 1, pp. 354–359). New York: Wiley.

Meyer, B. J. F. (1987). Reading comprehension and aging. In K. W. Schaie (Ed.), *Annual Review of Gerontology and Geriatrics* (Vol. 7, pp. 93–116). New York: Springer-Verlag.

Meyer, B. J. F., & Rice, G. E. (1989). Prose processing in adulthood: The text, the learner, and the task. In L. W. Poon, D. C. Rubin, & B. A. Wilson (Eds.), *Everyday cognition in adulthood and old age*. New York: Cambridge University Press (in press).

Meyer, B. J. F., Young, C. J., & Bartlett, B. J. (1989). *Memory improved: Reading and memory enhancement across the lifespan through strategic text strategies*. Hillsdale, NJ: Erlbaum.

Moscovitch, M., Winocur, G., & McLachlan, D. (1986). Memory as assessed by recognition and reading time in normal and memory-paired people with Alzheimer's Disease and other neurological disorders. *Journal of Experimental Psychology: General*, **115**, 331–347.

Murphy, M. D., Schmitt, F. A., Caruso, M. J., & Sanders, R. E. (1987). Metamemory in older adults: The role of monitoring in serial recall. *Psychology and Aging*, **2**, 331–339.

Neisser, U. (1985). Toward an ecologically oriented cognitive science. In T. M. Schlecter & M. P. Toglia (Eds.), *New directions in cognitive science* (pp. 17–32). Norwood, NJ: Ablex.

Neisser, U., & Winograd, E. (1988). *Remembering reconsidered: Ecological and traditional approaches to the study of memory*. New York: Cambridge University Press.

Niederehe, G., & Yoder, C. (1989). Metamemory perceptions in depressions of young and older adults. *Journal of Nervous and Mental Disease*, **177**, 4–14.

Park, D. C., Puglisi, J. T., & Smith, A. D. (1986). Memory for pictures: Does an age-related decline exist? *Psychology and Aging*, **1**, 11–17.

Park, D. C., Royal, D., Dudley, W., & Morrell, R. (1988). Forgetting of pictures over a long retention interval in young and older adults. *Psychology and Aging*, **3**, 94–95.

Perlmuter, L. C., Monty, R. A., & Chan, F. (1986). Choice, control, and cognitive functioning. In M. M. Baltes & P. B. Baltes (Eds.), *The psychology of control and aging* (pp. 91–118). Hillsdale, NJ: Erlbaum.

Poon, L. W. (1985). Differences in human memory with aging: Nature, causes, and clinical implications. In J. E. Birren & K. W. Schaie (Eds.), *Handbook of the psychology of aging* (2nd ed., pp. 427–462). New York: Van Nostrand Reinhold.

Poon, L. W. (Ed.) (1986). *Handbook for clinical memory assessment of older adults.* Washington, D.C.: American Psychological Association.

Poon, L. W., Rubin, D. C., & Wilson, B. A. (Eds.) (1989). *Everyday cognition in adulthood and old age.* New York: Cambridge University Press (in press).

Ratner, H. H., Padgett, R. J., & Bushey, N. (1988). Old and young adults' recall of events. *Developmental Psychology, 24*, 664–671.

Ratner, H. H., & Schell, D. A., Crimmins, A., Mittelman, D., & Baldinelli, L. (1987). Changes in adults' prose recall: Aging or cognitive demands? *Developmental Psychology, 23*, 521–525.

Rice, G. E. (1986a). The everyday activities of adults: Implications for prose recall—Part I. *Educational Gerontology, 12*, 173–186.

Rice, G. E. (1986b). The everyday activities of adults: Implications for prose recall—Part II. *Educational Gerontology, 12*, 187–198.

Rubin, D. C. (1985). Memorability as a measure of processing: A unit analysis of prose and list learning. *Journal of Experimental Psychology: General, 114*, 213–238.

Rubin, D. C. (Ed.) (1986). *Autobiographical memory.* London: Cambridge University Press.

Salomon, G., & Globerson, T. (1987). Skill may not be enough: The role of mindfulness in learning and transfer. *International Journal of Educational Research, 11*, 623–637.

Salthouse, T. A. (1985). *A theory of cognitive aging.* Amsterdam: North-Holland.

Salthouse, T. A. (1987). The role of experience in aging. In K. W. Schaie (Ed.), *Annual review of gerontology and geriatrics* (Vol. 7, pp. 135–158). New York: Springer.

Salthouse, T. A. (1988). The role of processing resources in cognitive aging. In M. L. Howe & C. J. Brainerd (Ed.), *Cognitive development in adulthood: Progress in cognitive develop-*

ment research (pp. 185–239). New York: Springer-Verlag.

Salthouse, T. A., Kausler, D. H., & Saults, J. S. (1988). Utilization of path-analytic procedures to investigate the role of processing resources in cognitive aging. *Psychology and Aging, 3*, 158–166.

Schacter, D. L. (1987). Implicit memory: History and current status. *Journal of Experimental Psychology: Learning, Memory, and Cognition, 13*, 501–518.

Schaie, K. W. (1983). The Seattle longitudinal study: A 21-year exploration of psychometric intelligence in adulthood. In K. W. Schaie (Ed.), *Longitudinal studies of adult psychological development* (pp. 64–135). New York: Guilford.

Sharps, M. J., & Gollin, E. S. (1987). Memory for object locations in young and elderly adults. *Journal of Gerontology, 42*, 336–341.

Shaw, R. J., & Craik, F. I. M. (1989). Age differences in predictions and performance on a cued recall task. *Psychology and Aging, 4*, 131–135.

Sinnott, J. D. (1986). Prospective/intentional and incidental everyday memory: Effects of age and passage of time. *Psychology and Aging, 1*, 110–116.

Sinnott, J. D. (1989). Prospective memory and aging: Memory as adaptive action. In L. W. Poon, D. C. Rubin, & B. A. Wilson (Eds.), *Everyday cognition in adulthood and old age.* New York: Cambridge University Press (in press).

Spilich, G. J. (1983). Life-span components of text processing: Structural and procedural differences. *Journal of Verbal Learning and Verbal Behavior, 22*, 231–244.

Spilich, G. J. (1985). Discourse comprehension across the span of life. In N. Charness (Ed.), *Aging and human performance* (pp. 143–190). New York: Wiley.

Stine, E. A. L., & Wingfield, A. (1987). Process and strategy in memory for speech among younger and older adults. *Psychology and Aging, 2*, 272–279.

Stine, E. A. L., & Wingfield, A. (1988). Levels upon levels: Predicting age differences in text recall. *Experimental Aging Research, 13*, 179–183.

Sunderland, A., Watts, K., Baddeley, A. D., & Harris, J. E. (1986). Subjective memory assessment and test performance in elderly adults. *Journal of Gerontology*, **41**, 376–384.

van Dijk, T. A., & Kintsch, W. (1983). *Strategies of discourse comprehension*. New York: Academic Press.

Weinert, F. E., Schneider, W., & Knopf, M. (1988). Individual differences in memory development across the lifespan. In P. B. Baltes, D. L. Featherman, & R. M. Lerner (Eds.), *Lifespan development and behavior* (Vol. 9, pp. 39–85). Hillsdale, NJ: Erlbaum.

West, R. L. (1986). Everyday memory and aging. *Developmental Neuropsychology*, **2**, 323–344.

West, R. L. (1988). Prospective memory and aging. In M. M. Gruneberg, P. E. Morris, & R. N. Sykes (Eds.), *Practical aspects of memory: Current research and issues* (Vol. 2, pp. 119–125). New York: Wiley.

West, R. L. (1989). Planning practical memory training for the aged. In L. W. Poon, D. C. Rubin, & B. A. Wilson (Eds.), *Everyday cognition in adulthood and old age*. New York: Cambridge University Press (in press).

Wilson, B. A. (1989). Designing memory therapy programs. In L. W. Poon, D. C. Rubin, & B. A. Wilson (Eds.), *Everyday cognition in adulthood and old age*. New York: Cambridge University Press (in press).

Wingfield, A., Stine, E. A. L., Lahar, C. J., & Aberdeen, J. S. (1988). Does the capacity of working memory change with age? *Experimental Aging Research*, **14**, 103–107.

Winocur, G., Moscovitch, M., & Freedman, J. (1987). An investigation of cognitive function in relation to psychosocial variables in institutionalized old people. *Canadian Journal of Psychology*, **41**, 257–269.

Yesavage, J. A., & Sheikh, J. I. (1989). Mnemonics as modified for use by the elderly. In L. W. Poon, D. C. Rubin, & B. A. Wilson (Eds.), *Everyday cognition in adulthood and old age*. New York: Cambridge University press (in press).

Zelinski, E. M. (1988). Integrating information from discourse: Do older adults show deficits? In L. L. Light & D. M. Burke (Eds.), *Language and memory in old age* (pp. 117–132). New York: Cambridge University Press.

Zelinski, E. M., & Gilewski, M. J. (1988). Memory for prose and aging: A meta analysis. In M. L. Howe & C. J. Brainerd (Eds.), *Cognitive development in adulthood: Progress in cognitive development research* (pp. 133–158). New York: Springer-Verlag.

Zelinski, E. M., & Light, L. L. (1988). Young and older adults' use of context in spatial memory. *Psychology and Aging*, **3**, 99–101.

Zelinski, E. M., & Miura, S. A. (1988). Effects of thematic information on script memory in young and old adults. *Psychology and Aging*, **3**, 292–299.

Sixteen

Interactions between Memory and Language in Old Age

Leah L. Light

It is very difficult to tell, especially in everyday life, when language comprehension leaves off and when processes involved in remembering begin. That is, remembering written or spoken information is most often simply a natural consequence of language comprehension, rather than of special strategic manipulations that occur after language comprehension is complete (Craik, 1983). Further, memory limitations affect not only comprehension and production of single sentences but also ability to establish the coherence of discourses through integrative processes, such as the determination of coreference and the generation of bridging inferences (e.g., Bock, 1982; Kintsch & van Dijk, 1978). Models of sentence comprehension assume that limitations in the amount of information that can be held in working memory are responsible for difficulties in comprehending complex syntactic structures. Also, forgetting of concepts mentioned earlier in a discourse can result in failure to understand expressions that refer back to these concepts.

Given the interdependence of language and memory, it is no surprise to find hypotheses that language comprehension difficulties underlie memory impairment in old age and that problems in language comprehension are due to age-related decrements in memory. The goal of this chapter is to analyze hypotheses about the relation between language and memory in old age. The chapter is divided into two sections. The first reviews evidence that impairment in language comprehension underlies age-related changes in memory. The second considers the role of memory in age-related changes in language comprehension.

I. Language Comprehension and Memory in Old Age

Perhaps the clearest formulation of the view that memory impairment in old age is due, in part, to impaired language comprehension is that of Craik and Byrd (1982). They postulated that aging is associated with "an attenuation or shrinkage in the richness, extensiveness, and depth

Handbook of the Psychology of Aging, Third Edition
Copyright © 1990 Academic Press, Inc. All rights of reproduction in any form reserved.

of processing operations at both encoding and retrieval," that "older subjects' encodings will contain less associative and inferential information," and "that an encoded event is less modified by the specific context in which it occurs for the older person and that this difference leads to a less distinctive (and thus less memorable) encoding of the event" (p. 208). These authors and others (e.g., Cohen, 1979) assume that comprehension deficits in old age arise because older adults have reduced processing resources (less attentional capacity or smaller working-memory capacity) or are slower to carry out mental operations (cf. McDowd & Birren, Chapter 13, this volume). However, studies using divided attention tasks do not support the hypothesis that older adults are at a special disadvantage when engaged in semantic encoding (Craik, Morris, & Gick, in press; Duchek, 1984; McDowd & Craik, 1988; but see Lorsbach & Simpson, 1988, for a different result). Nevertheless, the claim that comprehension problems are due to reduced processing resources and the claim that impaired semantic processing is responsible for memory impairment in old age are two different claims. That is, regardless of their origin, comprehension problems (if they exist) would be expected to affect memory.

The claim that comprehension problems underlie memory impairment in old age has been tested within the framework of network theories of memory (e.g., Anderson, 1983; Collins & Loftus, 1975). According to Anderson, all factual knowledge, both semantic and episodic, is organized in networks consisting of nodes, which stand for concepts or propositions, with these nodes being connected by associative pathways. When a concept is encountered, its node is activated, and activation also spreads along associative pathways to related nodes, making them more available for additional cognitive processing. Spreading activation is viewed as the mechanism underlying retrieval of both semantic and episodic information.

An important distinction in spreading activation models is that between automatic and attentional or effortful processes (Neely, 1977; Posner & Snyder, 1975). Automatic processes are believed to arise from a rapid spread of activation and are not subject to the influence of expectations, whereas attentional processes have a slow rise time and are driven by expectations.

Activation processes, both automatic and attentional, play an important part in natural language understanding. They have been implicated in perception of words in spoken or written form (McClelland & Rumelhart, 1981), in determining the syntactic structure of sentences (Tanenhaus, Dell, & Carlson, 1987) and in deriving the meaning of single sentences and entire discourses (Kintsch, 1988; Waltz & Pollack, 1985). Activation of pragmatic or general world knowledge embodied in schemata is necessary for making inferences, for establishing the topic of a discourse, and for determining the antecedents of pronouns. Hence, differences across age in the way knowledge is represented in memory or in the way activation proceeds could result in comprehension differences. Because it is the product of comprehension processes that is ultimately stored in memory (Anderson, 1983; Craik, 1983), age differences in comprehension would lead to age differences in retention. The remainder of this section is devoted to analysis of the specific claims that (1) older adults' encodings are less rich, extensive, and deep; (2) encoding deficits underlie memory problems; (3) older adults' encodings are more general in that they rely less on specific contextual information; and (4) older adults' encodings have less associative or inferential content.

A. Richness, Extensiveness, and Depth of Encoding

The terms *rich*, *extensive*, and *deep* can be understood in relation to network models of memory. Anderson (1983) has proposed that deep or elaborative processing involves increasing the number of associative pathways between ideas and that elaboration may involve activation of prior schemata or general world knowledge. Such elaborative encodings might be considered to be rich. The notion of extensiveness may similarly be construed in terms of number of pathways activated during encoding. Although Anderson equates depth and elaborativeness of processing, it is possible to think of these in slightly different ways. Elaborativeness and extensiveness may be viewed as referring to the number of pathways activated and depth to the specific contents that are activated. That is, activation of information related to meaning rather than to physical form could be taken as deeper processing (Craik & Lockhart, 1972). Age differences in encoding could arise either because the content or organization of knowledge is different in young and older adults, so that the pattern of connections in the network differs across age or because of differences in the nature of activation processes. If young and older adults do not share the same systems of meanings for words or the same general fund of pragmatic information, comprehension differences would not be surprising. Similarly, age differences in amount of activation, extent of activation, or rate of spread of activation could determine the likelihood that particular nodes receive activation from associated nodes. The available evidence, however, is consistent with the conclusion that neither the organization of concepts nor the characteristics of semantic activation vary with age.

1. Representation of Knowledge

Evidence about possible age differences in knowledge representation comes from studies employing a variety of experimental paradigms, including word association, similarity judgments, semantic priming in lexical decision and word naming tasks,

and category judgment tasks. There is clear evidence for stability in patterns of word associations when verbal ability is controlled (e.g., Burke & Peters, 1986; Howard, 1979a,b; Lovelace & Cooley, 1982). Category judgment latencies are equally affected by exemplar typicality in young and older adults, suggesting stable organization of the representation of categories across the adult years (e.g., Byrd, 1984; Howard, 1979a, 1980, 1983a; Mueller, Kausler, Faherty, & Oliveri, 1980). Also, there appear to be no age differences in the representation of scripted activities (Hess, 1985; Light & Anderson, 1983).

Evidence from other sources, however, is more difficult to interpret. For instance, older adults show age-related declines on some vocabulary tests (Salthouse, 1988a). Also, the quality of definitions offered by older adults on vocabulary tests has sometimes been said to be lower, in that older adults offer fewer good synonyms. However, this result is not always obtained (see Salthouse, 1982, for a review). Further, absence of synonyms could be simply a manifestation of the word-finding problems to which older adults are subject.

Although tasks that require judgments of global similarity of word meanings do not show age differences (Madden, 1985; Nebes & Brady, 1988), qualitative age differences in the basis for judgments of similarity sometimes show up in tasks requiring graded judgments (Howard, 1983a; Stine, 1986). Moreover, older adults are less likely than young adults to sort line drawings of common objects on the basis of taxonomic similarity, and they are more likely to make relational-thematic groupings by putting together things that are used in the same activity (Annett, 1959; Cicirelli, 1976; Kogan, 1973; Pearce & Denney, 1984). However, this outcome may be due to cohort differences in education or to the wording of instructions, inasmuch as Laurence and Arrowood (1982) found no age differences in type of sort when they asked highly educated people to put together objects that are "alike in some way" rather than using vague free sort instructions that may encourage variation in the way in which the task is construed (see also Smiley & Brown, 1979) even when the underlying knowledge base is the same. Cohort differences in education also may be responsible for declining performance on the WAIS Similarities subtest (Birren & Morrison, 1961; see Salthouse, 1982, for a review). Nonetheless, young adults outperform older adults on verbal analogies tests, which require retrieval of similarity information, even when age groups are equivalent on a multiple-choice test tapping knowledge of synonyms (e.g., Light & Albertson, 1988b; Riegel, 1959).

2. Spreading Activation

Studies of semantic priming in lexical decision (deciding whether a string of letters is a word), word naming, and judgments of semantic relatedness offer no evidence for age differences in extent or breadth of activation when type of association is varied (Howard, McAndrews, & Lasaga, 1981) or when strength of association between prime and target is varied (Balota & Duchek, 1988; Nebes, Boller, & Holland, 1986). In these tasks, the extent of priming is evaluated by comparing latencies when the target is preceded by a related prime to latencies and when the target is preceded by an unrelated prime or by a neutral prime. In lexical decision, the task most frequently used to assess age differences in priming, the results reveal remarkable similarity across age in the extent of priming, and no evidence for reduced benefits or costs when latencies following related and unrelated primes are compared to latencies following neutral primes (Bowles & Poon, 1985; Burke, White, & Diaz, 1987; Burke & Yee, 1984; Chiarello, Church, & Hoyer, 1985; Howard, 1983b; Howard et al., 1981; Howard, Shaw, & Heisey, 1986; Madden, 1986, 1988, 1989).

Benefits are believed to reflect a mix of automatic and attentional processes, whereas costs are believed to be the result of attentional processes only; thus these results point to the lack of age differences in either automatic or attentional components of activation.

One conflicting outcome was reported by Howard et al. (1986) who found that older adults showed facilitation from related primes only at long prime-target intervals. Because facilitation at short prime-target intervals is believed to arise solely from automatic processes, this result suggests an age-related slowing of automatic processes. However, other studies of lexical decision (Burke et al., 1987; Madden, 1989) and word naming (Balota & Duchek, 1988) have not observed interactions of age and prime-target interval.

Overall, then, there is little evidence for age-related differences in the organization of conceptual knowledge when studies use measures that are less responsive to the influence of strategies and equate subjects in education and verbal ability. In addition, the amount, breadth, and rate of spreading activation from concept to concept appear to be similar across ages. Nevertheless, there is evidence from a variety of sources that older adults experience increased difficulties in word finding that may be indicative of problems in activation of orthographic or phonological information from concepts. For instance, older adults have decreased output on verbal fluency tasks (McCrae, Arenberg, & Costa, 1987; Obler & Albert, 1985; Schaie & Parham, 1977), have more tip-of-the-tongue experiences (Burke, Worthley, & Martin, 1988; Cohen & Faulkner, 1986), are less accurate in naming to definition (Bowles & Poon, 1985), and show reduced performance in confrontation naming tasks (e.g., Albert, Heller, & Milberg, 1988; Borod, Goodglass, & Kaplan, 1980; Van Gorp, Satz, Kiersch, & Henry, 1986). Although age-related changes in the way in which concepts activate their orthographic and phonological representations cannot produce encoding difficulties, they may contribute to reduced performance on memory tests in old age by preventing lexical realization of concepts at the time of retrieval.

B. Encoding and Memory

Anderson (1983) has explicitly claimed that spreading activation is the mechanism of retrieval in both priming studies and in memory for new information. The view that older adults' memory problems are due to age differences in spreading activation predicts that studies examining memory for words involved in priming tasks should show reduced priming in the old whenever the old perform less well in recall or recognition. Of the studies that have examined both priming and subsequent retention, none show this pattern. Young adults score higher on recall and recognition than older adults despite age invariance in magnitude of semantic priming in lexical decision (Burke *et al.*, 1987; Burke & Yee, 1984; Howard, 1983b; Howard *et al.*, 1981; Howard, Shaw, & Heisey, 1986; Madden, 1986) and category judgment tasks (Mitchell & Perlmutter, 1986). Hence, reduced comprehension, as measured by priming, does not seem to be the cause of age-related differences in memory.

Thus, the evidence does not support any age-related changes in spreading activation that could affect encoding based on initial comprehension processes. Of course, it is possible that strategic processes coming into play after initial encoding takes place are responsible for age-related differences in memory (see Burke & Light, 1981; Craik, 1977; Craik & Rabinowitz, 1984; Poon, 1985, for reviews). However, the role of such processes in everyday life may be small inasmuch as young adults rarely report using deliberate mnemonic strategies (Harris, 1980; Intons-Peterson & Fournier, 1986).

Further, the representations on which such strategies presumably operate are those resulting from comprehension processes that appear to be invariant across age.

C. Encoding Inferences

Current models of discourse comprehension assume that inferences based on activation of general world knowledge are necessary for understanding (e.g., Kintsch, 1988); further, there is evidence from studies of young adults that certain kinds of inferences are made at the time that sentences or discourses are encountered (e.g., McKoon & Ratcliff, 1988; O'Brien, Shank, Myers, & Rayner, 1988). The question of interest here is whether aging affects the likelihood that such inferences will be made and, subsequently, stored.

When comprehension is examined during or immediately after a sentence is read, there is no evidence that young and older adults differ in how readily they draw inferences about the instruments with which verbs are used (Burke & Yee, 1984), the properties of nouns picked out by sentences (Burke & Harrold, 1988), the relevant grounds of metaphors (Light & Albertson, 1988b), the antecedents of pronouns (Light & Albertson, 1988a; Light & Capps, 1986), or the antecedents of noun–phrase anaphors (Light & Albertson, 1988a; Zelinski, 1988; but see Hasher & Zacks, 1988, for evidence that older adults may be slower here), or about the instance of a category implied by a sentence context (Light, Valencia-Laver, & Zavis, 1987). Even with longer passages or delays between study and test, age differences are not obtained invariably (Belmore, 1981; Hess & Arnould, 1986; Light & Anderson, 1983; Rebok, Montaglione, & Bendlin, 1988; Reder, Wible, & Martin, 1986; Zabrucky, Moore, & Schultz, 1987).

Studies that find age differences in the likelihood of drawing inferences typically do not use on-line procedures. For instance, some studies have used implicational cues for recall (Till, 1985; Till & Walsh, 1980). As pointed out by McKoon and Ratcliff (1988), these studies confound processes operating at storage with those operating at retrieval and do not permit inferences about encoding. Other studies reporting age differences have required people to hold some information in memory until other relevant facts are presented (Cohen, 1979, 1981; Hasher & Zacks, 1988; Light & Albertson, 1988a; Light & Anderson, 1985; Light & Capps, 1986; Light, Zelinski, & Moore, 1982; Zacks & Hasher, 1988; Zacks, Hasher, Doren, Hamm, & Attig, 1987), leaving open the possibility that forgetting of relevant information, inability to activate previously presented information when subsequent relevant information is given, and/or inability to combine unrelated facts when these are not presented in an optimal order contribute to problems in forming inferences. The results of these studies, taken as a package, strongly suggest that difficulties in drawing inferences on-line do not contribute to impoverished semantic encodings and poorer memory, but rather that, at least under some conditions, memory problems produce comprehension problems.

D. General Encoding

Rabinowitz, Craik, and Ackerman (1982) hypothesized that due to reduced attentional resources older adults might not form distinctive, contextually specific encodings of new information but rather would encode events "in the same old way" from one occasion to the next. In terms of network models, the suggestion is that when older adults encounter a concept, the pattern of activation does not depend on the specifics of the situation but only on the strength of preexisting associations. Evidence for this hypothesis comes from encoding specificity experiments

modeled after those of Thomson and Tulving (1970), who presented subjects with both weakly and strongly associated pairs to study and then tested them with either strong or weak associates as retrieval cues. Targets from both strongly and weakly associated pairs were better remembered when study and test cues were the same. Further, targets from the weak–weak condition were better remembered than those from the weak–strong condition, suggesting that strength of prior association is less crucial than compatibility of study and test cues in terms of activation at retrieval. Rabinowitz et al. (1982) found this pattern of results for their young subjects, but their older subjects' recall did not differ in the weak–weak and weak–strong conditions. Rather than simply treating these results as another instance of greater age differences in learning weak associates than strong associates (Salthouse, 1982), they interpreted their findings to mean that older adults do not have as distinctive encodings as younger adults and that core meanings of words are activated whenever they occur regardless of the context in which they occur. Simon (reported in Craik and Simon, 1980) presented young and older adults with sentences containing words from taxonomic categories. She found that the category names (which had not been presented) were better retrieval cues than other sentence words for these category members for older subjects, whereas sentence words were better cues for the young adults (see Perlmutter, 1979; Rabinowitz et al., 1982, for similar findings). This, too, is taken as evidence that older adults encode more generally than young adults.

There are, however, several problems with this conclusion. First, some studies purporting to find age differences in encoding specificity in fact did not obtain reliable interactions of context with age when appropriate indices of memory were used (Hess, 1984; Hess & Higgins, 1983). Second, young and older adults have been shown to have similar patterns of results, at least in some conditions, in replications of the Thomson and Tulving study (Puglisi, Park, Smith, & Dudley, 1988). Similarly, Light *et al.* (1987) found no age difference in the effectiveness of general and specific cues, either when these cues had been presented in sentences or when the context strongly implied them. Third, young and older adults show similar effects of context in studies of episodic priming; recognition is faster when a word is preceded by another word studied in close proximity to it originally (Hasher & Zacks, 1989; Howard, Heisey, & Shaw, 1986; Rabinowitz, 1986). Fourth, studies of word recognition and naming (e.g., Cohen & Faulkner, 1983; Nebes *et al.*, 1986; see Light, 1988, for a review) as well as studies of immediate memory for sentences (Wingfield, Poon, Lombardi, & Lowe, 1985) find that older adults rely at least as much as young adults on prior semantic and syntactic context. Fifth, the studies reviewed here that demonstrate that young and older adults are equally likely to make certain kinds of inferences during sentence comprehension offer no support for concluding that there are age differences in use of context to particularize word meaning. On the contrary, the evidence strongly suggests age constancy.

E. Summary

Review of the literature offers no support for the claim that deficits in semantic processing underlie memory problems in old age. The organization of knowledge is quite stable across the adult years. Moreover, none of the specific claims about the relation between language comprehension and memory hold water when immediate comprehension rather than memory is examined. Older adults do not seem to differ from young adults in rate, breadth, or amount of spreading activation, in likelihood of making inferences, or in use of context to particularize word meanings.

They do, however, differ in memory. Such results are embarrassing for network models that predict that age differences in memory should be accompanied by age differences in comprehension because the retrieval mechanisms involved in encoding and subsequent recall or recognition are the same. They also contradict models predicting such age differences because of reduced processing resources (see Light & Burke (1988) and Salthouse (1988b) for further discussion of processing resource explanations of cognition).

II. Memory and Language Comprehension in Old Age

Memory plays an important role in both sentence and discourse comprehension. Limitations in working memory capacity (the ability to simultaneously store and manipulate information for brief periods of time) affect comprehension of complex sentences (e.g., Bock, 1982). Integrative processes responsible for establishing discourse coherence also depend on the availability of related information in working memory (e.g., Clark & Haviland, 1977; Kintsch & van Dijk, 1978; Sanford & Garrod, 1981). There is evidence that older adults have decreased working memory capacity (e.g., Light & Anderson, 1985; Wingfield, Stine, Lahar, & Aberdeen, 1988; but see Hartley, 1986, for a different finding) so that less relevant information may be maintained in working memory. Hence, both sentence comprehension and integration of information in discourse would be expected to suffer in old age.

A. Sentence Comprehension

Some sentences are more syntactically complex than others. The contrast between *The race that the car that the people whom the obviously not very well dressed man called sold won was held last summer* and *The obviously not very well dressed man called the people who sold the car that won the race that was held last summer* (Miller, 1962) brings home this point. To understand the first, center-embedded sentence is more difficult because the words at the beginning must be held in memory for a longer period of time before a clause can be assembled, whereas each clause can be processed sequentially in the second, right-branching sentence. Limitations in working memory would be expected to differentially affect comprehension of syntactically more complex sentences in old age because of increased difficulty in storing early sentence elements and rearranging them when later elements become available.

The evidence suggests that this is so. Older adults score lower on the Token Test, which involves a series of commands of increasing syntactic and semantic complexity for manipulating a set of small pieces of plastic varying in size, shape, and color (Bergman, 1980; Emery, 1985; Lesser, 1976), though not all studies show this result (e.g., DeRenzi & Faglioni, 1978). Lesser (1976) reports that scores on the Token Test correlate with measures of short-term memory, suggesting that age-related declines on the Token Test are due to reduced working memory capacity in old age.

Experimental studies of the effects of syntactic complexity on comprehension in adulthood have sometimes used techniques that appear to directly tap comprehension (object manipulation, question answering, judging grammaticality, repairing ungrammatical sentences), and sometimes they have involved less obvious measures of sentence imitation or immediate recall. The results are quite consistent across studies and across paradigms. With the exception of Feier and Gerstman (1980) who found effects of age but no interaction of age with sentence complexity in an object manipulation task, studies of sentence imitation (Bergman, 1980; Kemper, 1986, 1988),

question answering (Emery, 1985; Light & Albertson, 1988a), and grammaticality judgments (Kemper, Rash, Kynette, Norman, & Rash, 1988) have all found the expected interaction. Those studies that also included measures of short-term memory report that comprehension correlates positively with span (Feier & Gerstman, 1980; Kemper, 1986, 1988). Thus, Kemper *et al.* (1988) found that complex but well-formed left-branching sentences were judged less grammatical by older adults and that digit span correlated more highly with judgments of grammaticality, especially for these left-branching sentences. However, the regression analyses that would permit clean dissection of the separate contributions of age and working memory (cf. Salthouse, 1985) were not reported, so the conclusion that working memory declines mediate comprehension declines with increasing age must remain a hypothesis.

These results are consistent with the view that reduced working memory capacity limits comprehension of complex syntactic structures in old age. There are, nonetheless, some discordant results. Increasing the propositional density of sentences of constant length does not differentially impair gist recall in the old (Stine, Wingfield, & Poon, 1986). Because propositional density and sentence complexity are probably confounded, age and propositional density would be expected to interact. Further, sentence complexity (whether sentences are positive or negative) has a disproportionate effect on sentence verification latency in the old, as would be predicted. However, contrary to prediction, varying the size of a concurrent memory load affects verification latencies to the same extent in young and old (Craik *et al.*, in press). Craik *et al.* suggest that different aspects of working memory (Baddeley, 1976) mediate sentence comprehension and retention of a memory load, with age-related processing differences in one of these (the central processor) but not the other (the articulatory loop). It is not clear, however, that such an account can explain the lack of an increased effect of propositional density in older adults.

B. Integration of Information in Discourse

Current models of discourse comprehension assign a major role to working memory (e.g., Kintsch, 1988; Kintsch & van Dijk, 1978; Sanford & Garrod, 1981; van Dijk & Kintsch, 1983). According to Kintsch and van Dijk (1978), construction of a coherent representation of a discourse proceeds in cycles. At the end of each cycle, there is too much information to be maintained in the short-term memory buffer, and propositions are carried over to subsequent processing cycles on the basis of importance and recency. The structure that emerges from this process is based on argument repetition. If propositions in the buffer do not contain overlapping arguments, a coherent representation cannot be formed, and two things can happen. Inferences based on general world knowledge may be made. Also, an effortful and fallible search of all recently processed propositions is made in the hope of locating some containing arguments overlapping with those in the short-term buffer. The network of coherent propositions that results is organized hierarchically with the most important propositions (i.e., those that have the most argument repetitions) at the highest level. It is well established that these more important propositions are better recalled, a phenomenon called "the levels effect."

This model permits several specific predictions with respect to aging. These predictions hinge on the assumptions that older adults have reduced working memory capacity and that they are more likely to forget recently processed propositions. First, older adults should show reduced recall of less important (lower level) propositions (Spilich, 1983). Decreased working memory capacity should reduce comprehension by limiting the number of propositions that can be processed in one cycle and by reducing the number of propositions that can be carried over from cycle to cycle. In addition, because older adults are less likely to remember recently processed propositions, the search for linking propositions is less likely to be successful. These factors would reduce the likelihood of a coherent structure developing. Assuming that young and older adults are equally able to select propositions for carryover based on importance (Mandel & Johnson, 1984; Petros, Tabor, Cooney, & Chabot, 1983), it is the lower level propositions that would be less likely to be reinstated, and therefore remembered, by older adults. This result is sometimes obtained, and sometimes it is not; variables mediating the different outcomes have yet to be fully identified (see reviews by Cohen, 1988; Hultsch & Dixon, 1984).

Second, older adults should exhibit greater distance effects. The ease with which new information can be integrated with prior information depends on the availability in working memory of the relevant prior information. Increasing the number of irrelevant propositions intervening between propositions to be linked should reduce the probability that the relevant propositions will be simultaneously in working memory and should increase the likelihood that time-consuming and error-prone searches of recently processed information would be initiated. Hence, it would be expected that older adults would be placed at a particular disadvantage by increasing the distance between relevant propositions. Indeed, Light and Capps (1986) found that young and older adults did not differ in ability to assign referents to pronouns when memory load was low (i.e., when there was no material intervening between a sentence containing a pronoun and a sentence containing its antecedent), but they did observe an age difference with two intervening sentences. Light and Anderson (1985), however, did not find that the old have a steeper distance effect for identifying the antecedents of pronouns. It is possible that this discrepancy arose because Light and Anderson used fairly long (12-sentence) paragraphs containing several possible referents. Young adults performed better than older adults on this task both when asked to recall the antecedent and when asked to pick out the antecedent from three possibilities offered on a recognition test. They were also more likely to recall or recognize specific facts that did not require anaphoric inferences. Hence, forgetting of relevant material may be a source of older adults' problems in establishing discourse coherence through inference.

Older adults also have been found to suffer more than young adults when information is not presented in an optimal order. Older adults have a greater decrement in prose recall when nonstandard sentence orderings are used (Smith, Rebok, Smith, Hall, & Alvin, 1983; but see Mandel & Johnson, 1984). Further, older adults are penalized more in reasoning tasks when information to be integrated is scrambled (Light et al., 1982). Scrambling has two possible effects. It may reduce the likelihood that related propositions will be processed in the same cycle or carried forward for processing in the next cycle. It also may make it more difficult to determine argument overlap for propositions that do appear in the same cycle. These problems would be exacerbated by reduced working memory capacity and, hence, it is no surprise that scrambling is particularly detrimental to the performance of older adults.

Third, older adults should experience greater difficulty in integrating information in discourse when relevant facts have been backgrounded by a topic change. Van Dijk and Kintsch (1983) have suggested that the importance of material is determined in large part by the extent to which it is in keeping with the current topic of a discourse. Hence, when the amount of material intervening between two sentences to be integrated is held constant, the likelihood that the initial material will remain in working memory is smaller when the intervening material backgrounds it. Successful integration then depends on retrieving recently processed propositions that may have been forgotten. Older adults are differentially hampered in detecting anomalies when relevant information is backgrounded, and the effect appears to be due to forgetting that relevant information (Light & Albertson, 1988a).

Fourth, age differences in integration of discourse could arise if the contents of working memory varied across age. Hasher and Zacks (1988) have suggested that, because of inefficient inhibitory mechanisms, older adults are more likely to entertain irrelevant thoughts (e.g., personally relevant thoughts, contextually inappropriate interpretations of words or phrases subject to multiple interpretation, and daydreams). This suggestion is based on the results of an experiment by Hamm (as cited in Hasher and Zacks, 1988) in which older adults were less likely to give up an inference made early in reading a passage that was rendered implausible by subsequent events related in the passage. Because older adults were more likely than young adults to have both correct and incorrect inferences available at the end of the passage, Hasher and Zacks suggest that the data contradict the view that working memory capacity declines with old age but support the idea that the contents of working memory are less likely to be goal path oriented in older adults. To the extent that this is true, age differences in establishing discourse coherence would be explained without invoking limitations in the amount of information held in working memory. This interesting hypothesis remains to be fully explored.

C. Summary

Although there are lacunae in the evidence, the findings discussed in this section are, on the whole, consistent with the view that working memory constraints are responsible in part for age differences in natural language understanding. As expected, older adults perform less well than young adults on tests of sentence comprehension involving complex syntactic structures. Age differences in integration of discourse are seen when working memory is taxed by the presence of large amounts of material, by the interpolation of irrelevant material, or by orderings of material that require complex mental operations. In addition, older adults may be more prone to forgetting earlier parts of a discourse, so that these are unavailable to serve as background against which to interpret new material. What cannot be remembered cannot be integrated. At this level, problems in memory may be caused by earlier interpretive failures because it is easier to remember what one has understood. However, the root of the problem is not deficient semantic processing at the level of single-word meanings. Instead, one memory failure leads to another downstream. Thus, older adults do not experience difficulty in extracting meaning from words or in drawing inferences unless they have forgotten prior information necessary to establish discourse coherence. They do not experience difficulty in determining the syntactic structure of sentences unless these are complex enough to tax working memory. Nevertheless, should such difficulties arise, older adults may have comprehension problems which result in subsequent memory problems.

References

Albert, M. S., Heller, H. S., & Milberg, W. (1988). Changes in naming ability with age. *Psychology and Aging*, **3**, 173–178.

Anderson, J. A. (1983). A spreading activation theory of memory. *Journal of Verbal Learning and Verbal Behavior*, **22**, 261–295.

Annett, M. (1959). The classification of instances of four common class concepts by children and adults. *British Journal of Educational Psychology*, **29**, 223–236.

Baddeley, A. D. (1976). *The psychology of memory*. New York: Basic Books.

Balota, D. A., & Duchek, J. M. (1988). Age-related differences in lexical access, spreading activation, and simple pronunciation. *Psychology and Aging*, **3**, 84–93.

Belmore, S. M., (1981). Age-related changes in processing explicit and implicit language. *Journal of Gerontology*, **36**, 316–322.

Bergman, M. (1980). *Aging and the perception of speech*. Baltimore: University Park Press.

Birren, J. E., & Morrison, D. F. (1961). Analysis of the WAIS subtests in relation to age and education. *Journal of Gerontology*, **16**, 363–369.

Bock, J. K. (1982). Toward a cognitive theory of syntax: Information processing contributions to sentence formulation. *Psychology Review*, **89**, 1–47.

Borod, J. C., Goodglass, H., & Kaplan, E. (1980). Normative data on the Boston Diagnostic Aphasia Examination, Parietal Lobe Battery, and the Boston Naming Test. *Journal of Clinical Neuropsychology*, **2**, 209–215.

Bowles, N. L., & Poon, L. W. (1985). Aging and retrieval of words in semantic memory. *Journal of Gerontology*, **40**, 71–77.

Burke, D. M., & Harrold, R. M. (1988). Automatic and effortful semantic processes in old age: Experimental and naturalistic approaches. In L. L. Light & D. M. Burke (Eds.), *Language, memory and aging* (pp. 100–116). New York: Cambridge University Press.

Burke, D. M., & Light, L. L. (1981). Memory and aging: The role of retrieval processes. *Psychological Bulletin*, **90**, 513–546.

Burke, D. M., & Peters, L. (1986). Word associations in old age: Evidence for consistency in semantic encoding during adulthood. *Psychology and Aging*, **1**, 283–292.

Burke, D. M., White, H., & Diaz, D. L. (1987). Semantic priming in young and older adults: Evidence for age-constancy in automatic and attentional processes. *Journal of Experimental Psychology: Human Perception and Performance*, **13**, 79–88.

Burke, D., Worthley, J., & Martin, J. (1988). I'll never forget what's-her-name: Aging and the tip of the tongue experience. In M. M. Gruneberg, P. Morris, & R. N. Sykes (Eds.), *Practical aspects of memory: Current research and issues* (pp. 113–118). New York: Wiley.

Burke, D. M., & Yee, P. L. (1984). Semantic

priming during sentence processing by young and older adults. *Developmental Psychology*, **20**, 903–910.

Byrd, M. (1984). Age differences in the retrieval of information from semantic memory. *Experimental Aging Research*, **10**, 29–33.

Chiarello, C., Church, K. L., & Hoyer, W. J. (1985). Automatic and controlled semantic priming: Accuracy, response bias, and aging. *Journal of Gerontology*, **40**, 593–600.

Cicirelli, V. G. (1976). Categorization behavior in aging subjects. *Journal of Gerontology*, **31**, 676–680.

Clark, H. H., & Haviland, S. E. (1977). Comprehension and the given-new contract. In R. O. Freedle (Ed.), *Discourse production and comprehension* (pp. 1-40). Norwood, NJ: Ablex.

Cohen, G. (1979). Language comprehension in old age. *Cognitive Psychology*, **11**, 412–429.

Cohen, G. (1981). Inferential reasoning in old age. *Cognition*, **9**, 59–72.

Cohen, G. (1988). Age differences in memory for text: Production deficiency or processing limitations? In L. L. Light & D. M. Burke (Eds.), *Language, memory, and aging* (pp. 171–190). New York: Cambridge University Press.

Cohen, G., & Faulkner, D. (1983). Word recognition: Age differences in contextual facilitation effects. *British Journal of Psychology*, **74**, 239–251.

Cohen, G., & Faulkner, D. (1986). Memory for proper names: Age differences in retrieval. *British Journal of Developmental Psychology*, **4**, 187–197.

Collins, A. M., & Loftus, E. F. (1975). A spreading-activation theory of semantic processing. *Psychological Review*, **82**, 407–428.

Craik, F. I. M. (1977). Age differences in human memory. In J. E. Birren & K. W. Schaie (Eds.), *Handbook of the psychology of aging* (pp. 384–420). New York: Van Nostrand Reinhold.

Craik, F. I. M. (1983). On the transfer of information from temporary to permanent storage. *Philosophical Transactions of the Royal Society of London, Series B*, **302**, 341–359.

Craik, F. I. M., & Byrd, M. (1982). Aging and cognitive deficits: The role of attentional resources. In F. I. M. Craik & S. Trehub (Eds.), *Aging and cognitive processes* (pp. 191–211). New York: Plenum.

Craik, F. I. M., & Lockhart, R. S. (1972). Levels of processing: A framework for memory research. *Journal of Verbal Learning and Verbal Behavior*, **11**, 671–684.

Craik, F. I. M., Morris, R. G., & Gick, M. L. (in press). Adult age differences in working memory. In G. Vallar & T. Shallice (Eds.), *Neuropsychological impairments of short-term memory*.

Craik, F. I. M., & Rabinowitz, J. C., (1984). Age differences in the acquisition and use of verbal information: A tutorial review. In H. Bouma & D. G. Bouwhuis (Eds.), *Attention and performance: X. Control of language processes* (pp. 471–499). Hillsdale, NJ: Erlbaum.

Craik, F. I. M., & Simone, E. (1980). Age differences in memory: The roles of attention and depth of processing. In L. W. Poon, J. L. Fozard, L. S. Cermak, D. Arenberg, & L. W. Thompson (Eds.), *New directions in memory and aging* (pp. 95–112). Hillsdale, NJ: Erlbaum.

DeRenzi, E., & Faglioni, P. (1978). Normative data and screening power of a shortened version of the Token Test. *Cortex*, **14**, 41–49.

Duchek, J. M. (1984). Encoding and retrieval differences between young and old: The impact of attentional capacity usage. *Developmental Psychology*, **20**, 1173–1180.

Emery, O. B. (1985). Language and aging. *Experimental Aging Research*, **11**, 3–60.

Feier, C. D., & Gerstman, L. J. (1980). Sentence comprehension abilities throughout the adult life span. *Journal of Gerontology*, **35**, 722–728.

Harris, J. E. (1980). Memory aids people use: Two interview studies. *Memory & Cognition*, **8**, 31–38.

Hartley, J. T. (1986). Reader and text variables as determinants of discourse memory in adulthood. *Psychology and Aging*, **1**, 150–158.

Hasher, L., & Zacks, R. T. (1988). Working memory, comprehension, and aging: A review and a new view. In G. H. Bower (Ed.), *The psychology of learning and motivation* (Vol. 22, pp. 193–225).

Hess, T. M. (1984). Efforts of semantically related and unrelated contexts on recognition memory of different-aged adults. *Journal of Gerontology*, **39**, 441–451.

Hess, T. M. (1985). Aging and context influences on recognition memory for typical and atypical script actions. *Developmental Psychology*, **21**, 1139–1151.

Hess, T. M., & Arnould, D. (1986). Adult age differences in memory for explicit and implicit sentence information. *Journal of Gerontology*, **2**, 191–194.

Hess, T. M., & Higgins, J. N. (1983). Context utilization in young and old adults. *Journal of Gerontology*, **38**, 65–71.

Howard, D. V. (1979a). *Category norms for adults between the ages of 20 and 80*. (Tech. Rep. NIA-79-1). Washington, DC: Georgetown University.

Howard, D. V. (1979b). *Restricted word association norms for adults between the ages of 20 and 80*. (Tech. Rep. NIA-79-2). Washington, DC: Georgetown University.

Howard, D. V. (1980). Category norms: A comparison of the Battig and Montague (1969) norms with the responses of adults between the ages of 20 ad 80. *Journal of Gerontology*, **35**, 225–231.

Howard, D. V. (1983a). A multidimensional scaling analysis of aging and the semantic structure of animal names. *Experimental Aging Research*, **9**, 27–30.

Howard, D. V. (1983b). The effects of aging and degree of association on the semantic priming of lexical decisions. *Experimental Aging Research*, **9**, 145–151.

Howard, D. V., Heisey, J. G., & Shaw, R. J. (1986). Aging and the priming of newly learned associations. *Developmental Psychology*, **22**, 78–85.

Howard, D. V., McAndrews, M. P., & Lasaga, M. I. (1981). Semantic priming of lexical decisions in young and old adults. *Journal of Gerontology*, **36**, 707–714.

Howard, D. V., Shaw, R. J., & Heisey, J. G. (1986). Aging and the time course of semantic activation. *Journal of Gerontology*, **41**, 195–203.

Hultsch, D. F., & Dixon, R. A. (1984). Memory for text materials in adulthood. In P. B. Baltes & O. G. Brim, Jr. (Eds.), *Life-span development and behavior* (Vol. 6, pp. 77–108). New York: Academic Press.

Intons-Peterson, M. J., & Fournier, J. (1986). External and internal memory aids: When and how often do we use them? *Journal of Experimental Psychology: General*, **115**, 267–280.

Kemper, S. (1986). Imitation of complex syntactic constructions by elderly adults. *Applied Psycholinguistics*, **7**, 277–288.

Kemper, S. (1988). Geriatric psycholinguistics. In L. L. Light & D. M. Burke (Eds.), *Language, memory, and aging* (pp. 58–76). New York: Cambridge University Press.

Kemper, S., Rash, S., Kynette, D., Norman, S., & Rash, S. (1988). *The judgment of grammaticality: Effects of age and syntactic complexity*. Unpublished manuscript, University of Kansas, Lawrence.

Kintsch, W. (1988). The role of knowledge in discourse comprehension: A construction-integration model. *Psychological Review*, **95**, 163–182.

Kintsch, W., & van Dijk, T. A. (1978). Toward a model of text comprehension and production. *Psychological Review*, **85**, 363–394.

Kogan, N. (1973). Creativity and cognitive style: A life-span perspective. In P. B. Baltes & K. W. Schaie (Eds.), *Life-span developmental psychology: Personality and socialization* (pp. 145–178). New York: Academic Press.

Laurence, M. W., & Arrowood, A. J. (1982). Classification style differences in the elderly. In F. I. M. Craik & S. Trehub (Eds.), *Aging and cognitive processes* (pp. 213–220). New York: Plenum.

Lesser, R. (1976). Verbal and non-verbal memory components in the Token Test. *Neuropsychologia*, **14**, 79–85.

Light, L. L. (1988). Language and aging: Competence versus performance. In J. E. Birren & V. L. Bengtson (Eds.), *Emergent theories of aging* (pp. 177–213). New York: Springer.

Light, L. L., & Albertson, S. (1988a). Comprehension of pragmatic implications in young and older adults. In L. L. Light & D. M. Burke (Eds.), *Language, memory, and aging* (pp. 133–153). New York: Cambridge University Press.

Light, L. L., & Albertson, S. A. (1988b). *Comprehension of novel metaphors in young and older adults*. Paper presented at the Second Cognitive Aging Conference, Atlanta, April.

Light, L. L., & Anderson, P. A. (1983). Memory for scripts in young and older adults. *Memory & Cognition*, **11**, 435–444.

Light, L. L., & Anderson, P. A. (1985). Working-memory capacity, age, and memory for discourse. *Journal of Gerontology*, **40**, 737–747.

Light, L. L., & Burke, D. M. (1988). Patterns of language and memory in old age. In L. L. Light & D. M. Burke (Eds.), *Language, memory, and aging* (pp. 244–271). New York: Cambridge University Press.

Light, L. L., & Capps, J. L. (1986). Comprehension of pronouns in young and older adults. *Developmental Psychology*, **22**, 580–585.

Light, L. L., Valencia-Laver, D., & Zavis, D. (1987). *General encoding in young and older adults*. Paper presented at the First Cognitive Aging Conference, Atlanta, May.

Light, L. L., Zelinski, E. M., & Moore, M. (1982). Adult age differences in reasoning from new information. *Journal of Experimental Psychology: Learning, Memory, and Cognition*, **8**, 435–447.

Lorsbach, T. C., & Simpson, G. B. (1988). Dual-task performance as a function of adult age and task complexity. *Psychology and Aging*, **3**, 210–212.

Lovelace, E. A., & Cooley, S. (1982). Free associations of older adults to single words and conceptually related word triads. *Journal of Gerontology*, **37**, 432–437.

Madden, D. J. (1985). Age-related slowing in the retrieval of information from long-term memory. *Journal of Gerontology*, **40**, 208–210.

Madden, D. J. (1986). Adult age differences in visual word recognition: Semantic encoding and episodic retention. *Experimental Aging Research*, **12**, 71–77.

Madden, D. J. (1988). Adult age differences in the effects of sentence context and stimulus degradation during visual word recognition. *Psychology and Aging*, **3**, 167–172.

Madden, D. J. (1989). Visual word identification and age-related slowing. *Cognitive Development*, in press.

Mandel, R. G., & Johnson, N. S. (1984). A developmental analysis of story recall and comprehension in adulthood. *Journal of Verbal Learning and Verbal Behavior*, **23**, 643–659.

McClelland, J. L., & Rumelhart, D. E. (1981). An interactive activation model of context effects in letter perception: Part 1. An account of basic findings. *Psychological Review*, **88**, 375–407.

McCrae, R. R., Arenberg, D., & Costa, P. T. (1987). Declines in divergent thinking with age: Cross-sectional, longitudinal, and cross-sequential analyses. *Psychology and Aging*, **2**, 130–137.

McDowd, J. M., & Craik, F. I. M. (1988). Effects of aging and task difficulty on divided attention performance. *Journal of Experimental Psychology: Human Perception and Performance*, **14**, 267–280.

McKoon, G., & Ratcliff, R. (1988). Contextually relevant aspects of meaning. *Journal of Experimental Psychology: Learning, Memory, and Cognition*, **12**, 82–91.

Miller, G. A. (1962). Some psychological studies of grammar. *American Psychologist*, **17**, 748–762.

Mitchell, D. B., & Perlmutter, M. (1986). Semantic activation and episodic memory: Age similarities and differences. *Developmental Psychology*, **22**, 86–94.

Mueller, J. H., Kausler, D. H., Faherty, A., & Oliveri, M. (1980). Reaction time as a function of age, anxiety, and typicality. *Bulletin of the Psychonomic Society*, **16**, 473–476.

Nebes, R. D., Boller, F., & Holland, A. (1986). Use of semantic context by patients with Alzheimer's disease. *Psychology and Aging*, **1**, 261–269.

Nebes, R. D., & Brady, C. B. (1988). Integrity of semantic fields in Alzheimer's disease. *Cortex*, **24**, 291–299.

Neely, J. H. (1977). Semantic priming and retrieval from lexical memory: Roles of inhibitionless spreading activation and limited-capacity attention. *Journal of Experimental Psychology: General*, **106**, 226–254.

Obler, L. K., & Albert, M. L. (1985). Language skills across adulthood. In J. E. Birren & K. W. Schaie (Eds.), *Handbook of the psychology of aging* (2nd ed., pp. 463–473). New York: Van Nostrand Reinhold.

O'Brien, E. J., Shank, D. M., Myers, J. L., & Rayner, K. (1988). Elaborative inferences during reading: Do they occur on-line? *Journal of Experimental Psychology: Learning, Memory, and Cognition*, **14**, 410–420.

Pearce, K. A., & Denney, N. W. (1984). A life-span study of classification preference. *Journal of Gerontology*, **39**, 458–464.

Perlmutter, M. (1979). Age differences in adults' free recall, cued recall, and recognition. *Journal of Gerontology*, **34**, 533–539.

Petros, T. V., Tabor, L., Cooney, T., & Chabot,

R. J. (1983). Adult age differences in sensitivity to semantic structure of prose. *Developmental Psychology*, **19**, 907–914.

Poon, L. W. (1985). Differences in human memory with aging: Nature, causes, and clinical implications. In J. E. Birren & K. W. Schaie (Eds.), *Handbook of the psychology of aging* (2nd ed., pp. 427–462). New York: Van Nostrand Reinhold.

Posner, M. I., & Snyder, C. R. R. (1975). Attention and cognitive control. In A. Solso (Ed.), *Information processing and cognition* (pp. 55–85). Hillsdale, NJ: Erlbaum.

Puglisi, J. T., Park, D. C., Smith, A. D., & Dudley, W. N. (1988). Age differences in encoding specificity. *Journal of Gerontology*, **43**, 145–150.

Rabinowitz, J. C. (1986). Priming in episodic memory. *Journal of Gerontology*, **2**, 204–213.

Rabinowitz, J. C., Craik, F. I. M., & Ackerman, B. P. (1982). A processing resource account of age differences in recall. *Canadian Journal of Psychology*, **36**, 325–344.

Rebok, G. W., Montaglione, C. J., & Bendlin, G. (1988). Effects of age and training on memory for pragmatic implications in advertising. *Journal of Gerontology: Psychological Sciences*, **43**, P75-78.

Reder, L. M., Wible, C., & Martin, J. (1986). Differential memory changes with age: Exact retrieval versus plausible inference. *Journal of Experimental Psychology: Learning, Memory, and Cognition*, **12**, 72–81.

Riegel, K. F. (1959). A study of verbal achievements of older persons. *Journal of Gerontology*, **14**, 453–456.

Salthouse, T. A. (1982). *Adult cognition: An experimental psychology of human aging*. New York: Springer-Verlag.

Salthouse, T. A. (1985). *A theory of cognitive aging*. Amsterdam: North-Holland.

Salthouse, T. A. (1988a). Effects of aging on verbal abilities: Examination of the psychometric literature. In L. L. Light & D. M. Burke (Eds.), *Language, memory, and aging* (pp. 17–35). New York: Cambridge University Press.

Salthouse, T. A. (1988b). The role of processing resources in cognitive aging. In M. L. Howe & C. J. Brainerd (Eds.), *Cognitive development in adulthood: Progress in cognitive development research* (pp. 185–239). New York: Springer-Verlag.

Sanford, A. J., & Garrod, S. C. (1981). *Understanding written language: Explorations of comprehension beyond the sentence*. New York: Wiley.

Schaie, K. W., & Parham, I. A. (1977). Cohort-sequential analyses of adult intellectual development. *Developmental Psychology*, **13**, 649–653.

Smiley, S. S., & Brown, A. L. (1979). Conceptual preferences for thematic or taxonomic relations: A nonmonotonic age trend from preschool to old age. *Journal of Experimental Child Psychology*, **28**, 249–257.

Smith, S. W., Rebok, G. W., Smith, W. R., Hall, S. E., & Alvin, M. (1983). Adult age differences in the use of story structure in delayed free recall. *Experimental Aging Research*, **9**, 191–195.

Spilich, G. J. (1983). Life-span components of text processing: Structural and procedural differences. *Journal of Verbal Learning and Verbal Behavior*, **22**, 231–244.

Stine, E. L. (1986). Attribute-based similarity perception in younger and older adults. *Experimental Aging Research*, **12**, 89–94.

Stine, E. L., Wingfield, A., & Poon, L. W. (1986). How much and how fast: Rapid processing of spoken language in later adulthood. *Psychology and Aging*, **1**, 303–311.

Tanenhaus, M. K., Dell, G. S., & Carlson, G. (1987). Context effects and lexical processing: A connectionist approach to modularity. In J. L. Garfield (Ed.), *Modularity in knowledge representation and natural-language understanding* (pp. 83–110). Cambridge, MA: MIT Press.

Thomson, D. M., & Tulving, E. (1970). Associative encoding and retrieval: Weak and strong cues. *Journal of Experimental Psychology*, **86**, 255–262.

Till, R. E. (1985). Verbatim and inferential memory in young and elderly adults. *Journal of Gerontology*, **40**, 316–323.

Till, R. E., & Walsh, D. A. (1980). Encoding and retrieval factors in adult memory for implicational sentences. *Journal of Verbal Learning and Verbal Behavior*, **19**, 1–16.

van Dijk, T. A., & Kintsch, W. (1983). *Strategies of discourse comprehension*. New York: Academic Press.

Van Gorp, W., Satz, P., Kiersch, M. E., & Henry, R. (1986). Normative data on the Boston

Naming Test for a group of normal older adults. *Journal of Clinical and Experimental Neuropsychology, 8*, 702–705.

Waltz, D. L., & Pollack, J. B. (1985). Massively parallel parsing: A strongly interactive model of natural language interpretation. *Cognitive Science, 9*, 51–74.

Wingfield, A., Poon, L. W., Lombardi, L., & Lowe, D. (1985). Speed of processing in normal aging: Effects of speech rate, linguistic structure, and processing time. *Journal of Gerontology, 40*, 579–585.

Wingfield, A., Stine, E. A. L., Lahar, C. J., & Aberdeen, J. S. (1988). Does the capacity of working memory change with age? *Experimental Aging Research, 14*, 103–107.

Zabrucky, K., Moore, D., & Schultz, N. R., Jr. (1987). Evaluation of comprehension in young and old adults. *Developmental Psychology, 23*, 39–43.

Zacks, R. T., & Hasher, L. (1988). Capacity theory and the processing of inferences. In L. L. Light & D. M. Burke (Eds.), *Language, memory, and aging* (pp. 154–170). New York: Cambridge University Press.

Zacks, R. T., Hasher, L., Doren, B., Hamm, V., & Attig, M. S. (1987). Encoding and memory of explicit and implicit information. *Journal of Gerontology, 42*, 418–422.

Zelinski, E. M. (1988). Integrating information from discourse: Do older adults show deficits? In L. L. Light & D. M. Burke (Eds.), *Language, memory, and aging* (pp. 117–132). New York: Cambridge University Press.

Seventeen

Intellectual Development in Adulthood

K. Warner Schaie

I. Introduction

The purpose of this chapter is to update the literature on adult intellectual development and to chart the directions of research that have become apparent since the last edition of this *Handbook*. The chapters on intelligence in the two previous editions differed markedly. Botwinick (1977) was concerned primarily with an exposition of research findings and methodological problems, whereas Labouvie-Vief (1985) elected to stress theoretical issues as well as the broader context of inquiry into adult intellectual development.[1] Although I intend to return the focus of my survey of the literature to primarily substantive and methodological topics, there are some meta-theoretical issues that are addressed briefly. These largely concern issues of definition, as well as a discussion of the implications of

theories of intelligence for the study of adult development. Thereafter, I intend to survey the empirical literature, emphasizing material published since 1983. I will first deal briefly with some methodological issues in the study of adult intellectual development, next consider what we now know about patterns of intellectual aging, and then address independent variables that affect the aging of intellectual abilities. I will then consider the relation between basic cognitive processes and products and the still somewhat nebulous topic of "practical" intelligence. The question of the reversability of intellectual deficit by means of educational training will be briefly considered, and the chapter will close with some comments on future directions for research and theory building in cognitive aging.

A. Intelligence and Cognition: Some Definitions

I will deal here primarily with what might be described as cognitive products rather than the cognitive processes that are

---

[1]Other extensive reviews of topics covered in this chapter may be found in Cunningham (1987), Denney (1982), Dixon, Kramer, and Baltes (1982), Jones (1959), and Schaie (1980).

Handbook of the Psychology of Aging, Third Edition
Copyright © 1990 Academic Press, Inc. All rights of reproduction in any form reserved.

favored by behavioral scientists interested in information processing (e.g., Rybash, Hoyer, & Roodin, 1986; Sternberg, 1977). The measurement of intelligence, whether global or differentiated into specific abilities, has traditionally been concerned with creating in the laboratory operations that would represent intelligent behaviors in the real world. As a consequence, I would argue that there is a natural hierarchy that leads from information processing, through the products measured in tests of intelligence, to what some call practical intelligence (e.g., Baltes, 1987; Sternberg & Berg, 1987). This is not to say that the understanding of the processes essential to intelligent behavior are not important or that theoretical models that attempt to account for the aging of such processes (e.g., Salthouse, 1988) are not relevant to the study of intelligence. In this *Handbook*, the literature on information processing and the development of expertise is presented elsewhere (see chapters by Light and Salthouse, this volume). It is my contention, however, that the products that characterize psychometric intelligence have had lasting value in directly predicting a variety of socially desirable outcomes; hence, they may be the most appropriate level of redundancy at which to assess adult intellectual development (Schaie, 1987a).

When we consider the aging of intellectual abilities, we are not simply concerned with intellectual development in the elderly; rather we are interested in the entire span from young adulthood into advanced old age. It is of interest to determine at what point intellectual development peaks as well as to note the rate and pattern of decline (cf. Schaie, 1980).

B. Implications of Theories of Intelligence for the Study of Adult Development

At the level of intelligence considered as products or performance variables, at least four influential theoretical positions have informed empirical research. The earliest influence stems from Sir Charles Spearman's work (1904) implying the existence of a general dimension of intelligence (g) that underlies all purposeful intellectual products, whose remainder would be viewed as task or item specific (s). This view is embodied empirically in the family of assessment devices originating from the work of Binet and Simon (1905), but the concept of a unidimensional form of intelligence has not been useful past adolescence, both because of the lack of a unidimensional validity criterion, such as scholastic performance, and because of convincing empirical evidence that differential life courses are found for different dimensions of intelligence (cf. Botwinick, 1977; Schaie, 1983).

More fruitful have been theories that are multidimensional in nature. The most prominent here has been E. L. Thorndike's view that there are different dimensions of intelligence but that their level of performance might be similar within individuals (cf. Thorndike & Woodworth, 1901). Wechsler's work (cf. Matarazzo, 1972) exemplifies this approach by specifying 11 operationally distinct scales derived from clinical observation and earlier mental tests that are combined into two broad dimensions: Verbal and Performance (non-verbal-manipulative) intelligence. These are then combined into a total IQ. Although enormously important because of its broad use in the clinical assessment of adults with psychopathology, one of the major limitations of the Wechsler Scales has been the fact that the factorial structure of the scales is not invariant across age (Cohen, 1957).

Dimensions that are factorially simpler were identified in the seminal work of Leon Louis Thurstone (1938). The primary mental abilities described by Thurstone have formed the basis for my own work, utilizing measurement instruments developed by Thurstone and Thurstone (1949), instruments developed by the Educational Testing Service (Ekstrom, French,

Harman, & Derman, 1976) based on the work of Thurstone and of Guilford (1967), as well as parallel forms developed in my laboratory (Schaie, 1985).

Although developed on children, the factorial structure of various subsets of the primary abilities is relatively simple and well described in numerous investigations of adults (e.g., Cornelius, Willis, Nesselroade, & Baltes 1983; Cunningham, 1987; Horn, 1982; Schaie, Willis, Hertzog, & Schulenberg, 1987; Schaie, Willis, Jay, & Chipuer, 1989). Moreover, second-order factor analyses of the primary abilities have resulted in the specification of higher order dimensions such as the concepts of fluid intelligence (applied to novel/eductive tasks) and crystallized intelligence (applied to acculturated information) popularized by Cattell (1963) and Horn (1982).

The introduction of Piagetian thought in America logically led some investigators to consider the application of Piagetian methods to the study of adult development. One limitation has been the relative paucity of the Genevan approach in its exploration of adult cognition (but cf. Commons, Richards, & Kuhn, 1982; Kramer, 1983; Piaget, 1972; Schaie, 1977/1978; Sinnott, 1984). Standardized assessment devices also have been limited, although there is recent work that might be applicable to the study of adults (e.g., Humphreys, Rich, & Davey, 1985). A review of some applications of Piagetian approaches to adults may be found in Hooper, Hooper, and Colbert (1984); it will not be addressed further in this chapter.

II. Methodological Issues

Although theories of intelligence have had important implications for the choice of assessment methods in the study of adult development, so have the introduction of methodological advances had major impact on determining how evidence on intellectual aging is to be collected. There has been a reciprocal effect of changes in

experimental paradigms informing theory development (cf. Abeles & Riley, 1987; Baltes, 1987; Baltes, Dittman-Kohli, & Dixon; 1984; Schaie, 1986, 1988c; Willis, 1985). Indeed, the study of adult intelligence has been one of the major battlegrounds for testing contentions regarding the design of studies and approaches to assessment that have broadly affected empirical work in gerontology.

A. Internal Validity Threats

There are two related but distinct objectives in the study of adult intelligence. Some investigators are concerned primarily with determining to what extent adults at different ages also differ in intellectual performance at a particular moment in historical time. To the extent that such information is needed for policy-relevant determinations, cross-sectional methods will suffice, particularly if due attention is paid to variability within and across age categories (cf. Schaie, 1988a,f). Those investigators, however, who are more concerned with determining how intelligence changes with age within individuals, and those who wish to study the antecedents that lead to individual differences in the course of adult development have discovered, to their consternation, that cross-sectional data are not suitable to answer these questions. As a consequence, there has been increased attention to the role of longitudinal data in understanding adult intellectual development, particularly as a number of longitudinal studies are now available that cover substantial age ranges (cf. Cunningham & Owens, 1983; Eichorn, Clausen, Haan, Honzik, & Mussen, 1981; Jarvik & Bank, 1983; Palmore, Busse, Maddox, Nowlin, & Siegler, 1985; Schaie, 1983; Schmitz-Scherzer & Thomae, 1983; Shock, Greulich, Andres, Arenberg, Costa, Lakatta, & Tobin, 1984; Siegler, 1983).

These and other studies have further focused our attention on the threats to the internal validity of both cross-sectional and longitudinal data for interpreting the evidence on intellectual change in adulthood. Because age cannot be assigned at random, studies of intellectual aging represent quasi-experiments (Campbell & Stanley, 1967). Seven different threats to the internal validity of such quasi-experiments have been identified. One of these, maturation, represents no threat to the validity of developmental studies, if their intent is to test hypotheses about effects of aging. The remaining six represent rival hypotheses to the effect of aging (i.e., maturational or age-specific changes). They involve the effects of history, testing (reactivity), instrumentation, statistical regression, experimental mortality (attrition), and selection. The consequences of these threats have been previously discussed (Schaie, 1977), and examples of their impact upon studies of adult intellectual development as well as research designs that control for their effects may be found in Schaie (1988d).

B. How Should We Measure Adult Intelligence?

Two major concerns will be addressed here: The first concerns the nature of appropriate assessment instruments; the second relates to the question whether our unit of analysis should be at the level of observable measures, or whether measurement needs to be conducted in terms of broadly marked estimates of latent constructs.

1. Assessment Instruments

The choice of assessment instruments is often informed by the theoretical model of intelligence subscribed to (see earlier discussion). The most commonly used instruments in the measurement of adult intelligence currently remain the Wechsler Adult Intelligence Scale and test batteries measuring various combinations of the primary mental abilities advocated by

Thurstone and Guilford. Norms for the recently revised form of the WAIS (through age 75) confirm the finding that there is relative stability for the verbal subtests but substantial negative age differences for the performance subtests that involve perceptual speed (cf. Sattler, 1982). Evidence for the stability of this pattern into advanced old age also has been documented (Field, Schaie, & Leino, 1988; Siegler, 1983).

Although the WAIS remains popular for cognitive assessment in clinical situations, its factorial complexity makes it less attractive for assessing intellectual changes across age and time. As a consequence, most recent studies of intellectual aging in community-dwelling populations have utilized samplars from the primary mental abilities (cf. Cunningham, 1987; Willis, 1985). The most extensive set of measures of primary mental abilities remains the Kit of Factor-Referenced tests published by the Educational Testing Service (Ekstrom et al., 1976). Increasing attention has been given to the confounding effects of the nature of test materials that do not take into account the requirements of older organisms (cf. Cornelius, 1984; Gonda, Quayhagen, & Schaie, 1981; Storandt & Futterman, 1982). These concerns have led to the development of batteries that include larger typefaces and other simplifications that make these tests more useful for work with the elderly (cf. Baltes & Willis, 1982; Schaie, 1985).

There also has been increasing interest in developing measures of the more pragmatic aspects of intelligence. A review of much of this work may be found in Sternberg and Wagner (1986). Furthermore, some of the test development related to the measurement of basic skills conducted by the Educational Testing Service (1977) has provided definitions of everyday tasks; the relationship of these tasks to intellectual aging having received some investigation (Willis & Schaie, 1986a).

For practical reasons, most assessment

instruments are at least slightly speeded. We will consider the effect of processing and perceptual speed upon intellectual aging later in this chapter but need to note here that speeded tests may adversely affect the elderly. It is not clear, however, whether extended time limits will necessarily reduce age differences. An emerging literature on testing the limits would actually argue to the contrary because the measured performance of older individuals is thought to be closer to their reserve capacity (Baltes, Dittmann-Kohli, & Kliegl, 1986). It could, of course, also be argued that a speedy response is an essential element of any substantive competent behavior, but the debate continues whether response speed should be measured directly or as part of substantive measures of intelligence.

2. Level of Measurement

In most work on intellectual aging, we are not so much concerned with age changes or differences in the specific measures but rather with the effects of intellectual aging on the underlying ability dimensions. Within the primary mental ability framework, there is a question whether our major interest should be in specific abilities or some higher order construct. Gustafson (1984), for example, described a hierarchical three-level model for intellectual abilities, which he claimed might fit most intellectual assessment systems. The first level represents the traditional matrix of primary mental abilities, a second order level would be akin to Horn's (1982) description of higher order factors involving fluid, crystallized, and visualization factors, and finally there is a third level of general intelligence (albeit most heavily identified with the fluid factor). Stankov (1988), moreover, used the concept of attention as a principle that would integrate all three levels. Nevertheless, it would seem that for the study of adult development, assessment is optimal at the pri-

mary level, especially because the role of g will become less central as expertise is developed in specific skills (Hoyer, 1987; Salthouse, 1984).

What is of concern here is not only that aging patterns differ for the primary (Schaie, 1983) or the second order factors (Horn, Donaldson, & Ekstrom, 1981) but also that some doubt has been shed on the equivalence of measures of intellectual functioning across age and time (Hertzog, 1985). Although the factor structure of abilities may be fairly stable across age, differences in factor covariances and particularly in the regression of the observed marker variables on the factors have been reported (cf. Cunningham, 1981; Hertzog, 1987; Hertzog & Schaie, 1986, 1988; Schaie et al., 1989). Most factor scores based on multiple markers can provide valid comparisons across age, but this is not necessarily the case for individual scales whose regression on a given ability factor may vary markedly from young adulthood into old age.

III. Patterns of Intellectual Aging

A. Estimates of Population Parameters

The progress of intellectual aging has been studied most intensively in the Seattle Longitudinal Study (Schaie, 1983, 1988d,f; Schaie & Hertzog, 1986). Throughout the study, subjects were assessed on five measures of psychological competence known as primary mental abilities (Schaie, 1985; Thurstone & Thurstone, 1949): *Verbal meaning*, the ability to comprehend words, a measure of recognition vocabulary; *spatial orientation*, the ability to mentally rotate objects in two-dimensional space; *inductive reasoning*, the ability to infer rules from examples that contain regular progressions of information; *number*, the ability to manipulate number concepts, as measured by checking simple addition problems, and *word fluency*, the ability to recall words according to a lexical rule. Various combinations of these abilities are prominently represented in virtually any meaningful activity of a person's daily living and work (Willis & Schaie, 1986a). The study has followed large numbers of individuals over each 7-year interval over the age range from 25 to 81 years. On average, there is gain until the late 30s or early 40s are reached, and then there is stability until the mid-50s or early 60s are reached. Average decrements from age 53 to 60 are quite small and are statistically significant only for number and word fluency. Beyond age 60, 7-year decrements are statistically significant throughout. These data suggest that average decline in psychological competence may begin for some as early as the mid-fifties, but that it is typically of small magnitude until the seventies are reached.

Although the prevalence of decline in mental abilities with advancing age has been reliably established for group data, there remains much controversy as to patterns of individual differences in such decline (cf. Hertzog, 1985; Schaie, 1989a). We can best examine this question by noting what proportion of individuals show particular patterns of decline over 7-year periods ending at age 60, 67, 74 and 81.[2] Figure 1 charts the resultant data in their positive form, that is, the proportion of individuals who maintain their level of functioning on specific abilities over the preceding 7-year period (Schaie, 1989c). Depending upon the age group, from 60 to 85% of all participants remain stable or improve on specific abilities. Note that the incidence of significant decrement is

[2]Statistically reliable decrement for individual study participants was defined by creating a 1 Standard Error of Measurement (SEM) confidence band about our participants' base scores (cf. Dudek, 1979). Those individuals whose 7-year change fell below this interval were considered to have reliably experienced age decrement; all others were considered to have maintained their previous level of performance. These criteria are described in more detail in Schaie (1989b) and Schaie and Willis (1986).

quite limited until age 60, affects less than a third of the study participants until age 74, and even by age 81 affects only between 30 and 40% of the persons studied.

B. Profiles of Individual Aging

Let us next consider the question of whether the decline in psychological competence is a global or a highly specific event. For this purpose, data are graphed in Figure 2 to show the cumulative proportions of study participants who maintain or improve their level of cognitive functioning in advanced age on one or more abilities. Very few individuals show global decline. It is particularly noteworthy that by age 60, 75% of the study participants maintained their level of functioning over 7 years on at least four out of the five abilities monitored and that this level of maintenance was true even at age 81 for slightly more than half of the sample. Virtually no individuals contained in our data set showed universal decline on all abilities monitored even by the 80s. It appears then that optimization of cognitive functioning in old age may well involve selective maintenance of some abilities but not others. Moreover, such optimization is individualized in nature (cf. Schaie, 1989a). Despite these encouraging data, it is clear that some reduction in psychological competence occurs in most persons as the 80s and 90s are reached. However, even at such advanced ages, competent behavior can be expected by many persons in familiar circumstances. Much of the observed loss in advanced age appears to be observable primarily in highly challenging, complex, or stressful situations (cf. Kliegl & Baltes, 1987).

C. The Role of Cohort Effects

Extensive research on adult intelligence has shown that there have been marked generational shifts in levels of performance on tests of mental abilities (Flynn,

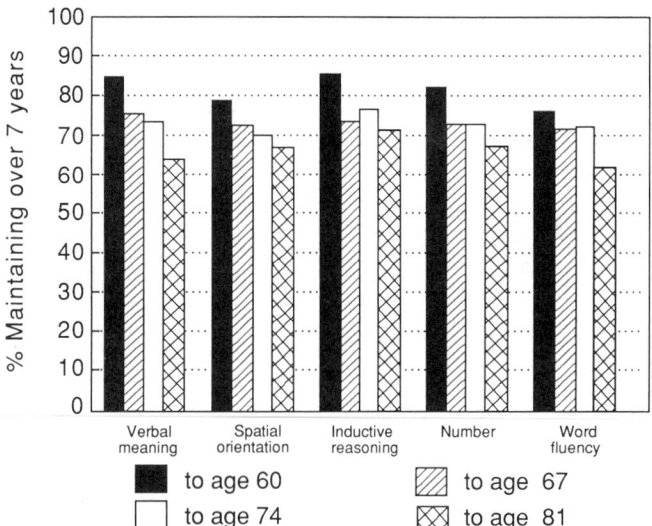

Figure 1 Proportion of individuals who maintain stable levels of performance over 7 years on five primary mental abilities.

1984; Schaie, 1983, 1989b; Willis, 1985). The usual empirical findings have been that later-born cohorts appear to be advantaged when compared with earlier cohorts at the same ages. This phenomenon has been explained by arguing that increased educational opportunities and improved life-styles, including nutrition and the conquest of childhood disease, have enabled successive generations to reach ever higher ability asymptotes, similar to the secular trends of improvement for anthropometric and other biological markers (Fries & Crapo, 1981; Shock *et al.*, 1984).

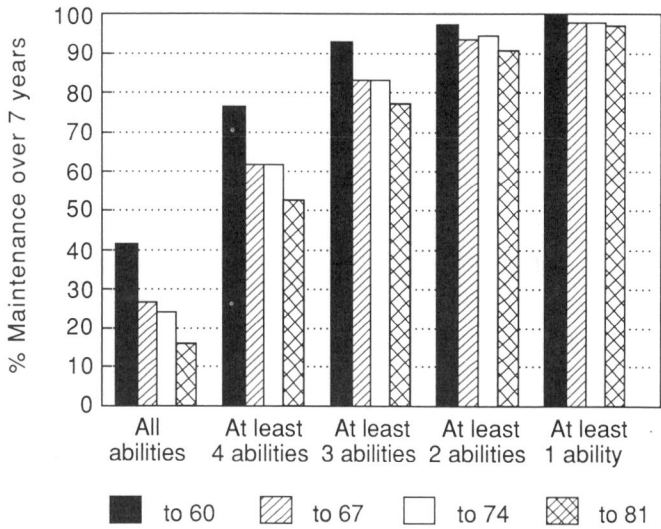

Figure 2 Proportion of individuals who maintain stable levels of performance over 7 years on multiple abilities.

Although linear trends have been found for some variables, there seems to be contrary evidence that suggests that such trends may have been time limited and domain or even variable specific (cf. Schaie, 1989b).

Accurate descriptions of patterns of cohort change in mental ability are important because they provide a foundation for gaining a better understanding of the manner in which productivity and competence shift over time in our society. Such data are also needed to understand how cohort differences in performance can lead to erroneous conclusions from age-comparative cross-sectional studies (cf. Schaie, 1977, 1988d). Because of the changing demographic composition of the population, it is of particular interest to assess differences in performance level at comparable ages for individuals representing eras that are characterized by differential fertility rates (e.g., contrasts of the pre-baby-boom, baby-boom, and baby-bust generations). Cohort shifts at older ages, moreover, are directly relevant to policy considerations regarding the maintenance of a competent work force that will contain increasing proportions of older workers as mandatory retirement becomes the relic of a biased past.

In addition, previous research (Schaie, 1983, 1989a; Schaie & Hertzog, 1986) has demonstrated differential cohort trends over time that are likely to influence the proportion of individuals of advanced age who may remain capable of significant late life accomplishments and that may impact upon the ability of older individuals to take advantage of recent technological developments (Schaie, 1988b).

Figure 3 shows cohort gradients for the abilities for which age trends were given before. Differences between successive cohorts as expressed in percentage of change in terms of the average of the total adult population were cumulated from the oldest cohort born in 1889 up to the most recently measured cohort born in 1959. The observed negative shift in some abilities for more recent cohorts may make many older persons more competitive with their younger peers than has been the case in the past. Because of the recent lev-

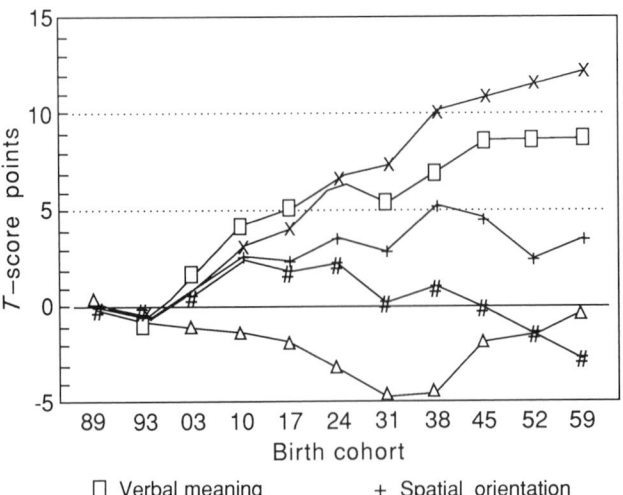

Figure 3 Cumulative differences on the primary mental abilities of verbal meaning, spatial orientation, inductive reasoning, number, and word fluency for cohorts born from 1889 to 1959.

eling off of some cohort changes and the curvilinear nature of cohort changes for some abilities, we can expect that the large ability differences between young and old adults that are observed currently will be much reduced. Indeed, for an ability such as numerical skill, we may expect a period of time when older adults will be advantaged as compared to younger persons. Conversely, the level reached by recent cohorts in educational attainment and positive life-styles may well be close to the limits possible within our society's resources and structures. The positive shifts in potential experienced in early old age by successive cohorts may consequently come to a halt by the end of this century.

IV. Factors That Affect Intellectual Aging

A. Normal versus Pathological Aging

It would seem reasonable to suspect that health status might be related to the rate of intellectual aging. Such analyses have been undertaken in both the Duke Longitudinal Study (Manton, Siegler, & Woodbury, 1986; Palmore et al., 1985) and in our Seattle Longitudinal Study. In the latter study, the relationship between cardiovascular disease and levels of performance on mental abilities was examined. Evidence was obtained that those individuals who were at risk from cardiovascular disease tended to decline earlier on average on all mental abilities studied than did individuals not so affected (cf. Hertzog, Schaie, & Gribbin, 1978). Particularly interesting is a recent analysis of the relationship between cardiovascular disease, significant decline over a 14-year period, and significant remediation of decline in a group of persons (ranging in age from 62 to 94) who received cognitive training on the Inductive Reasoning ability (Schaie, 1989b). Medical histories for these subjects were examined over the 7-year period preceding their pretraining evaluation. All incidents of clinic visits and illness episodes (continuous spells of illness) for these persons were recorded. Those who declined had significantly greater numbers of illness diagnoses, as well as visits for cardiovascular disease, whereas those who benefited from training had fewer disease incidents.

B. Speed of Performance and Intellectual Aging

There seems to be an abundant accumulation of evidence that decline in speed with age adversely affects performance on tests of intellectual abilities. Many questions remain, however, as to whether the behavioral slowing involves a single mechanism or multiple ones (cf. Salthouse, 1985). Slowing of performance has been shown to have differential effects depending not only on the cognitive processes or abilities involved but also on the format involved in the presentation of test materials (Berg, Hertzog, & Hunt, 1982; Hertzog, 1989). Moreover, although group data on age changes in reaction time or perceptual speed take quite linear form, analyses of individual differences tend to support patterns of change that more likely follow a stair-step pattern (Schaie, 1989d). There are even data that would support that the number of different components to be found in a battery of speeded tests may increase in advanced age (White & Cunningham, 1987).

Birren has argued for a long time that if one cannot think quickly, one cannot think well (cf. Birren chapter, this volume). Stankov (1988), in a factorial study of attention tasks, has shown that speed of search is related to processing information and manifests itself in a hierarchical structure of attention that is related to fluid and crystallized abilities. He showed further that when statistical adjustments are made for the effects of individual differences in attention, age differences in fluid abilities are markedly reduced, whereas crystallized abilities tend to show increases into later life.

C. Social Structures and Intellectual Aging

A number of structural variables have been identified that tend to effect the rate of cognitive decline (cf. Schaie, 1988e; Schooler & Schaie, 1987; Willis, 1989a). Positive factors that have been implicated range from the more obvious demographic variables of high levels of education, occupational status and income, to more subtle aspects such as high workplace complexity (Miller, Slomczynski, & Kohn, 1987; Schooler, 1987), intact marriage, exposure to stimulating environments, utilization of cultural and educational resources throughout adulthood (Gribbin, Schaie, & Parham, 1980; Schaie, 1984), or lengthy marriage to an intelligent spouse (Gruber & Schaie, 1986). Retirement has been found to have favorable cognitive sequelae for those retiring from routinized jobs but appears to accelerate decrement for those retiring from highly complex jobs (Dutta, Schulenberg, & Lair, 1986).

D. Personality Correlates of Intellectual Aging

Intellectual functioning is also substantially affected by a person's standing on some important personality traits and lifestyle variables. Modest relationships have been found between self-efficacy and intellectual functioning, although there is still some question whether this relationship is directional or reciprocal (Lachman, 1983; Lachman & Jelalian, 1984). Attribution of failure, primarily due to lack of confidence in one's ability to succeed, also has been implicated in the lowered performance of some older persons (Prohaska, Parham, & Teitelman, 1984). And Hayslip (1988) has argued that maintenance of higher levels of intellectual func-

tioning in later adulthood might be motivated by ego defense mechanisms that insulate older individuals from feelings of worthlessness and loss of control.

More securely established is the antecedent status of the personality characteristic of rigidity/flexibility. There are two aspects of this trait: motor-cognitive flexibility and attitudinal flexibility. Longitudinal studies suggest that one's lifelong standing on flexible behaviors is maintained for most persons into the 70s, whereas on average, people develop more rigid attitudes by the early 60s (cf. Schaie, 1983). It has been shown that those with flexible attitudes in midlife tend to experience less decline in psychological competence with advancing age than those who were observed to be fairly rigid at that life stage (Schaie, 1984).

Rigidity/flexibility also interacts with psychological energy and a variety of other demographic and life-style variables. For example, it has been noted that being interested in cultural and educational activities, being married, and being affluent at midlife are all characteristics that are positively related with the maintenance of high levels of psychological competence, energy, and attitudinal flexibility in young old age (Gribbin et al., 1980; Schaie, 1984). The same studies also conclude that high levels of motor-cognitive flexibility at the young-old stage are highly predictive of one's standing on numerical and verbal skills as well as psychological energy when reaching the old-old stage.

V. Practical Intelligence

A. Definitions of Practical Intelligence

The strong claim has been made that there is an aspect of intelligence that is not measured by conventional processing or psychometric approaches because it involves the pragmatics of applying intellectual skills to everyday activities, and further, that the activities involved therein may differ across the life course (e.g., Berg & Sternberg, 1985; Dixon & Baltes, 1986). There has been a proliferation of theoretical models (e.g. Baltes *et al.*, 1984; Cavanaugh, Kramer, Sinnott, Camp, & Markley, 1985; Sternberg & Wagner, 1986) that would add a whole new domain to the study of intellectual aging. Practical intelligence must be distinguished from highly specialized expertise (cf. Salthouse, Chapter 18, this volume) and from wisdom (cf. Clayton & Birren, 1980; Meacham, 1983; Smith, Dixon, & Baltes, 1988). The latter two expressions of complex behaviors involve high levels of intelligence as a necessary but not as a sufficient component. These topics are therefore not reviewed here.

We shall next review a number of different approaches that have been taken to discover what the dimensions of practical intelligence might be. They include judges' ratings, the identification of tasks of daily living, and the measurement of situationally linked competencies.

1. Judges' Ratings

One aspect of practical intelligence that has been considered is whether or not a person behaves in an "intelligent" manner (e.g., Goodnow, 1984). Such an approach, of course, requires the use of judges to rate for us such matters as the attributes of everyday competence at various life stages (Berg & Sternberg, 1985), ways in which people combine or organize information about everyday events (Goodnow, 1986), or psychologists' perceptions of their own intellectual functioning (Mason & Rebok, 1984). A general problem with such ratings is that attributes to be discovered may become increasingly specific to age, social class, work setting, and other contextual domains (cf. Scribner, 1984).

2. Everyday Tasks

There is a long history of developing measures that relate to the everyday experience of young, middle-aged, and older.

Examples of such work are the much neglected scales developed by Demming and Pressey (1957) or by Gardner and Monge (1977). Again, comparison across wide age ranges may be difficult if tasks are selected to favor experiences more common in the life space of older individuals than that of young adults, although it is at least as reasonable to test the appropriateness of materials developed on the elderly with younger subjects as it is to take the traditional stance of adapting methods developed for children to the need of older persons. The materials developed by the Educational Testing Service (1977) are attractive because they include many everyday tasks (e.g., interpreting medicine bottle labels, bus schedules, road maps, yellow page advertisements, warranties, and so on) that are of common concern across adulthood (cf. Willis & Schaie, 1986a). Longitudinal data are not yet available on this material, but a large-scale cross-sectional study showed age differences comparable to those seen for fluid abilities (Schaie, 1988f).

3. Situational Competencies

A quasi-ethnographic approach to practical intelligence involves the discovery of situations in which older adults are required to display competent behavior. This information can then be translated into a data language such as the Q-sort developed by Scheidt and Schaie (1978), which includes the situational dimensions of social-nonsocial, common-uncommon, supporting-depriving, and active-passive. The data language allows either the expression of perceived competence by the person to be described or judgments by other informants who are sufficiently familiar with the behavior of that person. Age differences in perceived competence have been reported with relative competence shifting in the direction of situations involving social, common, passive, and depriving elements (cf. Willis & Schaie, 1986a).

B. The Relationship of Psychometric and Practical Intelligence

What is the relationship between everyday competence and the traditional measures of psychometric intelligence? Although some theorists would posit these to be rather distinct domains (e.g. Sternberg & Berg, 1987), an alternate position can be taken that argues for a more hierarchical approach. That is, just as individual differences variance in a specific primary ability could be explained via componential analyses to reflect certain combinations of processing skills, so could everyday competence on specific tasks be explained by combinations of skills on relevant primary abilities. When this relationship is examined, it turns out that as much as 80% of individual differences variance in certain everyday tasks (the ETS Basic Skills Test) can be explained by individual differences on the primaries of figural relations, verbal ability, and social knowledge (Willis & Schaie, 1986b). At a behavioral level, high performance on fluid abilities has been shown to be predictive of the acquisition of computer skills in middle-aged and older adults (Garfein, Schaie, & Willis, 1988).

VI. Interventions in Adult Intellectual Development

A. Theoretical Significance

Empirical research on individual differences in intellectual change and the identification of antecedents for differential intellectual aging cast some doubt on the inevitability of general intellectual decline for all individuals. An even more potent source for such doubt is offered by the burgeoning cognitive intervention research that attempts to remediate intellectual decline in the elderly. Although there has been substantial evidence for some time that demonstrates selective training improvement in the elderly (cf. Baltes & Willis, 1982), it is only recently that several training interventions have been completed within the framework of longitudinal studies. Longitudinal studies make it possible to distinguish effects of training that serve to remediate observed age deficits in contrast to improving the performance of individuals beyond earlier obtained levels. The former outcome, however, is of particular theoretical interest because it suggests that much of the intellectual aging seen in community-dwelling elderly may be experiential in nature. Training studies conducted in a longitudinal context also permit the identification of antecedent conditions that serve to predict the likelihood of training success or failure (Willis, 1989b).

B. Empirical Findings

The literature on cognitive training and its implications for everyday competence has recently been reviewed by Willis (1987). Here I will simply summarize recent findings relevant to effects of training on psychometric abilities. Most of this work has been conducted either in the context of the ADEPT (Baltes & Willis, 1982) or the Seattle Longitudinal Studies (Schaie & Willis, 1986; Willis & Schaie, 1986b). Each of these studies involves pre–post test designs, with 5 hours of instruction in strategies at the ability level given in small groups in the ADEPT study and individually in the Seattle study. In the former study, significant training gains were demonstrated for subjects over age 60 for the primaries of figural relations and induction, whereas in the latter, significant training gains occurred for inductive reasoning and spatial orientation. In the Seattle study, moreover, significant gain was shown to occur for subjects who had declined as well as for those who had remained stable. Approximately 40% of the decline subjects were returned to the levels experienced some 14 years earlier. Gender effects have been noted that involve greater training effects for women on spatial orientation, and moreover, training seems to effect both speed and accuracy in women but primarily accuracy in men (Willis & Schaie, 1988). In both studies, near transfer was shown to occur for alternate markers within each ability, but there was no far transfer to other primary abilities.

Whether cognitive training might change the structural characteristics of the primaries involved has been investigated by confirmatory factor analyses of the pre- and posttest assessment batteries used in the Seattle study. Invariance of factor structure across training was confirmed in the training groups. Although there were some minor shifts in the factor loadings of the individual markers of the abilities trained, subsequently, training did not result in any of the markers loading on factors other than those hypothesized (Schaie et al., 1987). Findings from the ADEPT study have for the most part been replicated in a German sample (Baltes et al., 1986), as well as in a study by Blackburn, Papalia-Finlay, Foye, and Serlin (1988). Most recently, a long-term follow-up of the ADEPT study over a 7-year period has shown significant lower decline for those trained as compared to the control group (Willis, in press).

Cumulative magnitudes of cohort differences between those now in midlife and those in early old age are currently no greater than the training gains demonstrated for older adults who had not experienced age-related decline. It seems reasonable then to assume that much of the cohort-related aspect of older persons' intellectual disadvantage when compared with those at midlife may well be amenable to compensation by suitable educational interventions.

VII. Conclusions: Future Directions for Research on Intellectual Aging

The literature reviewed in this chapter suggests that there has been a turning from the simple definition of the extent and ability specificity of age differences and age changes in intelligence to a greater preoccupation with individual patterns of change and the identification of antecedent variables that might account for the vast array of individual differences. Significant progress has been made in identifying some of the social structural, health, and personality variables that account for such differences. The role of contextual variables has been treated previously primarily as a methodological confound and assessed primarily via the study of the index variable of cohort effects. We are beginning to see increasing efforts to decompose such effects in order to identify the precise influences that may permit the eventual prediction of individual hazards of intellectual decline and maintenance.

As the consequence of the apparent plateauing of cohort effects for some abilities, and negative effects for others, we can expect that age differences in adulthood may become more compressed over the next decade. The effects of population pressures on the aging of the baby-boom cohort therefore need to be monitored carefully and compared to the aging of earlier, perhaps more favored groups. Although our understanding of gender differences in abilities has increased markedly, we still have almost no comparative work on intellectual aging within minority groups in our country, nor useful cross-cultural comparisons with intellectual aging in other societies. This would be an extremely fertile area for future research, particularly because cross-cultural research allows variation in the timing of substantial environmental interventions (e.g., Great Depression, cultural revolution, and so on), that may effect intellectual aging.

Particularly noteworthy is the increased attention given to the field of practical intelligence. Much empirical work, however, needs to be done to identify the dimensions of practical intelligence, to develop taxonomies of situations and circumstances under which practical intelligence is expressed, as well as to examine the processes that link expressions of practical intelligence to the basic abilities, combinations and permutations of which are likely to remain the common denominators in any attempt to predict performance on everyday tasks, without moving into the quagmire of developing a differential psychology of situation-specific intelligence.

The empirical work on cognitive intervention has been successful in showing that intellectual decline in old age is not necessarily irreversible and has demonstrated that it may be possible to formalize intervention strategies that allow longer maintenance of high levels of intellectual function in community-dwelling older persons. This work holds future promise also as a technique for the early identification of individuals who may be at the threshold of cognitive impairment. To accomplish this, it will be necessary to continue the inquiry into health and environmental antecedents that distinguish those individuals who do or do not gain from cognitive interventions. To remove such techniques from the laboratory into a broader social context, it will also be necessary to investigate modes of intervention that are more indigenous to the daily experience of older persons (such as games and other activities that may be cognitively challenging) and to relate the effect of cognitive training to specific activities of daily living.

The past few years have brought a number of methodological advances that allow reconceptualization and reanalysis of existing data sets by techniques such as structural equation modeling, event history analysis, or latent growth models. It has been my observation that methodological innovations have made an especially strong impact upon research on adult intellectual development. I would expect that this trend will continue and that the application of the new techniques to this field will further expedite the emergence of more comprehensive theoretical formulations of adult intellectual development.

References

Abeles, R. P., & Riley, M. W. (1987). Longevity, social structure and cognitive aging. In C. Schooler & K. W. Schaie (Eds.), *Cognitive functioning and social structure over the life course* (pp. 161–175). New York: Ablex.

Baltes, P. B. (1987). Theoretical propositions of life-span developmental psychology: On the dynamics between growth and decline. *Developmental Psychology, 23,* 611–626.

Baltes, P. B., Dittman-Kohli, F., & Dixon, R. A. (1984). New perspectives on the development of intelligence in adulthood: Toward a dual-process conception and a model of selective optimization with compensation. In P. B. Baltes & O. G. Brim, Jr. (Eds.), *Life-span development and behavior* (Vol. 6, pp. 33–76). New York: Academic Press.

Baltes, P. B., Dittman-Kohli, F., & Kliegl, R. (1986). Reserve capacity of the elderly in aging-sensitive tests of fluid intelligence: Replication and extension. *Psychology and Aging, 1,* 172–177.

Baltes, P. B., & Willis, S. L. (1982). Enhancement (plasticity) of intellectual functioning in old age: Penn State's Adult Development and Enrichment Project (ADEPT). In F. I. M. Craik & S. Trehub (Eds.), *Aging and cognitive processes* (pp. 353–389). New York: Plenum.

Berg, C., Hertzog, C., & Hunt, E. (1982). Age differences in the speed of mental rotation. *Developmental Psychology, 18,* 95–107.

Berg, C., & Sternberg, R. (1985). A triarchic theory of intellectual development during adulthood. *Developmental Review, 5,* 334–370.

Binet, A., & Simon, T. (1905). Methodes nouvelles pour le diagnostic du niveau intellectuel des anormaux. *L'Année Psychologique, 11,* 191.

Blackburn, J. A., Papalia-Finley, D., Foye, B. F., & Serlin, R. C. (1988). Modifiability of figural relations performance among elderly adults. *Journal of Gerontology: Psychological Sciences, 43,* P87–P89.

Botwinick, J. (1977). Intellectual abilities. In J. E. Birren & K. W. Schaie (Eds.), *Handbook of the psychology of aging* (pp. 580–605). New York: Van Nostrand Reinhold

Campbell, D. T., & Stanley, J. C. (1967). *Experimental and quasi-experimental designs for research.* Chicago: Rand McNally.

Cattell, R. B. (1963). Theory of fluid and crystallized intelligence: A critical experiment. *Journal of Educational Psychology,* **54,** 1–22.

Cavanaugh, J., Kramer, D. A., Sinnott, J. D., Camp, C. J., & Markley, R. P. (1985). On missing links and such: Interfaces between cognitive research and everyday problems solving. *Human Development,* **28,** 146–168.

Clayton, V. P., & Birren, J. E. (1980). The development of wisdom across the life span: A reexamination of an ancient topic. In P. B. Baltes & O. G. Brim, Jr. (Eds.), *Life-span development and behavior* (Vol. 3, pp. 104–137). New York: Academic Press.

Cohen, J. (1957). The factorial structure of the WAIS between early adulthood and old age. *Journal of Consulting Psychology,* **21,** 283–290.

Commons, M. I., Richards, F. A., & Kuhn, D. (1982). Systematic and metasystematic reasoning: A case for levels of reasoning beyond Piaget's stage of formal operations. *Child Development,* **53,** 1058–1069.

Cornelius, S. W. (1984). Classic pattern of intellectual aging: Test familiarity, difficulty, and performance. *Journal of Gerontology,* **39,** 201–206.

Cornelius, S. W., Willis, S. L., Nesselroade, J. R., & Baltes, P. B. (1983). Convergence between attention variables and factors of psychometric intelligence in older adults. *Intelligence,* **7,** 253–269.

Cunningham, W. R. (1981). Ability factor structure difference in adulthood and old age. *Multivariate Behavioral Research,* **16,** 3–22.

Cunningham, W. R. (1987). Intellectual abilities and age. In K. W. Schaie (Ed.), *Annual review of gerontology and geriatrics* (Vol. 7, pp. 117–134). New York: Springer.

Cunningham, W. R., & Owens, W. A., Jr. (1983). The Iowa State Study of the adult development of intellectual abilities. In K. W. Schaie (Ed.), *Longitudinal studies of adult psychological development* (pp. 20–39). New York: Guilford.

Demming, J. A., & Pressey, S. L. (1957). Tests indigenous to the adult and older years. *Journal of Counseling Psychology,* **4,** 144–148.

Denney, N. W. (1982). Aging and cognitive changes. In B. B. Wolman (Ed.), *Handbook of developmental psychology* (pp. 807–827). Englewood Cliffs, NJ: Prentice-Hall.

Dixon, R. A., & Baltes, P. B. (1986). Toward life-span research on the functions and pragmatics of intelligence. In R. Sternberg & B. Wagner (Eds.), *Practical intelligence* (pp. 203–235). London: Cambridge University Press.

Dixon, R. A., Kramer, D. A., & Baltes, P. B. (1982). Intelligence: A life-span developmental perspective. In B. B. Wolman (Ed.), *Handbook of developmental psychology* (pp. 301–350). Englewood Cliffs, NJ: Prentice-Hall.

Dudek, F. J. (1979). The continuing misinterpretation of the standard error of measurement. *Psychological Bulletin,* **86,** 335–337.

Dutta, R., Schulenberg, J. E., & Lair, T. J. (1986). *The effect of job characteristics on cognitive abilities and intellectual flexibility.* Paper presented at the annual meeting of the Eastern Psychological Association, New York, April.

Educational Testing Service (1977). *Basic Skills Assessment Test: Reading.* Princeton, NJ: Author.

Eichorn, D. H., Clausen, J. A., Haan, N., Honzik, M. P., & Mussen, P. H. (1981). *Present and past in middle life.* New York: Academic Press.

Ekstrom, R. B., French, J. W., Harman, H., & Derman, D. (1976). *Kit of factor-referenced cognitive tests* (rev. ed.). Princeton, NJ: Educational Testing Service.

Field, D., Schaie, K. W., & Leino, E. V. (1988). Continuity in intellectual functioning: The role of self-reported health. *Psychology and Aging,* **3,** 385–392.

Flynn, J. R. (1984). The mean IQ of Americans: Massive gains 1932 to 1978. *Psychological Bulletin,* **95,** 29–51.

Fries, J. F., & Crapo, L. M. (1981). *Vitality and aging.* San Francisco: Freeman.

Gardner, E. F., & Monge, R. H. (1977). Adult age differences in cognitive abilities and educational background. *Experimental Aging Research,* **3,** 337–383.

Garfein, A. J., Schaie, K. W., & Willis, S. L.

(1988). Microcomputer proficiency in later-middle-aged and older adults: Teaching old dogs new tricks. *Social Behaviour*, **3**, 131–148.

Gonda, J., Quayhagen, M., & Schaie, K. W. (1981). Education, task meaningfulness and cognitive performance in young-old and old-old adults. *Educational Gerontology*, **7**, 151–158.

Goodnow, J. J. (1984). On being "judged" intelligent. *International Journal of Psychology*, **19**, 91–106.

Goodnow, J. J. (1986). Some lifelong everyday forms of intelligent behavior: Organizing and reorganizing. In R. J. Sternberg & R. K. Wagner (Eds.), *Practical intelligence: Origins of competence in the everyday world* (pp. 143–162). London: Cambridge University Press.

Gribbin, K., Schaie, K. W., & Parham, I. A. (1980). Complexity of life style and maintenance of intellectual abilities. *Journal of Social Issues*, **36**, 47–61.

Gruber, A. L., & Schaie, K. W. (1986). *Longitudinal-sequential studies of marital assortativity.* Paper presented at the annual meeting of the Gerontological Society of America, Chicago, November.

Guilford, J. P. (1967). *The nature of human intelligence.* New York: McGraw-Hill.

Gustafson, J. E. (1984). A unifying model for the structure of intellectual abilities. *Intelligence*, **8**, 179–203.

Hayslip, B., Jr. (1988). Personality-ability relationships in aged adults. *Journal of Gerontology: Psychological Sciences*, **43**, P79–P84.

Hertzog, C. (1985). An individual differences perspective: Implications for cognitive research in gerontology. *Research on Aging*, **7**, 7–45.

Hertzog, C. (1987). Applications of structural equation models in gerontological research. In K. W. Schaie (Ed.), *Annual review of gerontology and geriatrics* (Vol. 7, pp. 265–293). New York: Springer

Hertzog, C. (1989). The influence of cognitive slowing on age differences in intelligence. *Developmental Psychology*, **25**, 636–651.

Hertzog, C., & Schaie, K. W. (1986). Stability and change in adult intelligence: 1. Longitudinal covariance structures. *Psychology and Aging*, **1**, 159–171.

Hertzog, C., & Schaie, K. W. (1988). Stability and change in adult intelligence: 2. Simultaneous analysis of longitudinal means and covariance structures. *Psychology and Aging*, **3**, 122–130.

Hertzog, C., Schaie, K. W., & Gribbin, K. (1978). Cardiovascular disease and changes in intellectual functioning from middle to old age. *Journal of Gerontology*, **33**, 872–883.

Hooper, F. H., Hooper, J. O., & Colbert, K. C. (1984). *Personality and memory correlates of intellectual functioning.* Basel: Karger.

Horn, J. L. (1982). The theory of fluid and crystallized intelligence in relation to concepts of cognitive psychology and aging in adulthood. In F. I. M. Craik & S. Trehub (Eds.), *Aging and cognitive processes* (pp. 237–278). New York: Plenum.

Horn, H. L., Donaldson, J., & Ekstrom, R. (1981). Apprehension, memory and fluid intelligence decline in adulthood. *Research on Aging*, **3**, 33–84.

Hoyer, W. (1987). Acquisition of knowledge and the decentralization of g in adult intellectual development. In C. Schooler & K. W. Schaie (Eds.), *Cognitive functioning and social structure over the life course* (pp. 120–141). New York: Ablex.

Humphreys, L. G., Rich, S. A., & Davey, T. C. (1985). A Piagetian test of general intelligence. *Developmental Psychology*, **21**, 872–877.

Jarvik, L. F., & Bank, L. (1983). Aging twins: Longitudinal psychometric data. In K. W. Schaie (Ed.), *Longitudinal studies of adult psychological development* (pp. 40–63). New York: Guilford.

Jones, H. E. (1959). Intelligence and problem solving. In J. E. Birren (Ed.), *Handbook of aging and the individual* (pp. 700–738). Chicago: University of Chicago Press.

Kliegl, R., & Baltes, P. B. (1987). Theory-guided analysis of mechanisms of development and aging through testing-the-limits and research on expertise. In C. Schooler & K. W. Schaie (Eds.), *Cognitive functioning and social structure over the life course* (pp. 95–119). New York: Ablex.

Kramer, D. A. (1983). Post-formal operations? A need for further conceptualization. *Human Development*, **26**, 91–105.

Labouvie-Vief, G. (1985). Intelligence and cognition. In J. E. Birren & K. W. Schaie (Eds.), *Handbook of the psychology of aging* (2nd ed., pp. 500–530). New York: Van Nostrand Reinhold.

Lachman, M. E. (1983). Perceptions of intellectual aging: Antecedent or consequence of aintellectual functioning? *Developmental Psychology, 19,* 482–498.

Lachman, M. E., & Jelalian, E. J. (1984). Self-efficacy and attributions for intellectual performance in young and elderly adults. *Journal of Gerontology, 39,* 577–582.

Manton, K. G., Siegler, I. C., & Woodbury, M. A. (1986). Patterns of intellectual development in later life. *Journal of Gerontology, 41,* 486–499.

Mason, C. F., & Rebok, G. W. (1984). Psychologists' self-perception of their intellectual functioning. *International Journal of Behavioral Development, 7,* 255–266.

Matarazzo, J. D. (1972). *Wechsler's measurement and appraisal of adult intelligence* (5th ed.). Baltimore: Williams & Wilkins.

Meacham, J. A. (1983). Wisdom and the context of knowledge: Knowing that one doesn't know. In D. Kuhn & J. A. Meacham (Eds.), *Contributions to human development* (Vol. 8, pp. 111–134). Basel: Karger.

Miller, J., Slomczynski, K. M., & Kohn, M. L. (1987). Continuity of learning-generalization through the life span: The effect of job on men's intellectual process in the United States and Poland. In C. Schooler & K. W. Schaie (Eds.), *Cognitive functioning and social structure over the life course* (pp. 176–202). New York: Ablex.

Palmore, E., Busse, E. W., Maddox, G. L., Nowlin, J. B., & Siegler, I. L. (Eds.) (1985). *Normal aging III.* Durham, NC: Duke University Press.

Piaget, J. (1972). Intellectual evolution from adolescence to adulthood. *Human Development, 15,* 1–12.

Prohaska, T. R., Parham, I. A., & Teitelman, J. (1984). Age differences in attributions to causality: Implications for intellectual assessment. *Experimental Aging Research, 10,* 111–117.

Rybash, J. M., Hoyer, W. J., & Roodin, P. A. (1986). *Adult cognition and aging.* New York: Pergamon.

Salthouse, T. A. (1984). Effects of age and skill in typing. *Journal of Experimental Psychology: General, 113,* 345–371.

Salthouse, T. A. (1985). Speed of behavior and the implications for cognition. In J. E. Birren & K. W. Schaie (Eds.), *Handbook of the psychology of aging* (2nd ed., pp. 400–426). New York: Van Nostrand Reinhold.

Salthouse, T. A. (1988). Initiating the formalization of theories of cognitive aging. *Psychology and Aging, 3,* 3–16.

Sattler, J. M. (1982). Age effects on Wechsler Adult Intelligence Scale-Revised Tests. *Journal of Consulting and Clinical Psychology, 50,* 785–786.

Schaie, K. W. (1977). Quasi-experimental designs in the psychology of aging. In J. E. Birren & K. W. Schaie (Eds.), *Handbook of the psychology of aging* (pp. 39–58). New York: Van Nostrand Reinhold.

Schaie, K. W. (1977–1978). Toward a stage theory of adult cognitive development. *Aging and Human Development, 8,* 129–138.

Schaie, K. W. (1980). Intelligence and problem solving. In J. E. Birren & R. B. Sloane (Eds.), *Handbook of mental health and aging* (pp. 262–284). Englewood Cliffs, NJ: Prentice-Hall.

Schaie, K. W. (1983). The Seattle Longitudinal Study: A twenty-one year exploration of psychometric intelligence in adulthood. In K. W. Schaie (Ed.), *Longitudinal studies of adult psychological development* (pp. 64–135). New York: Guilford.

Schaie, K. W. (1984). Midlife influences upon intellectual functioning in old age. *International Journal of Behavioral Development, 7,* 463–478.

Schaie, K. W. (1985). *Manual for the Schaie-Thurstone Test of Mental Abilities (STAMAT).* Palo Alto, CA: Consulting Psychologists Press.

Schaie, K. W. (1986). Beyond calendar definitions of age, period and cohort: The general developmental model revisited. *Developmental Review, 6,* 252–277.

Schaie, K. W. (1987). Applications of psychometric intelligence to the prediction of everyday competence in the elderly. In C. Schooler & K. W. Schaie (Eds.), *Cognitive functioning and social structure over the life course* (pp. 50–59). New York: Ablex.

Schaie, K. W. (1988a). Ageism in psychological

research. *American Psychologist*, **43**, 179–183.

Schaie, K. W. (1988b). The delicate balance: Technology, intellectual competence, and normal aging. In G. Lesnoff-Caravaglia (Ed.), *Aging in a technological society* (Vol. 7, pp. 155–166). New York: Human Sciences Press.

Schaie, K. W. (1988c). The impact of research methodology on theory-building in the developmental sciences. In J. E. Birren & V. L. Bengston (Eds.), *Emergent theories of aging: Psychological and social perspectives on time, self and society* (pp. 41–58). New York: Springer.

Schaie, K. W. (1988d). Internal validity threats in studies of adult cognitive development. In M. L. Howe & C. J. Brainerd (Eds.), *Cognitive development in adulthood: Progress in cognitive development research* (pp. 241–272). New York: Springer-Verlag.

Schaie, K. W. (1988e). Introduction: Relating social structures and psychological aging processes. In K. W. Schaie & C. Schooler, (Eds.), *Social structure and aging: Psychological processes* (pp. 1–10). Hillsdale, NJ: Erlbaum.

Schaie, K. W. (1988f). Variability in cognitive function in the elderly: Implications for societal participation. In A. Woodhead, M. Bender, & R. Leonard (Eds.), *Phenotypic variation in populations: Relevance to risk management* (pp. 191–212). New York: Plenum.

Schaie, K. W. (1989a). Individual differences in rate of cognitive change in adulthood. In V. L. Bengston & K. W. Schaie (Eds.), *The course of later life: Research and reflections* (pp. 68–83). New York: Springer.

Schaie, K. W. (1989b). Late life potential and cohort differences in mental abilities. In M. Perlmutter (Ed.), *Late life potential*. Washington, DC: Gerontological Society of America.

Schaie, K. W. (1989c). The optimization of cognitive functioning in old age: Predictions based on cohort-sequential and longitudinal data. In P. B. Baltes & M. M. Baltes (Eds.), *Successful aging: Perspectives from the behavioral sciences*. London: Cambridge University Press.

Schaie, K. W. (1989d). Perceptual speed in adulthood: Cross-sectional and longitudinal studies. *Psychology and Aging*, **4**, (in press).

Schaie, K. W., & Hertzog, C. (1986). Toward a comprehensive model of adult intellectual development: Contributions of the Seattle Longitudinal Study. In R. J. Sternberg (Ed.), *Advances in human intelligence* (Vol. 3; pp. 79–118). Hillsdale, NJ: Erlbaum.

Schaie, K. W., & Willis, S. L. (1986). Can intellectual decline in the elderly be reversed? *Developmental Psychology*, **22**, 223–232.

Schaie, K. W., Willis, S. L., Hertzog, C., & Schulenberg, J. E. (1987). Effects of cognitive training upon primary mental ability structure. *Psychology and Aging*, **2**, 233–242.

Schaie, K. W., Willis, S. L., Jay, G., & Chipuer, H. (1989). Structural invariance of cognitive abilities across the adult life span: A cross-sectional study. *Developmental Psychology*, **25**, 652–662.

Scheidt, R. J., & Schaie, K. W. (1978). A taxonomy of situations for the elderly population: Generating situational criteria. *Journal of Gerontology*, **33**, 848–857.

Schmitz-Scherzer, R., & Thomae, H. (1983). Constancy and change of behavior in old age: Findings from the Bonn Longitudinal Study on Aging. In K. W. Schaie (Ed.), *Longitudinal studies of adult psychological development* (pp. 191–221). New York: Guilford.

Schooler, C. (1987). Cognitive effects of complex environments during the life span: A review and theory. In C. Schooler & K. W. Schaie (Eds.), *Cognitive functioning and social structure over the life course* (pp. 24–49). New York: Ablex.

Schooler, C., & Schaie, K. W. (Eds.) (1987). *Cognitive functioning and social structure over the life course*. Norwood, NJ: Ablex.

Scribner, S. (1984). Studying working intelligence. In B. Rogoff & J. Lave (Eds.), *Everyday cognition: Its development and social context* (pp. 9–40). Cambridge, MA: Harvard University Press.

Shock, N. W., Greulich, R. C., Andres, R., Arenberg, D., Costa, P. T., Jr., Lakatta, E. G., & Tobin, J. D. (1984). *Normal human aging: The Baltimore Longitudinal Study of Aging*. Washington, DC: Government Printing Office.

Siegler, I. C. (1983). Psychological aspects of the Duke Longitudinal Studies. In K. W. Schaie (Ed.), *Longitudinal studies of adult psychological development* (pp. 136–190). New York: Guilford.

Sinnott, J. D. (1984). Postformal reasoning: The

relativistic stage. In M. L. Commons, F. A. Richarda, & C. Armon (Eds.), *Beyond formal operations: Late adolescent and adult cognitive development* (pp. 298–325). New York: Praeger.

Smith, J., Dixon, R. A., & Baltes, P. B. (1988). Expertise in life planning: A new research approach to investigating aspects of wisdom. In M. L. Commons, J. D. Sinnott, F. A. Richards, & C. Armon (Eds.), *Beyond formal operations: Comparisons and applications of adolescent and adult developmental models*. New York: Praeger.

Spearman, C. (1904). "General intelligence": Objectively determined and measured. *American Journal of Psychology*, **15**, 201–292.

Stankov, L. (1988). Aging, attention and intelligence. *Psychology of Aging*, **3**, 59–74.

Sternberg, R. J. (1977). *Intelligence, information processing, and analogical reasoning: The componential analysis of human abilities*. Hillsdale, NJ: Erlbaum.

Sternberg, R., & Berg, C. (1987). What are theories of adult intellectual development theories of? In C. Schooler & K. W. Schaie (Eds.), *Cognitive functioning and social structure over the life course* (pp. 3–23). New York: Ablex.

Sternberg, R., & Wagner, B. (Eds.) (1986). *Practical intelligence*. London: Cambridge University Press.

Storandt, M., & Futterman, A. (1982). Stimulus size and performance on two subtests of the Wechsler Adult Intelligence Scale by younger and older adults. *Journal of Gerontology*, **37**, 602–693.

Thorndike, E. L., & Woodworth, R. S. (1901). Influence of improvement in one mental function upon the efficiency of other mental functions. *Psychological Review*, **8**, 247–261, 384–395, 553–564.

Thurstone, L. L. (1938). *Primary mental abilities*. Chicago: University of Chicago Press.

Thurstone, L. L., & Thurstone, T. G. (1949). *Examiner manual for the SRA Primary Mental Abilities Test*. Chicago: Science Research Associates.

White, N., & Cunningham, W. R. (1987). The age comparative construct validity of speeded cognitive factors. *Multivariate Behavioral Research*, **22**, 249–265.

Willis, S. L. (1985). Towards an educational psychology of the adult learner: Cognitive and intellectual bases. In J. E. Birren & K. W. Schaie (Eds.), *Handbook of the psychology of aging* (2nd ed., pp. 818–847). New York: Van Nostrand Reinhold.

Willis, S. L. (1987). Cognitive training and everyday competence. In K. W. Schaie (Ed.), *Annual Review of Gerontology and Geriatrics* (Vol. 7, pp. 159–188). New York: Springer.

Willis, S. L. (1989a). Cohort differences in cognitive aging: A sample case. In K. W. Schaie & C. Schooler (Eds.), *Social structure and aging: Psychological processes* (pp. 94–112). Hillsdale, NJ: Erlbaum.

Willis, S. L. (1989b). Improvement with cognitive training: Which dogs learn what tricks? In L. W. Poon (Ed.), *Everyday cognition in adult and late life*. New York: Cambridge University Press.

Willis, S. L. (In press). Long-term maintenance of cognitive training effects in the elderly. *Developmental Psychology*, in press.

Willis, S. L., & Baltes, P. B. (1981). Letter to the editor. *Journal of Gerontology*, **36**, 634–638.

Willis, S. L., & Schaie, K. W. (1986a). Practical intelligence in later adulthood. In R. J. Sternberg & R. K. Wagner (Eds.), *Practical intelligence: Origins of competence in the everyday world* (pp. 236–268). London: Cambridge University Press.

Willis, S. L., & Schaie, K. W. (1986b). Training the elderly on the ability factors of spatial orientation and inductive reasoning. *Psychology and Aging*, **1**, 239–247.

Willis, S. L., & Schaie, K. W. (1988). Gender differences in spatial ability in old age: Longitudinal and intervention findings. *Sex Roles*, **18**, 189–203.

Eighteen

Cognitive Competence and Expertise in Aging

Timothy A. Salthouse

In his concluding statement in a chapter concerned with the effects of aging on problem solving, Rabbitt (1977) suggested:

In view of the deterioration of memory and perceptual motor performance with advancing age, the right kind of question may well be not "why are old people so bad at cognitive tasks" but rather "how, in spite of growing disabilities, do old people preserve such relatively good performance?" (p. 623)

A major purpose of the current chapter is to examine salient issues related to Rabbitt's second question. Space limitations preclude an exhaustive review of the potentially relevant literature, and instead the emphasis is on conceptual distinctions and possible strategies of investigation relevant to this topic.

Rabbitt's question can be reformulated to focus on the reasons evaluations of cognitive competence and of cognitive ability have tended to lead to contradictory conclusions about the relation between increased age and effectiveness of cognitive functioning. That is, results from psychometric tests and experimental tasks designed to assess cognitive ability frequently reveal rather substantial age-related declines in the range from about 20 to 70 years of age (e.g., see reviews by Hultsch & Dixon, chapter 15, and by Light, chapter 16, this volume; and Kausler, 1982; Salthouse, 1982, 1985). On the other hand, adults in their 60s and 70s are seldom perceived to be less cognitively competent than adults in their 20s and 30s, and in fact, many of the most responsible and demanding leadership positions in society are routinely held by late middle-aged or older adults. Therefore, one of the greatest challenges in the field of psychology and aging is to account for the discrepancy between the inferred cognitive status of older adults based on their performance in psychometric testing situations and cognitive laboratories and that derived from observations of their successful functioning in everyday situations.

For the present purposes, *cognitive ability* will refer to the individual's intellectual level as measured by conventional tests of intelligence and cognitive functioning. Cognitive competence is more difficult to define, but it can be loosely in-

Handbook of the Psychology of Aging, Third Edition
Copyright © 1990 Academic Press, Inc. All rights of reproduction in any form reserved.

terpreted as the utilization of one's abilities—cognitive, interpersonal, and others—in adapting to particular situations. From this perspective, therefore, cognitive ability and cognitive competence are at least somewhat independent because it may be possible for a person with a low level of cognitive ability to achieve a high degree of competence by maximizing his or her usage of available abilities for functioning in specific situations.

The contrast between competence and ability is particularly striking when adults who are highly successful in cognitively demanding occupations are assessed with cognitive or psychometric procedures. An early example of this type of research is an important, but largely neglected, study by Sward (1945). The sample of participants in Sward's study consisted of 45 young adults (mean age 31.4, range 21 to 42 years) and 45 older adults (mean age 66.2, range 60 to 79 years), recruited from the faculty of two distinguished universities. Considerable effort was devoted to obtaining groups of individuals who were comparable with respect to socioeconomic status, field of professional specialization, frequency of election to college honor societies, and so on. Each participant was administered individually a battery of eight cognitive tests, with time limits imposed on only a few of the tests. Despite all participants being intelligent and presumably successful university professors, the younger faculty members performed significantly better than the older ones on six of the eight tests.

A more recent illustration of the discrepancy between cognitive test performance and inferred occupational competence was reported by Schludermann, Schludermann, Merryman, and Brown (1983). These investigators administered a battery of neuropsychological tests to 558 business executives of different ages. They summarized their results as follows: "The Old Executives seemed to function very adequately in high managerial positions which required judgment and complex decision making. Yet their performance level on neuropsychological tests, those measuring the most complex cognitive functions . . . was close to that of brain-damaged patients" (p. 153).

The preceding studies are but two instances of a common phenomenon in which results from laboratory studies and psychometric investigations seem to suggest that increased age is associated with lower levels of cognitive functioning, whereas observations of the same middle-aged and older adults outside of the laboratory generally reveal that they perform occupational and daily activities quite successfully. The complete explanation for this apparent paradox is not yet known, but four general categories of interpretation can be proposed. These attribute the discrepant age-related trends in cognitive ability and cognitive competence to differences in (a) the type of cognition being assessed; (b) the representativeness of either the behavioral observations, or the samples of individuals; (c) the sensitivity of the measurement or evaluation; and (d) the amount of relevant experience. Each of these categories will be discussed in turn.

I. Differences in the Type of Cognition

It is sometimes suggested that cognitive and psychometric psychologists have been preoccupied with a very narrow and limited range of cognitive functioning. According to this view, cognition is much more than the academic intelligence typically assessed in intelligence tests and cognitive tasks. Not much agreement exists concerning the exact nature of the alternatives to academic intelligence, but there seems little doubt that intelligence, at least as the construct has been assessed by existing tests, is only one of the determinants of success in many real-life activities.

Because cognitive competence is generally inferred from the capacity to perform familiar and ongoing activities, it is reasonable to propose that competence is the product of, among other things, the cumulative application of intellectual processes to specific situations. In this respect, therefore, cognitive competence might be considered to represent a compiled (Anderson, 1982), encapsulated (Rybash, Hoyer, & Roodin, 1986), or crystallized (Cattell, 1972; Horn, 1982) form of intelligence or cognitive ability.

One possible means of evaluating the view that the activities of one's occupation and of daily living involve a different type of cognition than that measured in typical psychometric tests or laboratory tasks is to examine patterns of correlations across the two sets of variables. Unfortunately, few studies of this type are available because of the difficulty of obtaining quantitative measures of real-world (i.e., outside the laboratory or testing situation) competence.

Some research has been conducted with surrogate measures of cognitive competence. For example, Willis and Schaie (1986) recently reported the correlations between measures of fluid and crystallized intelligence and scores on a paper-and-pencil test designed to assess skills of everyday living. One of the major findings from their project was that the best predictor of the performance of elderly adults in presumably everyday activities such as interpreting medicine bottle labels or understanding legal documents was the individual's performance on tests of fluid intelligence (e.g., reasoning and spatial relations). Because fluid intelligence is central to much of what is studied in contemporary cognitive psychology, this result seems inconsistent with the view that cognitive competence is determined by a different type of cognition than that evaluated by laboratory tasks and psychometric tests of cognitive ability. Further research on this issue is clearly warranted, however, if for no other reason than that the Willis and Schaie measure of cognitive competence was obtained with conventional psychometric test procedures (e.g., standardized paper-and-pencil tests), and only the content of the items distinguished this test from traditional assessments of cognitive or intellectual ability.

Suggestions that psychometric tests and laboratory tasks lack ecological validity, particularly for adults no longer in school, also seem to be based on the notion that competence (as reflected in ecologically valid activities) and ability (as measured in laboratory tasks) involve different types of cognition. However, these arguments are often weakened because the assessments of ecological validity are generally based on subjective judgments, rather than the application of well-specified empirical criteria. A more desirable procedure for evaluating the validity of cognitive ability tests, if appropriate criterion measures of cognitive competence could be identified, might be to conduct age-comparative validation studies to determine whether adults of varying ages have different patterns of correlations between measures of ability and measures of competence.

II. Differential Representativeness of Individuals or Observations

Incongruent evaluations of the effects of age on cognitive competence and on cognitive ability may also be a consequence of unrepresentative samples of individuals, or of behavioral observations, in one or both types of evaluations. For example, articles about aging and cognitive functioning in the popular press invariably include references to very old individuals who still are making remarkable musical, artistic, literary, or business achievements. Although these anecdotes are useful in promoting an optimistic perspective toward aging, and particularly in suggesting that the association between increased age and cognitive deterioration is not inevitable, they are often of very limited scientific value because of the unsystematic nature of the observations. That is, the mere fact that the individuals are selected for mention in this context suggests that they are probably not representative of their age peers. Furthermore, most anecdotal descriptions are highly selective, typically mentioning only a single aspect of a given individual's behavior, namely that which has led to his or her eminence, rather than being based on a comprehensive evaluation of the level of functioning across a broad range of cognitive dimensions. Because most people have at least some degree of control over the activities performed in everyday life and can avoid many of those that are perceived to be stressful or difficult, there is also the possibility of a positive selection bias in the sampling of behavioral observations of cognitive competence.

A similar selection bias may exist when cognitive competence evaluations are based on comparisons of young and old adults in the same occupation or profession. In this case, the considerable attrition that occurs in many occupations raises the possibility that only the most successful individuals survive in the occupation until late middle or old age. A probable consequence of this type of selective attrition is that the surviving members may not be as representative of their age peers as the young members.

Although the preceding comments have been primarily directed at assessments of cognitive competence, it should not be inferred that laboratory and psychometric studies of cognitive ability are free of these types of problems. Very few studies have involved samples of participants that accurately represent the entire population, and all can be criticized for neglecting potentially important aspects of cognition. For purposes of comparison, however, it is

the relative representativeness of individuals and behaviors across the two types of assessments that is important. Therefore, unless there is a similar sensitivity to the importance of unbiased samples and the assessment of many types of cognition in evaluations of cognitive competence and of cognitive ability, it may be impossible to rule out the hypothesis that what appear to be different age-related patterns in competence and ability are at least partially attributable to a lack of equivalence in the people, or range of behaviors, being evaluated.

III. Different Standards of Evaluation

A third possible interpretation of the apparent discrepancy in the adult age trends in cognitive competence and cognitive ability is that different standards of functioning might be used in the evaluations of competence and ability. This view has been succinctly stated by Bromley (1971) as follows:

Most of the ordinary demands of the adult life do not push the individual close to the limits of his mental abilities, just as they do not push him close to the limits of his physical capacities. Adult life tends to be geared to normal or low average levels of psychobiological functioning and to well-practised behaviour patterns, and hence the diminished fluid abilities of the elderly are not conspicuous. (p. 294)

According to this perspective, therefore, the discrepancy between what seems to be growth or maintenance of competence across adulthood and the age-related declines observed in tests of cognitive ability might be due to more rigorous or demanding standards imposed in the evaluation of cognitive ability compared with cognitive competence. This point can be elaborated by considering an analogy between the assessment of driving performance and the assessment of cognitive functioning. That is, driving performance is evaluated quite differently by government agencies responsible for granting driving licenses and by motor sports organizations attempting to establish a ranking of professional race car drivers. In the first case, the criterion is a relatively low level of proficiency, whereas in the latter case the goal is presumably to determine the ultimate behavior of which humans (in combination with automobiles) are capable.

Because it is often more important to know whether an individual can function within a specified set of environmental demands than to know how much above that level he or she could potentially function, the competence criterion may be more meaningful for many practical purposes. However, if one is interested in theoretical issues, and specifically understanding how and why increased age is associated with reduced levels of cognitive functioning, then evaluations of competence are less valuable because they may reflect the minimum, rather than the maximum, of which the individual is capable.

The different goals pursued by applied and theoretical researchers have probably contributed to some of the confusion about the magnitude, and practical significance, of age differences in cognitive functioning. Specifically, because theoretically oriented studies are designed to understand why age differences occur, they have quite naturally tended to emphasize situations exhibiting the greatest age-related differences in cognition. Although this strategy of concentrating on the most extreme or salient manifestations of a phenomenon is reasonable, it can result in distorted impressions about the frequency and importance of age-related differences in cognition for functioning outside the laboratory. On the other hand, researchers interested in devising interventions to maintain competent levels of functioning among older adults often tend to focus on the abilities that have been preserved instead of those that may have declined and to rely on minimum rather than maximum standards of functioning in their assessments.

It is obviously difficult to determine whether evaluations of different types of behaviors have comparable sensitivity. Nonetheless, without some means of ensuring that potential age-related differences can be detected as easily in assessments of cognitive competence as in cognitive ability, at least some of the apparent discrepancy in age trends might reasonably be attributed to differences in the standards of evaluation for the two types of cognitive functioning.

IV. Differential Amounts of Experience

The fourth category of explanation for the competence–ability discrepancy focuses on the disparate amounts of experience involved in measures of cognitive competence and measures of cognitive ability. Few behavioral measures seem immune to improvements with practice or experience, and it is often found that the within-individual changes in performance as a function of experience are much larger than the variations existing across different individuals at the same level of experience. Experiential effects of this type are relevant to the competence–ability discrepancy because age and experience are generally positively correlated in daily and occupational activities, and therefore high levels of competence might be achieved despite age-related declines in the novice, or unpracticed, level of proficiency in many cognitive abilities. In assessments of cognitive ability, on the other hand, special efforts are often deliberately employed to minimize the effects of past experience, for example, by using stimulus material that is equally novel and unfamiliar to all potential examinees.

It can be debated whether the "best" assessment of an individual's performance is obtained by allowing natural variations in amount of relevant experience or by attempting to make comparisons when everyone is assumed to be equally inexperienced in the activity of concern. Regardless of the merits of the two approaches, however, it seems likely that evaluations of cognitive competence and cognitive ability differ substantially in the extent of experiential influence. As suggested in an earlier context: "It is thus conceivable that contrasts in the laboratory involve near-novice levels of performance, while those in the activities of everyday life consist of older adult experts being compared with young adult novices" (Salthouse, 1987a, p. 143).

However, merely asserting that the effects of age might be minimal in activities in which individuals are highly experienced is inadequate unless there is also some specification of the mechanisms underlying the relation between age and experience. Research on this topic is still in its infancy, but several relevant issues can be identified.

An initial, and very fundamental, question is whether age effects are minimized only when age and experience are positively correlated or also are attenuated whenever people of different ages are compared after extensive, but equivalent, amounts of experience. Answers to this question are likely to be helpful in distinguishing among alternative interpretations of the relation between age and experience and in clarifying the exact nature of age effects in cognition.

For example, a discovery that age differences are reduced when people of all ages become more experienced with the relevant activities would imply that the age differences observed at early levels of experience with a task are attributable to short-term, easily modifiable, processes. Few cognitive studies with this type of Age × Skill interaction have apparently been reported. However an Age × Skill interaction in the opposite direction, with

the age effects most pronounced among the individuals with the highest degree of skill, and presumably experience, has been reported in analytical studies of performance in bridge (Charness, 1979) and in chess (Charness, 1981). These findings should probably be interpreted cautiously because they are based on relatively small samples of research participants. Nevertheless, they appear incompatible with the attenuated-age-difference interpretation and are more consistent with the speculations of Baltes and his colleagues (e.g., Baltes, 1987; Kliegl & Baltes, 1987) that, if it is assumed that increased age is associated with reductions in one's performance potential, then age differences might be expected to be greatest when everyone is functioning near the limits of his or her capabilities.

Many interesting questions also would remain if it were concluded that age effects were minimized only when age and experience were confounded, that is, when increased age was associated with greater amounts of experience. For example, at least four alternative interpretations could be proposed to account for a finding that age-related effects on measures of cognitive functioning are attenuated when age and amount of experience are positively correlated. Probably the simplest interpretation is that experience maintains or preserves abilities that would decline in the absence of this experience. This maintenance perspective would therefore suggest that people of different ages might exhibit similar levels of competency in a given activity domain because continuous and extensive experience has prevented declines in relevant abilities, and therefore equivalent degrees of competency are achieved with the same combination of abilities at all ages.

A second interpretation of the relationship between age and experience is that with increased experience, the individual learns to accommodate to his or her declining abilities by avoiding deficit-revealing situations. Accommodation to real or perceived declines in one's activities is a special case of experiential adaptation because competence is maintained across the adult years only by altering the activities in which one engages. Nevertheless, it may be quite effective because both self-assessed and external appraisals of competence might be maintained at high levels if the individual can adapt to his or her changing abilities by pursuing those activities in which relevant abilities have been preserved or increased and avoiding those in which relevant abilities have declined.

Two additional interpretations are relevant when equivalent levels of competence in the same activities are preserved throughout the adult years despite substantial declines in relevant cognitive abilities. One view is that although the initial development of competence may have been dependent upon efficient functioning of cognitive abilities, continued maintenance of the same level of competence no longer may require the same degree of efficiency in those abilities. Salthouse (1989) referred to this interpretation as the compilation perspective because of parallels to computer programs that have been assembled from subroutines, but once compiled, are no longer sensitive to changes in the efficiency of the constituent parts.

Preservation of competence in the face of declines in relevant abilities could also be interpreted as indicating that increased experience somehow leads to a compensation for declining abilities. The compensation interpretation has been quite popular, as documented by the sample of quotations in Table I containing a reference to the concept of compensation.

Although it is obvious from these quotations that many researchers believe in the idea of compensation, it is equally apparent that very few explicit proposals have yet been offered concerning the manner in which the hypothesized compensation occurs. This is a serious deficiency because in order to have confidence that compensation actually takes place, it is important that the specific mechanisms be identified that allow aging adults to achieve high levels of competence or proficiency in cognitive activities despite the declines that may be occurring in relevant cognitive abilities.

Because it is unlikely that the same

Table I
Representative References to the Concept of Compensation

Miles (1942, p. 772)
 . . . Well-formed and practiced mental habits plus the knowledge increment may tend to compensate in later age for the quickness in comprehension and action that typify early maturity.
McFarland (1956, p. 235)
 . . . one of the most important questions in the field of job placement and aging, is as follows: When in the aging process, is physiological and psychological deterioration no longer compensated for by past experience?
Welford (1958, p. 286)
 . . . older people have a remarkable ability to compensate for any changes which may tend to impair their performance and show an automatic and unconscious reordering of their activity to make the best use of what capacities they have . . . a process . . . we may call unconscious optimization.
Murrell and Griew (1965, p. 65)
 . . . experience gained over months or years of work . . . can, in many instances, fully compensate for decrease in biological capacity with age.
Schludermann, Schludermann, Merryman, and Brown (1983, p. 153)
 Compared to a young executive, the old executive may be a more effective decision maker, because he has acquired a much richer background of relevant experience. The more extensive experience of the old executive may more than compensate for any decline in "fluid intelligence."

---

compensatory mechanisms would be used across quite different activities, precise specification of compensatory mechanisms almost certainly will require detailed analyses of particular activities. It is nevertheless possible to propose some tentative guidelines to help in the identification of compensatory mechanisms, independent of the specific activity domain being investigated.

A first guideline is that although compensation implies the elimination of age differences, its usage probably should be limited to situations in which the individual takes an active role in the compensatory process. The individual's involvement need not be conscious, but without some requirement of active involvement it would be possible to claim that minimizing age differences by the removal of an obstacle or a barrier (e.g., providing eyeglasses to a visually impaired person) is an example of compensation. Because relevant cognitive processes probably do not change with these types of interventions, they might more appropriately be considered instances of accommodation rather than compensation.

A second guideline is that compensation should be inferred by the existence of a different composition of the overall activity, in the sense that similar levels of proficiency are achieved in different ways at different ages. From this perspective, therefore, compensation might be interpreted as a manifestation of age-specific expertise because the compensation concept implies that a comparable level of expertise is achieved in different ways at different ages. It is important to note that this functional definition of compensation as an age- or experience-related difference in the relative importance of various abilities to competence in a given activity does not imply a particular causal ordering of the declining abilities and the improving (compensatory) processes. The term *compensation* might therefore be applied to any temporal ordering of constituent

abilities and compensatory processes, although theoretical interpretations would probably differ considerably depending on whether the hypothesized compensatory processes begin to increase before, after, or simultaneous with the decline of relevant cognitive abilities.

A third guideline for the investigation of compensatory mechanisms is that the amount of relevant experience should be sufficient to allow plausible generalizations to real-world activities. The quantity of experience necessary to progress beyond a novice level obviously varies with the type of activity being performed, but one would rarely be considered competent in cognitively oriented occupations with less than at least a week of on-the-job experience. It therefore seems desirable that research on the relation between age and experience should involve a minimum of 40 hours of on-task experience, and preferably much more. This is not to say that it is impossible to identify differences in the manner in which an activity is performed with lesser amounts of experience but rather that it may not be plausible to attribute those differences to experientially based compensatory mechanisms.

What type of research might meet these guidelines and allow the maintenance, accomodation, compilation, and compensation interpretations of the age-experience relationship to be investigated? Because of the pragmatic constraints associated with providing sufficient amounts of practice in controlled laboratory settings, it seems likely that the research will attempt to capitalize on naturally occurring variations in experience. At least two strategies based on this idea have been proposed that could be used to examine the effects that experience might have on cognitive ability and cognitive competence.

One strategy, termed the Molar Equivalence–Molecular Decomposition strategy, involves selecting participants from a wide range of ages and experience levels but who, in the aggregate, exhibit no systematic relation between age and proficiency in the molar activity of interest. The molar activity then can be decomposed into molecular components, and the age trends examined in each component. The fundamental question of interest in this strategy is whether people of different ages achieve the same level of molar competency by means of the same molecular components (see Charness, 1981; and Salthouse, 1984, 1987a,b, 1989, for examples and further discussion of this strategy).

A second strategy is almost the converse of the former in that it involves selecting participants of different ages who do not differ in the efficiency or effectiveness of relevant component processes, and then examining whether there are age differences in the proficiency of a molar activity. This strategy, termed the Molar Analysis–Molecular Equivalence strategy (Salthouse, 1989), allows the investigator to determine whether there are age differences in the manner in which component processes are integrated or coordinated in complex activities. An interesting possibility, for example, is that experientially based compensation is manifested in a more efficiently organized or integrated assembly of component abilities, and if so, it should be apparent with the application of this strategy.

V. Summary

This chapter has been concerned with the topic of cognitive competence, defined as the degree of success in functioning within a specific environment. An issue of considerable importance within the psychology of aging is what is responsible for the apparent discrepancy in the age-related trends in cognitive competence (presumed to increase at least through middle adulthood) and in cognitive ability (often thought to decrease more or less continuously from early adulthood). Four hypotheses have been identified that might account for this discrepancy. These are that cognitive competence and cognitive ability might differ in (a) the type of cognition being assessed; (b) the representativeness of the behavioral observations or samples of individuals; (c) the sensitivity of the measurement or evaluation; and (d) the amount of relevant experience. Because age and experience are positively correlated in many real-life situations, it was suggested that a particularly promising direction for future research is the investigation of how age and experience interact to influence cognitive functioning. Process-oriented research aimed at distinguishing among the maintenance, accommodation, compilation, and compensation interpretations of the age-experience relation would be very informative in this respect and consequently is strongly recommended.

References

Anderson, J. R. (1982). Acquisition of cognitive skill. *Psychological Review*, **89**, 369–406.

Baltes, P. B. (1987). Theoretical propositions of life-span developmental psychology: On the dynamics between growth and decline. *Developmental Psychology*, **23**, 611–626.

Bromley, D. B. (1971). The effects of ageing on intelligence. *Impact of Science on Technology*, **21**, 291–301.

Cattell, R. B. (1972). *Abilities: Their structure, growth, and action*. Boston: Houghton-Mifflin.

Charness, N. (1979). Components of skill in bridge. *Canadian Journal of Psychology*, **33**, 1–16.

Charness, N. (1981). Aging and skilled problem solving. *Journal of Experimental Psychology: General*, **110**, 21–38.

Horn, J. (1982). The aging of human abilities. In B. B. Wolman (Ed.), *Handbook of developmental psychology*. Englewood Cliffs, NJ: Prentice-Hall.

Kausler, D. H. (1982). *Experimental psychology and human aging*. New York: Wiley.

Kliegl, R., & Baltes, P. B. (1987). Theory-guided analysis of mechanisms of development and aging through testing-the-limits and research on expertise. In C. Schooler & K. W. Schaie (Eds.), *Cognitive functioning and social structure over the life course*. Norwood, NJ: Ablex.

McFarland, R. A. (1956). Functional efficiency, skills and employment. In J. E. Anderson (Ed.), *Psychological aspects of aging*. Washington, DC: American Psychological Association.

Miles, W. R. (1942). Psychological aspects of ageing. In E. W. Cowdry (Ed.), *Problems of ageing*. Baltimore: Williams & Wilkins.

Murrell, K. F. H., & Griew, S. (1965). Age, experience, and speed of response. In A. T. Welford & J. E. Birren (Eds.), *Behavior, aging, and the nervous system*. Springfield, IL: Thomas.

Rabbitt, P. M. A. (1977). Changes in problem solving ability in old age. In J. E. Birren & K. W. Schaie (Eds.), *Handbook of the psychology of aging*. New York: Van Nostrand Reinhold.

Rybash, J. M., Hoyer, W. J., & Roodin, P. A. (1986). *Adult cognition and aging*. New York: Pergamon.

Salthouse, T. A. (1982). *Adult cognition*. New York: Springer.

Salthouse, T. A. (1984). Effects of age and skill in typing. *Journal of Experimental Psychology: General*, **113**, 345–371.

Salthouse, T. A. (1985). *A theory of cognitive aging*. Amsterdam: North-Holland.

Salthouse, T. A. (1987a). Age, experience, and compensation. In C. Schooler & K. W. Schaie (Eds.), *Cognitive functioning and social structure over the life course*. Norwood, NJ: Ablex.

Salthouse, T. A. (1987b). The role of experience in cognitive aging. *Annual Review of Gerontology and Geriatrics*, **7**.

Salthouse, T. A. (1989). Aging and skilled performance. In A. Colley & J. Beech (Eds.), *The acquisition and performance of cognitive skills*. New York: Wiley (in press).

Schludermann, E. H., Schludermann, S. M., Merryman, P. W., & Brown, B. W. (1983). Halstead's studies in the neuropsychology of aging. *Archives of Gerontology and Geriatrics*, **2**, 49–172.

Sward, K. (1945). Age and mental ability in superior men. *American Journal of Psychology*, **58**, 443–479.

Welford, A. T. (1958). *Ageing and human skill*. London: Oxford University Press.

Willis, S. L., & Schaie, K. W. (1986). Practical intelligence in later adulthood. In R. J. Sternberg & R. K. Wagner (Eds.), *Practical intelligence*. New York: Cambridge University Press.

Nineteen

Creativity and Wisdom in Aging

Dean Keith Simonton

I. Introduction

Human beings share numerous capabilities with other organisms, like the abilities to discriminate stimuli, learn concepts, and set goals. Indeed, many of these skills are found not only in advanced animals but in inanimate computers as well. Yet, our species can boast two abilities that fail to have proper counterparts elsewhere. Both are linked with our scientific designation, *Homo sapiens*, or "man the wise." The first capacity is *wisdom*. Rather than live from moment to moment with minimal reflection and even less foresight, human beings can acquire a broad perspective on life, discerning a larger view of life's meaning than permitted by a hand-to-mouth subsistence. Presumably such wisdom allows individuals to reach an equilibrium with themselves, others, and the world that smooths over the vicissitudes of mundane existence. The second capacity is *creativity*. A hallmark of our species is the ability to innovate, to change the environment rather than merely adjust to it in a more passive

sense. So, we create scientific theories, compose artistic masterpieces, and construct imaginative utopias. Whether such creative activities are necessarily wise is a profound question, yet we cannot deny that human creativity and wisdom have no close parallels among other organisms and machines. Perhaps because of this relative uniqueness, both concepts are very difficult to define and measure, and so at least a portion of this chapter will deal with how creativity and wisdom can be operationally defined. Yet the primary task of this essay is to discuss how these two special qualities change as a function of the aging process. This question, of course, has attracted much speculation over the centuries.

In ancient times, and in most traditional cultures and virtually all Eastern civilizations, the addition of years to one's life signified the accumulation of wisdom (see Clayton & Birren, 1980). In classical Western civilizations, for instance, Homer made Nestor the oldest but the wisest of the Greeks fighting the Trojans. Yet, since the Renaissance, the Western world began

Handbook of the Psychology of Aging, Third Edition
Copyright © 1990 Academic Press, Inc. All rights of reproduction in any form reserved.

to adopt a less respectful attitude toward the acquisitions of old age. Most conspicuous is the notion that creativity is the prerogative of youth, that aging is synonymous with a decrement in the capacity for generating and accepting innovations. Paul Dirac, who became a Nobel laureate at age 31 for work he published when merely 25, has expressed this belief in a rather extreme way:

> Age is, of course, a fever chill
> that every physicist must fear.
> He's better dead than living still
> when once he's past his thirtieth
> year.
> (quoted in Jungk, 1958, p. 27)

Thus, aging may entail counterpoised gains and losses. Wisdom might grow with advancing maturity but at the expense of the capacity for creativity.

How valid are these commonplace perceptions? Do wisdom and creativity really display opposite longitudinal trends over the life span? To address this question, the present chapter begins by briefly reviewing the central empirical findings of life-span changes in both creativity and wisdom. Next, an attempt is made to integrate these data by reviewing some empirical and theoretical results that seem germane to both characteristics.

II. Creativity

Creativity is a nebulous concept that does not lend itself to easy scientific assessment. For the most part, researchers have adopted one of two distinct approaches to evaluating this construct (Kogan, 1973; Romaniuk & Romaniuk, 1981). On the one hand, many investigators have devised psychometric measures of those cognitive processes most relevant to creativity, usually in the guise of standardized pencil-and-paper tests (e.g., Guilford, 1967; Mednick, 1962). Other researchers

have exploited biographical and historical data on actual creative achievements in order to define historiometric indices of the same construct (e.g., Dennis, 1966; Lehman, 1953).

A. Psychometric Indicators

There exists an abundance of measures that purport to assess some form of creativity. Although these instruments were first conceived for purposes of gauging individual differences in creative potential, it is evident that age-related fluctuations in performance on these tests may indicate how creativity changes with aging. The bulk of these measures gauge some type of "divergent thinking," as distinguished from the "convergent thinking" tapped by intelligence tests (Guilford, 1967). That is, the focus is on determining how well an individual can generate a multitude of alternative, novel responses to a given stimulus. Almost without exception, investigations into longitudinal changes in performance on these instruments show a decline with age (e.g., McCrae, Arenberg, & Costa, 1987), although sometimes a peak will appear before the decrement, indicating a curvilinear or nonmonotonic age function with an optimum somewhere around the late 30s of life (e.g., Alpaugh & Birren, 1977; McCrae et al., 1987; cf. Cornelius & Caspi, 1987). Moreover, even if not all creativity tests exhibit identical age-related trends (e.g., McCrae et al., 1987), in no instance can creative capacity be said to increase significantly with aging in the last half of life (cf. Cornelius & Caspi, 1987; Jaquish & Ripple, 1981). Thus the notion that creativity is the privilege of youth seems to possess some merit, at least as an expected longitudinal trend (Simonton, 1988a).

Admittedly, the last conclusion is somewhat weakened by two principal methodological difficulties often plaguing this research. First, longitudinal changes in creativity most frequently are inferred from cross-sectional data, a hazardous procedure that invites the confounding of age and cohort effects (e.g., Alpaugh, Parham, Cole, & Birren, 1982; Ruth & Birren, 1985). Fortunately, enough longitudinal studies have been conducted to suggest that the downward turn on most creativity measures cannot be dismissed simply as an artifact of cohort effects (e.g., McCrae *et al.*, 1987). Second, even if a psychometric measure has been labeled a *creativity test*, that does not automatically mean that such an indicator assesses real-life creativity. On the contrary, the validity coefficients for such instruments tend to be quite modest, even negligible (Simonton, 1988a; cf. Alpaugh *et al.*, 1982). The appropriate response to this potential objection is to resort to evaluations of actual creative performance, using tabulations of contributions over the life span.

B. Historiometric Indicators

Life-span developmental studies of creative achievement began with Quetelet in 1835, so that by the time of Lehman's 1953 book, *Age and Achievement*, this research formed a century-old tradition (see also Beard, 1874). This work has centered on three core topics: (a) the age curve that specifies how creative output varies over the course of a career, (b) the relation between quantity and quality of output (i.e., between "productivity" and "creativity"), and (c) the connection between productive precocity, longevity, and rate of output (Simonton, 1988a).

1. Age Curves

If one plots creative output as a function of age, productivity tends to rise fairly rapidly to a definite peak and thereafter tends to decline gradually (Cole, 1979; Dennis, 1966; Horner, Rushton, & Vernon, 1986; Lehman, 1953; Simonton, 1980, 1988a). Put approximately, if one tabulates the number of contributions

(e.g., publications, paintings, compositions, and so on) per time unit, the resulting longitudinal fluctuations may be described by an "inverted backward-J" curve. Typically, the peak of this nonmonotonic, concave downward curve comes somewhere in the late 30s or early 40s of life—about the same ages as observed in the psychometric inquiries. Assuming a normal life span, a creative individual in the last decade of his or her career will exhibit an output rate about half that observed at the career peak, although the rate will usually exceed that witnessed in the first career decade (Simonton, 1984a, 1988a).

To be more precise, the location of the peak, as well as the magnitude of the postpeak decline, tends to vary depending on the domain of creative achievement. At one extreme, some fields are characterized by relatively early peaks, usually around the early 30s or even late 20s in chronological units, with somewhat steep descents thereafter. This age-related pattern apparently holds for such endeavors as lyric poetry, pure mathematics, and theoretical physics (Dennis, 1966; Lehman, 1953; Simonton, 1975). At the contrary extreme, the typical trends in other endeavors may display a leisurely rise to a comparatively late peak, in the late 40s or even 50s chronologically, with a minimal, if not largely absent, drop-off afterwards. This more elongated curve holds for such domains as novel writing, history, philosophy, and general scholarship (Dennis, 1966; Lehman, 1953; Simonton, 1975). Of course, many disciplines exhibit age curves somewhat between these two outer limits, with a maximum output rate around chronological age 40, and a notable, if yet moderate, decline there after. Productive contributions in psychology, for example, tend to follow this pattern (Horner *et al.*, 1976). Whatever the specifics, these interdisciplinary contrasts do not appear to be arbitrary but instead have been shown to be invariant across different cultures and distinct historical periods (Lehman, 1962; Quetelet, 1835/1968; Simonton, 1975).

2. Quantity and Quality

A distinction can be made, of course, between quantity and quality of output: Quantity is mere productivity, whereas quality signifies true creativity. For some time in the empirical literature it was thought that the age curves for quantity and quality were far from identical, that the drop in output in the last decades was less pronounced when total productivity was assessed rather than restricting the tabulations to notable contributions (e.g., Dennis, 1966; Lehman, 1953). However, when suitable methodological precautions are taken, very different results emerge (Simonton, 1977a, 1984b, Chapter 6, 1985, 1988c, Chapter 4). First, if one calculates the age curves separately for major and minor works within careers, the resulting functions are basically identical. Second, if the overall age trend is removed from the within-career tabulations of both quantity and quality, minor and major contributions still fluctuate together. Those periods in a creator's life that see the most masterpieces also witness the most easily forgotten productions, on the average (e.g., Simonton, 1980). In other words, the "quality ratio," or the proportion of major products to total output per age unit, tends to fluctuate randomly over the course of any career. The quality ratio neither increases nor decreases with age, nor does it assume some curvilinear form (see Simonton, 1977a, 1985). What these two results signify is that if we select the contribution rather than the age period as the unit of analysis, then age becomes irrelevant to determining the success of a particular contribution (Oromaner, 1977; Over, 1988).

This longitudinal linkage between quantity and quality can be subsumed under the more general "constant-proba-bility-of-success model" of creative output (Simonton, 1977a, 1984b, 1985, 1988c, Chapter 4). According to this hypothesis, creativity is a probabilistic consequence of productivity, a relationship that holds both within and across careers. Within single careers, the count of major works per age period will be a positive function of total works generated each period, yielding a quality ratio that exhibits no systematic developmental trends. And across careers, those individual creators who are the most productive will also, on the average, tend to be the most creative: Individual variation in quantity is positively associated with variation in quality (Dennis, 1954a; Simonton, 1984b, Chapter 6, 1985, 1988c, Chapter 4).

3. Precocity, Longevity, and Output Rate

Individual differences in lifetime output are substantial (Simonton, 1984b, Chapter 5, 1988c, Chapter 4). So skewed is the cross-sectional distribution of total contributions that usually the top 10% of the most prolific elite can be credited with around 50% of all contributions, whereas the bottom 50% of the least productive workers can claim only 15% of the total work, and the most productive contributor is usually about 100 times more prolific than the least (Dennis, 1954a, 1955). Logically, there are three independent ways of achieving an impressive lifetime output: (1) the individual may exhibit exceptional precocity, beginning contributions at an uncommonly early age; (2) the individual may attain a notable lifetime total by producing until quite late in life, and thereby displaying productive longevity; (3) the individual may boast phenomenal output rates throughout a career, without regard to the career's onset and termination. These three components are mathematically distinct, and so may have almost any arbitrary correlation with each other, whether positive, negative, or zero, without altering their respective contributions to total productivity (Simonton, 1988a, 1988c, Chapter 4). When we look at the empirical data, we notice three things.

First, as might be expected, precocity, longevity, and output rate each are associated strongly with final lifetime output. That is, those who generate the most contributions at the end of a career also tend to have begun their careers at earlier ages, ended their careers at later ages, and produced at extraordinary rates throughout their careers (see, e.g., Albert, 1975; Cole, 1979; Dennis, 1954a,b; Lehman, 1953; Raskin, 1936; Simonton, 1977b; Zhao & Jiang, 1986).

Second, these three components are strongly linked with each other: Those who are precocious also tend to display longevity, and both precocity and longevity are positively associated with high output rates per age unit (see, e.g., Dennis, 1954ab; Horner et al., 1986; Simonton, 1977b). The relation between longevity and precocity becomes particularly evident when care is taken first to control for the impact of differential life span (Dennis, 1954b). Because those who are very prolific at a precocious age can afford to die young and still end up with a respectable lifetime output, a negative relation emerges between precocity and life span, necessitating that careers be equalized on life span before the correlation coefficients are calculated (Simonton, 1977b; Zhao & Jiang, 1986).

Third, despite the positive association of lifetime productivity with precocity, longevity, and high output rates, considerable empirical evidence demonstrates the age-related stability of the career peak (Simonton, 1988c, Chapter 4). That is, the age at which a creator generates the most contributions—which according to the constant-probability-of-success model is the age at which the best work is most likely to materialize—is a function of the discipline rather than the lifetime productivity or creative eminence of the given individual. In the sciences, for instance, the correlation between the eminence of psychologists and the age at which they contribute their most influential work is almost exactly zero (Zusne, 1976). And in the arts, such as literary and musical creativity, the age at which a masterpiece is generated is independent of the magnitude of the achievement (Simonton, 1975, 1977a,b). So, the expected age optimum generating quantity and hence quality of output is apparently dependent solely on the particular form of creative expression (also see Raskin, 1936).

III. Wisdom

Even if wisdom is an older notion than creativity, the subject has become a direct focus of psychological research only very recently. As a consequence, the literature on wisdom is far smaller than that on creativity. Moreover, relevant research is somewhat fragmented. On the one hand, several developmental psychologists have proposed theories that feature some implications for our understanding of wisdom. For instance, from the Piagetian school of thought emerged Kohlberg's (1973a) theory of moral development, a theory that may be interpreted as specifying the acquisition of ethical wisdom in a sequence of stages. Unfortunately, because moral development tends to cease in early adulthood, Kohlberg's scheme is not informative about the last years of life, when the accumulation of wisdom might even accelerate (however, see Kohlberg, 1973b). More directly applicable, therefore, is Erikson's (1959) theory of socioemotional stages that proceed all the way to advanced maturity. In this system, the latter part of life obliges the person to resolve a sequence of life crises. Most relevant is the final conflict between integrity and despair, the favorable resolution of which yields renunciation and wisdom. Although there is no theoretical guarantee that all persons will make the right choices at these nodal points in life-span development, those that do may be said to have grown in wisdom with age (see also Clayton, 1975).

On the other hand, empirical research on wisdom has been guided less by some overarching theory and instead devoted to preliminary spadework. Even if the results to date are by no means conclusive, such exploratory inquiries are probably essential if subsequent theorizing is to rest on a firm foundation. In any event, these empirical investigations are of two types. First, some researchers have attempted to assess how people generally perceive wisdom: Under what conditions can a person be judged wise? For example, Sternberg (1985) has examined the "implicit personality theories" underlying judgments regarding three affiliated but independent notions, namely intelligence, creativity, and wisdom. Others have discerned how concepts of wisdom differ for distinct age groups (e.g., Clayton & Birren, 1980). The upshot of these investigations is that a certain consensus exists on what sorts of personal attributes count as wisdom, with some shifts in particular components of the wisdom schema over the life span. For instance, older persons in comparison to younger persons are less likely to link wisdom with old age, perhaps itself an article of wisdom!

The second type of inquiry, though more rare by far, is much more germane to the topic of the current chapter. Rather than investigate how wisdom is perceived, some researchers have striven to assess directly the actual possession of wisdom by individuals. Here the bulk of the pertinent work has been conducted by Baltes and his coworkers at the Berlin Max Planck Institute for Human Development and Education, and most of it is quite new (see e.g., Baltes, 1987; Dittmann-Kohli & Baltes, 1989; Smith, Dixon, & Baltes, 1989). After operationalizing wisdom in terms of such attributes as a rich factual knowledge about life, life-span contextualism, and uncertainty of life, measures are devised that ask subjects to deal with concrete life issues, yielding protocols that can be scored for the expected attributes. Among the various aims of this research is to determine whether the possession of wisdom grows with age. More precisely, the expectation is that even though the acquisition of wisdom is by no means guaranteed among elderly citizens, the individuals who are most wise will be disproportionately found among the older subjects. This goal yet remains at a distance, although the approach holds immense promise. By defining measures of wisdom, developmental psychologists come closer to a fuller appreciation of the commonplace idea that wisdom is a gift of age.

IV. Integration

The literature reviewed so far suggests that life-span development in the later years may indeed witness a trade-off between a loss in creativity and a gain in wisdom. This conclusion is only reinforced by several theories of creative productivity that apparently imply an antithetical longitudinal relationship between these two skills. For instance, Mumford (1984) has explicated the age-decrement in creative output, such as those tabulated by Lehman (1953), in terms of a shift in "adaptive style"—from accommodation to realistic control (see also Mumford & Gustafson, 1988). In a similar vein, Simonton's (1988b,c) chance-configuration theory holds that creativity is driven by "self-organization" that over the life span, entails a gradual transformation in cognitive structure from an inefficient and disorganized "intuitive" mode to a more efficient and hierarchical "analytical" mode. Each of these hypothesized transformations may be considered age-related exchanges of creativity for wisdom.

Furthermore, this conversion may parallel the contrary age distributions of "fluid" versus "crystallized" intelligence (Horn & Cattell, 1972), where fluid intelligence entails the abstract capacity for problem solving (creativity), crystallized intelligence, the acquisition of practical experience and expertise (wisdom) (cf. Baltes, Dittmann-Kohli, & Dixon, 1984).

Nevertheless, not all theories concur that the linkage need be inverse. For example, Beard's (1874) two-factor theory holds that creative achievement is the product of enthusiasm, which peaks early in adulthood and then declines, and experience, which expands continuously with age. Although some endeavors, such as lyric poetry, may demand a dominating proportion of enthusiasm, other endeavors, such as philosophy, history, and scholarship, may require the significant infusion of experience. Because these last forms of creativity need more wisdom, contributions in these domains peak far later in life, and the age decrement in the later years is negligible (Dennis, 1966; Simonton, 1988a). These historiometric results are reinforced by psychometric findings as well: Even if performance on divergent-style tests declines in the latter half of life, tests that assess problem-solving ability regarding more everyday issues show an augmentation with age (Cornelius & Caspi, 1987). Thus some forms of creativity require the presence of life-accumulated experience, even wisdom. Indeed, in some instances, creativity may convert to a form of leadership, in which case the career peak may appear even later in life when contributions come to be made through others (cf. Simonton, 1988a).

Besides enhancing creativity in those domains that emphasize experience for full success, wisdom also may determine the course of creativity in the later years of life. As an example, content analyses of classic plays have indicated how the prevailing thematic material changes from the preoccupations of youth (e.g., love themes) to the concerns of wise maturity (e.g., spiritual issues) (Simonton, 1983, 1986). Even more suggestive, perhaps, is a recent empirical study of the "swan-song phenomenon" in the last works of 172 classical composers (Simonton, 1989). As musical creators approach their final years, a shift occurs in their compositional style such that they tend to produce works relatively brief and melodically simple yet rich in aesthetic significance and ultimate success. Such career swan songs appear imbued with a creative wisdom possibly propelled by some process of "life review" in which the composer must cope with the proximity of death. In any case, these historiometric inquiries show how creativity and wisdom can sometimes converge with age.

V. Conclusions

Creativity and wisdom are frequently viewed as exhibiting contrary relations with aging: Where the former is seen as a privilege of youth, the latter is seen as a prerogative of old age. Empirical research on longitudinal changes in both personal assets appear to support this commonplace perception. Whether we look at performance on psychometric tests or at actual achievements, creativity seems to peak in early or middle adulthood. According to historiometric findings, only three qualifications must be imposed on this generalization: (1) the precise location of the peak age as well as the magnitude of the postpeak decline varies according to the domain of creative achievements; (2) because quality of output tends to be a positive function of total quantity (i.e., the ratio of major to total works is constant throughout the career), on a contribution-for-contribution basis, aging is not associated with decline; (3) due to the positive relationships among the three components of lifetime productivity (precocity, longevity and output rate), those who begin their careers early and maintain a prolific level of output will be expected to continue productivity until late in life.

Although theories have emerged with implications concerning the life-span development of wisdom, empirical inquiry into this attribute is still at the initial stages. Nevertheless, recent work favors the notion that the accumulation of practical expertise may continue toward the very end of life. Finally, despite the apparent discrepancy between the longitudinal trends for creativity and wisdom, some studies suggest ways that the two phenomena may converge, including late-life changes in the content of creative products that evince the acquisition of wisdom (e.g., the "swan-song phenomenon"). Future research may do well to scrutinize further the ways that creativity and wisdom become more closely integrated during the process of aging. Does creativity generally adopt new forms in the later years, forms that place more emphasis on wisdom? Does the full appreciation of works produced late in a creator's life require that the potential appreciator has acquired the requisite amount of wisdom first? Are career changes in a creator's life but signs of ever growing wisdom? Can it ever prove wise not to create?

References

Albert. R. S. (1975). Toward a behavioral definition of genius. *American Psychologist*, **30**, 140–151.

Alpaugh, P. K., & Birren, J. E. (1977). Variables affecting creative contributions across the adult life span. *Human Development*, **20**, 240–248.

Alpaugh, P. K., Parham, I. A., Cole, K. D., & Birren, J. E. (1982). Creativity in adulthood and old age: An exploratory study. *Educational Gerontology*, **8**, 101–116.

Baltes, P. B. (1987). *Toward a psychological theory of wisdom*. Invited address presented at the annual convention of the American Psychological Association, New York, August.

Baltes, P. B., Dittmann-Kohli, F., & Dixon, R. A. (1984). New perspectives on the development of intelligence in adulthood: Toward a dual-process conception and a model of selective optimization and compensation. In P. B. Baltes & O. G. Brim, Jr. (Eds.), *Life-span development and behavior* (Vol. 6, pp. 33–76). New York: Academic Press.

Beard, G. M. (1874). *Legal responsibility in old age*. New York: Russell.

Clayton, V. (1975). Erikson's theory of human development as it applies to the aged: Wisdom as contradictory cognition. *Human Development*, **18**, 119–128.

Clayton, V. P., & Birren, J. E. (1980). The development of wisdom across the life span: A reexamination of an ancient topic. *Life-Span Development and Behavior*, **3**, 103–135.

Cole, S. (1979). Age and scientific performance. *American Journal of Sociology*, **84**, 958–977.

Cornelius, S. W., & Caspi, A. (1987). Everyday problem solving in adulthood and old age. *Psychology and Aging*, **2**, 144–153.

Dennis, W. (1954a). Bibliographies of eminent scientists. *Scientific Monthly*, **79**, 180–183.

Dennis, W. (1954b). Predicting scientific productivity in later decades from records of earlier decades. *Journal of Gerontology*, **9**, 465–467.

Dennis, W. (1955). Variations in productivity among creative workers. *Scientific Monthly*, **80**, 277–278.

Dennis, W. (1966). Creative productivity between the ages of 20 and 80 years. *Journal of Gerontology*, **21**, 1–8.

Dittmann-Kohli, F., & Baltes, P. B. (1989). Toward a neofunctionalist conception of adult intellectual development: Wisdom as a prototypical case of intellectual growth. In C. Alexander & E. Langer (Eds.), *Beyond formal operations: Alternative endpoints to human development*. New York: Oxford University Press (in press).

Erikson, E. H. (1959). Identity and the life cycle. *Psychological Issues*, **1**(1), 1–171.

Horn, J. L., & Cattell, R. B. (1972). Age differences in fluid and crystallized intelligence. *Acta Psychologica*, **26**, 103–129.

Horner, K. L. Rushton, J. P., & Vernon, P. A. (1986). Relation between aging and research productivity. *Psychology and Aging*, **1**, 319–324.

Guilford, J. P. (1967). *The nature of human intelligence*. New York: McGraw-Hill.

Jaquish, G. A., & Ripple, R. E. (1981). Cognitive creative abilities and self-esteem across the adult life-span. *Human Development*, **24**, 110–119.

Jungk, R. (1958). *Brighter than a thousand suns* (trans. J. Cleugh). New York: Harcourt.

Kogan, N. (1973). Creativity and cognitive style: A life-span perspective. In P. B. Baltes & K. W. Schaie (Eds.), *Life-span developmental psychology: Personality and socialization* (pp. 145–178). New York: Academic Press.

Kohlberg, L. (1973a). Continuities in childhood and adult moral development revisited. In P. B. Baltes & K. W. Schaie (Eds.), *Life-span developmental psychology: Personality and socialization* (pp. 179–204). New York: Academic Press.

Kohlberg, L. (1973b). Stages and aging in moral development—Some speculations. *Gerontologist*, **13**, 497–502.

Lehman, H. C. (1953). *Age and achievement*. Princeton, NJ: Princeton University Press.

Lehman, H. C. (1962). More about age and achievement. *Gerontologist*, **2**, 141–148.

McCrae, R. R., Arenberg, D., & Costa, P. T., Jr. (1987). Declines in divergent thinking with age: Cross-sectional, longitudinal, and cross-sequential analyses. *Psychology and Aging*, **2**, 130–137.

Mednick, S. A. (1962). The associative basis of the creative process. *Psychological Review*, **69**, 220–232.

Mumford, M. D. (1984). Age and outstanding occupational achievement: Lehman revisited. *Journal of Vocational Behavior*, **25**, 225–244.

Mumford, M. D., & Gustafson, S. B. (1988). Creativity syndrome: Integration, application, and innovation. *Psychological Bulletin*, **103**, 27–43.

Oromaner, M. (1977). Professional age and the reception of sociological publications: A test of the Zuckerman-Merton hypothesis. *Social Studies of Science*, **7**, 381–388.

Over, R. (1988). Does scholarly impact decline with age? *Scientometrics*, **13**, 215–223.

Quetelet, A. (1968). *A treatise on man*. New York: Franklin. (Reprint of 1842 Edinburgh translation of original 1835 publication.)

Raskin, E. A. (1936). Comparison of scientific and literary ability: A biographical study of eminent scientists and men of letters of the nineteenth century. *Journal of Abnormal and Social Psychology*, **31**, 20–35.

Romaniuk, J. G., & Romaniuk, M. (1981). Creativity across the life span: A measurement perspective. *Human Development*, **24**, 366–381.

Ruth, J.-E., & Birren, J. E. (1985). Creativity in adulthood and old age: Relations to intelligence, sex and mode of testing. *International Journal of Behavioral Development*, **8**, 99–109.

Simonton, D. K. (1975). Age and literary creativity: A cross-cultural and transhistorical survey. *Journal of Cross-Cultural Psychology*, **6**, 259–277.

Simonton, D. K. (1977a). Creative productivity, age, and stress: A biographical time-series analysis of 10 classical composers. *Journal of Personality and Social Psychology*, **35**, 791–804.

Simonton, D. K. (1977b). Eminence, creativity, and geographic marginality: A recursive structural equation model. *Journal of Personality and Social Psychology*, **35**, 805–816.

Simonton, D. K. (1980). Thematic fame, melodic originality, and musical zeitgeist: A biographical and transhistorical content analysis. *Journal of Personality and Social Psychology*, **39**, 972–983.

Simonton, D. K. (1983). Dramatic greatness and content: A quantitative study of 82 Athenian and Shakespearean plays. *Empirical Studies of the Arts*, **1**, 109–123.

Simonton, D. K. (1984a). Creative productivity and age: A mathematical model based on a two-step cognitive process. *Developmental Review*, **4**, 77–111.

Simonton, D. K. (1984b). *Genius, creativity, and leadership: Historiometric inquiries*. Cambridge: Harvard University Press.

Simonton, D. K. (1985). Quality, quantity, and age: The careers of 10 distinguished psychologists. *International Journal of Aging and Human Development*, **21**, 241–254.

Simonton, D. K. (1986). Popularity, content, and context in 37 Shakespeare plays. *Poetics*, **15**, 493–510.

Simonton, D. K. (1988a). Age and outstanding achievement: What do we know after over a century of research? *Psychological Bulletin*, **104**, 251–267.

Simonton, D. K. (1988b). Creativity, leadership and chance. In R. J. Sternberg (Ed.), *The nature of creativity* (pp. 386–426). Cambridge, MA: Cambridge University Press.

Simonton, D. K. (1988c). *Scientific genius: A psychology of science*. Cambridge, MA: Cambridge University Press.

Simonton, D. K. (1989). The swan-song phenomenon: Last-works effects for 172 classical composers. *Psychology and Aging*, **4**, 42–47.

Smith, J., Dixon, R. A., & Baltes, P. B. (1989).

Expertise in life planning: A new research approach to investigating aspects of wisdom. In M. L. Commons, J. D. Sinnott, R. A. Richards, & C. Armon (Eds.), *Beyond formal operations: Comparisons and applications of adolescent and adult development models*. New York: Praeger (in press).

Sternberg, R. J. (1985). Implicit theories of intelligence, creativity, and wisdom. *Journal of Personality and Social Psychology*, **49**, 607–677.

Zhao, H., & Jiang, G. (1986). Life-span and precocity of scientists. *Scientometrics*, **9**, 27–36.

Zusne, L. (1976). Age and achievement in psychology: The harmonic mean as a model. *American Psychologist*, **31**, 805–807.

Twenty

Personality and Aging

Nathan Kogan

I. Introduction

The present chapter builds upon the excellent review of the personality-and-aging literature published in the previous edition of this *Handbook* by Bengtson, Reedy, and Gordon (1985). Those authors reviewed almost all of the relevant research appearing in journals and books through 1982, with a sprinkling of references to work published in 1983 and 1984. Accordingly, this chapter will offer a 6-year progress report based on publications appearing since 1983 of relevance to the topic of personality and aging broadly conceived. Where necessary for clarity and coherence, reference will be made to work published prior to that 6-year period.

Bengtson *et al.* (1985) chose to organize their review within a social-psychological attitudinal framework with its tripartite division of cognitive, affective, and conative components. This threefold distinction will not be maintained in the present chapter. Though it obviously proved to be useful to Bengtson and his associates

in their effort to impose some order on what those authors termed the "litterature" of personality and aging, such a threefold division of studies is quite idiosyncratic and, furthermore, fails to do justice to the directions within the field over the past 6 years.

One major direction is toward increasing methodological sophistication. The era of isolated cross-sectional studies comparing diverse age groups on personality variables would appear to be waning. Use of cross-sectional methods is usually in the context of large-scale longitudinal projects, where the intent is to determine the relative influence of generational and maturational effects. An examination of the relevant literature over the past 6 years makes it clear that access to longitudinal data bases is of great advantage in the pursuit of significant research in the personality-and-aging field. In fact, a substantial portion of the research to be reviewed here represents the fruition of longitudinal projects initiated many years earlier. To the degree that the central issue

Handbook of the Psychology of Aging, Third Edition
Copyright © 1990 Academic Press, Inc. All rights of reproduction in any form reserved.

in the field concerns the extent and nature of personality stability and change over the life span, there is no alternative to the longitudinal method, whether or not combined with cross-sectional methods in cohort-sequential or time-sequential designs (e.g., Nesselroade & Labouvie, 1985).

Is it possible to discern any shifts in direction or emphasis in the personality-and-aging research published during the past 6 years? A qualified "no" would have to be given in answering the question, for the dominant traditions within the field— trait and developmental-stage models— were formulated many years ago. These two traditions continue to generate the majority of published works in the personality-and-aging domain. The former is considerably richer in empirically based research, the latter in theoretical contributions. Despite this evidence for continuity, however, some new directions appear to be emerging. Studies have begun to appear that explore linkages between trait and developmental-stage constructs (e.g., McCrae & Costa, 1980; Whitbourne, 1986, 1987).

An even more innovative development is the effort to relate personality to age-graded roles and to historical change. Neugarten (1977) stressed the need for such research on the topic of personality and aging, but it is only quite recently that studies have been carried out designed to deal with the complexity of the issues involved. Research in this tradition will be described later in this chapter under the heading of "contextual models."

II. Trait Models

Work published over the past 6 years clearly indicates that trait models are alive and well in the personality-and-aging realm. In addition to the continuous flow of empirically based articles, one can now point to specialized book chapters offering in-depth reviews and theoretical interpretations of the burgeoning trait-based personality-and-aging literature (Conley, 1985a; Costa, McCrae, & Arenberg, 1983). In addition, McCrae and Costa (1984) have authored a book that both describes the trait-oriented approach to personality in adulthood and argues for its scientific superiority over developmental-stage models.

Unfortunately, despite the obvious vigor of the trait approach to personality in adulthood, there is little hope that a complete convergence of outcomes ever can be achieved. Given that the major investigators in the area are tied to long-term longitudinal studies often initiated many years prior to their affiliation with the project, they are necessarily obligated to work with what they have (which, of course, may correspond with the choices they would have made in any case). Nevertheless, these researchers have inherited a set of instruments and procedures and a body of previously collected data that are unique to each setting.

An obvious example of discrepant approaches within the trait tradition is that of the normative/ipsative contrast. The former focuses upon interindividual differences, the latter upon intraindividual differences. Though one can employ such ipsative scores in interindividual analyses, one cannot be assured of comparability with outcomes based on normative approaches. Recently, however, McCrae and Costa (1987) have maintained that a five-factor model (neuroticism, extraversion, openness to experience, agreeableness, and conscientiousness) comprehensively encompasses the personality domain and that these same five factors (N,E,O,A, and C) also emerge from a factor analysis of the California Q-set (Block, 1978), the most widely used ipsatively based instrument in the personality field (McCrae, Costa, & Busch, 1986). Given the foregoing evidence, there is good reason to believe that any lack of comparability across studies may have more to do with the adequacy of the sampling of personality content than with the use of normative versus ipsative measurement procedures.

The ipsative-normative contrast is but one of the important distinctions that characterize the personality trait approach. Personality traits have their origins in natural language and can be viewed as the systematic reduction and classification (often through factor analysis) of person-descriptive adjectives culled from the dictionary (Allport & Odbert, 1936). In contrast to this inductive enterprise, another group of personality researchers has chosen the motive rather than the trait as the fundamental unit of personality (Murray, 1938). Veroff, Reuman, and Feld (1984) define a motive as "a disposition to find a class of incentives attractive; the stronger the motive, the more attractive that class of incentive is and the more attractive is any one incentive from that class" (p. 1144). Much of the seminal work in the Murray (1938) volume concerned the delineation of these motive-incentive (originally need-press) combinations. Self-report inventories have been constructed to assess the motives described by Murray (1938), and one of these—the Edwards Personal Preference Schedule (EPPS)—has been used in a long-term longitudinal study (Stevens & Truss, 1985). More recently, another such instrument assessing the Murray needs—Jackson's (1984) Personality Research Form—has been examined in respect to its overlap with the N,E,O,A, and C factors generated by Costa and McCrae (1988b). The results point to considerable overlap, suggesting that the Murray needs can be conceptualized as motivational traits and partially assimilated into the foregoing five-factor model. Others, however, (e.g., McClelland, 1980) have insisted that motives cannot be assessed via self-report instruments and instead require that thematic apperceptive content be coded for motivational imagery. The latter approach has led to the focused, intensive study of three motives—achievement, affiliation, and power—and these have been examined recently within a life-span perspective (Veroff et al., 1984).

A further fundamental contrast within the personality field relates to aims or goals. Some investigators consider their mission to be one of comprehensively charting the entire personality trait domain; others find it more profitable to fix upon a single or limited number of constructs that are deemed to have great theoretical fertility as well as predictive utility. As noted previously, the former group relies heavily on factor analysis to arrive at the optimal number of factors required to encompass the personality domain as a whole. The latter group, on the other hand, attempts to operationalize a theoretically derived construct. The resultant instrument is then used in predictive studies with a wide range of variables in what has come to be called "construct validation" (Cronbach & Meehl, 1955). A good example of the approach is the "locus of control" construct that was derived from Rotter's (1966) social learning theory. This construct has had a substantial impact on aging research, as reflected, for example, in a recently edited volume by Baltes and Baltes (1986).

In the remainder of the present section, I shall examine the evidence for stability and change on personality dimensions across the adult life span. Consideration will be given to interindividual stability at the level of specific traits and of correspondence in factor structures over the age continuum (structural invariance). I also shall discuss recent evidence regarding mean changes (or absence of such changes) across age on particular personality dimensions. The orientation of this chapter is life-span developmental rather than strictly gerontological, and hence much of the research described will encompass young and middle adulthood as well as old age.

A. Structural Invariance

Four longitudinal projects are responsible for the preponderance of literature published over the past 6 years that is concerned with the structural invariance of personality over time: (1) the Baltimore Longitudinal Study of Aging (Costa et al., 1983), a project initiated in 1958 and consisting of a community-dwelling well-educated sample of volunteers who have been repeatedly tested with a diversity of psychological and physiological procedures; (2) the longitudinal study initiated by Kelly (1955) during the period 1935–1938 involving 300 engaged couples followed up in 1954–1955, and again in 1979–1981 (Conley, 1984, 1985b); (3) the Cardiovascular Disease Project at the University of Minnesota begun in 1947 with cohorts of college students and middle-aged business and professional men and followed up 30 years later (Finn, 1986); and (4) the Oakland Growth Study and the Guidance Study in the files of the Institute for Human Development, University of California, Berkeley, projects in progress for more than 50 years and involving periodic measurements from childhood through late adulthood (Haan, Millsap, & Hartka, 1986).

Of particular interest is the fact that there is no overlap whatsoever in respect to the instruments employed to measure personality by the four projects in question. Such variation in measuring instruments across projects has both negative and positive implications. On the negative side, direct comparisons across projects are rendered more difficult at the level of individual personality scales, given the variation in item content even when scales carry similar labels. On the positive side, the use of factor analysis seems to be generating some agreement regarding the major constructs of personality. Hence, when comparable factors emerge from different instruments and these display comparable age effects across projects, generalizability is much enhanced, and confidence in the robustness of personality-and-aging effects is increased. Thus, the evidence is highly suggestive of a consensual five-factor structure within the personality trait domain across projects and over time within projects, and this structure bears a reasonable resemblance to the Costa and McCrae (1985) NEO-AC model. It is important to note that this five-factor structure is not new to the personality field, for it was uncovered in trait rating data more than 25 years ago (Norman, 1963; Tupes & Christal, 1961). In sum, the pattern of similarity in factor structure across different instruments, types of measurement, cohorts, and times of measurement is surely a powerful tribute to the structural invariance principle.

B. Long-Term Interindividual Stability

1. Multitrait Approaches

With the evidence in hand pointing to a five-factor structure within the personality trait domain, we can proceed to inquire how the five factors perform in respect to adults' interindividual stability over extended time periods. Costa and McCrae (1988a) offer some impressive evidence in this regard. Across the five factors, three- to six-year interindividual stability proved quite strong in regard to self-reports and spouse-ratings, and moderate in respect to self–spouse agreement.

In contrast to the 3 to 6-year interval characterizing the Costa and McCrae (1988a) research, the Conley (1984) self-report data are based on 20 and 45-year intervals. Such lengthy time intervals offer a strong challenge to a demonstration of interindividual stability, given the coverage of almost all of the adult life span. Nevertheless, factor-analytically derived neuroticism and extraversion measures generated significant stability coefficients across both adjacent assessments (20- to 25-year intervals) and the entire 45-year period. Further, the monotrait correlations over time always exceeded the heterotrait correlations across the same time periods.

In a subsequent report, Conley (1985b) expanded upon his prior study by including peer acquaintance and spouse rating data and incorporating these in a multitrait–multimethod–multioccasion analysis, an extension of the Campbell and Fiske (1959) model to longitudinal data. Good convergent and discriminant validity were obtained. The major contribution of Conley's (1984, 1985b) research is its demonstration that longitudinal stability is generalizable across methods of assessment, thus putting to rest the argument that long-term personality stability is nothing but consistency in the use of response sets in self-reports and/or the manifestation of consistent cognitive distortions or biases in raters.

In the results of the ipsative measurement procedures employed by Haan et al. (1986), correlations across age periods reflect intraindividual consistency in the relative salience of particular personality components. Seven age periods were examined—early childhood, late childhood, early adolescence, late adolescence, early adulthood, middle adulthood, and late adulthood. Median correlations across all of the personality components between adjacent age periods ranged from .40 to .60. The late adolescence to early adulthood transition yielded the lowest median, suggesting that the shifts involved in assuming work and family roles are accompanied by greater personality instability than is found elsewhere in the life span. Not surprisingly, correlations computed across the entire life span (early childhood to late adulthood) decline considerably (a median of .25 across the personality components). Though modest in size, these 50-year lifespan correlations are statistically significant at the .001 level and have not been corrected for unreliability of measurement.

An issue that has generated some controversy concerns the extent of interindividual stability at various portions of the life span. Testing Bloom's (1964) hypothesis that stability of personality is greater among older than younger adults, Finn (1986) found support for the hypothesis for selected MMPI scales. The absolute value of the r's ranged from .47 to .78 for higher-order factors of extraversion and neuroticism, evidence for strong interindividual consistency across a 30-year period.

Costa and McCrae (1988a) did not replicate Finn (1986) but note that they employed shorter time intervals (6 years) and that the youngest cohort in their study was not quite as young as that used by Finn. Haan et al. (1986) observed the greatest instability between the ages of approximately 17 to 35 years. Stability increased for older adult ages, an outcome supportive of Bloom (1964) and Finn (1986). Helson and Moane (1987) administered the California Psychological Inventory (Gough, 1987) and the Adjective Check List (Gough & Heilbrun, 1980) to female college seniors at age 21 and readministered it at ages 27 and 43. The evidence for interindividual stability was quite strong, with some indication that longitudinal studies commencing during the college years will generate lower stability coefficients than those beginning a few years later in the mid-20s. These outcomes are consistent with the Haan et al. (1986) and Finn (1986) findings discussed earlier and offer further support for Bloom's (1964) hypothesis of increasing interindividual stability over the adult life span. Finally, in research carried out by Stevens and Truss (1985), college students in the late 1950s and in 1965 filled out the EPPS, and then were retested 20 and 12 years later when they were approximately 40 and 30 years old, respectively. For the 15 scales comprising the ipsatively structured EPPS, stability coefficients were overwhelmingly significant for both cohorts, with almost half exceeding .45.

In sum, the evidence for long-term interindividual stability reviewed here must rank as among the most robust in the personality-and-aging field. Although stability coefficients, with few exceptions, tend to decline as the testing interval increases and tend to be somewhat weaker across the early adult years, they nevertheless remain statistically significant for intervals as long as 50 years. Variation in the magnitude of the effect across traits is relatively minor. Especially impressive is the extent of agreement across a diversity of studies.

2. Single Construct Approaches

As indicated earlier, the locus-of-control construct initially formulated by Rotter (1966) has captured the attention of life-span developmentalists, with the consequence that some relevant longitudinal data have been gathered and reported. The few published studies have been fairly short term, rarely exceeding 6 years. Nevertheless, the time interval is sufficient to offer some indication of the interindividual stability of the construct.

Lachman (1983, 1985) and Gatz and Siegler et al. (Gatz, Siegler, George, & Tyler, 1986; Siegler, 1983; Siegler & Gatz, 1985) have generated the bulk of the longitudinal data in the locus-of-control domain. The limited evidence suggests that the locus-of-control construct possesses satisfactory interindividual stability across time intervals extending from 2 to 6 years. The level of stability (particularly when corrections for attenuation are applied) approximates that achieved by the personality dimensions examined in the multitrait studies previously discussed. It should be noted that the trend in locus-of-control research toward domain-specific assessments (e.g., Gurin & Brim, 1984; Lefcourt, 1981) has not as yet been reflected in longitudinal projects. Ongoing research by Rodin (1987),

however, employs a longitudinal domain-specific approach and hence eventually should fill the significant gap in our knowledge regarding the relation between aging and locus of control.

C. Mean Level Personality Change and Stability with Age

1. Multitrait Approaches

Within the framework of personality trait models, the claims regarding personality change in adulthood run the full gamut from "trivial and insignificant," at the one extreme, to "substantial and meaningful," at the other extreme. Costa et al. (1983) and McCrae and Costa (1984) strongly endorse the former claim and have more recently argued that "if there are maturational changes in personality, they are likely to account for a change of less than one standard deviation during the full course of adult life" (Costa & McCrae, 1988a, p. 860). Given that the major portion of the variance is attributed to individual differences independent of age, those authors assert that we should seek out the sources of stability rather than concern ourselves with weak age-linked relationships to personality (Costa & Mc-Crae, 1986; Costa, McCrae, Zonderman, Barbano, Lebowitz, & Larson, 1986).

In this regard, Costa and McCrae would probably be sympathetically inclined toward the recent extension of the behavior-genetic approach to personality in the last half of the life span (Plomin, Pedersen, Mc-Clearn, Nesselroade, & Bergeman, 1988). Plomin et al. (1988) have worked with EAS traits (emotionality, activity, and sociability). They report average heritability estimates ranging from .23 to .48, suggestive of moderate genetic influence in samples of identical and fraternal Swedish twins reared together or apart, and averaging 59 years of age. In an extension of this work with the same sample (Pederson,

Plomin, McClearn, & Friberg, 1988), moderate heritability coefficients of .41 and .31 were obtained for extraversion and neuroticism, respectively. Contrary to what might be predicted from evidence of greater personality stability later in the life span, Pederson *et al.* (1988) observed that the foregoing coefficients are substantially lower than those found at younger ages. In support of Costa *et al.* (1986), only one weak but significant correlation ($r = -.12$) between the EAS traits and age was obtained (older individuals less active), despite an age range extending from 27 to 80+ (Plomin *et al.*, 1988).

Consider next those investigators who claim to find "substantial and meaningful" personality change in adulthood. Findings reported by Haan *et al.* (1986) undermine Costa and McCrae's claim of mean-level stability, but given the unique and relatively unfamiliar nature of the analytic procedures employed—componential analysis of ipsative Q-sort data (Meredith & Millsap, 1985)—a definitive resolution of the apparent disparity simply is not possible. As one moves away from the five-factor model to encompass other personality and motivational variables, the mean-level stability claim undergoes further challenges. Stevens and Truss (1985), working with the EPPS, observed longitudinal increases in achievement and dominance and decreases in affiliation and abasement. The weight of the evidence is in support of long-term maturational change.

With respect to the mean-level stability claim, it is important to note that the observed changes may well have occurred between the ages of 20 and 30. Such changes in college samples, in other words, may partially reflect significant role shifts—from student to employed adult, for example. In contrast, the data on which Costa and McCrae have based their argument for mean-level stability is derived from postcollege working samples with a lower age limit in the mid-20s. To the degree, then, that one excludes college from a longitudinal study, the likelihood of observing mean-level stability may be enhanced.

The longitudinal research of Helson and Moane (1987) provides an opportunity to test the foregoing hypothesis in a sample of women studied as college seniors in the late 1950s, and twice again when they were 27 and 43. If personality change is observed, is it largely confined to the 21 to 27 age interval, with little subsequent change from 27 to 43? The data fail to support such a distinction. If anything, more CPI scales are implicated in significant changes across the 27-to-43 age period.

In sum, the Helson–Moane outcomes offer a serious challenge to the view that mean-level personality change in adulthood is negligible. Of course, it is possible that little additional change will be observed in the Helson-Moane cohort, a possibility that is consistent with the view (Bloom, 1964; Finn, 1986) that the rate of change declines with increasing chronological age. Further longitudinal study of that cohort will be necessary to assist in resolving the issue, though it must be granted that the study of a single cohort of upper-middle-class women sharply limits generalization. Nevertheless, the examination of the relevant literature has clearly shifted the frame of reference from the question, "Is there mean-level personality change across the adult life span?" to the question, "How much mean-level personality change is found across the adult life span, and which personality traits exhibit greater or lesser change?"

2. Single Construct Approaches

As indicated earlier, it is the locus-of-control construct that has engaged the attention of gerontologists and life-span developmentalists. In part, such engagement has been inspired by the hypothesis that the elderly are buffeted by negative life events over which they have little control and hence should manifest a decline in beliefs of internal control and a concomitant increase in an external locus of control. Despite the rather compelling nature of the foregoing hypothesis, however, the accumulated evidence has not supported it (see Lachman 1986a,b).

Although cross-sectional studies obviously suffer from interpretational ambiguity, given the confounding of maturational and generational influences, Lachman (1986b) nevertheless has used the cross-sectional method to ask a different kind of question. Are age differences a function of the generality versus specificity of the instruments employed? In three independent replications involving comparisons of young and elderly cohorts, none of the generalized subscales (Levenson, 1974) generated significant age differences. These results contrasted sharply with those found in the domain-specific scales of health and intelligence, where the elderly exhibited significantly higher levels of external control.

Although the foregoing research has highlighted the advantage of domain-specific assessments, its cross-sectional design essentially rules out any definitive statement about age stability or change. Regrettably, longitudinal or cross-sequential research on locus of control is relatively scarce, and the few published studies have not employed domain-specific assessments. Lachman's (1983) 2-year longitudinal study of an elderly sample (ages 60 to 89), as well as the Siegler and Gatz (1985) 4-year longitudinal study of a sample aged 46 to 69, observed decreases in internality over time. On the other hand, the Lachman (1985) 4-year cross-sequential study of a 35- to 69-year-old sample found no age changes whatever. It can be argued that the three studies are not comparable, given the absence of any commonality in the assessment instruments employed.

III. Contextual Models

Contextual models do not so much represent an alternative to trait models as an expansion or elaboration of them. Within the framework of trait models, it is considered entirely adequate and informative to plot the trajectory of personality dimensions over extended intervals of time without giving much consideration to the sociocultural and historical parameters that distinguish the time intervals chosen. Included within such parameters are age-graded role transitions and events such as the Depression, World War II, the era of the 1960s, and so on, which represent possible situational influences during one's formative years. These parameters are presumed to interact, such that the transition from the single state to marriage, for example, might have different motivational or personality consequences for women during the 1950s in contrast to those in the 1960s.

A compelling feature of trait models is the nomothetic emphasis on the "behavior" of variables as opposed to persons. Thus we may find ourselves better informed about the trajectory of the extraversion factor over time than about the diverse ways in which extroverts select and respond to their surrounding environments over the life span. A contextualist orientation is more likely to have idiographic features, that is, to distinguish subtypes of persons and to trace their developmental paths over extended periods of time. Whereas trait models rely heavily on self-report and observer-rating data as the most valuable forms of information obtainable, investigators in a contextualist mode often strive to articulate personality with actual life events, for example, incidence of divorce, occupational status achieved, decisions regarding parenthood.

In the remainder of the present section, several studies will be described that illustrate the ways in which personality traits or motivational dispositions interact with age-graded roles and/or historical influences to produce personality change or stability and a diversity of life outcomes.

A. The Social Clock Project

For Helson, Mitchell, and Moane, "a major source of personality change in adulthood may be associated with adherence to or departure from social clock projects" (1984, p. 1081). Such projects in samples of female college seniors in 1958 and 1960 essentially reflect marriage, parental, and vocational plans. These women were studied again 5 and approximately 20 years later, and life events information obtained at those times was used to delineate a number of social clock patterns. These, in turn, were examined in relation to personality (CPI scales) at graduation and 20 years later.

Three broad categories were established: the feminine social clock (FSC), starting families by age 28; the masculine occupational clock (MOC), starting and advancing in a field of status potential by age 28; and women on neither of the foregoing clock projects by age 28 (NSC).

A rich array of findings was generated when the foregoing social clock patterns were considered in relation to CPI scales. It is possible to present only an illustration of these here. Within the MOC group, those women who persisted with that classification at age 42 proved to be significantly different from MOCs at 28 only on CPI scales (administered in college) indicative of assertive self-assurance. Within a contextualist perspective, one must keep in mind that the MOC track was an unconventional one in the early 1960s. Conceivably, the personality qualities indicated would not be so central within more recent cohorts of female college seniors launching professional careers.

In their more recent study, Helson and Moane (1987) examine normative changes on CPI scales over an extended interval (ages 21 to 43) for groups of women with different social-clock patterns. On the whole, women who initiated a social-clock project—whether FSC or MOC and whether fulfilled or disrupted—exhibited positive normative personality change of varying intensity. The trends, for example, pointed to increased dominance, independence, self-control, tolerance, and psychological mindedness. Only the NSC group of women failed to conform to the pattern described. All of this implies that the formulation and implementation of a social-clock project (or the failure to do so) can be viewed as an important *moderator* of subsequent personality change.

B. Temperament–Role Interaction

In a recent study, Caspi has argued that "the agenda for personality psychology is to examine how people confront, adapt, and make adjustments to age-graded roles and transitions" (1987, p. 1205). This agenda is implemented by Caspi and his associates (Caspi, 1987; Caspi, Elder, & Bem, 1987) through the study of members of the Berkeley Guidance Study (Eichorn, 1981) for whom both child and adult data were available. The personality dimension of interest concerns the severity and frequency of temper tantrums through age 10. The classification scheme netted 38% of the boys and 29% of the girls as having had a history of childhood tantrums. The remainder were classified as low in tantrums, and the two groups were compared on adult personality at age 30 and on a diversity of life outcomes at ages 30 and 40. A sociological perspective is brought to bear on an important personality dimension (traceable to childhood) through observing how that dimension impacts on a series of role transitions—education, military, work, marriage, and parenthood. For example, ill-tempered males experience difficulty in the work setting, whereas ill-tempered females adjust least well to the typically feminine role of parenting.

More recently, Caspi and his associates have employed the foregoing research paradigm to study life-course patterns of shy (Caspi, Elder, & Bem, 1988) and dependent (Caspi, Bem, & Elder, 1989) children.

C. Motives across the Adult Life Span

The research of Veroff et al. (1984) offers the unusual combination of the assessment of human motives through projective means (thematic apperception measures) and the use of survey methods to generate large samples (Ns of 1363 and 1208) representative of the American population. Further, by drawing two samples at two widely discrepant points in time (1957 and 1976), it becomes feasible to distinguish age from cohort effects (on the assumption that comparable age differences in the two cohorts are strongly suggestive of developmental trends).

Four motives were assessed by Veroff et al. (1984, p. 1145): achievement, affiliation, power as fear of weakness, and power as hope of power. Age trends consistent across both cohorts included declines in achievement and affiliation for women across the life span and a peaking of the hope-of-power motive in men at midlife. What places the research under the general heading of contextual models is the use of cohort differences and interactions with demographic variables to demonstrate how social-structural and historical factors influence age-linked motive patterns.

Consider, for example, the decline in achievement for women across the life span. The data indicated that high-school-educated women showed a steep decline at midlife rather than later. Further analysis revealed that the effect was confined to employed women, not housewives. Apparently, employed high-school-educated women begin with high career aspirations, but their educational background confines them to jobs offering little advancement and sense of accomplishment. Accordingly, the sharp decline in achievement motivation by midlife makes good intuitive sense.

Given the inconsistency of cohort effects across the 1957 and 1976 assessments, Veroff et al. (1984) suggest that the findings point to varying social contexts as the prime determinant of motive levels in adulthood. Such an interpretation stands in marked contrast to the genetic and early socialization explanations of personality trait stability.

IV. Developmental Stage Models

The idea of age-linked qualitative shifts in cognitive functioning has long been appealing to developmental psychologists, and it is, of course, best represented by the Piagetian tradition. Thus, the final cognitive stage—formal operations—emerges during the adolescent years and represents the end point of cognitive development. More recently, however, a small but dedicated group of developmentalists (e.g., Commons, Richards, & Armon, 1984) have argued the case for continued cognitive development in adulthood, with a possible stage beyond formal operations.

A. The Eriksonian Tradition

Has there been a development analogous to the cognitive domain within the personality field? The analogy in fact breaks down rather quickly, given the existence for many years now of Erikson's (1950) theory of eight ego-developmental stages extending from infancy to old age. A vivid descriptive account of the stage associated with old age has recently appeared (Erikson, Erikson, & Kivnick, 1986).

There has been limited empirical investigation from a developmental perspective

of Erikson's midlife and old-age stages—
generativity versus stagnation and integrity versus despair, respectively. There are
no longitudinal studies, for example, that
ask whether the achievement of generativity in midlife is a necessary precursor
for the achievement of integrity in the
later years. It is not that these stage constructs do not lend themselves to an operational definition. One group of investigators (Snarey, Son, Kuehne, Hauser, &
Vaillant, 1987) assessed generativity by interviewing married middle-aged men (at
age 47) and scoring for that characteristic if
there was evidence of "a definite capacity
for establishing and guiding the next generation, beyond raising their own children" (p. 596). In a distinctly different
approach, Ryff and Heincke (1983)
constructed "developmental personality
scales" of the self-report type to assess
both generativity and integrity. Though
the cross-sectional nature of their research
precludes a stage-type analysis, the results
are nevertheless supportive of Erikson's
theory. Further, their findings are quite
consistent with the view that personality
change is observed only when the measures employed in the study are of developmental relevance.

B. Loevinger's Model

The ego-developmental theory of Loevinger (1976) is one of the more popular stage
approaches, given the extensive measurement effort involved in the construction of
the assessment instrument—the Sentence Completion Test (Loevinger &
Wessler, 1970). Four stages are identified
across the adolescent and adult years—
conformist, conscientious, autonomous,
and integrated. Although these stages exhibit a modest correlation with chronological age, Loevinger is not particularly concerned with such a linkage. Rather, she
seems much more interested in examining
individual differences within particular
age cohorts. Thus it would be entirely fea-

sible to find the highest stage—integrated—represented in a college sample.
This is obviously quite different from
Erikson, for whom stages have some tie to
chronological age ranges across the adult
life span. In recent years, the ego-level
score on the Sentence Completion Test
has assumed the status of a trait measure
of developmental maturity (e.g., McCrae
& Costa, 1983; Helson & Wink, 1987; Labouvie-Vief, Hakim-Larson, & Hobart,
1987), and it has been shown to relate to
the trait index of openness to experience
(McCrae & Costa, 1980). In sum, it would
appear that the Loevinger developmental
model of personality has been put to use by
trait theorists for their own particular purposes. It is to Loevinger's credit, of course,
that unlike other developmental stage
theorists, she has developed a highly reliable measurement approach that renders
the model useful to investigators of diverse theoretical persuasions.

C. Levinson's Model

Consider finally the conception of adult
development offered by Levinson (1978,
1986). Of the various stage models, Levinson's is the most explicit in its linkage of
stages with relatively narrow chronological age intervals. This presumption of a
close linkage has been highly controversial (see McCrae & Costa, 1984). Further,
given the initial exclusive focus on males,
Levinson's work has been criticized by
Gilligan (1982) for its gender parochialism.
Such criticism is not warranted, however,
for Levinson (1986) has clearly indicated
that a comparable study of women is underway and will be published shortly. In
the meantime, Roberts and Newton (1987)
have reported the outcomes of four doctoral dissertations concerned with wom-
en's adult development in the Levinsonian
tradition. Those authors maintain that the
women in the four studies "progressed
through the same developmental periods
of early adulthood as the men in Levin-

son's sample and at roughly the same ages" (p. 160). Of particular interest is the substantial percentage of women who hold *split dreams*, believe that success is possible in both the occupational and family domains. Such a split is not evident in Levinson's occupationally successful men.

Though not specifically Levinsonian in orientation, the research of Reinke, Holmes, and Harris (1985) based on four cohorts of middle-class women aged 30, 35, 40, and 45 is of particular relevance. With retrospective interviews averaging approximately 2 hours in length, Reinke *et. al.* were able to obtain highly reliable clinical ratings of major psychosocial transitions in the lives of their respondents. Of special significance in the present context is the evidence that approximately 78% of the respondents were rated as beginning a major life transition between the ages of 27 and 30. Further, this transition was not linked to the phase of the family cycle, for it was observed in women with and without children. The transition is "characterized initially by personal disruption, followed by reassessment and a search for personal growth, and finally by a spurt in self-concept and psychological well-being." (Reinke *et al.*, 1987, p. 1361). This age 30 transition was also found consistently in the Roberts and Newton (1987) dissertation studies. As yet, however, the evidence for a midlife crisis in women around age 40 (comparable to that attributed to men by Levinson and others) is highly tentative.

Though the Levinson model is vulnerable to criticism on a number of grounds, there have been few empirically based attacks on the model. One of these is described by McCrae and Costa (1984), who developed a "midlife crises scale" and found that "there was not the slightest evidence of peaking of distress of midlife characteristics anywhere in the age range we studied" (p. 104). Those authors also report similar outcomes obtained in an in-terview study of a representative sample of middle-aged men (Farrell and Rosenberg, 1981). Levinson would offer the rejoinder, of course, that the interview as such is not sufficient; one must probe deeply for mid-life crises over a 10- to 20-hour series of sessions.

V. Summary and Conclusions

A. Trait Models

What does the trait approach tell us about personality stability and change across the adult life span? The answer is contingent upon how one chooses to operationalize stability or change. Thus, the evidence for structural invariance is quite strong both within and between studies. Consistent with the foregoing evidence is the indication that interindividual stability of specific traits across extended time periods is quite substantial. Individuals appear to retain their approximate rank order on diverse dimensions within their cohort across the adult life span, but the longer the time (and age) interval between assessments, the greater the instability (shifts in rank ordering) that is introduced. At the same time, there is now considerable evidence that stability across the latter half of the adult life span may be stronger than is found across the former half, but this issue has not been definitively resolved.

Much controversy continues to surround the matter of mean-level stability or change across the life span. The full range of opinion can be found from those who insist that the extent of change is trivial, at the one extreme, to those who maintain that the changes are sizable and psychologically significant, at the other extreme. The two extremes have focused on different personality constructs and different measurement procedures (ipsative versus normative), and this leads to a possible reformulation of the issue toward understanding which traits (or assessment procedures) generate a relatively high level of stability and which yield substantial change across the adult life span.

Whereas most of the research reviewed has made use of comprehensive multitrait instruments, the study of single constructs represents another important stream of work in the personality-and-aging tradition. The latter is exemplified by the locus-of-control construct. Generalizations about stability and change are limited by the relatively small number of studies currently available (the large majority of which are cross-sectional in design). There is good reason to believe, however, that individual differences in locus-of-control components are highly relevant to aging.

B. Contextual Models

Three illustrations have been provided of research that this writer has chosen to place under the rubric of "contextual models." The three are quite different in respect to the variables chosen for study and the methods selected to examine them. Yet all three are concerned with personality-motivational dimensions and their fate over time. At the same time, they clearly do not stop with conventional trait assessments but rather strive to locate those assessments within the particular sociocultural and historical context in which the respondents are living out their lives. One can make the case that contextual models are neutral with respect to the issue of stability versus change. However, the important question becomes one of understanding the sociocultural and historical contexts that contribute to stability, as in Caspi et al. (1987); to change, as in Helson et al. (1984); or to both stability and change, as in Veroff et al. (1984).

C. Developmental Stage Models

Three models of adult personality development have been discussed—those de-veloped by Erikson, Loevinger, and Levinson. These represent the models that are willing to venture beyond the period of early adulthood, though, as we have seen, Loevinger's levels of ego development are not directly tied to chronological age (especially in adulthood). Only the Erikson model offers a stage beyond midlife (integrity versus despair) that has clear psychological content. Levinson (1986) has extended his model beyond midlife, but he stops with the late adult transition (ages 60 to 65). It is evident that Levinson's current focus is on young and middle adulthood.

Loevinger's work is the most accessible to research given the availability of a measuring instrument that meets rigorous psychometric standards. Trait psychologists have used the measure (a sentence completion procedure) to assess developmental maturity within an individual-differences perspective. There is no reason, however, why the instrument could not be used to answer life-span developmental questions.

As we have seen, Erikson's mid- and late-adulthood stages can be operationalized. Given that Erikson's eight stages have been with us for almost 40 years, it is rather surprising that more empirically relevant work has not been carried out.

Finally, the Levinson model poses a serious conflict for adult developmentalists. There is no question but that a rich lode of personal material can be garnered from 10 to 20 hours of intensive interviewing. Such interviewing can never be completely bias free, of course, and given the impossibility of truly replicating Levinson's work, much will have to be taken on faith. As we have seen, efforts to locate the "midlife crisis" with scales and briefer interviews have not met with success. This is not at all troublesome to Levinson, who can always reply that his method is the only one appropriate to the project at issue. Within a scientific perspective, this poses a formidable problem.

D. Epilogue

The present chapter can make no claim of exhaustive coverage of the personality-and-aging literature published over the past 6 years. Conspicuous by its omission is a discussion of the role of personality as a predictor of life outcomes in late adulthood. Typical are studies in which the dependent variables concern life satisfaction, happiness, or well-being (e.g., Costa & McCrae, 1984; Mussen, 1985; Ogilvie, 1987), marital stability and satisfaction (e.g., Kelly & Conley, 1987), and coping and adaptation (e.g., Lieberman & Tobin, 1983; McCrae & Costa, 1986). One also finds studies in which personality is cast as the dependent variable to be predicted by early parental socialization practices (McCrae & Costa, 1988).

I regret that a more detailed exposition of the three classes of personality models was not feasible. Space limitations necessitated severe compression of the outlined topics and omission of personality relevant material that fell outside of those topics. Despite these shortcomings, the chapter does try to offer the reader more than a glimpse into some of the major issues in the personality-and-aging area over the past 6 years. It is my hope that the chapter will whet the reader's appetite for more and that the references provided will encourage an examination of the issues in greater depth.

References

Allport, G. W., & Odbert, H. S. (1936). Trait-names: A psycho-lexical study. *Psychological Monographs* (211).

Baltes, M. M., & Baltes, P. B. (Eds.) (1986). *The psychology of control and aging.* Hillsdale, NJ: Erlbaum.

Bengtson, V. L., Reedy, M. N., & Gordon, C. (1985). Aging and self-conceptions: Personality processes and social contexts. In J. E. Birren & K. W. Schaie (Eds.), *Handbook of the psychology of aging* (2nd ed., pp. 544–593). New York: Van Nostrand Reinhold.

Block, J. (1978). *The Q-sort method.* Palo Alto, CA: Consulting Psychologists Press.

Bloom, B. S. (1964). *Stability and change in human characteristics.* New York: Wiley.

Campbell, D. T., & Fiske, D. W. (1959). Convergent and discriminant validation by the multitrait-multimethod matrix. *Psychological Bulletin,* **56,** 81–105.

Caspi, A., (1987). Personality in the life course. *Journal of Personality and Social Psychology,* **53,** 1203–1213.

Caspi, A., Bem, D. J., & Elder, G. H., Jr. (1989). Continuities and consequences of interactional styles across the life course. *Journal of Personality,* **57,** 375–406.

Caspi, A., Elder, G. H., Jr., & Bem, D. J. (1987). Moving against the world: Life-course patterns of explosive children. *Developmental Psychology,* **23,** 308–313.

Caspi, A., Elder, G. H., Jr., & Bem, D. J. (1988). Moving away from the world: Life-course patterns of shy children. *Developmental Psychology,* **24,** 824–831.

Commons, M. L., Richards, F. A., & Armon, C. (1984). *Beyond formal operations: Late adolescent and adult cognitive development.* New York: Praeger.

Conley, J. J. (1984). Longitudinal consistency of adult personality: Self-reported psychological characteristics across 45 years. *Journal of Personality and Social Psychology,* **47,** 1325–1333.

Conley, J. J. (1985a). A personality theory of adulthood and aging. In R. Hogan & W. H. Jones (Eds.), *Perspectives in personality* (Vol. 1, pp. 81–115). Greenwich, CT: JAI Press.

Conley, J. J. (1985b). Longitudinal stability of personality traits: A multitrait-multimethod-multioccasion analysis. *Journal of Personality and Social Psychology,* **49,** 1266–1282.

Costa, P. T., Jr., & McCrae, R. R. (1984). Personality as a lifelong determinant of wellbeing. In C. Z. Malatesta & C. E. Izard (Eds.), *Emotion in adult development* (pp. 141–157). Beverly Hills, CA: Sage.

Costa, P. T., Jr., & McCrae, R. R. (1985). *The NEO personality inventory manual.* Odessa, FL: Psychological Assessment Resources.

Costa, P. T., Jr., & McCrae, R. R. (1986). Cross-sectional studies of personality in a national sample: 1. Development and validation of survey measures. *Psychology and Aging,* **1,** 140–143.

Costa, P. T., Jr., & McCrae, R. R. (1988a). Personality in adulthood: A six-year longitudinal study of self-reports and spouse ratings on the NEO personality inventory. *Journal of Personality and Social Psychology, 54*, 853–863.

Costa, P. T., Jr., and McCrae, R. R. (1988b). From catalog to classification: Murray's needs and the five-factor model. *Journal of Personality and Social Psychology, 55*, 258–265.

Costa, P. T., Jr., McCrae, R. R., & Arenberg, D. (1983). Recent longitudinal research on personality and aging. In K. W. Schaie (Ed.), *Longitudinal studies of adult psychological development* (pp. 222–265). New York: Guilford.

Costa, P. T., Jr., McCrae, R. R., Zonderman, A. B., Barbano, H. E., Lebowitz, B., & Larson, D. M. (1986). Cross-sectional studies of personality in a national sample: 2. Stability in neuroticism, extraversion, and openness. *Psychology and Aging, 1*, 144–149.

Cronbach, L. J., & Meehl, P. E. (1955). Construct validity in psychological tests. *Psychological Bulletin, 52*, 281–302.

Eichorn, D. H. (1981). Samples and procedures. In D. H. Eichorn, J. A. Clausen, N. Haan, M. P. Honzik, & P. H. Mussen (Eds.), *Present and past in middle life* (pp. 33–51). New York: Academic Press.

Erikson, E. H. (1950). *Childhood and society.* New York: Norton.

Erikson, E. H., Erikson, J. M., & Kivnick, H. Q. (1986). *Vital involvement in old age.* New York: Norton.

Farrell, M. P., & Rosenberg, S. D. (1981). *Men at midlife.* Boston: Auburn House.

Finn, S. E. (1986). Stability of personality self-ratings over 30 years: Evidence for an age/cohort interaction. *Journal of Personality and Social Psychology, 50*, 813–818.

Gatz, M., Siegler, I. C., George, L. K., & Tyler, F. B. (1986). Attributional components of locus of control: Longitudinal, retrospective, and contemporaneous analyses. In M. M. Baltes & P. B. Baltes (Eds.), *The psychology of control and aging* (pp. 237–263). Hillsdale, NJ: Erlbaum.

Gilligan, C. (1982). *In a different voice.* Cambridge, MA: Harvard University Press.

Gough, H. G., (1987). *Manual for the California Psychological Inventory.* Palo Alto, CA: Consulting Psychologists Press.

Gough, H. G., & Heilbrun, A. B., Jr. (1980). *The*

Adjective Check List manual. Palo Alto, CA: Consulting Psychologists Press.

Gurin, P., & Brim, O. G., Jr. (1984). Change in self in adulthood: The example of sense of control. In P. B. Baltes & O. G. Brim, Jr., (Eds.), *Life-span development and behavior* (Vol. 6, pp. 282–334). Orlando, FL: Academic Press.

Haan, N., Millsap, R., & Hartka, E. (1986). As time goes by: Change and stability in personality over fifty years. *Psychology and Aging, 1*, 220–232.

Helson, R., Mitchell, V., & Moane, G. (1984). Personality and patterns of adherence and non-adherence to the social clock. *Journal of Personality and Social Psychology, 46*, 1079–1096.

Helson, R., & Moane, G. (1987). Personality change in women from college to midlife. *Journal of Personality and Social Psychology, 53*, 176–186.

Helson, R., & Wink, P. (1987). Two conceptions of maturity examined in the findings of a longitudinal study. *Journal of Personality and Social Psychology, 53*, 531–541.

Jackson, D. N. (1984). *Personality Research Form manual* (3rd ed.). Port Huron, MI: Research Psychologists Press.

Kelly, E. L. (1955). Consistency of the adult personality. *American Psychologist, 10*, 659–681.

Kelly, E. L., & Conley, J. J. (1987). Personality and compatibility: A prospective analysis of marital stability and marital satisfaction. *Journal of Personality and Social Psychology, 52*, 27–40.

Labouvie-Vief, G., Hakim-Larson, J., & Hobart, C. J. (1987). Age, ego level, and the life-span development of coping and defense processes. *Psychology and Aging, 2*, 286–293.

Lachman, M. E. (1983). Perceptions of intellectual aging: Antecedent or consequence of intellectual functioning? *Developmental Psychology, 19*, 482–498.

Lachman, M. E. (1985). Personal efficacy in middle and old age: Differential and normative patterns of change. In G. H. Elder, Jr. (Ed.), *Life-course dynamics: Trajectories and transitions, 1968–1980* (pp. 188–213). Ithaca, NY: Cornell University Press.

Lachman, M. E. (1986a). Personal control in later life: Stability, change, and cognitive correlates. In M. M. Baltes & P. B. Baltes

(Eds.), *The psychology of control and aging* (pp. 207–236). Hillsdale, NJ: Erlbaum.

Lachman, M. E. (1986b). Locus of control in aging research: A case for multidimensional and domain-specific assessment. *Psychology and Aging*, **1**, 34–40.

Lefcourt, H. M. (Ed.) (1981). *Research with the locus of control construct: Assessment methods* (Vol. 1). Orlando, FL: Academic Press.

Levenson, H. (1974). Activism and powerful others: Distinctions within the concept of internal-external control. *Journal of Personality Assessment*, **38**, 377–383.

Levinson, D. J. (1978). *The seasons of a man's life*. New York: Knopf.

Levinson, D. J. (1986). A conception of adult development. *American Psychologist*, **41**, 3–13.

Lieberman, M. A., & Tobin, S. S. (1983). *The experience of old age*. New York: Basic Books.

Loevinger, J. (1976). *Ego development: Conception and theory*. San Francisco: Jossey-Bass.

Loevinger, J., & Wessler, R. (1970). *Measuring ego development 1. Construction and use of a sentence completion test*. San Francisco: Jossey-Bass.

McClelland, D. C. (1980). Motive dispositions: The merits of operant and respondent measures. In L. Wheeler (Ed.), *Review of personality and social psychology* (Vol. 1, pp. 10–41). Beverly Hills, CA: Sage.

McCrae, R. R., & Costa, P. T., Jr. (1980). Openness to experience and ego level in Loevinger's sentence completion test: Dispositional contributions to developmental models of personality. *Journal of Personality and Social Psychology*, **39**, 1179–1190.

McCrae, R. R., & Costa, P. T., Jr. (1983). Psychological maturity and subjective well-being: Toward a new synthesis. *Developmental Psychology*, **19**, 243–248.

McCrae, R. R., & Costa, P. T., Jr. (1984). *Emerging lives, enduring dispositions*. Boston: Little, Brown.

McCrae, R. R., & Costa, P. T., Jr. (1986). Personality, coping, and coping effectiveness in an adult sample. *Journal of Personality*, **54**, 385–405.

McCrae, R. R., & Costa, P. T., Jr. (1987). Validation of the five factor model of personality across instruments and observers. *Journal of Personality and Social Psychology*, **52**, 81–90.

McCrae, R. R., & Costa, P. T., Jr. (1988). Recalled parent-child relations and adult personality. *Journal of Personality*, **56**, 417–434.

McCrae, R. R., Costa, P. T., Jr., & Busch, C. M. (1986). Evaluating comprehensiveness in personality systems: The California Q-set and the five-factor model. *Journal of Personality*, **54**, 430–446.

Meredith, W., & Millsap, R. (1985). On component analysis. *Psychometrika*, **50**, 495–508.

Murray, H. A. (1938). *Explorations in personality*. London: Oxford University Press.

Mussen, P. (1985). Early adult antecedents of life satisfaction at age 70. In J. M. A. Munnichs, P. Mussen, E. Olbrich, & P. G. Coleman (Eds.), *Life span and change in a gerontological perspective* (pp. 45–61). Orlando, FL: Academic Press.

Nesselroade, J. R., & Labouvie, E. W. (1985). Experimental design in research on aging. In J. E. Birren & K. W. Schaie (Eds.), *Handbook of the psychology of aging* (2nd ed.), pp. 35–60). New York: Van Nostrand Reinhold.

Neugarten, B. L. (1977). Personality and aging. In J. E. Birren & K. W. Schaie (Eds.), *Handbook of the psychology of aging* (1st ed., pp. 626–649). New York: Van Nostrand Reinhold.

Norman, W. T. (1963). Toward an adequate taxonomy of personality attributes: Replicated factor structure in peer nomination personality ratings. *Journal of Abnormal and Social Psychology*, **66**, 574–583.

Ogilvie, D. M. (1987). Life satisfaction and identity structure in late middle-aged men and women. *Psychology and Aging*, **2**, 217–224.

Pederson, N. L., Plomin, R., McClearn, G. E., & Friberg, L. (1988). Neuroticism, extraversion, and related traits in adult twins reared apart and reared together. *Journal of Personality and Social Psychology*, **55**, 950–957.

Plomin, R., Pederson, N. L., McClearn, G. E., Nesselroade, J. R., & Bergeman, C. S. (1988). EAS temperaments during the last half of the life span: Twins reared apart and twins reared together. *Psychology and Aging*, **3**, 43–50.

Reinke, B. J., Holmes, D. S., & Harris, R. L. (1985). The timing of psychosocial changes in women's lives: The years 25 to 45. *Journal* of *Personality and Social Psychology*, **48**, 1353–1364.

Roberts, P., & Newton, P. M. (1987). Levinsonian studies of women's adult development. *Psychology and Aging*, **2**, 154–163.

Rodin, J. (1987). Personal control through the life course. In R. P. Abeles (Ed.), *Life-span perspectives and social psychology* (pp. 103–119). Hillsdale, NJ: Erlbaum.

Rotter, J. B. (1966). Generalized expectancies for internal versus external control of reinforcement. *Psychological Monographs*, **80** (1, Whole No.), 609.

Ryff, C. D., & Heincke, S. G. (1983). Subjective organization of personality in adulthood and aging. *Journal of Personality and Social Psychology*, **44**, 807–816.

Siegler, I. C. (1983). Psychological aspects of the Duke longitudinal studies. In K. W. Schaie (Ed.), *Longitudinal studies of adult psychological development* (pp. 136–190). New York: Guilford.

Siegler, I. C., & Gatz, M. (1985). Age patterns in locus of control. In E. Palmore, E. W. Busse, G. L. Maddox, J. B. Nowlin, & I. C. Siegler (Eds.), *Normal aging III* (pp. 259–267). Durham, NC: Duke University Press.

Snarey, J., Son, L., Kuehne, V. S., Hauser, S., & Vaillant, G. (1987). The role of parenting in men's psychosocial development: A longitudinal study of early adulthood infertility and midlife generativity. *Developmental Psychology*, **23**, 593–603.

Stevens, D. P., & Truss, C. V. (1985). Stability and change in adult personality over 12 and 20 years. *Developmental Psychology*, **21**, 568–584.

Tupes, E. C., & Christal, R. E. (1961). Recurrent personality factors based on trait ratings. *USAF ASD Technical Report* (61–97).

Veroff, J., Reuman, D., & Feld, S. (1984). Motives in American men and women across the adult life span. *Developmental Psychology*, **20**, 1142–1158.

Whitbourne, S. K. (1986). Openness to experience, identity, flexibility, and life change in adults. *Journal of Personality and Social Psychology*, **50**, 163–168.

Whitbourne, S. K. (1987). Personality development in adulthood and old age: Relationships among identity style, health, and well-being. *Annual Review of Gerontology and Geriatrics*, **7**, 189–216.

Twenty One

Psychosocial Factors and Effective Cognitive Functioning in Adulthood

Carmi Schooler

I. Introduction

The present chapter examines how, as individuals pass through the various stages of their adult lives, the effectiveness of their thinking is affected by their position in the social structure. Several types of research are relevant to dealing with this problem. Life-span psychologists have generally focused on how thinking processes have been affected by age. Cognitive psychologists have focused on developing models of cognitive functioning. Social psychologists (of either the sociological or psychological persuasion) have been concerned with whether or not environmental conditions determined by social structures affect levels of intellectual functioning. And cross-culturally oriented researchers have examined how cultural norms may affect thinking processes.

These disparate approaches have indeed been fruitful. Life-span psychologists have demonstrated that there is a near universal slowing of response time with age and that many, but not all individuals undergo quantitative and qualitative changes in

their cognitive functioning as they grow older. Social psychologists have succeeded in demonstrating that social-structurally determined conditions, such as occupational self-direction, can affect intellectual flexibility. Cognitive psychologists have developed models that successfully mimic individuals' cognitive functioning in various delimited areas. They also have demonstrated that the nature of thinking processes can be affected by experiences, such as practice with and training on various cognitive strategies, the likelihood of which is at least in part determined by the individual's place in the social structure. Cross-cultural research has provided evidence that historically determined cultural factors also affect the way people think.

The purpose of the present chapter is to briefly summarize and integrate the relevant findings in each of these disciplines and discuss their implications for understanding the dynamic linkages between social structure and the nature and processes of effective cognitive functioning as people move through the life course. We must know the answer to this problem if

Handbook of the Psychology of Aging, Third Edition
Copyright © 1990 Academic Press, Inc. All rights of reproduction in any form reserved.

we are to develop ways of keeping people productive and fulfilled throughout their lives.

II. Relevant Findings of Different Disciplines

A. Life-Span Psychology

I begin by briefly reviewing what we have learned from life-span psychologists about effective cognitive functioning in later life. The results of several studies suggest that the biological aging process may qualitatively change the way people process information (Kliegl & Baltes, 1987; Loftus, Traux, & Nelson, 1987). More definitive are the various findings that aging constrains the speed of individuals' cognitive functioning as well as their ability to cope with maximally demanding situations (Coper, Janicke, & Schulze, 1986; Kliegl & Baltes, 1987; Salthouse, 1987). Several strands of research, however, demonstrate that despite such losses, many elderly individuals develop mechanisms to deal with this decrement. They may, as Salthouse (1987) has demonstrated, adjust their mode of functioning to take into account their loss of speed (e.g., skilled typists as they age scan further ahead), or they may increase their efficiency or accuracy as their speed diminishes (Schaie, 1989; Willis, 1989).

One possible factor contributing to the maintenance, or even increase, of performance levels with age is the increase in expertise gained through experience in various domains. Cognitive researchers (for a review, see Hoyer, 1987) have demonstrated that such expertise results in a decrease in the amount of conscious processing involved and an increase in automaticized responses—responses that seem to be least affected by aging. What generally remains unexplored by life-span psychologists is the question of the social-structural and personality characteristics that increase the likelihood of individuals developing the expertise or other effective modes for dealing with the cognitive changes that accompany aging.

B. Social Psychology and Social-Structurally Determined Environmental Complexity

Social psychological research provides some clues about the social-structural and personality characteristics that lead to effective cognitive functioning during adulthood. One class of evidence is best organized heuristically by a rough-hewn hypothesis about the cognitive effects of environmental complexity (Schooler, 1984, 1987). According to this hypothesis, the complexity of an individual's environment is defined by its stimulus and demand characteristics. The more diverse the stimuli, the greater the number of decisions required, the greater the number of considerations to be taken into account in making these decisions, and the more ill defined and apparently contradictory the contingencies, the more complex the environment. To the degree that the pattern of reinforcement within such an environment rewards cognitive effort, individuals should be motivated to develop their intellectual capacities and to generalize the resulting cognitive processes to other situations. The aspect of cognitive functioning that is particularly likely to be affected in this way is intellectual flexibility—the ability to utilize an assortment of approaches and vantage points in confronting cognitive problems in a nonstereotypic way.

Many other strands of research lead to the same conclusions (for a review see Schooler, 1984, 1987). Substantial evidence about the effects of environmental complexity on adult cognitive functioning comes from a research program on the psychological effects of occupational conditions carried out over a 25-year period (Kohn & Schooler, 1983). The central cognitive finding of this program—revealed through linear structural equation analyses of longitudinal data from a representative sample of employed American men—is that job conditions that promote occupational self-direction (i.e., the use of initiative, thought, and independent judgment) increase men's intellectual flexibility, whereas jobs that limit occupational self-direction decrease men's intellectual flexibility. To the extent that the necessity for using initiative, thought, and independent judgment represent complex environmental demands, these findings provide strong empirical support for the hypothesis that environmental complexity on the job increases adult intellectual flexibility.

Other studies in the same research program strongly suggest that environmentally complex work conditions have similar cognitive effects on other adult populations. Miller, Schooler, Kohn, and Miller (1979) found that occupational self-direction is related to ideational flexibility in the same way in employed women as in employed men. Although longitudinal data are not available, linear structural equation analyses indicate that working in a substantively complex job increases women's intellectual flexibility, whereas working in a routinized job decreases it. Replications in Poland (Miller, Slomczynski, & Kohn, 1985) and Japan (Naoi & Schooler, 1985), indicate that substantively complex work has the same effects on men in those countries as in the United States.

Besides replication in different adult populations, there have been other forms of extension of the hypotheses about the cognitive effects of substantively complex work. Substantively complex housework has been shown to affect women the same way as substantively complex work done for pay (Schooler, Kohn, Miller, & Miller, 1983; Schooler, Miller, Miller, & Richtand, 1984). Further, the finding that substantively complex work increases the in-

tellectuality of both men's and women's leisure-time activity (Miller & Kohn, 1983) is powerful evidence that people generalize from job experience not only to their psychological functioning off the job but to the actual activities they perform in their leisure time.

There is also considerable evidence that exposure to a complex environment during childhood has effects on adult psychological functioning similar to the effects on adult functioning of exposure to environmentally complex occupational conditions during the middle of the life span. In an examination of the effects on adult psychological functioning of complexity and multifacetedness of childhood environment (Schooler, 1972), these factors were found to be linked to being young, having a well-educated father, and being brought up in an urban setting, in a liberal religion, and in a region of the country far from the South. Being raised in such complex environments was then shown to result in a relatively high level of adult intellectual functioning.

The Kohn–Schooler research program also specifically examined whether the cognitive effects of environmental complexity on adults differ with age (Miller *et al.*, 1985). In an analysis of the effects of substantively complex work on intellectual flexibility in different age cohorts in both the United States and Poland, it was found that in both countries the degree to which substantively complex work increases intellectual flexibility remains the same across the life span. What differs is the substantive complexity of the work done. In both countries, older workers do less substantively complex work. Thus, leaving aside the possible effects of retirement, part of the intellectual decrement reported in the elderly may result from the reduced complexity of their work environments.

Findings from other research programs also point to the importance of environmental complexity for the effective cognitive functioning of adults. Summarizing the results of his longitudinal analyses of intelligence changes in adulthood, Schaie (1980) concluded that "interindividual differences with regard to health and living conditions exert an influence on the development of intelligence . . . so significant, that one can hardly speak of a general process of intellectual development in adulthood" (p. 373). Among the living conditions that Schaie found to be important is environmental complexity.

Another longitudinal study by Owens (1966) links IQ changes in adulthood to specific life experiences. The subjects, 96 entrants to Iowa State University, were tested with the Army Alpha test in 1919, 1950, and again in 1961. Variables reflecting the complexity of the individuals' life experiences during the intervals between the initial and subsequent measures of IQ (e.g., amount of further education, field of college specialization, rural to urban migration, numbers of hobbies and recreational activities, and earned income) were found to be important correlates of temporal shifts in test score. "The demonstration that patterns of living moderate the relationships of age to mental ability implies that cognitive decline, like cognitive development, is conditioned to some extent on the nature and intensity of environmental stimulation" (p. 325). Results consonant with these conclusions also emerged from a second longitudinal study of complexity of life-style and intellectual functioning (Gribbin, Schaie, & Parham, 1980).

Although all of this research provides considerable evidence that the experience of environmental complexity generally improves intellectual functioning, neither the Kohn–Schooler research program nor the other literature surveyed provides more than a few clues about the nature of the mechanisms through which environmental complexity has such effects. Almost without exception, the studies that deal with the effects of environmental complexity regard the individual's cognitive functioning as a black box—the input and output of which might be measured, but the internal processes of which remain a mystery.

C. Cognitive Psychology

The work of cognitive psychologists provides some understanding about what takes place within adults when their cognitive processes are influenced by social-structurally affected environmental characteristics such as complexity. Unfortunately, the overwhelming majority of cognitive experiments are conducted on neither representative nor socially diverse samples. Even so, a wide range of cognitive studies has shown that not only the content but the nature of thinking processes can be affected by experiences, such as practice with and training on various cognitive strategies, the likelihood of which may well be a function of the individual's place in the social structure. Many types of thinking have been shown to be affected by training and/or practice. Among these are:

1. *Spatial thinking.* Pellegrino, Alderton and Regian (1984) have found that the three components of spatial ability—perceptual speed, spatial relations and spatial visualization—as well as "the ability to establish precise and stable representations of unfamiliar stimuli" can be dramatically improved by practice. In a further study, Regian, Shute and Pellegrino (1985) demonstrated that both high and low ability subjects show practice effects executing the encoding, comparison, and rotation processes estimated in mental rotation tasks and that these practice effects generalize to paper-and-pencil reference ability tests.

2. *Mathematical thinking.* Schoenfeld and Herrmann (1982) have demonstrated that faced with the task of classifying

nonstandard math problems, able novices differed from experienced experts by classifying problems according to surface features, whereas the experts classified them according to the general approach appropriate for their solution (e.g., analogy, induction). When half of the students were given a training course in mathematical problem solving, their approach became more similar to that of the experts.

3. *Statistical thinking.* Fong, Krantz and Nisbett (1986) have shown that both experimental training on the implications of the law of large numbers and training in statistics affect thinking about everyday problems, even when subjects are tested in situations and topics that are completely outside the training context.

4. *Logical thinking.* Cheng, Holyoak, Nisbett, and Oliver (1986) used a variety of experimental training procedures to test their hypothesis that people reason using abstract knowledge structures induced from ordinary life experience. The authors term these structures *pragmatic reasoning schemas* and see them as "a set of generalized context-sensitive rules which, unlike purely syntactic rules, are defined in terms of classes of goals . . . and relationships to these goals (such as cause and effect or precondition or allowable action)"(Cheng & Holyoak, 1985, p. 395). Their experimental findings indicate that, although training in purely abstract logic had almost no effect, training increases the logical level of reasoning when abstract principles are coupled with appropriate examples. Furthermore, even short periods of training in the use of pragmatic schema, as opposed to abstract logical principles, markedly improve performance.

5. *Expertise.* A variety of other studies have shown differences between novices' and experienced experts' problem-solving approaches in a wide range of fields:

Larkin, McDermott, Simon, and Simon (1980) for physics problems, Voss, Tyler, and Yengo (1983) for social science problems, and Scribner (1984) for the more mundane problems arising in work in a dairy processing plant. In fact, not only has much of the recent literature in cognitive science dealt with expert problem solving and information processing in limited domains, but so did some ground-breaking empirical work in psychology (Bryan and Harter's, 1899, studies on the acquisition of telegraphic language).

All of these findings show that not merely what people think, but how people think can be affected by the different experiences they undergo as a result of their different positions in the social structure. Furthermore, it seems likely that those in the more privileged sectors of society are more likely to be exposed to those environmental conditions that will lead them to develop their intellectual capacities (Bowles & Gintis, 1976; Kohn & Schooler, 1983).

D. Cross-Cultural Research

Cross-cultural comparisons strongly suggest that cultural processes also affect adult cognitive functioning. One piece of evidence that culture affects cognitive functioning is the finding (Schooler, 1976) that American men from ethnic groups with a recent history of serfdom show the non-self-directed orientation and lack of intellectual flexibility characteristic of American men working under conditions limiting the individual's opportunity for self-direction. These findings hold true even when the individual's other background characteristics and level of occupational self-direction are controlled. Although it is impossible to confirm each link in the causal chain from historical background to individual cognitive functioning, a model emphasizing the effects on ethnic groups' culture of historical conditions restricting the individual's autonomy seems a probable and parsimonious explanation of these ethnic differences in cognitive functioning.

There is suggestive evidence that both cultural and social structural factors may reduce the level of cognitive effectiveness of the elderly. Thus, a paper by Heise (1987) that juxtaposed potency and activity assessments of different lay categories of mental processing (e.g., understanding, speculating, guessing) with a cross-cultural comparison of potency and activity assessments of different life stages (e.g., baby, child, old person) suggests that "[p]sychological decrement among the aged may come about in part because western societies force the elderly into powerless roles that encourage them to give up potent thought." Congruent with such an hypothesis is the suggestive evidence that social and cultural attitudes leading to early retirement (Abeles & Riley, 1987) or nonchallenging work (Miller et al., 1985) are responsible for some of the loss of cognitive effectiveness in old age.

A number of cognitive scientists also have examined direct cultural effects on cognition. Some of this research has been done only on children. Thus, Kearins (1981) found that Australian aboriginal children performed better on visual spatial memory tests than did Australian white children. Furthermore, there seemed to be differences in strategy. "Aboriginal children attempted visual strategies, while most white children probably attempted verbal strategies" (p. 434). On the other hand, Piagetian investigators have found in their investigations of the development of logical concepts that not only Australian aboriginal children but also adults remote from European contacts demonstrate such concepts much later than is usual for Europeans, if at all. Aboriginal children living in urban communities,

however, perform like European children (Dasen, 1973). Somewhat similar findings on adults were obtained earlier by Luria (1976; but the research was carried out in the 1930s). In an attempt to test Vygotsky's (1962; Vygotsky & Luria, 1930) hypotheses about the importance of historically determined cultural factors, Luria found that the development of various logical concepts was directly related to the amount of exposure Central Asians had to European culture. Luria saw his results as supporting Vygotsky's view that language not only helps humans control their own behavior through mediational processes but also permits them to transmit what has been learned over time through the development of cultures. Other evidence of the effect of culture on cognitive processes can be found in the works of Berry and Dasen (1973) and Cole and Scribner (1974).

Perhaps the strongest evidence of the importance of culture as a determinant of cognitive processes can be found in the work of Hacking (1975). He convincingly demonstrated that the very concepts of statistical probability, whose prevalence has been used to test the cognitive competence of present-day college students, were only developed in the seventeenth century. He suggests that, although the history of gaming is ancient, anybody with a seventeenth-century knowledge of probability would probably have become very rich in classical Greece. Clearly, the nature of culturally available concepts places strong limits on the way people can think.

III. Self Direction and Cognitive Functioning

From the foregoing, it can be concluded that the findings of cross-cultural, social, and cognitive research indicate that the nature and effectiveness of adult cognitive processes are affected by social structurally and culturally determined experiences. This conclusion raises both theoretical and practical problems. A central theoretical problem is the nature of generalization. In order for social and cultural conditions to have their effects, what is learned in one set of circumstances must be generalized to others. For example, how does what is learned in one environment (e.g., work) come to be applied in another (e.g., a research interview or leisure time activity)? This problem has been dealt with from a number of different cognitive perspectives (for a review see Schooler, 1989a), but no general conclusion has been reached.

Findings from the Kohn–Schooler research program raise the dual possibilities that social structurally influenced, but noncognitive, psychological characteristics, such as self-directed values and orientations, are involved in cognitive generalization and that the nature of such generalization may be different at different stages of the life span. The evidence for such a difference comes in part from a study in which Miller, Kohn, and Schooler (1985, 1986) examined the processes by which students' educational experiences affect their psychological functioning. To do this, a linear structural equations analysis was performed on data from interviews conducted in 1974 with a subsample of the children of the respondents in the Kohn and Schooler study of work and personality. The results suggest that educational self-direction, in particular the substantive complexity of schoolwork, has a decided impact on students' intellectual flexibility. In addition, intriguing differences were found between the college and secondary-school respondents. For secondary-school students, a large proportion of the effect of educational self-direction on intellectual flexibility is direct. At the college level, however, the effect is mainly indirect, mediated by self-directedness of orientation. The effect of self-

directed work among employed workers also seems to be in large part indirect (Kohn & Schooler, 1983)—self-directed work leading to a self-directed orientation, which in turn leads to intellectual flexibility. The total pattern of findings suggests that the experience of self-direction may affect intellectual flexibility differently at different stages of education and later occupational career. More of the effect seems to be direct at the earlier stages, when the process may be more a matter cognitive training per se; more of the effect apparently being indirect in the later stages, when the process may become less a matter of cognitive training and more a matter of self-directedness and orientation.

A self-directed orientation may increase the effectiveness of cognitive functioning in adulthood in several different ways. One way may be by directly decreasing the rigidity and social stereotopy of the individual's cognitive responses. Such a possibility is not only strongly implied by the findings of the Kohn–Schooler research program but by several sociological theorists (Coser, 1975; Gabennesch, 1972). In fact, historical and cultural conditions that encourage individualistic self-directedness have been linked to cognitive flexibility and innovativeness that encourage technical and economic development (for a review, see Schooler, 1989b).

Self-directed orientations may also indirectly affect adult cognitive functioning by affecting motivation. Bandura's (1977) self-efficacy theory suggests that the belief in one's own efficaciousness should lead not only to decreased anxiety but also to increased effort and motivation and hence to better performance. Similarly, Seligman, Abramson, Semmel, and von Baeyer (1979) have argued that levels of cognitive performance are lowered by the experience of helplessness and inability to control the environment. This lowering of cognitive effectiveness is considered to occur because such experiences of helplessness lead to poor performance expectations—where even successes are seen as due to external, unstable causes, such as luck—that in turn produce anxiety and decrease motivation.

Empirical support for the belief that a sense of efficacy helps the cognitive functioning of the elderly comes from a variety of sources. Lachman, Steinberg, and Trotter (1987) have found greater increases (or smaller decreases) in performance among elderly who attribute their successful performance on an earlier memory test to internal, stable, and global factors compared to those who view their earlier success as due to luck or some other external cause. In terms of more general cognitive functioning, Rodin (1983) found a significant increase in problem-solving ability when nursing home residents are taught coping skills that enhance their sense of personal control and increase the control-relevant behaviors they can exercise. (For more extensive discussions of the effects of self-directedness on the psychological functioning of adults, see Baltes & Baltes, 1986; Rodin, Schooler, & Schaie, 1989; and Parmelee & Lawton, this volume.) Parmelee and Lawton make the point that, although much research has focused on the advantages of self-directedness and autonomy for the elderly not only in terms of their cognitive performance but also for many other aspects of their psychological and physical functioning, insufficient attention has been paid to the possible costs of such autonomy to the elderly and their sense of security.

Given our concern with effective cognitive functioning, the possibly deleterious cognitive effects of being on one's own in an environment more complex than one can effectively deal with should not be overlooked. Theories on the effects of complex environments (Schooler, 1984, 1987; Streufert & Streufert, 1978) indicate that individuals will exercise their potential for intellectually flexible and self-directed behavior as long as such behavior is rewarded. Environments can become so complex that individuals of a given ability level cannot deal effectively with the problems presented and such overload may result in a decrement of functioning. Individual differences in effectiveness in dealing with complex environments may result from the interaction of past environmental experience—much of which is determined by social-structural position—with genetic or other predispositions and, of course, with age. As we know, the elderly vary more than most populations in their ability to cope with environmental complexity. It should not be surprising, therefore, that there is a tendency among some of the elderly to seek environmental simplicity and security. What is less readily apparent is for whom and in what circumstances such reduced environmental complexity and personal autonomy is beneficial.

It is clear that social structure and culture play a part in determining the level of concern about self-directedness and the psychological consequences of its absence (for a review, see Schooler, 1989b). In Western and industrial societies, self-directedness is generally more valued by those in higher rather than lower social strata. These differences reflect the greater degree of occupational self-direction, the use of thought, and independent judgment, required by higher-status occupations (Kohn & Schooler, 1983). It may well be that those lower in the social hierarchy may be more readily able to tolerate a lack of control. It is also the case that cultures that share the level of concern over self-directedness and efficacy found in modern America are rather rare (Schooler, 1989b). It is an open empirical question whether feelings of self-directedness and efficacy would have the same effects on psychological functioning where self-direction and efficacy are not as valued, for example among Japanese or Iranians.

IV. Remedial Possibilities

The most immediate practical question raised by the research we have reviewed is whether, given our present level of knowledge, there are actions that societies can take that will increase adult cognitive effectiveness. The answer would seem to be yes. Furthermore, the demonstrated success of various interventions adds evidence to the empirical foundation of cognitive theorizing. The clearest evidence that actions societies may take can affect adult cognitive processes comes from the evaluation of various remedial interventions aimed at improving cognitive functioning of the elderly.

A goodly number of studies have demonstrated that remedial environmental manipulations, presently available to our society, can improve the intellectual functioning of older adults (for a review, see Willis, 1986). Studies of the performance of the elderly on Piagetian tasks have shown that levels of conservation, classification, avoidance of spatial egocentrism, and formal operations have been raised through training procedures. Concept formation and intellectual rigidity also have been modified through training, as have the psychometrically defined abilities of figural relations and inductive reasoning. Inductive reasoning, in fact, seems to be improved even by practice without feedback.

In an important methodological advance in the assessment of the nature of training generalization, Willis and Schaie (1986) have actually demonstrated that training on one indicator of a multiple-indicator-based latent factor resulted in significant training effects on other indicators of that factor. Such significant training effects were found at the factor score level for both Inductive Reasoning and Spatial Orientation.

Other experimental studies probed the environmental determinants of memory improvement in late adulthood (Langer, Rodin, Beck, Weinman, & Spitzer, 1979). The experimental manipulation involved increasing the cognitive demand of the environment and then varying the motivation of respondents to attend to and remember these environmental factors. In one study, motivation was manipulated by varying the degree of reciprocal self-disclosure offered by interviewers. In a second study, motivation to practice recommended cognitive activities was altered by varying whether positive outcomes were contingent on attending to and remembering these activities. In both studies, experimental subjects showed a significant improvement on standard short-term memory tests. They also improved on ratings of alertness, mental activity, and social adjustment, relative to controls. "Thus, restructuring the environment to make it more demanding, and then motivating elderly people to increase their cognitive activity leads to improvements in memory that are generalizable" (Rodin & Langer, 1980, p. 25). As has been noted already in the section on self-directedness, Rodin (1983) also demonstrated that interventions designed to increase the feelings of self-direction and control of the elderly improve their cognitive problem-solving ability.

V. Conclusion

Having reviewed a wide array of findings about the determinants of effective cognitive functioning at various states of the life course, we face the question of what we actually now know. From a practical perspective, we know that the effectiveness of some forms of remediation have been proven and that we have enough knowledge to develop others that are worth trying. Thus, we clearly now know enough to take steps that would substantially improve the cognitive effectiveness of people through their old age. Furthermore, there is good reason to believe that such remedial interventions would increase the levels of cognitive performance of individuals disadvantaged by their position in the social structure. Whether society has the resources or the desire to make the requisite effort is another matter.

From the perspective of scientific inquiry, it is clear that we have learned a lot. We know something about how people think, about the environmental conditions that affect the ways they think, and about changes in cognitive functioning during the life span, as well as something about how cognition, the life course, and the social environment affect each other. However, if we ask ourselves how much do we really know about how people think or about what the social antecedents of effective cognitive functioning are, the answer is that we do not know much of what we should or can know. Given the scope of the basic question—why one thought follows another—we have not come that much closer to plausible answers than we were in the days of Hume (1738). Lacking his genius, further progress toward a credible model of human thought would seem to require diligent empirically based theory building in each of the relevant disciplines, together with a more than occasional glance over disciplinary boundaries.

References

Abeles, R., & Riley, M. W. (1987). Longevity, social structure and cognitive aging. In C. Schooler & K. W. Schaie (Eds.), Cognitive functioning and social structure over the life course (pp. 161–175). Norwood, NJ: Ablex.

Baltes, M. M., & Baltes, P. B. (1986). The psychology of control and aging. Hillsdale, NJ: Erlbaum.

Bandura, A. (1977). Self-efficacy: Toward a unifying theory of behavioral change. Psychological Review, 84, 191–215.

Berry, J. W., & Dasen, P. R. (Eds.) (1973). Culture and cognition: Readings in cross-cultural psychology. London: Methuen.

Bowles, S., & Gintis, H. (1976). Schooling in capitalist America: Educational reform and the contradictions of economic life. New York: Basic Books.

Bryan, W. L., & Harter, N. (1899). Studies on the telegraphic language. The acquisition of hierarchy of habits. The Psychological Review, 6, 345–375.

Cheng, P., & Holyoak, K. J. (1985). Pragmatic reasoning schemas. Cognitive Psychology, 17, 391–416.

Cheng, P., Holyoak, K. J., Nisbett, R. E., & Oliver, L. M. (1986). Pragmatic versus syntactic approaches to training deductive reasoning. Cognitive Psychology, 18, 293–328.

Cole, M., & Scribner, S. (Eds.) (1974). Culture and thought. New York: Wiley.

Coper, H., Janicke, B., & Schulze, G. (1986). Biopsychological research on adaptivity across the life-span of animals. In P. B. Baltes, D. L. Featherman, & R. M. Lerner (Eds.), Life span development and behavior (Vol. 7, pp. 207–227). New York: Academic Press.

Coser, R. L. (1975). The complexity of roles as a seedbed of individual autonomy. In L. A. Coser (Ed.), The idea of social structure (pp. 237–251). New York: Harcourt.

Dasen, P. R. (1973). Piagetian research in central Australia. In G. E. Kearney, P. R. DeLacey, & G. R. Davidson (Eds.), The psychology of aboriginal Australians (pp. 381–408). Canberra: Wiley.

Fong, G., Krantz, D. H., & Nisbett, R. E. (1986). The effects of statistical training on thinking about everyday problems. Cognitive Psychology, 18, 253–259.

Gabennesch, H. (1972). Authoritarianism as world view. American Journal of Sociology, 77, 857–875.

Gribbin, K., Schaie, K. W., & Parham, I. A. (1980). Complexity of life style and maintenance of intellectual abilities. Journal of Social Issues, 36, 47–61.

Hacking, I. (Ed.) (1975). The emergence of probability: A philosophical study of early ideas about probability, induction and statistical inference. London: Cambridge University Press.

Heise, D. (1987). Sociocultural determination of mental aging. In C. Schooler & K. W. Schaie (Eds.), Cognitive functioning and social structure over the life course (pp. 247–261). Norwood, NJ: Ablex.

Hoyer, W. (1987). Acquisition of knowledge and the decentralization of g in adult intellectual development. In C. Schooler & K. W. Schaie (Eds.), *Cognitive functioning and social structure over the life course* (pp. 120–141). Norwood, NJ: Ablex.

Hume, D. (1738). *A treatise of human nature. Book I. Of the understanding* (Introduction by D. Macnabb, Ed.). New York: World Publishing, 1962.

Kearins, J. A. (1981). Visual spatial memory in Australian aboriginal children of desert regions. *Cognitive Psychology, 13*, 434–460.

Kliegl, R., & Baltes, P. (1987). Theory-guided analysis of mechanisms of development and aging through testing-the-limits and research on expertise. In C. Schooler & K. W. Schaie (Eds.), *Cognitive functioning and social structure over the life course* (pp. 95–119). Norwood, NJ: Ablex.

Kohn, M. L., & Schooler, C. (1983). In collaboration with J. Miller, K. A. Miller, C. Schoenbach, & R. J. Schoenberg, *Work and personality: An inquiry into the impact of social stratification.* Norwood, NJ: Ablex.

Lachman, M. E., Steinberg, E., & Trotter, S. D. (1987). Effects of control beliefs and attributions on memory self-assessments and performance. *Psychology and Aging, 2*, 266–271.

Langer, E. J., Rodin, J., Beck, P., Weinman, C., & Spitzer, L. (1979). Environmental determinants of memory improvement in late adulthood. *Journal of Personality and Social Psychology, 37*, 2003–2013.

Larkin, J. H., McDermott, J., Simon, D. P., & Simon, H. A. (1980). Models of competence in solving physics problems. *Cognitive Science, 4*, 317–345.

Loftus, G., Traux, P. E., & Nelson, W. W. (1987). Age-related differences in visual information processing: Qualitative or quantitative? In C. Schooler & K. W. Schaie (Eds.), *Cognitive functioning and social structure over the life course* (pp. 60–78). Norwood, NJ: Ablex.

Luria, R. (1976)(Ed.). *Cognitive development— Its cultural and social foundations.* Cambridge, MA: Harvard University Press.

Miller, J., Schooler, C., Kohn, M. L., & Miller, K. A. (1979). Women and work: The psychological effects of occupational conditions. *American Journal of Sociology, 85*, 66–94.

Miller, J., Slomczynski, K. M., & Kohn, M. L. (1985). Continuity of learning-generalization throughout the life span: The impact of job on intellectual processes in the United States. *American Journal of Sociology, 91*, 593–615.

Miller, K. A., & Kohn, M. L. (1983). The reciprocal effects of job conditions and the intellectuality of leisure-time activity. In M. L. Kohn & C. Schooler (Eds.), *Work and personality: An inquiry into the impact of social stratification.* (pp. 217–241). Norwood, NJ: Ablex.

Miller, K. A., Kohn, M. L., & Schooler, C. (1985). Educational self-direction and cognitive functioning of students. *Social Forces, 63*, 923–944.

Miller, K. A., Kohn, M. L., & Schooler, C. (1986). Educational self-direction and personality. *American Sociological Review, 51*, 372–390.

Naoi, A., & Schooler, C. (1985). Occupational conditions and psychological functioning in Japan. *American Journal of Sociology, 90*, 729–752.

Owens, W. A. (1966). Age and mental abilities: A second adult follow-up. *Journal of Educational Psychology, 57*, 311–325.

Pellegrino, J. W., Alderton, D. L., & Regian, J. W. (1984). *Components of spatial ability.* Paper presented at NATO Advanced Study Institute in Cognition and Motivation, Athens.

Regian, J. W., Shute, V. J., & Pellegrino, J. W. (1985). *The modifiability of spatial processing skills.* Paper presented at the 26th meeting of the Psychonomic Society, Massachusetts.

Rodin, J. (1983). Behavioral medicine: Beneficial effects of self-control training in aging. *International Review of Applied Psychology, 32*, 153–181.

Rodin, J., & Langer, E. (1980). Aging labels: The decline of control and fall of self-esteem. *Journal of Social Issues, 36*, 12–29.

Rodin, J., Schooler, C., & Schaie, K. W. (Eds.) (1989). *Self-directedness and efficacy: Causes and effects throughout the life course.* Hillsdale, NJ: Erlbaum (in press).

Salthouse, T. (1987). Age, experience and compensation. In C. Schooler & K. W. Schaie (Eds.), *Cognitive functioning and social structure over the life course* (pp. 142–157). Norwood, NJ: Ablex.

Schaie, K. W. (1980). Intelligence change in

adulthood (trans.). [Zeitschrift fuer Geron-
tologie,] **15**, 373–384.

Schaie, K. W. (1989). Late life potential and cohort differences in mental abilities. In M.
Perlmutter (Ed.), *Late life potentials*. Washington, DC: Gerontological Society of America (in press).

Schoenfeld, A. H., & Herrmann, D. J. (1982).
Problem perception and knowledge structure
in expert and novice mathematical problem
solvers. *Journal of Experimental Psychology*,
8, 484–494.

Schooler, C. (1972). Social antecedents of adult
psychological functioning. *American Journal of Sociology*, **78**, 299–322.

Schooler, C. (1976). Serfdom's legacy: An ethic
continuum. *American Journal of Sociology*,
81, 1265–1286.

Schooler, C. (1984). Psychological effects of
complex environments during the life span:
A review and theory. *Intelligence*, **8**, 259–
281.

Schooler, C. (1987). Cognitive effects of complex environments during the life span: A review and theory. In C. Schooler & K. W.
Schaie (Eds.), *Cognitive functioning and social structure over the life course* (pp. 24–49).
Norwood, NJ: Ablex.

Schooler, C. (1989a). Social structural effects
and experimental situations: Mutual lessons
of cognitive and social science. In K. W.
Schaie & C. Schooler (Eds.), *Social structure
and aging: Psychological process* (pp. 129–
147). Hillsdale, NJ: Erlbaum.

Schooler, C. (1989b). Individualism and the historical and social-structural determinants of
people's concern over self-directedness and
efficacy. In J. Rodin, C. Schooler, & K. W.
Schaie (Eds.), *Self-directedness and efficacy:
Causes and effects throughout the life
course*. Hillsdale, NJ: Erlbaum (in press).

Schooler, C., Kohn, M. L., Miller, K. A., & Miller, J. (1983). Housework as work. In M. L.
Kohn & C. Schooler (Eds.), *Work and personality: An inquiry into the impact of social

stratification* (pp. 242–260). Norwood, NJ:
Ablex.

Schooler, C., Miller, J., Miller, K. A., & Richtand, C. N. (1984). Work for the household:
Its nature and consequences for husbands
and wives. *American Journal of Sociology*,
90, 97–124.

Scribner, S. (1984). Studying working intelligence. In B. Rogoff & J. Lave (Eds.), *Everyday cognition: Its development in social
context* (pp. 9–40). Cambridge, MA: Harvard
University Press.

Seligman, M. E. P., Abramson, L. Y., Semmel,
A., & von Baeyer, C. (1979). Depressive attributional style. *Journal of Abnormal Psychology*, **88**, 242–247.

Streufert, S., & Streufert, S. D. (1978). *Behavior
in the complex environment*. New York:
Wiley.

Voss, J. F., Tyler, S. W., & Yengo, L. A. (1983).
Individual differences in the solving of social
science problems. In R. F. Dillon & R. R.
Schmeck (Eds.), *Individual differences in
cognition* (pp. 205–232). New York: Academic Press.

Vygotsky, L. S. (1962). *Thought and language*.
Cambridge, MA: MIT Press.

Vygotsky, L. S., & Luria, A. R. (1930). *Essays in
the history of behavior*. Moscow: State Publishing House.

Willis, S. L. (in press). Cognitive training in
later adulthood: Remediation vs. new learning. In L. Poon, D. Rubin, & B. Wilson
(Eds.), *Everyday cognition in adult and later
life* Cambridge, MA: Harvard University
Press.

Willis, S. L. (1989). Cohort differences in cognitive aging: A sample case. In K. W. Schaie
& C. Schooler (Eds.), *Social structure and
aging: Psychological processes* (pp. 95–112).
Hillsdale, NJ: Erlbaum.

Willis, S. L., & Schaie, K. W. (1986). Training
the elderly on the ability factors of spatial
orientation and inductive reasoning. *Psychology and Aging*, **1**, 239–247.

Twenty Two

Psychopathology and Mental Health in the Mature and Elderly Adult

Gene D. Cohen

The present chapter addresses three major areas: (1) the subtleties of recognizing mental disorders in the aged, including the distinction between normal aging and disorder; (2) the epidemiology of major mental disorders; and (3) the interaction of mental and physical health phenomena in aging, with attention to normal and abnormal brain and behavior relationships. Also presented is an overview of recent research bearing on practice. Throughout, there is an emphasis on implications for clinical practice that derive from the fact that elderly patients generally present multiple interacting disorders. The focus is essentially on individuals age 65 and older.

I. Mental Health in Later Life

Most older adults are in good mental health, cognitively, emotionally, and behaviorally (Birren & Renner, 1980; Busse, 1987; Cohen, 1988a). This is not to diminish the public health importance of the sizable elderly minority who have significant

mental health problems or psychopathology. Rather, the fact that stable mental health is the norm in later life highlights the need for the family, practitioner, and society to rigorously seek proper diagnosis and treatment for symptomatic aging individuals. Unfortunately, many symptoms caused by mental illness in later life are overlooked, dismissed as inevitable manifestations of the aging process. Poor understanding of the modifiability of mental disorder in later life compounds the problem.

II. Symptoms Signaling Possible Mental Disorder in the Elderly

There are a number of myths and stereotypes about aging that interfere with problem identification and treatment planning for psychopathology in older adults, and alter the way a wide range of clinical changes are perceived. Even symptoms of late life schizophrenia may be misinterpreted, viewed as eccentricity of old

Handbook of the Psychology of Aging, Third Edition
Copyright © 1990 Academic Press, Inc. All rights of reproduction in any form reserved.

age or misdiagnosed as "senility." Opportunities for effective interventions become lost.

A. Symptoms of Memory and Intellectual Difficulties in the Elderly

Marked change in intellectual functioning is becoming somewhat less likely to be dismissed as part of normal aging, given the heightened awareness of Alzheimer's disease. But there continues to be considerable underappreciation of the degree to which depression, anxiety, and psychopathology in general can interfere with cognition. Pseudodementia (e.g., depression or late-onset schizophrenia masquerading as dementia) represents an extreme form of this interference (Group for the Advancement of Psychiatry, 1988; Wells, 1979). For example, various studies have reported that as many as 15 to 20% of depressed older adults exhibit signs of transient cognitive impairment (Caine, 1981; Kaszniak, 1987; Roth, 1978; Thompson, Gong, Haskins, & Gallagher, 1987). Decremental change in memory or intellectual function can also result from various psychosocial and environmental influences, ranging from disuse of cognitive skills to stress factors.

B. Change in Sleep Pattern as a Symptom in an Older Adult

Older persons complaining of sleeping less are commonly assured that this is a normal part of aging, and not to worry. However, this is not necessarily so. Although a number of sleep studies have found that a reduction in total sleep time can occur in later life, others have not (Feinberg, 1968; Moran, Thompson, & Nies, 1988; Miller & Bartus, 1982). Clinically, it is safer to view such change as a group characteristic that does not apply to all individuals, and to note that any reduction that does occur is typically quite gradual. Consequently, sleep

changes in the elderly should not be taken for granted, especially if of recent onset. If an older person reports a noticeable reduction in sleeping—not just sleeping less at night because of having napped during the day—then an evaluation should be done. Apart from potential medical problems of arthritic, urologic, or cardiologic origin, mental disorders can induce sleep changes as hallmark symptoms. Early morning awakening may be an important clue to an underlying depression, whereas difficulty falling asleep or restless sleep with frequent awakenings may signal an anxiety disorder. Any of these problems responds to appropriate interventions.

C. Change in Sexual Interest or Capacity as a Symptom in an Elderly Individual

As with changes in sleep pattern, sexual complaints should prompt a similar approach to diagnosis. Again, one should separate group characteristics from the individual case. However, even as a group, healthy older men and women with a past history of normal sexual activity and a present situation of sexual opportunity demonstrate solid interest and capacity for sexual experience (Comfort, 1980; Dagon, 1988; Davidson, 1985; Verwoerdt, Pfeiffer, & Wang, 1970). Significant changes, particularly if more recent in onset, deserve a diagnostic work-up. Major areas of focus in an evaluation should include medical/surgical factors, drug side effects, and mental health problems. Men are more commonly affected than women by medical and drug influences because these factors can interfere with erectile and ejaculatory function. More common medical explanations for erectile dysfunction include metabolic and neurologic problems, such as diabetes mellitus, hypothyroidism, malnutrition, and Parkinson's disease. As part of a search for a possible drug role in sexual dysfunction, alcohol should also be considered; not only is alcohol a depressant in higher amounts, thereby negatively influencing sexual interest, it also can interfere with erectile and ejaculatory capacity. Moreover, alcohol abuse, which commonly accompanies mood disorder, can compound the effects of depression. Depression or anxiety can affect older men and women alike, lowering their motivation for romantic involvement and diminishing sexual satisfaction. Regardless of the cause, a substantial number of these problems can be ameliorated or eliminated with proper intervention (Butler, 1975; Comfort, 1980; Dagon, 1988; Masters & Johnson, 1981).

D. Dread of Death as a Symptom (Signal of Depression) in the Elderly

Research shows that whereas thoughts about death are more frequent in older persons, dread of death is less frequent in the elderly as compared to other age groups (Kalish, 1976; Kastenbaum, 1985; Reker, Peacock, & Wong, 1987). To be thinking or talking more about death is not the equivalent of fearing or dreading it. It should not be surprising that ideas or conversations about death are more common with the elderly. After all, older people are more likely to have peers and older relatives who have died or are dying. In contrast, *dread of death* as a normal phenomenon is found to be more likely to occur in middle age than in later life (Kalish, 1976). It is in middle age when one takes a phenomenologic turn in thinking for the first time about how much time is left, as opposed to how much has gone by. Once individuals start to think more deeply about their time remaining, they find themselves confronting an existential awareness of their own mortality.

To understand dread of death, one has to examine its context. Dread of death in later life is most common in an older person who *is dying or experiencing some major loss*. Typically, it is the presence of

a terminal illness, an underlying depression, or other emotional conflict—not the awareness of aging itself—that predisposes to death anxiety in certain elderly individuals. When one has a terminal illness or is suffering from depression, this brings an awareness of dying and can lead to despondency. But even here, the majority of individuals eventually come to terms with their fate and develop a reasonable acceptance of their condition (Brown, Henteleff, Barakat, & Rowe, 1986). The situation with depression is similar. Depression at any age clouds one's thinking. A depressed state increases the likelihood of thoughts about death. Depression at any age can, and should, be treated.

III. Atypical Presentations of Mental Disorder in the Elderly

Just as infection may be masked or present atypically in the elderly (e.g., without fever or an elevated white blood cell count), so, too, mental illness in older adults may become manifest in atypical forms. Depression in particular may wear many different masks in later life; *vague physical decline* and *multiple somatic complaints* represent two examples.

A. Vague Physical Decline

Physical decline in later life does not always represent the natural course of physiologic aging or the subtle progression of underlying physical illness. Commonly, one sees the impact of psychosocial factors aggravating medical problems with the elderly, at times precipitating a latent physical disorder. The nature and rate of physiologic change in later life, under the influence of depression, can reflect the will to live or die. For example, what may on the surface appear to be deterioration of overall health due to congestive heart failure may underneath represent the working of patient despair; a feeling of giving up may ensue, acted out via self-termination of medication, the covert suicidal behavior being missed.

B. Multiple Somatic Complaints

Many studies of depressed older persons describe them as having high frequencies of concern about their bodies (Cohen & Eisdorfer, 1985). One such study of 152 depressed patients over age 60 found somatic concerns in 62% of the women and 65.7% of the men (Busse & Blazer, 1980a). Although physical symptoms and multiple somatic complaints in the elderly require diligent general medical attention, the overall approach to the patient should include a search for underlying psychogenic factors. In time, the psychodynamic meaning of the patient's symptoms may become apparent. Depression can lead to social withdrawal or isolation, which are of greater risk in the elderly. In the process, energy that was invested in interpersonal interactions can be turned inward, with an exaggerated focus on oneself, allowing every ache and pain to become magnified. Older people with fewer friends and family may feel in a bind if they get into conflicts. They may have trouble dealing with their rage, fearing they will drive away the few social contacts that remain if they express their true feelings. Instead, they turn that anger inward, where it shows up as physical instead of emotional pain. The elderly are at increased risk of diverse losses (e.g., loss of spouse, economic status, physical health, overall independence); losses in certain vulnerable individuals can lead to diminished self-esteem and depression, as well as a disturbing sense of lost *control* over one's life in general. This may result in physical symptoms that represent maladaptive efforts to signal for help, gain attention, or *control* others.

These two examples of masked depression in the elderly also reflect the close connection between mental and physical health phenomena in the elderly, a topic to which we will return later.

IV. Research Opportunities and Controversies

A review of the epidemiological literature on mental illness in the elderly highlights, on the one hand, the large number of unanswered questions about the frequencies of various mental health problems in later life and, on the other hand, the many controversies that surround the classification of specific disorders. As a result, the research opportunities are myriad.

For example, it was not until 1987 that the revised third edition of the *Diagnostic and Statistical Manual of Mental Disorders* (DSM-III-R) allowed for the classification of "late-onset" schizophrenia—that is the onset of schizophrenia after age 45 (American Psychiatric Association, 1987). This was despite a sizable and reasonably long-standing literature base discussing late life schizophrenia (referred to by some as *paraphrenia*), including many cases with an onset after age 65 (Bridge & Wyatt, 1980a,b; Miller & Cohen, 1987; Post, 1980). Controversy has similarly surrounded the classification and reported prevalence of depression in later life, with some reports describing lower than expected rates in the elderly (Myers, Weissman, Tischler, Holzer, Leaf, Orvaschel, Anthony, Boyd, Burke, Kramer, & Stoltzman, 1984) and others providing different data and interpretations from the same overall study (Blazer, Hughes, & George, 1987). In fact, such controversy extends to major differences among reports on prevalence rates of mental disorders in general within the 65 and older age group (Kermis, 1986).

Even when there is relative agreement about the frequency of a certain problem, such as suicide in the elderly, much is unknown about the range or relative weight of factors contributing to its occurrence (Blazer, Bachar, & Manton, 1986). In many cases, neither the prevalence nor the genesis of the mental health problem or disorder is very well understood. Adding to the unknown is the limited knowledge of the natural history of these various mental health problems and disorders in later life. The cases of anxiety, alcohol abuse, and mania represent the few among many that stand out in this sense. This points to an immense and very fertile territory for the researcher. At the same time, the texts (Bergener, 1987; Birren & Sloane, 1980; Busse & Blazer, 1980b) and review chapters (Cohen & Eisdorfer, 1985; Gurland & Meyers, 1988; LaRue, Dessonville, & Jarvik, 1985) addressing knowledge and questions about psychopathology among older adults continue to accumulate.

Although the opportunity to advance knowledge about mental illness in later life by studying psychopathology in the elderly is clear, there is another opportunity of major importance. Through research on specific mental disorders in older adults, new findings may emerge that might add light to the understanding of these disorders independent of age. Consider once more the case of late-onset schizophrenia. Typically, schizophrenia has its onset in adolescence or early adulthood. Why is it then that some individuals have been able to live through so much of the life cycle, only to first suffer from the disorder late in life? What new clues about the disorder might we unlock by studying schizophrenia through this potential new window to the disorder? Thus research on mental disorders in later life may provide new pieces to puzzles about mental illnesses across the life cycle (Cohen, 1979, 1988a).

V. The Epidemiology of Mental Illness in the Elderly

A. Community and Nursing Home Populations

Mental health problems in later life are significant in frequency, in their impact on mental status, emotional state, and behavior in the elderly, and in their potential influence on the course of physical illness in older adults. During the first three quar-

ters of the twentieth century, epidemiologic studies documented the prevalence of mental disorders with serious symptomatology in those 65 years of age and older as ranging from 15 to 25% (Roth, 1976). Many reports since then have continued to document comparably high levels of major mental disorders, symptomatology, and suicide. The prevalence of mental disorders in the nursing home setting continues to rise (Harper & Lebowitz, 1986), as entering residents tend to be sicker now than in the past. Several studies have found as many as 70 to 80% of nursing home residents as experiencing psychiatric problems as a primary or secondary diagnosis (Teeter, Garetz, Miller, & Heiland, 1976); a more recent study identified 94% of the residents of a nursing home as having mental disorders according to DSM-III criteria (Rovner, Kafonek, Filipp, Lucas, & Folstein, 1986).

B. Specific Mental Disorders and Mental Health Problems

Organic mental disorders, among which Alzheimer's disease is the most frequent, affect more than 6% of those age 65 and older (Mortimer, 1983). Significant depressive symptomatology has been described in as many as 15% of community-dwelling elderly (Blazer, 1986; Blazer et al., 1987). Anxiety, like depression, refers to a spectrum of states, complicating the determination of its prevalence in older adults. There are reports, nonetheless, of it being diagnosed in 10% of elderly women and about 5% of elderly men (Gurland & Meyers, 1988). Reported rates of schizophrenia in the elderly vary considerably, with a median around 1% (Babigian & Lehman, 1987; Miller & Cohen, 1987). Reported prevalence rates of personality disorders have similarly varied, from 2.8 to 11% (LaRue et al., 1985; Sadavoy & Leszcz, 1987). The frequency of alcohol abuse in older adults, reported to be between 4 and 8% in one major study (Robins, 1984) has also been difficult to determine, but its prevalence is considered to be significantly higher than previously reported (Hartford & Samorajski, 1984; Maddox, Robbins, & Rosenberg, 1984). Other forms of substance abuse appear to be very low in frequency among the elderly (Myers *et al.*, 1984), although adequate research data are lacking and the future impact on late life prevalence from changing cohort groups who grew up during the rise of the drug culture is not clear.

1. Primary versus Secondary Depressions

When discrepancies between rates of depression in the elderly appear in different epidemiological studies, one important and often overlooked explanation is that different classifications of depression are being compared (Kermis, 1986). The lower prevalences typically describe only *primary* depressions—depressions that occur in the absence of physical disorders or drug side effects. The higher prevalences give a more accurate picture of depression in later life in that they include all depressions—both primary and secondary—the latter representing depressions that either accompany or result from somatic illness or adverse medication effects (Klerman, 1982). Because the elderly have both a much higher frequency of physical illness and the highest rate of medication usage among different age groups, they are more at risk for secondary depressions than any other age group.

2. Suicide in the Elderly

Suicide remains more frequent in the elderly than in any age group (Manton, Blazer, & Woodbury, 1987). Though suicides are carried out for different reasons, depression is among the most common. United States national data show that suicide rates among those 18 to 24 years of age increased significantly from 1970 to 1980. Nonetheless, the highest suicide rates in the country continue to be found among those age 65 and older. The differences are most striking among white males. Suicide is nearly 25% more common among white males age 65 to 74 as compared to those 18 to 24; and over 70% more common among white males 75 to 84 as compared to those 18 to 24. Apart from age differences, scrutiny is being directed to differences among cohort groups (population groups that grew up during different historical periods, such as the youth of the 1920s as contrasted to the youth of the 1940s). Different cohort groups appear to have different suicide rates in old age as well as during other phases in the life cycle (Blazer *et al.*, 1986).

In addition to direct or overt suicidal acts among the elderly, there are indirect or covert forms of suicidal behavior in older adults. The latter can make the diagnosis of suicidal potential a difficult one, an example of such covert suicidal behavior is provided below under Paradigm C of the paradigms for examining relationships between mental and physical health in the elderly.

VI. Interactions between Mental and Physical Health Phenomena in Aging

The interrelationship between mental and physical health is particularly significant in the elderly (see also Elias & Elias in the present volume). From a public health perspective, the relevance of this interrelationship is seriously underestimated. Consider the challenge of a frail older person attempting to manage several medications prescribed for various physical ailments; add a deep depression or psychosis to this, and the individual's ability to maintain clarity or organization of thought in managing these drugs may become impaired, with potentially serious consequences to overall health status. In this regard, there is a growing scientific literature and research delineating adverse effects of mental health problems on the course of physical illness in later life (Cohen, 1985). As a corollary, increasingly research is demonstrating the positive effect that mental health interventions have on the course of general medical and surgical problems in older adults; mental health consultation has been shown both to significantly reduce length of stay and improve clinical outcome (e.g., preventing institutionalization) in a large number of studies following hospitalized elderly cardiac and surgery patients (Levitan & Kornfeld, 1981; Mumford, Schlesinger, & Glass, 1982). Considering the high frequency of mental health problems that can accompany serious physical disorders in older patients, these findings become more understandable. One study, for example, found that 24% of 406 elderly men seen for physical health problems in a primary care setting complained of clinically significant depressive symptoms; other studies report even higher frequencies of depressive symptomatology in physically ill older adults (Boorson, Barnes, Kukall, Okimoto, Veith, Inui, Carter, & Raskind, 1986). Related data highlight the number of older patients in need of mental health interventions who present themselves to internists and family practice physicians. These data challenge the mental health field to develop new approaches to interact more effectively with primary care colleagues in assuring adequate patient care, and rank among the concerns of the emerging field of health psychology.

Clinical concerns and research questions pertaining to mental health aspects of physical health and illness in the elderly can be framed in a number of ways. A few models follow, illustrating the influence of mental health on physical health, the converse, and the effects of concurrent mental and physical disorders.

A. Paradigms for Examining Relationships between Mental and Physical Health

1. The impact of severe psychological stress leading to physical health consequences.

   Example: anxiety → gastrointestinal symptoms

   [The accurate diagnosis of gastrointestinal (GI) symptoms can be very difficult in the elderly, with research showing that as many as five out of nine older persons with GI trouble may be experiencing psychological problems that lead to their physical discomfort (Sklar, 1978).]

2. The effect of physical disorder that leads to mental disturbance.

   Example: hearing loss → onset of delusions

   [More than 25% of the elderly have a hearing impairment (Ruben, 1978); a sensory deprivation phenomenon may be at work in leading to psychotic symptoms in certain vulnerable individuals; an increased frequency of hearing loss also has been identified in older adults with late onset schizophrenia (Cooper, Kay, Curry, Garside, & Roth, 1974).]

3. The interplay of coexisting physical and mental disorders.

   Example: congestive heart failure + depression → further cardiac decline

   [Cardiac disorder and depression are two of the most common health problems of the elderly. A covert depression could bring about indirect suicidal behavior acted out by failure on the part of the patient to follow a proper schedule of medication; the resulting clinical picture then could be one of further deterioration in overall cardiac capacity.]

4. The impact of psychosocial factors on the clinical course of physical health problems.

   Example: diabetic with infected foot, living in isolation → increased risk of losing foot in absence of adequate social supports to help with proper medical management and follow-up

[One in three older women and one in seven older men live alone.]

There are, of course, many other ways in which research and clinical considerations can focus on the interaction of mental and physical health phenomena as they affect overall health. The preceding reflect the potential magnitude of public health problems brought about by such an interplay. Also, they reflect the role of mental health factors in that elusive "whole person," as he or she ages.

B. Is the Problem Mental or Physical?

Diagnosing an older patient depends not only on recognizing certain clinical changes as representing the manifestations of illness but on recognizing the right changes—the correct illness. The correct diagnosis can be especially challenging when it comes to differentiating psychogenic causes from physical ones. Consider the differential diagnosis of gastrointestinal (GI) complaints, where many clinicians have trouble seeing what they are looking at in the elderly patient. GI or abdominal complaints comprise a clinical situation eliciting competing stereotyped explanations as to what is causing the patient's problems. One stereotyped view holds that most GI complaints in the elderly have a psychogenic origin—a hypochondriachal explanation. The opposing stereotyped view asserts that most GI symptoms have a physical basis.

To resolve these discrepant views, an important study was conducted in which 300 patients over age 65 presenting with GI complaints at the outpatient department of a medical center received comprehensive assessments and were followed for at least a year after their initial visit (Sklar, 1978). Diagnoses that were identified and the percentage of patients possessing each diagnosis are listed next:

- 10% had gastrointestinal malignancy
- 8% had bladder disease
- 6% had duodenal ulcer
- 3% had gastric ulcer
- 3% had diverticulosis of the colon
- 14% had a wide variety of problems with an organic (physical) basis
- 56% had gastrointestinal distress associated with psychogenic factors, with no anatomical changes to account for them. This category included problems like irritable colon, spastic colitis, gastritis, heart burn, nausea, diarrhea, constipation, and other psychophysiologic problems

In short, the findings reveal that both psychogenic (56%) and physical factors (44%) play major roles in different patients with GI problems; the breakdown is nearly 50 : 50. The clinical significance of these results is that the responsibility of the practitioner—primary care physician or mental health specialist—is equally great to carry out comprehensive general medical and mental health work-ups in evaluating GI complaints in these patients. Different patients with GI symptoms often have very different diagnoses. The challenge to determine whether a symptom has a psychopathologic or a pathophysiologic genesis is a particularly geriatric one.

VII. Brain and Behavior Interactions Influencing Mental Health and Illness

The focus on interrelationships between mental and physical health phenomena in later life adds to our understanding of how biology influences behavior and how behavior influences biology in the elderly. Within this broader health and behavior context are brain and behavior interactions. Whereas the adverse effects of pathological brain changes on behavior are becoming increasingly recognized, little awareness exists of the potentially significant influence that behavior can have on the brain.

A. The Influence of Behavior on Brain Plasticity

Brain plasticity refers to the ability of brain tissue to be modified in a positive sense—to display functional growth or repair capacity. The concept of brain plasticity is relatively new, because for many years brain tissue was viewed as being static, unmodifiable, and unable to respond to damage. A new generation of brain research has altered these perceptions (Cohen, 1988a). For example, findings from studies of the effects of challenging and stimulating environments on the brains of rats are revealing (Diamond, Rosenzweig, Bennett, Lidner, & Lyon, 1972). Following such stimulation, the cerebral cortices (the part of the brain involved in higher cognitive functions) were found to have thickened, to have increased in weight, and to have contained greater activity of the enzyme acetylcholinesterase. That enzyme affects the metabolism of the neurotransmitter acetylcholine that has been found to influence memory and intellectual function. Later studies by Diamond (1983) replicated these young rat results in studies of aging ones. Diamond also examined the terminal dendrites of neurons in rats placed in enriched environments. Dendrites permit one neuron to communicate with numerous other neurons. Diamond's research demonstrated that the neurons of older rats exposed to more challenging stimuli had significantly longer dendrites than neurons of aged rats receiving less stimulation. This alteration in dendritic architecture raised the idea that improved communication resulted among existing neurons and that the capacity for these changes did not cease with aging.

These experiments have several ramifications: (1) they illustrate the plasticity of brain tissue and that this capacity does not disappear with the aging process; (2) they illustrate the influence of behavior on brain structure, including the structure of aging brains; (3) from at least a theoretical vantage point, they suggest that behavioral stimulation has a positive effect on the physical functional capacity of the aging brain. They suggest that sustained psychosocial stimulation can influence neuroanatomy and neurophysiology with aging. In response, the anatomical and physiological brain changes might then function in feedback fashion to exert influence on behavior in later life—perhaps enhancing behavioral responsiveness. By applying these speculative considerations to the *activity theory* versus *disengagement theory* debate (Passuth & Bengtson, 1988), perspective is added to the potential role of social activity in helping to better facilitate brain plasticity with aging and, in the process, behavioral plasticity. Hence, a feedback loop is suggested involving the effect of behavior on the brain, and the effect of resulting brain changes on mental health. The "use-it-or-lose-it" admonition about the aging mind takes on new scientific significance.

Building upon these experimental findings and associated theoretical considerations, there is mounting research interest and capacity to study the potential impact psychotherapy might have on the neuroanatomy and neurophysiology of the brain (Kandel, 1983; Reiser, 1984). The adverse impact of environmental stress on brain neuroanatomy and neurophysiology is suggested in the results of Kandel's (1983) molecular-level research on the giant marine snail, *Apiysia*. Kandel's studies suggest that chronic anxiety may result from a structural alteration in the number and size of vesicles on neurons that store and release neurotransmitters. Nerve cells communicate with one another via the release of neurotransmitters; anxiety may be associated with the increased release of certain of these chemical communicators following brain changes in response to stress. If nonsupportive environmental influences in the form of stress can adversely affect brain structure, might supportive influences, such as psychotherapy, have a positive effect on brain structure?

B. The Influence of Brain Disease on Pathological Behavior

One of the remarkable features of Alzheimer's disease (AD) is that although it is a devastating brain disorder with progressive neuropathological changes, most of the symptoms it produces for so much of its clinical course are behavioral in nature. This is a major reason why AD is so hard to diagnose, especially early in its progress. AD does not result in characteristic physical and laboratory changes; its primary clinical manifestations are behavioral in the broad sense of the term, with altered cognition, affect, and behavior. Hence, the National Institutes of Health Consensus Development Conference Statement on the Different Diagnosis of Dementing Diseases (U.S. Department of Health and Human Services, 1987) emphasized that "dementia is primarily a behavioral diagnosis" (see also Chapter 25 by Kaszniak, this volume, on the use of neuropsychological assessment). That the clinical diagnosis and predominant symptoms of AD are behavioral in nature explains why mental health interventions have such a critical role in the treatment of AD (Group for the Advancement of Psychiatry, 1988).

Pathological mood and thought content states define clinical subtypes of AD. AD with depression and AD with delusions represent two of four clinical subtypes of the disorder as listed in DSM-III-R. Because depression by itself can produce symptoms simulating dementia (i.e., pseudodementia), depression in combination with dementia clearly results in a degree of morbidity in excess of that attributed to the dementia alone; this clinical condition is referred to as the state of *excess disability*. Consequently, by treating excess disability, a remarkable clinical phenomenon can occur. That is, with the alleviation of excess disability, actual clinical improvement can occur at that point in time in the course of the dis-

order—despite the ongoing progression of underlying pathophysiology. The opportunity to treat excess disability states and to effect temporary clinical improvement in AD patients is considerably more common than generally recognized (Mace & Rabins, 1981; Reifler & Larson, 1988). This very much applies to treating the psychopathology of both depression and delusions in Alzheimer's disease.

VIII. Conclusion: Understanding and Treating Mental Disorders in the Elderly

From the foregoing it should be apparent that there are both new challenges and new opportunities for research into the nature and treatment of mental disorders in later life. We are moving beyond dichotomous psychosocial (Butler & Lewis, 1977) and somatic explanations (Salzman, 1984) as to what causes and what ameliorates mental illness in older adults. We are witnessing a new frontier of studies that are expanding our understanding of the interrelationships between biology and behavior as they affect both psychopathology and mental well-being with age (Cohen, 1988a,b). And as delineated here, this new knowledge is sharpening our ability to discern the many deceptive manifestations of mental disorder from normal mental and behavioral functioning in later life.

References

American Psychiatric Association, (1987). *Diagnostic and statistical manual of mental disorders* (3rd ed. rev.). Washington, DC: American Psychiatric Association.

Babigian, H. M., & Lehman, A. F. (1987). Functional psychoses in later life: Epidemiological patterns from the Monroe County psychiatric register. In N. E. Miller & G. D. Cohen (Eds.), *Schizophrenia and aging* (pp. 9–21). New York: Guilford.

Bergener, M. (Ed.) (1987). *Psychogeriatrics: An international handbook.* New York: Springer.

Birren, J. E., & Renner, J. (1980). Concepts and issues of mental health and aging. In J. E. Birren & R. B. Sloane (Eds.), *Handbook of mental health and aging* (pp. 3–33). Englewood Cliffs, NJ: Prentice-Hall.

Birren, J. E., & Sloane, R. B. (Eds.) (1980). *Handbook of mental health and aging.* Englewood Cliffs, NJ: Prentice-Hall.

Blazer, D. (1986). Depression. *Generations, 10,* 21–23.

Blazer, D. G., Bachar, J. R., & Manton, K. G. (1986). Suicide in late life. Review and commentary. *Journal of the American Geriatrics Society, 34,* 519–525.

Blazer, D., Hughes, D. C., & George, L. K. (1987). The epidemiology of depression in an elderly community population. *Gerontologist, 27* (3), 281–287.

Boorson, S., Barnes, R. A., Kukull, W. A., Okimoto, J. T., Veith, R. C., Inui, T. S., Carter, W., & Raskind, M. (1986). Symptomatic depression in elderly medical outpatients. *Journal of the American Geriatrics Society, 34* (5), 341–347.

Bridge, T. P. & Wyatt, R. J. (1980a). Paraphrenia: Paranoid states of late life. I: European research. *Journal of the American Geriatrics Society, 28,* 193–200.

Bridge, T. P., & Wyatt, R. J. (1980b). Paraphrenia: Paranoid states of late life. II: American research. *Journal of the American Geriatrics Society, 28,* 201–205.

Brown, J. H., Henteleff, P., Barakat, S., & Rowe, C. H. (1986). Is it normal for terminally ill patients to desire death? *American Journal of Psychiatry, 143,* 208–211.

Busse, E. W. (1987). Mental health. In G. L. Maddox (Ed.), *The encyclopedia of aging* (pp. 438–439). New York: Springer.

Busse, E. W., & Blazer, D. (1980a). Disorders related to biological functioning. In E. W. Busse & D. B. Blazer (Eds.), *Handbook of geriatric psychiatry.* New York: Van Nostrand Reinhold.

Busse, E. W., & Blazer, D. (Eds.) (1980b). *Handbook of geriatric psychiatry.* New York: Van Nostrand Reinhold.

Butler, R. N. (1975). Sex after 65. In L. E. Brown & E. O. Ellis (Eds.), *Quality of life: The later years.* Acton, MA: Massachusetts: Publishing Sciences Groups.

Butler, R. N., & Lewis, M. I. (1977). *Aging and mental health: Positive psychosocial approaches.* St. Louis: Mosby.

Caine, E. D. (1981). Pseudodementia: Current concepts and future directions. *Archives of General Psychiatry, 38,* 1359–1364.

Cohen, G. D. (1979). Research on aging: A piece of the puzzle. *Gerontologist, 19,* 503–508.

Cohen, G. (1985). Toward an interface of mental and physical health phenomena in geriatrics: Clinical findings and questions. In C. M. Gaitz & T. Samorajski (Eds.), *Aging 2000: Our healthcare destiny: Biomedical issues,* (Vol. 1). New York: Springer.

Cohen, G. D. (1988a). *The brain in human aging.* New York: Springer.

Cohen, G. D. (1986b). Disease models of aging: Brain and behavior considerations. In J. E. Birren & V. L. Bengtson (Eds.), *Emergent theories of aging* (pp. 83–89). New York: Springer.

Cohen, D. & Eisdorfer, C. (1985). Major psychiatric and behavioral disorders in the aged. In R. Andres, E. L. Bierman, & W. R. Hazzard (Eds.), *Principles of geriatric medicine* (pp. 867–908). New York: McGraw-Hill.

Comfort, A. (1980). Sexuality in later life. In J. E. Birren & R. B. Sloane (Eds.), *Handbook of mental health and aging* (pp. 885–892). Englewood Cliffs, NJ: Prentice-Hall.

Cooper, A. F., Kay, D. W. K., Curry, A. R., Garside, R. F., & Roth, M. (1974). Hearing loss in paranoid and affective psychoses of the elderly. *Lancet, 2,* 851–861.

Dagon, E. M. (1988). Sexuality and sexual dysfunction in the elderly. In L. W. Lazarus (Ed.), *Essentials of geriatric psychiatry* (pp. 41–64). New York: Springer.

Davidson, J. M. (1985). Sexuality and aging. In R. Andres, E. L. Bierman, & W. R. Hazzard (Eds.), *Principles of geriatric medicine.* New York: McGraw-Hill.

Diamond, M. C. (1983). The aging rat forebrain: Male-female left-right; Environment and lipofuscin. In D. Samuel, S. Algeris, S. Gershon, V. E. Grimm, & G. Toffan (Eds.), *Aging of the brain* (Vol. 22). New York: Raven.

Diamond, M. C., Rosenzweig, M. R. Bennett, E. L., Lidner, B., & Lyon, L. (1972). Effects of environmental enrichment and impoverishment on rat cerebral cortex. *Journal of Neu-rology*, 3, 47–64.

Feinberg, I. (1968). The ontogenesis of human sleep and the relationship of sleep variables to intellectual function in the aged. *Comprehensive Psychiatry*, 9, 138–147.

Group for the Advancement of Psychiatry. (1988). *The psychiatric treatment of Alzheimer's disease*. New York: Brunner/Mazel.

Gurland, B. J., & Meyers, B. S. (1986). Geriatric psychiatry. In J. A. Talbott, R. E. Hales, & S. C. Yudofsky (Eds.), *Textbook of psychiatry* (pp. 1117–1139). Washington, DC: American Psychiatric Press.

Harper, M. S., & Lebowitz, B. D. (Eds.) (1986). *Mental illness in nursing homes* (DHHS Publication No. ADM 86-1459). Washington, DC: Government Printing Office.

Hartford, M. S., & Samorajski, T. (Eds.) (1984). *Alcoholism in the elderly: Social and biomedical issues*. New York: Raven.

Kalish, R. A. (1976). Death and dying in a social context. In R. H. Binstock & E. Shanas (Eds.), *Handbook of aging and the social sciences*. New York: Van Nostrand Reinhold.

Kandel, E. P. (1983). From metapsychology to molecular biology: Explorations into the nature of anxiety. *American Journal of Psychiatry*, 140, 1277–1293.

Kastenbaum, R. (1985). Dying and death: A lifespan approach. In J. E. Birren & K. W. Schaie (Eds.), *Handbook of the psychology of aging* (2nd ed., pp. 619–643). New York: Van Nostrand Reinhold.

Kaszniak, A. W. (1987). Clinical neuropsychology and aging. In G. L. Maddox (Ed.), *The encyclopedia of aging* (pp. 481–482). New York: Springer.

Kermis, M. D. (1986). The epidemiology of mental disorder in the elderly: A response to the Senate/AARP report. *Gerontologist*, 26, 482–487.

Klerman, G. L. (1982). Affective disorders: Depressions and mania. In D. Oken & M. Lakovics (Eds.), *A clinical manual of psychiatry* (pp. 67–81). New York: Elsevier.

La Rue, A., Dessonville, C., & Jarvik, L. (1985). Aging and mental disorders. In J. E. Birren & K. W. Schaie (Eds.), *Handbook of the psychology of aging* (2nd ed., pp. 664–702). New York: Van Nostrand Reinhold.

Levitan, S. T., & Kornfeld, D. S. (1981). Clinical and cost benefits of liaison psychiatry. *American Journal of Psychiatry*, 138, 790–793.

Mace, N. L., & Rabins, P. V. (1981). *The 36-hour day*. Baltimore: Johns Hopkins University Press.

Maddox, G., Robbins, L. N., & Rosenberg, N. (1984). *Nature and extent of alcohol problems among the elderly*. Rockville, MD: Alcohol, Drug-Abuse, and Mental Health Administration DHHS Publication No. (ADM) 84-1321.

Manton, K. G., Blazer, D. G., & Woodbury, M. A. (1987). Suicide in middle age and later life: Sex and race specific life table and cohort analysis. *Journal of Gerontology*, 42 (2), 219–227.

Masters, W. H., & Johnson, V. E. (1981). Sex and the aging process. *Journal of the American Geriatrics Society*, 29, 385–390.

Miller, N. E., & Bartus, R. T. (1982). Sleep, sleep pathology, and psychopathology in later life: A new research frontier. *Neurobiology of Aging*, 3, 283–286.

Miller, N. E., & Cohen, G. D. (1987). *Schizophrenia and aging*. New York: Guilford.

Moran, M. G., Thompson, T. L., & Nies, A. S. (1988). Sleep disorders in the elderly. *American Journal of Psychiatry*, 145, 1369–1378.

Mortimer, J. A. (1983). Alzheimer's disease and senile dementia: Prevalence and incidence. In B. Reisberg (Ed.), *Alzheimer's disease* (pp. 141–148). New York: Free Press.

Mumford, E., Schlesinger, H. J., & Glass, G. V. (1982). The effects of psychological intervention on recovery from surgery and heart attacks: An analysis of the literature. *American Journal of Public Health*, 72, 141–151.

Myers, J. K., Weissman, M. M., Tischler, G. L., Holzer, C. E., III, Leaf, P. J., Orvaschel, H., Anthony, J. C., Boyd, J. H., Burke, J. D., Kramer, M., & Stoltzman, R. (1984). Six-month prevalence of psychiatric disorders in three communities: 1980 to 1982. *Archives of General Psychiatry*, 41, 959–967.

Passuth, P. M., & Bengtson, V. L. (1988). Sociological theories of aging: Current perspectives and future directions. In J. E. Birren & V. L. Bengtson (Eds.), *Emergent theories of aging* (pp. 333–355). New York: Springer.

Post, F. (1980). Paranoid, schizophrenia-like, and schizophrenic states in the aged. In J. E.

Birren & R. B. Sloane (Eds.), *Handbook of mental health and aging* (pp. 591–615). Englewood Cliffs, NJ: Prentice-Hall.

Reifler, B. V., & Larson, E. (1988). Excess disability in demented elderly outpatients: The rule of the halves. *Journal of the American Geriatrics Society, 36,* 82–83.

Reker, G. T., Peacock, E. J., & Wong, T. P. (1987). Meaning and purpose in life and well-being: A life-span perspective. *Journal of Gerontology, 42* (1), 44–49.

Reiser, M. F. (1984). *Mind, brain, body: Toward a convergence of psychoanalysis and neurobiology.* New York: Basic Books.

Robins, L. N. (1984). Introduction to the ECA project as a source of epidemiologic data on alcohol problems. In G. Maddox, L. N. Robins, & N. Rosenberg (Eds.), *Nature and extent of alcohol problems among the elderly* (DHHS Publication No. ADM 84-1321) (pp. 201–216). Washington, DC: U.S. Government Printing Office.

Roth, M. (1976). The psychiatric disorders of later life. *Psychiatric Annals, 6,* 57–101.

Roth, M. (1978). Diagnosis of senile and related forms of dementia. In R. Katzman, R. D. Terry, & K. L. Bick (Eds.), *Alzheimer's disease: Senile dementia and related disorders, Aging* (Vol. 7). New York: Raven.

Rovner, B. W., Kafonek, S., Filipp, L. Lucas, M. J., & Folstein, M. F. (1986). Prevalence of mental illness in a community nursing home. *American Journal of Psychiatry, 143,* 1446–1449.

Ruben, R. J. (1978). Otolaryngologic problems. In W. Reichel (Ed.), *The geriatric patient* (pp. 151–157). New York: HP Publishing.

Sadavoy, J., & Leszcz, M. (Eds.) (1987). *Treating the elderly with psychotherapy: The scope for change in later life.* Madison, CT: International Universities Press.

Salzman, C. (Ed.) (1984). *Clinical geriatric psychopharmacology.* New York: McGraw-Hill.

Sklar, M. (1978). Gastrointestinal diseases in the aged. In W. Reichel (Ed.), *Clinical aspects of aging.* Baltimore: Williams & Wilkins.

Teeter, R. B., Garetz, F. K., Miller, W. B., & Heiland, W. F. (1976). Psychiatric disturbances of aged patients in skilled nursing homes. *American Journal of Psychiatry, 133* (12), 1430–1434.

Thompson, L. W., Gong, V., Haskins, E., & Gallagher, D. (1987). Assessment of depression and dementia during the late years. *Annual Review of Gerontology and Geriatrics, 7,* 295–324).

U.S. Department of Health and Human Services (1987). Differential diagnosis of dementing disorders. *National Institutes of Health Consensus Development Statement, 6* (11), 1–27.

Verwoerdt, A., Pfeiffer, E., & Wang, H. (1970). Sexual behavior in senescence. In E. Palmore (Ed.), *Normal aging.* Durham, NC: Duke University Press.

Wells, C. E. (1979). Pseudodementia. *American Journal of Psychiatry, 136,* 895–899.

Part Four

Applications to the Individual and Society

Twenty Three

Psychological Intervention with the Aging Individual

Michael A. Smyer, Steven H. Zarit, and Sara H. Qualls

I. Introduction

The purpose of this chapter is to provide a framework for considering the efficacy of psychological interventions with older adults. In doing so, we review the research-based literature and offer suggestions for future directions in research and practice. The chapter is organized into three major sections: (1) a summary of essential issues affecting the development, implementation, and evaluation of interventions with older people; (2) a review of the array of treatments that have been used with older adults; and (3) professional and policy issues that affect who delivers services and which services and providers are reimbursed. We complete the chapter with a discussion of several broad themes that underlie psychological intervention (e.g., ethical issues, defining success in interventions, and the pressure to provide services in the absence of data on efficacy).

The chapter builds upon earlier discussions of psychological intervention, e.g., Gatz's (1988) master lecture on clinical psychology and aging, and Rechtschaffen's

(1959) classic discussion of psychotherapy, chapters in earlier handbooks (Eisdorfer & Stotsky, 1977; Gatz, Popkin, Pino, & VandenBos, 1985) and collections focused on mental health and aging (Birren & Sloane, 1980; Knight, 1986b; Steury & Blank, 1977). Our discussion of the historical roots of each topic will be necessarily brief, though our debts to earlier works are considerable.

The domain of psychological intervention can encompass a wide range of efforts (Seidman, 1983). Previous reviews (e.g., Gatz et al., 1985) have emphasized psychotherapy as a major psychological intervention with older adults. We will broaden the scope of psychological interventions to include planned processes of behavioral change that employ a deliberate application of psychological principles and theory to persons experiencing mental dysfunction or distress. This definition expands the range of concern beyond traditional therapist–client relationships to nontraditional approaches that highlight a broad range of settings for and providers of psychological interventions.

Handbook of the Psychology of Aging, Third Edition
Copyright © 1990 Academic Press, Inc. All rights of reproduction in any form reserved.

Two cautionary notes are important. First, the types of data and the accompanying research sophistication vary by area of inquiry. Thus, the level of analysis and the degree of confidence in results will vary also. For some topics, virtually the only type of information available is case studies, whereas for others, controlled intervention studies have been performed. In each section, we highlight the relative strengths and weaknesses of the domain, while emphasizing directions for future developments. Our review reflects a field still early in its conceptual and research development in which even in the most explored areas the research base is suggestive but not definitive.

A second area of caution concerns the relationship between psychological interventions and other treatment approaches. The range of interventions in human systems is varied (Ford, 1987). Possibilities include environmental and ecological modifications, political change such as alterations in the relation of the person to major institutions, biological intervention, and psychological interventions. Any of these manipulations may have an effect on mood, well-being, behavior, or even personality tendencies. Rather than assuming a priority for one type of intervention over another, we need to consider which is more effective under which conditions, or when combinations might be optimally effective. The research to date shows promise for a variety of psychological interventions with a variety of problems, indicating the need for more careful evaluation of the distinctive contributions of biological, psychological, social, political, and combined approaches.

II. Principles of Research and Evaluation of Psychological Interventions

The need for greater specificity and more rigorous testing of models is probably greater in this literature than in other fields of gerontological research. Not only are controlled studies rare, but much of the literature is characterized by a lack of precision in describing samples and settings. In this section, we highlight two sets of issues, the characteristics of the older person receiving treatment and the setting in which the intervention is carried out. Both elements affect choices of goals, procedures, and criteria for evaluating outcomes This discussion will provide a conceptual framework for evaluating the current literature.

A. Individual Characteristics

As knowledge of the aging process and mental disorders associated with aging has grown, it has become increasingly apparent that generalizations about "the elderly's" responsiveness to interventions are misleading or inaccurate. Today's older population is quite varied in demographic characteristics, past personal history, and current status of health and psychological functioning—all of which set the context for treatment of late-life problems. The choice and efficacy of interventions also depends on the nature of the older person's problem. Individual characteristics that should be considered in planning and implementing psychological interventions include cognitive functioning, diagnosis, lifelong pattern of adaptation, place of residence, social functioning, gender, health, and, finally, chronological age.

B. Cognitive Functioning

Perhaps the most serious methodological problem in intervention studies of older persons is the unsystematic way cognitive impairment has been evaluated. Historically, there was little effort to differentiate dementia patients from others with different problems. Subjects were included in samples by virtue of chronological age, even though there might have been substantial variability in current functioning and long-term prognosis. In other studies, the criteria and procedures used for differentiating cognitively impaired individuals from those who were relatively well functioning were imprecise or inaccurate (see Zarit & Anthony, 1986, for a review).

The importance to clinical studies of determining cognitive functioning, and in particular identifying subjects with dementia, should be apparent. The presence of dementia has specific implications for current functioning and long-term outcome. Because of their deficits in learning, memory, and other areas of cognitive functioning, dementia patients would be expected to respond differently to any intervention than would cognitively intact individuals. Identification of the probable type of dementia may also be relevant, depending on the intervention.

The most salient area of intervention where dementia makes a difference is the measurement of outcomes. Self-report measures of mood, morale, or life satisfaction, which are commonly used in intervention studies, depend on memory, particularly subjects' abilities to summarize their impressions of recent experiences. Given their deficits in recent memory, dementia patients cannot reliably recall this type of information and may consistently underreport problems while expressing globally positive feelings (Kahn & Zarit, 1974; Zarit & Anthony, 1986). At the same time, the patient's feelings of well-being may be a very important indicator of intervention outcome. Observational measures of mood and behavior are an alternative to self-report measures with this population.

In contrast to mood and well-being, cognitive impairment should be measured directly by psychological testing of patients, rather than through observation. Observational measures of cognition tend to be global or vague and do not necessarily have systematic procedures for sampling across time and situation. Observational items such as "patient looks more alert" do not give a clear indication of cognitive change. In general, claims that cognitive functioning has been improved should not be accepted without direct testing of patients, using valid and reliable indices of cognitive functioning.

C. Diagnosis and the DSM III-R

The appropriateness of DSM III-R diagnoses for problems other than dementia also needs to be considered in developing intervention studies. Use of operational criteria for establishing diagnosis enhances replicability of studies and their generalizability to clinical populations. Specificity of an intervention for a particular diagnostic group also can be established. On the negative side, however, diagnostic criteria that have been developed primarily with younger populations may not be appropriate for older samples. As an example, it has been suggested frequently that older people may not present depressive problems in similar ways as younger individuals (Blazer, Hughes, & George, 1987). There may also be considerable heterogeneity within diagnostic groups, which may have importance for treatment.

D. Lifelong Adaptation

Another feature on which samples in intervention studies have varied is lifelong adaptation. Prior adaptation may influence choice of treatment and expectations for acceptable outcomes. People are likely to differ in response to treatment depending upon their prior history of functioning, their experience of treatment success or failure, or their history of chronic, unremitting problems. As an example, goals of interventions for people with a history of chronic schizophrenic symptoms will be different than for older people with average or above average adaptation in earlier life who are now experiencing symptoms of depression.

Despite the importance of this issue, there has been only limited attention to its significance. In one of the earliest works on treatment of the elderly, Abraham (1953) advocated differentiating between the age of the patient and the age of the neurosis. He suggested that the history of the problem was a more significant prognostic indicator than age. Kahn and Zarit (1974) observed that pessimism among clinicians for treating older people derives in part from experience with chronic populations, such as older schizophrenics. In clinical studies, Post (1987) has suggested that persons with late-onset paranoid symptoms have relatively better outcomes than patients with onset of symptoms in early or middle adulthood. Recent studies of depression have indicated some relation of age of onset of symptoms with current symptomatology but not duration of episode (Meyers & Greenberg, 1989, Lewinsohn, Fenn, Stanton, & Franklin, 1986).

Lack of reliable measures to assess prior functioning has limited investigations of the significance of lifelong adaptation. One promising approach is the lifetime version of the Schedule for Affective Disorders and Schizophrenia, or SADS-L (Spitzer & Endicott, 1979). Use of an informant also may provide data with acceptable reliability in some circumstances. Application of assessment approaches for personality disorders for older populations provides another way of estimating long-term functioning and differentiating older subjects on the basis of prior adaptation (see Hyer & Harrison, 1986; Thompson, Gallagher, & Czirr, 1989).

E. Other Individual Characteristics

Community and clinical populations are likely to vary on several other characteristics that will affect psychological intervention, including socioeconomic status, race and ethnicity, social functioning, and health. Differences between men and women in reporting psychological problems and responsiveness to psychologically oriented intervention are important as well. Intervention studies, however, have given little systematic attention to these variables.

F. Age

An important question is the role of age in older adults' responsiveness to psychological intervention. In theory, age carries social and personal meanings that could affect the context of intervention. Several useful perspectives have been proposed that suggest the specific role of age (or stage of life) in interventions.

The work of Neugarten (1976; Neugarten & Hagestad, 1976) and others (Clausen, 1972; Elder, 1975) on the timing of events in the life cycle predicted more social support and anticipatory socialization for on-time events (Danish, Smyer, & Nowak, 1980), although on-time events may also be associated with greater pessimism, as in the case of a serious illness occurring in late life (Zarit & Kahn, 1975). Whitbourne (1985) extended this concept by suggesting that age norms contribute to the development of a psychological construct of the life span. She viewed coping and adaptation as an active process in which people appraise life events through their own interpretation of timing of events and their personal history or scenario. When events potentially challenge a person's scenario or self-esteem, coping processes are activated that may alter the individual's life story, aspirations and/or response to the event. The main point is that the relevance of "age" is viewed from the perspective of the individual's own life-span construct and scenario.

Finally, the question of the effectiveness of psychological interventions in later life can be viewed within the larger framework of life-span developmental psychology. In particular, we are guided by Baltes's model (1987) that stresses multiple patterns of development and change, recognizing that some skills continue to develop as other atrophy. The purpose of intervention is to minimize the effects of atrophy and to maximize development. Ability to use accumulated experience and knowledge wisely become a goal for intervention. Limitations of treatment are also suggested, including that therapists need to be less abstract, more tied to familiar experience, and need to allow for sufficient time for information to be processed (Knight, 1986b). In the broader context, generational and historical experiences will affect the attributions people make about life events and what psychological interventions they view as appropriate or relevant to their situations.

G. The Intervention Setting

Older adults experiencing psychological distress or dysfunction are likely to receive help in a variety of settings. Although the community mental health center system has improved its services for older adults (Lebowitz, 1988), the elderly continue to be underrepresented in the caseload of CMHCs (e.g., Flemming, Buchanan, Santos, & Rickards, 1984; Redick & Taube, 1980). Thus for those interested in psychological interventions with older adults, many nontraditional settings are important as mental health service settings for the elderly. Unfortunately, the research base focused on treatment settings is mainly descriptive, with few experimental or quasi-experimental studies of the comparative advantages of differing treatment settings or service packages in meeting the mental health needs of older adults. Few studies provide comparative information using randomly assigned older adults in different treatment programs or settings (see Pruchno, Boswell, Wolff, & Faletti, 1983, for a noteworthy exception). Lowy's (1980) summary of an earlier review is still apt: There is a paucity of good evaluation studies of programs and services to the aging. Most existing studies are based on "soft" data and tend to measure inputs or throughputs rather than outputs (p. 848).

The intervention setting must be considered in evaluating treatment goals, measures, or outcomes. The most obvious distinction is between community and institutional settings. In making comparisons across these settings, it cannot be assumed that interventions in community settings will necessarily generalize to an institutional site, and vice versa. The conditions of institutional life are sufficiently different that subjects from community or institutional settings cannot be mixed together without regard for place of residence.

Within institutional settings, special characteristics and contingencies affect behavior. Thus there needs to be differentiation of goals of treatment in institutional settings between addressing problems related to the setting (such as reinforcement of dependency) and problems that are independent of the institution. Additionally, although it is important in any intervention study to demonstrate maintenance of gains after completion of the intervention, it is especially so in institutional settings because of common contingencies that reinforce dependencies and other problems. Characteristics of noninstitutional settings should similarly be evaluated for possible effects on behavior.

1. Descriptive Studies

Examination of where older people do and do not receive treatment provides a starting point for consideration of the effects of settings. Shapiro (1986) reviewed data from the Epidemiologic Catchment Area (ECA) program of the National Institute of Mental Health (Regier, Meyers, Kramer, Robins, Blazer, & Hough, 1984). The ECA research program was designed to fill the gaps in epidemiological data existing at the time of the 1978 President's Commission on Mental Health. Drawing on data from the Baltimore area, Shapiro and his colleagues (German, Shapiro, & Kramer, 1986; Shapiro, Skinner, Kessler, Von Korff, German, Tishler, Leaf, Benham, Cottler, & Regier, 1984) documented that older adults are less likely to receive mental health services than those under age 65. When they did seek mental health services, they most often went to their primary care physician. Unfortunately, several studies have found that primary care physicians are unlikely to identify and treat psychiatric and psychological problems in older adults (e.g., Waxman, Carner, & Berkenstock, 1984) or to appropriately refer them to mental health professionals (Kucharski, White, & Schratz, 1979).

Although the ECA data are the most comprehensive and reliable source for describing older adults' service use patterns, similar impressions have emerged from smaller scale studies surveying CMHC staff (e.g., Fox, Swan, & Estes, 1986; Lebowitz, Light, & Bailey, 1987), as well as surveys of community dwelling elderly (e.g., Smyer & Pruchno, 1984; Wilson & Schulz, 1983).

2. Policy Studies

In addition to documenting patterns of service use, several studies have focused on the effects of policy changes in increasing the elderly's access to and use of mental health services. Estes and Wood (1984), for example, interviewed CMHC administrators to assess the effects of block grants on CMHC services. Similarly, Lebowitz and his colleagues (1987) assessed the effects of coordinating agreements between CMHCs and Area Agencies on Aging (AAAs). They concluded that such agreements improve the availability of services for older people. A recent report (Fox et al., 1986) indicated

that the growing decentralization of mental health policy, linked to the block grant mechanism and increased reliance on state funding for CMHCs, has allowed states increasing latitude in targeting services for populations of special concern. Not surprisingly, older adults are not emphasized in every state.

H. Nursing Homes

Recent epidemiological investigations have documented the significant level of mental health distress among nursing home residents (e.g., Burns, Larson, Goldstrom, Johnson, Taube, Miller, & Mathis, 1988; German et al., 1986; Kramer, 1986). In addition, clinical descriptive studies, using geropsychiatrists as interviewers with random samples of nursing home residents verified that the majority of nursing home residents are in need of psychiatric consultation (e.g., Rovner, Kofonek, Filipp, Lucas, & Folstein, 1986). As with other settings, most of the research in nursing homes has been descriptive, with little in the way of comparative investigation (Smyer, Cohn, & Brannon, 1988, provide a review of the setting and mental health treatment efforts).

I. Other Settings

Day care programs (e.g., Eskew, Sexton, Tars, & Wilcox, 1983; Mace & Rabins, 1984), neighborhood health care centers (e.g., Goldstrom, Burns, Kessler, Feuerberg, Larson, Miller, & Cromer, 1987), and in-home geriatric assessment teams (e.g., Knight, 1983) embody alternative programs. Other researchers have focused on reaching other types of service providers who ordinarily come in contact with the elderly, providing them with information about the psychology of later life and mental health issues. Target groups have included public utility meter readers (e.g., Raschko, 1985), as well as employees of more traditional social service agencies such as public housing and welfare agencies (e.g., Santos, Hubbard, Burdick, & Santos, 1983).

In summary, this section has emphasized the importance of both individual characteristics and setting characteristics as determinants of the outcomes of psychological interventions with older adults. Eventually, intervention research must focus on the combination of individual characteristics and setting characteristics that provide optional intervention success.

III. The Service Array: Types of Intervention for Older Adults

A variety of psychological interventions have been tried with older adults. They build upon a diversity of theoretical models and target a diversity of outcomes. This section begins with a discussion of individual psychotherapies with a focus on the three approaches that have been reported most often: psychoanalytic, behavioral, and cognitive-behavioral. Marital and sex therapy and group approaches will then be described. Although these treatments draw on the same theories of psychotherapy described in the section of individual psychotherapy, (e.g., psychoanalytic, behavioral), they share common properties and approaches that warrant consideration separately. Finally, we will consider environmental interventions and preventive efforts.

A. Individual Psychotherapy

Psychodynamic Therapy for the Elderly

Despite Freud's belief that the analysis of older adults was inappropriate due to their difficulty in learning and their long personal history, subsequent analysts have described numerous successful treatments (Nemiroff & Colarusso, 1985; Rechtschaffen, 1959; Sadavoy & Leszcz, 1987). However, the goals, as well as the process of treatment, may differ from traditional analysis. Many analysts question the appropriateness of engaging an older adult in a complete analysis. Restitution of ego functioning from crisis states is considered a viable goal for many elderly (Kahana, 1987). Goldfarb's therapy encouraged exaggeration, rather than resolution, of the transference for ill or cognitively impaired elderly by offering supportive therapy (Goldfarb, 1956). Recently, however, some analysts have begun to emphasize the viability of traditional analysis for older adults if patients are chosen with the same care as extended to young adults (Cath, 1983). Others (e.g., Horowitz, Marmar, Weiss, DeWitt, & Rosenbaum, 1984) have focused on short-term, time-limited adaptations of psychodynamic approaches.

Analysis of the transference, the basic process of psychoanalytic therapy, is considered to be particularly complex due to the patients' greater age. Although older adults may engage in "repetition compulsions" rooted in early childhood, there is increased recognition that the lengthy adult personal history may be both more cognitively salient (Nemiroff & Colarusso, 1985) and more important to the older adult's current construction of his or her world view than are events from earliest childhood (Cohler, 1980). Equally complex, countertransference issues may reflect the therapists' issues as parent, child, or grandchild.

Analysts embrace a developmental model for adulthood (Colarusso & Nemiroff, 1981). Two foci of development have been identified: social and physical losses and emerging capabilities. The most common focus is on themes of loss and dependence because they are increasingly salient due to the high rate of personal losses in later life (Nemiroff & Colarusso, 1985). In contrast, Gutmann (1980) proposed that late-life development includes the emergence of new capabilities and qualities. Gutmann's theory postulates that the second half of life is a continuation of individual development themes that were interrupted by the "chronic emergency" of parenting. The demands of parenting require parents to specialize, disrupting the balance of individual development. Traditional gender roles that emphasize male instrumentality and female expressivity in early adulthood set the stage for a predictable switch for males and females in the second half of adulthood. Psychopathology in later life is interpreted in the context of this developmental transition. Dysfunction reflects a block in the males' development of expressivity and the females' development of instrumentality.

There are very few systematic examinations of the efficacy of psychoanalytic or psychodynamic treatment of elderly patients. However, studies of the relationship between psychotherapy process and outcome are yielding information about critical ingredients of successful psychodynamic therapy with elderly clients. In a small sample of elderly psychotherapy patients in which an individualized outcome scaling technique was used to measure treatment gains, seven of eight patients experienced significant symptom improvement at the endpoint of treatment or at 6-month follow-up (Lazarus, Groves, Guttman, Ripekyj, Frankel, Newton, Gruner, & Havasy-Galloway, 1987). Analysis of videotapes of each treatment process led to the observation that the therapy was used consistently to "restore self-esteem and self-continuity and/or to consolidate diverse, disparate, or emergent aspects of the self into a more positive coherent sense of self" (Lazarus et al., 1987, p. 278). A more rigorous examination of the process-outcome relationship in psychodynamic therapy involved therapy of bereaved persons, many of whom were in the second half of life (Horowitz et al., 1984). Patient dispositional variables

(motivation and self-organization) interacted with process variables (therapeutic alliance and therapist action) in affecting outcome. Highly motivated and/or better organized patients benefitted more from exploratory actions, whereas supportive interventions were more effective with patients with low motivation and/or poor self-organization. These data may be viewed as supportive of the clinical lore that recommends careful selection of elderly patients for longer term, depth therapies.

Although psychoanalysts tend to rely upon case history studies, more traditional therapy outcome studies have provided support for the efficacy of time-limited psychodynamic therapy for depression (see description of Gallagher and Thompson's research).

B. Behavior Therapy

Behavior therapy involving application of principles of learning has been demonstrated to be effective with older persons for a variety of problems in a variety of settings. The most common research or case reports evaluate the effects of one or two procedures on a single problem, although more complex applications of behavioral approaches to multifaceted problems like depression, insomnia, and family caregiving also have been developed (see Bootzin, Engle-Friedman, & Hazelwood, 1983; Gallagher, Thompson, Baffa, Piatt, Ringering, & Stone, 1981; Green, Linsk, & Pinkston, 1986; Lewinsohn, Antonuccio, Steinmetz, & Teri, 1984; Hussian, 1986; Hussian & Davis, 1985; Haley, 1983; Pinkston & Linsk, 1984a,b). Given the relatively optimistic tone of behavioral therapy, it is perhaps surprising that the literature is not more extensive. Although experimental studies show some differences in learning between older and younger individuals, simple modifications of techniques (e.g., using errorless procedures, massed practice, or controlling for the anxiety or fatigue of older people) can reduce these problems (see Burgio & Burgio, 1986).

Much of the behavioral literature involves intervention in institutional settings. The theoretical and empirical work of Baltes and her colleagues (Baltes, 1982; Baltes & Baltes, 1986; Baltes, Honn, Barton, Orzech, & Lago, 1983; Baltes & Reisenzein, 1986; Baltes & Werner-Wahl, 1987) provided a context for these studies. Baltes *et al.* have demonstrated differential patterns of reinforcement of dependent and independent behavior within nursing homes, with staff generally providing social reinforcements for dependent behavior during self-care activities. These contingencies have been found to be reversed in family care settings. This work identified the mechanisms through which excess disabilities (Kahn, 1975; Kahn & Zarit, 1974) might develop in institutional settings. It also suggested that reversal of these contingencies and other changes in staff–patient interactions should be beneficial.

Several studies have demonstrated behavior change among institutionalized samples of elderly, including increased activity (MacDonald, Davidowitz, Gimbel, & Foley, 1982; O'Quin, O'Dell, & Burnett, 1982), increased attendance at therapeutic activities (Carstensen & Erickson, 1986; Gross & Martin, 1982), and increased exercise (Perkins, Rapp, Carlson, & Wallace, 1986). Burgio, Burgio, Engel, and Tice (1986) increased the degree of independence and distance of walking among nursing home residents. Patterson and his colleagues (McEvoy & Patterson, 1986; Patterson, Dupree, Eberly, Jackson, O'Sullivan, Penner, & Dee-Kelly, 1982; Patterson & Eberly, 1983) have developed a series of modules for training subjects in self-care, social skills, and cognitive tasks. Subjects included both older, long-term psychiatric patients and community residents at risk for institutionalization. The researchers proposed a link between social

skills and activities of daily living (ADLs), in that impairment in either domain may result in a breakdown of social supports needed to maintain an older person in the community or to achieve successful placement of formerly institutionalized patients. Results of their training program were generally positive, though they noted differences in learning between cognitively intact and impaired elderly, with the latter performing better on tasks that they can physically practice and less well on cognitive activities (McEvoy & Patterson, 1986).

Hussian (1981, 1982, 1986, 1987; Hussian & Davis, 1985) has contributed to the development of the behavioral interventions in institutional settings and specifically to management of severe behavior problems. He proposed that behaviors such as wandering and disorientation may be the result of ineffective stimulus control and reported that enhancing stimuli and pairing them with positive or aversive reinforcers can reduce these problems (Hussian, 1982, 1987).

Other specific problems that have been treated successfully in institutional settings using behavioral methods include chronic pain (Haley & Colce, 1986; Linoff & West, 1982; Miller & LeLieuore, 1982), tardive dyskinesia (Jackson & Schonfeld, 1982), and poor social interaction among elderly mentally retarded persons (Kleitsch, Whitman, & Santos, 1983). A particularly innovative intervention was conducted by Praderas and MacDonald (1986) who trained socially isolated nursing home residents in telephone conversational skills as a way to increase contacts with the outside world.

Another problem that has received considerable attention in both inpatient and outpatient settings is incontinence. Programs to reduce incontinence have included use of behavioral assessments to identify rates and possible antecedents and consequences, schedules, bladder training, contingency management, and biofeedback (Burgio & Engel, 1987; Sanavio, 1981; Schnelle, Traughber, Morgan, Embry, Binion, & Coleman, 1983; Spangler, Risley, & Bilyew, 1984). To an extent, regular verbal prompts of patients with limited mobility in nursing homes have been successful. Outpatient programs using a multimodal approach including self-monitoring, exercises, scheduled toileting, and biofeedback have demonstrated an 85% reduction of urinary incontinence and a 78% reduction of fecal incontinence (Burgio, Whitehead, & Engel, 1985; Whitehead, Burgio, & Engel, 1985).

C. Cognitive-Behavioral Therapy

Cognitive-behavioral therapy emphasizes the role of thoughts as mediators of behavior and emotions. In contrast to other approaches, researchers working with a cognitive-behavioral orientation have tended to compare their treatment with other approaches. A rich comparative literature has been emerging as a result. This trend is typified in the work of Gallagher and Thompson, who pioneered application of cognitive-behavior therapy with the elderly (Gallagher & Thompson, 1982, 1983; Thompson, Gallagher, & Breckenridge, 1987; Thompson, Davies, Gallagher, & Krantz, 1986). Gallagher and Thompson have conducted two major outcome studies of treatment of depression and have written extensively on clinical and research issues concerning cognitive-behavioral therapy.

In the initial study (Gallagher & Thompson, 1982), cognitive therapy was compared to two other time-limited approaches for treatment of depression: Lewinsohn's behavioral treatment (Lewinsohn et al., 1984) and short-term psychodynamic therapy based on the work of Bellack and Small (1965). Each treatment included 16 sessions. Subjects were interviewed with the Schedule for Affective Disorders and Schizophrenia (SADS) and

met research diagnostic criteria (RDC) for major depressive disorder. Results showed no initial differences between treatment conditions, but maintenance was better for subjects who had received either behavioral or cognitive psychotherapy.

Subsequent analysis (Gallagher & Thompson, 1983) examined the outcome in relation to initial presence or absence of endogenous features. The operational criteria for endogenous depression included presence of diurnal mood swings, loss of interest or pleasure in usual activities, irrational self-reproach, loss of appetite and weight loss, and insomnia. The presence of endogenous features at initial assessment was related to poorer outcome. Only one-third of those subjects who met the criteria for endogenous depression were symptom free at 1 year, compared to 80% of subjects who did not meet the criteria.

The second controlled study contrasted four conditions: behavioral, cognitive, brief psychodynamic, and a wait list control (Thompson et al., 1987). Subjects again met the RDC for major depression. The results showed that subjects in the three treatment groups improved, whereas wait list subjects did not. After completion of between 16 and 20 therapy sessions, 52% of the subjects who received treatment no longer met diagnostic criteria for depression, and another 18% had significant improvement. These gains were maintained after 1 year, with no differences in outcome among the three treatment conditions (Gallagher, Thompson, & Breckenridge, 1986). Thus all three structured, time-limited psychotherapies appear useful for treatment of depressed older people. Some common features of these psychotherapies, such as therapist qualities or the time limit on treatment, might account for these results. These positive findings stand out in contrast to relatively pessimistic statements about the prognosis of late-life depression made by other research teams.

Thompson et al. (1989) have recently

studied treatment failure in relation to premorbid level of adjustment. Subjects with evidence of a preexisting personality disorder were more likely to have a poor or incomplete response to psychotherapy.

Results of other research teams provide partial replication of the Gallagher and Thompson findings on effectiveness of treatment of depression, although with some important differences. Jarvik and her colleagues (Jarvik, Mintz, Steuer, & Gerner, 1982; Steuer, Mintz, Hammen, Hill, Jarvik, McCarley, Motike, & Rosen, 1984) reported somewhat more modest results for outcomes of cognitive therapy with depressed elderly. Comparing cognitive and psychodynamic therapy, they found that only 30% of all psychotherapy subject improved, although those who completed 9 months of treatment had rates of improvement comparable to the Gallagher and Thompson studies, with 40% in remission and another 40% with some symptomatic reduction. There are two important differences in the design of this study, however. Subjects were assigned to psychotherapy only after being judged ineligible for a drug study, usually because of medical contraindications for use of tricyclics, and psychotherapy was conducted in groups, rather than individually.

A research team headed by Beutler (Beutler, Scogin, Kirkish, Schretlen, Corbishley, Hamblin, Meredith, Potter, Bamford, & Levinson, 1987) compared group cognitive therapy to a supportive condition and to use of a medication (Alprazolam). They found improvements in all treated groups, with the most evidence for change among subjects who had received cognitive therapy. It should be noted that tricyclic medications are more frequently prescribed for depression than are minor tranquilizers like Alprazolam.

In a clinical paper, Thompson *et al.* (1986) suggested differences between cognitive therapy with the elderly and that with younger people. They posited that older people are, on average, more passive in therapy, that their depression is due to aging or medical problems, or solely the result of a loss, and that clients need to move at a slower pace. They also recommended that termination be done more gradually by tapering out the last sessions. Similar observations were made by Steuer and Hammen (1983).

Recently, Teri and Gallagher (1989) have suggested possible applications of cognitive therapy for mildly impaired dementia patients. Finally, Evans, Smith, Werkhoven, Fox, and Pritzl (1986) reported successful use of a cognitive therapy approach with group therapy via a conference call for disabled elders. Results showed decreased loneliness, improved mood, and attainment of goals for the treatment group, when compared to controls, although the control group was not described.

Taken as a whole, these studies represent the most extensive empirical inquiry into treatment outcome. Rather than suggesting that cognitive approaches are more effective, these studies indicate that structured, short-term psychotherapy of any type has impressive results with older people. The magnitude of improvement appears to be at least comparable to drug studies of similar patient groups (see Thompson *et al.*, 1987), although, as was noted, the one direct comparison with a medication did not test a commonly used drug. An underlying theme of much of this work is that psychotherapy could play a significant role in treatment of depression among the elderly. As Borson and Raskind (1986) observed, biologically based treatments are most appropriate for endogenous and other severe depressions, but large numbers of patients who might benefit from psychotherapy or other nonbiologic treatment often do not receive it.

D. Life Review

Another influential perspective has been developed by Butler and Lewis (Butler,

1963; Butler & Lewis, 1982). They proposed that life review may play a critical role in psychological adaptation in late life and suggested therapeutic procedures for enhancing this process, including use of multigenerational groups. Despite the popularity of this concept, there is no evidence to date of the usefulness of life review interventions or that it is a universal process (Kastenbaum, 1987).

E. Marital and Sex Therapy with Older Couples

Although the reasons older couples seek marital therapy may be unclear, the challenges faced by older couples in later life are apparent. Several of the tasks of later life require change in both members of the marital dyad: the exit (and reentry) of children, retirement, physical health decline, housing transitions, and severe disability of one or both members of the couple. Not only do these transitions require individual adjustments by both members of the dyad, but the couple frequently must alter mutual role expectations, share identities, and alter communication styles and strategies. The concept of developmental tasks for couples is receiving increasing support (Lee, 1986; Wolinsky, 1986). Wolinsky (1986) identified several marital developmental tasks that occur because of the increasing amounts of time couples spend together postretirement and because of the increased rate of illness and disability: redefining intimacy and roles; setting new goals; learning to live together without undue concern for the illness or death of the spouse; and developing the capacities to mourn self-losses, to nurture and to let go, and to view oneself as an individual.

There are a few published case studies but no controlled outcome studies of marital therapy. Case illustrations of the application of conjoint therapy with psychiatric patients (LaWall, 1981), paradoxical intervention in long-term conflicted couples (Gafner, 1987; Gilewski, Kuppinger, & Zarit, 1985), structural family therapy with depressed couples (Gallagher & Frankl, 1980), and insight-oriented couples therapy (Wolinsky, 1986) reflect the possibilities of applying many of the traditional marital therapy approaches to older couples.

Most therapists recognize the importance of distinguishing between couples who have experienced conflict throughout their marriages and those whose conflict is limited to the difficulties inherent to the negotiation of the major transitions of later life. Couples with long-term conflict may escalate the conflict in later life as they spend more time together and have more role overlap. Gilewski et al. (1985) presented a model for using paradoxical interventions with long-term conflicted couples whose poverty of mutual nurturance leaves both spouses resistant to investing in change processes.

Couples with no previous history of marital conflict may experience considerable distress because they do not recognize the extent of change required to adapt to the transitions of later life. Therapists may begin by offering information about the nature of the transitions and providing the couple with labels for their experiences. It is not uncommon for marital therapists to become involved in helping clients seek resources to help them cope with these challenges. The recent emphasis on caregiver functioning (see Gatz & Bengtson, this volume) reflects the growing awareness that both partners require support and emotional resources when one member is ill. Some previously well-functioning couples appear to lack sufficient communication skills to renegotiate roles of interaction patterns. Skills that were adequate for maintaining roles may be inadequate for transition periods. These couples may benefit from communication or problem-solving training.

Americans appear to be accepting sexuality as a normal part of older married life

(Roff & Klemmack, 1979). Therapists are encouraged to investigate the sexual functioning of older clients regardless of their diagnosis, as one would do with younger clients (Liptzin, 1984; Renshaw, 1984). In addition, therapists should be aware that sexual difficulties may arise as a result of chronic illness. Murphy, Hudson, and Cheung (1980) found a 20% incidence rate for sex-related problems in persons in the second half of life. Sexual problems and sexual dissatisfactions were both related to marital dissatisfaction in their sample (Murphy *et al.*, 1980). Case reports of sex therapy with older couples describe the use of traditional behavioral interventions with attention given to the developmental context of disorders and relationship dynamics (Apfel, Fox, Isberg, & Levine, 1984; Liptzin, 1984; Renshaw, 1984; Whitlatch & Zarit, 1989). One uncontrolled therapy outcome study reported the use of traditional behavioral interventions (education, communication exercises, and instruction in sexual techniques) with older married couples (Rowland & Haynes, 1978). The intervention was successful in reducing the amount of marital disagreement, in increasing the amount of sexual satisfaction, and in increasing the frequency of sexual behaviors.

F. Group Treatments

The use of groups as a therapeutic agent has had wide application. Groups have been based on the major therapeutic models that have been used in one-on-one therapy with older persons (e.g., psychodynamic, behavioral, cognitive-behavioral), although many groups are run in an atheoretical manner. In addition to therapy groups, self-help and psychoeducational groups have been popular intervention approaches. Work by Lieberman and his associates (Lieberman, 1983, 1987; Lieberman & Bliwise, 1985; Lieberman & Videka-Sherman, 1986) has been instrumental in characterizing differences in

processes of change between self-help and psychotherapy models of change, as well as in considering the effects of whether the leader is a professional or a peer. Similarly, Gallagher, Lovett, and Zeiss (1989) recently identified key features of psychoeducational approaches.

Lieberman noted that psychotherapy groups involve facilitation of change by focusing on interactions and experiences in the group setting. Both problem-focused and personal-growth (or self-actualization) groups share this emphasis, despite some differences in goals and techniques. In contrast, self-help groups provide interactions that lead to normalization of experiences and mutual support, including linking participants to a new social network. The type of leader (professional versus peer) does not necessarily determine the kind of group.

In psychoeducational groups, the main focus is on development of new skills to improve coping with stressors and to decrease adverse emotions, for example, depression or anger (Gallagher *et al.*, 1989). Features of these groups include helping participants break their global complaints into specific components, providing educational materials, and using guided exercises and homework. Here, an important hypothesized mechanism of change is improved self-efficacy. Thus this approach uses many cognitive and behavioral approaches, although in an educational format.

The boundaries among these three types of groups are not rigid, and groups may have some features of each type. Nonetheless, clear identification of prominent change mechanisms in different types of groups will help clinicians evaluate older clients for placement in groups and will guide researchers by suggesting what dimension or behaviors should change in a particular intervention.

Literature on psychotherapy groups has been the most limited in the past few years. Most papers are clinical, with only a few providing data and even fewer providing controlled outcome studies. The most detailed treatment protocol is provided by Yost, Beutler, Corbishley, and Allender (1986) who have adapted Beck's cognitive therapy for use in groups of older people. In outpatient settings, groups have been used with a variety of special populations. DeBor and Gallagher (1982) reported that a cognitively oriented group for widows, which emphasized reframing, encouragement of social activities, and relaxation training, was evaluated positively by participants. Leszcz (1987) proposed that group therapy has particular relevance because of the relative social isolation of many older people. He suggested that losses are a major theme of group discussions. A a result, leadership of the group must be flexible and supportive, so as to contribute to maintaining self-esteem in the face of losses.

Group programs have been found to be effective for involving people who do not respond to other interventions, for example, older female Hispanics (Franklin & Kaufman, 1982). Gilewski (1986) discussed possible group therapy interventions with cognitively impaired older adults. Reminiscence and life review groups continue to be popular in community settings, although as noted earlier, measurement of outcome remains problematic (see also Sherman, 1987; Molinari & Reichlin, 1984–1985).

In a rare controlled study, Scharlach (1987) compared involvement in a cognitive-behavioral group with that in a supportive condition and being on a wait list for relieving strain among middle-aged women in their relationships with elderly mothers. Subjects in the cognitive condition reported more reduction in feelings of burden and more improvement in the quality of their relationships with their mothers. A unique feature of this study was that the mothers of two thirds of the subjects were also interviewed. Mothers' feelings of loneliness decreased most when their daughters were in the cognitive condition.

One of the most innovative group programs is SAGE, which is based in northern California and offers interventions for older persons drawn from the human potential movement. Lieberman and Gourash (1979) evaluated SAGE groups compared to a wait list control, finding that treated subjects reported reductions of psychiatric symptoms and greater goal attainment. They also noted a discrepancy between the program's objective, which was to emphasize growth rather than repair, and the fact that many participants were experiencing levels of symptoms typical of patient populations.

Turning to group therapy in an inpatient setting, Moran and Gatz (1987) tested differences between a task-oriented group, in which participants would use or develop competencies; an insight-oriented group; and a wait list control group. Both therapy groups showed an increase in internal locus of control compared to controls. Members of the task group reported improved life satisfaction, whereas those in the insight group reported increased feelings of trust, compared to no change in the task group and a decrease of trust among wait list subjects. Although the sample size is small, this study is one of the few that examines theoretically interesting treatment dimensions that are linked to differential predictions about outcome.

Self-help groups have been investigated extensively by Lieberman and his associates (see Lieberman & Borman, 1979). These studies have not focused exclusively on groups for older people, but several programs included significant numbers of elderly, such as widows' groups. Lieberman (1987) noted, however, that older people tend to be underrepresented in these groups, compared to the proportion of older widows in the general population.

Outcomes of self-help groups are generally positive (Lieberman & Borman, 1979; Lieberman, 1987). In a study of widows' groups, Lieberman and Videka-Sherman (1986) found that participants showed more improvement over a 1-year period than nonparticipants, who were on the mailing list but did not attend groups or were part of a normative sample of widows. A key factor leading to change was making new social linkages through the group. Other mechanisms of change found to be important include normalization of one's experiences, support, and altruism, whereas the least helpful change mechanisms were expressions of strong emotions, revealing personal information, and receiving feedback from others (Lieberman, 1983).

Two studies have compared peer and professionally led groups. Lieberman and Bliwise (1985) reported that SAGE groups led by professionals resulted in more relief of psychiatric symptoms than did peer-led groups, although subjects in both conditions reported similar degrees of goal attainment. The researchers believed the poorer outcome of the peer-led groups was associated with the attempted implementation of a professional, rather than self-help model. Toseland, Rossiter, and Lebrecque (1987) compared caregiver support groups led by peers or professionals. As found by Lieberman and Bliwise, there was a general trend for subjects in professionally led groups to have more improvement in psychological functioning than those in peer led groups. Subjects in peer led groups, however, had more positive changes in their support network. This differential outcome appeared to be related to differences in group activities. There was a stronger emphasis on problem solving in the professionally led groups, whereas peer-led groups spent more time on socializing and sharing personal experiences. Overall, both groups were rated positively by participants.

The third type of group, psychoeducational, has been popular in part because it does not carry the same stigma as formal mental health services, yet these groups are able to attract participants with significant problems (see, for example, Thompson, Gallagher, Nies, & Epstein, 1983; Anthony-Bergstone, Zarit, & Gatz, 1988). The primary application of psychoeducational approaches has been with family caregivers. Although caregiver support groups have their origins in a self-help tradition, most published reports describe or evaluate programs with a significant psychoeducational component (an exception is Schmidt & Keyes, 1985, who use a psychotherapy model for dementia caregivers). A variety of programs have been described (e.g., Aronson, Levin, & Lipkowitz, 1984; Davies, Priddy, & Tinklenberg, 1986; Haley, Brown, & Levine, 1987; Greene & Monahan, 1987; Gallagher, Lovett, & Zeiss, in press; Glosser & Wexler, 1985; Zarit, Orr, & Zarit, 1985), with some preliminary outcome studies now appearing.

G. Milieu Approaches

Earlier reviews of milieu therapy (e.g., Gotestam, 1980; Raskin, 1976; Sherwood & Mor, 1980) have focused on two types of approaches encompassed by the term: One approach builds upon group dynamics and the development of a supportive social structure (e.g., Donahue, Hunter, & Coons, 1953; Gatz, Siegler, & Dibner, 1979–1980; Gottesman, Donahue, Coons, & Ciarlo, 1969); another approach builds explicitly upon behavioral principles to structure the physical and social environments (e.g., McClannahan & Risley, 1973, 1974, 1975; Patterson *et al.*, 1982). A few studies (e.g., Mishara, 1978) explicitly compared the two approaches.

In addition to these two general approaches, attempts to implement and evaluate reality orientation (RO) programs (Folsom, 1968) are sometimes included in discussions of milieu therapies. Outcome research on RO has been equivocal (Storandt, 1977). Although some have questioned its efficacy (Schwenk, 1979), a recent review concluded that RO is more effective than nonspecific treatments (Powell-Proctor & Miller, 1982). Kastenbaum (1987) summarized the literature on RO: "RO deserves more appropriate and capable research attention and, probably, also some continuing place in clinical gerontology" (p. 324).

The RO discussion exemplifies difficulties with the research literature on milieu approaches. Several problems are apparent in the general literature. First, many studies offer only a program description of a single intervention, with no comparison or control group. Second, even when control groups are present, random assignment to treatment is usually not possible, given the demands and constraints of service settings. Thus the groups contrasted are often not comparable at the outset of the experimental study. Third, many studies suffer from a lack of specificity regarding the outcomes desired or targeted. Fourth, some studies also focus on short-term changes, while not allowing for longer term consequences of interventions or contraindications of treatment (see Langer & Rodin, 1976; Rodin & Langer, 1977). As Gotestam (1980) noted, behavioral researchers generally have been better than researchers from other theoretical schools at designing and implementing rigorous evaluations of the effects of environmental approaches.

H. Preventive Interventions

In contrast to the service approaches described thus far, another type of intervention—preventive—is usually undertaken prior to the development of significant problems. Reviews of preventive interventions with older adults (e.g., Gatz, 1985; Kastenbaum, 1987; Rodin, Cashman, & Desiderato, 1986; Smyer, Gatz, & Pruchno, 1988) have highlighted three salient elements: the level of the intervention, the timing of the intervention, and the strategy of change.

Preventive efforts traditionally have focused on three broad levels of intervention: individual, family, or primary social group, and community or larger social group. Gatz (1985) emphasized three general targets for preventive interventions: those who are now old, families of impaired elderly, and the general public. Among the current elderly, three general areas have been highlighted as important targets of intervention: self-care capacity, including cognitive self-management strategies; social support and friendships; and self-management of medical and health-related problems (Gatz, 1985; Kastenbaum, 1987).

Timing has traditionally referred to whether the intervention occurs earlier or later in the problem process, similar to Caplan's (1964) distinction among primary, secondary, and tertiary preventions. Kastenbaum (1987) also emphasized the "tempo" of the intervention, a component of timing: "A prevention program is more likely to succeed when it receives a level of intensity and a rate of action (tempo) that matches the receptivity of its intended clientele and when it is introduced at a strategic moment" (p. 326).

Strategies of change reflect the specific types of interventions undertaken (e.g., education, consultation, developing support networks, advocacy). In addition, any specific approach can be implemented within a framework that assumes either deficits or competency on the part of the service recipient (Heller & Monahan, 1977).

Careful, systematic research with preventive interventions is sparse. Several questions must be answered in assessing the efficacy of preventive approaches: What is the specific target of the intervention? What are the essential, effective components of the intervention? What is the hypothesized outcome of the intervention? What are the short-term and long-term patterns of outcomes expected? Unfortunately, many of the preventive efforts in the literature are primarily descriptive in nature, with little attention given to the demands of experimental design. (See Smyer & Gatz, 1983, for a sample of program evaluations that reflect the varied level of research maturity in the field.)

IV. Professional and Policy Issues

The implementation of interventions depends on the interrelated issues of professionals who provide service and public policies that affect service delivery, reimbursement, and training of professionals.

A. The Professionals Who Provide Services

Psychological interventions are provided by professionals from many disciplines: nursing, social work, medicine, rehabilitation, psychology, and psychiatry, among others. Because psychological intervention often occurs outside of traditional outpatient and inpatient mental health settings, professionals and paraprofessionals from varied backgrounds will be called upon to intervene on behalf of the psychological well-being of their clients.

Several researchers have surveyed the extent to which professionals are involved in the mental health care of the elderly. Approximately 30% of psychologists see clients age 60+ for testing or therapy, and the actual number of elderly clients seen is quite small (Dye, 1978; VandenBos, Strapp, & Kilburg, 1981). Apparently much of this service occurs in institutions and hospitals. Only 2.7% of psychologists in office-based practices see elderly (Taube, Burns, & Kessler, 1984), compared with 15.7% of office-based psychiatrists.

Several reasons have been offered for the low rate of mental health professionals' involvement with elderly clients. Negative attitudes of mental health professionals toward elderly and negative expectations about treatment outcome have been demonstrated (Dye, 1978; Setting, 1982). In a careful analysis of the professional ageism hypothesis, Gatz and Pearson (1988) argued that attitudes toward elderly are complex and are only partially based on age-related biases. Their review of this literature suggested that a generalized age bias is less apparent among mental health professionals than specific beliefs about prevalence of diagnoses and treatment efficacy (see also, Knight, 1986c).

Another reason for low rates of mental health professional involvement is the lack of referrals from health care providers and community agencies. Nurses in long-term care tend not to refer patients with psychiatric symptoms for further evaluation despite their knowledge that the symptoms are likely to reflect psychological disorder (Caston, 1983). Similarly, physicians are unlikely to refer older patients for mental health consultation (Waxman et al., 1984).

A significant reason for lack of professional involvement with older clients is the difficulty of obtaining funding for mental health services and the low rates of Medicare reimbursement. Office-based psychologists receive less private payment for mental health services than psychiatrists (Taube et al., 1984), most likely due to psychologists' status as nonindependent providers under Medicare (other than in rural areas and CMHCs) and Medicaid (in many states), which makes it almost impossible for them to receive indirect (third party) payment.

The lack of training opportunities in geriatric mental health care is also a barrier to professional involvement with elderly clients. Only a limited range of programs provide aging-related courses in social work (Nelson, 1983), psychology (Storandt, 1977), and medicine (Satin, 1986); and even fewer offer fully credentialed specialty training in gerontology (Peterson, 1986). Community colleges have begun to offer associate degrees in gerontology that focus on "front-line" services (recreation/rehabilitation in health care settings and community services) that are involved with mental health needs (Mosher, 1983). Students completing training programs specializing in gerontology are successful in finding aging-related jobs (Connelly, 1986; Fruit, 1985; Peterson, 1985). However, the training programs simply cannot provide enough practitioners to meet the predicted demand.

A final factor contributing to lack of involvement with elderly clients is mental health organization variables. In recent years, many community mental health programs have been initiated [Knight, Reinhart, & Field, 1982; Parish & Landsberg, 1984; Ronch & Solomon, 1978; Selan & Gold, 1980; entire issue of *International Journal of Mental Health*, 1979–1980, **8** (3–4)], primarily as outreach programs serving elderly in nontraditional sites (e.g., senior centers, nutrition sites, homes) with the goal of preventing premature institutionalization. In an evaluation of the organizational factors in community mental health centers that influenced older adults' use of mental health services, Knight (1986a) found that the number of staff assigned to geriatric services predicted outpatient utilization, whereas the percentage of elderly advisory board members was an inverse predictor of inpatient utilization. These organizational variables were independent of population factors. Apparently, priorities for resources within institutions continue to be major determinants of service provision.

In light of most elderly's lack of access to mental health professionals, paraprofessional helpers have been considered as a viable alternative (Santos *et al.*, 1983). Although peer counselors and paraprofessionals are able to learn the social skills (Becker & Zarit, 1978) and behavioral principles (Linsk & Pinkston, 1984) involved in creating behavior change, it has been less clear that they produce the same effects on the clients. Gatz, Hileman, and Amaral (1984) concluded that paraprofessionals should be used to supplement rather than substitute for professionals.

The strongest evidence of paraprofessional effectiveness demonstrated that paraprofessionals had the same success rate as professionals in treating depressed elderly in "coping with depression" classes (Thompson *et al.*, 1983). Variability of success rates was only related to the willingness of the instructor to stay with the treatment protocol. Additional studies of paraprofessional effectiveness in a broad range of interventions are needed and apparently show considerable promise. Likely, mental health professionals can collaborate with paraprofessionals to extend the range of outreach efforts in a variety of institutional settings.

Interdisciplinary teams are touted as the appropriate way to address the complex interrelatedness of physical and mental health problems in older persons (Kerski, Drinka, Carnes, Golob, & Craig, 1987; VandenBos & Buchanan, 1983). Team-building tools have been identified (Czirr & Rappaport, 1984), and models of team functioning have been offered (Qualls & Czirr, 1988). Recently, evaluations of the efficacy and cost-effectiveness of team interventions have been accomplished with increasing rigor. In an exemplary true experiment, Zeiss and O'Karma (1984) randomly assigned patients in an arthritis clinic to one of four team conditions. They found that full team participation in clinical interviews with patients (in either an assessment and referral or a treatment model) and a model in which a case manager worked individually with each patient and used the team only for consultation were superior to a traditional physician-centered treatment model. Patients in the team conditions reported higher life satisfaction and lower depression scores, along with lower hospitalization rates and improved joint measures. The case manager model was most cost-effective and produced the best mental health outcome measures. This study illustrates the value of solid outcome research in testing the assumption that teams are a superior treatment model even as it identifies preferable procedures for teams to use. Apparently, although team assessments may be superior to traditional physician-centered evaluation, full team involvement in treatment may not be superior to a strong case management approach that involves team members as needed (Kerski *et al.*, 1987; Zeiss & O'Karma, 1984). Certainly, the cost of having several professionals involved with a single case is greater than the service system currently can bear (Satin, 1986).

B. Public Policy and the Funding of Psychological Interventions

An implicit theme in much of the discussion thus far is that the success of intervention depends upon making available appropriate services in appropriate modes at optimal times for targeted segments of the elderly population. Each of these components—service provider, service setting, timing of intervention, and service population—is affected by funding decisions regarding the availability and purpose of services. For psychological interventions, three major public funding streams provide a context for working with older adults: the Medicare program; the Medicaid program; and funding of community mental health centers (CMHCs).

Medicare was enacted in 1965 to insure older adults for the costs of acute illness. In 1985, the majority of Medicare expenditures (69%) went to hospitals, followed by physicians (25%), other care (5%) and nursing homes (1%) (U.S. Senate, 1986). In contrast, Medicaid was developed in 1966 as a collaborative effort by federal and state governments to provide medical assistance for needy citizens with low incomes, including the elderly. In 1985, more than two-thirds of the Medicaid budget was spent on nursing home care, primarily for older adults (U.S. Senate, 1986).

The third major public element influencing psychological services for older adults is the community mental health center system. CMHCs have traditionally focused on mandated services, including services for older adults (Bloom, 1975; Levine, 1981). A recurrent complaint, however, has been that CMHCs have traditionally underserved older adults. Two policy shifts—a move to block grants for federal funds in alcohol, drug abuse, and mental health services, and an increasing reliance on state support—have eliminated the mandated emphasis on older adults' services (Fox *et al.*, 1986). Thus there is continuing concern about the viability of CMHCs as a treatment site for mentally ill elderly. Recent analyses (e.g., Lebowitz *et al.*, 1987) indicate that categorical CMHC services targeted for older adults can make CHMCs more responsive to older adults' mental health service needs.

The net result of recent legislative changes in Medicare and Medicaid has been to increase the visibility of cost issues for services to older adults, while increasing state-level flexibility in determining which types of services will be paid for. Although there have been comprehensive suggestions for revising Medicare (e.g., Blumenthal, Schlesinger, & Drumheller, 1986), the decentralization of decision making that has marked aging services in general and mental health services in particular is likely to continue to affect the development and implementation of psychological services for older adults.

V. Conclusions

Apart from the specifics of an individual intervention approach in a particular setting, some general issues cut across all interventions and all settings: How do we define success? How do we take into account the variability of older adults? How do we accommodate the ethical dilemmas often posed by working with older adults? How do we improve upon the somewhat flawed research base? Finally, how do we undertake interventions in the absence of compelling or comprehensive data?

Defining success for psychological interventions may be difficult at times. In some instances, success may be avoiding excessive disability in the presence of an underlying deteriorating disease process (e.g., Alzheimer's disease). In other instances, success may be the development or restoration of functioning, rather than merely the maintenance of a previously developed set of skills. For those active in intervention, however, it is important to specify as clearly as possible both the expectations for and the limitations of an intervention's efficacy.

A key element in defining success or failure must be an acknowledgment of diversity between and within older individuals, what some have called inter- and intraindividual differences (e.g., Baltes, Reese, & Lipsitt, 1980). This element may make it difficult to accurately predict the changes in outcomes associated with a specific intervention. Similarly, it requires a more detailed descriptive phase of research to accurately portray the impact of diversity on intervention efficacy.

Working with older adults and their families also raises a number of ethical issues from both a service and research perspective (e.g., O'Donohue, Fisher, & Krasner, 1987). A primary consideration must be identifying who the appropriate participants are in either interventions or research: Who are the clients? Any answer to this query requires an analysis of issues of competence, autonomy, and the rights of individuals to determine their own involvement in research and interventions (see *Gerontologist*, 1988, for a special issue on this in nursing homes).

As pointed out earlier, in almost every area, there is a need for improved, systematic research that characterizes the effects of specific interventions on specific patterns of adjustment. The area of psychological interventions with older adults could benefit from an increased emphasis upon three elements: use of control groups, with random assignment to treatment or control; replications of findings from earlier studies to assess the stability and generalizability of trends; and longitudinal analyses to assess the stability or change of initial patterns of intervention effectiveness.

Finally, we should appreciate the dilemma of those who work directly with older adults and their families. They are often unable to delay intervening until the results of a definitive longitudinal study are completed. Oftentimes, they must balance demands for services with an understanding that our knowledge base is limited. Their dilemma reflects the urgency of improving the research base in the area of psychological interventions with older adults. It also underscores the importance of communicating research findings to both scholarly and practitioner-oriented audiences. Eventually, the relationship between psychological practice and research must be reciprocal, with each element informing the other.

Acknowledgments

We appreciate the helpful comments of Jim Birren, Margy Gatz, Bob Intrieri, Pat Piper, Jim Reid, Carmi Schooler, and Diana Spore on an earlier version of this chapter.

References

Abraham, K. (1977, orig. 1953). The applicability of psychoanalytic treatment to patients of advanced age. In S. Steury & M. L. Blank (Eds.), *Readings in psychotherapy with older people* (pp. 18–20). Rockville, MD: National Institute of Mental Health.

Anthony-Bergstone, C. R., Zarit, S. H., & Gatz, M. (1988). Symptoms of psychological distress among caregivers of dementia patients. *Psychology and Aging,* **3,** 245–248.

Apfel, R. J., Fox, M., Isberg, R. S., & Levine, A. R. (1984). Countertransference and transference in couple therapy: Treating sexual dysfunction in older couples. *Journal of Geriatric Psychiatry,* **17,** 203–214.

Aronson, M. K., Levin, G., & Lipkowitz, R. (1984). A community-based family/patient group program for Alzheimer's disease. *Gerontologist,* **24,** 339–342.

Baltes, M. M. (1982). Environmental factors in dependence among nursing home residents: A social ecology analysis. In T. A. Wills (Ed.), *Basic processes in helping relationships* (pp. 405–425). New York: Academic Press.

Baltes, M. M., & Baltes, P. B. (Eds.) (1986). *The psychology of control and aging.* Hillsdale, NJ: Erlbaum.

Baltes, M. M., Honn, S., Barton, E. M., Orzech, M., & Lago, D. (1983). On the social ecology of dependence and independence in elderly nursing home residents: A replication and extension. *Journal of Gerontology,* **38,** 556–564.

Baltes, M. M. & Reisenzein, R. (1986). The social world in long-term care institutions: Psychosocial control towards dependency? In M. M. Baltes & P. B. Baltes (Eds.), *The psychology of control and aging* (pp. 315–343). Hillsdale, NJ: Erlbaum.

Baltes, M. M., & Werner-Wahl, H. (1987). Dependence in aging. In L. L. Carstensen & B. A. Edelstein (Eds.), *Handbook of clinical gerontology* (pp. 204–221). New York: Pergamon.

Baltes, P. (1987). Theoretical propositions of life-span developmental psychology: On the dynamics between growth and decline. *Developmental Psychology,* **23,** 611–626.

Baltes, P. B., Reese, H. W., & Lipsitt, L. P. (1980). Life-span developmental psychology. *Annual Review of Psychology,* **31,** 65–110.

Becker, F., & Zarit, S. H. (1978). Training older adults as peer counselors. *Educational Gerontology,* **3,** 241–250.

Bellack, L., & Small, L. (1965). *Emergency psychotherapy and brief psychotherapy.* New York: Grune & Stratton.

Beutler, L. E., Scogin, F., Kirkish, P., Schretlen, D., Corbishley, A., Hamblin, D., Meredith, K., Potter, R., Bamford, C. R., & Levenson, A. I. (1987). Group cognitive therapy and alprazolam in the treatment of depression in older adults. *Journal of Consulting and Clinical Psychology,* **55,** 550–556.

Birren, J. E., & Sloane, R. B. (Eds.) (1980). *Handbook of mental health and aging.* Englewood Cliffs, NJ: Prentice-Hall.

Blazer, D., Hughes, D. C., & George, L. K. (1987). The epidemiology of depression in an elderly community population. *Gerontologist,* **27,** 281–297.

Bloom, B. L. (1975). *Community mental health: A general introduction.* Monterey, CA: Brooks/Cole.

Blumenthal, D., Schlesinger, M., Drumheller, P. D., & The Harvard Medicare Project. (1986). The future of Medicare. *New England Journal of Medicine,* **314**(11), 722–728.

Bootzin, R. R., Engle-Friedman, M., & Hazelwood, L. (1983). Insomnia. In P. M. Lewinsohn & L. Teri (Eds.), *Clinical geropsychology: New directions in assessment and treatment.* New York: Pergamon.

Borson, S., & Raskind, M. (1986). Antidepressant resistant depression in the elderly. *Journal of the American Geriatrics Society,* **34,** 245–249.

Burgio, K. L., Whitehead, W. E., & Engel, B. T. (1985). Urinary incontinence in the elderly: Bladder-sphincter biofeedback and toileting skills training. *Annals of Internal Medicine,* **103,** 507–515.

Burgio, L. D., & Burgio, K. L. (1986). Behavioral gerontology: Applications of behavioral methods to the problems of older adults. *Journal of Applied Behavioral Analyses,* **19,** 321–328.

Burgio, L. D., Burgio, K. L., Engel, B. T., & Tice, L. M. (1986). Increasing distance and independence of ambulation in elderly nursing home residents. *Journal of Applied Behavior Analysis,* **19,** 357–366.

Burgio, K. L., & Engel, B. T. (1987). Urinary incontinence: Behavioral assessment and treatment. In L. L. Carstensen & B. A. Edelstein (Eds.), *Handbook of clinical gerontology* (pp. 252–266). New York: Pergamon.

Burns, B. J., Larson, B. D., Goldstrom, I. D., Johnson, W. E., Taube, C. E., Miller, N. E., & Mathis, E. S. (1988). Mental disorder among nursing home patients: Preliminary findings from the national nursing home survey pretest. *International Journal of Geriatric Psychiatry,* **3,** 27–35.

Butler, R. (1963). The life review: An interpretation of reminiscence in the aged. *Psychiatry*, **26**, 65–76.

Butler, R. N., & Lewis, M. I. (1982). *Aging and mental health* (3rd ed.). St. Louis, MO: Mosby.

Caplan, G. (1964). *Principles of preventive psychiatry*. New York: Basic Books.

Carstensen, L. L., & Erickson, R. J. (1986). Enhancing the social environments of elderly nursing home residents: Are high rates of interaction enough? *Journal of Applied Behavioral Analysis*, **19**, 349–355.

Caston, R. J. (1983). The role of education and health care delivery structure in quality of nursing care for mentally ill patients in nursing homes. *Educational Gerontology*, **9**, 425–433.

Cath, S. H. (1983). Psychoanalysis and psychoanalytic psycho-therapy of the older patient. *Journal of Geriatric Psychiatry*, **15**, 43–53.

Clausen, J. A. (1972). The life course of individuals. In M. W. Riley, M. Johnson, & A. Foner (Eds.), *Aging and society: A sociology of age stratification* (Vol. 3). New York: Russell Sage Foundation.

Cohler, B. J. (1980). Adult development psychology and reconstruction in psychoanalysis. In S. I. Greenspan & G. H. Pollock (Eds.), *The course of life: Psychoanalytic contributions toward understanding personality development*: (Vol III). *Adulthood and the aging process*. Rockville, MD: National Institutes of Mental Health.

Colarusso, C. A., & Nemiroff, R. A. (1981). *Adult development: A new dimension in psychodynamic theory and practice*. New York: Plenum.

Connelly, J. R. (1986). Assessing gerontology personnel. *Educational Gerontology*, **12**, 531–547.

Czirr, R., & Rappaport, M. (1984). Tool kit for teams: Annotated bibliography on interdisciplinary teams: Its measurement and its effects. *Clinical Gerontologist*, **2**, 47–54.

Danish, S. J., Smyer, M. A., & Novak, C. A. (1980). Developmental intervention: Enhancing life event processes. In P. B. Baltes & O. G. Brim, Jr. (Eds.), *Life-span development and behavior* (Vol. 3). New York: Academic Press.

Davies, H., Priddy, J. M., & Tinklenberg, J. (1986). Support groups for male caregivers of Alzheimer's patients. *Clinical Gerontologist*, **5**, 385–395.

DeBor, L., & Gallagher, D. (1982). Groups counseling with bereaving elderly. *Clinical Gerontology*, **1**, 81–90.

Donahue, W., Hunter, W. W., & Coons, D. (1953). A study of the socialization of old people. *Geriatrics*, **8**, 656–666.

Dye, C. J. (1978). Psychologists' role in the provision of mental health care for the elderly. *Professional Psychology*, **9**, 38–49.

Eisdorfer, C., & Stotsky, B. A. (1977). Intervention, treatment, and rehabilitation of psychiatric disorders. In J. E. Birren & K. W. Schaie (Eds.), *Handbook of the psychology of aging*. New York: Van Nostrand Reinhold.

Elder, G. H., Jr. (1975). Age differentiation and the life course. *Annual Review of Sociology*, **1**.

Eskew, R. W., Sexton, R. E., Tars, S. E., & Wilcox, F. M. (1983). Day treatment program evaluation. In M. A. Smyer & M. Gatz (Eds.), *Mental health and aging: Programs and evaluations*. Beverly Hills, CA: Sage.

Estes, C. L., & Wood, J. B. (1984). A preliminary assessment of the impact of block grants on community mental health centers. *Hospital and Community Psychiatry*, **35**, 125–1129.

Evans, R. L., Smith, K. M., Werkhoven, W. S., Fox, H. R., & Pritzl, D. O. (1986). Cognitive telephone group therapy with physically disabled elderly persons. *Gerontologist*, **26**, 8–11.

Flemming, A. S., Buchanan, J. G., Santos, J. F., & Rickards, L. D. (1984). *Mental health services for the elderly: Report on a survey of community mental health centers* (Volumes I and II). Washington, DC: Action Committee to Implement the Mental Health Recommendations of the 1981 White House Conference on Aging.

Folsom, J. C. (1968). Reality orientation for the elderly mental patient. *Journal of Geriatric Psychiatry*, **1**, 291–307.

Ford, D. H. (1987). *Humans as self-constructing living systems: A developmental perspective on personality and behavior*. Hillsdale, NJ: Erlbaum.

Fox, P. J., Swan, J. H., & Estes, C. L. (1986). Trends in CMHC services to elderly populations. *Hospital and Community Psychiatry*, **37**(9), 937–939.

Franklin, G. S., & Kaufman, K. S. (1982). Group psychotherapy for elderly female Hispanic outpatients. *Hospital and Community Psychiatry*, **33**, 385–387.

Fruit, D. (1985). Are graduates of bachelor's degree programs in gerontology employed? A report of a national study. *Educational Gerontology*, **11**, 237–245.

Gafner, G. (1987). Paradoxical marital therapy and the discouragement meter. *Clinical Gerontologist*, **6**(3), 67–70.

Gallagher, D., & Frankl, A. S. (1980). Depression in older adults: A moderate structuralist viewpoint. *Psychotherapy: Theory, Research & Practice*, **17**(1), 101–104.

Gallagher, D., Lovett, S., & Zeiss, A. (1989). Interventions with caregivers of frail elderly persons. In M. Ory & K. Bond (Eds.), *Aging and health care: Social science and policy perspectives.* New York: Tavistock (in press).

Gallagher, D. E., & Thompson, L. (1982). Treatment of major depressive disorder in older adult outpatients with brief psychotherapy. *Psychotherapy: Theory, Research and Practice*, **19**, 482–490.

Gallagher, D. E., & Thompson, L. W. (1983). Effectiveness of psychotherapy for both endogenous and nonendogenous depression in older outpatients. *Journal of Gerontology*, **38**, 707–712.

Gallagher, D., Thompson, L. W., Baffa, G., Piatt, C., Ringering, L., & Stone, V. (1981). *Depression in the elderly: A behavioral treatment manual.* Los Angeles: University of Southern California.

Gallagher, D., Thompson, L. W., & Breckenridge, J. S. (1986). *Maintenance of gains versus relapse following brief psychotherapy for depression.* Paper presented at the meetings of the American Psychological Association, Washington, D.C.

Gatz, M. (1985). *Prevention and aging: Community programs.* Paper presented at the National Mental Health Association Commission on the Prevention of Mental and Emotional Disability. May 12th, Alexandria, VA.

Gatz, M. (1988). *Clinical psychology and aging.* Master lecture delivered at 96th annual convention of the American Psychological Association, Atlanta, August 15.

Gatz, M., Hileman, C., & Amaral, P. (1984). Older adult paraprofessionals: Working with and in behalf of older adults. *Journal of Community Psychology*, **12**, 347–358.

Gatz, M., & Pearson, C. G. (1988). Ageism revised and the provision of psychological services. *American Psychologist*, **43**, 184–188.

Gatz, M., Popkin, S. J., Pino, C. D., & Vanden Bos, G. R. (1985). Psychological interventions with older adults. In J. E. Birren & K. W. Schaie (Eds.), *Handbook of the psychology of aging* (pp. 755–785). New York: Van Nostrand Reinhold.

Gatz, M., Siegler, I. C., & Dibner, S. S. (1979–1980). Individual and community: Normative conflicts in the development of a new therapeutic community for older persons. *International Journal of Aging and Human Development*, **10**, 249–263.

German, P. S., Shapiro, S., & Kramer, M. (1986). Nursing home study of the Eastern Baltimore Epidemiological Catchment Area Study. In M. Harper & B. Lebowitz (Eds.), *Mental illness in nursing homes: Agenda for Research* (pp. 39–58). Rockville, MD: NIMH, U.S. Dept. of Health & Human Services.

Gilewski, M. J. (1986). Group therapy with cognitively impaired older adults. *Clinical Gerontologist*, **5**, 281–294.

Gilewski, M. J., Kuppinger, J., & Zarit, S. H. (1985). The aging marital system: A case study in life changes and paradoxical intervention. *Clinical Gerontologist*, **3**(3), 3–15.

Glosser, G., & Wexler, D. (1985). Participants' evaluation of educational support groups for families of patients with Alzheimer's disease and other dementias. *Gerontologist*, **25**, 232–236.

Goldfarb, A. I. (1956). Psychotherapy of the aged: The use and value of an adaptational frame of reference. *Psychoanalytic Review*, **43**, 65–81.

Goldstrom, I. D., Burns, B. J., Kessler, L. G., Feuerberg, M. A., Larson, D. B., Miller, N. E., & Cromer, W. J. (1987). Mental health services use by elderly adults in a primary care setting. *Journal of Gerontology*, **42**(2), 147–153.

Gotestam, K. G. (1980). Behavioral and dynamic psychotherapy with the elderly. In J. E. Birren & R. B. Sloane (Eds.), *Handbook of mental health and aging* (pp. 775–805). Englewood Cliffs, NJ: Prentice-Hall.

Gottesman, L. E., Donahue, W., Coons, D., & Ciarlo, J. (1969). Extended care of the aged: Psychosocial aspects. *Journal of Geriatric Psychiatry*, **2**(2), 220–237.

Green, G. R., Linsk, N. L., & Pinkston, E. M. (1986). Modification of verbal behavior of the mentally impaired elderly by their spouses.

Journal of Applied Behavior Analysis, **19,** 329–336.

Greene, V. L., & Monahan, D. J. (1987). The effect of a professionally guided caregiver support and education groups on institutionalization of care receivers. *Gerontologist,* **27,** 716–721.

Gross, A. M., & Martin, P. (1982). Increasing attendance to recreational therapy in a rehabilitation hospital. *International Journal of Behavioral Geriatrics,* **1**(3), 27–32.

Gutmann, D. L. (1980). Psychoanalysis and aging: A developmental view. In S. I. Greenspan & G. H. Pollock (Eds.), *The course of life: Psychoanalytic contributions toward understanding personality development.* (Vol III): *Adulthood and the aging process.* Rockville, MD: National Institutes of Mental Health.

Haley, W. E. (1983). A family-behavioral approach to the treatment of the cognitively impaired elderly. *Gerontologist,* **23,** 18–20.

Haley, W. E., & Colce, J. J. (1986). Assessment and management of chronic pain in the elderly. *Clinical Gerontologist,* **5,** 435–455.

Haley, W. E., Brown, S. L., & Levine, E. G. (1987). Group intervention for dementia caregivers. *The Gerontologist,* **27,** 376–382.

Heller, K., & Monahan, J. (1977). *Psychology and community change.* Homewood, IL: Dorsey.

Horowitz, M. J., Marmar, C., Weiss, D. S., DeWitt, K. N., & Rosenbaum, R. (1984). Brief psychotherapy of grief reactions. *Archives of General Psychiatry,* **41,** 439–448.

Hussian, R. A. (1981). *Geriatric psychology: A behavioral perspective.* New York: Van Nostrand Reinhold.

Hussian, R. A. (1982). Stimulus control in the modification of problematic behavior in elderly institutionalized patients. *International Journal of Behavioral Geriatrics,* **1,** 33–35.

Hussian, R. A. (1986). Severe behavioral problems. In L. Teri & P. M. Lewinsohn (Eds.), *Geropsychological assessment and treatment* (pp. 121–143). New York: Springer.

Hussian, R. A. (1987). Wandering and disorientation. In L. L. Carstensen & B. A. Edelstein (Eds.), *Handbook of clinical gerontology* (pp. 177–188). New York: Pergamon.

Hussian, R. A., & Davis, R. L. (1985). *Responsive care: Behavioral intervention with elderly persons.* Champaign, IL.: Research Press.

Hyer, L., & Harrison, W. R. (1986). Later life personality model: Diagnosis and treatment. *Clinical Gerontologist,* **5**(3/4), 399–416.

Jackson, G. M., & Schonfeld, L. I. (1982). Comparisons of visual feedback, instructional prompts and discrete prompting in the treatment of orofacial tardive dyskinesia. *International Journal of Behavioral Geriatrics,* **1,** 35–46.

Jarvik, L. F., Mintz, J., Steuer, J., & Gerner, R. (1982). Treating geriatric depression: A 26-week interim analysis. *Journal of the American Geriatrics Society,* **30,** 713–717.

Kahana, R. J. (1987). Geriatric psychotherapy: Beyond crisis management. In J. Sadavoy & M. Leszcz (Eds.), *Treating the elderly with psychotherapy.* Madison, CT: International Universities Press.

Kahn, R. L. (1975). The mental health system and the future aged. *Gerontologist,* **15**(1, Part 2), 24–31.

Kahn, R. L., & Zarit, S. H. (1974). Evaluation of mental health programs for the aged. In P. O. Davidson, F. W. Clark, & L. A. Hamerlynck (Eds.), *Evaluation of behavioral programs* (pp. 223–252). Champaign, IL: Research Press.

Kastenbaum, R. (1987). Prevention of age-related problems. In L. L. Carstensen & B. A. Edelstein (Eds.), *Handbook of clinical gerontology* (pp. 322–334). New York: Pergamon.

Kerski, D., Drinka, T., Carnes, M., Golob, K., & Craig, W. (1987). Post-geriatric evaluation unit follow-up: Team versus non-team. *Journal of Gerontology,* 42, 191–195.

Kleitsch, E. C., Whitman, T. L., & Santos, J. (1983). Increasing verbal interaction among elderly socially isolated mentally retarded adults: A group language training procedure. *Journal of Applied Behavior Analysis,* **16,** 217–233.

Knight, B. (1983). Evaluation of a mobile geriatric outreach team and aging: Programs and evaluation. In M. A. Smyer & M. Gatz (Eds.), *Mental health and aging: Programs and evaluations* (pp. 23–40). Beverly Hills, CA: Sage.

Knight, B. (1986a). Management variables as predictors of service utilization by the elderly in mental health. *International Journal of Mental Health*, **23**(2), 141–147.

Knight, B. (1986b). *Psychotherapy with older adults*. Beverly Hills, CA.: Sage.

Knight, B. (1986c). Therapist attitudes as explanations of under service of elderly in mental health: Testing an old hypothesis. *International Journal of Mental Health*, **22**(4), 261–269.

Knight, B., Reinhart, R., & Field, P. (1982). Senior outreach services: A treatment-oriented outreach team in community mental health. *Gerontologist*, **22**, 544–547.

Kramer, M. (1986). Trends on institutionalization and prevalence of mental disorder in nursing homes. In M. S. Harper & B. Lebowitz (Eds.), *Mental illness in nursing Homes: Agenda for research* (pp. 10–38). Rockville, MD: NIMH, U.S. Dept. of Health and Human Services.

Kucharski, L. T., White, R. M., & Schratz, M. (1979). Age bias, referral for psychological assistance and the private physician. *Journal of Gerontology*, **34**, 423–428.

Langer, E., & Rodin, J. (1976). The effects of choice and enhanced personal responsibility for ages: A field experiment in an institutional setting. *Journal of Personality and Social Psychology*, **34**, 191–198.

LaWall, J. (1981). Conjoint therapy of psychiatric problems in the elderly. *Journal of the American Geriatrics Society*, **29**, 89–91.

Lazarus, L. W., Groves, L., Gutmann, D., Ripekyj, A., Frankel, R., Newton, N., Gruner, J., & Havasy-Galloway, S. (1987). Brief psychotherapy with the elderly. A study of process and outcome. In J. Sadavoy & M. Leszcz (Eds.), *Treating the elderly with psychotherapy*. Madison, CT: International Universities Press.

Lebowitz, B. D. (1988). Practical Geriatrics: Correlates of success in community mental health programs for the elderly. *Hospital and Community Psychiatry*, **39**(7), 721–722.

Lebowitz, B. D., Light, E., & Bailey, F. (1987). Mental health center services for the elderly: The impact of coordination with area agencies on aging. *Gerontologist*, **27**(6), 699–702.

Lee, C. L. (1986). Developmental tasks affecting the marital relationship in later life. *American Behavioral Scientist*, **29**, 389–403.

Leszcz, M. (1987). Group psychotherapy with the elderly. In J. Sadavoy & M. Leszcz (Eds.), *Treating the elderly with psychotherapy: The scope for change in later life*, (pp. 325–350). Madison, CT: International Universities Press.

Levine, M. (1981). *The history and politics of community mental health*. New York: Oxford University Press.

Lewinsohn, P. M., Antonuccio, D. O., Steinmetz, J. L., & Teri, L. (1984). *The coping with depression course: Psychoeducational intervention for unipolar depression*. Eugene, OR: Castalia.

Lewinsohn, P. M., Fenn, D. S., Stanton, A. K., & Franklin, J. (1986). Relation of age at onset to duration of episode in unipolar depression. *Psychology and Aging*, **1**, 63–68.

Lieberman, M. A. (1987). Self-help groups and the elderly: An overview. In E. E. Lurie, J. H. Swan, & Associates (Eds.), *Serving the mentally ill elderly: Problems and perspectives*. Lexington, MA: Lexington Books.

Lieberman, M. A. (1983). Comparative analyses of change mechanisms in groups. In H. H. Blumberg, A. P. Hare, V. Kent, & M. Davies (Eds.), *Small groups and social interaction* (Vol. 2, pp. 239–252). New York: Wiley.

Lieberman, M. A., & Bliwise, N. G. (1985). Comparisons among peer and professionally directed groups for the elderly: Implications for the development of self-help groups. *International Journal of Group Psychotherapy*, **35**, 155–175.

Lieberman, M. A., & Borman, L. D. (1979). *Self-help groups for coping with crisis*. San Francisco: Jossey-Bass.

Lieberman, M. A., & Gourash, N. (1979). Evaluating the effects of change groups on the elderly. *International Journal of Group Psychotherapy*, **29**, 283–304.

Lieberman, M. A., & Videka-Sherman, L. (1986). The impact of self-help groups on the mental health of widows and widowers. *American Journal of Othopsychiatry*, **56**, 435–449.

Linoff, M. G., & West, C. M. (1982). Relaxation training systematically combined with music: Treatment of tension headaches in a geriatric patient. *International Journal of Behavioral Geriatrics*, **1**, 11–18.

Linsk, N. L., & Pinkston, E. M. (1984). Training gerontological practitioners in home-based family interventions. *Educational Gerontology*, **10**, 289–305.

Liptzin, B. (1984). Clinical perspectives on sexuality in older patients. *Journal of Geriatric Psychiatry*, **17**, 164–181.

Lowy, L. (1980). Mental health services in the community. In J. E. Birren & R. B. Sloane (Eds.), *Handbook of mental health and aging*. Englewood Cliffs, NJ: Prentice-Hall.

MacDonald, M. L., Davidowitz, J. J., Gimbel, B., & Foley, L. M. (1982). Physical and social environmental reprogramming as treatment for psychogeriatric patients. *International Journal of Behavioral Geriatrics*, **1**(1), 15–32.

Mace, N. L.,& Rabins, P. V. (1984). *A survey of day care for the demented adult in the United States*. Washington, DC: The National Council on the Aging.

McClannahan, L. E., & Risley, T. R. (1973). A store for nursing home residents. *Nursing Homes*, **22**, 10–11.

McClannahan, L. E., & Risley, T. R. (1974). Design of living environments for nursing home residents: Recruiting attendance at activities. *Gerontologist*, **14**, 236–240.

McClannahan, L. E., & Risley, T. R. (1975). Design of living environments for nursing home residents: Increasing participation in recreation activities. *Journal of Applied Behavior Analysis*, **8**, 261–268.

McEvoy, C. L., & Patterson, R. L. (1986). Behavioral treatment of deficit skills in dementia patients. *The Gerontologist*, **26**, 475–478.

Meyers, B., & Greenberg, R. (1989). Late-life delusional depression. *Journal of Affective Disorders*, in press.

Miller, C., & LeLieuore, R. B. (1982). A method to reduce chronic pain in elderly nursing home residents. *The Gerontologist*, **22**, 314–317.

Mishara, B. (1978). Geriatric patients in token economy and milieu treatments. *Journal of Consulting and Clinical Psychology*, **46**, 1340–1348.

Molinari, V., & Reichlin, R. E. (1984–1985). Life review reminiscence in the elderly: A review of the literature. *International Journal of Aging and Human Development*, **20**, 81–92.

Moran, J. A., & Gatz, M. (1987). Group therapies for nursing home adults: An evaluation of two treatment approaches. *Gerontologist*, **27**, 588–591.

Mosher, P. M. (1983). Gerontology career preparation at the associate degree level for the community-based practitioner. *Educational Gerontology*, **9**, 37–46.

Murphy, G. J., Hudson, W. W., & Cheung, P. P. L. (1980). Marital and sexual discord among older couples. *Social Work Research and Abstracts*, **16**(1), 11–16.

Nelson, G. M. (1983). Gerontological social work: A curriculum review. *Educational Gerontology*, **9**, 307–322.

Nemiroff, R. A., & Colarusso, C. A. (1985). *The race against time*. New York: Plenum.

Neugarten, B. (1976). Adaptation and the life cycle. *The Counseling Psychologist*, **6**, 16–20.

Neugarten, B. L., & Hagestad, G. O. (1976). Age and the life course. In R. Binstock & E. Shanas (Eds.), *Handbook of aging and the social sciences*. New York: Van Nostrand Reinhold.

O'Donohue, W. T., Fisher, J. E., & Krasner, L. (1987). Ethics and the elderly. In L. L. Carstensen & B. A. Edelstein (Eds.), *Handbook of clinical gerontology* (pp. 387–399). New York: Pergamon.

O'Quin, J. A., O'Dell, S. L., & Burnett, R. L. (1982). Effects of brief behavioral intervention on verbal interactions of socially inactive nursing home residents. *International Journal of Behavioral Geriatrics*, **1**, 3–9.

Parish, B., & Landsberg, G. (1984). Developing a geriatric mental health outreach unit in a rural community. *Journal of Gerontological Social Work*, **7**, 75–82.

Patterson, R. L., Dupree, L. W., Eberly, D. A., Jackson, G. M., O'Sullivan, J. J., Penner, L. A., & Dee-Kelly, K. (1982). *Overcoming deficits of aging: A behavioral treatment approach*. New York: Plenum.

Patterson, R. L., & Eberly, D. A. (1983). Social and daily living skills. In P. M. Lewinson & L. Teri (Eds.), *Clinical geropsychology: New directions in assessment and treatment* (pp. 116–138). New York: Pergamon.

Perkins, K. A., Rapp, S. R., Carlson, C. R., & Wallace, C. E. (1986). A behavioral intervention to increase exercise among nursing home residents. *Gerontologist*, **26**, 479–481.

Peterson, D. A. (1985). Employment experience of gerontology master's degree graduates. *Gerontologist*, **25**, 514–519.

Peterson, D. A. (1986). Extent of gerontology instruction in American institutions of higher education. *Educational Gerontology*, **12**, 519–530.

Pinkston, E. M., & Linsk, N. L. (1984a). Behavioral family intervention with the impaired elderly. *The Gerontologist*, **24**, 576–583.

Pinkston, E. M., & Linsk, N. L. (1984b). *Care of the elderly: A family approach*. New York: Pergamon.

Post, F. (1987). Paranoid and schizophrenic disorders among the aging. In L. L. Carstensen & B. A. Edelstein (Eds.), *Handbook of clinical Gerontology* (pp. 43–56). New York: Pergamon.

Powell-Proctor, L., & Miller, E. (1982). Reality orientation: A critical appraisal. *British Journal of Psychiatry*, **140**, 457–463.

Praderas, K., & MacDonald, M. L. (1986). Telephone conversational skills training with socially isolated, impaired nursing home residents. *Journal of Applied Behavior Analysis*, **19**, 337–348.

Pruchno, R. A., Boswell, P. C., Wolff, D. S., & Faletti, M. V. (1983). A community mental health program: Evaluating outcomes. In M. A. Smyer & M. Gatz (Eds.), *Mental health and aging: Programs and evaluations* (pp. 41–61). Beverly Hills, CA: Sage.

Qualls, S. H., & Czirr, R. (1988). Geriatric health teams: Classifying models of professional and team functioning. *Gerontologist*, **28**, 372–376.

Raschko, R. (1985). Systems integration at the program level: Aging and mental health. *Gerontologist*, **25**, 460–463.

Raskin, D. (1976). Milieu therapy re-examined. *Comprehensive Psychiatry*, **17**(6), 695–701.

Rechtschaffen, A. (1959). Psychotherapy with geriatric patients: A review of the literature. *Journal of Gerontology*, **14**, 73–84.

Redick, R. W., & Taube, C. A. (1980). Demography and mental health care of the aged. In J. E. Birren & R. B. Sloane (Eds.), *Handbook of mental health and aging*. Englewood Cliffs, NJ: Prentice-Hall.

Regier, D., Meyers, J. K., Kramer, M., Robins, L. N., Blazer, D. G., & Hough, R. L. (1984). The NIMH epidemiologic catchment area program: Historical context major objectives, and study population characteristics. *Archives of General Psychiatry*, **41**, 934–941.

Renshaw, D. C. (1984). Geriatric sex problems. *Journal of Geriatric Psychiatry*, **17**, 123–138.

Rodin, J., Cashman, C., & Desiderato, L. (1986). Psychosocial interventions in aging focusing on enrichment and prevention. In M. Riley, A. Baum, & J. Matarazzo (Eds.), *Perspectives on behavioral medicine IV: Biomedical and psychosocial perspectives of aging*. Orlando, FL: Academic Press.

Rodin, J., & Langer, E. J. (1977). Long-term effects of control-relevant intervention with the institutionalized age. *Journal of Personality and Social Psychology*, **35**, 897–902.

Roff, L. L., & Klemmack, D. L. (1979). Sexual activity among older persons: A comparative analysis of appropriateness. *Research on Aging*, **1**, 389–399.

Ronch, J. L., & Solomon, J. R. (1978). An outreach and prevention unit in a mental health center serving the elderly. *Hospital and Community Psychiatry*, **29**, 710–711.

Rovner, B. W., Kafonek, S., Filipp, L., Lucas, M. J., & Folstein, M. F. (1986). Prevalence of mental illness in a community nursing home. *American Journal of Psychiatry*, **143** (11), 1446–1449.

Rowland, K. F., & Haynes, S. N. (1978). A sexual enhancement program for elderly couples. *Journal of Sex and Marital Therapy*, **4**, 91–113.

Sadavoy, J., & Leszcz, M. (Eds.) (1987). *Treating the elderly with psychotherapy*. Madison, CT: International Universities Press.

Sanavio, E. (1981). Toilet retraining psychogeriatric residents. *Behavior Modification*, **5**, 417–427.

Santos, J., Hubbard, R., Burdick, D., & Santos, M. (1983). Mental health outreach and the elderly. In M. A. Smyer & M. Gatz (Eds.), *Mental health and aging: Programs and evaluations* (pp. 257–274). Beverly Hills, CA: Sage.

Satin, D. G. (1986). The future of geriatric and interdisciplinary education. *Educational Gerontology*, **12**, 549–561.

Scharlach, A. E. (1987). Relieving feelings of strain among women with elderly mothers. *Psychology and Aging*, **2**, 9–13.

Schmidt, G. L., & Keyes, B. (1985). Group psychotherapy with family caregivers of demented patients. *Gerontologist*, **25**, 347–350.

Schnelle, J. F., Traughber, B., Morgan, D. B., Embry, J. E., Binion, A. F., & Coleman, A. (1983). Management of geriatric incontinence in nursing homes. *Journal of Applied Behavior Analysis*, **16**, 235–241.

Schwenk, M. A. (1979). Reality orientation for the institutionalized aged: Does it help? *Gerontologist*, **19**, 373–377.

Seidman, E. (1983). Introduction. In E. Seidman (Ed.), *Handbook of social intervention*. Beverly Hills, CA: Sage.

Selan, B. H., & Gold, C. A. (1980). The late-life counseling service: A program for the elderly. *Hospital and Community Psychiatry*, **31**, 403–406.

Settin, J. M. (1982). Clinical judgment in geropsychology practice. *Psychotherapy: Theory, Research, and Practice*, **19**, 397–404.

Shapiro, S. (1986). Are elders underserved? *Generations*, **10**(3), 14–17.

Shapiro, S., Skinner, E. A., Kessler, L. G., Von Korff, M., German, P. S., Tishler, G. L., Leaf, P. J., Benham, L., Cottler, L., and Regier, D. A. (1984). Utilization of health and mental health services: 3 epidemiologic catchment area sites. *Archives of General Psychiatry*, **41** (10), 971–978.

Sherman, E. (1987). Reminiscence groups for community elderly. *Gerontologist*, **27**, 569–572.

Sherwood, S., & Mor, V. (1980). Mental health institutions and the elderly. In J. E. Birren & R. B. Sloane (Eds.), *Handbook of mental health and aging*. Englewood Cliffs, NJ: Prentice-Hall.

Smyer, M. A., Cohn, M. D., & Brannon, D. (1988). *Mental health consultation in nursing homes*. New York: New York University Press.

Smyer, M. A., & Gatz, M. (Eds.) (1983). *Mental health and aging: Programs and evaluations*. Beverly Hills, CA: Sage.

Smyer, M. A., Gatz, M., & Pruchno, R. A. (1989). Community psychology and aging. In M. S. Gibbs, G. R. Lachenmeyer, & J. Sigal (Eds.), *Community psychology: Theoretical and empirical approaches* (2nd ed.). New York: Cardner (in press).

Smyer, M. A., & Pruchno, R. A. (1984). Service use and mental impairment among the elderly: Arguments for consultation and education. *Professional Psychology*, **15**, 528–537.

Spangler, P. F., Risley, T. R., & Bilyew, D. D. (1984). The management of dehydration and incontinence in nonambulatory geriatric pa-

tients. *Journal of Applied Behavior Analyses*, **17**, 397–401.

Spitzer, R. L., & Endicott, J. (1979). *Schedule for affective disorders and schizophrenia—lifetime version* (3rd ed.). New York: New York State Psychiatric Institute.

Steuer, J. L., & Hammen, C. L. (1983). Cognitive behavioral group therapy for the depressed elderly: Issues and adaptations. *Cognitive Therapy and Research*, **7**, 285–296.

Steuer, J. L., Mintz, J., Hammen, C. L., Hill, M. A., Jarvik, L. F., McCarley, T., Motike, P., & Rosen, R. (1984). Cognitive behavioral and psychodynamic group psychotherapy in treatment of geriatric depression. *Journal of Consulting and Clinical Psychology*, **52**, 180–189.

Steury, S., & Blank, M. L. (1977). *Readings in Psychotherapy with older people*. Washington, DC: U.S. Department of Health, Education, and Welfare.

Storandt, M. (1977). Graduate education in gerontological psychology: Results of a survey. *Educational Gerontology*, **2**, 141–146.

Taube, C. A., Burns, B. J., & Kessler, L. (1984). Patients of psychiatrists and psychologists in office-based practice: 1980. *American Psychologist*, **39**, 1435–1447.

Teri, L. & Gallagher, D. (1989). Cognitive behavioral interventions for depressed patients with dementia of the Alzheimer's type. In T. Sunderland (Ed.), *Depression in Alzheimer's disease: Component or consequence*. New York: Grune & Stratton (in press).

Thompson, L. W., Davies, R., Gallagher, D., & Krantz, S. (1986). Cognitive therapy with older adults. *Clinical Gerontologist*, **5**, 245–279.

Thompson, L. W., Gallagher, D. E., & Breckenridge, J. S. (1987). Comparative effectiveness of psychotherapies for depressed elders. *Journal of Consulting and Clinical Psychology*, **55**, 385–390.

Thompson, L. W., Gallagher, D., & Czirr, R. (1989). Personality disorder and outcome in the treatment of late-life depression. *Journal of Geriatric Psychiatry*, in press.

Thompson, L. W., Gallagher, D., Nies, G., & Epstein, D. (1983). Evaluation of the effectiveness of professionals and nonprofessionals as instructors of "coping with depression" classes for elders. *Gerontologist*, **23**, 390–396.

Toseland, R. W., Rossiter, C., & Lebrecque, M. (1987). *The effectiveness of peer-led and professionally-led groups to support caregivers.* Paper presented at the meetings of the Gerontological Society of America, Washington, D.C.

U.S. Senate Special Committee on Aging (1986). *Developments in aging: 1985* (Vol. 3). Washington, DC: U.S. Government Printing Office.

VandenBos, G. R., & Buchanan, J. (1983). Aging, research on aging, and national policy: A conversation with Robert Butler. *American Psychologist*, **38**, 300–307.

VandenBos, G. R., Strapp, J., & Kilburg, R. R. (1981). Health service providers in psychology: Results of the 1978 APA Human Resources Survey. *American Psychologist*, **36**, 1395–1418.

Waxman, H. M., Carner, E. A., & Berkenstock, G. (1984). Physicians' recognition, diagnosis, and treatment of mental disorders in elderly medical patients. *Gerontologist*, **24**, 593–597.

Whitbourne, S. K. (1985). The psychological construction of the life span. In J. E. Birren & K. W. Schaie (Eds.), *Handbook of the psychology of aging* (pp. 594–618). New York: Van Nostrand Reinhold.

Whitehead, W. E., Burgio, K. L., & Engel, B. T. (1985). Biofeedback treatment of fecal incontinence in geriatric patients. *Journal of the American Geriatrics Society*, **33**, 320–324.

Whitlatch, C. J., & Zarit, S. H. (1989). Sexual dysfunction in an aged married couple: A case study of a behavioral intervention. *Clinical Gerontologist*, in press.

Wilson, K., & Schulz, R. (1983). Criteria for effective crisis intervention. In M. A. Smyer & M. Gatz (Eds.), *Mental health and aging: Programs and evaluations*. Beverly Hills, CA: Sage.

Wolinsky, M. A. (1986). Marital therapy with older couples. *Casework: The Journal of Contemporary Social Work*, **67**, 475–483.

Yost, E. B., Beutler, L. E., Corbishley, M. A., & Allender, J. R. (1986). *Group cognitive therapy: A treatment approach for depressed older adults.* New York: Pergamon.

Zarit, S. H., & Anthony, C. R. (1986). Interventions with dementia patients and their families. In M. L. M. Gilhooly, S. H. Zarit, & J. E. Birren (Eds.), *The dementias: Policy and management* (pp. 66–92). Englewood Cliffs, NJ: Prentice-Hall.

Zarit, S. H., & Kahn, R. L. (1975). Aging and adaptation to illness. *Journal of Gerontology*, **30**, 67–72.

Zarit, S. H., Orr, N. K., & Zarit, J. M. (1985). *The hidden victims of Alzheimer's disease: Families under stress.* New York: New York University Press.

Zeiss, A. M., & O'Karma, T. B. (1984). *Interdisciplinary team care for elderly arthritic patients: Research on treatment outcomes.* Paper presented at the Association for the Advancement of Behavior Therapy, Chicago.

Twenty Four

Caregiving Families

Margaret Gatz, Vern L. Bengtson, and Mindy J. Blum

In the past 5 to 7 years, there has been a surge of public and professional concern about family members who care for frail elderly relatives. Families have been recognized as providing enormous amounts of assistance to older relatives with physical and cognitive impairments (Brody, 1985). The reasons that older adults may require assistance are amply documented in other chapters in this volume (e.g., Cohen; Elias, Elias, & Elias). These writers present the epidemiological context in terms of chronic illnesses leading to physical disability and cognitive decrement, impairments that put large numbers of elders at risk of needing some assistance at some time.

Help is provided through formal and informal channels. The vast majority of frail older adults do not reside in institutions, but in the community, where the major channel for assistance is family members (Bass & Noelker, 1987). Family caregivers have been identified as the "hidden victims" (Crossman, London, & Barry, 1981; Zarit, Orr, & Zarit, 1985), experiencing burden secondary to their caregiving responsibilities. Interventions designed to support family members providing care to frail elders have taken on prominence.

The purpose of this chapter is to provide an overview of the research literature on caregiving that recently has become so visible in gerontological books and journals. Three themes are developed in this chapter that to date have not been emphasized elsewhere.

First, we argue that the situation is best construed as a family systems problem. The elder's decline in health generates dependency and need for assistance. That need and even the anticipation of that need create changes throughout the family, only one of which may be that one individual assumes primary responsibility for assuring whatever help is required. To focus only on the primary caregiver is to ignore much of the relevant process.

Second, elders who are the recipients of care have physical impairments or senile organic brain diseases; they typically do not have a history of mental disorder. Similarly, for the most part, their families had been functioning successfully until this

Handbook of the Psychology of Aging, Third Edition
Copyright © 1990 Academic Press, Inc. All rights of reproduction in any form reserved.

crisis developed; these are not a group of troubled families of the sort who would most often be seen for psychological treatment. Indeed, caregiving has been termed a *normative family stress* (Brody, 1985). To apply models from psychopathology is to ignore the essential strengths of both recipients and families.

Third, although caregivers and their burdens are now receiving well-justified attention, the perspective of the elder with increasing health impairments must be considered as well. To focus exclusively on the caregiver's perspective and stresses is to revictimize the first victim.

The scope of this chapter encompasses all older adults who need extra assistance due to health problems, and all family who provide that assistance. We focus on "family" caregivers—primarily spouses and adult children—recognizing that the literature is limited with regard to other relationships. However, similar issues of burden surely encompass other informal helpers, such as partners of gay or lesbian elders, individuals participating in communal living arrangements, and other close informal assistants. Furthermore, there is great variation in amount of assistance, from barely more than the sorts of help that family or close friends regularly offer one another, to full-time care. Our major focus is *changed* patterns of assistance in response to the elder's health-related dependency.

The chapter has three parts. First, any review of family caregiving must take as its context the demographic changes that describe the American family of the late 1980s. We begin with such an overview, showing how demographic considerations shape the demand for care.

Second, we turn to the caregiving literature, which we review in four sections: (1) who become family caregivers, (2) categories of assistance they provide, (3) consequences of caregiving and the nature of the stresses experienced by caregivers, and (4) effects of the situation for the entire fami-

ly. In the course of discussing this literature, we will refer to some alternative theoretical frameworks for understanding caregiving.

Third, we overview interventions designed to help caregivers, with particular attention to their conceptual bases and to research evaluating their effectiveness.

I. Aging Families

A. Changing Demographics

Four macrosocial aspects have contributed to making elder caregiving such a visible social issue. These trends and their implications are developed at greater length elsewhere (Bengtson, Rosenthal, & Burton, 1990; Hagestad, 1986). First, because of increases in life expectancy, today's middle-aged offspring are much more likely to have living parents—and grandparents—than were their counterparts in earlier eras. Nearly all middle-aged couples have one or more parents still living (Uhlenberg, 1980). When women born in the 1930s celebrate their 60th birthday, more than one-fourth will still have mothers living (Winsborough, 1980).

Second, because of fertility declines, aging parents have even fewer kin to call on for help than did their own parents. One consequence of longevity increases and fertility decreases is that, today, the average married couple has more living parents than living children (Preston, 1984), with some couples choosing to have no children. Another is that most middle-aged adults, having grown up in smaller families, have fewer brothers and sisters to share the support of aging parents and parents-in-law (Hagestad, 1986).

Third, the increase in female labor force participation implies more complex networks of roles and obligations for middle-aged women, who have long been the mainstay of family support systems for the aged. Today, over half of all married women aged 45 to 54 are in the labor force (Treas & Bengtson, 1987); the proportion is much higher for those not married.

Fourth, because of increased longevity, family structure has become more vertical—three, four, and five generations alive at one point in time, but with fewer members in each generation. For instance, Hagestad (1988) reports that 20% of women who died after the age of 80 in a Pennsylvania county had great-great-grandchildren, and 60% had great-grand-children. This "beanpole" family structure may mean that more grandchildren will be taking an active role in caring for family elders—a point so far largely ignored in the caregiving literature.

These demographic trends have three implications that are directly relevant to caregiving. The first is that middle generations in the "beanpole" family may be overburdened in caring for multiple dependents in other generations, both older and younger than itself. Indeed, it has been suggested that the modern family is severely overextended and that the elderly will be the victims (Callahan, 1987).

Second, it seems clear that there may be a greater intensity in intergenerational relations than in previous eras (Bengtson, 1986): as family members spend a greater proportion of their adult years with living parents and grandparents, expectations of mutual assistance may become even more salient. Far from its being the case that elders are abandoned by their families, it has been estimated that over one-third of older Americans will at some point live with an adult child (Horowitz, 1985). As will be reviewed later, the increased intergenerational intensity can have both positive and negative consequences for participants, especially as caregiving becomes more demanding.

Third, a substantial proportion of adult children caring for aging parents are themselves aged. For them, as is already true of spouses of frail older adults, the burden of giving care to older people becomes part of the stress of their own aging process.

B. Demographics of Caregiving

Two aspects of the caregiving literature currently limit our ability fully to describe family involvement in giving assistance to frail elderly relatives. The first is nonrepresentative samples; the second is reliance on cross-sectional studies.

Most caregiver research is based on volunteer samples (e.g., mailing lists from Alzheimer's Disease and Related Disorders Association [ADRDA]). Survey research based on representative, nonvolunteer samples is required to put what is learned from such purposive samples into demographic context. Two exceptions are Stone, Cafferata, and Sangl's (1987) study of caregiving using the 1982 National Long Term Care Survey (LTCS), and Tennstedt, McKinlay, and Sullivan's (1988) eastern Massachusetts survey. These studies provide the bulk of what we can surmise about the demographics of caregiving.

From the LTCS national probability sample, Stone et al. (1987) projected 2.2 million caregivers in the United States. Approximately 70% of respondents were "primary" caregivers, whereas the remainder assisted in secondary ways. Reflecting the aging of America, 21% of the recipients were aged 85 and older. Just over a third of these caregivers were spouses; another one third to 40% were adult children, of whom over 80% were female. In most purposive samples of primary caregivers, the proportion of spouses is somewhat higher; for example, in the Chenoweth and Spencer (1986) study based on an ADRDA mailing list, 55% of respondents were spouses.

The existence of competing demands is apparent; in the Stone et al. (1987) survey, 24% of the adult children caregivers had a child under age 18 residing in their home. Approximately half of the adult children caregivers were working; another 9% reported quitting work in order to provide care.

Eighty percent engaged in caregiving activities daily, whereas the average amount of care involved 4 days per week. Twenty percent had been giving care for 5 or more years. In the Stone et al. (1987) survey, 74% of the caregivers lived with recipients, presumably overlapping substantially with those engaging in daily care. By way of comparison, Tennstedt et al. (1988) reported that 46% of the frail elders in their study lived with the primary caregiver. Stone et al. (1987) found fewer than 10% of caregivers were assisted by a formal helper, such as a paid home health aide. In contrast, in Bass and Noelker's (1987) study of elders who lived with a relative, 51% used some nursing or aide services.

Stone et al. (1987) did not count relatives as caregivers once the frail elderly patient had been institutionalized, even if they continued to be involved in the patient's care. This group, however, accounted for 55% of the Chenoweth and Spencer (1986) sample and 41% of the spouses in the George and Gwyther (1986) sample.

The second limitation of the caregiving literature is that it tends to involve only one time of measurement. Without longitudinal data, it is difficult to generate a complete picture of changes in the family system, including the development of the role of caregiver, beginning before there was any caregiving crisis. One effort to capture such a picture over time is underway in the USC Longitudinal Study of Three Generations (Bengtson & Gatz, 1987; Gatz, Boyd, & Mellins, 1987; Richards, Bengtson & Miller, 1989). A sample of over 1300 individuals, representing three generations from 324 families, has been surveyed in 1971, 1985, and 1988, with plans for surveys in 1991 and 1994. In 1985, 144 respondents, representing 106 families, stated that they were caregivers to one or more elderly relatives (Martin,

Ko, & Bengtson, 1987). Thus in this large sample that was not selected for a study of caregiving, 33% of the families were involved in caring for elderly relatives. Members of 20 "caregiving" and 13 "noncaregiving" families, a sample of 101 individuals altogether, were interviewed in depth in 1986. Supplemented with additional families, they will be reinterviewed in 1990 and between future waves of the survey. The interview sample represents a group of caregivers who did not volunteer for a study of caregiving, and the longitudinal follow-up will inevitably include a subgroup who have taken on caregiving responsibilities between interviews. Throughout the chapter we will be reporting both published and previously unpublished data from this study.

II. Involvement of the Family in Caregiving

A. Who Become Caregivers

The person most likely to take on primary responsibility for the care of an elder in the community is the elder's spouse (cf. Zarit, Birkel, & MaloneBeach, 1989). If there is no spouse, there is a predictable sequence (described by Cantor, 1980; Shanas, 1979) of next most probable relatives to become primary caregivers, beginning with the adult daughter of the frail individual. In the USC Three Generations study, 18% of the caregivers were spouses, 38% were adult children, 3% were adult grandchildren, 4% were siblings, and 6% were nieces or nephews of the frail elder. The other 31%, including both men and women caregivers, were assisting a relative of their spouse (mother-in-law, father-in-law, spouse's aunt, spouse's sister, and so on). Of these, four caregivers continued to provide assistance despite divorce from their spouse. Additionally, 17 of the 144 caregivers assisted more than one elderly person, such as providing help to an uncle as well as to a mother.

Given more than one adult child, what factors predict which child will be nominated as primary caregiver? Horowitz (1985) summarizes possible factors, including geographical proximity and other role responsibilities, such as whether the adult daughter is married, whether she has young children, and whether she is employed. There are additional factors reflecting family history, such as which child has always been the one to whom the parent turned, which have competing commitments, and which of these are recognized by the parent and siblings as legitimately interfering with ability to give time to assisting the parent. In our interviews, we found that families seemed to view the person who becomes primary caregiver as more available than other relatives. For the most part, it was not an explicitly negotiated decision; responsibilities were simply assumed. As one 39-year-old granddaughter explained: "You see what needs to be done. . . . There's just things that have to be done. You just do it."

One obvious aspect of these rules for succession is that women are disproportionately elected as caregivers. A second aspect is that these descriptions present caregiving as a responsibility assumed by one member of the family. However, a handful of writers have begun to discuss the involvement of multiple family members in providing assistance (Brody & Schoonover, 1986; Gatz, Boyd, & Mellins, 1987; Stull, Montgomery, & Scarisbrick-Hauser, 1988; Tennstedt et al., 1988). Tennstedt et al. (1988) found that nearly three-quarters of the frail elders in their survey reported having more than one caregiver. In the interview sample from the USC Three Generations Study, one-third of the caregiving families indicated that two or more people shared primary caregiving responsibilities, and nearly a half of the families had highly involved secondary caregivers. Often *both* an adult

child and his or her spouse were making substantial contributions to caring for one of their parents (sometimes after having previously cared for the parent of the other spouse!) (Mellins, Boyd, & Gatz, 1988). Furthermore, when the caregiver was an elderly spouse, the adult children were often involved as well, if only to provide emotional support to a parent who was the primary caregiver (Fitting, Rabins, Lucas, & Eastham, 1986; Miller, 1987).

It seems likely that interviewing only the primary caregiver, or not asking the presumed primary caregiver about other family members, would lead to overlooking the extent to which multiple family members may contribute. In a rare study in which both caregiver and care recipient were interviewed, Townsend and Poulshock (1986) discovered that adult children caregivers see the helping network as larger than do the elders who are being assisted. On the other hand, in those caregivers seen in a clinic, or among caregivers seeking support through ADRDA, a frequent complaint is that others in the family cannot or do not help (Chenoweth & Spencer, 1986; Zarit et al., 1985).

Motivations to Assist

Why would a family member become a caregiver? Beyond responding to the obvious need and vulnerability of the elder who requires the assistance (Pratt, Schmall, & Wright, 1987), what motivates the depth and extensiveness of involvement typically required?

Using ideas derived from the helping literature in social psychology, Schulz, Biegel, Morycz, and Visintainer (1989) identified three theoretical possibilities: *altruistic motives*, such as feeling attachment and empathy; *social norms*, including reciprocity and moral duty; and *"self-serving" motives*, such as avoiding guilt or indebtedness. Several have questioned whether altruistic motives—warmth, love, affection, "feeling close"—are necessary to the decision to become a caregiver, although affection may well buffer the burden of caregiving (Jarrett, 1985; Walker, 1986). Instead, caregivers predominantly seem to be motivated by norms and moralisms of obligation, "filial responsibility," duty, and wanting to reciprocate (Bengtson & Kuypers, 1986; Brody, 1985; Fitting *et al.*, 1986; Jarrett, 1985). As well, "self-serving" motives are part of the inner experience, from guilt over not doing more to a sense of personal satisfaction derived from acting on an important value or moral good (Brody, 1985; Hanks & Settles, 1986).

B. Types of Assistance

What do family members do as caregivers? Assistance can be categorized by the type of impairment necessitating help or by the types of tasks performed. Absolute amount of assistance required often can be predicted by extent of functional disability (Brody & Schoonover, 1986). Beyond describing the help provided, writers have been concerned with identifying the most difficult aspects of caregiving. Two cautions should be noted. First, family help occurs in both directions. Even elders who require substantial assistance still contribute to younger generations in the family, especially through financial and other gifts, as well as through performing chores (Troll, 1986). Caregiving is not one way until there is extreme impairment. Second, the literature is almost entirely concerned with dementia and with the special problems of caring for demented elders. Comparatively little is written about caring for older individuals with chronic physical illnesses. In actuality, physical impairment is more common than cognitive disorders, and often both are present (Gatz, Pearson, & Weicker, 1987).

1. Impairments Requiring Assistance

Impairments can be characterized along a number of dimensions: the particular illness suffered by the patient, presence or extent of cognitive deficits, types of functional problems or difficulties in self-care, and special management problems.

Perhaps the most salient aspect of the patient's actual diagnosis is whether or not the patient has loss of cognitive capacity, for example, memory loss or disorientation associated with some type of dementing illness. The nature of the caregiving problem is profoundly different depending on whether or not the patient is demented. A physically incapacitated elder (e.g., hip fracture, severe emphysema) may know how to perform an activity but have to depend upon assistance because of his or her incapacities (Morycz, 1985; Silliman & Sternberg, 1988). By contrast, a cognitively impaired elder may be physically capable but unable to find his or her own way to the activity or unable to bear in mind the instructions for completing the activity. The ramifications for the daily life of a caregiver can be quite different. Especially often mentioned is the extent of constant vigilance required by the behavior problems associated with dementia (e.g., wandering) and the impossibility of scheduling caregiving activities (Zarit, 1989). Another aspect is the invisibility of the impairment; a demented individual often looks quite normal.

In addition to cognitive and functional problems, affective symptoms such as depression and personality changes (or accentuations of prior traits or neurotic tendencies) may be part of the picture (Niederehe & Fruge, 1984; Pearson, Verma, & Nellet, 1988; Poulshock & Deimling, 1984; Shomaker, 1987). Smyer and Birkel (1987) also draw attention to chronically mentally ill elderly, who constitute another uniquely challenging group for family caregivers.

2. Tasks Performed by Caregivers

Caregiving tasks are typically quantified in terms of categories of assistance, amount of help required with activities of daily living, and the amount of time required for meeting the elder's need for care.

Categories of types of help given by caregivers include (1) emotional support, advice; (2) direct instrumental assistance (meal preparation, housecleaning, laundry, shopping, transportation); (3) personal care (bathing; dressing; feeding; grooming; help with medicines, special diet, injections, bandages, colostomy; assisting with walking; help with transferring from bed to wheelchair to toilet and so on; toileting); (4) managing money; (5) making decisions about care and providing linkage to formal services (arranging for services in the home and at agencies and medical centers, supervising in-home help); and (6) providing direct financial assistance (Brody and Schoonover, 1986; Horowitz, 1985; Noelker, 1987; Townsend & Poulshock, 1986). Fischer and Eustis (1988) suggest that the role of the family caregiver as "case manager," linking to formal services, has increased due to changes in the health care system leading to faster discharge from hospitals. Often, secondary caregivers function as service brokers.

3. Most Difficult Types of Assistance

Contrary to conventional wisdom, neither absolute amount of assistance with activities of daily living nor severity of cognitive deficits has consistently predicted extent of difficulty or burden or the decision to institutionalize (Fitting et al., 1986; George & Gwyther, 1986; Niederehe & Funk, 1987; Silliman & Sternberg, 1988; Zarit, Todd, & Zarit, 1986). Instead, problem behaviors have emerged as the strongest correlates of burden, especially for caregivers of dementia patients (Niederehe & Funk, 1987). Deimling and Bass (1986) demonstrated that disruptive behavior and impaired interpersonal functioning were the best predictors of burden, with cognitive incapacity having an indirect effect through the other two. Noelker

(1987) found disruptive behaviors, number of personal care dependencies, and cognitive impairment, followed by incontinence, to predict stressfulness and institutionalization. In a 2-year longitudinal study, Zarit et al. (1986) reported that difficulties in dressing, bathing, and incontinence predicted institutionalization. The literature mentions many other sorts of problem behaviors, such as sleep disturbances, repetitive questions, following the caregiver around the house, difficulty handling money, agitated behavior or combativeness (Chenoweth & Spencer, 1986; Quayhagen & Quayhagen, 1988; Zarit et al., 1985). Finally, Cohler, Groves, Borden, and Lazarus's (1989) summary of the literature emphasized the patient's emotional distress as the most difficult problem for caregivers.

When dementia patients have been compared to other groups, amount of care has been found to be quite similar for cognitively and physically impaired aged (Birkel, 1987; Gatz, Boyd, & Mellins, 1987). Yet, Birkel (1987) found caregivers of dementia patients to be more stressed and to consider institutionalization more than caregivers of patients with physical illnesses. Employing a different contrast group, Liptzin, Grob, and Eisen (1988) found families of dementia patients equally burdened compared to families of depressed aged.

Three studies have converged on the counterintuitive finding of more burden or acute distress in early stages of the disease when the dementia patient is less impaired (Gatz, Boyd, & Mellins, 1987; Miller, 1987; Zarit et al., 1986). In contrast, for nondementia patients, extent of patient impairment, number of unpleasant caregiving events, and amount of time spent on giving care have been found to predict caregiver stress linearly (Deimling & Bass, 1986; Gatz, Boyd, & Mellins, 1987; Lovett & Gallagher, 1988). One explanation appears to lie in change in the nature of the stressors, with disruptive behavior peaking and then disappearing as a dementia patient becomes more and more impaired. Two and a half-year longitudinal data from Haley and Pardo (1987) generally support this picture.

An alternative explanation is that stress is heightened when Alzheimer's disease or a similar disorder is first diagnosed, and relatives must begin grieving the loss of the earlier person (Pruchno & Smyer, 1984). As decline proceeds, caregivers may begin to define the patient as no longer being the same person whom they once knew, or as no longer responsible for what he or she says or does (Gatz et al., 1987). This change in perception seems to reduce stress. As one caregiver explained, "My mother . . . knows no one, has no understanding at all. Her body exists, her soul departed many years ago. I loved her very much. . . . I miss her very much."

In sum, objective demands have not been found to be highly predictive of subjective sense of burden and institutionalization. Instead, most frequent reasons for institutionalization are caregivers' feeling overwhelmed by 24-hour caregiving, caregivers' becoming ill, or not having a secondary caregiver (Chenoweth & Spencer, 1986; Greene & Monahan, 1987). It seems that institutionalization can be predicted better by caregiver-related variables than by patient characteristics (Gwyther & George, 1986). Having supportive family members allows a frail or impaired elder to remain for a longer time in the community (Select Committee on Aging, 1987). It is to these caregiver variables that we turn in the next section.

C. Consequences of Caregiving

There is general agreement with the proposition that caregiving is stressful. What are the consequences of caregiving for the caregiver? What factors moderate negative effects? In this section we first provide a very general conceptual framework and then overview the empirical evidence. We rely in part on other recent reviews such as Cohler *et al.* (1989).

1. Framework

Most research on caregiver burden appears to operate on some sort of stress and coping model, whether explicit or—more often—implicit (Pearlin, Turner, & Semple, 1989; Schulz, 1988; Zarit, 1989). The elements of such models include: (1) the stressor or life event, (2) perceptions, appraisals, or attributions about the event and the demands created by the stressor, (3) mediators, or the coping skills and resources brought to bear on the situation, and (4) outcomes for the caregiver, such as level of morale. Stress and coping models were developed with an individual in mind. The McCubbin and Patterson (1982) "double ABCX" model is frequently cited by gerontologists (e.g., Cohler et al., 1989; Famighetti, 1986; Pruchno & Smyer, 1984; Schulz, 1988). Here, "A" is the stressful event, "B" is the family's resources, "C" is the family's perception of the crisis, and "X" is the sense of strain or amount of crisis. "Double" refers to the accumulation of additional problems secondary to the disruption caused by the initial crisis. "Double" further reflects the fact that stress results not only from the original event but also from the continuing combination of changes initiated by the elder's chronic illness.

A problem with stress-and-coping models is that they may be more useful heuristically than empirically. Part of the conceptual difficulty arises because the stressful event is typically a chronic situation. For instance, demands and consequences of the elder's health crisis can get very entangled and the idea of "burden" gets applied to both perceptions and outcomes. Next, we review the elements of stress and coping as they apply to caregiving. To help the reader organize the ideas visually, we have presented a depiction of the concepts we discuss in Figure 1.

The first element of the model is the *stressor*, which we discussed in the earlier presentation of impairments and tasks. The "double ABCX" idea may be a useful reminder that there are two crises or stressors: the health problem (the elder's crisis) and the caregiving problem (changes in the caregiver's life resulting from the health problem) (see Zarit, 1989). Drawing on ideas of role overload, the changes in the caregiver's life have been called "associated role strains" by Pearlin *et al.* (1989) to indicate their separate contribution to stressfulness. Among the competing demands are family, work, friendships, and finances. There is not time and energy for everything; the financial costs can be enormous, and adjustments must be made.

The second element of the model, *perceptions* or *appraisals*, also has two aspects. On the one hand are perceptions of the symptoms or behaviors, such as how upsetting and how manageable they are (Haley, Levine, Brown, & Bartolucci, 1987; Niederehe & Fruge, 1984; Zarit *et al.*, 1985). The other aspect is the caregiver's subjective sense of whether or not changes in his or her life due to caregiving are acceptable or unacceptable (Zarit, 1989) and how much he or she has available to contribute.

The third element of the model involves resources and coping skills, also referred to as mediators of the stressfulness of the situations. *Resources* include financial contributions, education, social support, and formal assistance. It should be noted perhaps that some resources may serve as both mediators and competing demands. For instance, work is described as an escape by some but as a competing pressure for time and attention by others. In the USC Three Generations study, one 52-year-old female caregiver explained during an interview: "I never would have believed that anyone would use Aircraft Engineering and Manufacturing Corporation

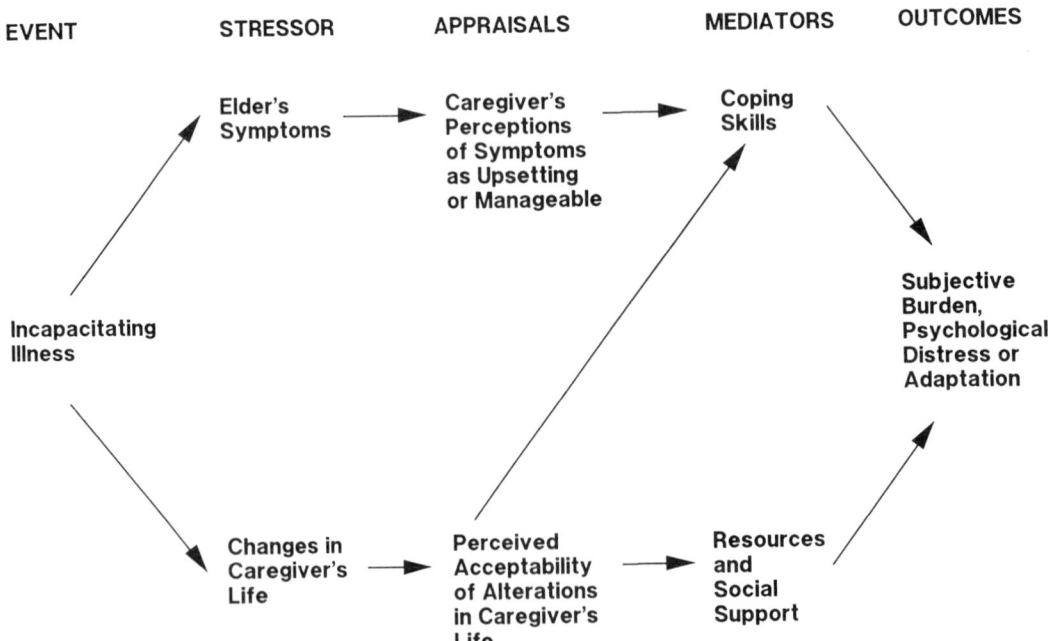

Figure 1 Conceptual framework for caregiver stress and coping.

for therapy, but I do. . . . I would never think of not going to work. . . . I go in there, I feel great." *Coping* encompasses (1) managing the situation (solving problems or seeking help), (2) modifying the meaning or appraisal of the situation (from focusing on one's own existential growth, to using humor, to refusing to think about the problem), and (3) managing stress symptoms (finding diversional activities, seeking social support, and finding a "safe place" to express frustration) (Pearlin *et al.*, 1989).

The fourth element of the model, *outcomes* for the caregiver, is generally referred to in terms of stress or burden. Indicators of stress include emotional distress, physical illness in caregiver, reduced social participation, altered relationship with the elder who is being cared for, and demands on finances (including secondary effects due to changing amount of time spent at work, or—for caregiving spouses —the potential of being obligated to pay for nursing care out of the couple's shared assets) (Schulz, 1988; Zarit, 1989). The term *burden* was initially used in this context. Currently, *objective burden* usually is employed to describe the actual changes in the life of the caregiver, such as having less time (Montgomery, Stull, & Borgatta, 1985), whereas *subjective burden* refers to feelings of distress, operationalized as the impact of the caregiving on various areas of the caregiver's life, as perceived by the caregiver. It should be noted that, although the literature emphasizes negative outcomes, positive consequences are possible, such as a sense of competence in managing the caregiving tasks, and self-respect or recognition by others for taking on caregiving duties.

The next sections summarize research findings applying these models. We begin with outcomes, in order to provide a clear summary of the consequences of caregiving. We then present findings about moderating factors, including perceptions, coping skills, and resources.

2. Outcomes

The connection of caregiving to lowered morale and physical health problems has been reviewed recently by Schulz (1988). As regards mental health outcomes, caregivers of dementia patients have been found to be significantly more distressed than normative noncaregiving populations on standard psychological assessment instruments (George & Gwyther, 1986). Lovett and Gallagher (1988) found 26% of their caregiver subjects to be experiencing a major depressive episode, and Haley, Levine, Brown, Berry, and Hughes (1987) found 43% of caregivers to be "clinically depressed" on a self-report measure. Anthony-Bergstone, Zarit, and Gatz (1988) also documented elevated depression but found anxiety and hostility to be even more apparent. Physical health consequences have received somewhat less attention, although self-reported deterioration in health was found by Haley, Levine, Brown, Berry, and Hughes (1987) and Bass and Noelker (1987).

However, there are inconsistent findings of morbidity effects, reflecting some of the limitations of the research (Schulz, 1988). For instance, spouse caregivers often are already in poor health. Further, studying nonrepresentative, volunteer samples may lead to exaggerated proportions of psychologically distressed caregivers. On the other hand, caregivers may have been selected for the role because of their good health and ability to cope with stress. Positive outcomes for some caregivers may counterbalance negative outcomes for others. Moreover, depressive symptoms may largely represent transient expressions of feeling burdened. In a rare longitudinal study of elders with a representative range of physical and cognitive impairments, Townsend, Noelker, Deimling, and Bass (1987) found that more caregivers became less depressed than became more depressed over time.

A number of instruments have been developed specifically to measure caregiver burden. The most widely employed is the Burden Interview (Zarit, Reever, & Bach-Peterson, 1981). Another frequently used scale by Poulshock and Deimling (1984) has subscales for two aspects of impact on caregivers: feelings of strain or resentment toward the elder and restrictions in activities. Lack of precision in the use of the construct of burden leads to questioning whether burden scales are measures of pure caregiver outcome (Schulz, 1988; Zarit, 1989). Nonetheless, burden scales seem to tap into something relevant about the phenomenon. In intervention studies, there usually has not been impressive reduction of scores on standard measures of psychological distress, whereas measures of "burden" have been more responsive. In a 2-year follow-up, Zarit et al. (1986) found that caregivers who were higher on burden at the first time of measurement were more likely to have placed their relative in a nursing home by the second time of measurement.

3. Appraisal

The appraisal factor in stress-and-coping models is typically measured with some form of behavior problem checklist where caregivers rate how tolerable or upsetting it is for their relative to exhibit the behaviors (Niederehe & Fruge, 1984; Zarit et al., 1985). Haley, Brown, and Levine (1987) and Zeiss, Gallagher, Lovett, and Rose (1987) expanded on this approach and, applying Bandura's (1982) self-efficacy theory to caregiving, asked caregivers to rate their confidence in managing problems. Haley, Levine, Brown, and Bartolucci (1987) tested all elements of a stress-and-coping model in predicting adaptation in dementia caregivers. Appraisal, coping, and social support were more important than objective stressor severity variables in predicting adaptation. In particular, depression was found in caregivers who appraised patient behaviors as more stressful

and appraised themselves as unable to manage the problems. Townsend et al. (1987) also found the caregiver's perceived effectiveness to mediate the relationship between caregiving stress and outcome, whereas Pagel, Becker, and Coppel (1985) found caregiver's perceived loss of control over a demented spouse's behavior to predict greater caregiver depression.

In describing the appraisal process, the social meaning of the diagnosis of dementia or Alzheimer's disease assumes importance (Cohler et al. 1989). Further, caregivers' coping may be affected by whether or not behavior changes are seen as deliberate stubbornness or as a consequence of the disease and by their understanding of the prognosis for their impaired relative (Deimling & Bass, 1986; Schulz, 1988).

Notions of control and meaning serve to organize the more qualitative observations often made about the caregiving situation. Whereas caregiving is presumed to some degree to reflect a voluntary choice, it constitutes a life event that is unscheduled, the tasks themselves are often unpredictable, and the duration is uncertain (Silliman & Sternberg, 1988). It is difficult for caregivers to feel control over their own lives. Furthermore, the needs and problem behaviors signify that the elder has declined to the point of no longer seeming to be the person he or she once was. There is a sense of loss and grief about the former person and former relationship, especially for demented or mentally disturbed patients who can no longer reciprocate affection or express gratitude (Pearlin et al., 1989; Smyer & Birkel, 1987). Brody (1985) captured the essence of change in meaning by pointing out that the adult child is now in the position of being depended upon by his or her parent.

4. Coping

Researchers who study coping with caregiving typically adapt coping strategy inventories or coding schemes from Lazarus and Folkman (1984) (e.g., Dundon, Cramer, & Nowak, 1987; Quayhagen & Quayhagen, 1988; Stephens, Norris, Kinney, Ritchie, & Grotz, 1988), from Moos and Billings (1981) (e.g., Niederehe & Funk, 1987), or from Pearlin et al. (1989).

In all three systems, major categories of coping strategies include *solving problems* and *modifying meaning.* Solving problems entails finding ways to manage the patient's symptoms. For example, Zarit et al. (1985) noted how ineffective it is to reason with a dementia patient. Haley, Levine, Brown, and Bartolucci (1987) found information seeking to be effective in lowering stress. Modifying meaning, that is, redefining stress as personal growth or reframing the situation in some other way, has been found to relate to more positive caregiver outcomes (Niederehe & Funk, 1987; Quayhagen & Quayhagen, 1988; Stephens et al., 1988), whereas escape-avoidance styles of coping are related to greater caregiver distress (Dundon et al., 1987).

5. Resources

Social support has proved consistently to be a powerful mediator of caregiving stress, with greater social support relating to higher morale and lower burden (Haley et al., 1987; Zarit et al., 1980). George and Gwyther (1986) found caregivers who lived with dementia patients to be more stressed than those who did not; however, according to Birkel's (1987) results, having more people in the household lowered stress in dementia cases.

Gender and generational (spouses compared to adult children) differences in caregivers have been widely researched. Spouses provide the most comprehensive care and keep the elder at home, out of an institution, longer (Greene & Monahan, 1987; Horowitz, 1985). At the same time, spouses appear to be more vulnerable to reduced well-being (George & Gwyther, 1986), although there is a reluctance to

complain of being burdened (Jarrett, 1985; Mellins et al., 1988).

Psychological morbidity and burden consistently have been found to be greater for women than for men (Fitting et al., 1986; Zarit et al., 1986). Anthony-Bergstone et al. (1988) compared male and female caregivers to respective age norms for each gender and found that older women, most of whom were wives, were more distressed than older men, younger women, or younger men.

Most researchers comment on gender differences in how the caregiving role is assumed. Women have been described as approaching caregiving similarly to child care (Miller, 1987). Men seem to approach it like a project, delegating tasks and recognizing limits, or like a teacher, trying to make contact with the remaining mental capacities of the dementing patient (Fitting et al., 1986). Men also have been found to be more comfortable seeking help and more able to maintain social contacts (Miller, 1987). Men are bothered by the personal care tasks (dressing, toileting) and housework, as well as by the loss of their wive's companionship (Miller, 1987; Zarit et al., 1986). Women seem more aware of the changed nature of the marital relationship; they are aware of their husband's dependency, bothered by embarrassments, and often have a hard time telling him what to do (Miller, 1987; Quayhagen & Quayhagen, 1988; Zarit et al., 1986).

6. Summary

The stress-and-coping framework has proved useful in organizing research about the consequences of caregiving for the caregiver. In particular, it highlights the salience of appraisals and mediators in determining what aspects are difficult, it allows for individual differences in interpreting and handling stressors, and it employs multiple indicators of adaptation. These models, however, have three limits. They focus on the individual caregiver's coping; positive outcomes are rarely recognized and explored, and the models make little provision for including the perspective of the elder.

The primary way in which the care recipient is included is through using some index of the quality of the relationship between the caregiver and the frail elder, as reported by the caregiver, as a mediating variable (e.g., Stull *et al.*, 1988). Certainly, however, physically frail elders are aware of their impairments and, in many cases, of the approach of death, and dementia patients, especially in earlier stages, are quite aware of their memory loss and its devastating implications (Cohler *et al.*, 1989). Thus, the elder, too, is engaged in processes of appraisal and coping. A relevant conceptual framework with regard to the elderly individual is Kuypers and Bengtson's (1973) social breakdown cycle, which warns against the potential vicious spiral of social labeling, induced helplessness, and exaggerated incompetence. Finally, the ways in which both the older adult patient and the caregiver manage the health-related dependency of the elder exist within a set of family interactions. These are addressed in the next section.

D. Effects on Family

The idea of a family system is that change anywhere affects the system. Applying this idea, the health-related dependency of the elder is best viewed as a family crisis (Creasey & Jarvis, 1989; Tubman, 1986). Pruchno, Blow, and Smyer (1984) have written about "life event webs." Their thesis is that there is interlinking among individual lives; when one person undergoes change, so must all of the "role partners" of the person. Thus when one person becomes ill, effects of that change radiate throughout all lives interlinked to the person. Taking a simple example, the elder becomes ill; therefore the adult child becomes a caregiver; therefore she has less time for her adolescent children.

Situations can get more tangled. Various family members are often undergoing their own problems or life transitions, separate from the caregiving, but contributing to the overall family pressure (Pruchno *et al.*, 1984). For example, within one family, a middle-aged woman may be caring for her frail mother, while she and her husband are dealing with tensions in their own marriage, and at the same time there are other difficulties, such as a drug problem, in their young adult offspring. Hagestad, Smyer, and Stierman (1984) have written about the even greater complexity when family members have divorced, remarried, and created step-families.

1. Interlinking Consequences

Family system factors can be incorporated into the stress-and-coping framework by regarding family solidarity as a mediator of the caregiver's stress (Niederehe & Funk, 1987; Tubman, 1986). Along similar lines, Stull *et al.* (1988) found that having a second caregiver reduced the negative effects of the situation on the primary caregiver's sense of well-being in instances when amount of time required by caregiving was large.

Greater shift to a family systems perspective is represented by studies of the extent to which strain has been shown to radiate to other family members. Creasey, Myers, Epperson, and Taylor (1989) compared couples with healthy or dementing parents. Both husbands and wives with a dementing parent were less satisfied with their relationships with the impaired parent; wives with dementing parents were less satisfied with their relationship with their own husbands; and burden was correlated with less satisfactory relationships with various family members. Problem behaviors in the dementia patients provoked family arguments. Creasey and Jarvis (1989) found that those children whose grandparents had dementia had less satisfactory relationships with their grandparents and that children with more burdened mothers had less satisfying relationships with their grandparents as well as with their fathers.

The work situation is part of the system of interlinked effects. Brody, Kleban, Johnsen, Hoffman, and Schoonover (1987) found that women who had quit work to care for their mothers experienced the most stress in terms of changes in their activities due to the caregiving and self-reported symptoms. When women caregivers still worked, there was more likely to be paid help, and others in the household or in the social network did significantly more assisting, for example, laundry and meal preparation. Last, the women who reported most interference of the caregiving with time for their husbands were those still working but conflicted about it.

Aspects of family stress provoked by the health-related dependency of the elder include (1) conflict between caregiving obligations and other family obligations (Brody *et al.*, 1987; Pratt *et al.*, 1987), (2) disagreements among family members about extent of contributions of each to caregiving and about the best form of care (especially, when to institutionalize) (Pearlin *et al.*, 1989), (3) readjustments in family roles, particularly as regards the balance of autonomy, dependency, and interdependency (Bengtson & Kuypers, 1986), and (4) emotional impact of the adversity in all members of the family, including heightened awareness of one's own vulnerability and finitude (Cohler *et al.*, 1989).

2. Effects of Dependency

The caregiving situation becomes the context for intensifying the inherent tension between personal autonomy and family interdependence (Cohler *et al.*, 1989). In couples, the dependency of one spouse on the other due to the illness alters the roles that the spouses had adopted or can so tax

the established marital roles as to reveal the weaknesses or limits of how the couple had chosen to manage their lives together. A parent's dependency can lead to a reversal of the balance of assistance that existed when the now-adult child was a youngster (Hanks & Settles, 1986; Zarit *et al.*, (1989).

Previously independent elderly adults are made dependent by illness, and they are forced to call upon children who had been sent away to live their own lives. Thereby, the caregiving situation often brings up old issues that adult children had thought were resolved (Niederehe & Fruge, 1984). Caregiving spouses may shield adult children from the severity of the other parent's impairment (Hanks & Settles, 1986). As well, more consideration should be given to the perception of the care recipient in these interactions; namely what it is like to be the patient—trying to maintain some sense of self in the face of physical and cognitive decline and fearing becoming a burden.

Several grandparents in the USC Three Generations Study alluded to family interdependence and their own issues of autonomy:

I know that my daughter is there, but I'm a very independent person and I don't call on my children as often as I should . . . . I try to do everything myself if I can . . . . I said, "I don't want to be a burden to you; I want you to put me either in a home or have someone . . . come and stay with me". . . . I think that's what I would do unless . . . . You know, there are some older people that . . . become so senile, and then their children have to take over.

My family do a lot of things for me that I can do myself. . . . I don't like it. . . . I think there's more tension with me than with them. I think it bothers me because I have always been so independent.

3. Positive Outcomes

Because family transitions occasioned by the health-related dependency of the elder represent developmental changes, they can have positive as well as negative outcomes. Only rarely does research address the satisfactions as well as the strains. Tennstedt et al. (1988), in discussing the increasingly common pattern of a nuclear family's being involved as a unit in caring for an older relative, suggest that the experience could either enhance cohesiveness or could concentrate and thereby increase the stress. Chenoweth and Spencer (1986) found a few families of dementia patients who described themselves as drawn closer, although the primary emphasis was on how "devastating" dementia was to the family. Some caregiving spouses of dementia patients report improvement in the marital relationship, and that they often recognize their own growth (Fitting et al., 1986; Miller, 1987).

In the USC Three Generations Study, these ideas were translated into a coding system for changes in the family system (Gatz, Boyd, & Mellins, 1987; Mellins et al., 1988). We anticipated and found that virtually every family member mentioned at least one relationship with another family member that had been altered by the health-related dependency of the elder (Mellins et al., 1988). A third of the families reported more positive than negative changes, with positive changes including increased closeness to one another and negative changes including tension between the primary caregiver and a relative who was less involved. We also found that at least one individual in each family, usually a person who was not in the caregiving dyad, described altered perspectives or meanings as a consequence of his or her awareness of the caregiving and the declining health of the elder. As a 50-year old woman whose parents each have many incapacitating ailments described, "I've got a few years behind me now, and the birth of my grandchildren and my parents being in need; I can see the whole broad view of a person being born and dying."

If family caregiving is a developmental process, then it must also be studied longitudinally (Brody, 1985; Tubman, 1986). When considering caregiving over time, the beginning point for adult children is before the parent needs a great deal more assistance. Marshall, Rosenthal, and Synge (1983) surveyed a representative sample of older parents and adult children in Canada. Over a third of the adult children were quite worried about their parents' future health and the possibility of the parents' losing their independence. Geographic distance was of great concern. Marshall et al. (1983) described these adult children as "watchful." A longitudinal design is necessary to establish the transition from worry to provision of care. Another common situation that requires longitudinal study is older adults' moving in and out of heightened need for assistance (e.g., during a period of recovery from surgery). Longitudinal research would permit actually studying the shifting family system and life event webs in relation to the elder's health-related dependency and decline.

III. Interventions to Aid Family Caregivers

There is beginning to be a distinctive literature in the area of interventions to aid family caregivers (see review by Gallagher, Lovett, & Zeiss, 1989). Much of the work tends not to be based on the theory or on the empirical findings highlighted in previous sections of this chapter. The field would benefit from increased conceptual rigor and from increased rigor of research evaluating the interventions. Two theoretical perspectives do have obvious relevance to conceptualizing this area: family therapy literature and writings in community psychology about preventive interventions (cf., Famighetti, 1986; Smyer, Gatz, & Pruchno, 1989); whereas Zarit (1989) has outlined the issues in conducting research on the efficacy of interventions with caregivers. The range of available interventions can be divided into family counseling, support groups for caregivers, and community services.

A. Family Counseling

The family systems and life event web perspectives argue for treating the family as a system and intervening at multiple points. Family sessions might involve not only the caregiver but also his or her spouse, their children, his or her siblings, their spouses and children, and the frail elder whose decline in health led to the concern (Qualls, 1988).

As Pruchno and Smyer (1984) remind us, these interventions do not have a traditional therapeutic goal, such as changing individual personality or behaviors from more pathological to less disturbed functioning. Instead, the idea is to help the family solve a situational problem. Some aspects of the health problem of the elder cannot be "fixed." Progressive dementia cannot be reversed. Unlike acute diseases, chronic physical illnesses create situations in which health cannot be totally restored. However, many of the problems precipitated by the caregiving crisis can be improved.

Qualls (1988) applies a cognitive-behavioral framework, challenging assumptions, expectations, and perceptions of the family that heighten their distress and impede effective caregiving. Herr and Weakland (1979) take the family through a stepwise process of problem solving. Seltzer, Ivry, and Litchfield (1987) arranged to teach families about community services. Therapists may suggest that family caregivers read one of the self-help books, such as Jarvik and Small (1988) as a general resource about parents' aging or Mace and Rabins (1981) for special information pertinent to caring for a demented relative. All writers in this area emphasize giving information to family members, in order to increase their control of the situation.

For relatives of dementia patients, there are many special issues for family counseling. These often represent tricky ethical dilemmas, especially in the arena of respecting the elder's autonomy and ability to make choices about his or her own care *versus* beneficence—acting in the elder's best interest as determined by the caregiver. For example, what decisions can the caregiver permit the elder to make and what cannot be permitted (e.g., driving, changing will, refusing surgery)? When should an adult child force the spouse of an impaired parent to assert more control over the patient's life? Then, caregivers have legitimate conflicts with other obligations—such as knowing they are neglecting their own children; and there are real problems about assets—such as how much to protect them or how to make choices between competing needs for family financial support. And finally, how does one set limits on caregiving (Pratt *et al.*, 1987; Rabins & Mace, 1986)?

Some caregivers do become clinically depressed. Especially to the extent that the problem represents a longstanding individual disorder, quite possibly reactivated by the stresses of the caregiving situation, some combination of individual psychotherapy for depression and family counseling for the current situation could be indicated (see chapter by Smyer, Zarit, & Qualls, in this volume).

B. Support Groups for Caregivers

Support groups emphasize both information and support, thus representing a psychoeducational intervention. In practice, groups often are specific to disorders and even to relationships (e.g., groups for spouses of dementia victims). Some are self-help groups; others are led or facilitated by a variety of professionals or paraprofessional staff. Some writers argue that a professional should be present in order to minimize the risk of support groups' becoming forums for the spread of misinformation (Davies, Priddy, & Tinklenberg, 1986). Whether the professional in support groups should be "on top" or "on tap" (a leader or a consultant) is a topic of some differences of opinion.

The need for psychoeducational support groups is documented by Chenoweth and Spencer (1986), who found that families of dementia patients tended not to get any adequate explanation of the disease from medical professionals. When Winogrond, Fisk, Kirsling, and Keyes (1987) conducted a group for caregivers of day hospital patients, they found resistance to psychotherapy among participants. Caregivers wanted a psychoeducational group.

In intervening with caregivers of dementia patients, Zarit et al. (1985) refer to a three-pronged approach including: giving information about the disease, providing social support in the group (and helping to identify substitute caregiving resources to increase support outside of the group), and exchange of ideas about how to manage behavior difficulties. Previously, teaching behavioral strategies had not been a part of the typical support group. Zarit (1989) suggests that a prime target of intervention is the caregiver's perception of the stressfulness of demands created by the patient's disease. Change in the appraisal of the problem may be achieved through teaching behavior management skills or educating the caregiver about the disease. It is useful to families if they are provided plausible explanations for the behavior and are told that behaviors are manifestations of the disease and are not volitional (Shomaker, 1987). Another form of appraisal consists of the caregiver's comparing his or her situation to the others.' Support groups may serve as well to provide a sense of meaning through transforming personal tragedy into a social cause (Pearlin et al., 1989).

Research evaluating the efficacy of support groups has rarely found strong or differential effects. Four studies will be described. Zarit, Anthony, and Boutselis (1987) compared support groups to family counseling as formats for providing similar treatments, that is, information about dementia, behavioral management skills, and how to increase the amount of support received by the caregiver. They found essentially equal reduction of burden and psychiatric distress in both treatment groups and in a waiting list control group. Haley, Brown, and Levine (1987) presented a controlled study of support groups for relatives of dementia patients, comparing support groups to support plus stress management, with a randomly assigned waiting list control group. They found participants to be enthusiastic about what they had learned; however, there was no reduction of depression or burden and no improved happiness or social participation. Lovett and Gallagher (1988) compared two psychoeducational group therapies for caregivers of frail elderly with various impairments: training in problem-solving skills (to manage problem behaviors of the patient) and cognitive/behavioral interventions for depression (e.g., increasing pleasant activities, challenging negative thoughts). Compared to a waiting list control group, participants in both types of groups increased in morale and showed reduced depression but did not report reduced stress. Greene and Monahan (1987) compared 34 support groups to a nonrandomly assigned sample of family caregivers not able to participate in the groups. The vast majority of impaired relatives had chronic physical illnesses and disabilities. Nursing home placement occurred more frequently among controls than support group participants.

In summary, some studies have demonstrated reductions in burden due to support group participation, but often objective indicators of the effectiveness of these interventions have not substantiated the enthusiastic perceptions of participants. Perhaps outcome measures are not always tapping the benefit that is presumed to result from the intervention. For example,

Haley, Brown, and Levine (1987) suggest that evaluations should begin measuring knowledge and coping skills instead of subjective well-being, particularly because most caregivers were not especially depressed at pretest. Finally, Zarit (1989) notes that effects of caregiver interventions on patients are rarely assessed. This omission is consistent with the pattern of not taking into sufficient account in caregiver research the perceptions of the elderly patient. Yet caregiving spouses still tend to construe themselves as part of a married couple, and they do not want services addressed just to the caregiver (Miller, 1987). Kuypers and Bengtson (1973) view the patient's involvement in planning his or her own care as crucial to arresting the vicious spiral of the social breakdown cycle.

C. Community Services

The service perhaps most frequently requested by caregiving families is "respite." The idea of respite encompasses in-home help that would let the caregiver leave the house, adult day care, and short-term residential placement that would give the caregiving family a vacation. Residential or inpatient respite has been a service of particular interest. Programs have been described by Miller, Gulle, and Mc-Cue (1986), Scharlach and Frenzel (1986), and Burdz, Eaton, and Bond (1988). Average length of stay varied from 7 to 15 days for these three studies.

The uses the families made of the respite time include taking a vacation or visiting relatives, simply getting a rest, and tending to personal needs (e.g., medical appointments). All three studies found positive perceptions of respite care. Burdz et al. (1988) reported improvement in behavior problems for respite patients—both dementia and physically impaired—as compared to control groups. Somewhat surprisingly, both Miller et al. (1986) and Scharlach and Frenzel (1986) found in-

creased likelihood of institutionalization for some patients. Apparently, in these instances, the respite program also functioned as a trial placement in anticipation of placing the patient in a nursing home.

Demographics of caregiving feed into public policy questions about whether incentives are needed to encourage families to do more: whether greater availability of formal community services would entice families to do less and whether financial assistance would alleviate family burden. On the whole, it appears that most families are doing all they can and that institutionalization is used as a truly last resort. Families are described as going "beyond their capacities" (Chenoweth & Spencer, 1986, p. 272). Especially spouses seem to continue care longer than seems strictly feasible, and there even may be reluctance to accept those formal services that could afford some backup.

IV. Conclusion

Demographic realities make caring for a frail dependent elder an expected, if unpredictable, part of adult family life. In this chapter we have reviewed the newly burgeoning literature about the strain experienced by family caregivers and about interventions designed to alleviate caregivers' burden. In the introduction to the chapter, we suggested three organizing themes, and through the various sections we pointed to aspects of the field that are in need of further development.

First, we have stressed that the caregiving situation involves the family system, not just a "primary caregiver." We showed how multiple family members become involved in sharing the tasks of caring for an impaired elder. Family relationship issues are reactivated and highlighted by the caregiving situation. Conversely, illness and health-related dependency provide a powerful context for studying adult development and family relations in response to life events. In order to fully investigate the phenomenon, it is necessary to conduct longitudinal research, including multiple generations and family members, on samples not selected because they were providing care.

The second theme is that family caregiving is a normative stress. Therefore, the premise of intervention should be that normal families are being helped through a crisis, and measures of outcome need to be selected taking this point of view into account. These measures should encompass both positive and negative outcomes. We offered a very general stress-and-coping framework to describe the caregiver's response to this normative stress. The conceptual framework includes appraisals and mediators that moderate negative effects and that point to intervention strategies. In psychological interventions with caregiving families, dimensions that seem most important are information and control. Information leads to greater perception of self-efficacy and personal control over the stressful situation.

The third and final theme is that the point of view of the elder must be incorporated in models of family stress and in intervention programs. We did not have much to say about this third theme because our message was that this issue has been overlooked. One bias that may help to account for this lack of attention to the care recipient is that much caregiving research has focused exclusively on dementia patients. Nonetheless, we expect that increased concern about personal autonomy will be reflected in research designs in the near future that take into more account the perspective of the care recipient. More generally, we predict continued intense interest in this field during the decade ahead.

Acknowledgments

Preparation of this chapter was facilitated by Grant No. 9 R37 AG07977 from the National Institute on Aging. We thank Linda Hall for her unstinting assistance and Michael Smyer for his comments on an earlier draft.

References

Anthony-Bergstone, C. R., Zarit, S. H., & Gatz, M. (1988). Symptoms of psychological distress among caregivers of dementia patients. *Psychology and Aging*, **3**, 245–248.

Bandura, A. (1982). Self-efficacy mechanisms in human agency. *American Psychologist*, **37**, 122–147.

Bass, D. M., & Noelker, L. S. (1987). The influence of family caregivers on elder's use of in-home services: An expanded conceptual framework. *Journal of Health and Social Behavior*, **28**, 184–196.

Bengtson, V. L. (1986). Sociological perspectives on aging, families and the future. In M. Bergener (Ed.), *Perspectives on aging: The 1986 Sandoz lectures in gerontology*. New York: American Press.

Bengtson, V. L., & Gatz, M. (1987). *A longitudinal study of generations and mental health*. Research Grant No. 9 R37 AG07977, National Institute on Aging.

Bengtson, V. L., & Kuypers, J. A. (1986). The family support cycle: Psychosocial issues in the aging family. In J. M. A. Munnichs, P. Mussen, & E. Olbrich (Eds.), *Life span and change in a gerontological perspective*. Orlando, FL: Academic Press.

Bengtson, V. L., Rosenthal, C. G., & Burton, L. M. (1990). Families and aging: Diversity and heterogeneity. In R. Binstock & L. George (Eds.), *Handbook of aging and the social sciences* (3rd ed.). San Diego: Academic Press.

Birkel, R. C. (1987). Toward a social ecology of the home-care household. *Psychology and Aging*, **2**, 294–301.

Brody, E. M. (1985). Parent care as a normative family stress. *Gerontologist*, **25**, 19–29.

Brody, E. M., Kleban, M. H., Johnsen, P. T., Hoffman, C., & Schoonover, C. B. (1987). Work status and parent care: A comparison of four groups of women. *Gerontologist*, **27**, 201–208.

Brody, E. M., & Schoonover, C. B. (1986). Patterns of parent-care when adult daughters work and when they do not. *Gerontologist*, **26**, 372–381.

Burdz, M. P., Eaton, W. O., & Bond, J. B. (1988).

Effect of respite care on dementia and nondementia patients and their caregivers. *Psychology and Aging*, **3**, 38–42.

Callahan, D. (1987). *Setting limits.* New York: Simon & Schuster.

Cantor, M. H. (1980). *Caring for the frail elderly: Impact on family, friends, and neighbors.* Paper presented at the annual meeting of the Gerontological Society, Washington, DC, November.

Chenoweth, B., & Spencer, B. (1986). Dementia: The experience of family caregivers. *Gerontologist*, **26**, 267–272.

Cohler, B. J., Groves, L., Borden, W., & Lazarus, L. (1989). Caring for family members with Alzheimer's disease. In E. Light & B. D. Lebowitz (Eds.), *Alzheimer's disease, treatment and family stress: Directions for research.* Washington, DC: National Institute of Mental Health. (DHHS Publication No. ADM 89–1569.

Creasey, G. L., & Jarvis, P. A. (1989). Grandchildren of grandparents with Alzheimer's disease: Effects of parental burden. *Family Therapy*, in press.

Creasey, G. L., Myers, B. J., Epperson, M. J., & Taylor, J. (1989). Grandchildren of grandparents with Alzheimer's disease: Perceptions of grandparent, family environment, and the elderly. *Merrill-Palmer Quarterly*, **35**, 227–237.

Crossman, L., London, C., & Barry, C. (1981). Older women caring for disabled spouses: A model for supportive services. *Gerontologist*, **21**, 464–470.

Davies, H., Priddy, J. M., & Tinklenberg, J. R. (1986). Support groups for male caregivers of Alzheimer's patients. In T. L. Brink (Ed.), *Clinical gerontology: A guide to assessment and intervention.* New York: Haworth.

Deimling, G. T., & Bass, D. M. (1986). Symptoms of mental impairment among elderly adults and their effects on family caregivers. *Journal of Gerontology*, **41**, 778–784.

Dundon, M. M., Cramer, S. H., & Nowak, C. A. (1987). *Distress and coping among caregivers of victims of Alzheimer's disease.* Paper presented at the annual convention of the American Psychological Association, New York, August.

Famighetti, R. A. (1986). Understanding the family coping with Alzheimer's disease: An application of theory to intervention. In T. L. Brink (Ed.), *Clinical gerontology: A guide to assessment and intervention.* New York: Haworth.

Fischer, L. R., & Eustis, N. N. (1988). DRGs and family care for the elderly: A case study. *Gerontologist*, **28**, 383–389.

Fitting, M., Rabins, P., Lucas, M. J., & Eastham, J. (1986). Caregivers for dementia patients: A comparison of husbands and wives. *Gerontologist*, **26**, 248–252.

Gallagher, D., Lovett, S., & Zeiss, A. (1989). Interventions with caregivers of frail elderly persons. In M. Ory & K. Bond (Eds.), *Aging and health care: Social science and policy perspectives.* Great Britain: Rutledge.

Gatz, M., Boyd, S., & Mellins, C. (1987). *Mentally or physically impaired elders: Family consequences.* Paper presented at the annual meeting of the Gerontological Society of America, Washington, DC, November.

Gatz, M., Pearson, C., & Weicker, W. (1987). Older persons and health psychology. In G. C. Stone, S. M. Weiss, J. D. Matarazzo, N. E. Miller, J. Rodin, C. D. Belar, M. J. Follick, & J. E. Singer (Eds.), *Health psychology: A discipline and a profession.* Chicago: University of Chicago Press.

George, L. K., & Gwyther, L. P. (1986). Caregiver well-being: A multidimensional examination of family caregivers of demented adults. *Gerontologist*, **26**, 253–259.

Greene, V. L., & Monahan, D. J. (1987). The effect of a professionally guided caregiver support and education group on institutionalization of care receivers. *Gerontologist*, **27**, 716–721.

Gwyther, L. P., & George, L. K. (1986). Caregivers for dementia patients: Complex determinants of well-being and burden. *Gerontologist*, **26**, 245–247.

Hagestad, G. O. (1986). The aging society as a context for family life. *Daedalus*, **115**, 119–139.

Hagestad, G. O. (1988). Demographic change and the life course: Some emerging trends in the family realm. *Family Relations*, **37**, 405–414.

Hagestad, G. O., Smyer, M. A., & Stierman, K. L. (1984). Parent-child relations in adulthood: The impact of divorce in middle age. In R. S. Cohen, B. J. Cohler, & S. Weissman (Eds.), *Parenthood: A psychodynamic perspective.* New York: Guilford.

Haley, W. E., Brown, S. L., & Levine, E. G. (1987). Experimental evaluation of the effectiveness of group intervention for dementia caregivers. *Gerontologist*, **27**, 376–382.

Haley, W. E., Levine, E. G., Brown, S. L., & Bartolucci, A. A. (1987). Stress, appraisal, coping, and social support as predictors of adaptational outcome among dementia caregivers. *Psychology and Aging*, **2**, 323–330.

Haley, W. E., Levine, E. G., Brown, S. L., Berry, J. W., & Hughes, G. H. (1987). Psychological, social, and health consequences of caring for a relative with senile dementia. *Journal of the American Geriatrics Society*, **35**, 405–411.

Haley, W. E., & Pardo, K. M. (1987). *Relationship of stage of dementia to caregiver stress and coping*. Paper presented at the annual convention of the American Psychological Association, New York, August.

Hanks, R. S., & Settles, B. H. (1986). *Theoretical questions and ethical issues in a family caregiving relationship*. Paper presented at the annual National Council on Family Relations Theory Construction and Research Methodology Workshop, Dearborn, MI, November.

Herr, J. J., & Weakland, J. H. (1979). *Counseling elders and their families: Practical techniques for applied gerontology*. New York: Springer.

Horowitz, A. (1985). Family caregiving to the frail elderly. In C. Eisdorfer (Ed.), *Annual Review of Gerontology and Geriatrics*, (Vol. 5). New York: Springer-Verlag.

Jarrett, W. H. (1985). Caregiving within kinship systems: Is affection really necessary? *Gerontologist*, **25**, 5–10.

Jarvik, L., & Small, G. (1988). *Parentcare: A commonsense guide for adult children*. New York: Crown.

Kuypers, J. A., & Bengtson, V. L. (1973). Social breakdown and competence. *Human Development*, **16**, 181–201.

Lazarus, R. S., & Folkman, S. (1984). *Stress, appraisal, and coping*. New York: Springer.

Liptzin, B., Grob, M. C., & Eisen, S. V. (1988). Family burden of demented and depressed elderly psychiatric inpatients. *Gerontologist*, **28**, 397–401.

Lovett, S., & Gallagher, D. (1988). Psychoeducational interventions for family caregivers: Preliminary efficacy data. *Behavior Therapy*, **19**, 321–330.

Mace, N. L., & Rabins, P. V. (1981). *The 36-hour day*. Baltimore: Johns Hopkins University Press.

Marshall, V. W., Rosenthal, C. J., & Synge, J. (1983). Concerns about parental health. In E. W. Markson (Ed.), *Older women*. Lexington, MA: Lexington Books.

Martin, M., Ko, C., & Bengtson, V. L. (1987). *Does filial responsibility run in families?* Paper presented at the annual meeting of the Gerontological Society of America, Washington, DC, November.

McCubbin, H. I., & Patterson, J. M. (1982). Family adaptation to crises. In H. I. McCubbin, A. E. Cauble, & J. M. Patterson (Eds.), *Family stress, coping and social support*. Springfield, IL: Thomas.

Mellins, C., Boyd, S., & Gatz, M. (1988). *Caregiving as a family network event*. Paper presented at the annual meeting of the Gerontological Society of America, San Francisco, November.

Miller, B. (1987). Gender and control among spouses of the cognitively impaired: A research note. *Gerontologist*, **27**, 447–453.

Miller, D. B., Gulle, N., & McCue, F. (1986). The realities of respite for families, clients, and sponsors. *Gerontologist*, **26**, 467–470.

Montgomery, R. J., Stull, D. E., & Borgatta, E. F. (1985). Measurement and the analysis of burden. *Research on Aging*, **7**, 137–152.

Moos, R. H., & Billings, A. G. (1981). Conceptualizing and measuring coping resources and processes. In L. Goldberger & S. Breznitz (Eds.), *Handbook of stress: Theoretical and clinical aspects*. New York: Macmillan.

Morycz, R. K. (1985). Caregiving strain and the desire to institutionalize family members with Alzheimer's disease. *Research on Aging*, **7**, 329–361.

Niederehe, G., & Fruge, E. (1984). Dementia and family dynamics: Clinical research issues. *Journal of Geriatric Psychiatry*, **17**, 21–56.

Niederehe, G., & Funk, J. (1987). *Family interaction with dementia patients: Caregiver styles and their correlates*. Paper presented at annual convention of the American Psychological Association, August.

Noelker, L. S. (1987). Incontinence in elderly cared for by family. *Gerontologist*, **27**, 194–200.

Pagel, M. D., Becker, J., and Coppel, D. B. (1985). Loss of control, self-blame, and depression: An investigation of spouse caregivers of Alzheimer's disease patients. *Journal of Abnormal Psychology*, **94**, 169–182.

Pearlin, L. I., Turner, H., & Semple, S. (1989). Coping and the mediation of caregiver stress. In E. Light & B. D. Lebowitz (Eds.), *Alzheimer's disease treatment and family stress: Directions for research*. Washington, DC: National Institute of Mental Health (DHHS Publication No. ADM 89–1569).

Pearson, J., Verma, S., & Nellet, C. (1988). Elderly psychiatric patient status and caregiver perceptions as predictors of caregiver burden. *Gerontologist*, **28**, 79–83.

Poulshock, S. W., & Deimling, G. T. (1984). Families caring for elders in residence: Issues in the measurement of burden. *Journal of Gerontology*, **39**, 230–239.

Pratt, C., Schmall, V., & Wright, S. (1987). Ethical concerns of family caregivers to dementia patients. *Gerontologist*, **27**, 632–638.

Preston, S. (1984). Children and the elderly: Divergent paths for America's dependents. *Demography*, **21**, 435–457.

Pruchno, R. A., Blow, F. C., & Smyer, M. A. (1984). Life events and interdependent lives. *Human Development*, **27**, 31–41.

Pruchno, R. A., & Smyer, M. A. (1984). *Therapeutic interventions with adult caregivers*. Paper presented at the Future of Natural Caregiving Networks in Later Life: Policy, Planning, Research and Intervention Workshop. Buffalo, NY, April.

Qualls, S. H. (1988). Problems in families of older adults. In N. Epstein, S. Schlesinger, & W. Dryden (Eds.), *Cognitive-behavioral therapy with families*. New York: Brunner/Mazel.

Quayhagen, M. P., & Quayhagen, M. (1988). Alzheimer's stress: Coping with the caregiving role. *Gerontologist*, **28**, 391–396.

Rabins, P. V., & Mace, N. L. (1986). Some ethical issues in dementia care. In T. L. Brink (Ed.), *Clinical gerontology: A guide to assessment and intervention*. New York: Haworth.

Richards, L. N., Bengtson, V. L., & Miller, R. B. (1989). The "generation in the middle": Perceptions of changes in adults' intergenerational relationships. In K. Kreppner & R. M. Lerner (Eds.), *Family systems and life-span development*. Hillsdale, NJ: Erlbaum.

Scharlach, A. E., & Frenzel, C. (1986). An evaluation of institution-based respite care. *Gerontologist*, **26**, 77–82.

Schulz, R. (1988). *Psychological perspectives on caregiving*. Invited address presented at annual convention of the American Psychological Association, Atlanta, August.

Schulz, R., Biegel, D., Morycz, R., & Visintainer, P. (1989). Psychological paradigms for understanding caregiving. In E. Light & B. D. Lebowitz (Eds.), *Alzheimer's disease treatment and family stress: Directions for research*. Washington, DC: National Institute of Mental Health (DHHS Publication No. ADM 89–1569).

Select Committee on Aging (1987). *Exploding the myths: Caregiving in America*. House of Representatives Comm. Pub. No. 99-611. Washington, DC: U.S. Government Printing Office.

Seltzer, M. M., Ivry, J., & Litchfield, L. C. (1987). Family members as case managers: Partnership between formal and informal support networks. *Gerontologist*, **27**, 722–728.

Shanas, E. (1979). The family as social support system in old age. *Gerontologist*, **19**, 169–174.

Shomaker, D. (1987). Problematic behavior and the Alzheimer patient: Retrospection as a method of understanding and counseling. *Gerontologist*, **27**, 370–375.

Silliman, R. A., & Sternberg, J. (1988). Family caregiving: Impact of patient functioning and underlying causes of dependency. *Gerontologist*, **28**, 377–382.

Smyer, M. A., & Birkel, R. C. (1987). *Research focused on intervention with families of the chronically mentally ill elderly*. Paper presented at the National Institute of Mental Health invitational conference on the chronically mentally ill, Orlando, FL, December.

Smyer, M. A., Gatz, M., & Pruchno, R. A. (1989). Community psychology and aging. In M. S. Gibbs, J. R. Lachenmeyer, & J. Sigal (Eds.), *Community psychology*. New York: Gardner (in press).

Stephens, M. A. P., Norris, V. K., Kinney, J. M., Ritchie, S. W., & Grotz, R. C. (1988). Stressful situations in caregiving: relations between caregiving coping and well-being. *Psychology and Aging*, **3**, 208–209.

Stone, R., Cafferata, G. L., & Sangl, J. (1987). Caregivers of the frail elderly: A national profile. *Gerontologist*, **27**, 616–626.

Stull, D. E., Montgomery, R. J. V., & Scarisbrick-Hauser, A. (1988). *Caregiver well-*

being: *The importance of two caregivers.* Paper presented at the meeting convention of the Gerontological Society of America, San Francisco, November.

Tennstedt, S. L., McKinlay, J. B., & Sullivan, L. M. (1988). *Informal care for frail elders: The role of secondary characteristics.* Presented at the annual meeting of the Gerontological Society of America, San Francisco, November.

Townsend, A., Noelker, L., Deimling, G., & Bass, D. (1987). *The longitudinal impact of caregiving on adult-child caregivers mental health.* Paper presented at the annual meeting of the American Psychological Association, New York, August.

Townsend, A. L., & Poulshock, S. W. (1986). Intergenerational perspectives on impaired elders' support networks. *Journal of Gerontology, 41,* 101–109.

Treas, J., & Bengtson, V. L. (1987). The family in later years. In M. B. Sussman & S. K. Steinmetz (Eds.), *Handbook of marriage and the family* (pp. 625–648). New York: Plenum.

Troll, L. E. (Ed.) (1986). *Family issues in current gerontology.* New York: Springer.

Tubman, J. (1986). *Family relations in parent care: Moving beyond the primary caregiver.* Paper presented at the annual National Council on Family Relations Theory Construction and Research Methodology Workshop, Dearborn, MI, November.

Uhlenberg, P. (1980). Death and the family. *Journal of Family History, 5,* 313–320.

Walker, A. J. (1986). *Conceptual issues in the study of parent caring.* Paper presented at the annual National Council on Family Relations Theory Construction and Research Methodology Workshop, Dearborn, MI, November.

Winogrond, I. R., Fisk, A. A., Kirsling, R. A., & Keyes, B. (1987). The relationship of caregiver burden and morale to Alzheimer's disease patient function in a therapeutic setting. *Gerontologist, 27,* 336–339.

Winsborough, H. H. (1980). A demographic approach to the life cycle. In K. W. Bach (Ed.), *Life course: Integrative theories and exemplary populations.* Boulder, CO: Westview.

Zarit, S. H. (1989). Issues and directions in family intervention research. In E. Light & B. D. Lebowitz (Eds.), *Alzheimer's disease treatment and family stress: Directions for research.* Washington, DC: National Institute of Mental Health (DHHS Publication No. ADM 89–1569).

Zarit, S. H., Anthony, C. R., & Boutselis, M. (1987). Interventions with caregivers of dementia patients: Comparison of two approaches. *Psychology and Aging, 2,* 225–232.

Zarit, S. H., Birkel, R. C., & MaloneBeach, E. (1989). Spouses as caregivers: Stresses and interventions. In M. Z. Goldstein (Ed.), *Family involvement in the treatment of the frail elderly.* Washington, DC: America Psychiatric Association (in press).

Zarit, S. H., Orr, N. K., & Zarit, J. M. (1985). *The hidden victims of Alzheimer's disease: Families under stress.* New York: New York University Press.

Zarit, S. H., Reever, K. E., & Bach-Peterson, J. (1980). Relatives of the impaired elderly: Correlates of feelings of burden. *Gerontologist, 20,* 649–655.

Zarit, S. H., Todd, P. A., & Zarit, J. M. (1986). Subjective burden of husbands and wives as caregivers: A longitudinal study. *Gerontologist, 26,* 260–266.

Zeiss, A., Gallagher, D., Lovett, S., & Rose, J. (1987). *Self-efficacy as mediator of caregiver coping: Developing an assessment model.* Paper presented at the annual meeting of the Association for the Advancement of Behavior Therapy, Boston, November.

Twenty Five

Psychological Assessment of the Aging Individual

Alfred W. Kaszniak

I. Introduction

Psychological assessment, as the term is employed within this chapter, refers to a collection of procedures whereby the mental and behavioral characteristics of an individual, within a particular situation and environment, are evaluated in order to answer specific questions. Psychological assessment encompasses such procedures as interviews, life history record and data review, tests, and situational observations. In the previous edition of this handbook, Zarit, Eiler, and Hassinger (1985) identified four prominent objectives of assessments: (1) determination of diagnosis, (2) assessment of broad patterns of behaviors, thoughts, or emotions, (3) evaluation of specific variables to assist in treatment planning, and (4) evaluation of the outcomes/effectiveness of interventions. The purpose(s) of a particular psychological assessment constrain the kinds of questions that are asked. In turn, the kinds of questions asked largely dictate the specific assessment procedures employed.

The present chapter reviews important recent research concerning psychological assessment of the aging individual. The focus is on assessment within clinical settings, for the purposes of differential diagnosis and treatment planning. Within this focus, neuropsychological assessment and functional psychometric assessment are emphasized as exemplifying approaches to addressing those most common questions within clinical settings serving older adults (persons age 60 and above). Greater emphasis is placed upon neuropsychological assessment because this area has not received as much attention in previous editions of this handbook or in other recent sources. This chapter does not attempt a comprehensive review of the numerous psychological assessment instruments appropriate for use with older adults. Rather, theoretic, methodologic, and practical issues that are common across various psychological assessment approaches are emphasized. These issues are given concrete consideration in examining recent research on a particularly common clinical problem, the assessment of memory complaints and difficulty.

Handbook of the Psychology of Aging, Third Edition
Copyright © 1990 Academic Press, Inc. All rights of reproduction in any form reserved.

First, however, it is necessary to review the rationale, indications, and general principles of the two assessment domains that form the focus of this chapter.

II. Neuropsychological Assessment

Neuropsychological assessment involves the application of various interview, observation, self-report, and cognitive-test procedures to the evaluation of persons with known or suspect cerebral disease. Neuropsychological evaluation plays an increasingly important role in the psychological assessment of older adults, particularly when dementing illness is suspected (Kaszniak, 1986, 1988; McKhann, Drachman, Folstein, Katzman, Price, & Stadlin, 1984).

Lezak (1983) identifies the three major purposes of neuropsychological assessment as including diagnosis, patient care planning and evaluation, and research. When employed in diagnosis, the various possible goals include assistance in distinguishing neurologic from psychiatric disorders, identifying possible neurologic disorders in nonpsychiatric patients and providing assistance in differentiating between neurologic syndromes (often including localization of the likely site of cerebral damage). Given these goals, it is not surprising that the most frequently employed criterion in external validation studies of neuropsychological tests is discrimination of patient groups formed on the basis of neurologic diagnosis or known location of cerebral damage.

Neuropsychological assessment of older adults requires particular knowledge specific to this age group. First is a basic understanding of the neurobiology, clinical neurology, pharmacology, clinical medicine, and psychology of aging. Second is a detailed understanding of the methodologic and conceptual issues that are relatively unique to the experimental and clinical neuropsychology of aging (Albert & Moss, 1988; Bayles & Kaszniak, 1987; Benton & Sivan, 1984). Third is a knowledge of the indications for (Albert, 1981) and practical aspects of (Kaszniak, 1987; Schear, 1984) neuropsychological assessment of older adults. Finally, there is a need for broad familiarity with neuropsychological assessment instruments and procedures (Lezak, 1983), particularly of those instruments with normative, reliability and validity data specific to older adults.

Approaches to neuropsychological assessment can be divided into two major traditions, one of which relies upon a fixed battery of standard tests and the other that employs a more flexible, individualized approach. The most popular of the neuropsychological test batteries are the Halstead–Reitan battery (HRB; Reitan & Wolfson, 1985) and the Luria–Nebraska battery (LNNB; Moses, Golden, Ariel, & Gustavson, 1983). Although neither approach is without significant psychometric limitations (see Hevern, 1980; Incagnoli, Goldstein, & Golden, 1986; Stambrook, 1983), they do represent the most developed of neuropsychological batteries.

Reitan and Wolfson (1986) provide a review of aging-related research with the HRB. Adult age is significantly related to performance on the majority of HRB subtests, indicating the necessity for age-group-specific normative data. Unfortunately, there are relatively few studies involving persons over the age of 70. HRB normative data has been provided for Veterans Administration patients through age 75 (Schear, 1988), for neurologically normal inpatients and outpatients through age 81 (Heaton, Grant, & Matthews, 1986), and for portions of the HRB employed with healthy nonpatient adults, aged 65 to 75 (Ernst, 1987, 1988). A serious limitation of these normative data bases is a reliance upon inappropriately wide age groupings. Schear (1988) groups all patients age 41 to

75 as "older" and Heaton *et al.* (1986) form one group of all individuals over the age of 60. Karzmark, Heaton, Grant, and Matthews (1984) do provide a validated regression equation for predicting the HRB Average Impairment Rating (a summary index) on the basis of age, education, race, sex, and occupation. However, similar equations are not available to estimate a given individual's probable premorbid performance on any of the individual HRB subtests.

HRB reliability data for older adult age groups is lacking. However, there has been a recent increase in the publication of HRB diagnostic validity studies using older adults (Bornstein, Paniak, & O'Brien, 1987; Hom, 1988; Schear, 1988). A significant practical drawback of the HRB is that its length (typically 5 hours) and the difficulty level of some of its subtests may make it inappropriate for some impaired and easily fatigued older adults. An abbreviated HRB, suitable for use with demented older adults, has been described (Storrie & Doerr, 1980), but additional normative, reliability, and validity studies would be necessary prior to recommending its clinical application.

As with the HRB, LNNB performance is significantly related to age, in a normal adult sample, for 11 out of its 16 scales (Vannieuwhirk & Galbraith, 1985). However, adequate normative data for older adults await development. Similarly, LNNB reliability data for older individuals are needed. Diagnostic validity studies, employing older age groups, recently have begun to appear (e.g., Burger, Botwinick, & Storandt, 1987). Although taking less time to administer than the HRB, the LNNB may still be too long (approximately 3 hours) for administration in one sitting, with impaired and easily fatigued older individuals. McCue, Shelly, and Goldstein (1985) describe an LNNB short form, suitable for use with older adults, that can be administered in under 1 1/2 hours. Additional research to establish normative, reliability, and validity data for this short form is needed.

Within flexible individualized approaches to neuropsychological assessment, the choice of particular tests is dependent upon the nature of the assessment question being asked. Among the most frequently included instruments is the Wechsler Adult Intelligence Scale, in its original (WAIS; Wechsler, 1958) and revised (WAIS-R; Wechsler, 1981) forms. The WAIS appears valid for the detection of intellectual deterioration in dementing illness (for review, see Kaszniak, 1986) and identification of likely hemispheric laterality of focal damage (Warrington, James, & Maciejewski, 1986). However, WAIS subtest score patterns do not appear to uniquely reflect the localization of damage within a cerebral hemisphere (Warrington *et al.*, 1986). Because the WAIS-R differs from the WAIS in both item content and stratified norming procedures, neuropsychologic validity of the WAIS-R cannot be assumed on the basis of that known for the WAIS. Accumulating validity data indicate that some patterns of performance established for the previous edition hold for the WAIS-R (Bornstein, 1987), although continued research is necessary.

The WAIS was standardized on previous generations of adults, and there have been cross-generational changes in IQ scores (Flynn, 1984). Thus, the WAIS is likely to overestimate the intellectual functioning of currently tested individuals, in comparison to the WAIS-R, by approximately 7 to 8 IQ points (Wechsler, 1981). This creates problems for any attempt to directly assess longitudinal changes (e.g., in a patient suspect of dementing illness), by comparison of WAIS and WAIS-R scores. Cross-validated procedures using demographic data to estimate premorbid WAIS (Goldstein, Gary, & Levin, 1986; Wilson, Rosenbaum, & Brown, 1979) and WAIS-R (Barona, Reynolds, & Chastain, 1984; Eppinger, Craig, Adams, & Parsons, 1987) IQ scores are helpful when prior testing is unavailable.

Other recent developments of particular interest include the validation of WAIS and WAIS-R profiles relatively specific to the cholinergic dysfunction characteristic of Alzheimer's disease (Brinkman & Braun, 1987; Fuld, 1984; Satz, Van Gorp, Soper, & Mitrushina, 1987). The relative specificity of this profile assists in differentiating among the various etiologies of dementia in older adults. However, its low sensitivity (Filley, Kobayashi, & Heaton, 1987) implies that a negative profile cannot be used to help rule out Alzheimer's disease.

Comprehensive reviews are available of other neuropsychological assessment instruments appropriate for evaluation of the older individual suspect of dementing illness (Albert & Moss, 1988; Bayles & Kaszniak, 1987; Riege & Metter, 1988; Spinnler & DellaSala, 1988) as well as for other purposes (Benton, Hamsher, Varney, & Spreen, 1983). The volume edited by Poon (1986) provides a number of chapters reviewing conceptual, methodologic, psychometric, and practical issues concerning memory assessment with older adults. However, special note should be taken of one particularly promising recent development.

The Wechsler Memory Scale (WMS; Wechsler, 1945) has been the most frequently employed clinical instrument for the assessment of memory, despite its numerous shortcomings (see Loring & Papanicolaou, 1987) and limited normative data for older adults. A new revision of the WMS (WMS-R; Wechsler, 1987) has been published, addressing many of the problems of the previous edition. First, the WMS-R was standardized on a nationally representative sample of adults, from ages 16 through 74, and the age-group-specific reliability of its various subtests has been established (Wechsler, 1987). Further, recently reported construct validity (Bornstein & Chelune, 1988; Delis, Cullum,

Butters, Cairns, & Prifitera, 1988; Roid, Prifitera, & Ledbetter, 1988) and diagnostic-group validity (Butters, Salmon, Cullum, Cairns, Troster, Jacobs, Moss, & Germak, 1988; Chelune & Bornstein, 1988; Ryan & Lewis, 1988) studies encourage its clinical application.

III. Functional Psychometric Assessment

In order to provide guidance in structuring interventions, as well as a baseline against which to measure intervention effectiveness, psychological assessment must evaluate a range of the older adult's functional strengths and deficits. Such assessment is necessarily multidimensional, taking into account "physical health status, mental and cognitive functioning, coping styles, social support systems, and other factors such as stressful events, morale and well-being, daily living skills, and adaptive skills" (Fry, 1986, p. 41). Although review of assessment approaches appropriate to each of these dimensions is beyond the scope of the present chapter, the importance of multidimensional assessment cannot be overemphasized. Comprehensive reviews are available (Brink, 1986; Fry, 1986; Kane & Kane, 1981).

Depression is the most frequently encountered mental disorder among older adults (Breslau & Haug, 1983). Reviews, comparing older adult normative, reliability, and validity data for depression assessment instruments are available (Fry, 1986; Gallagher, 1986a; Kaszniak & Allender, 1985; Thompson, Gong, Haskins, & Gallagher, 1987; Yesavage, 1986). Reviews of the aging-specific literature for particular instruments include those concerned with the Center for Epidemiologic Studies Depression Scale (Radloff & Teri, 1986), the Zung Self-Rating Depression Scale (Zung & Zung, 1986), the Beck Depression Inventory (Gallagher, 1986b), the D-scale of the Minnesota Multiphasic Personality

Inventory (Kaszniak & Allender, 1985, pp. 132–136), the Geriatric Depression Scale (Sheikh & Yesavage, 1986), and the Depression Adjective Check List and Multiple Affect Adjective Check List (Lubin & Rinck, 1986). The availability of reliability and validity data, specific for older adults, allows for informed choices of instruments best suited for a particular assessment question. Unfortunately, as is also true for neuropsychological assessment instruments, depression scale reliability and validity data for the old-old and very-old are not available (Weiss, Nagel, & Aronson, 1986). As recommended by various authors (e.g., Kaszniak & Allender, 1985; Thompson et al., 1987), the evaluation of suspected depression in older adults should include both self-report and behavior rating measures, in addition to information from medical examination, history and course of illness, and interview.

Although many have dismissed projective techniques as unreliable and lacking validity, recent meta-analytic reviews (Atkinson, 1986; Parker, Hanson, & Hunsley, 1988) have concluded that the reliability and validity of one projective technique, the Rorschach, is comparable to that of the Minnesota Multiphasic Personality Inventory (MMPI). Hayslip and Lowman (1986) have provided a comprehensive review of the use, with older adults, of techniques including the Rorschach, the Holtzman Inkblot Test, the Thematic Apperception Test, the Senior Apperception Test, the Geriatric Apperception Test, the Hand Test, and Sentence Completion techniques. Despite the persistent difficulties in determining the reliability and validity of projective techniques, their use with older adults has been recommended when information concerning psychodynamic constructs and processes is desired (Kahana, 1978), or when there "is little or no opportunity for more natural observation" (Gallagher, Thompson, & Levy, 1980, p. 29).

Applying the information contained within available reviews requires knowledge of those conceptual and methodologic issues particular to the assessment of older adults. The following section discusses a number of these issues.

IV. Critical Issues in the Psychological Assessment of Older Adults

The authors of related chapters in previous editions of this handbook (Schaie & Schaie, 1977; Zarit et al., 1985), among several others (e.g., Albert, 1981; Cunningham, 1986; Gallagher, 1986a; Kaszniak, 1988), have discussed various methodologic, psychometric, and practical issues in the psychological assessment of older adults. The present section will therefore briefly describe only the most salient of these issues.

A. Threats to Reliability and Validity

1. Reliability

a. Internal Consistency Reliability refers to consistency of measurement within and across occasions. Consistency within occasion is often measured by the average correlation among items within an assessment instrument (termed internal consistency) and is thus dependent upon both the adequacy of item sampling and the number of items. In the sampling of items for inclusion in an assessment instrument, attention must be given to whether items retain the same meaning across adult age groups. The experience of a given cohort with particular stimulus materials (e.g., printed questions versus computer displays) and language and phrasing of questions are relevant considerations. Possible age-group differences in such variables as the degree of social desirability response set (Klassen, Homstra, & Anderson, 1975) also indicate the need for age-group-specific internal consistency data. Further, because ill health in older age could be expected to increase variation in scores from item to item within an assessment instrument, knowledge of internal consistency reliability for particular diagnostic groups is desirable. Finally, although assessment instruments with larger numbers of items generally have higher levels of reliability, considerations of time requirements and fatigue may mitigate against the use of longer protocols.

b. *Interrater Reliability* Another criterion for evaluating consistency of measurement within occasion is that of interrater reliability. Although less relevant for measures of unambiguous response dimensions, this criterion is important for measures necessitating some subjective judgment on the part of the assessor. Interrater reliability can be increased by reducing *criterion variance* through clearly specified criteria to guide the examiner's judgment. This was a major motivating factor in the creation of the third edition of the *Diagnostic and Statistical Manual of Mental Disorders* (DSM-III, American Psychiatric Association, 1980) and its most recent successor, the DSM-III-R (American Psychiatric Association, 1987).

Interrater reliability also can be improved through reduction of *information variance*, by making the same observations or asking the same questions across all individuals being assessed. This was the rationale behind the construction of structured diagnostic interview procedures, such as the Schedule for Affective Disorders and Schizophrenia (SADS; Spitzer & Endicott, 1978), and the Diagnostic Interview Schedule (DIS; National Institute of Mental Health, 1979). DIS interrater reliability appears to be comparable when used with younger and older adults (Blazer, Hughes, & George, 1987).

c. *Test–Retest Reliability* Consistency between occasions is measured by test–

retest reliability. In applying the standard of test–retest reliability, it must be assumed that the behavior or construct being measured is itself consistent over time. For certain constructs, such as state anxiety or perceptual vigilance, this assumption is not supportable. Similarly, for certain clinical disorders, such as delirium or acute confusional state (Lipowski, 1987), marked fluctuation in behavior from one occasion to the next is expected. For those behaviors and constructs warranting the assumption of consistency over time, knowledge of age-group-specific and diagnostic-group-specific test–retest reliability is important.

Published information on the reliability of various assessment protocols for the young-old has increased substantially in recent years. However, there remains very little reliability information for such instruments when used with the old-old or very-old, and diagnostic-group-specific reliability information is far from complete.

2. Validity

Validity of an assessment procedure refers to both what is being measured and how well such measurement is accomplished. The question of what is being measured is asked in terms of face, content, and construct validity. The question of how well the measurement is accomplished is asked in terms of external validity. In assessing each of these aspects of validity, application to older adults poses some unique problems.

a. *Face Validity* Technically, face validity does not refer to the question of what an assessment procedure measures but rather what it "appears superficially to measure" (Anastasi, 1982, p. 136). Thus face validity is determined by the plausibility of the procedure, in the eyes of the individual being assessed. Given the likely impact upon degree of cooperation with a procedure, face validity is of importance in the assessment of persons of any age. However, older adults may be particularly sensitive to tasks or questions appearing to be childish or patronizing. Such sensitivity is likely to be even greater among those older individuals who are aware that they are experiencing cognitive difficulty. Careful consideration of face validity always should be given when a procedure originally developed for use with younger age groups is extended to use with older adults.

b. Content Validity Content validity is determined by the extent to which test items representatively sample the domain of interest. Representative sampling in item choice presumes a knowledge of the full domain of the construct or behavior of interest. One threat to content validity is possible age-related differences in the item domain of interest. Taking the example of a depression self-report inventory, it would thus be important to know whether depression symptoms differ between younger and older adults. Several investigators (Gallagher & Thompson, 1983; Gaylord & Zung, 1987; George, Blazer, Winfield-Laird, Leaf, & Fischbach, 1987) have concluded that depression in older and younger adults is essentially similar. However, other observers have suggested possible age-related differences in the frequency of particular somatic (Casper, Redmond, Katz, Schaffer, Davis, & Koslow, 1985) and cognitive (Blazer, 1982) symptoms.

c. Construct Validity Construct validation is typically conceptualized as an ongoing effort to identify the meaning of particular hypothetical constructs and their operationally defining measures. Nunnally (1978, p. 98) identifies three major aspects of the process of construct validation: (1) specification of the domain of possible observations related to the construct; (2) empirically and statistically (typically through factor analysis and re-

lated techniques) determining whether the observations tend to measure the same or different things; and (3) subsequent determination, through controlled experiments and/or individual difference studies, of whether the measures of the construct produce results predicted by theory concerning the construct.

Particularly for many psychological constructs (e.g., memory, depression), the consensually accepted domain of observables related to the construct undergoes continuous modification as basic and applied research data accumulate. The area of clinical memory assessment provides an easy example of this point. Current knowledge of the factorial complexity of the general construct of memory argues against reliance upon any single index (e.g., the WMS Memory Quotient) in memory assessment (cf., Butters, 1986).

Empirical determination of age-group-specific and diagnostic-group-specific construct validity is of importance. The factor structure of a given assessment instrument may not remain invariant across different age groups or clinical disorders. Using the WMS again as an example, there exist reports of a different factor structure for older, as compared to younger, patients undergoing evaluation for possible neurologic dysfunction (Larabee, Kane, & Schuck, 1983; Skilbeck, & Woods, 1980). Obvious threats to construct validity include measurement "contamination" by the contribution of age-related changes in sensory functioning. For many older adults, physical illness and drug-related symptoms create further complications.

Construct validity also may not be invariant over time for patients with a progressive dementia, such as Alzheimer's disease (AD). Different aspects of memory processing become impaired as AD patients progress from mild to moderately severe dementia (Kaszniak, Wilson, Fox, & Stebbins, 1986). As a range of cognitive functions becomes more severely impaired over time in AD, the operational measurement of a construct may become contaminated by other hypothetical processes, increasingly impaired in AD, but not significantly contributing to the task performance of healthy older adults (Wilson, Bacon, Fox, & Kaszniak, 1983; Wilson & Kaszniak, 1986). Caution is therefore necessary in the interpretation of what hypothetical psychologic process or construct a given task is actually measuring.

d. External Validity Kaszniak and Davis (1986) provide a discussion of the following questions that must be considered in external validation: (1) What are the justifications for selecting a particular external criterion? An explicit theoretic rationale, relating the assessment measure to the criterion, is needed. (2) What information is available concerning the reliability and validity of the criterion itself? If the criterion cannot be reliably measured, the associated error variance will attenuate the magnitude of any observed correlations between the criterion and assessment measures. (3) How will subject sampling affect external validity estimates? If subjects selected for study (e.g., AD patients) represent only a portion of the full range of a phenomenon of interest (e.g., either all mildly demented or all severely demented), this truncated range will affect correlations between an assessment measure and any eternal criterion.

The importance of selecting an external criterion appropriate to the assessment task at hand is illustrated by consideration of progressive dementia. Tests of verbal and visual secondary memory have known validity for differentiating mildly demented AD patients from their normal age cohort. Such tests would thus be appropriate for inclusion within a diagnostic battery. However, these same tests lack validity for tracking dementia progression, due to floor effects (Kaszniak, Wilson, Fox, & Stebbins, 1986). Other tests, such as those of visual confrontation naming and au-ditory comprehension, do not adequately differentiate mildly demented AD patients from normal individuals. However, the later tests are valid for tracking deterioration, as they reflect impairment with disease progression and do not show floor effects until quite late in the illness.

Various subject characteristics may affect external validity estimates. For example, consider clinical memory tests that are often used to assist in differentiating normal from pathological memory functioning in older adults. The degree of age relationship for different memory tasks is substantially modulated by subject variables such as socioeconomic status, education, verbal intelligence, and certain personality characteristics (e.g., Arbuckle, Gold, & Andres, 1986). Older adult normative data for memory and other cognitive tests seldom allow for adequate subdivision by these relevant subject variables. Consequently, psychological assessment results need to be interpreted cautiously, weighing the possible impact of an individual's characteristics.

Similar considerations would apply to the application of clinical memory tests in assisting to differentiate possible etiologies of memory deficit. Limitations in group discriminative validity (Kaszniak, Poon, & Reige, 1986; Tierney, Snow, Reid, Zorzitto, & Fisher, 1987) must be taken into account, as well as interpretation of test scores always supplemented with clinical history and observation of discriminating qualitative aspects of behavior and test performance (Gurland & Toner, 1983; Milberg, Hebben, & Kaplan, 1986).

V. Assessing Complaints of Memory Difficulty

The practical importance of the reliability and validity issues detailed here can be appreciated best through consideration of a common assessment problem. One of the more frequent reasons for referral of an older adult for psychological assessment is complaint of memory difficulty. Although the focus here is upon assessment of memory difficulty, the issues discussed generalize to many other assessment problems.

A. Memory Complaint and Memory Impairment

Research employing questionnaires to assess the subjective frequency of everyday memory failures has shown older adults to complain of memory difficulty more than younger adults (see Zelinski, Gilewski, & Thompson, 1980). However, correlations between these questionnaire assessments and performance on verbal memory tests have varied for normal older adults (Larrabee & Levin, 1986; Riege, 1982; Sunderland, Watts, Baddeley, & Harris, 1986; Zelinski et al., 1980). As reviewed by Gilewski and Zelinski (1986), memory complaint questionnaires used in studies of older adults have shown test–retest reliability coefficients from .22 to .64 and internal consistency coefficients from .61 to .93.

Thus, older adults' complaints of memory difficulty, even when assessed with carefully constructed questionnaires, may not be reliable or valid predictors of objective memory task performance. However, comparing memory complaint with objective memory task performance can provide important information to assist in differential diagnosis. Depressed older adults tend to complain about memory difficulty, even though they may show no memory performance deficits (Kahn, Zarit, Hilbert, & Niederehe, 1975; Larrabee & Levin, 1986). Conversely, moderately and more severely demented patients with AD show clear memory performance impairment but subjectively overestimate their memory ability (Reisberg, Gordon, McCarthy, Ferris, & de Leon, 1985). Mildly demented patients with AD show memory performance deficits and report com-

mensurate awareness of memory problems (Reisberg et al., 1985).

B. Accuracy and Sources of Error in Differential Diagnosis

Although comparison of memory complaint with memory performance can assist in differential diagnosis, this approach alone is not sufficient. To gain an understanding of the importance of other considerations, it is helpful to briefly review current data on diagnostic accuracy and sources of error in differential diagnosis. AD and vascular dementia are the most frequent diagnoses made of patients referred for neurologic assessment because of memory complaints (Thal, Grundman, and Klauber, 1988). Thus a focus upon accuracy in the diagnosis of dementia is appropriate.

Inaccurate diagnoses of dementia in the general medical population have been reported to range from 10% to over 50% (Gurland & Toner, 1983; National Institute on Aging Task Force, 1980). Many of these misdiagnoses are false negative errors (failing to diagnose the syndrome of dementia when it is present). Increasingly, however, false positive error in the diagnosis of dementia, particularly overdiagnosis of AD, is becoming a concern (Gatz & Pearson, 1988). A large number of medical and neurologic disorders can present with a dementia syndrome (Cummings, 1987), many of which are potentially reversible. One of the most frequent types of false positive errors is diagnosis of irreversible dementia in an older person actually suffering from depression (Garcia, Reding, & Blass, 1981).

C. Depression, Cognitive Deficit, and the "Dementia Syndrome of Depression"

Why should the differentiation of depression from irreversible dementia be difficult? As already discussed, depressed older adults frequently complain of memory difficulty. In addition, depressed older adults may score in a range similar to mildly demented AD patients on tasks evaluating concentration and speed of performance (Hart, Kwentus, Wade, & Hamer, 1987). Some depressed older adults also demonstrate memory and other cognitive deficits on tasks for which speed of performance does not affect scoring. In some cases, cognitive deficit may be sufficiently severe as to warrant the term *dementia syndrome of depression* (Folstein & McHugh, 1978), or *pseudodementia* (Kiloh, 1961). Further, a number of the DSM-III symptom criteria for depression also may occur as concomitants of normal aging or illness (including dementia) in older adults. These include changes in sleep pattern, appetite changes, fatigue, behavioral slowing or agitation, and complaints of diminished ability to think or concentrate. Similarities also exist between certain behavioral features of depression and dementia (see Kaszniak, 1987; Kaszniak, Sadeh, & Stern, 1985). For example, the dementia patient may be careless in personal grooming, suggesting the possibility of depression-related apathy. Similarly, decreased variability of facial expression in dementia may be interpreted as the loss of interest or pleasure seen in depression.

The prevalence of the dementia syndrome of depression remains unknown. A prerequisite for reliable prevalence data would be further development and validation of clear diagnostic criteria (e.g., Rabins, Merchant, & Nesladt, 1984). Lists of identifying features (e.g., Wells, 1983) have been proposed, but the validity of these remains to be established. As reviewed by Niederehe (1986), the research literature concerned with memory and other cognitive functioning in depressed middle-aged and older adults has yielded contradictory results. Some studies report depression and cognitive impairment to be significantly associated, whereas other studies find few significant differences between depressed patients and healthy controls. There is also controversy concerning the question of whether cognitive impairment is more likely in older, than in younger, depressed patients.

Attempts have been made at resolving apparent controversies in this literature, providing the clinician with some guidance in assessment result interpretation (see Johnson & Magaro, 1987). As suggested by Kelly (1986), depressed older individuals may show deficit in recall of neutral or positive material, whereas recall of material with negative themes may be preserved. At this time, standardized memory assessment instruments, allowing for systematic manipulation of the mood congruency of mnemonic stimuli, do not exist. However, thematic valence of to-be-remembered material should be given consideration in the interpretation of memory assessment results. For example, it is of interest to note that the WMS and WMS-R contain predominantly negative themes in their paragraph recall subtests.

Reviews of the literature on depression and memory in older age (Niederehe, 1986; Raskin, 1986) also have suggested that higher probability of memory impairment is related to inpatient status, greater severity of depression, poor premorbid social competence, and low premorbid intelligence. Further, as illustrated in a series of studies by Weingartner and his colleagues (Weingartner, 1986), cognitive processes presumed to require greater effort are the ones most impaired in depression. Recent data showing depressed older adults to be impaired (relative to age-matched controls) on recall but not recognition memory testing have been interpreted as consistent with decreased effort of memory processing in depression (Blau & Ober, 1988). In contrast, mildly to moderately demented AD patients show deficit in both recall and recognition memory (Kaszniak, Poon, & Riege, 1986).

The new WMS-R, with its normative

data for adults through age 74, provides measures of both recall and recognition memory for both verbal and nonverbal stimuli. The Recognition Memory Test (RMT; Warrington, 1984) provides separate measures of recognition memory for words and for faces. Normative data for adults through age 70 is provided for the RMT, and sensitivity to the memory impairments of patients with diffuse and with various focal cerebral lesions has been demonstrated (Warrington, 1984). However, determination of WMS-R or RMT specificity in distinguishing demented from depressed older adults awaits future research.

Comparison of recall and recognition memory task performance thus may be helpful in attempting to differentiate the memory impairments of AD from those of the dementia syndrome of depression. It also appears that qualitative analysis of error patterns in recognition memory task performance may be helpful. Several investigators (Corwin, Peselow, & Dash, 1988; Miller & Lewis, 1977; Niederehe, 1986) have found evidence for a conservative response bias in older adult depressed patients. In contrast, AD patients have been reported to show an abnormally liberal response bias with both verbal (Branconnier, Cole, Spera, & De Vitt, 1982) and pictorial recognition memory tasks (Snodgrass & Corwin, 1988). The recently developed California Verbal Learning Test (Delis, Freeland, Kramer, & Kaplan, 1988) provides for standardized assessment of verbal recognition response bias.

As already noted, there are some data indicating that depressed patients learn and remember less than normal controls only under conditions that demand effortful processing. However, depressed individuals might show normal storage, as reflected by rate of forgetting, once initial learning of new information is equated to that of controls. In contrast, AD patients show abnormally rapid forgetting, even

under conditions where initial learning is optimized (Moss, Albert, Butters, & Payne, 1986). Hart, Kwentus, Taylor, and Harkins (1987) directly tested rate-of-forgetting differences between age-matched depressed older adults, mildly demented AD patients, and normal controls. Depressed and AD patients showed learning impairments, but only the AD group showed rapid forgetting in the first 10 minutes after learning to criterion. These results are of particular clinical interest because the depressed and AD patients performed similarly on most of a set of commonly employed neuropsychological tests.

Thus even when mildly demented AD patients and cognitively impaired depressed older adults cannot be differentiated on the basis of standard neuropsychological testing, examination of rate of forgetting might be helpful. It should be noted, however, that AD patients may not reveal evidence of rapid forgetting when they are not equated to normals for initial learning (Becker, Boller, Saxton, & McGonigle-Gibson, 1987), or when rate of forgetting is evaluated over the interval of from 10 minutes to 1 week after initial learning (Kopelman, 1985). Future research will need to resolve issues concerning the intervals over which forgetting is measured. There is also the need for additional research on the impact of stimulus exposure time (or other ways of equating initial learning; cf., Martone, Butters, & Trauner, 1986), before the diagnostic validity of rate of forgetting can be uncritically accepted.

Standardized memory assessment instruments that allow a distinction to be made between the hypothetical memory processes of storage and retrieval also have been shown to have validity in distinguishing dementia from depression. One such instrument is the Buschke Selective Reminding Test (SRT; Buschke & Fuld, 1974). AD patients obtain lower scores than age-matched controls on SRT measures of storage and retrieval from long-term memory (Weingartner, Kaye, Smallberg, Ebert, Gilin & Sitaram, 1981). These measures also appear to be more sensitive than the WAIS or WMS subtests in discriminating mildly demented AD patients from normals (Larrabee, Largen, & Levin, 1985). Acceptable alternate-form and test–retest reliability, as well older adult norms, have recently been reported for the SRT (Branconnier, Harto, McNiff, Kilpatrick, Torre, & Spera, 1987). Hart, Kwentus, Taylor, and Hamer (1987) found that depressed older adults, although impaired relative to controls on a recall measure from the SRT, could be differentiated from AD patients on the basis of storage and recognition memory measures. Another test, allowing a similar distinction between storage and retrieval, is the Fuld Object Memory Evaluation (OME; Fuld, 1980). OME scores correlate with both the neuropathologic (Fuld, Dickson, Crystal, & Aronson, 1987) and the neurochemical (Fuld, Katzman, Davies, & Terry, 1982) characteristics of AD. The OME has recently been shown to be a better discriminator of depressed versus demented older adults than various other commonly employed memory tests (LaRue, D'Elia, Clark, Spar, & Jarvik, 1986).

Finally, mention should be made of the enhanced cued recall procedure of Grober and Buschke (Grober, Buschke, Crystal, Bang, & Dresner, 1988). This procedure was developed to minimize the impact of inefficient encoding due to insufficiently effortful processing in memory. The cued recall measures are superior to the free recall measures from this procedure in discriminating demented from nondemented older adults, showing a high degree of sensitivity and specificity (Grober et al., 1988). The cued recall procedure would appear well-suited for further research to determine its validity in differentiating AD patients from older adults with the dementia syndrome of depression.

D. Depression and Depressionlike Symptoms in Dementing Illness

Another factor contributing to difficulty in differentiating dementia from depression is the coexistence of depression and cognitive deficit in some AD patients (Lazarus, Newton, Cohler, Lesser, & Schweon, 1987). Further complicating matters is the fact that dementia may initially present as apparent depression, without marked cognitive deficit, in some cases. Mortsyn, Hochanadel, Kaplan, and Gutheil (1982) have referred to this as *pseudodepression*. Reding, Haycox, and Blass (1985), in a 3-year follow-up study, showed that 16 (57%) of 28 depressed patients, not initially thought to be demented, went on to develop frank dementia. Retrospective analysis of other data obtained on these patients suggested the following risk factors for the development of dementia in depressed older adults: older age; evidence of cerebrovascular, extrapyramidal, or spino-cerebellar disease; confusion or somnolence in response to low doses of tricyclic antidepressant medication; or a score under 8 on a 10-item mental status questionnaire. Mortsyn *et al.* (1982) argue for the important contribution of comprehensive neuropsychological assessment in identifying these patients. However, prospective data concerning the accuracy of neuropsychological assessment in predicting the development of dementia in depressed older adults is not available. At this point, the most prudent approach would appear to be frequent reevaluation of those depressed older adults presenting with the risk factors described by Reding *et al.* (1985).

VI. Conclusions and Future Directions

Research on the psychological assessment of the aging individual has progressed at an accelerating pace during recent years. This chapter has concentrated upon important developments in this progression, particularly in the areas of neuropsychological evaluation and the use of psychological assessment to assist in differentiating dementia from depression. In concluding their chapter on clinical assessment within the previous edition of this handbook, Zarit *et al.* (1985) recommended that clinicians carefully investigate the reliability, validity, norms, and appropriateness of neuropsychological and other clinical assessment instruments before adopting their use with older persons. Among the most significant of recent developments has been the increase in publication of normative, reliability, and validity data specific to older adults, for a variety of assessment instruments. This gives the clinician a breadth of choice more closely approximating the range of assessment questions that he or she faces. Despite the progress made in this area, there remains a lack of reliability, validity, and normative data relevant to old-old and very-old individuals. Thus even the very carefully determined representative sampling frame employed in standardization of the WMS-R (Wechsler, 1987) excluded persons 75 years of age and older. As increasing numbers of persons within this age group are referred for psychological assessment, the need for data concerning them grows.

Of equal importance has been the developing recognition of the specific threats to reliability and validity encountered in psychological assessment of older adults. As illustrated by the problems in assessing memory complaints, an appreciation of the limits of, and variables affecting, the reliability and validity of assessment tools provides the guidance necessary for informed assessment decisions and interpretation.

Finally, it is particularly gratifying to observe the recent contributions being made to psychological assessment research and practice by experimental cognitive psychology and neuropsychology. Further cross-fertilization between experimental and clinical research approaches should result in the information necessary for increasingly sophisticated, and accurate, psychological assessment of the aging individual.

References

Albert, M. S. (1981). Geriatric neuropsychology. *Journal of Consulting and Clinical Psychology*, **49**, 835–850.

Albert, M. S., & Moss, M. B. (Eds.) (1988). *Geriatric neuropsychology*. New York: Guilford.

American Psychiatric Association (1980). *Diagnostic and statistical manual of mental disorders* (3rd ed.). Washington, DC: Author.

American Psychiatric Association (1987). *Diagnostic and statistical manual of mental disorders* (3rd ed. revised). Washington DC: Author.

Anastasi, A. (1982). *Psychological testing* (5th ed.). New York: Macmillan.

Arbuckle, T. Y., Gold, D., & Andres, D. (1986). Cognitive functioning of older people in relation to social and personality variables. *Psychology and Aging*, **1**, 55–62.

Atkinson, L. (1986). The comparative validities of the Rorschach and MMPI: A meta-analysis. *Canadian Psychology*, **27**, 238–247.

Barona, A., Reynolds, C. R., & Chastain, R. (1984). A demographically based index of premorbid intelligence for the WAIS-R. *Journal of Consulting and Clinical Psychology*, **52**, 885–887.

Bayles, K. A., & Kaszniak, A. W. (1987). *Communication and cognition in normal aging and dementia*. Boston: College-Hill/Little, Brown.

Becker, J. T., Boller, F., Saxton, J., & McGonigle-Gibson, K. L. (1987). Normal rates of forgetting of verbal and nonverbal material in Alzheimer's disease. *Cortex*, **23**, 59–72.

Benton, A. L., Hamsher, K. de S., Varney, N. R., & Spreen, O. (1983). *Contributions to neuropsychological assessment: A clinical manual*. New York: Oxford University Press.

Benton, A. L., & Sivan, A. B. (1984). Problems and conceptual issues in neuropsychological research in aging and dementia. *Journal of Clinical Neuropsychology, 6,* 57–63.

Blau, E., & Ober, B.A. (1988). The effect of depression on verbal memory in older adults. *Journal of Clinical and Experimental Neuropsychology, 10,* 81.

Blazer, D. G. (1982). *Depression in late life.* St. Louis, MO: Mosby.

Blazer, D., Hughes, D. C., & George, L. K. (1987). The epidemiology of depression in an elderly community population. *Gerontologist, 27,* 281–287.

Bornstein, R. A. (1987). The WAIS-R in neuropsychological practice—boon or bust. *The Clinical Neuropsychologist, 1,* 185–190.

Bornstein, R. A., & Chelune, G. J. (1988). Factor structure of the Wechsler Memory Scale-Revised. *The Clinical Neuropsychologist, 2,* 107–115.

Bornstein, R. A., Paniak, C., & O'Brien, W. (1987). Preliminary data on classification of normal and brain-damaged elderly subjects. *The Clinical Neuropsychologist, 1,* 315–323.

Branconnier, R. J., Cole, J.O., Spera, K. F., & De Vitt, D. R. (1982). Recall and recognition as diagnostic indices of malignant memory loss in senile dementia: A Bayesian analysis. *Experimental Aging Research, 8,* 189–193.

Branconnier, R. J., Harto, N.E., McNiff, M. E., Kilpatrick, K., Torrey, C., & Spera, K. F. (1987). The Buschke Selective Reminding Test: The norms. *Journal of Clinical and Experimental Neuropsychology, 9,* 280.

Breslau, L., & Haug, M. (1983). *Depression and aging.* New York: Springer.

Brink, T. L. (1986). *Clinical gerontology: A guide to assessment and intervention.* New York: Haworth.

Brinkman, S. D., & Braun, P. (1984). Classification of dementia patients by a WAIS profile related to central cholinergic deficiencies. *Journal of Clinical Neuropsychology, 6,* 393–400.

Burger, M. C., Botwinick, J., & Storandt, M. (1987). Aging, alcoholism, and performance on the Luria-Nebraska Neuropsychological Battery. *Journal of Gerontology, 42,* 69–72.

Buschke, H., & Fuld, P. A. (1974). Evaluating storage, retention, and retrieval in disordered memory and learning. *Neurology, 24,* 1019–1025.

Butters, N. (1986). The clinical aspects of memory disorders. In T. Incagnoli, G. Goldstein, & C. Golden (Eds.), *Clinical application of neuropsychological test batteries* (pp. 361–382). New York: Plenum.

Butters, N., Salmon, D. P., Cullum, C. M., Cairns, P., Troster, A. I., Jacobs, D., Moss, M., & Cermak, L. S. (1988). Differentiation of amnesic and demented patients with the Wechsler Memory Scale-Revised. *The Clinical Neuropsychologist, 2,* 133–148.

Casper, R. C., Redmond, D. E., Katz, M. M., Schaffer, C. B., Davis, J. M., & Koslow, S. H. (1985). Somatic symptoms in primary affective disorder. *Archives of General Psychiatry, 42,* 1098–1104.

Chelune, G. T., & Bornstein, R. A. (1988). WMS-R patterns among patients with unilateral brain lesions. *The Clinical Neuropsychologist, 2,* 121–132.

Corwin, J., Peselow, E., & Dash, S. (1988). Effects of depression on response bias, and explicit and implicit memory tasks. *Journal of Clinical and Experimental Neuropsychology, 10,* 81.

Cummings, J. L. (1987). Dementia syndromes: Neurobehavioral and neuropsychiatric features. *Journal of Clinical Psychiatry, 48,* (5, Suppl.), 3–8.

Cunningham, W. R. (1986). Psychometric perspectives: Validity and reliability. In L. W. Poon (Ed.), *Handbook for clinical memory assessment of older adults* (pp. 27–31). Washington, DC: American Psychological Association.

Delis, D. C., Cullum, C. M., Butters, N., Cairns, P., & Prifitera, A. (1988). Wechsler Memory Scale-Revised and California Verbal Learning Test: Convergence and divergence. *The Clinical Neuropsychologist, 2,* 188–196.

Delis, D. C., Freeland, J., Kramer, J. H., & Kaplan, E. (1988). Integrating clinical assessment with cognitive neuroscience: Construct validation of the California Verbal Learning Test. *Journal of Consulting and Clinical Psychology, 56,* 123–130.

Eppinger, M. G., Craig, P. L., Adams, R. L., & Parsons, O. A. (1987). The WAIS-R index for estimating premorbid intelligence: Cross-validation and clinical utility. *Journal of Consulting and Clinical Psychology, 55,* 86–90.

Ernst, J. (1987). Neuropsychological problem-solving skills in the elderly. *Psychology and Aging, 2*, 363–365.

Ernst, J. (1988). Language, grip strength, sensory-perceptual, and receptive skills in a normal elderly sample. *The Clinical Neuropsychologist, 2*, 30–40.

Filley, C. M., Kobayashi, J., & Heaton, R. K. (1987). Wechsler Intelligence Scale profiles, the cholinergic system, and Alzheimer's disease. *Journal of Clinical and Experimental Neuropsychology, 9*, 180–186.

Flynn, J. (1984). The mean IQ of Americans: Massive gains 1932 to 1978. *Psychological Bulletin, 95*, 29–51.

Folstein, M. F., & McHugh, P. R. (1978). Dementia syndrome of depression. *Aging, 7*, 87–93.

Fry, P. S. (1986). *Depression, stress, and adaptations in the elderly: Psychological assessment and intervention.* Rockville, MD: Aspen Systems.

Fuld, P. A. (1980). Guaranteed stimulus processing in the evaluation of memory and learning. *Cortex, 16*, 255–271.

Fuld, P. A. (1984). Test profile of cholinergic dysfunction and of Alzheimer-type dementia. *Journal of Clinical Neuropsychology, 6*, 380–392.

Fuld, P. A., Dickson, D., Crystal, H., & Aronson, M. K. (1987). Primitive plaques and memory dysfunction in normal and impaired elderly persons. *New England Journal of Medicine, March 19*, 756.

Fuld, P. A., Katzman, R., Davies, P., & Terry, R. D. (1982). Intrusions as a sign of Alzheimer dementia: Chemical and pathological verification. *Annals of Neurology, 11*, 155–159.

Gallagher, D. (1986a). Assessment of depression by interview methods and psychiatric rating scales. In L. W. Poon (Ed.), *Handbook for clinical memory assessment in older adults* (pp. 202–212). Washington, DC: American Psychological Association.

Gallagher, D. (1986b). The Beck Depression Inventory and older adults: Review of its development and utility. *Clinical Gerontologist, 5*, 149–163.

Gallagher, D., & Thompson, L. (1983). Depression. In P. Lewinsohn & L. Teri (Eds.), *Clinical geropsychology* (pp. 7–37). New York: Pergamon.

Gallagher, D., Thompson, L. W., & Levy, S. M. (1980). Clinical psychological assessment of older adults. In L. W. Poon (Ed.), *Aging in the 1980s: Psychological issues* (pp. 19–40). Washington, DC: American Psychological Association.

Garcia, C. A., Reding, M. J., & Blass, J. P. (1981). Overdiagnosis of dementia. *Journal of the American Geriatrics Society, 29*, 407–410.

Gatz, M., & Pearson, C. G. (1988). Ageism revised and the provision of psychological services. *American Psychologist, 43*, 184–188.

Gaylord, S. A., & Zung, W. W. K. (1987). Affective disorders among the aging. In L. L. Carstensen & B. A. Edelstein (Eds.), *Handbook of clinical gerontology* (pp. 76–95). New York: Pergamon.

George, L. K., Blazer, D. G., Winfield-Laird, I., Leaf, P. J., & Fischbach, R. (1987). Psychiatric disorders and mental health services use in later life: Evidence from the Epidemiologic Catchment Area program. In J. Brody & G. Maddox (Eds.), *Epidemiology and aging* (pp. 189–219). New York: Springer.

Gilewski, M. J., & Zelinski, E. M. (1986). Questionnaire assessment of memory complaints. In L. W. Poon (Ed.), *Handbook for clinical memory assessment of older adults* (pp. 93–107). Washington, DC: American Psychological Association.

Goldstein, F. C., Gary, H. E., & Levin, H. S. (1986). Assessment of the accuracy of regression equations proposed for estimating premorbid intellectual functioning on the Wechsler Adult Intelligence Scale. *Journal of Clinical and Experimental Neuropsychology, 8*, 405–412.

Grober, E., Buschke, H., Crystal, H., Bang, S., & Dresner, R. (1988). Screening for dementia by memory testing. *Neurology, 38*, 900–903.

Gurland, B., & Toner, J. (1983). Differentiating dementia from nondementing conditions. In R. Mayeux & W. G. Rosen (Eds.), *The dementias* (pp. 1–17). New York: Raven.

Hart, R. P., Kwentus, J. A., Taylor, J. R., & Hamer, R. M. (1987). Selective reminding procedure in depression and dementia. *Psychology and Aging, 2*, 111–115.

Hart, R. P., Kwentus, J. A., Taylor, J. R., & Harkins, S. W. (1987). Rate of forgetting in dementia and depression. *Journal of Consulting and Clinical Psychology, 55*, 101–105.

Hart, R. P., Kwentus, J. A., Wade, J. B., & Hamer, R. M. (1987). Digit symbol performance in mild dementia and depression.

Journal of Consulting and Clinical Psychology, **55**, 236–238.

Hayslip, B., & Lowman, R. L. (1986). The clinical use of projective techniques with the aged: A critical review and synthesis. *Clinical Gerontologist*, **5**, 63–94.

Heaton, R. K., Grant, I., & Matthews, C. G. (1986). Differences in neuropsychological test performance associated with age, education, and sex. In I. Grant & K. M. Adams (Eds.), *Neuropsychological assessment of neuropsychiatric disorders* (pp. 100–120). New York: Oxford University Press.

Hevern, V. W. (1980). Recent validity studies of the Halstead-Reitan approach to clinical neuropsychological assessment: A critical review. *Clinical Neuropsychology*, **2**, 49–61.

Hom, J. (1988). Differential diagnostic ability of the HRB in Alzheimer's and cerebrovascular dementias. *Journal of Clinical and Experimental Neuropsychology*, **10**, 64.

Incagnoli, T., Goldstein, G., & Golden, C. J. (Eds.) (1986). *Clinical applications of neuropsychological test batteries*. New York: Plenum.

Johnson, M. H., & Magaro, P. A. (1987). Effects of mood and severity on memory processes in depression and mania. *Psychological Bulletin*, **101**, 28–40.

Kahana, B. (1978). The use of projective techniques in personality assessment of the aged. In M. Storandt, I. C. Siegler, & M. F. Elias (Eds.), *The clinical psychology of aging* (pp. 145–180). New York: Plenum.

Kahn, R. L., Zarit, S. H., Hilbert, N. M., & Niederehe, G. (1975). Memory complaint and memory impairment in the aged. *Archives of General Psychiatry*, **32**, 1569–1573.

Kane, R. A., & Kane, R. L. (1981). *Assessing the elderly: A practical guide to measurement*. Lexington, MA: Lexington Books.

Karzmark, P., Heaton, R. K., Grant, I., & Matthews, C. G. (1984). Use of demographic variables to predict overall level of performance on the Halstead-Reitan Battery. *Journal of Consulting and Clinical Psychology*, **52**, 663–665.

Kaszniak, A. W. (1986). The neuropsychology of dementia. In I. Grant & K. M. Adams (Eds.), *Neuropsychological assessment of neuropsychiatric disorders* (pp. 172–220). New York: Oxford University Press.

Kaszniak, A. W. (1987). Neuropsychological consultation to geriatricians: Issues in the assessment of memory complaints. *The Clinical Neuropsychologist*, **1**, 35–46.

Kaszniak, A. W. (1988). Cognition in Alzheimer's disease: Theoretic models and clinical implications. *Neurobiology of Aging*, **9**, 92–94.

Kaszniak, A. W., & Allender, J. (1985). Psychological assessment of depression in older adults. In G. M. Chaisson-Stewart (Ed.), *Depression in the elderly: An interdisciplinary approach* (pp. 107–160). New York: Wiley.

Kaszniak, A. W., & Davis, K. L. (1986). Instrument and data review: The quest for external validators. In L. W. Poon (Ed.), *Handbook for clinical memory assessment of older adults* (pp. 271–276). Washington, DC: American Psychological Association.

Kaszniak, A. W., Poon, L. W., & Riege, W. (1986). Assessing memory deficits: An information-processing approach. In L. W. Poon (Ed.), *Handbook for clinical memory assessment of older adults* (pp. 168–188). Washington, DC: American Psychological Association.

Kaszniak, A. W., Sadeh, M., & Stern, L. Z. (1985). Differentiating depression from organic brain syndromes in older age. In G. M. Chaisson-Stewart (Ed.), *Depression in the elderly: An interdisciplinary approach* (pp. 161–189). New York: Wiley.

Kaszniak, A. W., Wilson, R. S., Fox, J. H., & Stebbins, G. T. (1986). Cognitive assessment in Alzheimer's disease: Cross-sectional and longitudinal perspectives. *Canadian Journal of Neurological Sciences*, **13**, 420–423.

Kelly, C. M. (1986). Depressive mood effects on memory and attention. In L. W. Poon (Ed.), *Handbook for clinical memory assessment of older adults* (pp. 238–243). Washington, DC: American Psychological Association.

Kiloh, L. G. (1961). Pseudo-dementia. *Acta Psychiatrica Scandinavica*, **37**, 336–351.

Klassen, D., Homstra, R. K., & Anderson, P. B. (1975). Influence of social desirability on symptom and mood reporting in a community survey. *Journal of Consulting and Clinical Psychology*, **43**, 448–453.

Kopelman, M. D. (1985). Rates of forgetting in Alzheimer-type dementia and Korsakoff's syndrome. *Neuropsychologia*, **23**, 623–638.

Larabee, G. L., Kane, R. L., & Schuck, J. R. (1983). Factor analysis of the WAIS and Wechsler Memory Scale: An analysis of the construct validity of the Wechsler Memory Scale. *Journal of Clinical and Experimental Neuropsychology*, **5**, 159–168.

Larabee, G. J., Largen, J. W., & Levin, H. S. (1985). Sensitivity of age-decline resistant ("Hold") WAIS subtests to Alzheimer's disease. *Journal of Clinical and Experimental Neuropsychology*, **7**, 497–504.

Larabee, G. L., & Levin, H. S. (1986). Memory self-ratings and objective test performance in a normal elderly sample. *Journal of Clinical and Experimental Neuropsychology*, **8**, 275–284.

LaRue, A., D'Elia, L. F., Clark, E. O., Spar, J. E., & Jarvik, L. F. (1986). Clinical tests of memory in dementia, depression, and healthy aging. *Psychology and Aging*, **1**, 69–77.

Lazarus, L. W., Newton, N., Cohler, B., Lesser, J., & Schweon, C. (1987). Frequency and presentation of depressive symptoms in patients with primary degenerative dementia. *American Journal of Psychiatry*, **144**, 41–45.

Lezak, M. D. (1983). *Neuropsychological assessment* (2nd ed.). New York: Oxford University Press.

Lipowski, Z. J. (1987). Delirium (acute confusional states). *Journal of the American Medical Association*, **258**, 1789–1792.

Loring, D. W., & Papanicolaou, A. C. (1987). Memory assessment in neuropsychology: Theoretical considerations and practical utility. *Journal of Clinical and Experimental Neuropsychology*, **9**, 340–358.

Lubin, B., & Rinck, C. M. (1986). Assessment of mood and affect in the elderly: The Depression Adjective Check List and the Multiple Affect Adjective Check List. *Clinical Gerontologist*, **5**, 187–191.

Martone, M., Butters, N., & Trauner, D. (1986). Some analyses of forgetting of pictorial material in amnesic and demented patients. *Journal of Clinical and Experimental Neuropsychology*, **8**, 161–178.

McCue, M., Shelly, C., & Goldstein, G. (1985). A proposed short form of the Luria-Nebraska Battery oriented toward assessment of the elderly. *The International Journal of Clinical Neuropsychology*, **7**, 96–101.

McKahnn, G., Drachman, D., Folstein, M., Katzman, R., Price, D., & Stadlin, E. M. (1984). Clinical diagnosis of Alzheimer's disease: Report of the NINCDS-ADRDA work group under the auspices of the Department of Health and Human Services Task Force on Alzheimer's disease. *Neurology*, **34**, 939–944.

Milberg, W. P., Hebben, N., & Kaplan, E. (1986). The Boston process approach to neuropsychological assessment. In I. Grant & K. M. Adams (Eds.), *Neuropsychological assessment of neuropsychiatric disorders* (pp. 65–86). New York: Oxford University Press.

Miller, E., & Lewis, P. (1977). Recognition memory in elderly patients with depression and dementia: A signal detection analysis. *Journal of Abnormal Psychology*, **86**, 84–86.

Mortsyn, R., Hochanadel, G., Kaplan, E., & Gutheil, T. G. (1982). Depression vs. pseudodepression in dementia. *Journal of Clinical Psychiatry*, **43**, 197–199.

Moses, J. A., Golden, C. J., Ariel, R., & Gustavson, J. L. (1983). *Interpretation of the Luria-Nebraska neuropsychological battery* (Vol. 1). New York: Grune & Stratton.

Moss, M. B., Albert, M. S., Butters, N., & Payne, M. (1986). Differential patterns of memory loss among patients with Alzheimer's disease, Huntington's disease, and alcoholic Korsakoff's syndrome. *Archives of Neurology*, **43**, 239–246.

National Institute on Aging Task Force (1980). Senility reconsidered: Treatment possibilities for mental impairment in the elderly. *Journal of the American Medical Association*, **244**, 259–263.

National Institute of Mental Health (1979). *The Diagnostic Interview Schedule*. Washington, DC: National Institute of Mental Health, Center for Epidemiological Studies.

Niederehe, G. (1986). Depression and memory impairment in the aged. In L. W. Poon (Ed.), *Handbook for clinical memory assessment of older adults* (pp. 226–237). Washington, DC: American Psychological Association.

Nunnally, J. C. (1978). *Psychometric theory*. New York: McGraw-Hill.

Parker, K. C. H., Hanson, R. K., & Hunsley, J. (1988). MMPI, Rorschach and WAIS: A meta-analytic comparison of reliability, stability, and validity. *Psychological Bulletin*, **103**, 367–373.

Poon, L. W. (Ed.) (1986). *Handbook for clinical memory assessment of older adults*. Washington, DC: American Psychological Association.

Rabins, P. V., Merchant, B., & Nesladt, G. (1984). Criteria for diagnosing reversible dementia caused by depression: Validation by 2-year follow-up. *British Journal of Psychiatry*, **144**, 488–495.

Radloff, L. S., & Teri, L. (1986). Use of the Center for Epidemiological Studies-Depression Scale with older adults. *Clinical Gerontologist*, **5**, 119–136.

Raskin, A. (1986). Partialling out the effects of depression and age on cognitive functions: Experimental data and methodologic issues. In L. W. Poon (Ed.), *Handbook for clinical memory assessment of older adults* (pp. 244–256). Washington, DC: American Psychological Association.

Reding, M., Haycox, J., & Blass, J. (1985). Depression in patients referred to a dementia clinic: A three-year prospective study. *Archives of Neurology*, **42**, 894–896.

Reisberg, B., Gordon, B., McCarthy, M., Ferris, S. H., & de Leon, M. J. (1985). Insight and denial accompanying progressive cognitive decline in normal aging and Alzheimer's disease. In B. Stanley (Ed.), *Geriatric psychiatry: Ethical and legal issues* (pp. 37–79). Washington, DC: American Psychiatric Press.

Reitan, R. M., & Wolfson, D. (1985). *The Halstead-Reitan Neuropsychological Test Battery: Theory and clinical interpretation*. Tucson, AZ: Neuropsychology Press.

Reitan, R. M., & Wolfson, D. (1986). The Halstead-Reitan Neuropsychological Test Battery and aging. *Clinical Gerontologist*, **5**, 39–61.

Riege, W. H. (1982). Self-report and tests of memory aging. *Clinical Gerontologist*, **1**(2), 23–36.

Riege, W. H., & Metter, E. J. (1988). Cognitive and brain imaging measures of Alzheimer's disease. *Neurobiology of Aging*, **9**, 69–86.

Roid, G. H., Prifitera, A., & Ledbetter, M. (1988). Confirmatory analysis of the factor structure of the Wechsler Memory Scale-Revised. *The Clinical Neuropsychologist*, **2**, 116–120.

Ryan, J. J., & Lewis, C. V. (1988). Comparison of normal controls and recently detoxified alcoholics on the Wechsler Memory Scale-Revised. *The Clinical Neuropsychologist*, **2**, 173–180.

Satz, P., Van Gorp, W. G., Soper, H. V., &

Mitrushina, M. (1987). WAIS-R marker for dementia of the Alzheimer type? An empirical and statistical induction test. *Journal of Clinical and Experimental Neuropsychology*, **9**, 767–774.

Schaie, K. W., & Schaie, J. P. (1977). Clinical assessment and aging. In J. E. Birren & K. W. Schaie (Eds.), *Handbook of the psychology of aging* (pp. 692–723). New York: Van Nostrand Reinhold.

Schear, J. M. (1984). Neuropsychological assessment of the elderly in clinical practice. In P. E. Logue & J. M. Schear (Eds.), *Clinical neuropsychology: A multidisciplinary approach* (pp. 199–236). Springfield, IL: Thomas.

Schear, J. M. (1988). Attempt to cross-validate norm-based dysfunction scores in young and older neuropsychiatric patients. *The Clinical Neuropsychologist*, **2**, 57–66.

Sheikh, J. I., & Yesavage, J. A. (1986). Geriatric Depression Scale (GDS): Recent evidence and development of a shorter version. *Clinical Gerontologist*, **5**, 165–173.

Skilbeck, C. E., & Woods, R. T. (1980). The factorial structure of the Wechsler Memory Scale: Samples of neurological and psychogeriatric patients. *Journal of Clinical Neuropsychology*, **2**, 293–300.

Snodgrass, J. G., & Corwin, J. (1988). Pragmatics of measuring recognition memory: Applications to dementia and amnesia. *Journal of Experimental Psychology: General*, **117**, 34–50.

Spinnler, H., & DellaSala, S. (1988). The role of clinical neuropsychology in the neurological diagnosis of Alzheimer's disease. *Journal of Neurology*, **235**, 258–271.

Spitzer, R. L., & Endicott, J. (1978). *NIMH Clinical Research Branch Collaborative Program on the Psychobiology of Depression: Schedule for Affective Disorders and Schizophrenia (SADS)*. New York: New York State Psychiatric Institute, Biometrics Research Division.

Stambrook, M. (1983). The Luria-Nebraska Neuropsychological Battery: A promise that may be partly fulfilled. *Journal of Clinical Neuropsychology*, **5**, 247–269.

Storrie, M. C., & Doerr, H. O. (1980). Characterization of Alzheimer type dementia utilizing an abbreviated Halstead-Reitan Battery. *Clinical Neuropsychology*, **2**, 78–82.

Sunderland, A., Watts, K., Baddeley, A., & Harris, J. E. (1986). Subjective memory assessment and test performance in elderly adults. *Journal of Gerontology, 41*, 376–384.

Thal, L. J., Grundman, M., & Klauber, M. R. (1988). Dementia: Characteristics of a referral population and factors associated with progression. *Neurology, 38*, 1083–1090.

Thompson, L. W., Gong, V., Haskins, E., & Gallagher, D. (1987). Assessment of depression and dementia during the late years. *Annual Review of Gerontology and Geriatrics, 7*, 295–324.

Tierney, M. C., Snow, W. G., Reid, D. W., Zorzitto, M. L., & Fisher, R. H. (1987). Psychometric differentiation of dementia: Replication and extension of the findings of Storandt and coworkers. *Archives of Neurology, 44*, 720–722.

Vannieuwhirk, R. R., & Galbraith, G. G. (1985). The relationship of age to performance on the Luria-Nebraska Neuropsychological Battery. *Journal of Clinical Psychology, 41*, 527–532.

Warrington, E. K. (1984). *Recognition memory test manual*. Windsor, England: NFER-Nelson.

Warrington, E. K., James, M., & Maciejewski, C. (1986). The WAIS as a lateralizing and localizing diagnostic instrument: A study of 656 patients with unilateral cerebral lesions. *Neuropsychologia, 24*, 223–239.

Wechsler, D. A. (1945). A standardized memory scale for clinical use. *Journal of Psychology, 19*, 87–95.

Wechsler, D. (1958). *The measurement and appraisal of adult intelligence* (4th ed.). Baltimore: Williams & Wilkins.

Wechsler, D. (1981). *Wechsler Adult Intelligence Scale-Revised manual*. New York: The Psychological Corporation.

Wechsler, D. (1987). *Wechsler Memory Scale-Revised manual*. New York: The Psychological Corporation.

Weingartner, H. (1986). Automatic and effort-demanding cognitive processes in depression. In L. W. Poon (Ed.), *Handbook for clinical memory assessment of older adults* (pp.218–225). Washington, DC: American Psychological Association.

Weingartner, H., Kaye, W., Smallberg, S. A., Ebert, M. H., Gilin, J. C., & Sitaram, N. (1981). Memory failures in progressive idiopathic dementia. *Journal of Abnormal Psychology, 90*, 187–196.

Weiss, I. K., Nagel, C. L., & Aronson, M. K. (1986). Applicability of depression scales to the old old person. *Journal of the American Geriatrics Society, 34*, 215–218.

Wells, C. E. (1983). Differential diagnosis of Alzheimer's dementia: Affective disorder. In B. Reisberg (Ed.), *Alzheimer's disease: The standard reference* (pp. 193–197). New York: Free Press.

Wilson, R. S., Bacon, L. D., Fox, J. H., & Kaszniak, A. W. (1983). Primary memory and secondary memory in dementia of the Alzheimer type. *Journal of Clinical Neuropsychology, 5*, 337–344.

Wilson, R. S., & Kaszniak, A. W. (1986). Longitudinal changes: Progressive idiopathic dementia. In L. W. Poon (Ed.), *Handbook for clinical memory assessment of older adults* (pp. 285–293). Washington, DC: American Psychological Association.

Wilson, R. S., Rosenbaum, G., & Brown, G. (1979). The problem of premorbid intelligence in neuropsychological assessment. *Journal of Clinical Neuropsychology, 1*, 49–53.

Yesavage, J. A. (1986). The use of self-rating depression scales in the elderly. In L. W. Poon (Ed.), *Handbook for clinical memory assessment of older adults* (pp. 213–217). Washington, DC: American Psychological Association.

Zarit, S. H., Eiler, J., & Hassinger, M. (1985). Clinical assessment. In J. E. Birren & K. W. Schaie (Eds.), *Handbook of the psychology of aging* (2nd ed., pp. 725–754). New York: Van Nostrand Reinhold.

Zelinski, E. M., Gilewski, M. J., & Thompson, L. W. (1980). Do laboratory tests relate to self-assessment of memory ability in the young and old? In L. W. Poon, J. L. Fozard, L. S. Cermak, D. Arenberg, & L. W. Thompson (Eds.), *New directions in memory and aging* (pp. 519–544). Hillsdale, NJ: Erlbaum.

Zung, W. W. K., & Zung, E. M. (1986). Use of the Zung Self-Rating Depression Scale in the elderly. *Clinical Gerontologist, 5*, 137–148.

Twenty Six

Human Factors and Design for Older Adults

Neil Charness and Elizabeth A. Bosman

I. Human Factors and Age

Human factors (ergonomics, human engineering) is the discipline that tries to optimize the design of living and working conditions (Kantowitz & Sorkin, 1983; Sanders & McCormick, 1987). Due to the many changes associated with aging, the optimal environments and tools for people will change over the life span (Koncelik, 1982). Planners and designers are now confronted with a population in which the fastest growing segment consists of older people. The credo for good design is "know the user." This *Handbook* and its predecessors are ideal sources for learning about the capabilities of older adults.

Human factors specialists deal with issues that span microlevels, such as finding the best font for characters on computer screen, to macrolevels, such as discovering the best layout for a nuclear power station. The ideal situation for designers is to be able to consult a reference such as the *Handbook of Human Factors* (Salvendy, 1987) to extract guidelines for appropriate design, such as letter sizes for signs that

will be seen by 95% of the sighted population. Unfortunately, information about the specific capabilities of older adults is either nonexistent or of dubious quality in such sources. There is also a paucity of data on the performance of the very old: those in their 80s and above. Because physical disability increases strikingly in old age, it is obvious that barrier-free designs (e.g., Carstens, 1985; Government of Canada, 1987) are needed when planning for the 80+ age range.

Traditional human factors analyses tend to focus on the work environment and how productivity and safety can be enhanced. When there is concern for the everyday world (e.g., kitchens), the emphasis is usually on safety, though functionality and aesthetics may be equally important to older consumers. Discovering the goals of older consumers is an important challenge for this discipline.

The chapter is organized in four sections. First we will introduce a heuristic model of information processing developed by Card, Moran, and Newell (1983) as a useful source for low-level design deci-

Handbook of the Psychology of Aging, Third Edition
Copyright © 1990 Academic Press, Inc. All rights of reproduction in any form reserved.

sions. Then we will look at aspects of visual and auditory performance, examine anthropometry, and finally, we will end with an examination of some issues related to home and work environment. Given space limitations, we have left untouched issues in design of large-scale environments, such as nursing homes or apartment complexes, topics covered partially in Parmelee and Lawton (this volume) and in Koncelik (1976). Excellent sources of information on housing are Canada Mortgage and Housing Corporation (1988) and Regnier and Pynoos (1987).

II. The Older Information Processor

The goal embraced by Card *et al.* (1983) was to provide information-processing constants for human factors engineers to aid their design decisions. A brief sketch of features of their model is given in Table I. Although their approach is considered controversial, it is the only one that attempts to make quantitative predictions that could be useful in design decisions. (One obvious problem is that it does not deal well with attention, nor with the sensory systems underlying balance, taste, touch, or smell.) We have supplemented their model by providing age-relevant information as constants and regression equations in Table II. Because most experimental studies of aging do not sample representatively from the population, further research with representative samples is needed to refine these estimates.

How would designers make use of this information? A hypothetical example might be the design of a sign scheme for an airport access road. Consider either putting up a single sign with two statements: "Left lane for arrivals, right lane for departures," or two signs, each containing half the message. Assume that signs are large enough to be perceived at a distance of 40 meters by any licensed driver (less likely

for older drivers under low light conditions: Sivak, Olson, & Pastalan, 1981). Assume that if signs are read by the time that drivers reach them (i.e. within 40 meters), the correct lane change can be made safely. Assume all drivers travel at 17 meters/s (60 kilometers/hour). Which is the better choice for a 20-year-old versus a 70-year-old driver?

Although the eye fixation times from Table II are not based on text reading, they do provide a conservative estimate. Assuming one fixation (or attention shift, for foveal displays) covers each word pair in the sign, the predicted reading times for the 20-year-old in the single sign situation is 528 ms/fixation × 4 word pairs = 2.1 seconds. For the 70-year-old, the estimate is 706 ms/fixation × 4 word pairs = 2.8 seconds. If cars are traveling 17 m/s, there will be sufficient reading time for the younger (17 m/sec × 2.1 s = 36 m) but not for the older driver (48 m) with a single sign. In the two-sign condition, reading times/distances are halved, and both drivers will read the messages in time to change lanes safely.

An important restriction on the parameters provided in the tables is that they are based mostly on data derived from inexperienced performers. As Salthouse (1984) has shown with typists, older experts can sometimes compensate for age-related slowing. Nonetheless, it is usually safer to underestimate rather than overestimate capabilities.

Case Analysis: Intersection Crossing

Determining valid parameters for human performance as a function of age can be critical. Sterns, Barrett, and Alexander (1985) and Svanborg (1984) noted that the majority of pedestrian accidents are cases where older pedestrians are struck by vehicles at intersections. Both papers speculated that light crossing times may be inadequate.

Walking speed declines with age,

Table I
Model Human Processor

I. Model Components
   A. Subsystems
      The human information-processing system consists of three interdependent subsystems, a **perceptual system** that processes incoming information from the senses, a **cognitive system** that utilizes information from the senses and in memory to reach decisions regarding the available information, and a **motor system** that executes responses.
   B. Processors
      Each subsystem possesses a processor that operates upon the information available to its associated system. The critical parameter describing the activity of each processor is its **cycle time**, which defines the time required to process a minimum unit of information.
      For example, the cycle time of the perceptual processor represents the amount of time required to process a perceptual event. It should be noted that perceptual events occurring during a cycle of the perceptual processor will not be perceived. With regards to the motor processor, movement is assumed to be discontinuous, consisting of a series of discrete micromovements whose duration corresponds to the cycle time of the motor processor. Tapping a finger once requires two cycles of the motor processor. The cycle time of the cognitive processor represents the amount of time required to recognize an item in **Long-Term-Memory (LTM)**, or to encode a stimulus.
      An additional parameter that describes the activity of the perceptual system is **eye movement duration**.
   C. Memory Stores
      The perceptual and cognitive systems each possess memory stores. The critical parameters describing each memory store are (1) the **storage capacity**, (2) the **decay constant** that defines the duration of information in the store, and (3) the **main code type** that defines how information in each store is coded.
      Memory Stores of the Perceptual System
         The perceptual system contains two memory stores, the **Visual Information Store (VIS)** and the **Auditory Information Store (AIS)**. Both are limited capacity, highly transient stores that retain the information obtained from the brief presentation of a stimulus.
      The **capacity** of each store is defined by the number of items that can be correctly reported after a brief stimulus presentation. The **decay constant** is defined by the time interval during which information can be obtained from each store. The **code type** for **VIS** and **AIS** is physical.
      Memory Stores of The Cognitive System
         The cognitive system contains two memory stores, **Long-Term Memory (LTM)** and **Working Memory (WM)**.
         LTM is the store containing all the knowledge the individual has acquired. The **capacity** of **LTM** is assumed to be infinite. It is assumed that items do not **decay** from **LTM** but that they become functionally inaccessible. The **code type** for **LTM** is semantic.
         WM holds information currently being operated upon as part of ongoing information processing. The information contained in **WM** is obtained from the memory stores of the perceptual system and **LTM**. The **capacity of WM** is measured in chunks of information. Without augmentation from **LTM**, the capacity is of **WM** is defined by the capacity of primary memory. With augmentation from **LTM**, capacity is defined by digit span. The **decay constant** defines the rate at which a chunk of information decays from **WM**. The **code type** for **WM** is visual and acoustic.
II. Principles of Operation
   A. General Principals of Operation
      Rationality Principle
         People work to obtain their goals through rational action. The actions they take are determined by the structure of the task, the available information, and the limitations of their knowledge and information-processing capabilities.
      Problem Space Principle
         The rational activity people use to solve a problem can be described in terms of (1) a set of states of knowledge, (2) operators for changing from one state into another, (3) constraints on the application of operators, and (4) knowledge of the order in which to apply operators.

(continued)

Table I   (*Continued*)

B. Factors Affecting Processor Operation
 Variable Perceptual Processor Rate
  The cycle time of the perceptual processor varies inversely with stimulus intensity.
 Variable Cognitive Processor Rate
  The cycle time of the cognitive processor diminishes with practice and when greater effort is applied.
 Recognize Act Cycle of the Cognitive Processor
  On each cycle of the cognitive processor, the contents of **WM** initiate actions associatively linked to the contents in **LTM.** Via this process the contents of **WM** are continuously updated.
C. Factors Affecting Retrieval from LTM
 Encoding Specificity
  The operation performed during encoding determine what is stored and which retrieval cues will be most effective.
 Discrimination Principle
  The difficulty of retrieval is determined by the candidates that exist in memory, relative to the retrieval cues.
D. Aimed Hand Movements
 Fitts' Law
  The time, T_{pos} to move the hand to a target of size S that lies a distance D away is given by:

$$T_{pos} = I_M \log_2 (D/S + .5); \text{ where } I_M = \text{ms/bit.}$$

E. Choice Reaction Time
 Hick's Law
  Decision time T increases with uncertainty about the decision to be made, and is given by:

$$T = I_C H; \text{ where } I_C = \text{rate of information transfer in ms/bit;}$$
$$H = \log 2 (n + 1) \text{ for equiprobable signals.}$$

F. Effect of Practice
 Power Law of Practice
  The time T_n to perform a task on the nth trial follows a power law given by:

$$T_n = T_1 n^{-a}; \text{ where } a \text{ is the exponent describing improvement with practice.}$$

Source: Card *et al.* (1983).

particularly walking "as fast as possible" (e.g. Cunningham, Rechnitzer, Pearce, & Donner, 1982). Svanborg (1984) cites walking speed data from a Swedish study by Rundgren that used a representative sample. In that study, "fast walking speeds" at age 79 were 1.21 m/s for males and 1.05 m/s for females.

The assumed walking speed for intersections in Sweden (Svanborg, 1984) was cited as 1.4 m/s. In most of Canada in 1988, the assumed walking speed for intersections used by seniors and schoolchildren was 1.0 m/s, and for regular intersections, 1.2 to 1.25 m/s walking speed. Green light time values (in seconds) of 0.82 times intersection width (m) are widely cited in North American standards, for example, *Uniform Traffic Control Devices for Canada* (1976).

Apparently, all intersection crossing times ought to be calibrated to a walking speed *no greater that 1 m/s* to allow adults in their 80s to cross intersections safely.

III. Designing the Visual and Auditory Environments

Guidelines have been developed to reduce the deleterious effects of the changes in visual and auditory perception that accompany normal aging. A brief summary of guidelines for modifying the visual and auditory environment appears in Tables III and IV, respectively. These guidelines

Table II
Age Differences for the Model Human Processor

Model component	Value	Source
A. Perceptual system[a]		
Visual information store		
Capacity	Young: 3 to 4 items Elderly: 2 to 3 items	Cerella, Poon, and Fozard (1982)
Readout rate[b]	Young: 27 ms/item Elderly: 35 ms/item	Cerella, Poon, and Fozard (1982)
Perceptual processor		
Cycle time (ms)		
Light–dark ratio = 98%	$Y' = 104.16 + 1.05(age)$, $SE = 12.91$	McFarland, Warren, and Karis (1958)
Light–dark Ratio = 2-95%	$Y' = 38.31 + .12(age)$, $SE = 13.28$	
Eye movement duration	$Y' = 457 + 3.56(age)$, $SE = 203$	Hess (1988)
B. Motor system		
Motor processor		
Cycle time (ms)	$Y' = 33.9 + .67(age)$	Salthouse (1984, Study 1)
C. Cognitive system[c]		
Working memory		
Capacity (items or chunks)		
Not augmented by LTM	Young: $Mean = 3.5$, $Sd = 1$ Elderly: $Mean = 3.5$, $Sd = 1$	Craik (1968); Wright (1982)
Augmented by LTM		
Forward digit span	$Y' = 7.34 - .01(age)$, $SE = .50$	Botwinick and Storandt (1974); Bromley (1958); Caird (1966); Kriauciunas (1968); Light and Anderson (1985); Smith (1975)
Backward digit span	$Y' = 6.15 - .02(age)$, $SE = .50$	Botwinick and Storandt (1974); Bromley (1958); Light and Anderson (1985)
Decay constant	See Inman and Parkinson (1983)	
Cognitive processor		
Cycle time (ms)	$Y' = 18.49 + .66(age)$, $SE = 16.23$	Anders and Fozard (1973); Anders, Fozard, and Lillyquist (1972); Eriksen, Hamlin, and Daye (1973); Madden and Nebes (1980); Salthouse and Somberg (1982)
D. Principles of operation		
Fitts' Law		
I_M	$Y' = 60.68 + 1.86(age)$, $SE = 14.49$	Welford (1977)
Hick's Law		
I_C	$Y' = 179.92 + 1.64(age)$, $SE = 49.95$	Fozard, Thomas, and Waugh (1976); Goldfarb (1941) as cited in Welford (1977); Rabbitt and Vyas (1980); Simon (1967); Simon and Pouraghabagher (1978)
Power Law of Practice		
Exponent	Young: $Mean = .67$, $Sd = .3$ Elderly: $Mean = .70$, $Sd = .3$	Beres and Baron (1981); Charness and Campbell (1988); Falduto and Baron (1986); Grant, Storandt, and Botwinick (1978); McDowd (1986); Salthouse and Somberg (1982)

[a] Age differences for the auditory information store (AIS) have not been determined (Crowder, 1980).
[b] Given the nature of the available data, readout rate is substituted for the decay constant.
[c] Age differences for LTM are not discussed, but it is known that with increased age items in LTM are more likely to become functionally inaccessible.

were drawn principally from the following sources: Boyce (1980), Fozard and Popkin (1978), Hughes and Neer (1981), *The Illumination Engineering Society Lighting Handbook* (1981a,b), Regnier and Pynoos (1987), and Sanders and McCormick (1987). A more detailed discussion of the guidelines can be found in these sources. Where possible, quantitative guidelines developed for older adults have been supplied. In some instances, it was necessary to supply quantitative guidelines developed for the population in general, rather than for older adults in particular. These values should be regarded as defining a minimum acceptable standard and could very likely be inadequate for older adults. The accuracy of the guidelines developed for older adults is unknown. Many are based upon a limited number of studies, and some have not been verified empirically.

Many of the guidelines are proscriptive, rather than quantitative in nature. The difficulty with a proscriptive guideline is that it does not provide a strong basis for making design decisions. For example, although it is useful to know that background noise should be minimized for older adults, it would be even more useful to know what is the desirable maximal level of background noise. In the absence of a quantitative guideline, the designer must engage in extensive testing before reaching a design decision or make an educated guess. The former can be prohibitively time consuming and expensive, whereas a design decision based upon an educated guess may not be adequate.

Another feature of the guidelines in Table III is that they deal with aspects of the visual and auditory environment individually, rather than in combination. The critical point is that different features of the environment interact to determine performance. For example, Boyce (1980) reported a study in which the color discrimination of older adults was improved by increasing the level of illumination.

Similarly, it does not seem safe to assume that increased illumination alone will compensate for age-related declines in acuity. Instead, some combination of increased illumination and increased size of important visual detail is required for optimal performance. The question of how to optimize different aspects of the visual and auditory environment has not been addressed.

Of the guidelines cited in Table III, required level of illumination has been studied most extensively. The relationship between task performance and illumination level follows the law of diminishing returns. The level of illumination at which performance asymptotes depends upon the difficulty of the task, with greater gains achieved with increases in illumination for more difficult visual tasks (Boyce, 1980). It is well established that for the same task older adults require more light than younger adults in order to perform well (Boyce, 1973, 1980; Hughes & McNelis, 1978; Hughes & Neer, 1981; Ross, 1978; Sanders & McCormick, 1987), although there is no consensus on how much more illumination is required. Further, it is not clear how level of illumination should vary with age and task characteristics. Some guidelines, like those presented in Table III, assume a positive linear relationship between age and level of illumination and between task difficulty and level of illumination. Whether or not these assumptions are correct is unclear. For example, Ross (1978) concluded that increasing illumination above 500 lux results in little improvement in performance. Ross (1978) also concluded that once an illumination level of 10 to 20 footlamberts was established, the variables of contrast and age had a greater impact upon performance than the level of illumination.

Given the difficulty of specifying the optimal level of illumination, Fozard and Popkin (1978) suggested that lighting level be left under the control of the individual.

Table III
Guidelines for Optimizing the Visual Environment

1. Increase levels of illumination for older adults

   The most extensive guidelines for establishing illumination levels for older adults are those of the Illuminating Engineering Society (IES) (1981a,b). Less extensive guidelines can be found in Regnier and Pynoos (1987), and the Government of Canada (1987). The following was drawn from these sources.

	Lux
General	75–100, min of 50
Corridors	75–200
Elevators	150–200
Stairs	150–200
Tops and bottoms of stairs, all changes in level	300
At signs	500–600
Library	300–1000
Reading	300–1000
Bedroom	200
Bathroom	150–500
Kitchen	300–1000
Dining	150–300

2. Accommodate for decreased rate and final level of dark adaptation

   Avoid sudden and pronounced shifts in the level of illumination.

   Have levels of emergency illumination adequate for older adults.

   The IES (1981a,b) makes the following recommendations regarding emergency illumination for the general population:

       illumination not less than 1% of normal amount, min of 5 lux;

       min illumination of 30 lux at all doors and hazards;

       hazards should be light in color and contrast with surroundings.

3. Control glare

   Shield light fixtures.

   Use nonreflectant materials on walls, floors, and ceilings.

   Position furniture away from glare sources.

   Architectural modifications

       Overhangs on windows.

       Avoid windows at places likely to be the site of falls, such as on stairways and other changes in level.

   Borderline between comfort and discomfort glare (BCD) index

       The BCD indicates the level of illumination at which a light source will produce discomfort glare for individuals of different ages (Bennett, 1977)

           BCD (foot lamberts) $= 25000/age(yr)$

4. Eliminate difficult color discriminations

   Avoid discriminations in the blue–green range.

   Avoid discriminations among colors of the same hue.

   A list of colors from the Munsell Color Test that are equally discriminable among the general population appears in Woodson (1981), pp. 523–525.

5. Increase the size of important visual objects

   Print

       The IES (1981a,b) makes the following recommendations for the general population:

           min acceptable font size is 8;

           for prolonged reading font size is 10 or 12.

   Signs

       The Government of Canada (1987) recommends the following letter sizes be used on signs to be read by older adults:

           min 15 mm;

           ratio of letter size to reading distance $= 1:100$.

(continued)

Table III *(Continued)*

6. Increase contrast
   Blackwell and Blackwell (1971) suggest that the target luminance necessary to achieve sufficient contrast for different age groups can be determined by multiplying the natural log of the background luminance by the following contrast multipliers.

Age	Contrast multipliers
30–40	1.17
40–50	1.20
50–60	1.86
60–70	2.51

   The following luminance ratios for the general population have been drawn from the IES *Handbook* (1981a,b), and from Woodson (1981):

	Luminance Ratio
Task to immediate darker surroundings	3 : 1
Task to more remote darker surroundings	10 : 1

   Use contrast to emphasize changes in level and other hazards in the enrironment.

Some studies report that people prefer the level of illumination that results in optimal performance (Hughes & McNelis, 1978), and others indicate that they do not (Boyce, 1980). The practical implication is that leaving lighting level under the control of the older adult may not result in optimal illumination levels.

IV. Anthropometry

Anthropometry is concerned with measuring the dimensions and physical characteristics of the human body (Sanders & McCormick, 1987). Structural or static anthropometry deals with measuring body dimensions while the individual is standing or sitting still. Functional or dynamic anthropometry focuses on measuring the range of movement, and the strength of these movements when the body is engaged in different activities in a variety of positions. Examples of the types of measurements taken are functional reach of limbs, the range of motion of different joints, and the strength that can be exerted with a particular movement from a given

Table IV
Guidelines for Modifying the Auditory Environment

1. Control background noise
   Eliminate where possible constant sources of background noise such as piped in music, air conditioning, etc.
   Use sound-absorbing materials on walls, floors, ceilings, and windows.
   Eliminate reverberation and echos.
2. Avoid high frequency (4000 Hz plus) sounds
   For warning signals and other important sounds use low frequency (1000Hz–2000Hz) sounds that have reverberation.
3. Increase the volume of important sounds
   Estimates of age- and gender-related differences in auditory threshold can be found in Olsho, Harkins, and Lenhardt (1985, p. 351).
4. Facilitate use of visual cues when speaking and listening
   Arrange furniture in a circular, or semicircular manner.
   Use furniture that can be easily moved.
   Restrict the size of conversation groups to between four and six persons.

Table V

Average Weight, Height, and Selected Body Dimensions by Age Group and Gender

Males	Age Group					
	25–34	35–44	45–54	55–64	65–74	75–79
Weight (lb)	171 (114–248)[a]	172 (121–244)	172 (116–241)	166 (112–230)	160 (99–225)	150 (99–212)
Height (in)	69.1 (62.6–76.0)	68.5 (62.3–74.1)	68.2 (62.3–74.0)	67.4 (61.2–73.5)	66.9 (60.8–72.0)	65.9 (57.7–72.6)
Sitting height: erect in)	36.0 (32.5–39.0)	35.9 (32.2–38.9)	35.7 (32.8–38.9)	35.2 (31.4–38.7)	34.7 (31.3–37.7)	34.2 (27.7–37.6)
normal (in)	34.4 (31.0–37.8)	34.2 (30.8–37.7)	34.1 (30.8–37.7)	33.8 (30.2–36.9)	33.4 (30.1–36.4)	33.0 (26.7–36.7)
Knee height (in)	21.6 (19.0–24.6)	21.4 (18.4–24.4)	21.3 (18.2–23.9)	21.1 (18.1–24.0)	21.0 (18.2–23.7)	20.6 (18.0–23.3)
Popliteal height (in)	17.6 (15.1–20.6)	17.3 (15.0–19.9)	17.2 (14.7–19.9)	17.1 (14.9–19.8)	17.0 (14.2–19.8)	16.6 (15.0–19.3)
Elbow rest height (in)	9.7 (7.0–12.6)	9.7 (6.5–12.6)	9.5 (7.0–12.0)	9.3 (6.0–12.2)	9.0 (6.1–11.9)	8.6 (5.7–11.0)
Thigh clearance height (in)	5.8 (4.1–7.9)	5.8 (4.1–7.8)	5.6 (4.1–7.1)	5.5 (4.0–7.4)	5.4 (4.0–7.0)	5.2 (3.9–7.2)
Buttock–knee length (in)	23.6 (20.8–26.8)	23.3 (20.3–26.2)	23.3 (20.4–26.1)	23.0 (19.6–25.8)	23.0 (20.1–25.9)	22.7 (20.2–24.9)
Buttock–popliteal length (in)	19.6 (16.6–23.1)	19.4 (16.5–22.7)	19.4 (17.0–22.0)	19.3 (16.4–22.2)	19.2 (16.3–21.9)	18.9 (16.2–22.1)
Elbow to elbow breadth (in)	16.4 (13.1–21.4)	16.8 (13.1–21.5)	16.9 (13.2–21.8)	16.8 (13.2–22.0)	16.9 (13.2–21.0)	16.4 (12.4–20.7)
Seat breadth (in)	14.0 (11.7–17.4)	14.1 (12.0–17.1)	14.1 (11.5–16.9)	14.0 (11.6–16.9)	13.9 (11.4–16.6)	13.7 (11.4–16.5)
Right arm skinfold (cm)	1.4 (0.4–5.4)	1.4 (0.4–4.0)	1.3 (0.4–3.8)	1.2 (0.4–3.3)	1.2 (0.3–3.2)	1.1 (0.4–3.0)
Infrascapular skinfold (cm)	1.5 (0.5–4.1)	1.6 (0.6–4.2)	1.6 (0.6–3.9)	1.5 (0.6–4.0)	1.5 (0.5–3.5)	1.3 (0.5–3.3)
Right arm girth (in)	12.3 (9.6–15.6)	12.4 (9.8–15.6)	12.3 (9.5–15.3)	11.9 (9.0–15.00)	11.6 (8.0–14.5)	10.9 (8.0–13.5)
Chest girth (in)	39.1 (32.5–47.8)	39.6 (33.2–47.0)	39.8 (33.3–47.5)	39.3 (49.2–32.6)	38.9 (32.3–47.2)	37.9 (29.8–45.4)
Waist girth (in)	34.1 (26.6–45.8)	35.0 (27.3–46.3)	36.0 (27.9–46.7)	36.6 (27.5–47.6)	36.5 (26.9–47.7)	35.7 (25.8–46.2)
Biacromial diameter (in)	15.8 (13.8–17.8)	15.7 (13.6–17.5)	15.6 (13.8–17.3)	15.4 (13.5–17.7)	15.2 (13.4–16.7)	14.7 (12.4–16.2)

Females	25–34	35–44	45–54	55–64	65–74	75–79
Weight (lb)	136 (92–236)	144 (100–238)	147 (95–240)	152 (95–244)	146 (92–214)	138 (74–205)
Height (in)	63.7 (58.1–69.0)	63.5 (57.6–69.0)	62.9 (57.3–68.7)	62.4 (56.0–68.7)	61.5 (55.8–67.0)	61.1 (46.8–68.2)
Sitting height: erect (in)	33.7 (30.3–36.8)	33.7 (30.3–36.8)	33.4 (30.1–36.4)	33.0 (30.0–36.4)	32.1 (28.6–35.8)	31.7 (17.8–35.7)
normal (in)	32.6 (28.9–35.9)	32.6 (29.2–34.8)	32.2 (28.7–35.5)	31.9 (28–35.4)	31.1 (27.0–34.9)	30.5 (14.8–35.0)
Knee height (in)	19.7 (17.2–22.5)	19.7 (17.2–22.4)	19.5 (17.1–22.5)	19.4 (16.6–21.9)	19.3 (17.1–22.0)	19.4 (16.3–21.5)
Popliteal height (in)	15.7 (13.2–18.2)	15.6 (13.1–17.9)	15.5 (13.1–18.3)	15.4 (13.1–17.9)	15.3 (13.0–17.9)	15.5 (9.6–17.8)
Elbow rest height (in)	9.3 (6.1–11.9)	9.4 (6.7–12.0)	9.2 (6.4–12.1)	8.9 (5.9–11.9)	8.4 (5.4–11.30)	8.2 (2.8–10.7)
Thigh clearance height (in)	5.4 (4.0–7.7)	5.5 (4.0–7.8)	5.5 (4.0–7.7)	5.4 (3.5–8.3)	5.3 (3.4–7.0)	5.2 (3.2–6.9)
Buttock–knee length (in)	22.4 (20.0–25.6)	22.5 (20.0–25.9)	22.3 (19.4–25.5)	22.3 (19.4–25.7)	22.2 (19.4–25.9)	22.0 (18.5–24.7)
Buttock–popliteal length (in)	18.9 (16.1–21.9)	18.9 (16.2–22.4)	18.9 (15.8–22.0)	18.9 (16.1–22.0)	18.8 (16.1–21.9)	18.6 (14.7–20.8)
Elbow to elbow breadth (in)	14.5 (11.4–20.6)	15.3 (11.7–21.5)	15.8 (11.6–21.7)	16.4 (12.3–21.8)	16.4 (12.4–20.8)	15.8 (12.3–19.8)
Seat breadth (in)	14.2 (11.5–19.0)	14.6 (12.0–19.2)	14.7 (12.0–19.0)	14.8 (12.1–18.7)	14.7 (12.1–18.2)	14.2 (9.8–17.1)
Right arm skinfold (cm)	2.1 (0.7–4.7)	2.3 (1.0–4.6)	2.4 (0.8–4.8)	2.5 (1.0–4.7)	2.4 (0.8–4.7)	2.0 (0.3–3.9)
Infrascapular skinfold (cm)	1.5 (0.5–4.6)	1.8 (0.6–4.3)	2.0 (0.6–4.6)	2.2 (0.6–4.9)	2.0 (0.6–4.1)	1.7 (0.4–4.3)
Right arm girth (in)	10.8 (8.4–15.5)	11.4 (8.7–16.0)	11.7 (8.5–16.4)	11.9 (8.3–16.3)	11.5 (8.2–15.3)	11.0 (7.9–14.6)
Chest girth (in)	33.7 (28.9–43.2)	34.7 (29.4–43.6)	35.3 (29.5–43.8)	36.2 (30.1–43.7)	35.7 (29.0–42.2)	34.8 (29.6–42.2)
Waist girth (in)	28.3 (22.5–41.0)	29.7 (23.6–44.6)	31.1 (23.5–44.9)	32.7 (24.5–47.2)	33.1 (24.4–43.5)	32.8 (23.9–42.0)
Biacromial diameter (in)	14.0 (12.3–15.6)	14.1 (12.3–15.8)	14.0 (15.8–12.4)	13.9 (12.3–15.6)	13.7 (12.2–15.7)	13.6 (12.1–14.9)

Source: Stoudt, Damon, McFarland, and Roberts (1965, 1973).
[a]Values in parentheses are 1st and 99th percentiles.

position. Such information is used in designing everything from chairs to kitchens to nuclear power stations.

The most extensive source of anthropometric data is the *Anthropometric Source Book* compiled by NASA (1978) that provides an invaluable bibliography of existing anthropometric studies. A review of the studies included in this book indicates that very few have systematically examined the effect of age. Further, most studies that have examined the effects of age have been concerned with static anthropometry. Very few studies have examined the functional anthropometry of older adults.

The National Health Examination Survey (Stoudt, Damon, McFarland, & Roberts, 1965, 1973) conducted in the United States in 1962 is the most extensive study on age and static anthropometric measurements. Some of the information from this survey is presented in Table V. As is the case for all cross-sectional studies, age and cohort trends are confounded. People in developed countries have shown gains in height and weight over the years. Today's older cohorts may be somewhat different than those measured earlier.

Given the lack of information regarding the functional anthropometry of older adults, the literature sometimes suggests that the first percentile for young adults be used as the design standard for older adults. Inspection of Table V indicates that for static anthropometric measures, this approach would only accommodate older adults some of the time. This may also be the case for functional measures. Further, the segment of the population not accommodated by this approach is most often the frail elderly, individuals who are most vulnerable to poor design. An alternative is to correct the first percentile for

Table VI
Age Differences for Selected Measures of Functional Anthropometry

Mean Functional Reach (In) of the Elderly by Gender
(standard deviation in parentheses when available)

Males (age range 72–91 yrs)	
Forward arm reach	34.21 (1.51)[a]
Females (approximate age range 65–80)	
Sitting on 17 in chair	
Distance from back of thorax to gripped pencil, arm horizontal	28.56 (1.67)[b]
Distance from back of thorax to gripped pencil, arm straight, hand 11 in above seat	25.35 (1.84)[b]
Standing	
Distance from abdomen to gripped pencil, arm horizontal	18.54 (2.4)[b]
Distance from abdomen to gripped pencil, arm on 34-in table	13.96 (2.34)[b]
Height reached, arm upward	68[c]
Height reached, arm horizontal	49[c]
Height reached, arm downward	29.5[c]

Combined Right and Left Hand Grip Strength (kg) by Gender and Age[d]
(5th and 95th percentiles in parentheses)

	20–29	30–39	Age Group 40–49	50–59	60–69
Males	107 (81–139)	107 (81–135)	104 (76–128)	97 (74–119)	88 (62–111)
Females	62 (47–78)	62 (48–80)	61 (46–80)	56 (42–72)	52 (39–67)

Sources: [a]Damon and Stoudt (1963); [b]Roberts (1960); [c]Grandjean (1973); [d]Canadian Standardized Test of Fitness, 3rd Edition (1986).

younger adults with an age factor, though the value of this factor still needs to be determined. Table VI presents some functional anthropometric data for individuals of different ages. The small number of measures and the unknown representativeness of the samples reduce the utility of the functional reach measures in Table VI. The strength data were drawn from the 1981 Canada Fitness Survey (Canadian Standardized Test of Fitness, 3rd ed., 1986) and can be considered representative of the population.

There is a dearth of relevant dynamic strength information. Can a typical 80-year-old female safely push open an emergency exit door in a theatre, or twist open a standard vacuum-sealed food jar? Practical questions of this nature still need to be addressed. A good review of motor changes with age appear in Pirozzolo and Letta (1982).

V. Design for the Home

Design principles should encompass safety as well as productivity. Accidents, particularly falls, are a serious threat to older adults (Stern et al., 1985). Although there are many suggestions for how to design to avoid accidental injury (e.g., Product Safety and the Older Consumer, 1988), there has been virtually no research to support the claims.

Human factors textbooks have perennially outlined problems about the design of ovens/stovetops (placement of controls, mapping of controls to burners), baths and showers (placement and mapping of hot water controls), counter heights, and so on, not even mentioning older users. Obviously, these problems are exacerbated for older adults who suffer from physical impairments and medication side effects.

Take the lowly stepstool as an example. It is an essential piece of equipment for those less than 6 feet tall who want to reach standard kitchen cabinets, yet loss of balance while using the stepstool can lead to serious injury. Accident analyses suggest that railings might be added and steps might be widened.

A simpler solution is to bring the cabinets down to the user. There are, for instance, Scandinavian-designed kitchens with cabinets mounted on motorized railings. The user can adjust the height of cabinets and working surfaces with electric panel switches. Such systems are ideal for those in wheelchairs, but their cost, even with government subsidies, is too high for most seniors.

The authors have seen and read about many other suggested improvements: gas-detecting sensors over gas ranges; cutoff switches or timers on burners, ovens, and heating pads; better labeling of hot water controls and/or installation of temperature regulators to prevent scalding water from being delivered; glare-resistant coverings for instrument panels. Manufacturers and designers need to be made more aware of these problems and solutions. Ideally, better designs would be adopted for economic (profit) reasons, though government regulation may prove necessary. At the least, cost/benefit analyses are needed to address these issues.

VI. The Design
of Microcomputer Systems

Today's prototypical product for human factors research is the computer system. Desktop systems, virtually unknown only 10 years ago, have become an essential component of many work environments. Probably because there were so few older workers in the labor force until recently, little attention has been given to designing for them. Nonetheless, the labor force, much like the population as a whole, is aging (Denton, Feaver, & Spencer, 1986, estimate the 1990 median age to be 39 years in Canada). Older computer users will change from a rarity to a routine occurrence.

Computers stress the perceptual, cognitive, and motor capabilities of their users. Hardware design flaws commonly observed in office systems are difficult-to-read characters on displays and nonstandard keyboard designs with dubious tactile or auditory feedback. Many people over age 50 with bifocals suffer neck strain as they peer at elevated monitors through the lower halves of their glasses. (Flexible placement of the monitor or special reading glasses can help overcome this problem.) Glare from light sources and distracting background noise (e.g., from dot matrix printers) are additional problems in many environments.

On the software side of the equation, young and old alike have to contend with difficult-to-learn programs and interfaces. Training programs for major software packages often consist of minimal tutorials, and there is little, if any, formal evaluation of their effectiveness. Even basic issues, for example, whether people learn more quickly with a command line interface or an icon-based, menu-driven system, are unresolved. Few of these issues have been addressed from an aging perspective (see Tobias, 1987).

Studies mostly have explored applications such as word processing (Czaja, Hammond, Blascovich, & Swede, 1986; Elias, Elias, Robbins, & Gage, 1987; Gomez, Egan, & Bowers, 1986; Gomez, Egan, Wheeler, Sharma, & Gruchacz, 1983; Hartley, Hartley, & Johnson, 1984; Zandri & Charness, in press) and spreadsheets (Garfein, Schaie, & Willis, 1988; Gist, Rosen, & Schwoerer, 1988).

A few useful parameters come from these studies. In the studies that taught word processing, older adults were either no different (Hartley et al., 1984), 1.5 times slower (Elias et al., 1987, with trained typists), or 2.5 times slower (Zandri & Charness, with nontypists) than young adults in proceeding through the self-paced tu-torials or test sessions. The range of 1.5 to 2 times as slow fits well with rates observed in studies of list learning in a trials to criterion procedure (e.g., Kausler, 1982, Chap. 8).

In short, if you anticipate training naive older adults to learn a new software package, you should set aside about twice as much time as that normally allocated for young adults. It would also make sense to use self-paced rather than lecture-style training procedures with an age-heterogeneous group of learners. The issue of whether there are age-by-training technique interactions has not been adequately explored. Gist et al. (1988) failed to find an interaction between age and technique (modeling + tutorial, tutorial alone) for spreadsheet learning. Czaja et al. (1986) reported no interactions in their word-processing training study. Zandri and Charness (in press) found an interaction for final performance score using parts of Borland's desktop utility, Sidekick; older adults were relatively insensitive to the manipulation of training in pairs or alone, but young adults performed better when partnered. Older partnered adults needed more help in the final session, however, than older adults learning alone.

Studies of VDT characteristics and input devices (Charness, Graham, Bosman, & Zandri, 1988) yielded information congruent with theoretical predictions. Age and display color interacted to predict oral reading speed for text paragraphs. Display colors, equated for foreground/background contrast ratio, were blue, green, cyan, white (all on a black background), and black on a white background. For young readers, there were no differences in reading speed (average = 315 ms/word). For the middle-aged, black-on-white characters were read more quickly (331 ms/word) than all other combinations (353 ms/word). In this condition only, the middle-aged people read as quickly as the young. For the old, who were significantly slower than the young and the middle-aged, black on white (374 ms/word) was superior to blue on black (407 ms/word), with all other combinations no different (averaging 390 ms/word).

The finding of an advantage for black on white in the middle-aged and the old argues in favor of the adoption of black on white as a standard display type for monochrome displays, subject to the usual concerns about choice of character font, contrast, and so on (Helander, 1987).

Another study examined the effectiveness of cursor keys versus a mouse as an input device. It found that age differences in the speed of target acquisition were minimized by using a mouse. Particularly for older individuals who do not type well, a menu-driven interface with a mouse may prove to be the most effective solution. A caveat is that some older adults appeared to have difficulty with exact (character size) positioning (perhaps due to hand tremor), so the use of large targets (per Fitts' Law) seems necessary.

The video display terminal is becoming commonplace. There is an urgent need to establish the impact of its design characteristics on older adults.

A. High Technology versus Low Technology Solutions

Questions are being raised about the potential usefulness of microcomputers and robots in the home, and even in the nursing home. Although the authors admit to being enthusiastic users of this remarkably powerful technology, there are real limits to its applicability to the lives of retired adults.

Take the case of the family matriarch who maintains addresses, phone numbers, anniversaries, and birthdays on index cards or in a diary. We wonder whether the expense and learning time involved in translating this information to an electronic database is worthwhile.

Good design need not meet needs completely. It may be useful to challenge someone's capabilities in a way that could foster growth. Providing an impaired older person with a cane may lead to more self-reliance than offering them a "high-tech" wheelchair.

Even when a "high-tech" solution is desirable, it need not build in all the overhead associated with a typical computer system. A good example often referred to (e.g., Syndulko, Crooks, Wang, & Tourtellotte, 1984) is the problem of forgetting appointments or failing to take prescription drugs at prescribed times. Ironically, older adults may not have any more difficulty than younger adults with such prospective remembering tasks (West, 1988).

A cheap solution to pill taking is an inexpensive digital wristwatch with an alarm. However, setting current inexpensive watch alarms requires too high a degree of dexterity for the impaired or arthritic older adult. Further, the alarm frequency, a high-pitched chirp of about 50 dB, is probably inaudible for some older adults. Wristwatch-sized computers with better interfaces could serve as adjunct memory systems (if the user remembers to program them in the first place). However, a question that needs to be addressed first is: Is such technology acceptable to the older user? Brickfield's (1984) cross-sectional interview study demonstrated that technology use declined with age in current older cohorts. You can introduce seniors to technology, but you cannot make them use it.

B. Involving Older Adults in Design

If designers heed the admonition to "know the user," it becomes essential to involve older adults as product testers. Designers are no less prey to the same memory constraints as other humans, tending to design for the most representative and available case (Kahneman & Tversky, 1973): themselves.

We urge all designers to put at least one older adult into their test panels. We suspect that many design flaws that plague the entire population could be quickly weeded out. Such testing, together with data from future parameter estimation studies, should prove to be a powerful tool for design. Involving older people in design may not be a panacea. It is all too common for people having problems to blame themselves, rather than the environment: the "I-must-be-stupid" syndrome observed so often around computer equipment (see Norman, 1988).

VII. Conclusions

We see the following challenges for the disciplines of human factors and design. First, normative data from representative samples should be gathered to provide the parameter estimates needed to simplify low-level design decisions. Studies are needed to verify, supplement, and in many cases, replace the contents of Tables II through VI. Good places to start would be discovering how combinations of factors (such as luminance, size, and contrast) constrain visual performance. Further, both static and dynamic anthropometric data should be gathered for older adults both to see whether there are cohort-related changes and to set standards. If designers are to produce better products and environments (home and work) they must have the requisite data.

Second, design must be conceptualized as a cycle of design, *evaluation*, and modification. Most products in the marketplace have undergone minimal, if any, evaluation of their functionality for older adults (though governments now force safety evaluation). In principle, the consumer determines marketability, but in practice, many products have no competitors (e.g., city airports or public transportation vehicles), and older consumers have minimal influence on selection or design decisions. Designers should solicit feedback from older users.

Finally, older adults must also enter into the feedback loop at the level of *goal definition* to ensure that design is with, not just for, older adults. It is all too easy for human factors specialists to make decisions based on what they think will be appropriate. The wishes of older adults need to be incorporated into the design process.

Acknowledgments

This work was supported by grants from the Natural Sciences and Engineering Research Council of Canada (NSERC A0790), Bell Northern Research, and DEC Canada. We thank Tom Hess for providing the eye movement fixation data. We are grateful to Cameron Camp for providing the addresses for many researchers on Bitnet, facilitating our information gathering. Barbara Gilmour (Regional Municipality of Waterloo) provided assumed walking speeds for traffic lights. Thanks also to Tim Moore, James Birren, and two anonymous reviewers for comments on earlier drafts.

References

Anders, T. R., & Fozard, J. L. (1973). Effects of age upon retrieval from primary and secondary memory. *Developmental Psychology*, **9**, 411–415.

Anders, T. R., Fozard, J. L., & Lillyquist, T. D. (1972). Effects of age upon retrieval from short-term memory. *Developmental Psychology*, **6**, 214–217.

Bennett, C. A. (1977). The demographic variables of discomfort glare. *Lighting Design and Application*, **7**, 22–24.

Beres, C. A., & Baron, A. (1981). Improved digit symbol substitution by older women as a result of extended practice. *Journal of Gerontology*, **36**, 591–597.

Blackwell, O. M., & Blackwell, H. R. (1971). Visual performance data for 156 normal observers of various ages. *Journal of the Illuminating Engineering Society*, **1**, 3–13.

Botwinick, J., & Storandt, M. (1974). *Memory, related functions and age*. Springfield, IL: Thomas.

Brickfield, C. F. (1984). Attitudes and perceptions of older people toward technology. In P.

K. Robinson & J. E. Birren (Eds.), *Aging and technological advances* (pp. 31–38). New York: Plenum.

Bromley, D. B. (1958). Some effects of age on short term learning and remembering. *Journal of Gerontology*, **13**, 398–406.

Boyce, P. R. (1973). Age, illuminance, visual performance and preference. *Lighting Research and Technology*, **5**(3), 125–144.

Boyce, P. R. (1980). *Human factors in lighting*. Essex, England: Applied Science Publ.

Caird, W. K. (1966). Aging and short-term memory. *Journal of Gerontology*, **21**, 295–299.

Canada Mortgage and Housing Corporation (1988). *Older people and their homes: A tool to examine potential environmental improvements*. CMHC Publications, Ottawa, Ontario, Canada K1A 0P7.

Canadian Standardized Test of Fitness, (3rd ed.) (1986). Published by the Minister of State, Fitness and Amateur Sport (FAS 7378), 365 Laurier Ave. W., Ottawa, Ontario K1A0X6.

Card, S. K., Moran, T. P., & Newell, A. (1983). *The psychology of human-computer interaction*. Hillsdale, NJ: Erlbaum.

Carstens, D. Y. (1985). *Site planning and design for the elderly: Issues, guidelines, and alternatives*. New York: Van Nostrand Reinhold.

Cerella, J., Poon, L. W., & Fozard, J. L. (1982). Age and iconic read-out. *Journal of Gerontology*, **37**, 197–202.

Charness, N., & Campbell, J. I. D. (1988). Acquiring skill at mental calculation in adulthood: A task decomposition. *Journal of Experimental Psychology: General*, **117**, 115–129.

Charness, N., Graham, J., Bosman, E., & Zandri, E. (1988). Computer technology and age. Poster presented at the Atlanta Conference on Cognitive Aging, April.

Craik, F. I. M. (1968). Two components in free recall. *Journal of Verbal Learning and Verbal Behavior*, **7**, 996–1004.

Crowder, R. G. (1980). Echoic memory and the study of aging memory systems. In L. W. Poon, J. L. Fozard, L. S. Cermak, D. Arenberg, & L. W. Thompson (Eds.), *New directions in memory and aging*, Proceedings of the George A. Talland Memorial Conference (pp. 181–204). Hillsdale, NJ: Erlbaum.

Cunningham, D. A., Rechnitzer, M.D., Pearce,

M. E., & Donner, A. P. (1982). Determinants of self-selected walking pace across ages 19 to 66. *Journal of Gerontology*, **37**, 560–564.

Czaja, S. J., Hammond, K., Blascovich, J. J., & Swede, H. (1986). Learning to use a word-processing system as a function of training strategy. *Behaviour and Information Technology*, **5**, 203–216.

Damon, A., & Stoudt, H. W. (1963). The functional anthropometry of old men. *Human Factors*, **5**, 485–491.

Denton, F. T., Feaver, C. H., & Spencer, B. G. (1986). Prospective aging of the population and its implications for the labour force and government expenditures. *Canadian Journal on Aging*, **5**, 75–95.

Elias, P. K., Elias, M. F., Robbins, M. A., & Gage, P. (1987). Acquisition of word-processing skills by younger, middle-age, and older adults. *Psychology and Aging*, **2**, 340–348.

Eriksen, C. W., Hamlin, R. M., & Daye, C. (1973). Aging adults and rate of memory scan. *Bulletin of the Psychonomic Society*, **1**, 259–260.

Falduto, L. L., & Baron, A. (1986). Age-related effects of practice and task complexity on card sorting. *Journal of Gerontology*, **41**, 659–661.

Fozard, J. L., & Popkin, S. J. (1978). Optimizing adult development: Ends and means of an applied psychology of aging. *American Psychologist*, **33**, 975–989.

Fozard, J. L., Thomas, J. C., & Waugh, N. C. (1976). Effects of age and frequency of stimulus repetitions on two choice reaction time. *Journal of Gerontology*, **31**, 556–563.

Garfein, A. J., Schaie, K. W., & Willis, S. L. (1988). Microcomputer proficiency in later-middle-age and older adults: Teaching old dogs new tricks. *Social Behavior*, **3**, 131–148.

Gist, M., Rosen, B., & Schwoerer, C. (1988). The influence of training method and trainee age on the acquisition of computer skills. *Personnel Psychology*, **41**, 255–265.

Gomez, L. M., Egan, D. E., & Bowers, C. (1986). Learning to use a text editor: Some learner characteristics that predict success. *Human-Computer Interaction*, **2**, 1–23.

Gomez, L. M., Egan, D. E., Wheeler, E. A., Sharma, D. K., & Gruchacz, A. M. (1983). How interface design determines who has difficulty learning to use a text editor. *Proceedings of the CHI'82 Conference on Human*

Factors in Computer Systems, 219–222. New York: ACM.

Government of Canada (1987). Housing an aging population: Guidelines for development and design. National Advisory Council on Aging. Ministry of Supply and Services Canada, ISBN: 0-662-15640-4, Catalogue: H-71-3/6-1987E.

Grandjean, E. (1973). Ergonomics of the home. New York: Wiley.

Grant, E. A., Storandt, M., & Botwinick, J. (1978). Incentive and practice in the psychomotor performance of the elderly. Journal of Gerontology, 33, 413–415.

Hartley, A. A., Hartley, J. T., & Johnson, S. A. (1984). The older adult as computer user. In P. K. Robinson & J. E. Birren (Eds.), Aging and technological advances (pp. 347–348). New York: Plenum.

Helander, M. G. (1987). Design of visual displays. In G. Salvendy (Ed.), Handbook of human factors (pp. 507–548). New York: Wiley.

Hess, T. (1988). Personal communication, based on "Age differences in scene memory: The effects of organization and typicality on attention and memory," 2nd Cognitive Aging Conference, Atlanta.

Hughes, P. C., & McNelis, J. F. (1978). Lighting, productivity, and the work environment. Lighting Research and Design, 8, 32–40.

Hughes, P. C., & Neer, R. M. (1981). Lighting for the elderly: A psychobiological approach to lighting. Human Factors, 23(1), 65–85.

Illuminating Engineering Society (1981a). IES lighting handbook: Application volume. New York: Waverly.

Illuminating Engineering Society (1981b). IES lighting handbook: Reference volume. New York: Waverly.

Inman, V. W., & Parkinson, S. R. (1983). Differences in Brown-Peterson recall as a function of age and retention interval. Journal of Gerontology, 38, 58–64.

Kahneman, D., & Tversky, A. (1973). On the psychology of prediction. Psychological Review, 80, 237–251.

Kantowitz, B. H., & Sorkin, R. D. (1983). Human factors: Understanding people-system relationships. New York: Wiley.

Kausler, D. H. (1982). Experimental psychology and human aging. New York: Wiley.

Koncelik, J. A. (1976). Designing the open nursing home. Stroudsburg, PA: Dowden, Hutchinson & Ross.

Koncelik, J. A. (1982). Aging and the product environment. New York: Van Nostrand Reinhold.

Kriauciunas, R. (1968). The relationship of age and retention-interval activity in short-term memory. Journal of Gerontology, 23, 169–173.

Light, L. L., & Anderson, P. A. (1985). Working-memory capacity, age, and memory for discourse. Journal of Gerontology, 40, 737–747.

Madden, D. J., & Nebes, R. D. (1980). Aging and the development of automaticity in visual search. Developmental Psychology, 16, 377–384.

McDowd, J. M. (1986). The effects of age and extended practice on divided attention performance. Journal of Gerontology, 41, 764–769.

McFarland, R. A., Warren, A. B. & Karis, C. (1958). Alterations in critical flicker frequency as a function of age and light : dark ratio. Journal of Experimental Psychology, 56, 529–538.

National Aeronautics and Space Administration (NASA) (1978). Anthropometric source book (Vol. 1) Anthropometry for designers; (Vol. 2) A handbook of anthropometric data; (Vol. 3) Annotated bibliography (NASA Ref. Pub. 1024).

Norman, D. A. (1988). The psychology of everyday things. New York: Basic Books.

Olsho, L. W., Harkins, S. W., & Lenhardt, M. L. (1985). Aging and the auditory system. In J. E. Birren & K. W. Schaie (Eds.) Handbook of the psychology of aging (2nd ed., pp. 332–377). New York: Van Nostrand Reinhold.

Pirozzolo, F. J. & Letta, G. J. (Eds.) (1982). The aging motor system. New York: Praeger.

Product Safety and the older consumer (1988). What manufacturers/designers need to consider. COMSIS Corporation, available from U. S. Consumer Product Safety Commission, Washington, DC 20207.

Rabbitt, P., & Vyas, S. M. (1980). Selective anticipation for events in old age. Journal of Gerontology, 35, 913–919.

Regnier, V., & Pynoos, J. (1987). Housing the aged. New York: Elsevier.

Roberts, D. F. (1960). Functional anthropometry of elderly women. Ergonomics, 3, 321–327.

Ross, D. K. (1978). Task lighting—yet another view. *Lighting Design and Applications*, **8**, 37–43.

Salthouse, T. A. (1984). Effects of age and skill in typing. *Journal of Experimental Psychology: General*, **13**, 345–371.

Salthouse, T. A., & Somberg, B. L. (1982). Skilled performance: Effects of adult age and experience on elementary processes. *Journal of Experimental Psychology: General*, **111**, 176–207.

Salvendy, G. (Ed.) (1987). *Handbook of human factors*. New York: Wiley.

Sanders, M. S., & McCormick, E. J. (1987). *Human factors in engineering design* (6th ed.). New York: McGraw Hill.

Simon, J. R. (1967). Choice reaction time as a function of auditory S-R correspondence, age, and sex. *Ergonomics*, **10**, 659–664.

Simon, J. R., & Pouraghabagher, A. R. (1978). The effects of aging on the stages of processing in a choice reaction time task. *Journal of Gerontology*, **33**, 553–561.

Sivak, M., Olson, P. L., & Pastalan, L. A. (1981). Effect of driver's age on nighttime legibility of highway signs. *Human Factors*, **23**, 59–64.

Smith, A. D. (1975). Aging and interference with memory. *Journal of Gerontology*, **30**, 319–325.

Sterns, H. L., Barrett, G. V., & Alexander, R. A. (1985). Accidents and the aging individual. In J. E. Birren & K. W. Schaie (Eds.), *Handbook of the psychology of aging* (2nd ed. pp. 703–724). New York: Van Nostrand Reinhold.

Stoudt, H. W., Damon, A., McFarland, R. A., & Roberts J. (1965). *Weight, height, and selected body dimensions of adults. Vital and health statistics*, Series 11, No 8. Rockville, MD: Public Health Service.

Stoudt, H. W., Damon, A., McFarland, R. A., & Roberts J. (1973). *Skinfolds, body girths, biacromial diameter and selected anthropometric indices of adults. Vital and health statistics*, Series 11, No 35. Rockville, MD: Public Health Service.

Svanborg, A. (1984). Technology, aging and health in a medical perspective. In P. K. Robinson & J. E. Birren (Eds.), *Aging and technological advances* (pp. 159–168). New York: Plenum.

Syndulko, K., Crooks, V., Wang, R., & Tourtellotte, W. W. (1984). Computer based memory training and memory prosthesis in older adults. In P. K. Robinson & J. E. Birren (Eds.), *Aging and technological advances* (pp. 359–361). New York: Plenum.

Tobias, C. L. (1987). Computers and the elderly: A review of the literature and directions for future research. *Proceedings of the Human Factors Society 31st annual meeting, New York*, **2**, 866–870.

Uniform traffic control devices for Canada, (1976). Roads and Transportation Association of Canada, 1765 St. Laurent Boulevard, Ottawa, Ontario K1G3V4.

Welford, A. T. (1977). Motor performance. In J. E. Birren & W. K. Schaie (Eds.), *Handbook of the psychology of aging* (pp. 450–496). New York: Van Nostrand Reinhold.

West, R. L. (1988). Prospective memory and aging. In M. M. Gruneberg, P. E. Morris, & R. N. Sykes (Eds.), *Practical aspects of memory: Current research and issues* (Vol. 2). New York: Wiley.

Woodson, W. E. (1981). *Human factors design handbook*. New York: McGraw Hill.

Wright, R. E. (1982). Adults age similarities in free recall output order and strategies. *Journal of Gerontology*, **37**, 76–79.

Zandri, E., & Charness, N. (in press). Training older and younger adults to use software. *Educational Gerontology*.

Twenty Seven

The Design of Special Environments for the Aged

Patricia A. Parmelee and M. Powell Lawton

Psychologists' concern for the significance of environment for aging people was crystallized in Kleemeier's (1959) chapter in the early predecessor to this *Handbook*. Later editions surveyed the burgeoning research in this area (Lawton, 1978) and focused more specifically on theoretical developments (Scheidt & Windley, 1985) and contextual aspects linking physical and psychosocial dimensions (Moos & Lemke, 1985). It seems fair to observe that the bulk of empirical research in this area was framed by the predecessor and second edition of this *Handbook*. Since then, there have been more applications of person–environment knowledge to policy and practice than new theoretical concepts, interesting research methodologies, or major new research findings.

Several factors may be responsible for the lull in empirical research during the past decade. One possible explanation is the relative standstill in federally assisted housing program development since 1980. Similar factors are the relatively small trickle of new nursing home construction and the slowing of community develop-

ment funds, both of which spurred the research of the 1970s. Another trend that resulted at least partly from diminished federal funds was the somewhat belated interest of the policy and housing services professions in older persons living in ordinary communities. The tradition of person–environment research was to study environments planned and designed for a specific population. The research community was slow to apply the same outlook to unplanned housing (Lawton & Hoover, 1981).

Another explanation for the slack in relevant research may be the failure of new concepts and methods to emerge in a way that could pace new research. Person–environment relations was founded on theory-driven attempts by psychologists, geographers, and architects to specify some of the links between people and their environments (cf. Kates & Wohlwill, 1966). A major portion of research since then, however, has come from applied fields such as architectural and interior design, urban planning, public administration, and many of the service professions.

Handbook of the Psychology of Aging, Third Edition
Copyright © 1990 Academic Press, Inc. All rights of reproduction in any form reserved.

Although much useful knowledge has been produced, such research neither utilized nor generated much theory; the low demand for theory-based research simply may have failed to reinforce development of theory, which in turn became less and less available to generate more productive research. Similarly, research methods familiar to the disciplines from which the research emanated were applied to this new area—behavior observation, survey research, psychological tests, and qualitative analysis, for example. Few attempts to develop environment-specific methods have been reported. In sum, the environmental innovations that stimulate research have lessened, and the type of research that would generate need for new concepts and methods has slowed.

Although applications to housing design are promising, research and theory development have dwindled and innovations are relatively few. In many ways, the study of aging and environment, particularly with respect to special housing, stands at a crossroad; its future richness may well depend upon which direction it takes. We attempt in this chapter to trace how the field has come to this crossroad during the decade of the 1980s and to outline the major points that will influence its further development. The chapter begins by proposing an organizing theme—the dialectic between autonomy and security—by which the relationships between older people and the variety of environments in which they live may be viewed. How this theme is played out in many types of environments is then discussed. A primary focus is on the social environment, a topic that can benefit from integration of existing knowledge with that gained from other types of environmental research. The third section will review research generated by various approaches designed to accommodate the complexities of the person–environment system and identify how advances in these areas might lead to better, more usable research. Although the chapter will be concerned with application, the underlying theme will be the reciprocal influences among theory, method, and practice.

I. Autonomy versus Security

In reviewing the literature on environment and aging—or for that matter, on the elderly in general—one is stuck by the emphasis on autonomy. Although terms differ (for example, *agency, competence, control, mastery*), much recent theory and research has emphasized older people's need to maintain perceived and exerted independence as they move from private residences into special housing environments. Let us therefore begin by defining *autonomy* as a state in which the person is, or feels, capable of pursuing life goals by the use of his or her own resources; there is thus minimal need to call upon other people's resources. The implication is not, of course, freedom *from* responsibilities, social ties, and so forth, but freedom *of* choice, action, and self-regulation of one's life space—in other words, the perception of and capacity for effective independent action.

Although this orientation has strong intrinsic conceptual merits and potential for design-relevant application, it tends to accentuate the positive functions of autonomy while downplaying the very real benefits that ostensibly choice-limiting design factors may offer. A specific goal of many special environments for the elderly is to promote *security:* a state in which pursuit of life goals is linked to, limited by, and aided by dependable physical, social, and interpersonal resources. The term thus emphasizes not only physical safety or psychological peace of mind but also the communality rather than separateness of the person. We shall argue that autonomy for the aged in special environments is no more—and no less—critical than security and that autonomy and security together form a dialectic that lies at the heart of person–environment relations in late life. First, however, it will be helpful to review the conceptual and empirical evidence on which this dialectic is posited.

A. Aging, Environment, and Autonomy: Control Theory

The concept of a basic human need for competence was first elaborated in depth by White (1959) in his treatise on *effectance*—the need to feel competent in transactions with one's environment—as a central motivational force underlying much of human behavior. Subsequent formulations have centered on subjective assessments of controllability of events and outcomes from both perceptual (Rotter, 1966) and experiential perspectives (Deci, 1980). Perhaps the most influential work in this area has been that of Seligman (1975) and his colleagues on *learned helplessness:* the notion that repeated exposure to uncontrollable situations leads to a generalized sense of inefficacy manifested by behavioral passivity, apathy, and inability to distinguish controllable from uncontrollable situations. More recent, cognitively oriented formulations have emphasized attributions of failure to stable, generalized aspects of the self as a hallmark of learned helplessness and consequent performance deficits and psychological disorders, most notably chronic depression (see Peterson & Seligman, 1984, for review and discussion). Gerontological theorists have similarly long acknowledged the benefits of a sense of personal mastery (Lowenthal, 1977) and the negative effects of dependency (Baltes & Wahl, 1987; Kalish, 1969) for the elderly.

This emphasis on autonomy and a sense of control is also evident in theory and research on environment and aging. The now-classic experimental studies of Langer and Rodin (1975; Rodin & Langer, 1977) and of Schulz (1976) vividly demonstrated the substantial positive impact of minor increments in control of personal activities and social contacts, as well as the negative effects of loss of such control (Schulz & Hanusa, 1978), for elderly nursing home residents. These pioneering efforts have subsequently been replicated conceptually in both nursing homes (Schulz & Hanusa, 1979) and retirement communities (Slivinske & Fitch, 1987). The ecological validity of such experimental interventions is confirmed by a stream of correlational research relating the environmental constraints of institutional settings to low morale or life satisfaction (Saup, 1986) and external locus of control (Carstensen & Whitbourne, 1978). Similarly, perceived lack or external locus of control has been associated with poorer adjustment, activity, and physical health among older persons living independently in the community (Mancini, 1980), in nursing homes and congregate housing (Parmelee, 1982; Ziegler & Reid, 1983), and among those making the transition between private and institutional living environments (Arling, Harkins, & Capitman, 1986).

Several authors have sought to refine the concept of control as it applies to the aged and to elucidate the effects of environment on perception and exercise of autonomy. An important differentiation is that of *personal efficacy*—perceived ability to act effectively—from expectations for *environmental responsiveness* to such action (see Bandura, 1982). Although studies reviewed here suggest that environment can affect perceived control, research on stability of control perceptions as a function of age per se has yielded, at best, conflicting results (Lachman, 1986; Morganti, Nehrke, Hulicka, & Cataldo, 1988). Gurin and Brim (1984) suggest that whereas sense of personal efficacy remains fairly stable, perceptions of environmental responsivity to control efforts may change markedly across time and situations. Specifically, in order to maintain a sense of self as causal agent, the older person may attribute failures or deficits of control to environmental or other external causes. Presumably, this protects against the helplessness caused by self-attribution of failures; it may also contribute to the greater importance of environment for older people postulated by Lawton and Nahemow (1973).

In a related vein, Kuhl (1986) distinguishes *actual* behavioral control from *passive* control, the generalized perception of self-efficacy in the absence of active control attempts. Kuhl argues that although institutional settings and other factors in the social environments of the elderly inhibit exercise of actual control, persons may retain a state-oriented sense of general causal agency. That is, they may *feel* competent even though both individual capacity and environmental affordances for active control may be quite limited. Similarly, Rothbaum, Weisz, and Snyder's (1982) notion of *secondary control* suggests that such postulated tactics as predictive power, identification with powerful others, or concepts of fate or a higher will may be equally as beneficial as direct control for frail aged in institutional settings. Unfortunately, as White and Janson (1986) point out, few empirical studies expressly have examined such indirect control tactics and their effects among older people in such environments.

Thus, although theory on autonomy and perceived control is developing nicely, empirical research thus far has been conducted from a rather narrow perspective. Autonomy has generally been viewed unidimensionally and positively; little attention has been given to individual differences in the desire for control, tactics for its expression, or its benefits (see, however, Morganti et al., 1988; Zeigler & Reid, 1983). Neither has adequate attention been paid to the social relativity of autonomy—for example, social class differences within a culture or differences among cultures (Kalish, 1969). As Sampson (1977) has noted, individualism and independence are distinctly American—specifically, contemporary middle-class American—ideals. In addition, variations in familial patterns, expectations, and living arrangements undoubtedly influence not only the importance of autonomy for the elderly but its very meaning as well. Thus the salience of autonomy for elderly of differing cultures, social backgrounds, and cohorts merits further exploration.

B. Aging, Environment, and Security: Design and Application

Like theorists, designers recognize the importance of autonomy, but their practical work places equal if not greater emphasis on *security* as a primary need. The term, as used here as well as in the literature, spans a variety of conditions presumed to contribute to (or by their absence, detract from) freedom from risk, danger, concern, or doubt—that is, to enhance both physical safety and peace of mind. At the physical level, several recent studies of design preferences have identified personal safety and security as a major concern of the elderly (Brennan, Moos, & Lemke, 1988; Regnier, 1987) and a strong contributor to their residential satisfaction (Carp & Carp, 1982; Carp & Christensen, 1986a; Lawton, 1980). Both empirical studies and practical design guides emphasize the importance of visual orientation, reduced risk of accidents, environmental familiarity, and neighborhood integration as contributors to older persons' physical safety and psychological well-being in community and congregate settings (Howell, 1980; Hunt & Roll, 1987). Security may also include ready access to health care and emergency services. Among a sample of upper-income elderly living in private homes in the community, access to home health and round-the-clock nursing services were frequently endorsed preferences for congregate housing (Regnier, 1987). On the psychological side, Carp (1987) reported that one of the most frequently cited advantages of the move to planned housing was an increased sense of security, in terms not only of physical safety but also of simply knowing one had found an environment suitable for the remainder of one's life. Security also has interpersonal aspects, in terms of a sense of community with neighbors and ready availability of contact, support, and assistance in time of need (Sheehan, 1986; Sullivan, 1986).

Thus, in addition to design and prosthetics to maximize autonomy, the applied literature places strong emphasis on physical, social, and emotional security. The juncture of concerns about autonomy and security is nicely illustrated by Carstens's (1985) delineation of four issues in environmental design for older people: (1) autonomy, independence, and usefulness; (2) personalization and control of private space; (3) predictability and control of space; and (4) safety and security.

C. The Autonomy–Security Dialectic

Whereas Carstens's analysis presents autonomy and security as distinct design concerns, they may be viewed more parsimoniously as poles of a dialectic. The move to a residential facility is in most cases a trade-off: Gains in security, in the form of increased access to health care and other services, a more manageable environment, and a relatively dense social-supportive environment, are achieved at the cost of some loss of choice and independence. We posit that although this trade-off becomes especially salient when people consider or effect a change of environment, it is an ongoing dynamic of old age. The normal aging process makes physical security a primary need; psychological feelings of safety, stability, and social communality are important concerns. Yet, as the control literature demonstrates, effective adaption requires that individuals maintain a sense of self-efficacy appropriate to their resources and competencies. Thus person–environment relations in old age may be conceptualized as an ongoing dynamic between autonomy and security.

As with any dialectic approach, this notion assumes that autonomy and security form a single continuum, the poles of which coexist in a dynamic equilibrium between forces pulling the organism toward each extreme. Specifically, psychological motives for autonomy and for security, although equally important, create conflicting behavioral demands. Satisfaction of autonomy needs is presumed to produce a positive state of emotional activation that eventuates in a sense of self as an effective causal agent. Frustration of such needs may lead immediately to boredom and eventually to apathy and reduced self-efficacy. The immediate effect of adequate security is passive personal contentment and satisfaction with one's environment; frustration of security needs should be evidenced as anxiety or depression. Thus, achievement of a proper balance along with autonomy–security continuum should result in both general satisfaction as well as a sense of mastery or agency. The dynamic nature of the dialectic is such that any balance achieved is short lived; ascendance of one pole over the other at any specific time or in a given environmental context is highly likely. Lawton (1989a) has described this process in detail and related it to the ecological model proposed earlier (Lawton & Nahemow, 1973). Overly secure environments produce boredom, apathy, and withdrawal; too much autonomy (i.e., in the absence of security) leads to stress and its documented effects.

Table I details how specific attributes of the physical and social environments are hypothesized to affect the autonomy–security dialectic. The environmental attributes (left-most column) represent environmental aspects of Lawton's (1982) competence hierarchy. A dialectic between security and autonomy in relation

Table I
Some Hypothesized Dimensions of the Autonomy–Security Dialectic

Environmental Attribute	Security	Autonomy
Orienting quality (e.g., familiarity, environmental knowledge)	Physical and psychological security of knowledge of time, place and person / Prescription for life-maintaining behaviors / Place identity/sense of place	Novelty, complexity, curiosity
Safety (e.g., visual orientation, pathways clear)	Minimize risk of accidents	Unlimited behavioral options
ADL affordance	Facilitate performance of everyday tasks	Sharpen and develop skills
Interpersonal resources (e.g., sociopetal vs. sociofugal; open/closed)	Sharing, loving support	Independence, privacy, autonomy
Cultural integrative (community/privacy)	Normative behavior regulation / Sense of community	Individuality, nonconformity

Note: Entries under security and autonomy are ideal behavioral and psychological outcomes presumed to result from adequate satisfaction of each motive.

to each of these environmental attributes may be hypothesized. Acting to maximize the security aspects of that attribute results in one outcome, while maximizing the autonomy aspects results in another, sometimes conflicting, outcome. For every person–environment transaction, the tension between security and autonomy operates continuously so that any period of apparent equilibrium is short lived.

The basic concepts of this model are well represented by previous research on environment and aging. Perhaps the most notable examples are models based on the concept of person–environment (P-E) congruence or fit—the match between characteristics of the individual and his or her physical environment—such as Lawton's (1982, 1985; Lawton & Nahemow, 1973) *environmental docility* model and Kahana's (1982) *P–E fit* approach. The basic tenet of these models, that performance and adaption are maximized where characteristics of the environment are consonant with individual needs and preferences and complementary of deficits,

implicitly affirms the importance of both autonomy and security for normal functioning.

A recent variant on the P-E fit approach is that of Carp (1987; Carp & Carp, 1984), who suggests that fit must be considered from two perspectives. At the first level are lower order life-maintenance needs such as foot, water, and adequate shelter. Fulfillment of these basic needs depends upon the degree of *complementarity* between personal resources (e.g., ADL skills) and environmental affordances: If resources are limited, additional environmental affordances are needed to ensure need satisfaction. At a higher level, Carp suggests that higher order psychological needs such as affiliation, order, and privacy are facilitated by *similarity* between personality (which presumably determines strength of a particular need) and environmental affordances for need satisfaction. Thus, in the case of affiliation, P-E congruence would be represented where a person with a strong desire for interpersonal contact lived in an environment that afforded high degrees of contact with others. This situation was illustrated by Carp and Carp's (1980) follow-up of Victoria Plaza residents. As compared with a group who did not move to the new apartment facility, movers displayed significant gains over 8 years in a variety of types of social activity. However, these gains were greatest among those who had scored highest in sociability before the move; persons who had initially been least socially active displayed even lower levels of socializing after moving. Presumably, those inclined toward interpersonal pursuits took full advantage of the opportunities offered by the new environment. Those for whom the "close quarters" of age-segregated housing were incongruent with personal preferences withdrew and became even more isolated.

At least two studies suggest that P-E congruence may moderate effects of age density among aged living independently in the community. Lawton, Moss, and Moles (1984), in a secondary analysis of two national surveys, examined age density (percentage of persons over 65) of the residential environment as well as preference for age segregation. Controlling for effects of demographic characteristics, they found that congruence of actual and preferred age mix slightly but significantly increased explained variance in morale beyond that accounted for by the two factors separately. Their data also revealed that more socially deprived groups—for example, the poor, less educated, or minority elderly—were more likely to prefer the relative security of age-segregated residential environments. Usui and Keil (1987), controlling for demographic characteristics, found that age density bore a small but significant *negative* relation to life satisfaction. This was especially true among persons who reported high levels of contact with friends living outside the neighborhood. In contrast, participation in voluntary organizations reduced the nega-

tive association between age density and life satisfaction. And where extra neighborhood contacts were low and organizational membership high, the relation of age density to life satisfaction was reversed to a positive one. Thus for those whose friendship activities were focused outside the neighborhood, having a large proportion of older people in the residential environment was a negative factor. But formal organizational participation, an indicator of integration in the local area, was congruent with age concentration and therefore bore a positive relation to life satisfaction.

Carp's bilevel approach reinforces our proposed distinction between security and autonomy as primary environmental motives in old age. Of course, it does not reflect a dialectic view, because Carp includes what one would consider security needs at both lower (e.g., shelter) and higher (order, harmavoidance) levels. But by distinguishing life-maintaining from psychological needs, Carp's formulation helps integrate previous congruence concepts that emphasized *either* functional competence (e.g., Lawton, 1982) *or* personality traits (Kahana, 1982) and emphasizes the breadth of factors that must be considered when assessing person–environment relations among the elderly.

Lawton's (1989a) recent expansion of his environmental docility model more clearly reflects the concepts underlying the proposed dialectic. By incorporating the notion of *proactivity*, the individual's active shaping of his or her environment, Lawton has introduced a component of self-directed, planful behavior that was lacking in previous P-E congruence models. That is, the individual is viewed not simply as reacting passively to environmental conditions but also as shaping his or her environment by acting on it directly. This acknowledgement of the proactive orientation of White (1959) and other early effectance theorists implicitly redefines aging in terms not only of functional deficits but also of capabilities, psychological needs, and continued agency.

II. Special Types of Environments: Autonomy and Security

The variety of environments inhabited by older people reflects the autonomy–security dialectic inasmuch as differing housing types afford differing balances between autonomy and security. A brief review of major types of residential environments will demonstrate that they vary greatly in their ability to afford P-E congruence in people of any particular level of competence, as well as in the breadth of the autonomy–security continuum they offer. A dominant theme is that of *aging in place*—the mutual process whereby both the older person and the environment change, the only constant being geographic location. As we shall see, aging in place can create disequilibrium, in some cases impeding the individual's ability to achieve a satisfactory balance between autonomy and security needs.

A. Unplanned Ordinary Communities

About 85 to 88% of all older people live in ordinary homes in ordinary communities; 75% of this group own their own homes (Lawton & Hoover, 1981). For the majority of older people who are not physically impaired, such housing clearly affords the maximal range of autonomy and security. Many observers (Altman & Gauvain, 1981; O'Bryant, 1982; Rowles, 1984; Rubinstein, 1989) have noted that home affords the freedom to allocate space, to decide what behavior should occur when, to avoid public scrutiny, and other functions that clearly represent psychological autonomy and efficacious action. On the other hand, home is also a shelter from the elements, a haven from crime, and a venue for interpersonal contact, relaxation, and other security-inducing activity. Thus maximum options are available for creating one's preferred mix of autonomy and security. Incongruence arises primarily where reduced competence creates excess demand for coping with environmental barriers to performance of everyday activities. Yet even very impaired people may justify remaining in their homes in terms of their freedom to retain some level of control there.

B. Adapted Housing

One response to the reduced security consequent to impairment is modification of existing private housing to meet changing needs. Struyk (1987), using data from the 1978 Annual Housing Survey, estimated that of households headed by an individual over 65 and in which at least one elderly member had health or mobility limitations, about 10% had been modified in some way. Handrails and grab bars were by far the most common addition; less frequent adaptations were made to accommodate wheelchair access and sensory deficits. However, the modal number of adaptations was one, and about 865,000 households that could benefit from such modifications had none. Using the same data set, Newman (1985) concluded that 17% of elderly who suffer significant mobility limitations inhabit dwellings that do not meet HUD standards—a figure almost twice the 9.9% rate for persons who have no such limitations. These and similar figures have prompted Struyk and others (Steinfeld, 1987; Pynoos, Cohen, Davis, & Bernhardt, 1987) to suggest that as federal monies for constructing new housing for older people continue to shrink, existing funds may usefully be funneled into improvement and modification of existing homes to accommodate needs of residents as they age in place.

C. Planned Independent Housing

This is an ill-defined category of environments distinguished by the fact that they were planned without supportive services and intended to house fully independent older people. Almost all of the 600,000 elderly occupied federal public housing units, the majority of other federally assisted housing programs, and the great bulk of all privately developed retirement villages and new towns fall into this category. Because they are age-segregated and subject to varying degrees of organizational control and managerial oversight, such environments afford somewhat less autonomy than does unplanned housing. A modicum of greater security is offered by a few basic built-in housing modifications, reasonably good physical security, and a social milieu of concern for beginning frailty. However, aging in place may require renegotiation of the initial congruence attained by originally healthy residents, generally due to increased security concerns. Kramek, Hoffman, and Baker's (1986) survey of a large retirement town revealed that complaints, although generally few, often focused on the lack of on-site medical facilities and in-home services. Ten percent of the respondents felt that their community was not well-suited to the needs of the very old, the frail, or those without adequate incomes.

The reality of aging in place was documented by Lawton, Moss, and Grimes (1985), who reexamined five housing sites 10 to 12 years after their initial study as newly occupied environments. Although health had declined only marginally, there had been an increase of 5 years in mean age and an overall decline in level of social activity or engagement. Lawton *et al.* estimated that 17% of tenants were impaired and in need of services but only 7% were both impaired and not receiving appropriate services. Thus, the segment whose aging in place had led to enforced autonomy with deprived security was small.

However, this is a group in major need—one that may grow as more people age in place in planned housing.

D. Alternative Housing

Over the past decade, a number of nontraditional forms of housing have appeared, including accessory apartments, small congregate facilities, and shared housing (see Eckert & Murrey, 1984, for a detailed discussion). Most such housing puts major constraints on autonomy but can under some conditions enhance security. For example, of 699 applicants to a San Diego home-sharing program, almost half of the homeowners providing housing cited need for assistance from the renter as a primary motive (Pritchard, 1983). Companionship was also an important motive for owners and some tenants. Given the inherent problems in asking people about preferences for situations they have not experienced, it is difficult to interpret survey estimates that 7% of older people were interested in home sharing and 8% in remodeling their homes to include an accessory apartment (Turner & Mangum, 1982), or that 12% would "consider" these alternatives (American Association for Retired Persons, 1987). Because many participants in shared housing are motivated by need for assistance, alternative housing is probably not a first choice for many people. However, for the small group of elderly who have a combination of high security need, low income, limited choices, and the willingness to compromise autonomy, alternative housing may be exactly the right choice.

E. Congregate Housing

Congregate housing is planned housing that offers a package of diverse supportive services, always including meals in a common dining room. No estimate of the number of such units is available. However, it appears that although only a tiny number of public housing sites and a minority of other subsidized housing falls into this category, a large but unknown amount of private for-profit and not-for-profit housing does.

On the autonomy–security continuum, security is probably consistently higher in congregate housing than in housing forms reviewed above, with autonomy being mildly compromised by an overseeing managerial style and ready availability of meals and other assistance. Earlier research indicated that people with higher security needs selectively chose congregate housing (Lawton, 1969); they benefitted psychologically but declined in some forms of autonomous behavior, such as interacting with the community outside the housing (Lawton, 1976). Of course, in some instances the simple desire for amenities and services may lead people to congregate housing with no implication of reduced capacity for an autonomous life-style. Thus, much congregate housing may have one subgroup of tenants with high autonomy and another with high security needs.

In a study of five congregate environments, Lawton et al. (1985) did find accommodation of the housing environment to the increased needs of aging tenants. They documented, in the absence of organized site-sponsored services, the development of a "patchwork of services" delivered to some tenants in poorly coordinated, sometimes overlapping form by local service agencies. Services were fairly well targeted to those tenants most in need and served as a useful (though improvable) proxy for site-sponsored services. It is, however, very unlikely in most cases that just the right level of security-inducing services will be targeted to a tenant population of just the right degree of competence, particularly given tenant diversity and differing rates of change in competence. Therefore, the major requirements for a viable housing setting are, first, a context that affords personal choice and control and second, a light, elective,

and selectively applied service provision system.

F. Continuing Care Retirement Communities (CCRCs)

Formerly referred to as "life care," this class of environments offers a continuum from moderately high autonomy to the utmost in security: from independent or congregate housing through full nursing home care (see Sherwood, Ruchlin, & Sherwood, 1989, for a complete description). Continuing care is the equivalent of a long-term care insurance policy: A large initial lump sum payment is supplemented by monthly maintenance fees that may vary with inflation but not with level of care. Thus, life care offers total reassurance that needs will be met as one ages in place. Other forms of CCRCs offer less total security because they charge for actual services received or allow upward rate readjustment for higher levels of care.

Despite the long history of CCRCs, most research on such housing is descriptive and focuses particularly on financial aspects of such care (Cohen, Tell, Greenberg & Wallack, 1987; Winkelvoss & Powell, 1984). Sherwood et al. (1989) showed definitively that clientele wait until very late in life to enter CCRCs (average age of entry in the late 70s) and are more likely than the population at large to be unmarried and childless. Given their age, CCRC residents also represent an elite in education, income, involvement and interests, and health. Thus it seems fair to characterize the goal of the CCRC as that of affirming autonomy, activity, and engagement to a degree substantially beyond that typical for this age group, while providing the security of knowing that future, greater needs will be met. The subjective aspect of the balance is illustrated by Sherwood et al.'s (1989) identification of a mix of reasons for desiring life care that reflected simultaneous desires for access to services and continued independence.

G. Residential Care Homes

This class of residences for older people who need some assistance but do not require intensive supervision or skilled nursing includes facilities variously referred to as board and care, domiciliary care, adult foster care, and the current generic type, residential care homes. These licensed facilities, which are usually (though not necessarily) relatively small, typically provide room and board plus personal care and some supervision. Surveys by Mor, Sherwood, and Gutkin (1986) and Newcomer and Grant (1989) indicate that there are around 300,000 such adult beds, although these authors view this as a probable underestimate. Unlicensed facilities are impossible to count, but they constitute another resource for people who fall short of needing full nursing home care (Eckert, Namazi, & Kahana, 1987).

H. Nursing Homes

Nursing homes remain a major resource for moderately to severely disabled elderly: On any given day, about 1.3 million elderly are living in skilled and intermediate nursing facilities (National Center for Health Statistics [NCHS], 1987). This figure, like earlier ones, represents only about 5% of all Americans over 65; however, because of the growth of the elderly population as a whole, it reflects a 17% increase in number of nursing home residents since 1977. Not surprisingly, the very old are overrepresented among nursing home residents: 22% of persons over age 85 live in such facilities, and this group accounted for much of the increase in nursing home occupancy between 1977 and 1985. Their presence is also at least partly responsible for the increased dependency of present nursing home residents relative to those of past decades, although functional dependency is greater even when age is held constant (NCHS, 1987).

One troubling trend is the apparent increase over the past several years in the number of elderly psychiatric patients occupying nursing home beds, attributable at least partly to the deinstitutionalization movement of the 1960s and 1970s. Currently, 3% of all nursing home residents were admitted from mental health facilities; for those under age 75, this figure rises to 7.6% (NCHS, 1987). Unfortunately, few skilled nursing facilities offer in-house psychological or psychiatric services. Findings such as these, along with epidemiological studies of the prevalence of psychiatric disorders in nursing homes (Parmelee, Katz, & Lawton, 1989), have led to increased concern with the social milieu of nursing homes and with provision of psychiatric and social services as well as physical health care.

Residential care and nursing home care represent the extreme of environmental accommodation to the security needs of impaired people. However, viewing security as residents' dominant need too often leads to the conclusion that no autonomy is possible. Research on personal control and institutional dependency belies this mistaken conclusion, again indicating that a dynamic tension, rather than an end state, exists between the two poles of the dialectic.

III. The Social Environments of Residential Types

Although the conceptual importance of other people as an aspect of the phenomenological environment has long been acknowledged (Lawton, 1982; Lewin, 1951), much previous work on environments of the aged treated the interpersonal realm superficially if at all. But thanks to renewed interest in social relationships and social support (Cohen & Syme, 1986), as well as to the central position given aspects of the social environment by Moos and Lemke in the last edition of this *Handbook* (Birren & Schaie, 1985), a closer look is being given interpersonal relationships of older people in special environments.

Much of this work has taken place in nursing homes, addressing patterns and quality of social ties both within and outside the facility. A number of studies have documented the generally low levels of interaction and lack of close relationships among residents (Noelker & Poulshock, 1980; Tesch & Whitbourne, 1981). Social integration is especially poor among the physically and cognitively impaired, for whom the limitations imposed by functional deficits are compounded by ostracism by more able residents (Stephens, Kinney, & McNeer, 1986). Furthermore, whereas relationships with residents and staff are few and only minimally related to well-being, ties with family and others outside the institution are strong positive correlates of adjustment to nursing home life (Parmelee, 1982).

Research in congregate apartments reveals somewhat higher but still relatively low rates of interaction among neighbors (Kaye & Monk, 1987). Over a 10-year span, five housing sites showed measurable decreases in amount of social interaction among residents (Lawton *et al.*, 1985); aging in place of both tenants and the housing community may have been responsible. Social stratification appears also to occur in congregate housing, leading to greater contact and social support among persons with similar functional abilities (Sheehan, 1986) and among demographic majorities (Kaye & Monk, 1987). Although social integration appears to be unrelated to family or friendship ties outside the residential milieu, at least one study suggests that among retirement community residents, neighbors may be preferred over relatives as sources of support (Sullivan, 1986).

The Social Environment of Institutions: A Threat to Autonomy?

Recent research and theory in this area have incorporated concepts of control outlined earlier. Stemming from early research on dependency (Kalish, 1969), a growing body of work attempts to describe and explain the interpersonal origins and reinforcement of psychological and behavioral helplessness among the elderly.

In their *social breakdown syndrome* model, Kuypers and Bengtson (1973) argued that normal decrements of aging, in combination with negative attitudes and stereotypes, place the elderly at particular risk of decreased sense of competence. A similar but more psychologically oriented view is offered by Langer, Rodin, and their colleagues. Early formulations (reviewed in Rodin, 1986), closely following that of Kuypers and Bengtson, addressed the negative implications of social labels (e.g., *old*, *sick*) and attributions upon social status, perceived control, and behavioral performance of the elderly. Institutional environments are presumed to exacerbate this problem (Langer & Avorn, 1982; White & Janson, 1986) due to the exigencies of care and residents' assumption of the sick role (Parsons, 1951). More recently, Langer and her colleagues (Piper & Langer, 1986) have suggested that the fact of institutionalization, along with the physical setting and the process of health care in nursing homes and similar environments, constitutes multiple cues indicating that the individual is in fact helpless. These cues, coupled with environmental overpredictability and lack of opportunities for autonomous behavior, may contribute to residents' "mindless" acceptance of, and behavior in accordance with, the implication that they are incompetent and dependent upon others. Thus, simply by doing their jobs, nursing home staff may unwittingly be contributing to the physical and psychological dependency of their charges.

A more sinister view of staff's role in fostering dependency is provided by Baltes and her colleagues (reviewed in Baltes & Reisenzein, 1986). Using behavioral observation techniques, Baltes has repeatedly demonstrated that whereas nursing home staff consistently reward dependency in self-care activities, they do not respond or may even terminate interaction when residents display competent, self-determinative behavior. Although other types of constructive behaviors (e.g., reading, playing games with other residents) may receive positive attention, such rewards are irregular at best. Further analysis (Baltes, Kindermann, Reisenzein, & Schmid, 1987) indicates that this is not due to help seeking by the older person; more than 80% of all dependent self-care behaviors were categorized as compliance or cooperation with directives of staff. Comparing these data with observations of institutionalized children, Baltes and Reisenzein (1986) concluded that residents' old age per se, rather than the desire to complete self-care routines quickly or efficiently, may be the primary factor underlying staff's dependency-inducing reward contingencies.

Of course, these kinds of behavior cannot be attributed to any direct or ill-intentioned attempt by staff directly to undermine residents' feelings of self-worth. But whereas health care staff favor patients whose disorders are treatable and whose behavior is manageable, many of the health problems of aging are by implication untreatable and for staff, manageability translates as passivity and dependency (Timko & Rodin, 1985). Timko and Rodin further cite staff burnout as a contributor to their reinforcement of dependency: Having observed the futility of rehabilitative efforts in "curing" age-related decline, staff may be blinded to what can be done to help aged patients maintain and hone existing capabilities.

Despite this compelling evidence that dependency is reinforced in these settings, one must recognize that providing security is the major goal of institutional care. Naturally, staff behavior leading to presumed security will tend to be reinforced. Thus, righting the balance to afford residents autonomy and control where appropriate may well be approached through staff training designed to increase awareness of the continuous and dialectic nature of autonomy and security. The work of deCharms (1976) with elementary-school teachers indicates that such interventions might lead not only to direct changes in staff's attitudes and behavior but also to "trickle-down" increments in residents' sense of autonomy. Unfortunately, no such intervention has yet been undertaken with an elderly institutional population.

Finally, it must be noted that our understanding of the intricacies of social relationships in age-segregated environments remains somewhat limited. A number of studies of aged living independently in the community have yielded in-depth analyses of social network structure, function, and support among that population (Kahn & Antonucci, 1980). Unfortunately, because these perspectives and techniques have not been systematically extended to specially designed environments, much current knowledge of social ties in such settings remains couched in somewhat rudimentary terms of number or frequency of contacts.

IV. How Can Empirical Research Accommodate the Complexity of Person–Environment Relations?

The foregoing review of research that has examined elements of the person, the social environment, and the physical setting makes clear the complexity of the total system. Studies that have focused on one or a few personal and environmental attributes have provided useful knowledge but usually conclude by identifying multiple additional factors that need to be considered as possible conditioning factors. If we conceive of person–environment relationships as being arranged in hierarchical order of complexity, the specificity of a relationship confirmed on one level may not be preserved on the next. Thus the units of causal relationships at lower levels are frequently transformed into more complex units that include the lower level units but require new concepts or methods. Inevitably, such units invoke more abstract concepts and become more difficult to operationalize. This section will use a methodological, rather than substantive, focus to review research that has attempted to deal with several levels of complexity in person–environment (P–E) relations. Of course, choice of research method bears a rough relationship to the environmental scale of the phenomenon under study, and every level of complexity has its own potential for generating useful knowledge. But we shall argue that the more complex levels require more global concepts and that, for the present, qualitative approaches to empirical research are better able to deal with such concepts.

Research that attempts to operationalize discrete aspects of person and environment in order to predict some hypothesized outcome may be referred to as *interactional*. Interactionism thus deals with person–environment stimulus–response patterns, often in combination; sometimes a combination results in a new level of complexity, such as person–environment congruence.

By contrast, another environmental perspective moves beyond the concept of interaction toward what Altman and Rogoff (1987) term the *transactional* perspective as a more appropriate representation of P–E processes. According to Altman and Rogoff, the transactional approach to psychology is the study of "changing relations among psychological and environmental aspects of holistic unities . . . composed not of separate elements but [of] a *confluence* of inseparable factors that depend upon one another for their very definition and meaning" (p. 24). Thus personal and environmental processes are impossible to separate at this level, and the only appropriate unit of study is the reciprocal P–E transaction. The transactional model further stresses the dynamic, changing quality of P–E relations rather than static characteristics of individuals and their physical worlds. The underlying assumption is that as the individual reacts to (or acts on) his or her environment, not only the person and/or the environment but the relation between the two is changed. This focus on change highlights a third emphasis—time as a crucial variable in the P–E system.

A. Interactional Research

The great bulk of research in environment and aging has been done in interactional form. Indeed, there is no substitute for such research, and there can be no call for abandonment of these nonholistic conceptions of person and environment. Human factors research is the prototype of microlevel study, where the stimulus–response (S–R) paradigm has considerable validity. A typical approach is to identify an environmental variable that bears some predictable relationship to a behavioral or subjective outcome. Czaja, Hammond, and Drury (1982), for example, determined the location and the precipitating environmental trigger for a large number of accidents experienced by older people. Although their data did not detail all possible causal factors, at least a partial depiction of the increased risk associated with some environmental features was derived. (A review of human factors research is found in Chapter 26 of this *Handbook*.)

It is also possible to design S–R research that relates to larger and more complex aspects of the environment. For example, Hunt and Roll (1987) compared older groups without knowledge of a (nursing home) building to those who had had either a site visit or exposure only to a model with simulated tours (Hunt & Roll, 1987). The simulation group performed best by several criteria; the site visit group did less well but better than controls. Another nursing home study simultaneously altered the social and physical arrangement of activity and mealtime environments (Gotestam & Melin, 1988). Improvement in observed communication and eating behavior was observed in a multiple-baseline experimental versus control group study.

Housing satisfaction has been a common dependent variable in interactional research. The joint contributions of various person factors and environmental factors to housing satisfaction recently have been confirmed in studies of community populations (Butterfield & Weidemann, 1987; Carp & Carp, 1981). In one such study, a new class of interactional variable, stimulus seeking, was included among predictors of housing satisfaction (Golant, 1982). Though this scale measures a characteristic of the person, it also has the external environment as its referent. Interestingly, older people who expressed a greater need for novelty and new kinds of stimulation were less satisfied with their housing. Another contribution was made by O'Bryant (1982), who developed a scale of subjective attitudes toward home ownership that yielded four factors: competence, family traditions or memories, status, and cost versus comfort tradeoff. Although these are subjective rather than objective environmental attributes, the fact that they added considerably to the variance in satisfaction accounted for by objective housing deficits and personal characteristics give impetus to pursue the concept of the psychological functions of home.

Two other studies are noteworthy because, unlike most research in this area, they used physical environmental attributes as predictors of satisfaction. Lawton (1980) used a set of objective housing descriptors and indicators of housing deficiencies from the Annual Housing Survey as predictors of housing satisfaction of a national sample of 12,000 older households. Although many were nonpredictive or redundant, about 20% of the variance in satisfaction was predicted by such attributes as number of bathrooms and heating characteristics.

Carp and Carp (1982), who refer to characteristics that can be determined by observation and a minimum of interpretation as *technical environmental assessments*, have been most active in attempting to organize and measure the objective environment. They confirmed that scales based on such attributes were substantially related to a series of subjectively evaluated attributes of the environment. In a later study, Carp and Christensen (1986a) formed 16 multi-item, objectively countable technical environmental assessment instruments (TEAIs). With personal factors controlled, TEAIs relevant to the needs for harmavoidance, noxavoidance and affiliation accounted for 28% of the housing satisfaction of 88 community resident older women. TEAIs were also significant predictors of neighborhood satisfaction. In another report (Carp & Christensen, 1986b), similar scales relating to the local area, in concert with the housing TEAIs, accounted directly for variance in two indicators of psychological well-being.

A different genre of interactional research inquires descriptively about a very broad range of personal and environmental phenomena. The Annual Housing Surveys (since 1983 the biennial American Housing Survey) have been reported in many secondary analyses of older community residents' housing (for example, Newman, 1985; Struyk, 1987). Large samples of other housing types such as board and care of domiciliaries, foster homes, congregate housing, continuing care retirement communities, public housing, and residential homes have been studied with varying mixes of data relating to residents, administration and staffing, organizational environment, financial aspects, and turnover (see Lawton, 1989b for a review). Unfortunately, the physical aspects of these environments have been less comprehensively detailed; additionally, the interactions between person and environment are likely to be addressed by implication rather than directly. In some instances these data sets are available to other investigators for secondary analysis. All of these housing forms, plus others even more neglected, such as mobile home parks (Haley, 1986) and the various forms of alternative housing (Eckert & Murrey, 1984), are important resources for some subgroups. Thus, the need is clear for further, longitudinal research to capture the processes of aging in place in these settings.

A particular type of interactional study attempts to specify desirable environmental features by studying people's subjective preferences or by observing and evaluating the behavioral outcomes of environmental variations. Because the data tend to be descriptive or unidimensionally evaluative, the introduction of qualitative analytic methods is necessary to integrate such data. Two studies, by Duffy, Bailey, Beck, and Barker (1986) and Brennan et al. (1988), are the most sophisticated of recent user preference studies because they allow us to contrast preferences of older clients with those of experts. Results are sobering in showing low expressed need by older consumers for features that experts judged to be essential according to person–environment principles, but the meaning of this lack of agreement is ambiguous. Brennan et al. (1988) point out that older consumers may wish not to express preferences that deviate from existing features (which were strongly criticized by design experts), or they may actively reject making environmental concessions to their own disability. It may also be that because of their training, experts possess an environmental awareness that many older research subjects lack.

Many publications contain useful lists of physical features, amenities, and services generated from preference studies of older subjects (cf. Brennan et al., 1988; Regnier, 1987). Some rely equally or even exclusively on direct observation of older users of residential or nursing home environments (Peace, Kellaher, & Willcocks, 1982; Steinfeld, 1987). Some home design alterations made by older people themselves have been described by Saperstein, Moleski, and Lawton (1985), Pynoos et al. (1987), and Windley and Scheidt (1980). There are now enough such studies to warrant some attempt to determine the range of consensus among different observers and integrate the findings for design application. Zeisel and his colleagues, in their study of low-rise buildings (Zeisel, Epp, & Demos, 1977) and their later one of mid-rise buildings (Zeisel, Welch, Epp, & Demos, 1983), produced usable compendia of design-relevant directives generated by an expert panel. Each expert judged whether a potential directive was based firmly on empirical research findings, on generally consistent findings, simply on consensual conjecture, or was without basis.

Several design guides published in the past 5 years assembled state-of-the-art consensus in a less formal manner than did Zeisel et al. 1977, 1983), but they carry the applied science further in invoking theory-based rationales for their suggestions (Carstens, 1985; Hoglund, 1986). In nursing home design, Calkins (1988) used conceptual and applied knowledge regarding senile dementia to treat the design of special care units for such patients systematically for several functional requirements (for example, self-maintenance or social behavior) and space types (halls, bedrooms, and so on). Emphasis on the large proportion of people living in unplanned community housing and particularly the confluence of functional impairments and diminished housing quality (Newman, 1985) has led to some highly specific guides to home improvement useful to both the service sector and older occupants themselves (Canada Mortgage and Housing Corporation, 1987). These guides and related articles tend to focus more on safety, perception, and cognition of the environment, and to some extent on activities of daily living, and less on more complex activities such as time use, social behavior, or aesthetic considerations.

B. Transactional Research

Qualitative research in the transactional realm is relatively sparse. The research of Carp and Carp (1984), discussed earlier, is a good example of transactionalism. Their operationalizations of the many elements and subelements of a very complex model have confirmed the relations between personal needs and objective environment (Carp & Christensen, 1986a,b) in determining psychological outcomes.

The research program of Moos, Lemke, and associates was recently reviewed in integrative form (Moos, Lemke, & David, 1987). These authors conceive of the residential environment as an open system with components of physical and architectural features, policy and program factors, aggregate resident and staff characteristics, and the social climate of subjective attitudes and goals (such dimensions as cohesion, independence, physical comfort). Much of their research has demonstrated the interdependence among these systems. The environmental system, in turn, is related to many factors in the personal system, and their covariation under differing conditions is associated with stability and change over time. Thus, empirical research has demonstrated consistency among environmental features and their relationship to personal and social aspects of sheltering environments. For example, the activities of residents of such environments were predicted by differential combinations of personal competence and environmental features in ways predicted by both the Lawton and Nahe-

mow (1973) competence–press model and the Carp & Carp (1984) complementarity/congruence model (Lemke & Moos, 1989). These authors also developed measures of residential quality (for example, comfort, security, staff richness). They found considerable variance, with larger facilities and those with nonprofit sponsors tending to be of higher quality. This stream of research comes closest to the transactional ideal in emphasizing the covariation of a variety of aspects of the environment. On the other hand, although individual behavioral outcomes have been studied, mental health outcomes have not been well represented.

A thoroughly transactional environmental analysis was reported by Streib and his colleagues (LaGreca, Streib, & Folts, 1985; Streib, Folts, & LaGreca, 1985; Streib, LaGreca, & Folts, 1986). They studied 36 retirement communities, chosen to represent a range and variety of places in several favorite retirement states, using primarily qualitative interviews with residents, staff, and local neighbors or municipal officials, as well as archival materials. Their focus was on the community as a whole; personal outcomes were represented only in aggregates such as the "viability" of the entire community or its ability to meet threats to stability arising from either external or internal forces. Results indicated that ownership of the land was a critical determining characteristic of the life history of communities. Tenant-owned communities, when stressed, generally have their stability threatened by internal conflicts over governance or policies. Developer-owned communities experience threats more when change of owners or owners' goals raises other issues such as concern over the continued age homogeneity of the community (LaGreca et al., 1985).

Another report focused on autonomy and decision making (Streib et al., 1985), showing conclusively that autonomy was higher in tenant-owned communities, particularly the older ones. Streib *et al.* found little evidence that autonomy was strongly associated with community well-being. They emphasize that stability is a more evident need and suggest that autonomy may be latent: That is, it may be the potential for, rather than actual exercise of, autonomy that is important. However, they also note that the aging in place of the population in the resident-owned community is a threat to self-government; thus, one measure needed to ensure viability is an admission policy that brings in a stream of younger and more able new residents. Streib's research thus illustrates the congruence of personal and community dynamics on an aggregate level. This research throws into relief how social environmental forces may be similar or dissimilar to individual needs, or in turn, congruent or incongruent with individuals' preferred mixes of opportunities for autonomy and security.

Despite the centrality of the person as an element in the transaction, the research reviewed here has told us little about the relationships between personal, social, and physical space. Are there parallels in the interior of the person to the constriction of social space, as exemplified in protected living situations or in reductions in geographic locomotion, that come about as the result of retirement, income loss, or physical illness? Behavior, subjective perspective, and physical space expand and contract as health and life circumstances change. This is understandable within the concept of "life space" as articulated many years ago by Lewin (1951). A few very illuminating studies reflecting this concept have recently appeared, all using qualitative individual case methods. The meaning of home was studied by Rubinstein (1989) among a small group of elderly community residents. He observed that people created meaning in their everyday lives through socially based conceptions of how their home environments should be ordered and how the home is related to personal history, life course, and the body (i.e., comfort, self-care). Extensive use of case material traced the processes by which person and environment literally form one another. Kalymun (1985) was concerned with the allocation of space in the home among members of multigenerational households. Her descriptions of the parallel nature of social exchanges and spatial negotiations within families illustrate above all the unity of such household P–E transactions. Lawton (1985) and colleagues (Saperstein *et al.*, 1985) observed the proactive behavior of highly impaired older people, some of whom arranged their grossly limited physical worlds in a way that maximized the amount of information, stimulation, and control of their space. These individuals' "control centers" consisted of a well-chosen chair placed in the living room to monitor the front door and view of the street from the window, with objects relevant to continued engagement (e.g., television, letters or photos, food, medicine) placed within hand's reach. These observations suggest the need for quantitative research to determine the personal, social, and environmental contexts in which control centers are and are not created.

Finally, the most complete program of such idiographic research has been performed by Rowles, a geographer. His study of older people in a small town of Appalachia (Rowles, 1983, 1984) illustrated how changing ability to participate physically in a setting resulted in gradual constriction of spatial range. In turn, cognitions of space were reduced to a point where the perceived zone of "intense involvement" became limited to the home and the "surveillance zone," the visual range that could be monitored from the home. Finally, the affective side of environment is represented by attachments to places, differentiating the "inside" zones of involvement (including those from the past that are kept alive by environmental fantasy) from those "outside" with lesser degrees of affective involvement.

In summary, research that captures the complexity of the person–environment transaction is in a very early stage. The type of cataloging that characterizes housing surveys, preference studies, and design guides is a necessary beginning. Moos, Streib, and others have shown that traditional social science methods can be applied to transactional research, although the resources required to gather such large amounts of data are substantial. The qualitative approach has best succeeded so far in allowing important new concepts to emerge, such as environmental fantasy and the control center.

The risks of qualitative research need no recounting. Little qualitative research has subjected its important constructs to even basic reliability analysis. In keeping with the goals of both fortifying consensuality and amplifying the contributions of different disciplines to our knowledge, continuation of such research by teams of two or more observers seems indicated. This is a first step that with multiple observers or coding from tapes is totally feasible without destroying the opportunity to distill meaning from a very broad person–environment field.

V. Conclusion

We stated at the beginning of this chapter that research on special environments for the aged stands at a crossroad. That crossroad has been reached through a confluence of factors: theoretical developments in the areas of personal control and person–environment congruence; design and policy emphases on safety and security; increased focus on the social environment and, perhaps most influential, changing conceptions of the nature of

person–environment relations. In many ways, the environmental psychology of late life faces today a crisis similar to that acknowledged by social psychologists in the late 1960s (McGuire, 1967). Calls for more holistic and more integrative theory are contraposed against a pressing need for practical design guides. The generalizability of research conducted in institutional "laboratories" to the majority of older community residents has been called into question; yet few large-scale studies of unplanned housing have examined person–environment relations at the individual level. Researchers recognize that traditional research paradigms and methodologies may be inadequate but are reluctant to borrow from other, unfamiliar perspectives and disciplines.

There are no ready solutions to these dilemmas, but recognition that they exist creates rich opportunities for continued evaluation and development of the field. As control theory continues to be developed and refined, it will, we hope, enjoy further integration with existing models of person–environment fit; here, differentiation of active from passive control and of self-efficacy from environmental responsivity seem especially promising areas. The leads provided by control-relevant research on the social environment of residential settings are also fertile territory, particularly in terms of interventive efforts.

But perhaps the most exciting prospects for innovation lie in the area of methodology, drawing specifically from the diversity of perspectives that have begun to permeate research in this area. We see no reason why the constructs derived from qualitative study should not be subjected to quantitative use, as have some of those used by Moos and Streib. We also find it perfectly reasonable that the same data generated to explore human action in transactional style can also be used to test more traditional linear hypotheses using outcomes such as behavior or subjective well-being. None of the qualitative studies noted have been longitudinal, a design necessary for outcomes most appropriately to be assessed. Thus whether the focus is the autonomy–security dialectic, the social environment, or the transactional context in its broadest form, a longitudinal design with a mix of qualitative and quantitative methods that allows person and environment to be measured both separately and transactionally offers the best opportunity to move the field beyond its current languishing state.

References

Altman, I., & Gauvain, M. (1981). A cross-cultural and dialectic analysis of homes. In L. Liben, A. Patterson, & N. Newcome (Eds.), *Spatial representation and behavior across the life span* (pp. 283–320). New York: Academic Press.

Altman, I., & Rogoff, B. (1987). World reviews in psychology: Trait, interactional, organismic, and transactional perspectives. In D. Stokols & I. Altman (Eds.), *Handbook of environmental psychology* (Vol. I, pp. 7–40). New York: Wiley.

American Association of Retired Persons (1987). *Understanding senior housing.* Washington, DC: Author.

Arling, G., Harkins, E. B., & Capitman, G. A. (1986). Institutionalization and personal control: A panel study of impaired older people. *Research on Aging, 8,* 38–56.

Baltes, M. M., Kindermann, T., Reisenzein, R., & Schmid, U. (1987). Further observational data on the behavioral and social world of institutions for the aged. *Psychology and Aging, 2,* 390–403.

Baltes, M. M., & Reisenzein, R. (1986). The social world in long-term care institutions: Psychosocial control toward dependency? In M. M. Baltes & P. B. Baltes (Eds.), *The psychology of control and aging* (pp. 315–343). Hillsdale, NJ: Erlbaum.

Baltes, M. M., & Wahl, H. W. (1987). Dependence in aging. In L. L. Carstensen & B. A. Edelstein (Eds.), *Handbook of clinical gerontology* (pp. 204–221). New York: Pergamon.

Bandura, A. (1982). Self-efficacy mechanism in human agency. *American Psychologist, 37,* 122–147.

Brennan, P. L., Moos, R. H., & Lemke, S. (1988). Preferences of older adults and experts for physical and architectural features of group living facilities. *Gerontologist, 28,* 84–90.

Butterfield, D., & Weidemann, S. (1987). Housing satisfaction of the elderly. In V. Regnier & J. Pynoos (Eds.), *Housing the aging: Design directives and policy considerations* (pp. 133–152). New York: Elsevier.

Calkins, M. (1988). *Design for dementia.* Owings Mills, MD: National Health Publ.

Canada Mortgage and Housing Corporation (1987). *Specific disabilities and home modifications for independing living.* Ottowa: Author.

Carp, F. M. (1987). Environment and aging. In D. Stokols & I. Altman (Eds.), *Handbook of environmental psychology* (Vol. I, pp. 329–360). New York: Wiley.

Carp, F. M., & Carp, A. (1980). Person–environment congruence and sociability. *Research on Aging, 2,* 395–415.

Carp, F. M., & Carp, A. (1981). Age, deprivation and personal competence: Effects on satisfaction. *Research on Aging, 3,* 279–298.

Carp, F. M., & Carp, A. (1982). A role for technical assessment in perceptions of environmental quality and well-being. *Journal of Environmental Psychology, 2,* 171–191.

Carp, F. M., & Carp, A. (1984). A complementarity/congruence model of well-being or mental health for the community elderly. In I. Altman, M. P. Lawton, & J. Wohlwill (Eds.), *Elderly people and the environment* (pp. 279–336). New York: Plenum.

Carp, F. M., & Christensen, D. L. (1986a). Technical environment assessment predictors of residential satisfaction: A study of elderly women living alone. *Research on Aging, 8,* 269–287.

Carp, F. M. & Christensen, D. L. (1986b). Older women living alone: Technical environmental assessment predictors of psychological well-being. *Research on Aging, 8* 497–425.

Carstens, D. Y. (1985). *Site planning and design for the elderly.* New York: Van Nostrand-Reinhold.

Carstensen, L., & Whitbourne, S. (1978). *Variations in locus of control and morale by institutional totality in an elderly sample.* Paper presented at the annual meeting of the

Gerontological Society of America, Dallas, November.

Cohen, M. A., Tell, E. J., Greenberg, J. N., & Wallack, S. S. (1987). The financial capacity of the elderly to insure for long-term care. *Gerontologist*, *27*, 494–502.

Cohen, S., & Syme, L. (1986). *Social support and health*. Orlando, FL: Academic Press.

Czaja, S. J., Hammond, K., & Drury, C. G. (1982). *Accidents and aging*. Final report. Buffalo, NY: BOSTI.

deCharms, R. (1976). *Enhancing motivation in the classroom*. New York: Halstead.

Deci, E. C. (1980). *The psychology of self-deter-mination*. Lexington, MA: Heath.

Duffy, M., Bailey, S., Beck, B., & Barker, D. G. (1986). Preferences in nursing home design: A comparison of residents, administrators, and designers. *Environment and Behavior*, *18*, 246–257.

Eckert, J. K., & Murrey, M. (1984). Alternative modes of living for the elderly. In I. Altman, M. P. Lawton, & J. Wohlwill (Eds.), *Human behavior and the environment: The elderly and the physical environment*. New York: Plenum.

Eckert, J. K., Namazi, K., & Kahana, E. (1987). Unlicensed board and care homes: An extra-familial living arrangement for the elderly. *Journal of Cross-Cultural Gerontology*, *2*, 377–393.

Golant, S. M. (1982). Individual differences un-derlying the dwelling satisfaction of the el-derly. *Journal of Social Issues*, *38*, 121–133.

Gotestam, K. G., & Melin, L. (1988). Improving well-being for patients with senile dementia by minor changes in the ward environment. In L. Levi (Ed.), *Society, stress, and disease* (Vol. 5, *Old Age*, pp. 295–297). New York: Oxford University Press.

Gurin, P., & Brim, O. G., Jr. (1984). Change in self in adulthood: The example of sense of control. In P. B. Baltes & O. G. Brim, Jr. (Eds.), *Life-span development and behavior* (Vol. 6, pp. 281–334). New York: Academic Press.

Haley, B. A. (1986). Are mobiles a solution to the housing problems of low-income elders? In R. J. Newcomer, M. P. Lawton, & T. O. Byerts (Eds.), *Housing an aging society* (pp. 217–228). New York: Van Nostrand Rein-hold.

Hoglund, D. (1986). *The intangible qualities of housing*. New York: Van Nostrand Reinhold.

Howell, S. (1980). *Design for aging*: *Patterns of use*. Cambridge, MA: MIT Press.

Hunt, M. D., & Roll, M. K. (1987). Simulation in familiarizing older people with an un-known building. *Gerontologist*, *27*, 169–175.

Kahana, E. (1982). A congruence model of per-son-environment interaction. In M. P. Law-ton, P. G. Windley, & T. O. Byerts (Eds.), *Aging and the environment: Theoretical ap-proaches* (pp. 97–121). New York: Springer.

Kahn, R. L., & Antonucci, T. C. (1980). Con-voys over the life course: Attachment, roles and social support. In P. B. Baltes & O. G. Brim (Eds.), *Life-span development and be-havior* (Vol. 3, pp. 254–286). New York: Aca-demic Press.

Kalish, R. A. (1969). *The dependencies of old people*. Ann Arbor, MI: Institute of Geron-tology, University of Michigan.

Kalymun, M. (1985). *The intergenerational ecology of households*. Paper presented at the annual meeting of the Environmental Design Research Association, Atlanta, April.

Kates, R. W., & Wohlwill, J. F. (Eds.) (1966). Man's response to the physical environment. *Journal of Social Issues*, *22*(4).

Kaye, L. W., & Monk, A. (1987). *Social network reciprocity in enriched housing for the aged*. Paper presented at the annual meeting of the Gerontological Society of America, Wash-ington, DC, November.

Kleemeier, R. W. (1959). Behavior and the orga-nization of the bodily and the external en-vironment. In J. E. Birren (Ed.), *Handbook of aging and the individual* (pp. 400–451). Chi-cago: University of Chicago Press.

Kramek, L. M., Hoffman, T. J., & Baker, M. W. (1986). *Stability and change in the Sun City retirement community: Findings from the 1984 follow-up study*. Tucson, AZ: Arizona Long Term Care Gerontology Center.

Kuhl, J. (1986). Aging and models of control: The hidden costs of wisdom. In M. M. Baltes and P. B. Baltes (Eds.), *The psychology of con-trol and aging* (pp. 1–34). Hillsdale, NJ: Erlbaum.

Kuypers, J. A., & Bengtson, V. L. (1973). Social breakdown and competence. *Human Devel-opment*, *16* 181–201.

Lachman, M. E. (1986). Locus of control in aging research: A case for multi-dimensional and domain-specific assessment. *Psychology and Aging*, *1*, 34–40.

LaGreca, A. J., Streib, G. F., & Folts, W. E. (1985). Retirement communities and their life stages. *Journal of Gerontology, 40*, 211–218.

Langer, E. J., & Avorn, J. (1982). Impact of the psychosocial environment of the elderly on behavioral and health outcomes. In R. D. Chellis, J. F. Seagle, Jr., & B. M. Seagle (Eds.), *Congregate housing for older people* (pp. 15–25). Lexington, MA: Lexington Books.

Langer, E. J., & Rodin, J. (1975). The effects of choice and enhanced personal responsibility for the aged: A field experiment in an institutional setting. *Journal of Personality and Social Psychology, 34*, 191–198.

Lawton, M. P. (1969). Supportive services in the context of the housing environment. *Gerontologist, 9*, 15–19.

Lawton, M. P. (1976). The relative impact of congregate and traditional housing on elderly tenants. *Gerontologist, 16*, 237–242.

Lawton, M. P. (1978). The impact of environment on aging and behavior. In R. L. Binstock & E. Shanas (Eds.), *Handbook of the psychology of aging* (2nd ed., pp. 276–301). New York: Van Nostrand Reinhold.

Lawton, M. P. (1980). Housing the elderly: Residential quality and residential satisfaction. *Research on Aging, 2*, 309–328.

Lawton, M. P. (1982). Competence, environmental press, and the adaptation of older people. In M. P. Lawton, P. G. Windley, & T. O. Byerts (Eds.), *Aging and the environment: Theoretical approaches* (pp. 33–59). New York: Springer.

Lawton, M. P. (1985). The elderly in context: Perspectives from environmental psychology and gerontology *Environment and Behavior, 17*, 501–519.

Lawton, M. P. (1989a). Behavior-relevant ecological factors. In K. W. Schaie & C. Schooler (Eds.), *Social structure and aging: Psychological processes* (pp. 57–78). Hillsdale, NJ: Erlbaum.

Lawton, M. P. (1989b). Knowledge resources and gaps in housing for the aged. In D. Tillson & C. J. Fahey (Eds.), *Support of the frail elderly in residential environments*. Glenview, IL: Scott Foresman (in press).

Lawton, M. P., & Hoover, S. (Eds.) (1981). *Community housing choices for older Americans*. New York: Springer.

Lawton, M. P., Moss, M., & Grimes, M. (1985).

The changing service needs of older tenants in planned housing. *Gerontologist, 25*, 258–264.

Lawton, M. P., Moss, M., & Moles, E. (1984). The suprapersonal neighborhood context of older people: Age heterogenity and well-being. *Environment and Behavior, 16*, 89–109.

Lawton, M. P., & Nahemow, L. (1973). Ecology and the aging process. In C. Eisdorfer & M. P. Lawton (Eds.), *Psychology of adult development and aging* (pp. 619–674). Washington, DC: American Psychological Association.

Lemke, S., & Moos, R. H. (1989). Personal and environmental determinants of activity involvement among elderly residents of congregate facilities. *Journal of Gerontology, 44*, S139–S148.

Lewin, K. (1951). *Field theory in social science.* New York: Harper.

Lowenthal, M. F. (1977). Toward a sociological theory of change in adulthood and old age. In J. E. Birren & K. W. Schaie (Eds.), *Handbook of the psychology of aging.* New York: Van Nostrand-Reinhold.

Mancini, J. (1980). Effects of health and income on control orientation and life satisfaction among aged public housing residents. *International Journal of Aging and Human Development, 12*, 215–220.

McGuire, W. J. (1967). Some impending reorientations in social psychology: Some thoughts provoked by Kenneth Ring. *Journal of Experimental Social Psychology, 3*, 124–139.

Moos, R. H., & Lemke, S. (1985). Specialized living environments for people. In J. E. Birren & K. W. Schaie (Eds.), *Handbook of the psychology of aging,* (pp. 864–889). New York: Van Nostrand Reinhold.

Moos, R. H., Lemke, S., & David, T. G. (1987). Priorities for design and management in residential settings for the elderly. In V. Regnier & J. Pynoos (Eds.), *Housing the aged: Design directives and policy considerations* (pp. 179–205). New York: Elsevier.

Mor, V., Sherwood, S., & Gutkin, C. (1986). A national study of residential care for the aged. *Geronotologist, 26*, 405–417.

Morganti, J. B., Nehrke, M. F., Hulicka, I. M., & Cataldo, J. F. (1988). Life-span differences in life satisfaction, self-concept, and locus of control. *International Journal of Aging and Human Development*, **26**, 45–56.

National Center for Health Statistics (1987). Use of nursing homes by the elderly: Preliminary data from the 1985 National Nursing Home Survey. *Advance data from vital and health statistics* No. 135. DHHS Pub. No. (PHS) 87–1250. Hyattsville, MD: Public Health Service.

Newcomer, R., & Grant, L. (1989). Residential care facilities: Understanding their role and improving their effectiveness. In D. Tillson & C. J. Fahey (Eds.). *Support of the frail elderly in residential environments*. Glenview, IL: Scott Foresman (in press).

Newman, S. J. (1985). Housing and long-term care: The suitability of the elderly's housing to the provision of in-home services. *Gerontologist*, **25**, 35–40.

Noelker, L. S., & Poulshock, S. W. (1980). *Intimacy: Factors affecting its development among members of a home for the aged*. Paper presented at the annual meeting of the American Sociological Association, New York, August.

O'Bryant, S. (1982). The value of home to older persons: Relationship to housing satisfaction. *Research on Aging*, **2**, 349–363.

Parmelee, P. A. (1982). Social contacts, social instrumentality, and adjustment of institutionalized aged. *Research on Aging*, **4**, 269–280.

Parmelee, P. A., Katz, I. R., & Lawton, M. P. (1989). Depression among institutionalized aged: Assessment and prevalence estimation. *Journal of Gerontology*, **41**, M22–M29.

Parsons, T. C. (1951). Social structure and dynamic process: The case of modern medical practice. In T. C. Parsons (Ed.), *The social system*. New York: Free Press.

Peace, S. M., Kellaher, L. A., & Willcocks, D. M. (1982). *A balanced life? A consumer study of residential life in a hundred local authority old people's homes*. Research Report No. 14. Polytechnic of North London, London.

Peterson, C., & Seligman, M. E. P. (1984). Causal explanations as a risk factor for depression: Theory and evidence. *Psychological Review*, **91**, 347–374.

Piper, A. I., & Langer, E. J. (1986). Aging and mindful control. In M. M. Baltes & P. B. Baltes (Eds.), *The psychology of control and aging* (pp. 71–89). Hillsdale, NJ: Erlbaum.

Pritchard, D. C. (1983). The art of matchmaking: A case study in shared housing. *Gerontologist*, **23**, 174–179.

Pynoos, J., Cohen, E., Davis, L. G., & Bernhardt, S. (1987). Home modifications: Improvements that extend independence. In V. Regnier & J. Pynoos (Eds.), *Housing the aged: Design directives and policy considerations* (pp. 277–303). New York: Elsevier.

Regnier, V. (1987). Programming congregate housing: The preferences of upper-income elderly. In V. Regnier & J. Pynoos (Eds.), *Housing the aged: Design directives and policy considerations* (pp. 207–226). New York: Elsevier.

Rodin, J. (1986). Health, control and aging. In M. M. Baltes & P. B. Baltes (Eds.), *The psychology of control and aging* (pp. 139–165). Hillsdale, NJ: Erlbaum.

Rodin, J., & Langer, E. (1977). Long-term effects of a control-relevant intervention. *Journal of Personality and Social Psychology*, **35**, 897–902.

Rothbaum, F., Weisz, J., & Snyder, S. (1982). Changing the world and changing the self: A two-process model of perceived control. *Journal of Personality and Social Psychology*, **42**, 5–37.

Rotter, J. B. (1966). Generalized expectancies for internal vs. external control of reinforcement. *Psychological Monographs*, **80** (Whole No. 609).

Rowles, G. D. (1983). Geographical dimensions of social support in rural Appalachia. In G. D. Rowles & R. J. Ohta (Eds.), *Aging and milieu: Environmental perspectives on growing old* (pp. 111–130). New York: Academic Press.

Rowles, G. D. (1984). Aging in rural environments. In I. Altman, M. P. Lawton, & J. F. Wohlwill (Eds.), *Elderly people and the environment* (pp. 129–157). New York: Plenum.

Rubinstein, R. L. (1989). The home environments of older people: A description of psychosocial processes linking person to place. *Journal of Gerontology*, **44**, S45–S53.

Sampson, E. E. (1977). Psychology and the American ideal. *Journal of Personality and Social Psychology*, **35**, 767–782.

Saperstein, A., Moleski, W. H., & Lawton, M. P. (1985). Determining housing quality: A guide for home-health care. *Pride Institute Journal*, **4**, 41–51.

Saup, W. (1986). Lack of autonomy in old age homes: A stress and coping study. *Journal of Housing for the Elderly*, **4**, 21–36.

Scheidt, R. J., & Windley, P. G. (1985). The ecology of aging. In J. E. Birren & K. W. Schaie (Eds.), *Handbook of the psychology of aging* (pp. 245–258). New York: Van Nostrand Reinhold.

Schulz, R. (1976). Control, predictability, and the institutionalized aged. *Journal of Personality and Social Psychology*, **33**, 563–573.

Schulz, R., & Hanusa, B. H. (1978). Long-term effects of control and predictability-enhancing interventions: Findings and ethical issues. *Journal of Personality and Social Psychology*, **36**, 1194–1201.

Schulz, R., & Hanusa, B. H. (1979). Environmental influences on the effectiveness of control- and competence-enhancing interventions. In L. C. Perlmuter & R. A. Monty (Eds.), *Choice and perceived control* (pp. 315–337). Hillsdale, NJ: Erlbaum.

Seligman, M. E. P. (1975). *Helplessness*. San Francisco: Freeman.

Sheehan, N. W. (1986). Informal support among the elderly in public senior housing. *Gerontologist*, **26**, 171–175.

Sherwood, S., Ruchlin, H. S., & Sherwood, C. C. (1989). CCRCs: An option for aging in place. In D. Tillson & C. J. Fahey (Eds.), *Support of the frail elderly in residential environments*. Glenview, IL: Scott Foresman (in press).

Slivinske, L. R., & Fitch, V. L. (1987). The effect of control enhancing intervention on the well-being of elderly individuals living in retirement communities. *Gerontologist*, **27**, 176–181.

Steinfeld, E. (1987). Adapting housing for older disabled people. In V. Regnier & J. Pynoos (Eds.), *Housing the aged: Design directives and policy considerations* (pp. 307–339). New York: Elsevier.

Stephens, M. A. P., Kinney, J. M., & McNeer, A. E. (1986). Accommodative housing: Social integration of residents with physical limitations. *Gerontologist*, **26**, 176–180.

Streib, G. F., Folts, N. E., & LaGreca, A. J. (1985). Autonomy, power, and decision-making in 36 retirement communities. *Gerontologist*, **25**, 403–409.

Streib, G. F., LaGreca, A. J., & Folts, W. E. (1986). Retirement communities: People, planning, prospects. In R. J. Newcomer, M. P. Lawton, & T. O. Byerts (Eds.), *Housing an aging society* (pp. 94–103). New York: Van Nostrand Reinhold.

Struyk, R. J. (1987). Housing adaptions: Needs and practices. In V. Regnier & J. Pynoos (Eds.), *Housing the aging: Design directives and policy considerations* (pp. 259–276). New York: Elsevier.

Sullivan, D. A. (1986). Informal support systems in a planned retirement community: Availability, proximity, and willingness to utilize. *Research on Aging*, **8**, 249–267.

Tesch, S., & Whitbourne, S. (1981). Friendship, social interaction and subjective well-being of older men in an institutional setting. *International Journal of Aging and Human Development*, **13**, 317–327.

Timko, C., & Rodin, J. (1985). Staff-patient relationships in nursing homes: Sources of conflict and rehabilitation potential. *Rehabilitation Psychology*, **30**, 93–108.

Turner, L. A., & Mangum, E. (1982). *Report on the housing choices of older Americans*. Washington, DC: National Council on Aging.

Usui, W. M., & Keil, T. J. (1987). Life satisfaction and age concentration of the local area. *Psychology and Aging*, **2**, 30–35.

White, C. B., & Janson, P. (1986). Helplessness in institutional setting: Adaptation or iatrogenic disease? In M. M. Baltes & P. B. Baltes (Eds.), *The psychology of control and aging* (pp. 297–313). Hillsdale, NJ: Erlbaum.

White, R. W. (1959). Motivation reconsidered: The concept of competence. *Psychological Review*, **66**, 297–323.

Windley, P. G., & Scheidt, R. J. (1980). Person-environment dialectics: Implications for competent functioning in old age. In L. Poon (Ed.), *Aging in the 1980s* (pp. 407–423). Washington, DC: American Psychological Association.

Winkelvoss, H., & Powell, A. V. (1984). *Continuing care retirement communities: An empirical, financial, and legal analysis*. Homewood, IL: Pension Research Council, The Wharton School, Richard D. Irwin Press.

Zeisel, J., Epp, G., & Demos, S. (1977). *Low-rise housing for older people: Behavioral criteria for design* (HUD Publication No. 483). Washington, DC: U.S. Government Printing Office.

Zeisel, G., Welch, P., Epp, G., & Demos, S. (1983). *Mid-rise elevator housing for older people*. Boston, MA: Building Diagnostics.

Ziegler, M., & Reid, D. (1983). Correlates of changes in desired control scores and in life-satisfaction scores among elderly persons. *International Journal of Aging and Human Development*, **16**, 135–146.

Twenty Eight

Ethical Issues in Gerontological Research and Services

Douglas C. Kimmel and Harry R. Moody

Psychological research and the delivery of professional services that involve older persons raise ethical issues that may differ from those ordinarily considered because of age-related stereotypes and bias based on age or gender. Moreover, standard issues related to informed consent and confidentiality can raise special concerns both in the conduct of research and in the delivery of psychological services to older populations. Ethical issues may be especially complex when dealing with samples of frail or dementing persons of any age or with persons receiving long-term care.

This chapter suggests relevant issues and recommendations for use by researchers and clinicians who are relatively new to the field of psychology and aging. It also may be relevant to more experienced gerontologists, including review committees for papers at professional meetings, textbook authors, and those teaching about aging, age-related issues, or social bias. It is intended to alert researchers to issues and potential problems in research on aging, some of which reflect problems in the field of gerontology. However, the considerations described here are not a criterion for evaluating "good" or "ethical"

research and practice. They should be considered only as an adjunct to existing standards.[1] The sections of this chapter that focus on research issues are based on discussions of the Task Force to Develop Non-Ageist Guidelines for Research sponsored by the American Psychological Association Board of Social and Ethical Responsibility and the Board of Scientific Affairs.[2]

[1] These include *Ethical Principles of Psychologists* (APA, 1981), *Ethical Principles in the Conduct of Research with Human Participants* (APA, 1982), and *General Guidelines for Providers of Psychological Services* (APA, 1987). Other documents may also be relevant: for example, *Guidelines for Avoiding Sexism in Psychological Research* (Denmark, Russo, Frieze, & Sechzer, 1988), *Guidelines for Ethical Research in Long Term Care Settings* (Cassel, 1988), *Avoiding Heterosexist Bias: Guidelines for Ethical and Valid Research* (APA Committee on Lesbian and Gay Concerns, 1987).

[2] Douglas C. Kimmel, Chair; Martha T. Mednick, Lillian E. Troll, K. Warner Schaie, members. The Board of Social and Ethical Responsibility Subcommittee on Ageism was responsible for the creation of this task force and also stimulated the publication of a series of relevant articles on ageism in the *American Psychologist* (Gatz & Pearson, 1988; Kimmel, 1988; Roybal, 1988; Schaie, 1988; see also Rodeheaver & Datan, 1988).

Handbook of the Psychology of Aging, Third Edition
Copyright © 1990 Academic Press, Inc. All rights of reproduction in any form reserved.

I. Ethical Issues in Psychological Research on Aging

Much of the discussion in this section seeks to identify for research in psychology and aging those ethical principles that promote fairness and respect for human dignity and autonomy (Denham, 1984). This discussion may strike some researchers as mainly a list of warnings and dangers to avoid. In fact, most discussions of ethics and research in aging *are* one-sided. Cassel (1985) has pointed out that most documents on the ethics of experimentation with human participants are preoccupied with protecting the vulnerable from harm or exploitation. If the ethical difficulties of doing research on aged people are greater than with other groups, it may prove easier simply to avoid these studies. Thus the effect of this preoccupation with the vulnerabilities of older persons unwittingly has been to exclude large segments of the elderly population—for example, those in nursing homes or those with dementia—because of strong criteria for informed consent (Cassel, 1987; Ratzan, 1980, 1981). There remain serious ethical issues in conducting dementia research (Gilhooly, 1986; Mahendra, 1984). However, the one-sided preoccupation with harm to research participants may need to be balanced by attention to the *benefits* of participation in research projects, including both biomedical research and behavioral research.

Limiting the discussion here only to nontherapeutic psychological or behavioral research on the elderly, we can identify a number of benefits in such participation such as (1) individual benefits of new knowledge gained by being a participant at the time of debriefing; (2) general societal benefits arising from cumulative advancements in knowledge; (3) improved information about subpopulations of the elderly often excluded from research studies; and (4) improved morale and feelings of self-worth as a result of playing a contributive role in an important social enterprise. For many elderly, particularly the frail or those with few opportunities for social participation, the experience of serving as a research participant can be an extremely positive and beneficial element in their lives. The proper concern to avoid exploitation or coercion must be balanced by due recognition of these positive benefits of the research enterprise itself; likewise, the power of these benefits needs to be considered with regard to potential coercion (Cassel, 1988).

In the next section, we make recommendations with regard to issues that affect the research participant directly: informed consent, confidentiality, and debriefing. In the following section, we focus on more general issues regarding psychological research on topics related to aging. The final section discusses concerns regarding psychological services.

A. Ethical Issues Relevant to Individual Participants

1. Informed Consent

The principle of respect for persons in our society involves acknowledgement of individual *autonomy:* That is, individuals may not be subjects in treatment or experimentation without their free and informed consent. Informed consent, in its legal definition, requires that a decision be voluntary, knowledgeable, and made by a mentally competent individual. It is this last requirement that poses an ethical dilemma in some gerontological research because of the diversity within the population of older adults. Some may require ethical considerations similar to those that apply to persons of any age who are cognitively impaired or institutionalized (see APA, 1982, pp. 33–34, 44–46, respectively). Others may be unusually vulnerable to pressure for participation. Most, however, probably require only appropriate informed consent procedures (see Cohen-Mansfield, Kerin, Pawlson, Lipson, & Holdridge, 1988, for an illustrative model and an empirical exploration of relevant issues).

Because the incidence of mental impairment and dementia rises significantly with very advanced age and is particularly likely in health care settings, it is often reasonable to scrutinize the participant's capacity to give informed consent. At the same time, this extra scrutiny holds a peril of its own. Ageist biases are all too often at play when an elderly person is infantalized or viewed as incompetent simply because of momentary confusion or an insignificant gap in short-term memory. A more appropriate ethical stance on the mental capacity issue would involve a prima facie degree of caution in obtaining consent, particularly among the old-old or those with signs of mental frailty. This caution does not undercut the legal and ethical imperative of presuming people to be competent unless proved otherwise. In short, the prima facie position of caution must be accompanied by a strong burden of proof in evidence to demonstrate impaired capacity (cf. Cassel, 1988). Likewise, if the study focuses on the dementing elderly, several special issues regarding informed consent arise (cf. Gilhooly, 1986).

The Task Force to Develop Non-Ageist Guidelines for Research sponsored by the American Psychological Association suggested the following minimum recommendations: (1) Ensure that informed consent is fully honored and means the same for all age groups in the study. (2) Do not accept permission by nonqualified "authorities" or pressure on participants. (3) Do not treat older persons in general as if they were legally incompetent with regard to informed consent. (4) If relevant, develop procedures to find out who can give consent and for reconfirming that consent with the participant if possible; know the state statutes governing power of attorney and guardianship.

2. Confidentiality

Although often promised, absolute confidentiality cannot be fully guaranteed in social science research because it is not legally protected by "doctor–patient" privilege (Gray & Melton, 1985). Steps can be taken to maximize the guarantee of confidentiality, and these are especially important in socially sensitive research on topics, such as AIDS, that pose a conflict between individual privacy and public health (Melton & Gray, 1988). Ordinary protections of confidentiality are probably adequate for most gerontology research. Nonetheless, institutionalized persons may require special consideration because an institution (or other health care service) may want or need to know information obtained to better care for those involved in the study (cf. Cassel, 1988).

3. Debriefing

Procedures for explaining the project to the participants can be especially important in aging research. For example, if any ageist stereotypes were employed in the study, participants should be debriefed regarding those stereotypes so that they do not leave the study with any greater age bias than they had at the beginning. In addition, some studies involve experimental conditions that are in themselves rewarding to the participants (such as friendly contact with the researcher in a nursing home). Care should be given to debriefing when the study is completed to minimize, or replace, the loss of some positive benefit from the study protocol (see also point 4 in the next section). Moreover, the debriefing may be a benefit to the participant in its own right.

4. General Concerns

The Task Force to Develop Non-Ageist Guidelines for Research made several specific recommendations regarding more general aspects in the conduct of research. (1) Avoid patronizing or infantilizing older persons (e.g., use of first names only or the use of childish language, or "dearie," and so on). (2) Be aware that some individual differences may affect the results (such as immigration status, illegal drug use, alcohol use, financial circumstances, or sexual orientation); these differences, if relevant, might involve potentially intrusive questions that can raise ethical considerations involving concerns about privacy and confidentiality balanced against the need to know this information. (3) Health assessment, which can raise methodological questions if it is self-reported, may involve ethical considerations if medical reports or tests are used (e.g., confidentiality, release of information to the participant, and access to the information by family or institutions). (4) In studies where there is a risk of death (e.g., relocation of institutionalized aged), psychological damage when the experimental treatment ends (e.g., visitors to home bound or institutionalized persons for the duration of the study), or in research where a treatment has been found to be beneficial and a "control" group is needed to assess an alternative treatment, careful consideration of professional responsibility needs to inform the experimental protocol and follow-up after the study ends. For example, instead of a "treatment versus no treatment" study, comparing a new treatment with a proven beneficial treatment is advised, and when the results are clear, both groups should receive the most beneficial treatment after the study is concluded.

B. Issues Relevant to Psychological Research on Age-Related Topics

In this section we discuss research that poses little ethical concern regarding the participants—such as answering a questionnaire or participating in a laboratory experiment involving learning and memory—but that may produce findings that are sufficiently biased as to be harmful to the older population. This may be caused by an inappropriate choice of a research topic, flawed design or methodology, and problems in data analysis or interpretation. These issues are similar to those that arise with regard to gender and racial bias in research. Often, the lack of attention to these issues simply leads to unintentionally dull or irrelevant studies. The following considerations are offered as suggestions to make good research better and to avoid pitfalls that may raise ethical issues (cf. Schaie, 1988).

1. Choice of Research Topic

The ethical concerns in the choice of a research topic involve a balance between practical concerns, theoretical issues, interests of the participants, and curiosity of the researcher. Surely, few researchers would choose a topic for research that deliberately raised ethical questions, yet few begin a study by asking the participants what questions they want the study to answer. Because researchers usually choose the topic, the Task Force identified several relevant concerns and recommendations to consider in this process.

1. *Concern:* Absence of a theoretical perspective and focusing instead on purely descriptive studies, or on "age" as the cause of differences or changes without a theoretical rationale. Lack of awareness of relevant work in the existing literature, including perspectives that are not age related ("developmental") or associated with aging. *Recommendation:* Consider a life-span view in formulating topics and selecting relevant theories or constructs. Consider why the particular age studied is appropriate from the life-span perspective. Consider multidisciplinary approaches to encourage a broad theoretical perspective and consideration of relevant variables.

2. *Concern:* Adopting an inappropriate

or simplistic model, such as decrement or decline, without considering more complex models that include an appreciation of individual or group differences. *Recommendation:* Recognize that the aged are a diverse population. Stress their heterogeneity; consider their gender, ethnicity, socioeconomic status, education, immigration history, geographic location, sexual orientation, and life-style. Moreover, consider the implications of the topic selected. Could it promote a stereotyped view of any particular age group? Is that a necessary risk that is offset by the scientific merit of the study? Likewise, consider whether the study could contribute to a reduction of age bias.

3. *Concern:* Choice of topic from among a small list of overstudied areas (e.g., decline, deterioration, dependency, or disability) instead of from relatively neglected areas such as those that involve positive or nondecremental changes and those that can affect persons of any age. *Recommendation:* Consider the perspectives, interests, and concerns of the age subpopulation studied. What questions, implicit theories, or hypotheses are important to them? For example, research on Alzheimer's disease and other "overstudied" topics can be approached from this perspective without contributing to age bias.

In general, researchers are urged to review critically previous research and theory on the topic, noting relevant alternative perspectives and also examples of age bias—which can apply to any age, not only those who are old (Kimmel, 1988).

2. Design and Methodology

Good research uses a design and methods that follow from the question that the study asks. The choice of topic alone, however, does not guarantee an adequate design. The Task Force suggested that the following considerations may help ensure

that the design and choice of methods are appropriate for studies in gerontology.

1. Evaluate the use of age as a variable in the study. Examine the choice and definition of hypotheses that imply an inference that age or aging is the cause of hypothesized changes or differences. Do not assume that everyone, regardless of differences in demographic, life-style, and other interactive variables, responds similarly to age-related issues. Consider whether chronological age is the most relevant variable. Consider the interaction of age, sex, culture, and other social variables in which groups in the population may differ by age. Would other variables be more appropriate than age, such as educational level, income, duration of marriage, retirement status, generational position? The main effect of age may be less interesting than the interaction of age with other variables. Consider cohort and historical effects that covary with chronological age. Avoid inconsistent criteria for groupings by age; "old" samples may vary considerably in age (from the 60s to 90s), whereas middle-aged and young samples often are more uniform in age. Recognize that a convenient sample, although of a particular age, is not necessarily an appropriate group for the question studied. Recognize diversity (race, gender, class, and so on) in sample selection. Describe the sample characteristics, method of recruitment, and method of age assessment used.

2. Seek ways to prevent frequent problems in the choice of a sample. Avoid inadequate operational definition of the age variable, such as using groups that are overly global or inclusive (e.g., under age 65 versus over age 65). Avoid use of inappropriate comparison groups or control subjects; for example, college students differ from members of senior citizen centers on many variables beside age. Precisely matched groups also may not be appropriate; for example, matching

on the absolute level of formal education would produce a much more selective sample among older persons than among younger persons. Control for extraneous variables that may vary by age such as reaction time, sensory acuity, and so on; in computerized testing, for example, these factors may affect performance. Consider possible effects of survivorship and dropout rates. Survivors or dropouts may have been different at the beginning. This applies not only to longitudinal studies (such as IQ change) but also to any study where the sample, by definition, consists of those who have survived to the age studied. Assess the health status of the respondents if this may be relevant to the focus of the study. Distinguish between normal age changes and disease. Recognize the limitations of possible generalizations from the study if health status is used to select the sample—for example, in generalizing to the entire population from a subset of it or in comparing healthy young with healthy old, when very different proportions of the young and old populations are being studied.

3. Examine the constructs and measures in the study carefully. Consider whether the constructs mean the same thing at different ages. For example, might dependency and aggression be expressed differently or mean something different at age 20 compared with age 50 or 80? Be sensitive to experimenter bias about how questions are asked of various age groups. Think through the implications of "tactful" questions on presumed sensitive topics; does making the question "tactful" change its meaning? Consider using pilot studies to explore these issues. Examine previous research to determine whether the validity of the measures has been established for the sample to be studied and whether the present sample is sufficiently similar to suggest that the measure would be valid; if necessary, check validity. Use appropriate measures; for example, if family concern is the issue, consider that the number of family visits to an elderly person reflects in part the number of surviving family members—therefore, a lower number of visitors to very old residents in a nursing home may reflect a low number of surviving relatives, not necessarily rejection by the family. Check the norms of tests used for age-cohort bias; standardized tests may have been based on different cohorts—cohorts with different backgrounds from the ones in the present study.

4. Exercise sensitivity to potential age bias and stereotypes. Empirically evaluate instruments to ensure that they do not contain explicit or implicit age bias; check for inappropriate or offensive items. Avoid a priori assumptions like because of their age, respondents would be more (or less) sensitive to questions about topics such as sexuality, death, bereavement, menopause, body image, or love. This does not mean that sensitive topics should be avoided but that they need to be evaluated carefully. For example, is the measure and language used appropriate for each age group in the study? Are the hypotheses influenced by negative or positive age bias? Is there an assumption that senility is caused by living a long time, or that long-term marriages reflect marital satisfaction. Consider the sex, age, and other relevant characteristics of the interviewers or confederates for possible effects on respondents or subjects and for subtle manifestations of positive or negative ageist assumptions. Design the study to evaluate possible confounding effects, if relevant. Recognize also the possibility of positive age bias that hides individual differences; for example, in studies of care giving, whereas some older people are rejected by mean-spirited families, others are rejected by family members because the old person has a long history of being unpleasant.

5. Researchers should be aware of any relevant policy implications that might be drawn from the research so that the design of the study will allow meaningful recommendations to be made.

3. Data Analysis and Interpretation

Problems in analyzing and interpreting data from research in gerontology also may raise special issues, in particular when the topic is relevant to social policy (e.g., occupational qualifications) or deals with socially sensitive issues (e.g., Alzheimer's disease). Among the potential problems the Task Force identified are the following:[3]

1. Individual differences, group variance, and contextual variables in studies of age-related change are sometimes ignored. For example, because of the increasing proportion of individuals showing decline with age on memory tests and thus declines in average scores with age, it is incorrectly concluded that everyone will inevitably decline in memory ability as they get older. Researchers are urged to consider the increasing range of individual differences with age, and to avoid inferences of universal age change based on averages. Older persons are generally *more*, not less, diverse than younger populations. If the sample was screened by health status or matched on some variables, note the effects this may have on the generalizability of the findings. In addition, the effects of contextual and intervening variables should be ruled out before attributing observed group differences to age. In all cases, use caution in generalizing from results.

2. When behavioral characteristics are assessed with scales that have good psychometric quality, statistically reliable age-group differences can be found, but the absolute size of these differences may

be so small as not to justify public policy decisions. For example, the well-documented slowing of reaction time with age actually amounts to less than 1 second for those between 60 and 70 years of age, compared with those 20 to 30 years old. Therefore, the magnitude of age changes should not be ignored. Researchers should consider how much difference a difference makes, especially when the data are relevant to public policy or may affect an individual's situation, such as occupational fitness. Many age changes have little or no practical effect. Also, consider compensatory mechanisms; for example, older expert typists may use a strategy of looking farther ahead while typing and thus maintain a high rate of accurate performance despite slower reaction time.

3. Absence of differences relevant to ageist stereotypes may not be reported. If no difference is found, the inability to determine the significance of a null hypothesis may inhibit its being reported despite its importance. However, instead of testing a null hypothesis, researchers can stipulate the expected age difference and test that hypothesis so that a finding of little or no age difference can be statistically meaningful.

4. Age differences found accidentally (where age is included as a variable in the analysis without a clear rationale) are reported as findings. A more appropriate interpretation is that these are issues deserving further systematic study.

5. Age-related and time-dependent or duration effects are not distinguished. It may be noted that time-dependent changes may have different ages of onset. Thus calender age is not necessarily relevant in all developmental studies.[4] For example, if executive burnout is the issue, duration effects, such as length of time on the job, may be the important dimension. This may be spuriously

---

[3]For more detailed discussion see Schaie (1988).

[4]See Schroots and Birren, Chapter 3, this volume

correlated with calendar age because of similar ages of starting to work but would be uncorrelated with age in a population where career entry occurs over a wide age range. Thus, the term *age related* should be restricted to those processes that have age-specific onset, asymptote, or rates of change. By contrast, those processes that imply developmental change but that have wide latitude in age of onset or progression would better be labeled as *time dependent*.

6. Ageist assumptions and models may have been used in data analysis and interpretation. An implied irreversible decrement model (such as the Gompertz curve) may be unduly restrictive; it does not allow for the recursive or lagged phenomena so characteristic of development and aging. The unidirectionality of time-ordered observations does not necessarily imply that the process under study is unidirectional. Although there are many age-related processes that may be unidirectional at best over limited portions of the life-span, others may generally take cyclical or recursive forms. Likewise, value-laden language should be avoided (e.g., age *decrement* versus age *difference*).

7. In socially significant areas (such as productivity in employment, Alzheimer's disease, memory loss) consider the impact of the research on people, institutions, and social policy.

II. Ethical Issues in Psychological Services for the Aged

Just as in research, there are multiple ethical issues that arise in psychological services for the aged. As psychologists become more actively involved in aging services, they will be compelled to face questions, some familiar and applicable to younger age groups and others arising from distinctive characteristics of the last stage

of life. The ethical issues in geriatric services have stimulated a growing literature on the subject (Cassel & Meier, 1986). But far less attention has been given to ethics and psychological services for the aging. Some of the most important issues in psychological services for the aging are discussed next.

A. Psychological Testing

Psychologists provide many kinds of services for older people, but one of the distinctive contributions of psychology lies in testing and assessment. Despite the seeming objectivity and value neutrality of tests and measurements, in fact, psychological testing with older people presents some important ethical issues that need to be considered.

We should be especially cautious in interpreting any psychometric test results for older people for two reasons. First age-related declines in test performance may sometimes be related to speed as well as power factors. Because of age-related slowing in reaction time, anxiety, or unfamiliarity with the test equipment (e.g., computers), test performance may not accurately reflect underlying ability. Second, because of culturally shared negative images of aging, older people are likely to be especially fearful of age-related decrements in mental ability or memory. Whatever gerontologists may say, the public still accepts many stereotypes that suggest advanced age invariably leads to mental decline or even senility. Both factors of test design and fears about aging argue for an extra degree of caution in communicating and interpreting results of psychological tests or other assessments to older clients. Nonetheless, in some cases, the individual needs to know so that effective legal and financial planning can be undertaken (cf. Overman & Stoudemire, 1988).

Psychologists who are skilled in testing also can play an important role in providing information about the mental status of individuals when there is doubt about their competency to consent to treatment (Roth, Meisel, & Lidz, 1977).

B. Legal Determinations of Competence

We should be very reluctant to deny elderly patients the right to make crucial decisions simply because of vague or sweeping interpretations of their behavior. This line of argument underscores the crucial importance of professional psychological assessment in making judgments of mental competency in the clinical arena. This point applies to *ethical* decisions rendered on an everyday basis by both informal judgments and professional psychological assessment. But the point becomes even more crucial when we move to the *legal* arena: for example, when a proxy or surrogate decision maker is to be appointed (Buchanan, 1981). In fact, a determination of incompetence is not a psychological but rather a legal or judicial decision, though of course the term is used loosely in practice. However, both psychologists and psychiatrists can be placed in a strategic position when it comes to assessing a patient's mental status or providing expert information about mental capacity (Baker, Perr, & Yesavage, 1986). This is a very serious ethical situation because testimony can contribute to a judicial determination of incapacity resulting in an individual being declared permanently incompetent, with irrevocable consequences, such as civil commitment (Brock, 1980). The same issues arise in matters of conservatorship and guardianship. Proof of diminished capacity may have serious legal as well as medical consequences and, therefore, this puts a special ethical burden on the sensitivity and professional skill of psychologists.

The problem, of course, is that in rendering services we are seeking an appropriate balance: to avoid the extremes of unrealistic ascription of autonomy, on the one hand, or diminished incapacity and paternalism, on the other. A solution to this dilemma may come about through research. Indeed, some psychologists argue that the ideal of autonomy for older adults can best be achieved by devising more accurate psychometric instruments to measure mental capacity along functional rather than global terms (Stanley, 1986). More research is certainly called for. However, even if better mental status instruments become available, there will remain problems of interpretation, communication, and balancing of competing interests in applying the results to practical problems.

The question of consent and clinical decision making is by no means resolved by more accurate test results alone. For one thing, results are often ambiguous (Caplan, 1985). Even in the case of demonstrable loss of decisional capacity, a different set of ethical dilemmas appears. These dilemmas can be summed up as the complexity of "negotiated consent" among family members who serve as surrogate decision makers (Moody, 1988). Psychologists or social workers often are called in for consultation when a family is trying to reach a difficult decision—for example, a decision to terminate life-sustaining treatment in a deteriorating geriatric patient—and when family dynamics or psychological factors, such as guilt or projection, seem to destroy the capacity to reach a reasonable decision or actually disrupt family communication patterns. The same kinds of decision or communication problems arise in many other contexts: for example, decisions about placing an elderly relative in a nursing home, disputes about money or inheritance, or paternalistic intervention in cases of diminished mental capacity. There are no simple rules that can resolve these ethical dilemmas.

C. Psychotherapy

There is considerable evidence that psychotherapy is routinely less available to older people than to younger (U. S. General Accounting Office, 1982). This situation is troubling but should be viewed in proper perspective. First, members of the current cohort of older adults grew up in a period when psychotherapy was more stigmatized and less acceptable then today, and therefore older people may have greater inner barriers to seeking psychotherapeutic assistance; this may change with future cohorts. Second, the phenomenon that Kastenbaum (1965) described as the "reluctant therapist" is still in evidence today. The reasons go back at least to Freud (1924) and his legendary pessimism about the possibilities of psychological change or the benefits of therapy in later life. However, Gatz and Pearson (1988) challenge the idea that ageism on the part of professionals accounts for the insufficient mental health services that are available and point out that the issues are more complex; for example, they assert that the overemphasis and overdiagnosis of Alzheimer's disease may be a particularly significant manifestation of ageism today that deflects attention away from other psychological problems. Third, there are financial incentives that tend to inhibit the availability of psychotherapy to older people (Roybal, 1988). Reimbursement for psychotherapy under Medicare is very limited, and reimbursement incentives go in the direction of psychopharmacology or other medical, rather than psychosocial, interventions.

D. Interdisciplinary Collaboration

Psychologists have a professionally based inclination to promote psychologically oriented treatments. This inclination can be especially helpful in the geriatric environment. Indeed, geriatric health care as a field of practice offers great promise for the emerging field of developmental health psychology (Siegler, 1989). However, at present the reality is that, in clinics, nursing homes, hospitals, and other settings, the medical model remains dominant, both in terms of professional authority or control and in terms of the reimbursement incentives mentioned before. This condition means that the normative imperative of "interprofessional collaboration," so frequently endorsed in the literature of gerontology and geriatrics, becomes a very problematic ideal. How can collaboration be genuinely collegial and multidisciplinary when the bias and control channels remain skewed *away from* psychological intervention by patterns of organizational authority and reimbursement structure?

This problem of bias and control creates some serious ethical dilemmas for psychologists who try to honor the imperative of collaboration and doing what is best for the patient. For example, one ethical dilemma involves truth telling: how to communicate information to patients, how much to divulge about disagreements among members of the professional team, how much to alter the facts in order to obtain reimbursement or eligibility for medically defined services. Other ethical dilemmas focus on relationships among professionals and institutions: for example, the dilemma of loyalty or "carrying out orders" versus dissent and disobedience. Here the status of the psychologist (as employee or consultant) may be a significant factor in the way the dilemma is framed. The ethical dilemma of the "professional-as-employee" is a familiar one with no clear-cut answers (Abramson, 1985).

E. Behavioral Intervention

A plausible argument can be made that the most profound improvements in longevity and quality of life in old age have come about through behavioral and psychological change rather than medical interventions (Sagan, 1987). Even if this claim is exaggerated, there can be no doubt that clear behavioral changes like exercise, giving up smoking, or modification of diet play a profound role in health or sickness. In addition, apart from etiology and prevention, even from a strictly medical point of view, successful therapy depends on psychological elements. For example, there is growing evidence of the problem of patient compliance with medical regimens. Moreover, there is increased recognition of the importance of psychological factors in pain control and in the management of chronic illnesses (Melamed, 1984). All of these recent trends underscore the importance of psychological services in the care of the aged.

At the same time, these trends raise serious questions about the limits of psychological intervention in matters of health and well-being. One problem is the familiar dilemma of autonomy and paternalism. To take one example, if behavior is linked with health, to what extent should we hold individuals responsible for the consequences of their actions—for example, charge higher insurance premiums for people who fail to adopt "correct" behavior? If society pays the bill for unhealthy behavior, does that mean society has a right to intervene and modify that behavior? Psychology is likely to play a major role in promoting more healthful, and less costly, behavior through education and other methods of behavior change. Thus, it will be confronted with the ethical issues involved (cf. Morin, 1988).

The dilemma is most acute in matters of life and death. One of the most difficult examples here is the problem of suicide and the aged. As a practical matter, most psychologists and other health professionals would probably agree that, when in doubt, one should err on the side of preserving life and, in particular, aggressively treating depression. But when intervention takes the form of aggressive paternalism, troublesome ethical issues arise (Bromberg & Cassel, 1983). It is here that the background issue of ageism is important to remember. An ethical presumption

for more aggressive intervention may well be justified in a society where the negative stereotypes of ageism abound and where older people themselves are likely to share those stereotypes: for example, where people who are "useless" (e.g., widowed, unemployed, dependent, and so on) are inclined to be depressed. In these situations, how can we have confidence that a "rational" decision for suicide is truly free? On the other hand, how can we intervene in such cases while still respecting patient autonomy?

III. Conclusion

Ethical questions and issues of individual autonomy do not arise in a vacuum, but in a specific social context. For example, the recent preoccupation with cost containment in health care among policymakers is matched by a new interest among professionals in behavioral medicine and a continuing interest among the public in self-help activities of all kinds. Further, successive cohorts of older people have higher levels of education and show more familiarity and acceptance of psychology. They are likely to make use of psychological services, particularly where third-party payment makes these services more accessible. A final trend is the aging of the population itself, especially the rapid growth of the old-old among whom dementing illnesses, with their psychological problems, are more prevalent.

The combined effect of all these trends in the future is likely to be an environment where psychological research and services achieve heightened importance for policymakers, health care practitioners, and the elderly and their families. But higher levels of utilization and greater acceptance of psychological services in geriatric care make it still more important that we continue to address the ethical issues of psychology and aging. The discussion has barely begun.

References

Abramson, M. (1985). Caught in the middle: The professional as employee and colleague. *Generations*, **10**(2), 35–37.

American Psychological Association (1981). Ethical principles of psychologists. *American Psychologist*, **36**, 633–638.

American Psychological Association (1982). *Ethical principles in the conduct of research with human participants*. Washington, DC: Author.

American Psychological Association (1987). General guidelines for providers of psychological services. *American Psychologist*, **42**, 712–723.

APA Committee on Lesbian and Gay Concerns (1987). *Avoiding heterosexist bias: Guidelines for ethical and valid research*. Washington, DC: American Psychological Association.

Baker, F. M., Perr, I. N., & Yesavage, J. A. (1986). *An overview of legal issues in geriatric psychiatry* (Task Force Report 23). Washington, DC: American Psychiatric Association.

Brock, D. W. (1980). Involuntary civil commitment: The moral issues. In B. A. Brody & H. T. Englehardt (Eds.), *Mental illness: Law and public policy*. Dordrecht: Reidel.

Bromberg, S., & Cassel, C. (1983). Suicide in the elderly: The limits of paternalism. *Journal of the American Geriatrics Society*, **31**, 698–703.

Buchanan, A. (1981). The limits of proxy decision making for incompetence. *UCLA Law Review*, **29**.

Caplan, A. (1985). Let wisdom find a way: The concept of competency in the care of the elderly. *Generations*, **10**(2), 10–14.

Cassel, C. K. (1985). Ethical issues in research in geriatrics. *Generations*, **10**(2), 45–48.

Cassel, C. K. (1987). Informed consent for research in geriatrics: History and concepts. *Journal of the American Geriatrics Society*, **35**, 542–544.

Cassel, C. K. (1988). Ethical issues in the conduct of research in long term care. *Gerontologist*, **28** (Suppl.), 90–96.

Cassel, C. K., & Meier, D. E. (1986). Selected bibliography of recent articles in ethics and geriatrics. *Journal of the American Geriatrics Society*, **34**, 399–409.

Cohen-Mansfield, J., Kerin, P., Pawlson, G.,

Lipson, S., & Holdridge, K. (1988). Informed consent for research in a nursing home: Processes and issues. *Gerontologist*, **28**, 355–359.

Denham, M. J. (1984). The ethics of research in the elderly. *Age and Aging*, **13**, 321–327.

Denmark, F., Russo, N. F., Frieze, I. H., & Sechzer, J. A. (1988). Guidelines for avoiding sexism in psychological research: A report of the Ad Hoc Committee on Nonsexist Research. *American Psychologist*, **43**, 582–585.

Freud, S. (1924). On psychotherapy. In *Collected papers*, (Vol. 1). London: Hogarth.

Gatz, M., & Pearson, C. G. (1988). Ageism revised and the provision of psychological services. *American Psychologist*, **43**, 184–188.

Gilhooly, M. L. M. (1986). Legal and ethical issues in the management of the dementing elderly. In M. L. Gilhooly, S. H. Zarit, & J. E. Birren (Eds.), *The dementias: Policy and management* (pp. 131–160). Englewood Cliffs, NJ: Prentice-Hall.

Gray, J. N., & Melton, G. B. (1985). The law and ethics of psychosocial research on AIDS. *Nebraska Law Review*, **64**, 637–688.

Kastenbaum, R. J. (1965). The reluctant therapist. In R. J. Kastenbaum (Ed.), *New thoughts on old age* (pp. 139–145). New York: Springer.

Kimmel, D. C. (1988). Ageism, psychology, and public policy. *American Psychologist*, **43**, 175–178.

Mahendra, B. (1984, March). Some ethical issues in dementia research. *Journal of Medical Ethics*, **10**, 29–31.

Melamed, B. G. (1984). Health intervention: Collaboration for health and science. In B. L. Hammonds & C. J. Scheirer (Eds.), *Psychology and health* (Master Lecture Series No. 3, pp. 49–119). Washington, DC: American Psychological Association.

Melton, G. B., & Gray, J. N. (1988). Ethical dilemmas in AIDS research. *American Psychologist*, **43**, 60–64.

Moody, H. R. (1988). From informed consent to negotiated consent. *Gerontologist*, **28**(Suppl.), 64–70.

Morin, S. F. (1988). AIDS: The challenge to psychology. *American Psychologist*, **43**, 838–842.

Overman, W., Jr., & Stoudemire, A. (1988). Guidelines for legal and financial counseling of Alzheimer's disease patients and their families. *American Journal of Psychiatry*, **145**, 1495–1500.

Ratzan, R. M. (1980). Being old makes you different: The ethics of research with elderly subjects. *Hastings Center Report*, **10**(5), 32–42.

Ratzan, R. M. (1981). The experiment that wasn't: A case report in clinical geriatric research. *Gerontologist*, **21**, 297–302.

Rodeheaver, D., & Datan, N. (1988). The challenge of double jeopardy: Toward a mental health agenda for aging women. *American Psychologist*, **43**, 648–654.

Roth, L. H., Meisel, A., & Lidz, C. W. (1977). Tests of competency to consent to treatment. *American Journal of Psychiatry*, **134**, 279–284.

Roybal, E. R. (1988). Mental health and aging: The need for an expanded Federal response. *American Psychologist*, **43**, 189–194.

Sagan, L. (1987). *The health of nations*. New York: Basic Books.

Schaie, K. W. (1988). Ageism in psychological research. *American Psychologist*, **43**, 179–183.

Siegler, I. C. (1989). Developmental health psychology. In M. Storandt & G. R. VandenBos (Eds.), *The adult years: Continuity and change* (Master Lecture Series No. 8, pp. 119–142). Washington, DC: American Psychological Association.

Stanley, B. (Ed.) (1986). *Geriatric psychiatry: Ethical and legal issues*. Washington, DC: American Psychiatric Press.

U. S. General Accounting Office (1982). *The elderly remain in need of mental health services*. (GAO/HRD-82-112, September 16). Washington, DC: Author.

Author Index

518

McArdle, W. D., 186, *199*
McArthur, L. Z., 268, *272*
McBride, O. W., 72, *77*
McCallum, W. C., 139, *146*
McCarley, T., 385, *402*
McCarthy, M., 435, *444*
McClannahan, L. E., 389, *400*
McClearn, G. E., 67, 68, 69, 71, 72, 73, 74, 75, 76,
78, 335, 336, *345*
McClelland, D. C., 174, *181*, 332, *345*
McClelland, J. L., 202, 219, *220*, 276, *288*
McCormick, D. A., 237, 240, *255, 256*
McCormick, E. J., 446, 451, 453, *463*
McCrae, R. M., 31, 37, *42*
McCrae, R. R., 48, *60*, 73, 76, 87, 94, 95, 96, 98, 128,
130, 172, 173, 174, 175, 176, *180, 181*, 278, *288*,
321, 322, 328, 331, 332, 333, 334, 335, 336, 336,
340, 341, 343, *344, 345*
McCubbin, H. I., *424*
McCue, F., 421, *424*
McCue, M., 429, *443*
McDermott, J., 351, *357*
McDonald, C. S., 138, *149*
MacDonald, M. L., 383, *400, 401*
McDonald, R. P., 21, 33, 37, 38, 41, *42*
McDowd, J. M., 222, 223, 230, 232, 276, *288*, 450,
462
McEvoy, C. L., 383, *400*
Mace, N. L., 368, *370*, 380, *400*, 419, *424, 425*
McFarland, R. A., 151, *167*, 316, 319, 450, 455, 456,
462, 463
McFarland, R., 48, *61*
McGaugh, J. L., 242, 247, 254, *255*
McGee, N. D., 158, *167*
McGeer, E. G., 141, *147*
McGeer, P. L., 141, *147*
McGhie, A., 224, *232*
McGlinchey, R. E., 90, 91, *101*
McGonigle-Gibson, K. L., 437, *439*
McGrath, C., 155, *168*
McGrath, J. E., 49, 52, 59, *61*
McGue, M., 75, *78*
McGuire, W. J., 481, *485*
McHugh, P. R., 436, *441*
Maciejewski, C., 429, *445*
McIntyre, J. S., 262, 268, *272*
McKahnn, G., 428, *443*
McKenzie, C. A., 224, 225, *231*
Mackenzie, R. A., 139, *147*
McKinlay, J. B., 406, 408, 418, *425*
McKoon, G., 279, 280, *288*
McLachlan, D., 260, *272*
McMahon, A. W., *61*
McNaughton, B. L., 247, *252*
McNeer, A. E., 475, *487*
McNelis, J. F., 451, 453, *462*
McNiff, M. E., 438, *440*
MacRae, H., 195, *200*
MacRae, P., 194, 195, *199, 200*

Madden, D. J., 90, *101*, 156, 157, 158, 159, *167, 168*,
220, 223, 227, 228, 232, 277, 278, 288, 450, *462*
Maddox, G., 293, 299, 307, 364, *370*
Maehr, M. L., 175, *181*
Magaro, P. A., 436, *442*
Maggini, C., 137, *146*
Mahanand, D., 142, *145*
Mahard, R. E., 114, *121, 122*
Mahendra, B., 490, *500*
Maier, H. W., 8, *19*
MaloneBeach, E., 407, 412, 417, *425*
Man'kovskii, N. B., 141, *147*
Mancini, J., 466, *485*
Mandel, R. G., 283, 284, *288*
Mandler, G., 173, *181*
Mangum, E., 472, *487*
Manton, K., 37, 38, 43, 106, 107, 108, 109, 117, 118,
122, 123, 298, 307, 362, 364, *369, 370*
Margulis, M. K., 161, *166*
Markides, K. S., *122*
Markley, R. P., 301, *305*
Marmar, C., 381, 382, *398*
Marriott, J. G., 248, *255*
Marsden, C. D., 91, 92, *101*
Marsh, G. R., 135, 140, *147*, 158, *167*, 225, *233*
Marsh, H. W., 37, *42*
Marshall, J., 92, *100*
Marshall, V. W., 418, *424*
Martin, G. A., 173, 176, *181*
Martin, J., 262, 270, 278, 279, 285, *289*
Martin, J. E., 88, *98*
Martin, M., 407, *424*
Martin, N. G., 37, *41*
Martin, P., 383, *398*
Martinez, D. R., 264, *272*
Martone, M., 437, *443*
Mason, C. F., 301, *307*
Mason, R., 39, *41*
Masters, W. H., 361, *370*
Matarazzo, J. D., 94, *101*, 292, *307*
Mathers, R. A., 45, *62*
Mathis, E. S., 380, *395*
Matousek, M., 140, *147*
Matsueda, R. L., 37, *42*
Matsuyama, S. S., 88, *100*
Matthews, C. G., 428, 429, *442*
Matthews, K., 76, *78*
Matthews, K. A., 95, *100*
Mauldin, W. M., 151, 152, *167*
Mayeux, R., 93, *102*
Mazur, J. E., 205, 214, *220*
Meacham, J. A., 262, *272*, 301, *307*
Medicine and Science in Sports and Exercise, *199*
Medinger, F., 116, *123*
Mednick, S. A., 321, 322, *328*
Meehl, P. E., 332, *344*
Meier, D. E., 496, *500*
Meisel, A., 497, *501*
Melamed, B. G., 499, *500*

Subject Index

Abilities, 266–68, 320: crystallized, 16, 73, 300; discriminate stimuli, 320; fluid, 16, 73, 300; goal setting, 320; learning and, 15, 320; problem-solving, 354; verbal, 267

Absolute time, 45: definition of, 51

Abstract intelligence, 219

Accidents: chronic diseases, stress and, 108

Accumulated knowledge, 266

Achievement, 322: intellectual functioning and, 115; life-span perspective of, 332; power and, 339

Achievement Anxiety Test, 174

Acquisition curve, 214

Action and behavior: theory of, 9

Activation: components of, 278–279

Activities, 119, 195, 264: age-related differences in, 263; daily living, of, 73, 183, 184, 193, 195, 263, 409, 430, 480; health-promoting, 109; leisure, 265; physical work capacity and, 184; professional, 265; restrictions in, 107–108, 110, 414; self-help, 499

Activity theory, 367

Acute diseases, 419: confusional state, 432

Adaptation, 156, 412: dementia caregivers, in, 414; gentling and, 241; lifelong patterns of, 376–378; multiple indicators of, 415; noise, to, 162; roles of, 115; skills and, 115; stimulus, 156; strategies, 16; styles, 325

Adjective Check List, 334

Administration on Aging (AOA), 14

ADEPT study, 302–303

Adolescence, 6

Adult children, 405, 406, 417: caregivers, as, 406, 408, 414

Adult development, 258, 292–293, 340: child development and, 5, 6; course of, 6, 70–71, 160, 173; family relations and, 421; psychology of, 57; theory of, 11
    See also Aging

Adult family life, 421

Adult grandchildren, 407

Adult life span, 172, 204, 332, 333, 339, 341: personality across, 332

Aerobic capacity, 186, 195

Affect, 365, 409

Affiliation, 332: needs for, 176–177; life-span perspective, within a, 332

Age, 12, 21–23, 32, 45, 46, 49, 50–53, 56, 70, 71, 80, 85, 92, 94–95, 114, 116–118, 130, 137, 151, 154, 155, 162, 183, 187, 203, 209, 210, 216, 258, 267, 325, 335, 429: accuracy in, 263; advanced, 81; age-by-occasion matrix, 36; association of variables with, 6; attention and, 16; behavior and, 13, 22, 65, 190; bias and stereotypes, 494; biological, 47–48, 51; calendar, 45, 53, 496; changes, 11–15, 23–24, 39, 52, 67, 70–71, 75, 117, 151, 155, 160–61, 187, 337; chronological, 29, 46–47, 49, 51, 56, 106; cohorts and, 24–28, 46, 322; cross-sectional, comparison, 69; decrements, 260; deficits, 216, 219, 223, 261; definition of, 106; density, 470; diabetes and, 91; differences, 23, 67, 73, 75, 222–225, 237–241; dynamic instability with, 58; effects of, 34, 36, 73, 171, 210, 260, 263–266, 456; electrophysiologic differences, 135; exercise and, 195–196; experience and, 315; expertise and, 470; factor, 467; faculties, 4; familiarity, 269; functional, 47, 51; functions of, 69, 70; groups, 24, 26, 35–37, 428, 431; homogeneity, 480; information and, 447; information processing and, 200–202; latency as a function of, 30, 203; linear, 30–33; metabolic, 49, 56; misreporting, 107; motivation, 171, 176–178; motor performance and, 188–189; network, 202, 210, 215; norms, 52; performance and, 267; population, of, 15; productivity with, 16; psychological, 51; ranges, 36; segregation, 37, 470; skill and, 315; social, 51; speed of response and, 189–194;

531